T0292815

Cyberlibertarianism

Cyberlibertarianism

The Right-Wing Politics of Digital Technology

DAVID GOLUMBIA

UNIVERSITY OF MINNESOTA PRESS

MINNEAPOLIS · LONDON

Published by the University of Minnesota Press
111 Third Avenue South, Suite 290
Minneapolis, MN 55401-2520
http://www.upress.umn.edu

ISBN 978-1-5179-1813-2 (hc)
ISBN 978-1-5179-1814-9 (pb)

A Cataloging-in-Publication record for this book is available from the
Library of Congress.

Printed in Canada on acid-free paper

The University of Minnesota is an equal-opportunity educator and employer.

33 32 31 30 29 28 27 26 25 24   10 9 8 7 6 5 4 3 2 1

Contents

Publisher's Note

At the time when David Golumbia was diagnosed with an aggressive cancer in summer 2023, his completed manuscript for *Cyberlibertarianism* had been through peer review and approved for publication by the Faculty Editorial Board of the University of Minnesota Press. David intended to make minor revisions and to write a brief preface that would bring the work up to date, but regrettably his treatment did not allow him to do so. He died on September 14, 2023. The publisher gratefully acknowledges the help of David's friend and interlocutor of long standing George Justice, provost of the University of Tulsa, for advising us on David's final wishes and reviewing the copyedited manuscript and proofs.

Foreword

George Justice

Cyberlibertarianism: The Right-Wing Politics of Digital Technology is the result of years of research, from the author's practical, lived experience as a software engineer to his deep reading in philosophy, critical theory, fiction, and poetry and his analysis of hours and hours of watching movies and TV and listening to music, constantly and intensely. David Golumbia (1963–2023) lived a life steeped in culture and thought. He shared the results of his analysis with students at the University of Pennsylvania, the University of Virginia, and Virginia Commonwealth University; with his family and friends; and with his growing number of readers, who watched him in intellectual battle with friend and foe in his books, articles, voluminous blogs (first at Uncomputing.org and then on Medium.com), and tweets. I was a close friend of David and had the benefit of thousands of hours of conversation with him over thirty-five years.

This book is the culmination of his life's work, the previous milestone of which was his first book, *The Cultural Logic of Computation* (2009), with *The Politics of Bitcoin* (2016) serving as a midway check-in that garnered attention for its lucid description of the inextricability of the blockchain and right-wing ideology. *Cyberlibertarianism* takes a broad look at the links between computers (always, entirely cultural) and political thought (very dangerous at the current moment!). In this book you will read a cultural and political history of the Western world (particularly the United States) from the 1950s to the present, written by the most optimistic pessimist you could ever meet.

For these pages are dark in their insistence that the technologies we deploy in nearly all aspects of our lives have been built on fundamentally antidemocratic, *antihuman* premises. It's not just that digital technologies can be used for nefarious purposes—their very constitutive elements are built on a nihilism that denies human flourishing. This book is a scary read, but its premise is optimistic: We human beings can read, we can write, we can create art and poetry and, above all (for David), music. We can connect with each other, with animals, with our environment. David Golumbia always expected the worst, but the richness of his thought betrays an essentially hopeful belief in the powers of the human mind to contemplate, understand, and attempt to change the world for the better.

There's a photo that circulated on the internet a couple of months before David died. At the center is Jerry Garcia, the guitarist, songwriter, and singer of the Grateful Dead, a very familiar image to many people on X (formerly known as Twitter, as the newspapers all say). Next to Garcia is a typical preppy youth of the 1980s or 1990s, identifiable by perhaps even more millions as a young Tucker Carlson, right-wing firebrand and television talking head. Carlson, who had recently been kicked off Fox News, was hawking his new rogue media presence and (seemingly) auditioning for the VP spot on the Trump 2024 ticket. How shocking, right? The hippie Garcia and the right-wing Tucker Carlson (pre–bow tie, which also predated his hard turn to Trumpism) hanging out in what looks like a fancy hotel lobby.

On the phone, David laughed gleefully and said, "Yes, that's exactly it. The Grateful Dead and that whole scene are deeply tied in with the entire cyberlibertarian movement and always were." And, David went on to tell me, it wasn't just John Perry Barlow, songwriting partner of Dead guitarist Bob Weir and cofounder of the Electronic Freedom Foundation, which David takes to task in the following pages. Barlow was just one representative of a deep and persistent connection among the cultures of the Grateful Dead, Silicon Valley, and right-wing politics. Think Burning Man. Think rich, mostly white people smugly convinced that their self-indulgent journeys through music, drugs, and camping in the Nevada desert would lead to a new world of unending freedom—for themselves at least.

The thing is, David was himself one of the most knowledgeable and committed "Deadheads" I have ever known. He loved the music, and he might even have been attracted to certain subcultures associated with the band. It was, after all, John Perry Barlow's words that brought alive one of David's favorite Grateful Dead songs, "Black-Throated Wind." (David claimed that

Barlow and Weir must have written this song before they jumped too deeply into libertarian bullshit.) He probably wished, at some level, that he could have attended and enjoyed Burning Man. David was able to maintain seemingly contradictory elements in his thinking and his practice. He would never have been so naive as to see a realm of culture dissociated from ideology. But he was certainly fascinated by, and perhaps even "loved," aspects of culture, whether in music, writing, or film, in which he could identify dangerous, undemocratic strains of thought and through which forces exercised undemocratic control over human lives.

As a matter of fact, some of our first conversations in 1988 were about the Grateful Dead. It would be fair to say that he was my teacher about the Grateful Dead over decades of close friendship. I never heard him happier than when, a few years ago, he greeted me on the phone with the simple command "Listen" and played, with an aspirational fidelity, the rhythm guitar part of "Scarlet Begonias," a song we both loved. In later years he pursued things like playing the guitar and getting tattoos, neither of which he did when we met in graduate school. Indeed, in the weeks before he died David was still directing me to both obscure and famous shows—available through Archive.org, a robust repository that houses live recordings of Dead shows as well as hosting the Wayback Machine, which aims to ensure that web pages never die. Archive.org was the kind of digital tool on which David relied for information and entertainment. As skeptical as *Cyberlibertarianism* shows him to be about "free" things on the internet and tech's self-interested assault on copyright, he was happy to enjoy bootlegged recordings of the musicians he loved wherever he could find them.

I briefly met David Golumbia in August 1988 at the orientation for new doctoral students in the Department of English at the University of Pennsylvania. Two days later, we ran into each other in a stairwell in what was then called Bennett Hall, which was the department's home. A quick hello turned into one of the most compelling forty-five-minute conversations I have ever had, ranging from books to music to politics to personal matters. And pretty much every conversation I had with David from that day until our last conversation in August 2023, thirty-five years later, covered the same territory. I wouldn't be the person I am today without those conversations, which were endlessly interesting to me.

We both came to Penn planning to study eighteenth-century literature. David was fascinated with Daniel Defoe, who possessed an intellect and set of sometimes contradictory wide-ranging opinions and commitments similar to David's. Each of us chose Penn to work with John Richetti, whose brilliant *Defoe's Narratives: Situations and Structures* applied literary theory to Defoe's novels. David had done his first year of graduate school at the University of Michigan and then transferred to Penn. He didn't stick to the eighteenth century, and his path through the doctoral program was a bit bumpy. As his project developed—and by "project," I mean his broad intellectual effort to bring his research into linguistics, literature, digital technology, philosophy, and literary theory together with his deep personal and political commitments to both individual freedom and the common good—advisers shied away from working with him. His work wasn't exactly literary, but it certainly wasn't—well, it wasn't anything else, either. It didn't help that he knew a lot more about many things than anyone else in the department, including the faculty.

So here are things we talked about.

Music: I still have the incredible mixtapes he made for me. I've tried to translate some of them to Apple Music playlists, but there were many obscure post-punk tracks he acquired on vinyl that have never been digitized, so my playlists are at best a pale imitation. We went to see the Fall at the space that used to house Studio 54 in New York (incredible show), and we saw Neil Young (with Sonic Youth opening) kick off his set with an incredible rendition of "Blowin' in the Wind." David loved Bob Dylan and the whole Anglo-American popular music scene from 1960 to the present.

Books: Everything from novels and poetry to literary theory and the political journalism of the day, whatever the day was. David had read so much, and he had an uncanny knack for both understanding others' arguments on a deep level and combining those arguments with his own deep critique of the world. Despite being an impecunious graduate student, he bought books, all books, all the time. His apartment even then was filled with stacks and stacks of books.

Games: He loved computer games from the beginning and played them quite a bit. Although I never really played the games myself, he would spend quite a bit of time telling me about the games he played, including online games when they became available, including *Magic: The Gathering*, which he played online for hours and hours.

Movies and TV: David was ahead of the curve in loving television before the great series of the early 2000s. He watched situation comedies and drama alike, always finding what was funnier in the comedies than the shows themselves understood and what was ironic or tragic beyond the ostensible plots and situations of the dramas.

Although I believe I gained the most from them, our conversations weren't one-sided. What I lack in David's encyclopedic knowledge and analytical brilliance I might make up for in general competence at navigating the world, particularly academia. It wasn't my job to make David any different from the quixotic polymath who was continually shocked that people shared neither his intellectual abilities nor his moral and political commitments. That would have involved betrayal of who he was at his core. But I did take it as a responsibility (and a deep pleasure) to give him a bit of insight into the world as many (most?) people experience it. Was I helpful? I hope so. Was he helpful to me? Absolutely.

David knew *a lot* more than I did. When I got depressed because I couldn't understand a book bringing together Lacanian psychoanalysis and eighteenth-century philosophy, he patiently talked me through it—for hours. I grew dependent on his interpretations of the theory that we read together, and I took for granted his explanations of analytic philosophy and contemporary linguistics.

We talked quite a bit about computers back in the day when we both came to Penn lugging our Macintosh Plus desktop machines. He explained things to me along the way, from getting my first modem and using Gopher to find information (and look at early dating sites), to deeper forms of information as the World Wide Web got up and running. He had distinctive handwriting that I am convinced achieved some of its shape and clarity through an imitation of Apple's Geneva font (I was more a New York kind of guy). He was an early practitioner of computer art, which he pursued seriously along with the L=A=N=G=U=A=G=E poetry he wrote (and published) all while building his career in teaching and literary criticism.

David didn't find academic employment after finishing his studies. Instead, he moved to New York and worked on Wall Street as a software developer while his partner (and then spouse) Suzanne Daly pursued her PhD in the English department at Columbia University. His years working in software gave him additional knowledge about how computers had become indispensable, in sometimes uncomfortable ways, to culture and commerce. He began to develop a knowledgeable skepticism about what computers could and should (as well as shouldn't) do. He understood and appreciated the importance of the digital and was proficient in hardware and software alike; but throughout his life he adhered to the power and primacy of the analog. He wanted the real thing, whether in music or in people. He saw the digital not as a more faithful version of the truth, but as a sometimes-unhelpful translation of the things that make us human and give life meaning.

His career was precarious. He didn't stay in New York or in software development. Instead, he was hired to one of the first "digital humanities" jobs in the country, as an assistant professor at the University of Virginia. Virginia was home to important projects that brought together computers and the humanities, including archival repositories centered on William Blake and Dante Gabriel Rossetti. These were the kinds of endeavors he could get behind: he always saw himself as a critic and theorist, not as a zealot for the transformational change that computing might bring to what the humanities are and what they can do.

As digital humanities (DH) developed it betrayed its initial ethos of *serving* humanists through bringing new tools to our evergreen commitment to analysis and interpretation. David felt increasingly at odds with both DH and colleagues who became enthusiasts for technology merely because it could do things that seemed cool. The greater the claims for the ascendance of digital humanities, the more alarmed David became. DH scholars seemed happy to let the computers do the thinking, whereas to David the thinking was the important thing. At that time, he was working on his first monograph (largely unrelated to his doctoral dissertation), *The Cultural Logic of Computation,* published by Harvard University Press in 2009. The book's project was to demonstrate that computers were always cultural. Using tools from philosophy, linguistics, critical theory, and cultural studies, along with a deep knowledge of how programming actually works, David sounded a warning. Computers could not only be used for ill, but indeed in important ways are predisposed to do ill—to ourselves as individuals and to our communities, our culture, and our democracy.

The book alarmed his technophile senior colleagues at Virginia. They initially thought they had hired a fellow traveler who, with the greater practical knowledge he had developed, could help them pursue their DH dreams—and grants. When, despite the big Harvard book, he was denied tenure, he took it as a serious betrayal of the university's ideals. To be sure, he could be cranky, and he was never a "go along to get along" kind of person. But in the end (and he did understand this), colleagues who were committed to mainstream thinking about the wonders of technology and the future of the digital humanities fundamentally and forcefully rejected his analysis of computing and culture. Without their really knowing it, these colleagues were enthralled—as so many political progressives are—with the miracle of tech. Even if such people abhor Ayn Rand, they subscribe, implicitly and sometimes even explicitly, to cyberlibertarianism, the approach to technology that David explains, and rejects, in the pages that follow.

Over the course of his career David was equally frustrated with his fallible colleagues and his tyrannical universities. At the same time, he enjoyed being in academic communities and loved the full life of research, teaching, and service at the heart of a faculty career. He was hired at Virginia Commonwealth University, where he earned tenure and became a beloved teacher of both graduate students and undergraduates. While he was never an easy colleague, Catherine Ingrassia, his chair and then dean, gave him enough space to read, write, and think, while keeping him engaged with the department in meaningful ways. The symposium held in spring 2024 by colleagues and former students of David's at VCU was a revelation to me—not of David's intellect and care for others, but of how he made a profound difference in the lives of his students.

It was at VCU that David developed the big ideas that this book expresses so powerfully. In 2016 he published with the University of Minnesota Press an installment in its Forerunners series, *The Politics of Bitcoin: Software as Right-Wing Extremism*. Here David made a powerful intervention in the world, combining his deep academic and practical knowledge with a sharply pointed argument about not just the uses of but also the nature of cryptocurrencies. This short book continues to be discussed widely. Cheered by some, treated with contempt by others, the work allowed David to develop the voice that carried *Cyberlibertarianism*: knowledgeable, engaged, sometimes deeply polemical. *The Politics of Bitcoin* was not a mere academic exercise, nor is *Cyberlibertarianism*, despite its deeply serious research and argumentation.

As cynical as David could be about colleagues and institutions of higher learning, he was a true believer in the potential of academic culture and the idea of the university. He valued friends outside of academic life, but he found sustenance within the walls of academia, misunderstood as he was. Despite loathing the world of the digital humanities, he continued to participate in debates over its meaning, including in 2016 cowriting (with Daniel Allington and Sarah Brouilette) a remarkable piece for the *Los Angeles Review of Books,* "Neoliberal Tools (and Archives): A Political History of Digital Humanities," followed by an interview a month and a half later in the same publication, "The Digital in the Humanities: An Interview with David Golumbia." In 2021 he published an interview with Dorothy Kim, "Digital Humanities and/as White Supremacy," in *Alternative Historiographies of the Digital Humanities.*

David found community with a few colleagues at VCU but also with a much larger network across the country (brought together, of course, by the digital technology of which he was so suspicious). Like his beloved rescue pit bulls, David sought shelter and love. He wasn't a misanthropist. At the same time, he perhaps found that shelter and love more with his dogs than with his fellow human beings. Some of my favorite conversations in the past decade with David came during trips to Erie, Pennsylvania, home to Presque Isle State Park and its beach for dogs. He would call from the Red Roof Inn there, which he visited with Lucky multiple times per year, often while traveling back and forth to visit his parents, Art and Linda, as well as friends in his native Michigan. But sometimes he and Lucky would go to Erie just to get a break, so that Lucky could play in the Great Lake. Before Lucky, there had been Scout. His love for these dogs grounded him even when romance foundered, his career seemed stymied, or he wrestled with his personal demons.

Indeed, David had close relations with many friends, including myself. He also had loving relationships with many partners, including Suzanne Daly, to whom he was married for several years, and, at the end of his life, his very good friend Caren Freeman, who was at his side at the end. Indeed, it was Caren who worked with the University of Minnesota Press and me to secure his final assent to the contract that allowed this book to be published. Caren visited David in hospice. The nurses decreased for a short while his pain medications. She asked him to agree, with voice or a squeeze of the hand, to the contract that press editor Doug Armato, who has worked with David on this major project since his time at Virginia and through *The Politics of Bitcoin,* had sent him a few months earlier. David squeezed Caren's hand, perhaps his last conscious gesture before he died.

David would have wanted to acknowledge a few critical people and academic communities, including *boundary 2,* led by the renowned scholar and editor Paul Bové, a prominent intellectual who finally *got* David—not because their work was identical or even similar, but because Bové appreciated who David was and how David thought. David helped build *b2 Online,* and he cherished his relationships with the entire editorial collective at *boundary 2,* especially Hortense Spillers. He would also have wanted me to mention his beloved friend of many years, Lisa Alspector, and his collaborator and great friend in more recent years, Chris Gilliard. These are only a few of the people. David was known to so many, reflected in the fact that my post on X that David died has received, at this writing, more than 284,000 views: by far the most well-read (and likely well-appreciated) piece of writing I will ever produce.

I end with another mention of the Grateful Dead's "Scarlet Begonias." David and I talked about this couplet when I was sick with stage 3 rectal cancer from 2015 to 2016, and we revisited it in the weeks before his death:

Once in a while you get shown the light
In the strangest of places if you look at it right

For thirty-five years, David Golumbia showed me the light about so many things about our world, its culture, and its politics. Here, in *Cyberlibertarianism,* his magnum opus, he shares the light, writing with complexity and power about things he understood better than nearly anyone else: how software works; how language and culture work; how human beings deceive themselves, but more brutally deceive others, sometimes for profit and other forms of exploitation, at other times out of zealous adherence to delusional principles. There's a bit of both of those things in the right-wing ideology he associated with "computationalism" throughout his career and here explains in greater detail and deeper pockets of thought. He lived for his academic work, and I know he would have loved himself to contribute to the conversation, and the controversy, this book is sure to spark.

Tulsa, Oklahoma
April 6, 2024

Preface

The Critique of Cyberlibertarianism

From free and open-source software to free culture and "internet freedom"; from net neutrality to "censorship" to demands for unbreakable encryption and absolute anonymity: these and many other terms serve as rallying cries for digital activists from across the political spectrum. Raising questions about what the terms might actually mean, let alone what might be the arguments for and against the causes they seem to represent, is to stand in the way of progress. To oppose the favored position is to be idiotic, a Luddite, or morally inferior. Freedom and justice lie only on the side of the cause that advocates promote.

These claims should give those of us outside the hothouse of digital advocacy pause. Given the urgency with which digital enthusiasts tell us that projects like open-source software and internet freedom are vital political causes, it is odd that we find such a lack of detailed discussion of positions supporting and opposing them, or demonstration of the ways they fit into the rest of our politics. It is difficult, and maybe even impossible, to find complete descriptions of the various nuanced positions and their pros and cons in digital advocacy, as there are for other political issues. Instead, one finds work after work recommending just one position, or at best slight variations of that one position. These works often seem as if they are copy-pasted from each other, with very little interest in articulating the underlying and foundational questions that the topics seem to entail. Free software pioneer Richard Stallman's famous assertion that in "free software," "free" means "free as in free speech, not as in free beer" (2002, 43), is almost always taken to be clear and sufficient. Yet even cursory reflection will show that what the free software movement recommends has almost nothing in common with what "free" means in "free speech." Further, to the limited degree that software is analogous to speech, it automatically has the same protections as do other forms of speech. It is nearly impossible to find free software advocates reflecting on this or providing anything like the detailed analyses that would be required to connect free speech to free software.

While these topics are often discussed and promoted as political, their relationship to non-digital political issues and orientations is at best opaque. "Privacy," "rights," "free," and "freedom" are frequently repeated in the names given to these issues. However, it is often unclear how we should compare them to other non- or pre-digital uses of these terms. When encryption advocates demand that governments be unable to surveil or retrospectively examine electronic communications even with a legal warrant because of what they call "privacy," it is difficult to find any digital enthusiast reflecting on the fact that "privacy" has to mean something different in that context than it does in what lawyers, judges, and legislators use the term to mean.

This is because the term has rarely, if ever, been used in any prior democratic context to mean that law enforcement and legislators should never be able to serve properly executed warrants. It is not a matter of whether the encryption promoters were providing an accurate analysis, but rather that the fundamental questions regarding privacy, which have been debated in the United States and every other democracy for hundreds of years, are being ignored in favor of a dogma that prevents such discourse. Despite the fact that quite a few lawyers, judges, legal scholars, and democracies other than the United States take a different approach to this complex question, we hear repeatedly that everyone should be in favor of absolute freedom of speech. We believe we understand the principle of "freedom of speech," but when we are told that everyone should be in favor of more or less absolute "internet freedom" because it is "freedom of speech for the internet," or some similar formulation, these deep and abiding questions suddenly fall away.

"Cyberlibertarianism" is a term (introduced in Winner 1997) that scholars and journalists have developed to highlight and understand this phenomenon. Although useful, the term has potentially misleading connotations. The incorporation of the word "libertarian" may suggest that it is meant to point at the widespread presence of overt libertarian politics in digital culture. It does mean that, to an extent, but also points at a wider phenomenon that may not be immediately obvious from the word itself.

At its narrowest core, cyberlibertarianism is a commitment to the belief that digital technology is or should be beyond the oversight of democratic governments—meaning democratic political sovereignty. Frequently, the sentiment can be reduced to the view that democratic governments cannot or must not regulate the internet—or to flip this formulation on its head, that the internet should be a place to which laws do not (or cannot) apply. Even in this narrow form, cyberlibertarianism is openly self-contradictory. This is most visible in its alternation between the view that governments are unable to use laws to regulate digital technology and the view that governments must not be allowed to use laws in this way. These two ideas are incompatible. Despite this, many digital enthusiasts subscribe to this contradictory set of ideas as a core, unassailable principle, impervious to critical investigation. It has become an article of faith, the central tenet of both the most famous statement articulating what we now call cyberlibertarianism, John Perry Barlow's 1996 "Declaration of the Independence of Cyberspace," and 1994's "Cyberspace and the American Dream: A Magna Carta for the Knowledge Age" crafted by antidemocratic luminaries George Gilder and Alvin Toffler (who were working closely with Newt Gingrich at the time), which was the immediate spur for Winner's original cyberlibertarianism essay.

Since Winner's original analysis in the late 1990s, cyberlibertarian dogma has grown into a set of tropes and rhetorical strategies that shape public discourse. This approach discourages rigorous research into the nature of claims made and fails to ask who may benefit from the policies being proffered. In general, it does not support the work of deliberative democracy. It is a remarkable irony that tools advertised as promoting "democratization," the accessibility of knowledge, and the wide dispersal of information can be conjoined to a belief system that seems designed precisely to prevent the exercise of those values.

To call cyberlibertarianism a "belief system," is to give it too much credit. This implies there is a coherent body of doctrine available that can be articulated in terms of the grounding of its premises and the way its elements proceed from those premises. Cyberlibertarianism can claim no such coherence: many of its most cherished principles directly contradict one another, even when they can be specified in adequate detail, which they often cannot.

For example, the values of privacy (which might be the same thing as secrecy) and openness (which might be the same thing as publicity or transparency) are ones that, under various names, have long been discussed in a wide range of philosophical and political venues, from political philosophy to legal scholarship to jurisprudence. Thinkers across the political spectrum widely acknowledge that privacy and openness can conflict with each other in important ways. Maximum privacy would suggest that nothing is ever put out in the open, while maximum openness would suggest that everything must be. Sober thinking about these topics recognizes that both privacy and openness are important values. They may conflict with each other, and it is the job of politics—government, the citizenry, thinkers, judges, and lawyers—to carefully weigh these values and others like them in specific cases. While there are certainly cases that nearly everyone would acknowledge should be ruled almost entirely by privacy (a child's medical records—but should those records be available to emergency room doctors even without the parents' consent, to save the child's life?) and others ruled almost entirely by openness (legislative proceedings—but should that prohibit confidential discussion of diplomatic and military matters that are confidential matters of state?), the majority of cases fall in between.

In cyberlibertarian writings on these questions, answers are presented as obvious, unproblematic absolutes, even when they conflict with one another. Everything should be maximally private, we will read from them on one day; everything must be maximally open, we will read the next. There are no contradictions, digital evangelists insist: it is obvious that everything must be private and that everything must be open, and further, it is obvious where and how each of these contradictory principles apply.

Such assertions require more skeptical consideration than they have received until now. Non-dogmatists have every justification in demanding they be grounded in direct engagement with the foundational ideas that they seem to touch on the surface, while typically not doing so in practice. For example, they should explain how "democratization" intersects with actually existing democratic institutions and democratic theory. They should also push back on the idea that democratically enacted laws are somehow inapplicable when computers are involved. They should reject the notion of a radical break with all existing institutions and thought, coupled with the simultaneous assertions that all the hopes those institutions and thoughts represent are somehow being realized in the new disruptive digital ones as they gleefully attack and destroy existing structures and values built to promote them.

Cyberlibertarian dogma has a related but less visible effect that profoundly deforms the rest of politics. Despite the propagandistic assertions that open-source software, end-to-end encryption, and anti-copyright efforts are themselves profoundly political causes that also rise above ordinary politics, the activism and agitation around these concepts affects ordinary political concepts that most digital enthusiasts rarely talk about. These include the ability of capital to capture and bypass regulation; the relatively stable regimes of law and jurisprudence on which democracy depends; consent of the governed; many of the rights encoded in documents like the Universal Declaration of Human Rights (other than the hypertrophied version of "freedom of speech" championed by both digital activists and the far right), such as equality under the law and due process; and the very ability of democratic governments to pass laws to regulate economic activity. Thus one of the signal dangers of cyberlibertarianism is a kind of sleight of hand: we seem to be talking about one thing, but in fact we are talking about something far more important and consequential than our apparent subject. We seem to be talking about copyright, freedom of speech, or the "democratization" of information or some technology. But if we listen closely, we hear a different conversation that questions our right and ability to govern ourselves.

One of cyberlibertarianism's chief effects is to minimize or eliminate the power of democratic governments to choose which technologies fit their vision of a healthy society. In practice, this means quieting or altogether muting the voices of those who insist that democracies must have the power to decide which technologies are beneficial for their citizens. For democracy to mean anything, there must be actual political mechanisms (legislative, regulatory, and judicial) through which governments can exercise this power beyond the almost exclusively deregulated free markets that cyberlibertarianism advocates. Some versions of democratic oversight of technology take the form of abolition (Benjamin 2019; Selinger and Hartzog 2019; Stark and Hutson 2022); others, heavy regulation (Bracha and Pasquale 2008; Pasquale 2016, 2020) or licensure (Pasquale 2021). These approaches have been so thoroughly muted by cyberlibertarian discourse that many of us do not even appreciate that they are possible. Not only are they possible, but the future of democracy depends on the ability of citizens to reclaim that power from the companies and technologists that have so effectively undermined it.

Chapter 1 provides an overview of the scholarly critique of cyberlibertarianism. Chapter 2 delves more deeply into the history of the phenomenon, contextualizes it in terms of other right-wing political campaigns,

and demonstrates how it manifests in current discussions of digital technology. Chapter 3 explores in detail two of the most direct policy manifestations: the role of Section 230 of the U.S. Communications Decency Act
of 1996 and the promotion of so-called multistakeholderism in global governance. In chapters 4–6 I present cyberlibertarianism in its core rhetorical
functions: the deployment of tropes, comparisons, stories, and rhetorical
strategies that serve to shape and frame public discussion and governmental
oversight of technology. Finally, in chapter 7 I show how cyberlibertarianism has always been linked to far-right politics, how cyberlibertarian dogma
both creates openings for and directly supports protofascist and fascist politics, and how that dogma too often serves to obscure the far-right politics
of digital technology.

PART I

CYBERLIBERTARIANISM IN THEORY AND PRACTICE

The Dogma of Cyberlibertarianism

Langdon Winner, one of the world's leading philosophers of technology, coined the term "cyberlibertarianism" in his 1997 article "Cyberlibertarian Myths and the Prospects for Community." The ideas he expressed there were also developing elsewhere around the same time, including in a much-cited essay called "The Californian Ideology" by media studies scholars Richard Barbrook and Andy Cameron (1995, 1996). While scholars and other commentators use the label "Californian Ideology" as a near synonym for cyberlibertarianism, the first term can suggest that the system of thought only operates in California (or even only in the Bay Area), and thus risks confusion. A third work, *Cyberselfish* (2000) by Paulina Borsook, is a semi-ethnographic account by a journalist who was once a somewhat enthusiastic supporter of the digital revolution as a writer for the central digital utopian publication, *Wired*. In that book Borsook uses the term "technolibertarianism" in a very similar way to Winner's and Barbrook and Cameron's terms, but her term lacks the specifically digital connotations of the *cyber-* prefix. The term cyberlibertarianism continues to turn up with some regularity in scholarship (e.g., Chenou 2014; Dahlberg 2010), journalism, and social media. Although these terms are not used in other critical work, it still shows how right-wing ideas are deeply embedded in digital evangelism (Morozov 2013d; Schradie 2019).

Winner describes cyberlibertarianism as "a collection of ideas that links ecstatic enthusiasm for electronically mediated forms of living with radical, right-wing libertarian ideas about the proper definition of freedom, social life, economics, and politics" (1997, 14). The two prongs of this statement are crucial: on the one hand, an ecstatic enthusiasm for digital technology itself—something that is of course found pervasively throughout our culture, especially in Silicon Valley—and on the other, right-wing libertarian ideas about the proper definition of core terms like freedom.

CYBERLIBERTARIANISM

Winner writes that these views about digital–technological progress are too often characterized by a "whole hearted embrace of technological determinism. This is not the generalized determinism of earlier writings on technology and culture, but one specifically tailored to the arrival of the electronic technologies" (1997, 14). That technological determinism, typically framed as apolitical, insists that "the experiential realm of digital devices and networked computing offers endless opportunities for achieving wealth, power, and sensual pleasure. Because inherited structures of social, political, and economic organization pose barriers to the exercise of personal power and self-realization, they simply must be removed" (15).

It is this attitude toward the "inherited structures of social, political, and economic organization," especially the construal of them as "barriers," that characterizes cyberlibertarianism as a political force. This kind of language pervades the writings of not just overt right-wing figures like Eric Raymond, Paul Graham, and Peter Thiel but also those with nominally left-of-center political leanings like Clay Shirky and Yochai Benkler. These latter writers often take as given right-wing definitions of social freedom, the role of government, and the place of institutions, while occasionally paying what is mostly lip service to the political goals of non-libertarians. By doing so, they actively promote the idea that digital technology is irresistibly destroying our current social structures. We have no ability to preserve them, and these explosions are largely, if incoherently, good for democracy. Therefore, they recommend that we let technology take the lead: social institutions and governments can try to catch up, ponder, and perhaps adjust to what technology has done only afterward, if social institutions and governments continue to exist at all.

Many of the best investigations have studied how digital culture has tried to solve social problems, especially Fred Turner's *From Counterculture to Cyberculture* (2006a) and Adam Curtis's documentaries, especially his *All Watched Over by Machines of Loving Grace* (2011) and *The Trap: What Happened to Our Dream of Freedom* (2007). In these works, we see people who believe they are working toward "social justice" or a vaguely 1960s-inspired flower power vision of world improvement, but who become entranced by the "possibilities" of digital technology. They transfer their social beliefs into technological ones without careful reflection on whether these goals are compatible. One need look no further for an example of this pattern than to Apple cofounder Steve Jobs, whose pursuit of "insanely great" technology via the empowerment of individuals was marked by counterculture radicalism. Jobs's crowning achievement, the iPhone, might even be argued to escape certain typical limitations of commercial products and have some kind of socially beneficial effect. However, it is hard to see how these effects are much more than marginal. It is even harder to see why discussions of the prosocial features of the iPhone should preclude our talking about aspects of the product that may be antisocial or antidemocratic.

It is a huge leap from the social justice pursuits associated with the civil rights campaigns of the 1960s to the design, manufacturing, and distribution of one of the most successful commercial products of the twenty-first century. The iPhone primarily serves the interests of Apple's Board of Directors, senior executives, and shareholders. Further, the intense self-involvement and lack of engagement with the immediate social world, often thought to be predictable by-products of consumer technology, are far removed from the egalitarian values of the 1960s. From Jobs's perspective, the radical impetus of the 1960s to help the world by turning away from self and commerce, and toward other people and their needs, appears to have been warped into something that looks almost like its polar opposite. The situation would be less remarkable if there were not such a tenacious insistence on the continuity between the two projects, despite the obvious lack of fit between them.

The confluence of 1960s social activism and digital utopianism resulted in a profound shift whose consequences remain under-examined to this day. Built on top of the civil rights and antiwar movements, much of 1960s activism was predicated on the notion that democratic government is and should be the *primary* guarantor of social equality, in terms of both the rights of minorities (which pure majoritarian democracy will inherently fail to protect) and the attempts to realize through government certain principles found in the U.S. Constitution and Bill of Rights, as might best be understood via the Supreme Court's actions in the 1954 *Brown v. Board of Education* decision. This focus on equality has been a bedrock principle of left politics, ranging from the moderate insistence on voting rights and public education to the farther-left demands for economic equality across the board via communism. During the social movements of the 1960s, equality in its various forms was a hallmark that was hard to miss. It was, in fact, the natural target of many conservative forces that opposed such activism.

The personal computer drew early digital enthusiasts together, as they saw an easy alliance between egalitarian goals and the provision of technology (along with Turner 2006a and 2006b, Markoff 2005 is devoted in particular to the countercultural claims of the personal computer movement). Making computing power available to individuals, rather than confining it to businesses, the military, and governments, is certainly a step toward egalitarian goals. Steve Jobs, Steve Wozniak, Bill Gates, and Paul Allen are all exemplary individuals who used materials available at hand to empower not only themselves but other individuals in their milieu. That does not necessarily mean they understood the ultimate ends to which their creations would be put.

It is striking that cyberlibertarianism not merely enjoys but stubbornly insists on a countercultural, utopian social orientation while being, in seemingly contradictory ways, yoked to one of the most aggressive corporatist and deregulatory agendas in recent history. The imposition of that agenda—anti–social welfare, anti–civil rights, anti–New Deal—has resulted in some of the deepest economic and even social inequality seen in the United States, and to some extent worldwide, for at least a hundred years. The story of social liberation has been grafted onto the story of business success and innovation. The Silicon Valley marketing plan insists on its social mission even as it appears to work toward many of the precise oppressive political goals that the 1960s social movements emerged to combat. It has become difficult to disentangle the stories of "utopian social orientation" and "corporatist and deregulatory agendas" from each other: when critics emphasize that Silicon Valley promotes the business success attained by technology simply in those terms (and not projects of social beneficence), they are accused of extreme dystopianism and negativity. These accusations typically come from business executives and tech workers themselves, who, one might think, should be perfectly happy for their successes to be characterized in terms of business. Somehow, instead, Silicon Valley business success can't be just that: it has to be linked with a countercultural aim.

Yet the business interests remain paramount, aligning the ubiquitous spread of computerization with right-wing political aspirations. The values of computerization, and the definitions that inform them, characterize cyberlibertarianism, which becomes as notable for what it pushes aside as for what it embraces. Many people who are individually opposed to right-wing politics and political libertarianism find themselves advocating for individual rights and economic freedom and championing markets as the solution to social problems, as they fight against government regulation and defend the rights of companies like Google to do as they please, leaving behind public education, civil rights, labor conditions, the social safety net, and proper regulation of business. This is how cyberlibertarianism works: it is not so much about party politics as it is about controlling the terms of discourse and the conversation itself. This ensures that only variations in rightist political formations ever get on the table, and all concerns are subsumed under a general faith that digital technology will inevitably make things better, even if "better" is never precisely defined.

Barbrook and Cameron write that what they call the "Californian Ideology . . . simultaneously reflects the disciplines of market economics and the freedoms of hippie artisanship. This bizarre hybrid is only made possible through a nearly universal belief in technological determinism" (1996, 50). Along with that technological determinism—the belief that digital technology inevitably leads toward political progress—what binds the apparently disparate politics of cyberlibertarianism is an "anti-statism" that "provides the means to reconcile radical and reactionary ideas about technological progress." "The Californian ideologues," write Barbrook and Cameron, "preach an anti-statist gospel of hi-tech libertarianism: a bizarre mishmash of hippie anarchism and economic liberalism beefed up with lots of technological determinism" (56).

The context in which the mishmash occurs is one built and sustained by capital. Thus, even the apparently left and anti-corporate energies among digital utopians are easily diverted to capitalist ends, especially when these ends are not clearly labeled as such. As we shall see, movements like "open source," "open access," "piracy," "hacking," "open government," and even "free software" all have clear lineages in and ongoing connections to important pillars of right-wing political doctrine. However, they are often recommended as if pointing in the opposite direction—and advocates strongly resist efforts not just to describe these foundations, but to provide any foundational support for the doctrines at all.

Cyberlibertarianism is especially dangerous because, like other libertarian anti-philosophies, it speaks in the name of an individual or "negative" freedom that takes advantage of rhetoric based in values like democracy, rights, and equality while at the same time agitating strongly against all of the structures and institutions that democracies build to protect those values. For example, the term "digital rights" (see chapter 2) is one with wide currency in cyberlibertarian discourse. To the untrained ear, it may sound like it refers to advocacy for human and civil rights in digital contexts, and sometimes it does mean this. In its initial deployments, however, the phrase meant something entirely different: the idea that copyright and intellectual property should have different meanings on computers than off of them. It even carried the connotation that the "right" to obtain works of intellectual property without compensation to their creators was in some way aligned with human rights. The poster child for this movement was always Wikipedia, which has been portrayed as an unalloyed human good. However, the nonprofit organization that runs the site has consistently disparaged the idea that creators, especially academics, should have property interests in their work. Even academic treatments of "digital rights" (Herman 2013; Postigo 2012; see also chapter 2) offered little space to the view that *creator rights* might have any grounding in or relationship to *human rights.* To the contrary, the ambiguity in the word "rights" in this context consistently blurs the line between its narrow and legalistic meaning in terms of "ownership" of intellectual property versus its wider sense in "human rights."

Wikipedia and other nonprofits are often portrayed as the main beneficiaries of the anti-copyright movement, prioritizing the user interests of intellectual property (IP) consumers over the ability of creators to earn a living from their hard work. Pop music artists from Metallica to Dr. Dre who attempt to assert their rights to be compensated for work are often ridiculed in the name of a nebulous idea of the "rights" of listeners. Meanwhile, writers like Cory Doctorow, Lawrence Lessig, and others are celebrated for their thinly reasoned arguments about the selfishness of creators who want to be paid for their work.

It would be wrong to suggest that the legions of Reddit, Y Combinator, and X (formerly Twitter) writers attacking the interests of creators are willing participants in a nefarious plot to direct profits toward an unseen commercial entity, let alone one in which those individuals have a vested interest. However, the proliferation of arguments in favor of file sharing via torrent and other forms of "digital piracy" (Mueller 2019) suggest that individual interests in those materials do indeed play a significant role. It is also the case that companies that profit directly from IP belonging to others (especially Google and its YouTube platform) may be working explicitly to seed these discussions. Nevertheless, the ideology of "open" and "free" pervading these discussions is broader than the commercial or consumer interests of those who advance them.

This is part of why organizations like the Electronic Frontier Foundation (EFF), the Center for Democracy and Technology (CDT), and Fight for the Future that have direct histories with commercial entities are of such great concern, as are quasi-academic bodies with strong industry ties—like the MIT Media Lab, Stanford's Internet Observatory, the Berkman Center at Harvard, and the Data and Society Institute (originally sponsored by Microsoft Research). And these are only slightly more concerning than nonprofit organizations like Mozilla, the Internet Archive, Wikipedia, and the Linux Foundation, which have more distant relationships, even though corporate capital does use and profit from these resources. All these organizations and many others, and the many individuals informed by them, are characterized by their power to advance a dogma that exerts tremendous pressure against reasoned debate. "Open," "free," "democratize": who could argue against movements to which these labels are applied? Yet when such labels point in the opposite direction of the values they seem to name, we must demand a precise explanation of how they fit into more widely explicable articulations of those values. It cannot be enough to assert that there are things called "digital rights" and that, by dint of the sound of that term, they are part of "human rights." We need to understand if there really are direct, substantive, and meaningful connections between canons of human rights and the interests advanced in the name of "digital rights." Too often, the main function of cyberlibertarian discourse is to deflect demands to see clearly such connections by making such demands seem at least unreasonable, even ludicrous.

POLITICAL LIBERTARIANISM VERSUS CYBERLIBERTARIANISM

Cyberlibertarianism is not simply a combination of political libertarianism and digital utopianism. The specific point of this analysis of cyberlibertarianism is not that technology attracts people to join one of the libertarian parties, to vote for early 2010s Tea Party candidates, or to campaign against Democrats. Despite their association with cyberlibertarianism, these effects are not the ones this book aims to uncover. For the most part, political libertarians understand themselves to be libertarians and may even belong to one of the libertarian parties, vote for libertarian candidates, and so on. "Cyberlibertarianism" is not the name of a political movement or party; it is (with minor exceptions) a set of positions to which people knowingly subscribe, although usually without using that term. It is an *analytical* category: it describes widespread beliefs and practices that require investigation to accurately attribute to individuals.

Paulina Borsook's *Cyberselfish* (2000) provides the most trenchant discussion we have of the differences between cyberlibertarianism (or what she calls "technolibertarianism") and political libertarianism itself. She is explicit that her inquiry describes a phenomenon that goes far beyond what is typically meant by the term "libertarian." Borsook writes that "technolibertarianism manifests in two forms: political and philosophical" (10). Political technolibertarianism, already more specific than political libertarianism tout court, "takes the shape of a convenient obliviousness to the value of social contract and governance." Despite this, compared to ordinary political libertarians who identify as such, "technolibertarianism is far more of a political way of being in the world than an actual voting pattern." "Because of their conceptual dismissal of government," she writes, "technolibertarians typically can't be bothered to engage in conventional political maneuvers" (11).

In contrast to political technolibertarianism, what Borsook calls *philosophical* technolibertarianism is a "scary, psychologically brittle, prepolitical" phenomenon that "bespeaks a lack of human connection and a discomfort with the core of what many of us consider it means to be human." Because "computers are so much more rule-based, controllable, fixable, and comprehensible than any human will ever be," she writes, these philosophical or lifestyle technolibertarians "make a philosophy out of a personality defect." This is the primary political–psychological substrate out of which cyberlibertarianism is built; its very incoherence is what marks it as less a belief system and more an ideology that does not understand its own parameters and foundations. As Borsook writes:

If you were born in twelfth-century France you might be only half-aware of the ways that Christianity influenced every move that you made—and so it

is with the philosophical libertarianism in high tech. I can't count the number of times I've gotten into a discussion with a thoughtful sweet high tech
guy about something where he will snort disdainfully about how he's not a
libertarian (meaning, he's not like those crazy people over there) and then
will come right out with a classic libertarian statement about the el stewpido
government or the wonders of market disciplines or whatever. (15)

In no small part because it is not a designation of formal party membership, the distinction between philosophical and political cyberlibertarianism cannot be taken as fixed. This is why it is essential to understand
cyberlibertarianism as a set of ideological commitments and not as a coherent belief system. The actual voting political behavior of many who can
be accurately described as philosophical cyberlibertarians may map fairly
well onto those of ordinary Democrats or Republicans. Those same people
may spend a lot of time advocating positions on issues they see as "apolitical" or "scientific" without much awareness of how these opinions map onto
the political landscape.

The policy position called "internet freedom," is a prime example of this
phenomenon. Digital enthusiasts of all stripes champion it as the "digital
equivalent of the First Amendment," but it is actually a nebulous phrase
whose policy implications are no less clear than the principles from which
it is said to emerge. Major support for this policy comes from industry-tied
advocacy groups like EFF and notably from Google and the U.S. Department of State, which uses "telecommunications laws and information-
technology related exports to promote US political economic interests
around the world" (Powers and Jablonski 2015, 22).

Borsook suggests that philosophical cyberlibertarianism itself comes in
two distinct varieties (she calls them "cultural moieties, or perhaps sects";
15), which she calls "ravers" and "gilders." I view the distinction between
political and philosophical cyberlibertarianism as a spectrum rather than a
binary choice. Therefore it does not seem important to stick too closely to
either distinction in understanding how cyberlibertarianism continues to
operate. But as with the other distinction, Borsook's descriptions are both
incisive and instructive even a quarter century after she constructed them.

Ravers, she writes, "are neohippies whose antigovernment stance is more
hedonic than moral, more lifestyle choice than policy position. Keep your
laws off my body: Let's hear it for drugs, sex, and rock 'n' roll!" (15–16).

While the use of the term "neohippie" needs to be complicated by Turner's distinction between New Communalists and the New Left—in fact, there is a great deal of overlap between Turner's New Communalists and Borsook's ravers—it is easy enough to identify the sort of individual Borsook means to pick out here. In fact, Borsook gives us a specific individual as the exemplary raver, Grateful Dead lyricist and EFF cofounder John Perry Barlow, whose 1996 "Declaration of the Independence of Cyberspace" famously begins:

> Governments of the Industrial World, you weary giants of flesh and steel, I come from Cyberspace, the new home of Mind. On behalf of the future, I ask you of the past to leave us alone. You are not welcome among us. You have no sovereignty where we gather.
>
> We have no elected government, nor are we likely to have one, so I address you with no greater authority than that with which liberty itself always speaks. (28)

One notes the poetic, exultant register of these statements, which, despite being peppered with terms and ideas familiar in political libertarianism, nonetheless eclipses the more focused statements of Hayek or Nozick. The Declaration contains many statements whose rhetoric eclipses the practical sense that can be made of it, such as the idea that governments are "weary giants of flesh and steel," while cyberspace is made of some other, ineffable material. The florid use of metaphors and inexact characterizations of "governments" as opposed to the "us" who make up "cyberspace" helps to obscure the fact that Barlow's text, as media studies scholar Aimée Hope Morrison has written in a careful analysis, offers "an idealized but otherwise easily recognizable online version of liberal individualism" that can only be understood as something else through a "certain rhetorical violence, evidenced in the text by the wild proliferation of loaded metaphors and some tricky pronoun usage" (2009, 61). This aspect of "raver" cyberlibertarianism becomes critical for the ideology's success, as its very haziness and rhetorical power serves as a rallying cry especially for those who prefer to take their policy prescriptions in sweeping, programmatic form.

At the other end of the spectrum, Borsook posits a group she calls "gilders," named after the once prominent digital culture figure George Gilder, coauthor of another founding cyberlibertarian document, "Cyberspace and the American Dream: A Magna Carta for the Knowledge Age" (Dyson et al. 1994)—that Langdon Winner also analyzed in his foundational cyberlibertarianism essay. The "Tory leader of the *Wired* technolibertarian revolution," Borsook writes, Gilder is a "former Republican Party speechwriter and is a family-values Cotton Mather" (2000, 140–141) who shared with *Wired* founder Louis Rossetto an anti-feminist, arguably misogynist perspective on women's rights long before he found computers. (Borsook points out that he is "singled out for special vivisection in Susan Faludi's *Backlash.*") An ardent supporter of supply-side economics during the Reagan era, born-again Christian, and proponent of the creationist pseudoscientific theory of intelligent design, Gilder might be thought an odd figurehead for a movement that purports to be based in scientific and technological progress. Nevertheless, the profoundly right-wing nature of Gilder's overall belief system (in addition to Borsook, Gerard 2022 provides a thorough analysis of Gilder's more recent thought) turns out to be critical for understanding how cyberlibertarianism functions.

While many cyberlibertarians earn their livings from disseminating that dogma—including Jeff Jarvis, Clay Shirky, and Cory Doctorow, who make enormous speaking and consulting fees for spreading the gospel of digital disruption—Gilder deserves Borsook's special categorization for the ways his economic and political theories about digital transformation play transparently and even deceitfully into his personal fortunes. At just the moment he was being prominently featured repeatedly in *Wired,* Gilder was writing and publishing one of the leading technology-focused investment newsletters in the United States, the *Gilder Technology Report.* Investment newsletters exist in a contradictory segment of investment advice where it can be hard to reconcile the adviser's advertised expertise in investing with their preference for selling that advice rather than following it themselves. Such publications are often said to survive on the hype they generate to sell copies. Gilder was selling his advice at top dollar while at the same time hyping the radical success of technology firms as an ostensibly objective "forecaster." Of course, that top dollar was mostly available due to what is now called the "dot-com bubble" of the late 1990s, whose spectacular popping in 2000–2001 took Gilder along with it.

As reads a portrait of Gilder published in 2002 in *Wired* itself, after he and Rossetto, his strongest supporter, were no longer affiliated with the magazine:

For a short stretch during the late 1990s, Gilder's newsletter made him a very wealthy man. Anyone taking a cursory look at it might wonder why. Every issue is densely freighted with talk of lambdas, petahertz, and erbium-doped fiber amplifiers. The eighth and final page, however, explains how so geeky a publication attained, at its zenith, an annual subscription base of $20 million. It's on the back page that Gilder lists the stocks he has dubbed "telecosmic"—companies that have most faithfully and fully embraced the "ascendant" telecom technologies in which he believes so wholly and deeply. "For a few years in row there, I was the best stock picker in the world," Gilder says ruefully. "But last year you could say"—here, for emphasis, he repeats each word as a sentence unto itself—"I. Was. The. Worst." Most of the companies listed have lost at least 90 percent of their value over the past two years, if they're even in business anymore. (Rivlin 2002)

As his use of the nonce term "telecosmic"—also the title of one of Gilder's mid-1990s books—suggests, Gilder's stock picking was integral to his techno-utopianism. Many who follow "gilder" cyberlibertarianism share his crypto-religious view of technological progress—which must be reconciled with his anti-scientific beliefs in creationism, evangelical Christianity, and deep biological differences between the sexes—propelling humanity toward a transcendent climax. This end point was referred to as the "New Economy" in the 1990s, but it actually represented a self-interested belief in the overcoming of the forces typically associated with the word "economy." As Rivlin writes, the theory of the New Economy "that created its own set of rules represented no great leap for this man who was inclined to see history as the determined march from savage to enlightened being."

Gilder's peculiarities are themselves resonant for much of cyberlibertarian culture. But Borsook draws attention to him for his philosophical cyberlibertarianism, which may be at odds with the "raver" portrait more familiar to the general public. "Ravers," as Borsook sees it, are likely to attend the Burning Man festival, admire Timothy Leary, and spend a great deal of time fantasizing about sex, drugs, music, and video games when they aren't thinking about coding. Gilders, on the other hand, may well enjoy the sybaritic pleasures but tend to spend more time focused on how digital technology can directly increase their material wealth. They are social traditionalists (for the most part, perhaps with the exception of those places where such attitudes might interfere with their own enrichment) with politics "similar to those of the conservative branch of the Republican Party and are suspicious of the government for many of the same reasons" (Borsook 2000, 17; it's worth noting how different the "conservative branch of the Republican party" was in the 1990s from what it is today). No doubt, this description is similar to political libertarianism, but it is distinguished by its strong focus on economics, particularly the self-interested pursuit of wealth, over libertarianism as a political party or praxis. While gilders may identify as Republicans, they may also desire to move the party away from regulation. True political libertarians, such as members of the (former) Tea Party and Ron Paul and Rand Paul and their followers, identify as libertarians and are able to articulate the finer points of libertarian doctrine as political principles to which they attempt to adhere.

The strongest distinguishing factor between political and philosophical cyberlibertarians may be their propensity to identify as libertarian. One of the most powerful ways ideologies function is to obscure their deepest commitments and social functions in psychological and cultural clothing, so that adherents may have no need to—or may even be discouraged from—understanding their beliefs' true political effects. This is most evident in phenomena such as rightist attacks on "immigrants" as the cause of economic damage to the working class. It is possible that those who feel most strongly about their loss of economic power may be completely unaware of the ways in which they are being seduced into voting to empower the very people and institutions who are in fact responsible for that economic damage. While this is an especially deliberate and egregious example, the very propensity of philosophical libertarians not to grasp the politics to which they are committed is an important source of its power. People can declare themselves not to be libertarians but still consider the state to be largely a force for evil. They can consider labor unions nothing but a terrible drag on economic growth. They can work hard to develop or aggressively promote software systems that are built to bypass lawfully enacted regulations and democratic governance (as in the cases of sharing economy companies like Uber and Airbnb), and can work hard to deny governments the power to enforce laws on their citizens (via lawful surveillance) while raising nowhere near the same level of concern about private corporate power manipulating and surveilling people without hint of warrant and to far greater extent than government could ever even propose. This shows cyberlibertarianism's power as an ideological force. Many philosophical cyberlibertarians may support women's rights and gay rights and vote Democratic. However, their failure to see the political ramifications of many of their other beliefs only underscores the importance of identifying and enumerating them.

There is one more concrete reason to talk about cyberlibertarianism as a formation related to political libertarianism. Rather than being a clear set of principles, political libertarianism, except in the hands of its most sophisticated promoters, is not a coherent doctrine. This sets it apart from all major forms of democratic theory, as well as from the theories of monarchy and feudalism that democracy replaced. In those theories, relations of power and authority, though noxious to modern sensibilities, were at least clear. Libertarianism has often been characterized as something like an excuse for power: a set of myths propagated by those who have accumulated a great deal of power to themselves, and now wish to pull up the bridge behind them (see Haworth 1994). As articulated by its most fervent spokespeople, from Ayn Rand to Murray Rothbard to Hans-Hermann Hoppe, libertarianism depends on both prevarication over terms and false background presumptions about the nature of society.

DEMOCRACY: THE ENEMY OF CYBERLIBERTARIANISM

Barbrook and Cameron speak of "anti-statism" as a core philosophical foundation for cyberlibertarianism, which is fair enough. But it is also possible to understand the foundation as something closer to "anti-democracy," as it is democratic governance that cyberlibertarian dogma puts squarely in its sights. Although cyberlibertarian discourse occasionally criticizes authoritarian governments, it closely follows the anarcho-capitalist view that *all* governments are inherently authoritarian, regardless of their claims or the actual appearance of democratic consent. Of course political libertarianism speaks out of both sides of its mouth: it frequently claims to support some kind of abstract and better democracy while making its major target not just governments per se but democratic governments in particular. Political libertarianism marshals a group of stories, most deeply dishonest, about the nature of democracy. It uses words like "liberty" and "tyranny" to characterize political power in deceptive ways, relying on a willful misreading of the sociologist Max Weber. Weber wrote in a brief 1919 essay, "Politics as a Vocation," that "a state is a human community that (successfully) claims the *monopoly of the legitimate use of physical force* within a given territory" (2004, 33). Weber was largely trying to develop an account of state *legitimacy,* which is why the word occurs in the formula; he goes on to write that "the state is considered the sole source of the 'right' to use violence." Weber provided little argument or empirical evidence to support this novel definition, and indeed it has been challenged by more recent scholars (see Giddens 1985, 17–34). Nevertheless, Weber's statement persists as one of the most common definitions of the state, although it is typically presented in some version of the form given by anarcho-capitalists like Murray Rothbard: "The State is that organization in society which attempts to maintain a monopoly of the use of force and violence in a given territorial area; in particular, it is the only organization in society that obtains its revenue not by voluntary contribution or payment for services rendered but by coercion" (2000, 57).

All talk of "legitimacy" and "right" has been removed and replaced with a wholesale, a priori rejection of the basic premises of democracy. Government itself is "coercion" when it exerts control over economic activity. It takes only a few steps from this kind of unsupported assertion to the form found throughout online discussions of the state and government. For example, according to billionaire tech entrepreneur Elon Musk in 2021, "government is simply the biggest corporation, with a monopoly on violence and where you have no recourse" (Wolfe 2021). It is only natural to proceed from there to one of the pillars of far-right antigovernment and militia movement dogma: everything governments do is "violence," while actions by nongovernment entities are exempt from this categorization. That is, government is uniquely evil, usually based on some kind of recourse to natural rights or fundamentalist philosophy: Rothbard's essay is collected in a volume called *Egalitarianism as a Revolt against Nature,* which could not put his rejection of democratic politics more clearly.

To most supporters of democracy, the major difference between government power and other forms is that the former expresses (by proxy) the will of the governed, and that power can be checked by the members of a democratic polity. Political libertarianism is on its face committed to a conspiracy theory about democracy per se, in which it is always illegitimate and all its claims to popular sovereignty are automatically false. Supporting this position leaves the adherent in an uncomfortable position, making it nearly impossible to judge which claims to legitimacy or power can be taken seriously. If voting, representative deliberation, and input into public policy do not constitute legitimate democratic power, it is hard to see what could. Because political libertarianism is largely a conspiracy theory used by those who already have significant economic and political power to prevent democratic governance from limiting that power, it can produce no coherent account of what forms of power would be legitimate or democratic. It is no accident that at the edges of political libertarianism—such as the sovereign citizens movement, Christian Identity, and other forms of right-wing extremism (see Belew 2019)—we find massively contradictory appeals to an absolute authoritarian power, stemming from the purported absolute freedom of the individual.

Political libertarianism and cyberlibertarianism join in their antipathy for democracy. Nearly all the political causes on which cyberlibertarianism activism focuses have as their proximate target the actions or the very existence of democratic sovereignty. That cyberlibertarianism cloaks itself in the language of democracy while attacking democracy is in keeping with the ruse of political libertarianism. Since the advent of cyberlibertarianism and the rise of digital technology, we have witnessed a remarkable growth in antidemocratic propaganda and a notable weakening of democratic institutions and polities. Democracy is under attack as it has never been before, from the anti-vax movement that was already deeply destructive prior to the Covid-19 pandemic and became nearly genocidal in scope during it; climate change denial, "gun rights" in the United States, GamerGate, the Tea Party, and the full-throated conspiracism of QAnon; the Brexit and Trump elections of 2016 and the rise to power of fascist and protofascist leaders worldwide (Bolsonaro, Orban, Putin); and the Stop the Steal movement and the resulting January 6, 2021, attempted insurrection against the U.S. government. At every juncture, digital media and the political program of cyberlibertarianism have played decisive roles.

Antidemocratic movements have never been more powerful or influential worldwide than in the last decades, and not since World War II has democracy been understood to be so close to the brink of collapse (Appelbaum 2021; Snyder 2017), to be replaced by any number of authoritarian, fascist, and dictatorial forms of power, some of them explicitly invoking the monarchical and feudal forms of government that the democratic revolutions of the Enlightenment were thought to have permanently displaced. Despite its claims to promote "democratization," cyberlibertarian political power is directly implicated in these antidemocratic movements, insisting that democratic governance is impossible but at the same time that digital technology is providing "real" democracy. Of course, any attempt to ground those claims in existing theory about what real democracy is or should be can be dismissed out of hand due to the antidemocratic foundations we start with. Any claim to expertise or knowledge is rejected out of hand as less democratic than the alternative of "doing your own research," a libertarian-tinged slogan that means exactly the opposite of what it says. In the 2020s, we have learned just how vital to democracy it is for societies to have some mechanisms by which we develop some shared sense of what real history and real science and real knowledge look like, and how democracy relies on them for its very existence. Digital media tells us it is vital to that project, too, yet evidence continually shows us the opposite: that the institutions and methods we relied on for democracies to function are specifically what digital media destroys.

Few ideas are more contested than that of "right-wing politics." This is due to the moderate success of relatively disinterested scholarship, journalism, and activism, along with their overtly interested counterparts, which repeatedly expose significant gaps and contradictions in the very concept. Although the notion of right-wing politics depends on a meaningful split between the right and left wings, the term "right-wing politics" is not entirely identical with everything that goes onto the right-hand side of a right–left split. Despite not intending to do so, "right wing" can appear to gesture exclusively at the extremes of the right (in a way parallel to the connotations of "left wing"). Of note is the open question of whether what is typically described as "mainstream conservatism," or even more specifically as "Burkean conservatism," should be understood as right-wing politics. If we are drawing a binary contrast—as we often must in politics—between right and left, then Burkean conservatism falls on the right. But as the split between the pro-Trump (and pro–Tea Party) and anti-Trump factions in the U.S. Republican Party showed, factionalization and sectarianism are always possible within these high-level categorizations. The past few decades in the United States and the United Kingdom seem to have solidified splits that were only hazily visible during the regimes of Reagan and Thatcher. The extreme right wing came to dominate to the degree that what had once been the mainstream now became exiled almost entirely. It is no longer clear whether what we once called "conservatism" has much in common with "right-wing politics" at all.

Complicating these problems is one occasionally remarked on by political theorists but hard to ignore: the political theories of the Enlightenment, on which much of our current political understanding is based, were themselves ambiguous in specific ways, often deliberately, but have become lost to us over time. This is most especially true when we consider the idea of "liberalism," an overarching term for post-Enlightenment political philosophy that does not endorse one of the specific dissenting forms of politics critical of it, including Marxism and fascism. In the late twentieth-century United States, "liberal" became a generic term for left-wing politics that stood back from socialism or communism. At the same time, "economic liberalism" was a common phrase in international relations, referring to the expansion of free market doctrine and the relaxing of regulation. Although not exclusively, Republican administrations were more likely to advocate for this than their Democratic counterparts. In this sense "liberal" seems to point in two contradictory directions: toward the use of governmental power on the one hand, and against it on the other hand. Those associated with the Neoliberal Thought Collective and the Mont Pelerin Society (Mirowski 2009, 2013), the political actors furthest to the right, could berate liberalism as the very name for all that they thought was worst in society while describing themselves as "classical liberals." They often pointed at the same figures (especially John Stuart Mill) from whom those on the left might also take inspiration for specific purposes.

As in the case of trade liberalization, economic liberalism seems to point almost exclusively at capitalism as its goal, whereas political liberalism is far more interested in political freedoms and rights. To some of the founding theorists of liberalism like Adam Smith and John Locke, it might appear that capitalism and political liberalism go hand in hand, although read closely even these two thinkers express cautions about this equation. As Ishay Landa puts it:

> Liberalism was the socioeconomic doctrine with which the ascending European bourgeoisie of the late eighteenth and early nineteenth century challenged the nobility. It began optimistically, a "progressive" movement which

demanded political "freedoms," such as constitutional and representative government which, in turn, were seen as undergirding a market society emancipated from antiquated burdens of feudal and absolutist protectionism, mercantilism, etc. But in the course of the nineteenth century it became clear that the demand for popular representation is a political weapon that cuts both ways: wielded by the bourgeoisie in the name of the people against the aristocracy, it was effective in bringing about and consolidating bourgeois society. But once "the people" wished to dispense with their bourgeois proxies and speak and act for themselves, demanding, as a necessary first step, that the suffrage be universally extended, popular representation threatened to encroach upon bourgeois prerogatives and interests. (2010, 21)

As Landa explains, for Locke in particular, what we today call liberalism was not intended as an independent political formation: "The whole purpose of the liberal civil society from a Lockean point of view was to shore up nascent capitalist property and production" (22). "Rather than being limited by a political framework," Landa goes on, "liberal capitalism was in fact equipped with a built-in option to bail out of constitutionalism and revert to the rule of force, upon seeing its economic interests imperiled" (24). This resurgence of economic liberalism to displace democracy is visible everywhere today, especially in cyberlibertarian discourse.

CYBERLIBERTARIAN DOGMA: THE NARROW FORM

These grounding political commitments of cyberlibertarianism are rarely made explicit. Another set of beliefs and opinions is often stated in public, asserted as fact, and whose relationship to the underlying cyberlibertarian principles may not be obvious. These beliefs and opinions constitute the attractive philosophy that particularly captures young people as they encounter, contemplate, and use digital technologies. One of the more frustrating parts of digital culture is watching them be "discovered" over and over again, as if they are either complex conceptual problems the writer has just worked out, or startling new insights, rather than canards that can be found repeated ad nauseum in a variety of well-known writings. These surface cyberlibertarian principles include the following (for related though not identical lists of such principles, see Levy 2010, 28–34; Liu 2004, 242–51). Note that in many cases the words in these principles should be understood as more specialized points of dogma than literal terms of reference and thus deserve to be read in scare quotes:

- Everything in the world is being changed utterly, almost always for the better, by the advent of digital technology.
- Anything that existed prior to the digital needs total or near-total transformation.
- What existed prior to the digital was closed and private; digital phenomena are, in contrast, open and public.
- Digital technology democratizes; the internet is fundamentally democratizing.
- Everything can be or should be open.
- Information wants to be free.
- Despite the ubiquitous transformations created by digital technology, whatever is essential or important to any given phenomena will remain part of the transformed thing.
- Creators should have few or no ownership rights over the materials they produce.
- The internet is democratizing culture in a way that is just as profound as the impact of the printing press.
- Networked and peer-to-peer connections are distinctive marks of the digital.
- Networked and peer-to-peer connections constitute a fundamental transformation of human communications and social organization.
- People who resist any technological change or request any other means of regulating change than the one just mentioned do so only out of fear, jealousy, or lack of understanding.
- Widespread adoption and use of a technology is prima facie proof that the technology is beneficial.

It is remarkable the degree to which we find this set of beliefs—or dogmatic and vague articles of faith—coexisting in the same people, despite the many contradictions among them. This is true even when those people have little to no investment in the overarching issue except when it has a digital component. Further, it is notable how little what sounds like ordinary politics enters into these statements. The only nod at ordinary politics would appear to come in the idea that digital technology is "democratizing," which sounds like it should mean promoting democratic political systems over nondemocratic ones but does not.

Adherents cling to these propositions or slogans dogmatically, with little ability to articulate the reasoning that explains why they should be thought to be true. These ideas are assumed to follow from facts about the "computer revolution" that are so obvious there is no point in questioning them. And yet it is remarkable that these propositions need to be rediscovered on a regular basis, and each time they are rediscovered they are presented as entirely new. These include the obvious works by the nominally non-right-wing thinkers Clay Shirky, Jeff Jarvis, and others discussed below, along with books by right-leaning writers like Nicholas Negroponte's *Being Digital* (1996), Esther Dyson's *Release 2.0* (1997), and Glenn Reynolds's *Army of Davids* (2006). Similar to these but in some ways even more extreme are works like Jane McGonigal's *Reality Is Broken* (2011), Marina Gorbis's *The Nature of the Future* (2013), Eric Schmidt and Jared Cohen's *The New Digital Age* (2013), and the many works of Don Tapscott and his son Alex such as *The Blockchain Revolution* (2018), all of which repackage venture capitalist jargon with vague, depoliticized pronouncements about "revolution." Perhaps even more concerning are overtly left-leaning works like Violet Blue's *How to Be a Digital Revolutionary* (2017), Heather Brooke's *The Revolution Will Be Digitised* (2011), and Paul Mason's *Why It's Kicking Off Everywhere* (2012), which ground their political analysis in assertions about digital technology and the politics that emerge from it that were developed and are promoted by the far right.

In one sense, cyberlibertarianism as it is practiced across the political spectrum can be summarized into a single, paradoxical tenet: mass adoption of ubiquitous computerization produces social and political freedom. Therefore, in the name of freedom, this story goes, society has no choice about whether to exercise its power by any means other than markets (or market-like mechanisms). The greatest tool to produce freedom in our time, then, *requires* us to abandon all nonmarket forms of political power.

This tenet indicates the two primary reasons "cyberlibertarian" remains the best term for the phenomenon: first, *-libertarian* denotes "freedom," and computerization must be presumed to produce freedom; second, computerization itself is depicted as delegitimizing nonmarket forms of political power, which thus realizes a—perhaps *the*—central principle shared by libertarianism and neoliberalism. It is an article of faith that nominally nonmarket forms of choice found throughout the digital realm—free and open-source software, "copyleft" and other anti-copyright perspectives on intellectual property, and peer-to-peer and various forms of sharing—actually live up to the rhetoric of existing beyond or outside market-based choice.

Perhaps more important than the positive political points embraced by cyberlibertarianism are its negative points. These elements are rarely discussed in the context of digital media "revolution"; if they are addressed, they are dismissed with judgments that surprisingly echo those of the far right. Notably, these judgments are often accepted by individuals who may not see themselves as partisans of the political right, and may well even vote for candidates of the British Labour or U.S. Democratic parties. Many of these topics are notable for their absence in literature about the digital revolution, despite being common in discussions of related political subjects. Other topics are notable for the ease with which people who do not identify with the political right insist on obviously right-wing judgments (e.g., the destructive effects of labor unions).

Cyberlibertarian dogma requires treating activities that are understood to be conducted "online" or via the "digital" in a manner entirely different from the way they are treated in other facets of experience. We are led to believe that using computers to take certain actions is heroic, not the actions themselves. This less-than-explicit aspect of the cyberlibertarian dogma undergirds much of what passes for thought and informed inquiry, especially in online discussion forums. When a computer is involved, different standards apply. The use of the computer is itself heroic, inherently destabilizing to bad authorities and bad power, and requires no self-examination as to whether computer users are engaging in bad acts or serving those same authorities and that same power. Recently, members of certain online groups have taken on the role of law enforcement. These individuals, much like the Sovereign Citizens and other right-wing militia movements, begin their actions by invoking legal, constitutional, and ethical principles they believe other actors have failed to conform with. They then use tactics and principles that, if applied to society as a whole, would be among the least free imaginable.

Cyberlibertarian discourse is characterized by its dismissal of not only the practice, but the very idea that politics is a subject worthy of study on its own. Furthermore, the deep intellectual subjects surrounding politics and democracy are considered unworthy of study, let alone that one might want to study these subjects prior to actively engaging in attempting to change the political and governmental structures under which we live. Instead, "civic hackers" and others push forward, "doing" instead of "talking." They are sure that their unexamined ideas about core political concepts are so solid as not even to admit of analysis—despite the fact that most of us familiar with those concepts find that even on close examination their exact meanings and consequences are rarely transparent. Inherent in the "civic hacking" project generally and the "Code for America" project specifically is a shiny, well-designed optimism for "citizen engagement" with the levers and pulleys of democracy. These initiatives neither encourage nor require participants to familiarize themselves with the actual American system of government. Such engagement would impede the direct action encouraged by such projects. It is unsurprising that these movements, as discussed below, fail to achieve authentic political engagement, instead often disparaging the project of government and seeking to monetize public resources for private interests. This is usually done with the explicit proviso that such monetization should not be reflected back on government or the citizens responsible for the resource in the first place.

These projects are highly effective in steering public and civic impulses for private benefit through implicitly belittling political expertise. However, this implicit belittlement is overshadowed by the typically explicit disdain expressed by digital enthusiast communities for the social, political, philosophical, economic, and military expertise on which our democratic institutions rely. The self-identified "cypherpunks" routinely wax authoritatively on matters on which they have no background whatsoever, such as diplomacy, intelligence, military operations, and state security. Such lack of context might be excusable were they autodidacts who engaged deeply with the wide range of materials and personal expertise available on these topics; instead, they typically dismiss such knowledge with a variety of business-derived, conspiratorial rhetorical gestures involving "gatekeepers," "incumbents," and the like.

CYBERLIBERTARIAN DOGMA: THE WIDE FORM

"Cyberlibertarianism" cannot be understood as the name for a serious, coherent philosophical or political position. While some "proper" libertarians (or, as they often called themselves, "classic liberals")—Friedrich von Hayek, Ludwig von Mises, Milton Friedman, Robert Nozick, and others—might be thought to follow a consistent political philosophy, many contemporary self-styled libertarians, including followers of the Tea Party and other groups like it, do not. Figures like Murray Rothbard, Ron Paul and Rand Paul, Hans Herman Hoppe, and even contemporary economists like Tyler Cowen and Robin Hanson (who work at Koch-funded academic institutions; see Mayer 2017) are instead the products of deliberate corporate and oligarchic manipulation of people and their thoughts. This is done in the interests of the richest and most powerful members of society, without regard for the truth or coherence of their claims.

Some of the tenets of political libertarianism that occur with surprising frequency in most discussions of digital technology include the following:

- Government is illegitimate.
- Democracy is a fraud.
- Companies and the market are better guarantors of human rights than are democratic governments.
- Equality of outcomes is an entirely illegitimate goal to pursue.
- Power in society is largely distributed through merit.
- Technology and commercial power are essentially outside of politics.
- The world as we have it is politically "neutral"; "bias" is attributable to "bad actors" whose influence can be uprooted via more neutrality.
- Government is inherently far more destructive—and even "evil"—than commercial or financial power can ever be.
- The "mainstream media" cannot be trusted at all.
- The real, exposed existence of secret government programs means that all information associated with "government" can be discounted as propaganda.

Cyberlibertarianism is a part and product of what some have called the "post-fact" or "post-truth" society, where maintaining consistency for the sake of rallying one's political constituency is no longer necessary. The climate change denial movement is the most well-known and effective example of the post-fact society. Despite glaring inconsistencies and incoherence, partisans continue to advance completely ludicrous positions. These points appear entirely ungrounded in fact, reason, or previous thought, but always conveniently promote points of view that harmonize with the moneyed backers of the movement. More diffuse, but just as poisonous, are the multiple blatant contradictions among the Tea Party and its allied extreme right-wing political factions. The ideas promoted by the movement—such as the health insurance legislation known as "Obamacare," the theory of the "unitary executive," the constitutional philosophy of "judicial restraint," the notion that it is treasonous to question the judgment of a president during times of war—can be turned on their heads or altogether ignored when they no longer serve.

Cyberlibertarianism is different from the Tea Party and climate denial in that it is not directly and specifically articulated by right-wing funding bodies like the Koch brothers, Richard Mellon Scaife, Karl Rove, and others. It is also not primarily concerned with the nuts and bolts of legislation and executive policy (although it is more interested in these than may seem obvious at first). Where climate denial and the Tea Party require a great deal of priming to function, cyberlibertarianism in many ways runs on its own power. Cyberlibertarianism works by processes of identification and attraction, in part because it does not appear to be constituted as a force contrary to views which have widespread social support.

Cyberlibertarians (with few exceptions) do not refer to themselves by that name; there is (as yet) no political movement that calls itself cyberlibertarianism. Cyberlibertarians do not have to advertise their wares with great specificity. And unlike the case with the Tea Party and climate denial, the borders of cyberlibertarianism do not have to be policed. Nevertheless, for all its viral amorphousness, cyberlibertarianism is widespread, distinctly powerful, unified despite its deep incoherence, and committed to its core (contradictory) principles. However, like the Tea Party and climate denial, when it comes down to money, cyberlibertarians almost always end up on the side of those with the most access to and most investment in tools of power.

There is one notable exception to the lack of self-identified cyberlibertarians: a pamphlet produced by the Technology Liberation Front, whose name itself points at the movement's faux-populist politics. The organization is a project run by Adam Thierer, an affiliate and executive at several of the furthest-right lobbies and academic centers in the United States, including the Heritage Foundation, the Cato Institute, the Federalist Society, and the Mercatus Center at George Mason University. Along with another right-wing technology activist, Berin Szóka, Thierer wrote "Cyber-Libertarianism: The Case for Real Internet Freedom," which grounds cyberlibertarianism in the same genealogy provided by Winner and others: Austrian economists (Hayek, Mises, Rothbard, Sowell), other anarcho-capitalists (Friedman, Rand, Nozick, Epstein), and technology promoters (de Sola Pool, Toffler, Gilder, Negroponte, Barlow, even Section 230 defender Eric Goldman; see chapter 3) (Thierer and Szóka 2009). Thierer and Szóka contrast these cyberlibertarians with those whom, following very typical far-right discourse, they term "cyber-collectivists," including Lawrence Lessig, Tim Wu, Yochai Benkler, Jonathan Zittrain, the Berkman Center, and New America. They then provide the usual quotations from Barlow, Gilder, and so on, but fail to note that those they call "cyber-collectivists" endorse most of the same principles of "internet exceptionalism" (here, used to mean that the internet is or should be ungovernable) that they claim characterize cyberlibertarianism. This typology is not exactly coherent, but that is typical of most species of libertarianism, which function as excuses for the accretion of concentrated power rather than coherent political theories.

Indeed, this incoherence in the service of power is what marks cyberlibertarianism *as* species of libertarianism, and libertarianism as a whole is perhaps the most striking example of Philip Mirowski's (2013) "shells" or "Russian dolls" in right-wing political discourse (see chapter 2). Despite appearing to be a "grassroots" movement, U.S. libertarianism is directed by "inner shell" figures like the Koch brothers. Evidence suggests that the Koch brothers are more identifiable as neoliberals than as libertarians. However, they support and stoke movements like the Tea Party because of the way those groups lubricate U.S. politics for neoliberal policies. The Kochs use the nationalism, populism, and other social issues important to nonwealthy Americans to create affective cultural attachments to the political–economic doctrine they actually endorse.

In fact, they only agree on a few fundamental points, but these points are important to those in the "inner shell." Such agreement provides the explanation for neoliberal support and promotion of libertarianism. In particular, there is hostility toward government itself as an expression of democratic will. More specifically, the shared view is that the most important expression of "individual freedom" is found in the individual's ability to profit. All attempts to interfere with that profit, from antitrust enforcement to taxes to environmental and workplace safety laws, must be opposed because they are affronts to "freedom."

Neoliberals don't care much about freedom of expression, gay marriage, privacy, or even Obamacare. They know that these highly emotional issues add fuel to the fire they do care about, which is the one that views government as "the problem." This view doesn't oppose government in toto, but instead promotes the virtual ownership of government by for-profit, "free market" interests. These entities engage in large-scale projects of wealth redistribution and social engineering, of which radical inequality is not merely an inadvertent product but the implicit and sometimes explicit goal.

Again, it is less the obvious, interested advocacy of right-wing politics by openly libertarian figures like David Friedman, Peter Thiel, or Eric Raymond that is of primary concern here. Instead, the same pro-business, anti-government perspectives inherent in discourse of "the digital" are subtly embedded within broader right-wing ideology. In this respect, cyberlibertarianism is best understood as a magician's trick. The magician directs the audience to look at one hand, which usually holds a flashy object or performs some kind of dramatic action. Meanwhile, the magician carries out the mechanics of the trick with their other hand, while the audience is distracted. In cyberlibertarianism, the hand holding the flashy object is our talk about digital technology; the other hand, to which nobody is paying attention, is doing the work.

This analogy is a bit misleading, though, because it implies a level of willfulness on the part of those expressing cyberlibertarian beliefs. Such individuals may not ever understand the nature of what they are doing. They are focused on the digital object, program, app, or event and therefore do not see that it is not really doing the work it appears to be doing. They rarely notice that how they refer to core values like "freedom," "equality," and "democracy" may no longer resemble the way they used those terms before.

The analogy is also misleading because it suggests there is somebody who is consciously guiding the whole presentation. That is, neither Jeff Jarvis nor Clay Shirky acknowledges the ways they substitute discussion of digital technologies for discussions of the core values they seem to be talking about; and neither one of them receives direct orders from Karl Rove, the Koch brothers, Peter Thiel, or Eric Raymond to put one over on their audiences (although, to be fair, both Jarvis and Shirky do receive a fair amount of money from the very corporate sources that benefit from cyberlibertarian practices).

This is what makes cyberlibertarianism more dangerous than overt libertarianism informed by digital technologies. At least when Peter Thiel or Elon Musk speaks, audiences can be clear about what politics they endorse and what policies might emerge from them. More careful attention needs be paid to writers like Jarvis, Shirky, Doctorow, and other promoters of "internet freedom," "digital liberation," "liberation technologies," and "Twitter revolutions." These voices tend to allow descriptions of technology to overwhelm and displace discussions of the politics they appear to be describing. This lack of close attention to politics results in either a lack of resistance or an explicit acceptance of identifiably neoliberal prescriptions for governments, society, and the economy.

The neoliberal agenda is no secret. Critics from the political left have been exploring this idea for decades, particularly in the 1990s and since 2000. It is also evident in the writings and speeches of far-right political thinkers and politicians. This idea has its roots in the work of Friedrich Hayek and Ludwig von Mises, who participated in the Mont Pelerin Society (Mirowski 2009). It resurged in the philosophy of Robert Nozick in the early 1970s and the practices of Chicago School economists like Milton Friedman beginning in Pinochet's Chile in 1973. The idea was most notably put into practice in the West by Ronald Reagan in the United States and Margaret Thatcher in the United Kingdom in the 1980s. Both leaders steered their countries in an economic direction that had been considered too far to the right for any reasonable democracy to follow just a decade earlier. The profound change in political outlook is exemplified by the transition from Abraham Lincoln's 1863 Gettysburg Address, which describes the American system of government as "of the people, by the people, for the people"—"by," notably, entailing that the U.S. system of representative democracy means that in a legal and political sense government *is* the people—to Ronald Reagan's first inaugural address in 1981, where he famously stated that "government is the problem." At the time it was little noted—because it was hard to believe it could be true—that Reagan represented a doctrine according to which "government," meaning "the people," could be "the problem" in a democracy, and that this formulation could be acceptable from an elected president, let alone be seen as a welcome articulation of political principle.

Cyberlibertarianism functions as a less explicit outer shell of neoliberalism. Unlike political libertarianism, it has few overt proponents. Its supporters tend instead to rally around specific terms like "free" and "open," "internet freedom," and "copyright monopolies." Their concerns appear neither nationalistic nor especially populist; they sometimes embrace a far more progressive social agenda than do libertarians. Yet on the matters about which adherents are most likely to have significant political impact, cyberlibertarian doctrine is identical with those points of contact between neoliberalism and libertarianism: Government is the problem. It is incompetent and illegitimate. Attempts to ensure "equality" other than via the invisible hand of the market are automatically the same thing as Soviet-style social planning (a theme directly out of Hayek's 1944 work). Government should stay out of the way of "digital innovation," whether that means enforcing the copyrights of legitimate creators or interfering with the "disruptive innovations" of "sharing economy" startups like Lyft, Airbnb, and Uber or the massive rewriting of world legal frameworks undertaken by Google. Public goods are there for the taking and are best seen as resources for profitable enterprises to exploit. Law itself is largely illegitimate, and "digital natives" could do a better job—thus producing the bizarre, anarchic paradox that the world would be more lawful if there were no rules to follow.

As with libertarians, the powerful neoliberal interests aligned with the most concentrated and unequal exponents of capital do not actually care about the specifics of cyberlibertarianism. But they care a great deal about its main pillars, which "just happen" to be identical with their program of "structural adjustment" and forced privatization of public goods. Finally, but just as important, labor, in particular organized labor, is the enemy of freedom—because "freedom" means the freedom of capitalists to concentrate and maximize profits. Even basic forms of labor organization are viewed as redistributionist class warfare, while neoliberal "shock doctrine" techniques are seen as promoting freedom, despite extracting public resources and wages from the lower classes to enrich those who already have much more than the rest of us.

A notable imbalance in digital discourse is the conflict between governmental and private entities regarding abrogations of rights, particularly the right to privacy. For employees of corporations, in no small part due to digital technology, nearly all the putative benefits of cyberlibertarian utopianism are overturned. As a general rule, employees have few rights to privacy or free expression; are subject to complete, invasive surveillance; have no ownership over their work products; and, thanks to pressure against labor laws, often have little legal recourse for mistreatment. Sometimes employees even lose the right to sell their skills in the marketplace when separated from their employer. They have little or no input over the capitalist owners of the enterprise offshoring significant parts of the company's labor needs to cut costs, as is famously the case with virtually all the resource procurement and manufacturing associated with digital technologies. Yet much of the promotion of "digital rights" ignores most of these issues, while magnifying the issue of "government surveillance" as the signal evil of our times.

CYBERLIBERTARIANISM IN PRACTICE I:
THE CAMPAIGN AGAINST SOPA AND PIPA

One of the most prominent examples of cyberlibertarianism in action is the activism against the SOPA and PIPA U.S. legislation in the early 2010s. PIPA—the PROTECT IP (Preventing Real Online Threats to Economic Creativity and Theft of Intellectual Property) Act—was introduced to the U.S. Senate by Patrick Leahy (D-Vt.) in May 2011; the related SOPA—the Stop Online Piracy Act—was introduced to the U.S. House of Representatives in October 2011 by Lamar Smith (R-Tex.). Both were intended, according to their sponsors, to protect the economic rights of content creators to profit from their work. The bills were explicitly pro-business and, to start, enjoyed wide bipartisan support. PIPA was eventually cosponsored by forty senators from both parties ("PROTECT IP Act" 2020); SOPA had over thirty bipartisan sponsors ("Stop Online Piracy Act" 2020). As their names imply, the bills were intended to "provide law enforcement and rights holders with an increased ability to protect American intellectual property" (Leahy 2011). The legislation was designed to address unauthorized distribution of copyrighted materials, including films, videos, and computer games, as well as counterfeit consumer goods. These issues were considered significant problems by both individual creators and businesses that rely on the sale of their products. Initially, the bills had broad support from the motion picture production companies, their lobbying arms, producers of consumer products that were being heavily counterfeited, and the labor unions representing workers in those industries. Groups as varied as Ford Motor Company, Nike, the Better Business Bureau, the U.S. Chamber of Commerce, the American Federation of Musicians, the Directors Guild of America, and the National Basketball Association voiced their support ("Stop Online Piracy Act" 2020).

The nature and intensity of the eventual opposition to SOPA/PIPA is remarkable, as is the fact that it was easily portrayed and understood as a grassroots, democratic, and even "progressive" movement. Opposition to SOPA/PIPA was widely seen as the "little guys" against the "copyright behemoths," and as such, a movement against corporate profiteering and illicit exploitation. Even then, it was clear that such resistance was part of a corporate-funded and coordinated campaign conducted by the largest technology monopolies, especially Google, Facebook, Twitter, and others, along with their lobbyists. These companies share a direct commercial interest in exploiting creative labor for their own profits. All of them, especially Google (via YouTube), routinely feature and profit from copyrighted material without compensating the rights holders—and did so even more brazenly when SOPA/PIPA was a live issue.

Despite Google's involvement, even today most commentators consider the defeat of SOPA/PIPA to be a demonstration that "the familiar left–right, single-axis paradigm sometimes breaks down, frequently so in the civil liberties and Internet freedom space" (Segal 2013, ix). Moreover, this is seen as a politically emancipatory development that does not require examination of the political science behind claims that "the familiar left–right paradigm breaks down" (since this is almost always a claim associated with fascism; see chapter 2) or that civil liberties advocacy does not always follow the liberal–conservative divide.

The volume of internet-based activism generated against SOPA/PIPA was remarkable. While some of the activism opposed specific provisions of the bills, a far louder chorus of voices declared that their passage would "end the internet as we know it," one of the hallmarks of cyberlibertarian dogma (again, see chapter 2). This activism far surpassed the actual content of the bills. Aggressive, self-righteous, and certain, activists imputed to legislators a host of conspiratorial motives. Perhaps most famously, Wikipedia imposed a "blackout": "The English Wikipedia blackout occurred for 24 hours on January 18–19, 2012. In place of articles (with the exception of those for SOPA and PIPA themselves) the site showed only a message in protest of SOPA and PIPA asking visitors to 'Imagine a world without free knowledge.' It is estimated in excess of 160 million people saw the banner" ("Stop Online Privacy Act" 2020).

Yet in truth, the claims of the activists were at best overstatement and at worst outright disinformation. Since the two bills had not yet been reconciled, let alone passed, any assertions about what they *would* do were highly conjectural. In the ordinary process of legislation, real concerns would have been considered during the later stages of bill drafting. Wikipedia's threat that the bill's passage would have led to its blackout was dishonest. This claim was not the intended effect of the bill, and if it were likely, the legislation would have been redrafted to fix the problem. Several organizations, both commercial and noncommercial, threatened to or did participate in similar blackouts. Along with many individual activists, the widespread consensus was that SOPA/PIPA were part of a desire by the evil "government" to "censor" the internet.

These "hyperbolic mistruths" (Sherman 2012) misrepresented not just the contents of the law but the intentions of the legislators. They made it impossible to ask what should have been important questions: "When the police close down a store fencing stolen goods, it isn't censorship, but when those stolen goods are fenced online, it is?" (Sherman 2012). They repeatedly referred to something conspiratorially called "copyright monopoly" and the "copyright industry," imputing illicit motives to copyright holders, as if their pecuniary interests in the law were not abundantly clear on the surface. Cui bono? is always a central question to ask with any law or regulation. Yet the vehemence of their rhetoric and performative activism prevented them from being asked the question of who benefits from the relatively easy use of copyrighted material without paying royalties. Who benefits from the sale of counterfeited goods?

These questions were almost off the table, even though their answers happened to align exactly with the interests of those stoking the protests. This is easy enough to see in the commercial sector. At the height of the controversy, for example, Google's public policy director Bob Boorstin said, "YouTube would just go dark immediately" (Pepitone 2012). Although Senator Patrick Leahy, the legislator who introduced PIPA, stated that websites like Wikipedia and YouTube would not be subject to the provisions of the bill, it was clear that major commercial interests were concerned that this legislation would cut into their profits. In a characteristic trick of cyberlibertarian propaganda, even the sponsors of the legislation, along with its plain text, were rejected as authorities about its meaning—even though U.S. courts often refer to statements by legislators to determine ambiguous parts of the meaning of a law.

While the SOPA/PIPA protests were widely promoted as triumphs of the "digital commons," they are better understood as triumphs of the propaganda machine surrounding digital technology companies. Google was found to be heavily involved in generating and encouraging digital activism against not just SOPA/PIPA, but also against any attempt to rewrite them in order to avoid any real problems that might have been present in the bills. Many of the apparently grassroots "digital rights" organizations, including EFF, CDT, and Fight for the Future, were involved as well. Beyond these players, a surprisingly wide range of activists joined in. As journalist Yasha Levine put it:

> Facebook, Yahoo, Amazon, eBay, Mozilla, Reddit, PayPal, Twitter, and scores of smaller tech companies went into battle mode to oppose SOPA and PIPA. They framed the legislative dispute as a fight between freedom and totalitarianism and launched a frenzied public relations and lobbying campaign to kill the laws. The overheated rhetoric of the anti-SOPA tech moguls resembled nothing so much as the take-no-prisoners agitprop of the National Rifle Association—right down to the claim that, even if a regulatory curb on the criminal abuse of tech platforms were to pass, it would prove useless in execution and enforcement, just as Wayne LaPierre and Oliver North insist that curbs on untrammeled gun ownership would do precisely nothing to curb determined criminals from flouting such regulations. (2018a)

All of this might be less problematic if it had been clear just what the activists wanted. Google, Facebook, Yahoo, and others would certainly be affected by governments scrutinizing their business practices, which has become more apparent since SOPA/PIPA. Yet the aims of nominally non-industry activists is less clear, because what they rallied around was demonstrably false—a pattern that has continued to haunt nearly every effort by democracies to constrain the power of digital technology. David Newhoff, a filmmaker and copyright activist who has emerged as one of the leading critics of digital astroturf, wrote that it was fair to compare "the belief that SOPA threatens free speech with a belief in healthcare death panels; and I am more than willing to insult my friends to make the point. Both fears are irrational, both fears have been ginned up and funded by corporate interests, and both fears lead the electorate away from a sober effort to address a tangible problem" (2012). The outrage about "censorship" and against "copyright monopolies" was shouting about something that was unlikely to happen.

David Lowery, musician and copyright activist, suggested to Levine in 2018 that groups like EFF and Fight for the Future are, in Levine's words, "Silicon Valley front-groups that masquerade as edgy and enlightened defenders of freedom on the internet." Lowery told Levine, "They're spreading the hyperbolic claims and outright misinformation that Google and other Silicon Valley firms can't be seen to be spreading"; as Levine put it, "their funding structure is designed to obfuscate Silicon Valley's involvement" (Levine 2018a; see also Tech Transparency Project 2017a, 2017b).

Internet activism is not as coordinated and funded by dark money as climate change or tobacco denialism, but it is still a significant political force. It is a force that is not fully aware of the world it claims to understand, and Google and Facebook have learned to use it to their advantage. As one commentator put it during the SOPA/PIPA blackouts: "What the Google and Wikipedia blackout showed is that it's the platforms that exercise the real power. Get enough of them to espouse Silicon Valley's perspective, and tens of millions of Americans will get a one-sided view of whatever the issue may be, drowning out the other side" (Sherman 2012).

The frenzied attacks on SOPA and PIPA represent an extreme of cyberlibertarianism in action but also a clear example of how the dogma works. There are to this day many activists who feel they defeated "censorship" or "totalitarianism," but they cannot provide any thoughtful grounding for those claims in the underlying political thought or actual facts that those terms designate. They will argue that this kind of activism indicates some kind of higher political cause that can't be summed up in left–right thinking. Despite the fact that SOPA and PIPA were unusually bipartisan to begin with—the real form of cooperation in democracies—their defeat served the interests of some of the world's most powerful actors whose products and platforms have been consistently implicated in tearing at the fabric of democracy itself.

CYBERLIBERTARIANISM IN PRACTICE II: FACEBOOK AND META

No organization is more emblematic of cyberlibertarian agitation than Facebook, which rebranded in 2021 as Meta. CEO Mark Zuckerberg is known for his reserved stance on politics, unlike other technology CEOs and venture capitalists with overt right-wing political profiles like Peter Thiel, Elon Musk, Marc Andreessen, Balaji Srinivasan, Larry Ellison, and Travis Kalanick. Journalists have characterized Zuckerberg as a liberal (Burns and Haberman 2013), and conservative activists, journalists, and politicians have done the same (Riccardi 2021; Tenney 2021; Williamson 2021; Yates 2020). However, groups with liberal or left leanings, including employees inside the company itself, have seen both Zuckerberg and the platform as far too accommodating toward Republican and right-wing causes (Lee 2016; Newton 2020; Seetharaman and Glazer 2020). Zuckerberg has claimed that he is neither a Democrat nor a Republican (Murse 2020; Seetharaman and Glazer 2020) and instead leans toward a political syncretism (see chapter 2). However, he appears to be unwilling or unable to reflect on the history and location of this syncretism within political science.

When pressed on his political opinions, Zuckerberg characteristically responds with crafted remarks about the "neutrality" of platforms and invokes core cyberlibertarian tropes. "I'm pro–knowledge economy" he said in 2013, in a statement that tacitly endorses the right-wing reconfiguration of social and cultural phenomena into free market terms. Zuckerberg frequently references "community" and "connection" in both public and internal corporate communications, without situating these ambiguous, value-laden terms in a more ordinary political frame (Hoffmann, Proferes, and Zimmer 2018; Rider and Wood 2019). This is especially relevant to criticisms of Facebook that focus on the platform's rebukes to and destructive impact on democracy. In later years Zuckerberg's own discourse has tended to concentrate on the importance of freedom of expression and even freedom of the press to democracy, especially in his fall 2019 speech at Georgetown University (Romm 2019). He ignores how the political right has learned to turn certain specialized definitions of free speech toward the expansion of corporate and market power and against democratic governance (see chapter 6).

In that same Georgetown speech, Zuckerberg invoked two of the most important Black figures in U.S. history, and proffered that Facebook is important, maybe even necessary, for civil rights. He suggested that the world needs Facebook for the same reason we need civil rights leaders: "Throughout history, we've seen how being able to use your voice helps people come together. We've seen this in the civil rights movement. Frederick Douglass once called free expression 'the great moral renovator of society.' He said 'slavery cannot tolerate free speech.'" Later he invokes Martin Luther King Jr. and Eugene V. Debs: "We saw this when Martin Luther King Jr. wrote his famous letter from Birmingham Jail, where he was unconstitutionally jailed for protesting peacefully. We saw this in the efforts to shut down campus protests against the Vietnam War. We saw this way back when America was deeply polarized about its role in World War I, and the Supreme Court ruled that socialist leader Eugene Debs could be imprisoned for making an anti-war speech." He also touched on two of the best-known progressive causes that have had social media components:

> We now have significantly broader power to call out things we feel are unjust and share our own personal experiences. Movements like #BlackLivesMatter and #MeToo went viral on Facebook—the hashtag #BlackLivesMatter was actually first used on Facebook—and this just wouldn't have been possible in the same way before. 100 years back, many of the stories people have shared would have been against the law to even write down. And without the internet giving people the power to share them directly, they certainly wouldn't have reached as many people. With Facebook, more than 2 billion people now have a greater opportunity to express themselves and help others. (Romm 2019)

It may take some reflection to understand the immense offensiveness of Zuckerberg's arguments, particularly in his suggestion that Facebook, or social media in general, is essential for the most important efforts to protect democracy and advance civil rights. He also employs sleight of hand by casting these as matters of "speech" while ignoring the ways Facebook and social media have contributed to the destruction of the democratic social fabric, the destabilization of journalism's critical function in democracies, and the promotion of hate and disinformation using the same "tools" Zuckerberg claims spread civil rights.

His disingenuous use of civil rights causes and leaders to advance the interests of his platform came under immediate attack from sources that should have been revealing. In an op-ed for the *Washington Post,* Sherrilyn Ifill, president and director–counsel of the NAACP Legal Defense Fund, wrote that Zuckerberg's speech depended on "a profound misreading of the civil rights movement in America. And a dangerous misunderstanding of the political and digital landscape":

> The civil rights movement was not fought to vindicate free speech rights under the First Amendment. It was a fight to fulfill the promise of full citizenship and human dignity guaranteed to black people by the 14th Amendment. To

use the struggle of those extraordinary heroes as a rationale for protecting Facebook users who seek to incite the same kind of division and violence those heroes faced turns that history on its head.

Facebook must do more than stand in the reflected glory of those who sacrificed much to create our modern democracy. It must stand in the harsh light of truth and confront the enormous responsibility of stewarding a platform that influences hundreds of millions of people and the potential uses of that platform that threaten our democracy. (Ifill 2019)

Ifill was not the only civil rights advocate to point out how Zuckerberg was misusing the language of civil rights and free speech to advance an antidemocratic agenda. Rather than free speech, Martin Luther King Jr.'s daughter Bernice focused on Facebook's proven role in worldwide disinformation campaigns, writing that she would "like to help Facebook better understand the challenges #MLK faced from disinformation campaigns launched by politicians. These campaigns created an atmosphere for his assassination" (Oreskovic 2019).

Alicia Garza, one of the founders of the Black Lives Matter movement, was even more pointed: "If #BlackLivesMatter to Mark Zuckerberg, then he should ensure that Black users are not targeted with misinformation, harassment and censorship on his platform and stop cozying up to anti-Black forces. Until then, his company will be remembered as an enabler of white supremacy." She argued that Zuckerberg was being "deceptive" in his deployment of BLM to support Facebook: "It really lacks integrity for Mark Zuckerberg to even invoke @Blklivesmatter in this kind of insidious way. Not interested in being your mule. You're being deceptive + it needs to stop." Rashad Robinson, president of the civil rights organization Color of Change, expressed something similar: "'These comments and comparisons, it's not surprising but deeply disappointing,' Robinson said. 'These are the kind of arguments against which I've been pushing back now for years. The idea that you can bask in a delinquent idea of freedom of expression without some kind of rules of the road is just, well, bankrupt.'" Facebook offered a predictable, evasive response to these remarks through a spokesperson: "We respect and appreciate the comments made by some of the nation's foremost civil rights leaders. Their perspectives are critically important and we are committed to continuing the ongoing dialogue. Our work is far from over" (Ross 2019).

These criticisms were not only directed at the cynical rhetoric Zuckerberg uses to promote Facebook. After all, these comments came in 2019, long after the platform had been implicated in scandals involving the promotion of hate, disinformation, violence, and antidemocratic sentiment worldwide. Facebook played a central role in sowing racial hatred and discord, which was instrumental in the election of Donald Trump in the 2016 U.S. presidential election and the 2016 UK Brexit referendum result (Cadwalladr 2019). Many concerned citizens and politicians had examined Facebook's role in these developments, and individuals as well as organizations had directly intervened to get it even to recognize, let alone confront, its corrosive effects on democracy and civil rights.

Prior even to addressing the deeper issues of disinformation and hate, there is Facebook's role in suppressing the vote. As Ifill remarks in her op-ed, the NAACP Legal Defense Fund she heads is one of many civil rights organizations that has tried to address this problem: "Facebook insists it does not allow voter suppression on its platform. But that statement is more aspiration than fact. After nearly two years of conversations between the company and our groups, I am convinced that Facebook simply is ill-equipped to define what constitutes voter suppression—especially at the local level. To help Facebook understand, we have provided the company with multiple examples of voter suppression practices we have seen at the local level that would survive their policies" (Ifill 2019).

Despite the long-standing efforts of civil rights organizations and voting advocates to highlight the usefulness of Facebook for those who want to suppress the vote, the platform appears to be either unable or unwilling to address the problem. A detailed *ProPublica* report found that even in 2020, Facebook remained "rife with false or misleading claims about voting, particularly regarding voting by mail, which is the safest way of casting a ballot during the pandemic. Many of these falsehoods appear to violate Facebook's standards yet have not been taken down or labeled as inaccurate" (McCarthy 2020). A *Media Matters* report found similar problems earlier that year: "Even though Facebook claims that its policies are 'helping to protect the 2020 US elections,' the social media platform is still earning revenue on Trump's ads that promote his right-wing misinformation about voter fraud." In part due to its own policies, Facebook continued to allow ads that made false claims. These policies were enacted in October 2019, the same month Zuckerberg made his "civil rights" speech (Gogarty 2020).

Facebook's characteristic response to these analyses—that "a total of 2.2 million ads on Facebook and Instagram have been rejected and 120,000 posts withdrawn for attempting to 'obstruct voting' in the upcoming US presidential election" (Agence France-Presse 2020)—only begs the question: Why is a platform like Facebook so attractive for voter suppression, unless these efforts are successful? And why should democracies agree to tolerate a company and platform that attract so very much antidemocratic energy and effort?

Voter suppression deserves particular attention because it is so toxic for democracy. Facebook has paid lip service to dealing with the problem and devoted significant resources to managing it. Whether we agree that those efforts are or ever could be adequate is another question. But when we move beyond that issue to other central civil rights concerns, if anything the picture gets worse. Facebook has long been targeted by civil rights groups for the role it plays in seeding and promoting hate around the world. The NAACP, Color of Change, the Anti-Defamation League, and more recently the Center for Countering Digital Hate (CCDH) have been leading the way in both public activism and private efforts with Facebook and later Meta to curtail the use of its platforms to spread hate speech. In 2018, the law firm Relman Colfax, "at the behest and encouragement of the civil rights community and some members of Congress, proceeded with Facebook's cooperation" (Murphy et al. 2020, 3) and conducted a civil rights audit of the platform. Despite the audit having been undertaken in part at Facebook's request and with its participation, and despite noting "a number of positive and consequential steps that the company has taken," the auditors reported they were "concerned that those gains could be obscured by the vexing and heartbreaking decisions Facebook has made that represent significant setbacks for civil rights" (8).

The report authors specifically "expressed significant concern" about Facebook's use of civil liberties rhetoric to expand its economic and political power, noting "the company's steadfast commitment since Mark's October 2019 Georgetown speech to protect a particular definition of free expression, even where that has meant allowing harmful and divisive rhetoric that amplifies hate speech and threatens civil rights" (9). Regarding white nationalist content, the authors shared that in a preliminary version of their audit they "restrained their praise for Facebook's then-new ban on white nationalism and white separatism because, in the Auditors' view, the policy is too narrow in that it only prohibits content expressly using the phrase(s) 'white nationalism' or 'white separatism,' and does not prohibit content that explicitly espouses the very same ideology without using those exact phrases" (50). The auditors then suggested that Facebook "look to expand the policy to prohibit content which expressly praises, supports, or represents white nationalist or separatist ideology even if it does not explicitly use those terms." At the time of the final report, Facebook had "not made that policy change" (51).

Instead, the authors wrote, Facebook created a multidisciplinary team that "brings together subject matter experts from policy, operations, product, engineering, safety investigations, threat intelligence, law enforcement investigations, and legal." The team includes "350 people who work exclusively on combating dangerous individuals and organizations, including white nationalist and separatist groups and other organized hate groups." Facebook stated that "the collective work of this cross-functional team has resulted in a ban on more than 250 white supremacist organizations from its platform, and that the company uses a combination of AI and human expertise to remove content praising or supporting these organizations. Through this process, Facebook states that it has learned behavioral patterns in organized hate and terrorist content that make them distinctive from one another, which may aid in their detection" (51). This sounds good on the surface—if anything it seems like Facebook may be going out of its way to confront the use of its platform for hate. But the auditors were not satisfied.

Among other points, they rightly noted that the public and even the auditors themselves are repeatedly faced with Facebook's own accounts of the shocking amounts of hate they remove from the site but given no way to assess its significance: "In its May 2020 Community Standards Enforcement Report, Facebook reported that in the first three months of 2020, it removed about 4.7 million pieces of content connected to organized hate—an increase of over 3 million pieces of content from the end of 2019. While this is an impressive figure, the Auditors are unable to assess its significance without greater context (e.g., the amount of hate content that is on the platform but goes undetected, or whether hate is increasing on the platform overall, such that removing more does not necessarily signal better detection)" (51). Even the auditors do not confront the question whether products that attract so much hate (much as Facebook and other social platforms attract enormous amounts of child sexual abuse material; see Hitt 2021) belong in democratic polities to begin with. Cyberlibertarian agitation is organized to keep this question off the table.

Facebook's lack of cooperation with civil rights groups is even more disturbing. The auditors noted that Facebook still seems unable or unwilling to deal with a great deal of hate content on the platform: "Civil rights groups have challenged the accuracy and effectiveness of Facebook's enforcement of these policies; for example, a 2020 report published by the Tech Transparency Project (TTP) concluded that more than 100 groups identified by the Southern Poverty Law Center and/or Anti-Defamation League as white supremacist organizations had a presence on Facebook" (51). This is partly true because the company does not use the hate group definitions developed by experts in the field: "Because Facebook uses its own criteria for designating hate organizations, they are not in agreement with the hate designation of organizations that are identified by the TTP report. In some ways Facebook's designations are more expansive (e.g., Facebook indicates it has designated 15 US-based white supremacist groups as hate organizations that are not so-designated by the Southern Poverty Law Center [SPL] or Anti-Defamation League [ADL]) and in some ways civil rights groups feel that Facebook's designations are under inclusive." On this topic, the audit's authors concluded that "the company should be doing more" and expressed concern that Facebook "has not implemented the Auditors' specific recommendation that it work to prohibit expressly—even if not explicit—references to white nationalist or white separatist ideology" (52).

The 2020 audit appeared to bend over backward to give the company the benefit of the doubt; the report conducted by TTP released just a few months earlier was far more critical. TTP researchers "conducted searches on Facebook for the names of 221 white supremacist organizations that have been designated as hate groups by the SPLC and the ADL, two leading anti-hate organizations." Their research found that "of the 221 designated white supremacist organizations, more than half—51%, or 113 groups—had a presence on Facebook"; that "many of the white supremacist Pages identified by TTP were created by Facebook itself. Facebook auto-generated them as business pages when someone listed a white supremacist or neo-Nazi organization as their employer"; that "Facebook's 'Related Pages' feature often directed users visiting white supremacist Pages to other extremist or far-right content"; and that "in addition to the hate groups designated by SPLC and ADL, TTP found white supremacist organizations that Facebook had explicitly banned in the past" (Tech Transparency Project 2020).

TTP, SPLC, ADL, and CCDH, along with governmental officials, have long been urging Facebook to confront the usefulness of its platform for far-right extremism. The TTP report notes that "Facebook's Community Standards have included rules against hate speech for years, but in the past three years the company has expanded its efforts"; however, despite these efforts, overt, obvious uses of the platform for hate-motivated violence continue: "Despite the policy update, Facebook didn't immediately take down an event page for the 'Unite the Right' rally, which SPLC had tied to neo-Nazis. According to one media report, Facebook only pulled the listing the day before the rally." This was 2017, and after Unite the Right Facebook again announced it would redouble efforts to prevent racist hate and violence. Yet

> Facebook scrambled again in early 2019 following the Christchurch attack, in which a gunman used Facebook to stream the massacre of 51 people at a pair of mosques in New Zealand. As the killings made headlines around the world, the company said it would ban "white nationalist" content along with the previously banned category of white supremacism. Facebook Chief Operating Officer Sheryl Sandberg also said a handful of hate groups in Australia and New Zealand would be banned.
>
> Two months after the New Zealand attack, however, *BuzzFeed News* found that extremist groups Facebook claimed to have banned were still on the platform. (Tech Transparency Project 2020, with an internal link to Lytvynenko, Silverman, and Boutilier 2019)

BuzzFeed quotes extremism researcher Megan Squire, who often works with SPLC, as saying "Facebook likes to make a PR move and say that they're doing something but they don't always follow up on that" (Lytvynenko, Silverman, and Boutilier 2019); and TTP echoes this sentiment.

They are not alone. A coalition of civil rights groups launched Stop Hate for Profit after Zuckerberg's 2019 speech, the 2020 civil rights audit, and other instances of hate-based violence in which Facebook was implicated. The campaign's name suggests what many are hesitant to say out loud: Facebook is aware that its product suppresses democracy and promotes hate.

The company puts its own power and economic welfare above the civil rights and democracy it claims to support. ADL, Common Sense, NAACP, Color of Change, and other civil rights organizations are all part of the campaign coalition. On June 17, 2020, the coalition explains, "we asked businesses to temporarily pause advertising on Facebook and Instagram in order to force Mark Zuckerberg to address the effect that Facebook has had on our society. Following an incredible groundswell of support, Mr. Zuckerberg asked to meet with Stop Hate for Profit coalition leaders on July 7th 2020." Facebook's civil rights audit was released the next day. Yet during the July 7 meeting, Zuckerberg "made clear he had no intention of taking any steps to tackle our requests." And things did not improve: "One year later, Facebook's progress toward these demands [had] been minimal at best" (Stop Hate for Profit 2021).

In the wake of the meeting, participants noted the strategic and repetitive nature of Facebook's claims about suppressing hate: "'We've seen over and over again how it will do anything to duck accountability by firing up its powerful PR machine and trying to spin the news,' said Jessica J. González, co-CEO of Free Press, a nonprofit organization that lobbies technology and media companies on behalf of people of color and underserved communities." Despite Facebook's claims of having large internal teams working on the matter, researchers at civil rights organizations are able to locate hate material with relative ease. This material is only taken down after the organizations present the data in public, as one participant pointed out: "Derrick Johnson, the president and chief executive of the NAACP, told NBC News in an interview, that Facebook only acted to take down white supremacist groups after they were alerted rather than doing it proactively. 'They have the technology to prevent racial hate speech'" (Byers and Atkinson 2020). Other meeting participants were equally frank. Color of Change executive director Rashad Robinson said that Facebook "showed up to the meeting expecting an A for attendance." ADL CEO Jonathan Greenblatt stated, "We had 10 demands and literally we went through the 10 and we didn't get commitments or timeframes or clear outcomes." Jessica González of Free Press went further: we "didn't hear anything today to convince us that Zuckerberg and his colleagues are taking action. Instead of committing to a timeline to root out hate and disinformation on Facebook, the company's leaders delivered the same old talking points to try to placate us without meeting our demands" (Graham and Rodriguez 2020).

The world is inundated with antidemocratic propaganda and racist and ethnic hatred, which frequently leads to violence on a scale unthinkable as recently as a decade ago. In most of these movements, social media has not only been implicated but arguably has been part of a long chain of causes. Facebook and other social platforms have empowered various antidemocratic movements: QAnon; Flat Earth; anti-vaccine propaganda; climate change denial; hatred and violence organized around race, gender, ethnicity, sexuality, and sexual identity; MAGA; Stop the Steal; and the January 6 insurrection at the U.S. Capitol. Whether this is due to affordances of the platform structure itself, as some suspect, or merely its ability to amplify and connect, is an open question. Yet two facts are abundantly clear: democracies existed and even prospered prior to social media, and Facebook and similar companies are unwilling or unable to lock their platforms to ensure they do not produce corrosive antidemocratic effects. Facebook continues to use the cyberlibertarian rhetoric of "democratization," "community," "voice," "access," and "engagement" to promote its activities. This is accepted far too readily by many in the public, despite being repeatedly exposed as false or, at best, misleading public relations.

Over the years, writers and activists have exposed Facebook's direct promotion of antidemocratic and far-right political values over competing values more consistent with democratic government. Journalists like Sheera Frankel and Cecilia Kang explain in detail how throughout Facebook's history, there was one

> core libertarian refrain Zuckerberg would return to again and again: the all-important protection of free speech as laid out in the First Amendment of the Bill of Rights. His interpretation was that speech should be unimpeded; Facebook would host a cacophony of sparring voices and ideas to help educate and inform its users. But the protection of speech adopted in 1791 had been designed specifically to promote a healthy democracy by ensuring a plurality of ideas without government restraint. The First Amendment was meant to protect society. And ad targeting that prioritized clicks and salacious content and data mining of users was antithetical to the ideals of a healthy society. (2021, 16–17)

"Libertarian" here should be interpreted as the cyberlibertarian or political libertarian translation of central democratic values into economic values that oppose them.

The efforts of Frankel, Kang, and others have been supplemented by a series of whistleblowers from the company itself. In early 2021, Sophie Zhang, a former data scientist who worked with Facebook's "integrity" unit to detect "fake" and "inauthentic" activity, provided internal corporate documentation to *The Guardian* and other publications about what she called "harm being done on Facebook that is not being responded to because it is not considered enough of a PR risk" (Wong 2021). Zhang focused on countries outside North America and Europe. She found that especially in smaller countries with authoritarian leaders, Facebook was slow to act and sometimes reversed whatever measures it did impose. Framed one way, Facebook fails to confront antidemocratic politics; framed another way, Facebook supports authoritarian politics. The company always portrays itself as doing the former, but the latter is arguably more credible.

Later in 2021, Frances Haugen, another former Facebook data scientist and product manager, released documents and testified before American, British, and European Union governmental bodies. Her files echoed criticisms and revelations made by journalists and civil rights groups. Despite Facebook's continual claims of doing everything that is reasonable to confront the "misuse" of its platforms, Haugen's disclosures, like Zhang's, suggested that the situation is much worse than most of Facebook's critics had feared. In short, what some commentators and Facebook itself call "misuse" is more accurately described as "use."

Haugen's documents showed that despite the company's vaunted efforts to stem Covid-19 disinformation, in many areas it remained unable or unwilling to address the problem. One area of particular concern is the spread of anti-vaccine sentiment in Facebook comments: "One document dated March 2021 shows an employee raising the alarm about how unprepared the platform was. 'Vaccine hesitancy in comments is rampant,' the memo reads. 'Our ability to detect vaccine-hesitant comments is bad in English, and basically non-existent elsewhere. We need Policy guidelines specifically aimed at vaccine hesitancy in comments.'" In October 2021, almost two years after the Covid-19 pandemic started, Facebook took "some steps . . . to address misinformation in comments," but "those changes came more than six months after the alarm had been raised internally and after Facebook had publicly expressed anxiety about the impending leak" (Brandom, Heath, and Robertson 2021). Predictably, because the company in policy director Nick Clegg's words is "fundamentally committed to free expression," in 2022 Facebook asked its Oversight Board to determine "whether or not the COVID-19 misinformation removal policy is hurting that mission" (Wille 2022).

Other items covered in Haugen's documents included the fact that "Apple threatened to pull Facebook and Instagram from iOS on October 23rd of 2019" due to work by journalists: "Apple had been tipped off by a BBC News Arabic report that found domestic workers being sold via Instagram and other apps" (Brandom, Heath, and Robertson 2021). In India, an especially important market for several Facebook platforms including WhatsApp, "inflammatory content on Facebook spiked 300% above previous levels at times during the months following December 2019, a period in which religious protests swept India," according to Facebook's own internal report released by Haugen. The report goes on to note that "rumors and calls to violence spread particularly on Facebook's WhatsApp messaging service in late February 2020, when communal violence in Delhi left 53 dead"; "Hindu and Muslim users in India say they are subjected to 'a large amount of content that encourages conflict, hatred and violence on Facebook and WhatsApp.'" "There is 'so much hatred going on' on Facebook," wrote two *Wall Street Journal* journalists covering Haugen's disclosures, quoting from the reports themselves, "one Muslim man in Mumbai was quoted as telling the researchers, saying he feared for his life. 'It's scary, it's really scary'" (Purnell and Horwitz 2021).

Facebook's response to these and other disclosures is always the same. Even though the company's own spokesperson acknowledges that "hate speech against marginalized groups, including Muslims, is on the rise globally," Facebook itself plays no important role in that increase: "everything that is good, bad, and ugly in our societies will find expression on our platform" (Purnell and Horwitz 2021). Despite Facebook's frequent marketing claims about "community" and "connection," which are always depicted as positive and even transformative powers to change society, it is never responsible for its negative effects. "We don't benefit from hate" its spokesperson says, repeating Nick Clegg's (2020) infamous declaration in response to the Stop Hate for Profit campaign.

Clegg and other Facebook spokespeople routinely elaborate on this claim with a positive endorsement of community: "We have absolutely no incentive to tolerate hate speech. We don't like it, our users don't like it, advertisers understandably don't like it. . . . We benefit from positive human connection—not hate" (Duffy 2020). These crafted words deliberately distort obvious facts. They segment what civil rights leaders call "hate" from what many Facebook users do not see as "hate" at all, pretending that those who practice and transmit hate are not "users" with "likes." We know this is false. KKK members, MAGA extremists, ISIS recruiters, Hindu nationalists, and others typically identified as hate groups all see themselves as bound not by intolerance but by love of "family" and others close to them. We know from many lines of research that some members of these communities are the most active users of communications technologies, and often at their vanguard (see Belew 2019; and chapter 7, below). Facebook benefits from having U.S. MAGA and Donald Trump supporters on its platforms, even if they constitute at most a quarter of the population. In other countries, the percentage of users fundamentally committed to hate may be even higher. There are many examples of nations made up of "communities" largely constituted by hatred of one another. Through this very narrow perspective, one might even ask whether some on the left "hate" the MAGA right, whether Facebook can or should try to mitigate this "hate," or whether both the community-building and anger-generating aspects of these groups fit right into the company's business model. Though Clegg says the company does not "profit from hate," in-group identification and out-group anger may be its primary product.

These clear affordances of Facebook and other platforms have led some researchers to talk about "polarization." While this may be a useful frame in some instances, it seems to risk a "both sides" analysis that is fundamentally political. Driving society into extremes, encouraging science denial, jeopardizing democratic fundamentals, and ignoring political realities—all phenomena of the contemporary and historical political right—are directly associated with the rise of Facebook and other social media platforms. While we don't think of it this way, the majority of past and present science and reality denial campaigns have been clearly identified with the right, particularly when they align with deregulation and the extremes of free market capitalism. From climate change denial to its close bedfellow, tobacco "science" (Oreskes and Conway 2010), to the range of conspiracy theory movements presently active, most aim to expand right-wing political power, the interests of concentrated capital that wants to avoid political accountability and constraint, or some combination of the two. Financial interests associated with the fossil fuel industry emerge at the bottom of many of these movements.

While its critics have rightly called out Facebook for promoting hate, most of them step back from connecting these dots in the most straightforward way: that Facebook is a knowing and active promoter of rightwing politics. Yet the evidence for this is substantial. Another revelation from Haugen's leaked documents is Facebook's own employees stating on its internal message boards that "the company was allowing conservative sites to skirt the company's fact-checking rules, publish untrustworthy and offensive content and harm the tech giant's relationship with advertisers." Staff questioned the presence of far-right propaganda site *Breitbart* on Facebook's News tab; Facebook kept the listing, despite its own researchers determining that it "was the least trusted news source, and also ranked as low quality, among several dozen it looked at across the US and Great Britain." In 2020, a "Facebook engineer gathered up a list of examples he said were evidence that Facebook routinely declines to enforce its own content moderation rules for big far-right publishers like Breitbart, Charlie Kirk, PragerU and Diamond and Silk" (Hagey and Horwitz 2021). Around the same time, a Facebook spokesperson defended the platform's conservative bias by saying that "right-wing populism is always more engaging." As a former Facebook employee working at the liberal Center for American Progress said in response, "Facebook is not a mirror—the newsfeed algorithm is an accelerant" (Thompson 2020; also see Edelson et al. 2021). It is difficult to reconcile these facts with the company's claim that "hate" is unwelcome on the platform.

Add to this Facebook's work with lobbyists, most of them from the deregulatory far right, especially the American Edge Project, a business lobby that, despite comprising twenty-four member organizations, is described by the Tech Transparency Project (2022) as having been solely founded by the social media giant. TTP claims that Facebook's support for relatively minor tech industry regulations, which Facebook would help write, is partly meant to conceal the company's opposition to antitrust efforts. Such large-scale government action would threaten the concentration of wealth and power on which Facebook thrives. Further, "Facebook has an active Republican operative—vice president of public policy Joel Kaplan . . . who repeatedly sided with right-wing misinformation peddlers." In particular, Kaplan helped to drive both right-wing disinformation on Facebook *and* the narrative that Facebook is biased against the right: "Kaplan made an effort to 'protect' Breitbart's account from being downsized in the news feed despite its distribution of harmful misinformation. Kaplan reportedly defended keeping up a network of fake news pages because removing them would 'disproportionately affect conservatives.' Kaplan also reportedly defended basing Facebook's algorithm on 'super-sharers'—who are mostly extremely partisan—instead of regular Facebook users. And Kaplan shut down efforts to address polarization and extremism on the platform." Angelo Carusone, president and CEO of Media Matters for America, notes that Kaplan was one of the Republican operatives who tried to interfere with the infamous Florida recount in the 2000 U.S. presidential election, suggesting "that the key decision-maker at Facebook for election-related matters once engaged in a partisan effort to literally stop votes from being counted in order to affect the outcome of an election should alarm everyone both inside and outside of Facebook" (Carusone 2020).

That effort to portray Facebook and other social media as having a bias against conservatives remains a remarkable and telling disinformation project. Its goal is clearly not to expose "bias" but to shift the public and political conversation to pressure Facebook (and its advertisers) to allow not only "conservative" but far-right hate and antidemocratic extremism to flourish on the platform (Kraus 2020). As many commentators have pointed out, it is not those we used to call "ordinary" conservatives who get flagged for misuse of the platform: it is those who spread far-right hate, denialism, and conspiracy theory, which remains on the platform or is removed long after it should be (Binder 2021).

Put these analyses alongside Facebook's role in the 2016 Brexit and Trump campaigns, the role in those efforts of Cambridge Analytica and many other data broker and analysis companies (Halpern 2018; Wylie 2019), and their own funding by the far-right Mercer family (Cadwalladr 2017); the fact that far-right agitator Ben Shapiro and his propaganda platform the *Daily Wire* even now typically receive "more likes, shares and comments on Facebook than any other news publisher by a wide margin" (Parks 2021); and that Zuckerberg is reported to have had long personal meetings with far-right commentators including Shapiro himself (Bertrand and Lippman 2019) and Tucker Carlson (Glaser 2019), when he seems to have no parallel engagement with leaders on the moderate left, to say nothing of progressives. The picture that emerges is one aptly described by journalist Brian Feldman in 2020: "Facebook has always been right-wing media." Yet the rhetoric of cyberlibertarianism and its variety of studied techniques for digital denialism mean that unlike *Breitbart,* the *Daily Wire,* the *Washington Times,* Facebook is somehow seen as something different from what it is.

THE FORCE OF CYBERLIBERTARIANISM

One way of understanding the debates surrounding digital technology is to see them as cast between two parties of relatively equal power and status: "optimists" versus "pessimists," "utopians" versus "dystopians," "cyber-enthusiasts" versus "cyber-skeptics." While not entirely false, this orientation obscures the profoundly unbalanced playing field on which the two sides play. As Evgeny Morozov writes:

> To listen to Silicon Valley and its cheerleaders, to talk technology today is to talk innovation, progress, emancipation. By analogy, to talk anti-technology is to succumb to a reactionary, anti-progressive view that offends the very spirit of Enlightenment. It is to be a Luddite and an enemy of human betterment.
>   This framing explains why the contemporary opposition to the policy imperialism of Silicon Valley is so ineffective and impotent. (2013b)

That this framing is invalid is obvious, but that must not obscure its power. Unlike many academic and even political debates, those over the politics of the digital are conducted between one side that directly represents the interests of existing and new businesses and the accumulation of capital more generally; the "other" side consists of academics and other writers who believe the ideas at issue are fundamentally questionable. Further, nonprofits like the Mozilla Foundation and the Open Society Foundation—to say nothing of NGOs with explicit tech-lobbying roots like EFF, CDT, and the parts of ACLU that focus on digital technology (see Franks 2019a), which on the surface looks as if it could not possibly be pro-business—provide critical propagandistic power for the unfettered development of technology. For contrast, truly pro-regulation and pro-democracy NGOs like the Electronic Privacy and Information Center tend to promote much more skeptical and well-considered platforms but receive much less attention than do the others.

Morozov (2013a) refers to the promoters of what he calls "solutionism" as "Silicon Valley." This is a useful figure of speech to describe the large collection of businesses (Google, Facebook, Apple, Twitter, Airbnb, Intel,

Cisco, Acxiom, etc.) that profit from the ongoing proliferation of digital technology. Additionally, venture capitalists (such as Andreessen Horowitz, Sequoia Partners, Founders Fund, and Kleiner Perkins Caufield & Byers), consultants, and even academics benefit no less from the growth and development of digital businesses. Even many of those with no apparent stake in business profits—such as free and open-source software developers, various other "hackers," and even directors of nonprofit enterprises like Wikipedia—have much to gain in the proliferation of digital industries. This leads to an uncomfortable asymmetry between organizations traditionally associated with "rights" of various sorts, such as Amnesty International, the ACLU, and Human Rights Watch. They are typically made up almost entirely of disinterested academics and activists with no commercial stake in the positions for which they fight. In contrast, organizations that have sprung up in the digital age, such as EFF and the CDT, have deep and sustained ties to industry. Despite *seeming* like rights organizations, they more closely resemble lobbying organizations for digital-industry businesses. Many of their boards and even staff members hold such direct stakes.

The pro-digital side often accuses critics of promoting their own self-interest, thus negating discussion of the stake either side has in the debate. At its most absurd, this response accuses a writer like Evgeny Morozov of "profiting" from the proliferation of his views, trying to "get rich" off "people's fear of technology." This objection is ludicrous, of course. It is no truer of Morozov or myself than it is of any authors or speakers that proliferation of their views might lead to personal benefit. Rejecting the views of *all* commentators because of their interest in promoting their perspective would be required if this argument held any weight.

This response is truly bizarre because it both accepts and rejects the analysis with which we began: that we should read (Google executive chairman, ex-CEO, and major shareholder) Eric Schmidt and (Google Ideas director) Jared Cohen's *New Digital Age* (2013), for example, with an eye toward the enormous profits available to Google if the book's recommendations were enacted. This parallels the bizarre and disingenuous attacks on climate scientists for being interested in their analysis due to theoretical profits from carbon credits, a view promulgated by huge multinational energy companies that stand to benefit if action on climate change is stalled and to lose if the world takes action. If all Schmidt and Cohen gained from people reading their book were sales and speaking fees, it might be fair to compare their "interestedness" with that of Morozov. What Morozov lacks is the far greater—enormous, in fact—profit that Google and other Silicon Valley ventures earn via the promotion of views like those of Schmidt and Cohen. If personal bias in one's analysis is a valid concern, then huge financial interest should be our primary concern.

Morozov offers an apt analysis of the stakes of this debate:

> For the true and democratically minded critic, "technology" is just a slick, depoliticized euphemism for the neoliberal regime itself. To attack technology today is not to attack the Enlightenment—no, it is to attack neoliberalism itself.
>
> Consider the outlines of a digital world that is rapidly coming into existence. All the achievements of social democracy—public health, public education, public transportation, public funding for the arts—are being undermined by the proliferation of highly personalized app-based solutions that seek to get rid of bureaucratic institutions and replace them with fluid and horizontal market-based interactions.

Morozov writes that in the eyes of Google, health information providers, and "sharing economy" companies like Airbnb, Uber, and Lyft, the smartphone is becoming "a buzzing real-time calculator of what our life is worth—and of what it might be worth if we make the right trades at the right time. To think that this is anything but an extension of neoliberal logic to the most private corners of our existence—what the historian of economic thought Philip Mirowski calls 'everyday neoliberalism'—is naïve. 'Technology' is just a sweet euphemism here" (2013b).

So on the one hand, we have a significant percentage of the world's most mobile and aggressive capital profoundly invested in promoting the beneficence of the "digital revolution" *whether what it's promoting is correct or not.* On the other hand, a small group of academics and writers who believe that much of that promotion is misguided, and at best stand to gain no more from sharing their ideas than Clay Shirky and Jeff Jarvis stand from offering theirs. This is not a fair or balanced debate, but rather one where 99 percent of the resources, energy, and potential gain accrue to one side.

While terms like "digital utopian" and "digital enthusiast" can point at the rhetorical content of certain pieces of writing and the beliefs many people hold, it is important to understand them in their proper context. We are not talking about two neutral, disinterested parties having a rational debate about whether "the digital" is leading in positive or negative directions. Rather, there is a tremendous amount of built-in resistance to even considering the critique of technological proliferation, especially when that critique appears to entail governmental (i.e., democratic) limits on what corporate capital can do. Even when "digital enthusiasts" have no stake in business outcomes, their arguments must be properly contextualized in the commercial environment in which we live.

CHAPTER 2

The Forms and Functions of Cyberlibertarianism

M uch of the character of cyberlibertarianism emerges from its distinctive origins, crossing ideological lines from the begin- ning, which turns out to be essential to its current function. Despite its current reputation (especially among conservatives) for being "liberal," Silicon Valley and computer culture in general emerge from the right. For a long time this was neither contested nor particularly note- worthy. Especially during the first flush of computer development, digital technology was primarily associated with the military, the defense indus- try, and the Cold War corporate and governmental establishment. As path- breaking works like Paul Edwards's *The Closed World* (1997), Alex Abella's *Soldiers of Reason* (2008), Philip Mirowski's *Machine Dreams* (2002), and S. M. Amadae's *Rationalizing Capitalist Democracy* (2003) show, the tight connections between the development of digital computers and conserva- tive U.S. politics were taken for granted. To many political radicals of the 1960s, computers were among the most potent symbols of the conservative political machine they opposed, and sometimes even served as targets for direct political action (Larson, forthcoming).

While some on the left saw computers as a political threat, few (if any) saw them as a site for political hope. The story of how that changed is both remarkable and underrepresented. Histories like Markoff's *What the Dor- mouse Said* (2005) and especially Turner's *From Counterculture to Cybercul- ture* (2006a) show how a part of the 1960s counterculture came to embrace digital technology, especially in the "friendly face" of the personal com- puter. Turner in particular shows how this part of the counterculture had little to do with leftist political activism. Yet even Turner's detailed account

57

of Stewart Brand and others does not account in wider sociopolitical terms how—or even whether—digital technology accomplished its apparent flip from conservative to liberal politics.

Seen in retrospect, the advent of the politics surrounding digital technology resembles those surrounding some of the most intense corporate–political issues of our time: tobacco science, climate change, and the economic program associated with the Chicago School and the Neoliberal Thought Collective (Mirowski 2013; Mirowski and Plehwe 2009). Yet it stands out from them, too. Rather than a set of relatively centralized and concentrated think tanks and funders producing industry-supporting propaganda (i.e., astroturfing), the digital technology propaganda is, true to form, "decentralized" and far less coordinated. In part this is due to the far deeper penetration of digital tools into every facet of our social lives. Digital tools themselves, including social media, are often used to spread cyberlibertarian dogma. This is done by technologists and others who have no direct connection with think tanks, right-wing funding bodies, or even technology companies. It would not be wrong to label these people as "true believers" in the cyberlibertarian cause, but they seem unable or unwilling to locate their beliefs in the political foundations to which they claim to adhere.

While cyberlibertarianism is distinct from other conservative, deregulatory, and antidemocratic campaigns, it uses many of the same devices to realize its ideological goals—namely a series of rhetorical moves, including metaphors and other tropes, argumentative strategies, and narratives, all of which disrupt challenges to the political power of technology. Many of these strategies divert attention from the political foundations of digital technology, substituting vague syncretisms for thorough political analysis. Despite the nearly inevitable contradictions of cyberlibertarian dogmatists, their shifting tactics and multiple nodes mean there are always rhetorical moves available to draw attention away from close analysis of the politics on offer. Of course those politics are not a unified bloc. But on balance, cyberlibertarian dogma works to stave off or at best shape regulation; to dismiss serious concerns about the political impact of digital technology while sometimes framing that impact as pro-democracy despite manifest evidence otherwise; and in fact to insist on the continued expansion of power of a set of interlocking technologies and corporate interests that a half century ago were seen as contrary to democratic political interests they now claim to have always championed.

THE POLITICAL HISTORY OF CYBERLIBERTARIANISM

As documented by Turner, Winner, Barbrook, and Cameron, cyberlibertarianism emerged as a political force from the conjunction of political turmoil and technological development, particularly in the culture of Silicon Valley and the Bay Area in the late 1960s. The generalized "counterculture" features of cyberlibertarianism, embodied in figures like Stewart Brand and Timothy Leary, can seem straightforward. They are part of a general left-oriented politics that is likely to support democracy and civil rights because at least some parts of 1960s activism put these values at their hearts.

Yet this appearance is foundational for the antidemocratic politics that came to characterize cyberlibertarianism. Neither Brand nor Leary had much truck with democracy, especially when it came to democratic regulation and oversight of economic activity; neither of them spent much energy on core democratic activities such as voting protections and other civil rights. Brand, especially, was far more focused on economic growth than democratic values.

Further, the technological development of cyberlibertarianism makes strange bedfellows with the apparently left-wing radicalism of 1960s counterculture. After all, Silicon Valley itself was a primary nexus point for the "military–industrial complex" that even Republican president Dwight Eisenhower famously condemned. Stanford University was one of the academic headquarters for this kind of activity, often described along with MIT as the academic heart of the complex (Leslie 1993). Silicon Valley was named after the transistor circuits that originated at Stanford University. Stanford was the birthplace of many of the leading digital technology companies, including Google, Instagram, Yahoo, Fairchild Semiconductor, HP, and Cisco.

It was also a major U.S. center for the promotion of eugenics, and one of Silicon Valley's founding figures, who ran the lab that "put the silicon in Silicon Valley" (Moffitt 2018), was a particularly vehement racist—William Shockley. It would be churlish to insist that the views of one founder somehow inform all that follows. Yet the connection between white supremacist and fascist thinking in Silicon Valley libertarianism (see chapter 7) and the promotion of racist IQ theories in digital culture should give any dispassionate thinker pause. This must especially be true given Silicon Valley's shift from developing and selling military technology to insisting that what it offers is both culturally and politically welcome and even necessary to the health of democratic societies.

No less vital to the analysis of cyberlibertarianism is the political history of the computing industry. This includes works by journalists (Levy 1985; Markoff 2005; Frank 1997; Levine 2018b; Curtis 2011) and academics (Roszak [1969] 1995, 1986a, [1986b] 1994; Gitlin 1993; Edwards 1997; Turner 2006a). Taken together, they detail the connection of politics, the military, and industry to the development of computers and culture that forces us to reconsider some of the popular narratives about the 1960s. The United States is believed to have shifted significantly to the political left during the 1960s, partly in response to the bureaucratic nature of organizations such as industrial, military, and governmental bodies that were prevalent in the 1950s. This transformation included both the well-known civil rights initiatives, which focused on race and gender, and widespread anti-war movements. Lifestyle revolutions in the Western world during the same period were characterized by changes in fashion, sexual mores, popular music, and drug use. These shifts were embodied by events such as the Summer of Love of 1967, figures like Timothy Leary and the Grateful Dead, slogans like "turn on, tune in, drop out," and the development of self-actualization programs like Erhard Seminars Training and the back-to-the-land commune movement.

Gitlin, Roszak, and Turner demonstrate that despite popular perceptions, this constellation of forces comprises at the very least two movements that span the political spectrum. It is familiar to associate the 1960s with the idea of a "New Left," but these critics ask us to look carefully at the countercultural movements to see whether that label is appropriate. A relatively natural divide appears, according to which some figures (e.g., Gitlin himself, Robert F. Kennedy, Martin Luther King Jr., Malcolm X, Students for a Democratic Society, the Revolutionary News Service) clearly aligned themselves with left politics, whereas others (e.g., many of the most famous exponents of 1960s culture like Leary, Ken Kesey, Stewart Brand, the Merry Pranksters, the Grateful Dead, Jerry Rubin, the be-ins)—advocated a pro-business, anti-communist, anti-left politics whose public face focused on lifestyle as opposed to actual politics. Rather than working for a more equal society, retreat to a commune; rather than working for women's emancipation, construe "free love" as inherently liberatory; rather than work for civil rights for minorities, listen to Motown.

Obviously there was a great deal of traffic between the two sides, and no doubt many ordinary participants in the counterculture found it easy and natural to participate in both. Frank and others have shown that industry played a deep role in the generation of culture through entertainment companies, as well as in the Madison Avenue generation of cultural forms through advertising and branding. This suggests that the revolutionary energies of 1960s radicals were quickly and effectively channeled into life-style radicalism, which can seem like the opposite of the politics offered.

Turner calls the part of the counterculture not explicitly committed to leftist politics the "New Communalists":

> Even as their peers organized political parties and marched against the Vietnam War, this group . . . turned away from political action and toward technology and the transformation of consciousness as the primary sources of social change. If mainstream America had become a culture of conflict, with riots at home and war abroad, the commune world would be one of harmony. If the American state deployed massive weapons systems in order to destroy faraway peoples, the New Communalists would deploy small-scale technologies—ranging from axes and hoes to amplifiers, strobe lights, slide projectors, and LSD—to bring people together and allow them to experience their common humanity. (2006, 4)

To illustrate the orientation and influence of the New Communalists, Turner draws attention to the life and work of Stewart Brand, publisher of the *Whole Earth Catalog*, whose appearance at so many vital moments in computing and the counterculture writ large is remarkable. Associated with but not a "member" of the Merry Pranksters, the archetypal anti-political countercultural group, Brand played key roles in promoting the back-to-the-land, small-farmer, neo-agrarian alternative to direct political action. Even in the late 1960s Brand was demurring from left politics and expressing quiet sympathy for the right. Brand appears repeatedly in the development of the utopian view of computing due to a number of direct connections between the *Whole Earth Catalog* and the developing personal computer community. In 1968, he ran and designed the audiovisual aspects of the so-called Mother of All Demos in San Francisco, where computer pioneer Douglas Engelbart "dealt lightning with both hands" by show-casing an integrated computer hardware and software system. This event helped to galvanize the computer-centric parts of the Valley into its self-image as quasi-political revolutionaries.

The combination of the personal computing revolution and the New Communalist movement has effectively remapped the cultural landscape, rendering it today almost invisible and unthinkable. This is the view that "centralized authority" and "bureaucracy" are somehow emblematic of concentrated power, whereas "distributed" and "nonhierarchical" systems oppose that power. As Turner explains, one of the main sources for the idea of flattened and distributed networks comes not from the political left, but instead from

> the social and rhetorical tactics by which the defense engineers of World War II and the cold war had organized and claimed legitimacy for their own work. Much like Norbert Wiener and the scientists of the Rad Lab, Stewart Brand had made a career of crossing disciplinary and professional boundaries. Like those who designed and funded the weapons research laboratories of World War II, Brand had built a series of network forums—some face-to-face, such as the Hacker's Conference, others digital, such as the WELL, or paper-based, such as the *Whole Earth Catalog*. Like the Rad Lab, these forums allowed members of multiple communities to meet, to exchange information, and to develop new rhetorical tools. Like their World War II predecessors, they also facilitated the construction and dissemination of techno-social prototypes. Sometimes, as in the case of the *Catalog* or the WELL, Whole Earth productions themselves would model the sorts of relationships between technology, information, the individual, and the community favored by network members. (2006, 249–50)

At the heart of these changes is a profound series of developments in computer technology. The early critiques of computers as tools of technocracy focused on the computer as a machine that resided in institutions; frequently entire rooms and even wings of buildings were required just to house the hardware. The journalist John Markoff highlights the importance of remembering that a great deal of vision, ingenuity, and perseverance was required to create computers that were designed for individuals and eventually became mobile. The transition from institutional to personal computing tracks precisely with the shift from countercultural beliefs in the computer as an instrument of dehumanizing power to the computer as an instrument for *expanding* human power.

The critique of institutionalized computing was partly based on the accurate depiction of computing power as physically separate from human bodies. There was a very strong sense that computers were remote collectors and sorters of data about us. This was done in service of powerful institutions that could manipulate us via the knowledge they gained through computing. The countercultural idea of computing promulgated by Stewart Brand, Douglas Engelbart, Steve Jobs, Bill Gates, and others, was that individuals should have the power of computing in their hands. It is important to note that these entrepreneurs had a personal financial interest in this idea. But this vision of computing, which reversed the power dynamic entirely, tells only a small part of the story.

That is, giving computing power to individuals does not take it away from institutions; in many ways, the technological revolutions associated with personal computing depended on expanded institutional power. Nowhere is this more evident than in the quick rise of self-identified rebel hackers—individuals Levy (2010) called "hackers" and "heroes of the computer revolution"—to become the richest and most powerful figures in the world's leading industries.

Being physically separated from computing machines does not insulate us from their most pernicious effects. The location of computing power has been variable. Sometimes it is mediated by "dumb" terminals communicating with powerful central machines, and at other times it places much of that power in user devices. Today's smartphones possess enormous computing power but at the same time depend on communication with powerful networks and servers. They convey extremely rich data about us back to institutions that process that data for political control. This includes both the narrow, party/electoral sense of the term and a broader sense of social control. In other words, the personal computing revolution has been succeeded by a global computing revolution made up of bureaucratic, centralized infrastructures. However, these infrastructures obscure themselves by putting data-collecting and -processing devices directly into the hands of users.

CYBERLIBERTARIANISM AS DIGITAL DENIALISM

To understand how cyberlibertarianism functions, it is especially useful to compare it with two other disinformation campaigns associated with the public's understanding of corporate and capitalist power: "tobacco science" and climate change denial. Naomi Oreskes, the Harvard historian of science, is the most forceful analyst of these practices and the connections between them. In her 2010 book with Erik Conway, *Merchants of Doubt: How a Handful of Scientists Obscured the Truth on Issues from Tobacco Smoke to Global Warming*, she explains how the tobacco industry discovered it "could use science against itself. 'Doubt is our product,' ran the infamous memo written by one tobacco industry executive in 1969, 'since it is the best means of competing with the "body of fact" that exists in the minds of the general public'" (34). The power of convincing the public that the link between smoking and lung cancer was unproven was exercised indirectly. The U.S. surgeon general was able to place warnings on cigarette packages, which might be thought to be a direct political effect. However, consumers were subtly encouraged to discount the expertise of scientists, to doubt the scientific enterprise itself, and to see their consumption of tobacco as a matter of "freedom." All of these actions accomplished the tobacco industry's goals of remaining in business and diminishing the likelihood of preventative regulation and litigation.

Certainly, in some localities electoral politics were affected. In tobacco-growing states, tobacco anti-science was one element of a suite of political movements that kept politicians supporting the tobacco industry regardless of party affiliation. It would be a mistake to stand above this set of facts and declare that Big Tobacco's propaganda efforts were politically ineffective just because many in those states voted for Democratic presidential candidates.

It would be similarly inaccurate to see climate denialism simply as a device used to maintain the dominance of one party over another. Instead, its effect is to deform the very shape of the political debate, seeding a range of frankly ridiculous "doubts" in the public discourse. Industry propaganda becomes a quasi-religious belief that resists testing against evidence and is adhered to with venomous force. Climate deniers are often convinced by propaganda and write as if they are defending "science" because climate scientists fail to follow the "evidence." Yet it is next to impossible to find any of these denialists indicating what they consider reasonable standards of evidence to test the hypotheses of climate change. They do not say, "Your climate science fails to meet X standard of proof"; they say, "No evidence could *ever* support your conclusions."

Both tobacco anti-science and climate denialism promote anti-scientific thinking *as if it were* science itself. Those who promote these views are doing so in part because they *do* believe the science and are trying to forestall the natural political effects of widespread belief in what they *know* the science shows. This enables partisans (think Sean Hannity or Mark Levin) to declare that, while they are not scientists, they are in position to show that scientists themselves are not being scientific. The production of anti-science denialism has the side effect of undermining the foundations of scientific political formations. This can lead to the belief that vaccines cause autism; that AIDS, Ebola, or Covid-19 were genetically engineered by the pharmaceutical industry and government; or that the science of evolution is a fraud.

These movements help to consolidate the power of the right and sow doubt about government regulation and democratic power. This is done through electoral politics and the maintenance of a level of political force and affect that exists outside the direct management of those who benefit from it most. The force exists outside of them but remains untapped, ready to be used when it benefits one or another political effort. Perhaps just as important, it creates political "events" that overwhelm the ability of the electorate to focus on other issues.

The anti-vax movement is an effective example of how falsified research by a small group of scientists can have unforeseeable consequences. It is unlikely that the anti-science propagandists deliberately started the movement. Their motivations for being suspicious of vaccines is difficult or even impossible to pin down. The movement is routinely dismissed by scientists across the board and is rarely embraced by politicians. Yet, it sticks in the public imagination with a fierce tenacity despite how thoroughly it has been discredited. It helps promulgate a set of anti-government, anti-science beliefs that are accessible to those who need it, when they need it. Despite anti-vax thought harming public health, it remains useful to those who prefer to manage public opinion by emotional subterfuge rather than informed debate.

Cyberlibertarianism resembles these movements but also differs in important ways. Its effects line up with theirs in surprising ways. Cyberlibertarianism was not produced by a coterie of scientists or political operatives; instead, it emerged organically from the work and writings of some of the most prominent figures in digital culture. Stewart Brand's *Whole Earth Catalog* and members of the nascent cyberculture were involved in something more than productive cross-fertilization. As Fred Turner narrates the story:

In 1968 Brand brought members of the two worlds together in the pages of one of the defining documents of the era, the *Whole Earth Catalog*. In 1985 he gathered them again on what would become perhaps the most influential computer conferencing system of the decade, the Whole Earth 'Lectronic Link, or the WELL. Throughout the late 1980s and early 1990s, Brand and other members of the network, including Kevin Kelly, Howard Rheingold, Esther Dyson, and John Perry Barlow, became some of the most-quoted spokespeople for a countercultural vision of the Internet. In 1993 all would help create the magazine that, more than any other, depicted the emerging digital world in revolutionary terms: *Wired*. (2006a, 3)

These original promulgaters of the "Californian Ideology" are among the most telling exemplars of cyberlibertarianism. They occupy a "nontraditional" space on the political spectrum and are frequently taken to be advocates of left-wing as well as right-wing values. However, they are better-known as promoters of a liberation through computing that is construed as being "above" or "beyond" traditional politics. These views somewhat "swamp" their ordinary political positions. Nonetheless, the overt political libertarianism of Barlow and Brand informs much of their writing and philosophy.

It is unclear if anyone told these people what to say. There may be no equivalent of the Koch brothers for cyberlibertarianism. They developed their philosophy themselves and, to a greater or lesser extent, seem to believe in it. Dyson and Rheingold, at least occasionally, make statements that fit into typical left-wing political points of view. However, these recommendations remain subordinate to their overall conviction that computerization is inherently progressive. Barlow, Brand, and Kelly see the computer as leading to a kind of "liberation" that is far more obviously right-wing than left-wing.

All of them oppose the idea that democratic polities should manage or regulate the development of digital technology. Instead, they endorse a Hayekian market approach to technological change. Kelly's view is that the market is a biological organism whose development might be threatened by too much parental intervention. None of them has much tolerance for views that question corporate power or the range and sway of capitalism. Brand, an avowed right-wing libertarian, encourages companies to work toward eco-friendly solutions because the market rewarding such solutions is the most effective way to achieve them. This view is sometimes called green capitalism. While no doubt many of its exponents have a sincere and committed orientation toward what may be our planet's most serious problem, green capitalism nevertheless rejects the view of most left-wing environmentalists that unbridled capitalist development is the signal cause of environmental destruction and therefore must be confronted for these effects to be mitigated.

Turner goes on:

> By the mid-1990s, throughout much of the mainstream press and in busi-
> ness and government as well, the networked entrepreneurship of the Whole
> Earth group and its self-evident financial and social success had become
> evidence for the transformative power of what many had begun to call the
> "New Economy." According to a raft of politicians and pundits, the rapid
> integration of computing and telecommunications technologies into inter-
> national economic life, coupled with dramatic rounds of corporate layoffs
> and restructuring, had given rise to a new economic era. Individuals could
> now no longer count on the support of their employers; they would instead
> have to become entrepreneurs, moving flexibly from place to place, sliding
> in and out of collaborative teams, building their knowledge bases and skill
> sets in a process of constant self-education. The proper role of government
> in this new environment, many argued, was to pull back, to deregulate the
> technology industries that were ostensibly leading the transformation, and,
> while they were at it, business in general. (2006a, 7)

The popular perception of these figures is that they are hippies. However, like the Grateful Dead, for whom Barlow wrote lyrics, their left-wing sur-face conceals a pro-business, anti-government, Hayekian worldview. "Do your own thing" is the guiding principle, which is as much a business mantra as it is a statement of political tolerance. It is no surprise then that Brand and his colleagues became successful entrepreneurs. Brand, along with sev-eral other entrepreneurs and corporate leaders, formed a practice in the late 1980s called the Global Business Network, among whose later "net-work members" were Clay Shirky and Kevin Kelly. Today GBN is owned by Deloitte, one of the world's major business consulting organizations. It is not difficult to see how the hippie mantra of "live and let live" has been transformed into the neoliberal "don't regulate what companies do."

THE SYNCRETIC AND INCHOATE POLITICS
OF CYBERLIBERTARIANISM

Cyberlibertarianism presents itself as a political force, offering a means for organizing the world and social action to benefit many, though perhaps not most, of us. It offers critiques of existing political structures, especially democratic institutions, as inadequate for the tasks the world presents. This condition is said to result from the changes wrought by technology, which are both inevitable and overwhelmingly beneficial, even for democracy, despite the relative impotence of democracies to do anything about them.

Despite the political nature of its fundamental claims, cyberlibertarian dogma has specific modes of intervention into politics, suggested by its core insight that posits technological progress as a force for positive social change. However, social change is predicated largely on right-wing ideas about society itself. By this, we do not mean some of the most hot-button ideas about left-right politics, especially social ideas. To the contrary, many of those who endorse cyberlibertarian dogma may well oppose the most obvious exponents of right-wing politics. They may support abortion rights and public education, accept the reality of climate change, and be in favor of higher taxes on corporations and the wealthy. To those of us with left-leaning politics, this is all to the good.

Many followers of cyberlibertarian dogma are unaware of the ways such precepts serve right-wing political power. If platforms like Facebook, X, and YouTube have played fundamental roles in shifting U.S. and global politics to the right, then efforts to prevent that power from being curtailed may well serve the right wing. This argument is especially legible concerning Section 230 of the Communications Decency Act of 1996 (see chapter 3), which enjoys persistent support across the political spectrum, especially among digital enthusiasts and even tech workers, who may see the law in terms of "freedom" and "openness" and accept the mainstream Silicon Valley story about its positive influence.

Cyberlibertarian politics are both *inchoate* and *syncretic*. Inchoate refers to the fact that the preeminent cyberlibertarians frequently refuse to wear their narrow politics on their sleeves. They suggest that anyone and everyone should support "internet freedom" and "free expression online" because such causes embody core political commitments, even though right and left very rarely agree on what these core commitments are.

Free expression defenders argue that digital platforms like X and Facebook should be governed by the same commitment to absolute free speech found in the last hundred years of U.S. Supreme Court doctrine. Supporters of both left and right politics believe that all politics will be harmed if *platforms* (and perhaps governments at a second-order level, through their power to regulate platforms) are understood to have the power to decide legitimate speech practices within their specific domains. This suggests that these platforms exert little or no influence over the political views conveyed through them, which has provoked significant arguments between partisans of left politics and free expression promoters. These arguments parallel arguments between absolutist free speech advocates in general and others, especially from critical legal studies and critical race theory, who have questioned whether the specific form of free speech absolutism found in U.S. legal doctrine treats all actors equally, or whether it too inherently favors the political right (see chapter 6).

Evangelists who promote an absolute position on free speech for digital platforms as obviously salutary for advocates across the political spectrum advance an *inchoate* doctrine. They take for granted its political orientation while not being able to show how or why the political consequences it claims for itself actually follow.

Syncretic politics, related to but not identical with inchoate politics, is a more disturbing phenomenon. In political theory, syncretism has a specific meaning. It is used especially in the context of "red–brown syncretism," a key idea in the theory of fascism. In that formulation, "red" represents socialism or communism and "brown" represents fascism, through association with Nazi brownshirts. Chapter 7 discusses syncretism as an on-ramp to fascism. Here, we can employ the term in a slightly looser fashion while not losing sight of its fascist overtones.

Two key insights emerge from studies of syncretic politics. First, they advocate a kind of politics that is "above left and right," sometimes referred to as "third positionism" (Berlet 2016; Griffin 1995; Southern Poverty Law Center 2015). Second, despite this claim, they nearly always serve as supports for the right. Sometimes this advocacy may be something that emerges over time, suggesting that the original claims to be "beyond left and right" were sincere if misguided. At other times, the syncretic formations are more open, including deliberate attempts to obscure the power and force of right-wing politics.

As the political scientist and analyst of right-wing politics Chip Berlet noted as early as 1990, "Third Position adherents actively seek to recruit from the left. . . . The fascist right has wooed the progressive left primarily around opposition to such issues as the use of U.S. troops in foreign military interventions, support for Israel, the problems of CIA misconduct and covert action, domestic government repression, privacy rights, and civil liberties." He goes on to note, "There is nothing intrinsically wrong with building coalitions with conservatives or libertarians around issues of common concern, but a problem does arise when the persons seeking to join a coalition have racist, anti-Jewish or anti-democratic agendas. Besides being morally offensive, these persons often peddle scapegoating theories that can divide existing coalitions." I have previously argued (Golumbia 2016d) and will reiterate in chapter 7 that the far right has a more direct influence on the development of digital technology and its supporting ideology than many non-supporters may realize (see also Belew 2019; Schradie 2019).

When Winner, Barbrook and Cameron, and others critique cyberlibertarianism for putting a digital face on right-wing beliefs, they do not imply that these attitudes are transformed into something other than what they are. Syncretism is not always engaged in the recruitment of those with left politics to the right. It is more generally a way of marshaling political energies and force that their adherents believe to be genuinely on the left toward often unwitting support for right-leaning politics.

The Tea Party is one of the best-known examples of third positionism in recent U.S. politics. It continues to be felt even after Trump left office in 2021. The Tea Party at first insisted on being "beyond left and right." One of the first books published on the movement, *Mad as Hell,* by right-leaning pollster Scott Rasmussen and Douglas Schoen, a former Democratic Party consultant who in the 2010s served as a political analyst and commentator for Fox News and Newsmax, was subtitled *How the Tea Party Movement Is Fundamentally Remaking Our Two-Party System.* The book begins with an epigraph from a Tea Party rally participant: "I'm not a Republican, I'm not a Democrat, I'm American. I'm here because I believe we need to do something about what is happening in our country" (Rasmussen and Schoen 2010, 1). The authors go on to dispute the view among some media commentators that "these protests were by no means spontaneous, that the Tea Party movement was not a legitimate grassroots movement. Rather, it was being fueled by conservative talk radio and cable television" (3). They insist that it is "patently false" that "elements of the Republican Party . . . had maneuvered" the Tea Party movement into existence (4); instead, they claim, it is a "genuine grassroots phenomenon" that has "unprecedented broad-based support" (5).

In the years since, the original clams that Rasmussen and Schoen dispute have all been shown to be true by far more reputable and rigorous scholars and journalists. Lepore (2010) and Skocpol and Williamson (2012) had already demonstrated the manufactured far-right nature of the movement. More recently, Costley White draws attention to the Tea Party as a brand whose primary functions were found in the media:

> By conveying shifting identities of the Tea Party as a social movement and political party, the news media gave the Tea Party brand a narrative fungibility that allowed it to function as a multiple signifier: sometimes as a third political party and other times as a social movement that took up the tropes of historical civil rights struggles. In relaying brand attributes through a collective emphasis on particular attributes, newsmakers specifically highlighted race, gender, and class (among other qualities like militarism, religiosity, and anger) as primary Tea Party characteristics. The Tea Party was often portrayed as a white working-class movement, while Tea Party women were used to brand the Tea Party as a form of modern conservatism. (2018, 184)

The Tea Party can be seen as having led to the right-wing populism that helped to elect Donald Trump in 2016. Originally seen as being other than right wing, its functions in the media as a brand that "took up the tropes of historical civil rights struggles" help to show how and why the political right frequently relies on causes and language that obscure their political commitments. The underlying movement serves in powerful ways to galvanize and enact right-wing political goals.

Glenn Greenwald, whose contribution to cyberlibertarian dogma via the WikiLeaks and Edward Snowden revelations is particularly telling, appeared interested in blurring the right-wing commitments of the Tea Party. In early 2010, Greenwald wrote a piece for *Salon* that referred to the Tea Party "movement" in quotation marks, called it "totally incoherent," and described it as "at bottom, nothing more than a cynical marketing attempt to re-brand the right wing of the Republican Party under the exact same policies and principles which defined it for the last couple of decades."

However, Greenwald wrote in the same publication almost a year later that "it's long been clear that the best (and perhaps only) political hope for civil liberties in the US is an alliance that transcends the standard Democrat v. GOP or left v. right dichotomies" (2011). He praised Rep. Dennis Kucinich (D-Ohio) for asking the Tea Party to join him in opposing the extension of the Patriot Act and Rep. Ron Paul (R-Tex.) and other libertarians for their apparent interest in protecting civil liberties. He ignored all the other aspects of their politics that might give pause to those on the political left in making common cause with them. Greenwald has since then been quick to diminish, belittle, and attack critics of his approach by using canned right-wing themes like "the establishment." He also praised a "genuine left–right alliance" in Britain that was in fact just another way for the Conservative party to use the Liberal Democrats against their primary Labour opposition.

CYBERLIBERTARIANISM AS DISINFORMATION

Neoliberalism, as described by Mirowski, incorporates disparate doctrinal features. Its exoteric doctrines feature government as pure violence, the individual as supreme, and wealth and power as correlatives of rights. These can be related to its esoteric doctrines, namely government as power to be used by those with other forms of wealth and power; wealth and power as supreme, even to the expense of the individual; and "rights" as essentially meaningless. It is less clear how the relationship between neoliberal economic goals and its esoteric and exoteric doctrines regarding the self and the person, and the relation of these to society at large, contribute to neoliberalism's larger goals. Why should neoliberalism, in either its esoteric or exoteric doctrines, promote the kind of self-formation typified by Howard Roark in Ayn Rand's *The Fountainhead,* realized as variously as the quasi-fascism of weev, the arrogant demeanor of Julian Assange (see chapter 7), or the condescending, dismissive global cultural analyses of Clayton Christensen, Clay Shirky, Jane McGonigal, Marina Gorbis, or Jeff Jarvis?

In addition to promoting a consumerist, narcissistic conception of personhood, where politics is construed almost entirely in terms of personal "empowerment," neoliberalism thrives on actively rejecting the older ideas of a consistent or stable selfhood, critical to the views of John Locke, for example, the political philosopher to whom writers like Hayek and Rothbard sometimes point for foundational support. Instead, neoliberalism favors an ungrounded, "flexible" conception of personhood that

> lays waste to older distinctions between production and consumption rooted in the labor theory of value, and reduces the human being to an arbitrary bundle of "investments," skill sets, temporary alliances (family, sex, race), and fungible body parts. "Government of the self" becomes the taproot of all social order, even though the identity of the self evanesces under the pressure of continual prosthetic tinkering; this is one possible way to understand the concept of "biopower." Under this regime, the individual displays no necessary continuity from one "decision" to the next. The manager of You becomes the new ghost in the machine. (Mirowski 2013, 59)

One of the distinctly exoteric consequences of this doctrine is that Neoliberal Thought Collective (NTC) and Mont Pelerin Society (MPS) members read widely and pontificate on their own interpretations of critical figures and issues in political thought. However, holding onto such ideas is actively resisted among the most public and functional institutions dear to neoliberalism. The Tea Party studiously avoids sustained relationship with foundational texts and issues from the Revolutionary Boston period that would cast doubt on many of its critical precepts. Anti–climate change advocates have developed an entire intellectual sphere in which anti-science reasoning is vociferously advanced as science itself, over the objections of actual working scientists. Maintaining political force like this requires ignorance of a special kind that actively resists engagement with material that would call its precepts into question.

Mirowski points out that this studied ignorance is not an incidental feature of neoliberals' esoteric motives. Rather, it is a central part of their teaching. Perhaps the most important tenet of their philosophy is that human beings are not merely constitutionally ignorant but fundamentally ignorant. We can and do know very little (despite the obvious contradiction that Hayek and Mises certainly seem to think that they know a lot); *only the market knows*. "The market," whatever that is, is intelligence that can be conveyed to human beings *only in the form of the imperfect information known as "price"* (although in some circumstances, such as the "marketplace of ideas," certain variables other than price can also be construed as meaningful information). Such a view is not only coincidentally emergent with the advent of digital technology, but inextricably tied to it, because *"the market" itself is a very special kind of computer.* "In the popular Hayekian account," writes Mirowski, "the marketplace is deemed to be a superior information processor, so therefore all human knowledge can be used to its fullest only if it is comprehensively owned and priced" (2013, 65). Part of the "double truth" of neoliberalism is that despite being "dedicated to rational discourse about a market conceived as a superior information processor," the most influential members of the NTC "ended up praising and promoting ignorance" (70).

This is not a minor complaint, but rather central to the public dogma of these thinkers, although only critics point out the brute contradictions it entails:

> Hayek is noteworthy in that he placed ignorance at the very center of his political theory: "the case for individual freedom rests chiefly on the recognition of the inevitable ignorance of us all." Most commentators tend to interpret this as an appeal to ignorance as some kind of primal state of mankind; but I think they need to expand their horizons. The distinction begins to bite when we take note that Hayek harbored a relatively low opinion of the role of education and discussion in the process of learning, and notoriously, an even lower opinion of the powers of ratiocination of those he disparaged as "the intellectuals." These, of course, were the mirror image of his belief in the market as a superior information processor: "Nor is the process of forming majority opinion entirely, or even chiefly, a matter of discussion, as the overintellectualized conception would have it . . . Though discussion is essential, it is not the main process by which people learn. Their views and desires are formed by individuals acting according to their own designs . . . It is because we normally do not know who knows best that we leave the decision to a process we do not control." (Mirowski 2013, 78, quoting Hayek's *Constitution of Liberty*)

This prompts Mirowski, again sticking closely to Hayek, to declare that "neoliberalism masquerades as a radically populist philosophy, one that begins with a set of philosophical theses about *knowledge* and its relationship to society" (82), emphasizing that *"the major ambition of the Neoliberal Thought Collective is to sow doubt and ignorance among the populace"* (83).

Wherever we declare that some aspect of society cannot be governed by rational actors but only by the superior intelligence of markets, we insist that ignorance trumps knowledge. Those of us who use our knowledge to follow what the market appears to tell us—despite the fact that we are, by stipulation, not knowledgeable enough to discern just what that is—should be praised for following our ignorance, rather than pursuing other seeming routes to truth or insight. This line of thinking, as contradictory and self-dealing as it appears, is not to be extended outside the market proper. Hayek's own essay on "The Use of Knowledge in Society" (1945) is a particular example to guide us. While Hayek's main target is efforts to construct a rational economic order (519)—that is, the "centralized" economic planning that is often the explicit target of the Austrian economists and their adherents, and that remains a rhetorical target of their allies even today—the title itself tells us that Hayek ends up having bigger game in his sights.

Thus, while Hayek tells us that "the peculiar character of a rational economic order is determined precisely by the fact that the knowledge of the circumstances of which we must make use never exists in concentrated or integrated form, but solely as the dispersed bits of incomplete and frequently contradictory knowledge which all the separate individuals possess" (519), the problem becomes "a problem of the utilization of knowledge not given to anyone in its totality" (520). In this early phase, Hayek is willing to grant that "the position will be different with respect to different kinds of knowledge." "So far as scientific knowledge is concerned, a body of suitably chosen experts may be in the best position to command all the best knowledge available" (521).

Yet the boundaries between "scientific," "social," and "economic" knowledge are more permeable than Hayek's language allows. He ultimately repudiates the idea that "all such [economic] knowledge should as a matter of course be at the command of everybody" (522), which is suggestively used in much of the libertarian rhetoric surrounding digital media. Practical economic knowledge, as opposed to statistics "arrived at by abstracting from minor differences" among things in the world, "by its nature cannot enter into statistics and therefore cannot be conveyed to any central authority in statistical form." "The economic problem of society is mainly one of rapid adaptation to changes in the particular circumstances of time and place," he writes, and only "some form of decentralization" can "ensure that the knowledge of the particular circumstances of time and place will be promptly used" (524).

While it is probably true that Hayek intended this line of thinking to be nominally constrained to the economic sphere, in later years no such restraint has been observed. It should come as little surprise that Jimmy Wales, who has said that Ayn Rand's thought "colors everything I do and think" ("Free-Knowledge Fundamentalist" 2008), and who named his daughter after a character in *Atlas Shrugged* (Chozick 2013), drew inspiration for Wikipedia from Hayek's article:

> Read Hayek's "The Use of Knowledge in Society" as an undergraduate; deep impact on thinking. Game-theoretic, rule-making within society, how people interact; basic ideas, e.g., simply making a rule doesn't make anything happen, but just changes the costs and benefits. At the time ongoing debate in economics on the efficacy of a centrally planned economy versus the efficacy of a market economy. Hayek's point in the essay was that this is a question of information: is it more effective to communicate all the information inward to a central authority who will use that information to make a decision, or is it more efficient to leave the information where it is and push decision-making out to the endpoints? . . . is it better to gather all the world's information into a group of experts who then make editorial decisions, or to push the decision making out to the endpoints, the people who have the information? (Roberts 2009)

Despite Hayek's explicit refusal to apply his analysis outside of central economic planning, Wales generalizes and expands on it, to the point of documenting the totality of human knowledge to which Wikipedia aspires.

In fact, despite Wikipedia's aspirations, Mirowski has constructed an elegant argument that suggests a main function of the site is to promote ignorance, providing a central resource for spreading uncertainty over the historical record and the reliability of experts. Noting that "many on the contemporary left seem to be flummoxed when it comes to grasping some basic facts of the modern neoliberal regime" (2009, 422), Mirowski points out that Wikipedia is constantly changing. This occasionally lauded feature of the "encyclopedia anyone can edit" means it "can't manage to get much of *anything* straight for very long." This follows directly from Wales's implementation of the misapplied Hayekian economic dictum to the world of knowledge at large: "The conviction that the truth 'emerges' from random interactions of variously challenged participants in the precincts of Wiki-world . . . only holds water if we are allowed great latitude in the definition of 'truth'" (424).

Noting Wikipedia's destructive effects on "encyclopedias, journals, and newspapers"—exactly those organs to which democracies turn in their pursuit of knowledge—Mirowski argues that Wikipedia disparages the very notion of knowledge it claims to champion. While the site's philosophy, like that of the overall NTC project, "appears to be a radical levelling philosophy, denigrating expertise and elite pretensions to hard-won knowledge," it "appeals to the vanity of every self-absorbed narcissist, who would be glad to ridicule intellectuals as 'professional secondhand dealers in ideas'" (425, quoting Hayek's Studies in Philosophy, Politics and Economics). As in the culture of Wikipedia, so in the NTC: "Attacks on 'intellectuals' were a common refrain in the history of Mont Pelerin and were not restricted to Hayek" (448n12).

"But of course," Mirowski notes, "the neoliberals didn't renounce *all* expertise—just the stuff they don't like" (448n12). This "double truth" goes hand in hand with another core neoliberalism contradiction. "For outsiders, neoliberal thinkers are portrayed as plucky individual rebel blooms of rage against the machine, arrayed against all the forces of big government and special interests" (Mirowski 2013, 75–76), but the truth is that "once initiated into the mysteries of the thought collective, only the organization men rise to the top, and they know it" (76). This means that, despite all appearances, neoliberalism is comfortable with authoritarian forms of governance: Mirowski quotes Hayek in a 1966 address to the MPS: "It is at least possible in principle that a democratic government may be authoritarian and that an authoritarian government may act on liberal principles" (57). As the neoliberals' dalliance with Chilean dictator Augusto Pinochet suggests, the public is supposed to understand neoliberalism (and its more public variant, contemporary libertarianism) as philosophies of freedom in general. However, they entail that "freedom" for those closest to the center, which results in massive curtailments of freedom for those at the margins. The appearance of distributed and decentralized democracy satisfies the masses. But there is a studied ignorance of the nature of the actual, operating form of power, which is closer to plutocracy or oligarchy than to representative democracy. Attempts to bring these facts to light, no matter how thorough or well-documented, fail to "stick" against the smooth wall of ignorance neoliberalism cultivates.

It may be surprising to discover that despite its claims to decentralization and horizontal power, Wikipedia is in practice what its doubly ironically titled "benevolent dictator for life" (Chozick 2013) Jimmy Wales claims to loathe: a "strict hierarchy, in which higher levels exist to frustrate and undo the activities of participants at lower levels" (Mirowski 2009, 422). "What looks like a libertarian paradise is in fact a thinly veiled totalitarian hierarchy," and "in the spaces where spontaneous participation is permitted, knowledge in fact degrades rather than improves" (426). All of this "adds up to a 'double truth' doctrine: one truth for the masses/participants and another for those at the top."

Study after study has shown that the demographic of Wikipedia editors is very narrow, and that a large percentage of all writing and editing is performed by them (Oberhaus 2017). In many cases, these editors seem to relish their positions of power, especially when they get to rebuff the suggestions of experts who attempt to weigh in directly on topics to which they have devoted many years of study. A recent quantitative paper shows that "instead of functioning as digital 'laboratories of democracy,' peer production projects may conform to Robert Michels' 'iron law of oligarchy'" (Shaw and Mako Hill 2014, 1). Shaw and Mako Hill note that this problem is inherent not just to Wikipedia, but to the very wiki form that is promoted as conducive to nonhierarchical power relations: "We find strong evidence that, on average, as wikis become larger, a small group—present at the beginning—monopolizes positions of formal authority in the community and accounts for more administrative activity while also using their authority to restrict contributions from experienced community members. The wikis in our sample are not indicative of robustly democratic, participatory institutions. This is true despite the relative lack of formal bureaucratic structure or clearly-defined roles within many wikis" (3).

In cyberlibertarian practice, the marketing labels attached to a project are more important in establishing its public reputation than actual evidence of the thing in operation. "Anyone can edit," we are told: despite evidence that the results of anyone being able to edit are not a closer approximation to useful knowledge than the former model of letting experts write about what they know, the counterfactual marketing story maintains itself in the public mind. This is especially true in the minds of pundits and advocates

(Benkler 2007; Shirky 2008a; Tapscott and Williams 2013), many of whom continue to point to Wikipedia as the exemplar of what distributed, non-hierarchical power can achieve.

In *What the Dormouse Said*, John Markoff writes that computing pioneer "Alan Kay observed that you could divide the pioneers of personal computing into two camps: those who read and those who didn't" (2005, 179). In a 2013 interview, Kay observes:

> It is not a huge exaggeration to point out that electronic media over the last 100+ years have actually removed some of day to day needs for reading and writing, and have allowed much of the civilized world to lapse back into oral societal forms (and this is not a good thing at all for systems that require most of the citizenry to think in modern forms).
>
> For most people, what is going on is quite harmful. (Greelish 2013)

A wealth of data suggests that how we read online is less conducive to deep intellectual engagement than how we engage with books. It is not unreasonable to worry that we are trading deep engagement for surface engagement. There is no evidence that one accomplishes the same goals as the other. Giving up deep reading, on which so much of our political and social institutions are based, in favor of products promoted by the very neoliberal capital that reading deeply often calls us to question, is not justifiable for any reason beyond the immediate pleasures we get from engagement with digital devices and media.

Furthermore, we occasionally see the promotion of the nearly ubiquitous short-form texts in digital media as not just the apotheosis of long-form texts, but also the replacement for them. Such rhetoric of replacement is widespread, significantly under-motivated by evidence, and *ideological,* dismissing the notion that reading books is critical to society. While there are undoubtedly instances of what appear to be culturally conservative "defenses of reading" (e.g., Birkerts 2006) that are routinely dismissed in cyberlibertarian rhetoric as "romantic" or "traditional," the vitriol that digital utopians have toward the very kind of practice—the reading of long texts—that produced the democracy they appear to be championing is striking and deserves more scrutiny.

I am not suggesting active conspiracy. Clay Shirky, Jeff Jarvis, Howard Rheingold, Tim Berners-Lee, Jimmy Wales, and Nicholas Negroponte are not part of a coordinated Koch brothers program developed to disparage reading—which does not mean some of them have not accepted some of that dark money. They are not being paid or even encouraged to disparage higher education—although there is a certain amount of circulation between the academics who promote the digital replacement of higher education like Shirky and Clayton Christensen and the business, corporate consulting, and venture capitalists who stand to benefit from it.

But "the digital" exists in a cultural context widely permeated by neoliberal propaganda, which includes the disparagement of intellectuals and intellectual practice as well as the promotion of ignorance. The fact that so much of the digital environment happens to align with this profoundly ideological assault on the project of an informed citizenry is paradoxical and ironic. This attack often happens under the banner of "information wants to be free" and "default open," which is why we must be much more attentive to the contexts in which cyberlibertarian rhetoric appears and the larger political contexts in which its recommendations circulate.

CYBERLIBERTARIANISM AS FRAMING

The dogma of cyberlibertarianism frames debates. "Framing" is a social-scientific concept that sets out a range of acceptable answers to questions. It is much subtler than direct argumentation and determines what is considered reasonable and unreasonable when approaching a given topic. One of its most important effects is to depict alternatives A, B, and C as the "solution" to a problem, which disqualifies alternatives D and E as options.

Digital advocates appear to have learned a lot about framing from climate change denialists, who learned a lot in turn from the tobacco industry. As Philip Mirowski, Jeremy Walker, and Antoinette Abboud put it in 2013 regarding climate change, "One reason neoliberals have triumphed over their ideological rivals is because they have ventured beyond a single 'fix' for any given problem, instead deploying a broad spectrum of policies from the most expendable short-term expedients, to medium-term politics, to long-horizon utopian projects. While these may appear as distinct and contradictory policies, they are in fact integrated in such a way as to produce eventual capitulation to the free market." In the case of climate change denial, the "short-term expedients" are forms of raw science denialism; the medium-term come in the form of emissions credits; and the long-term as massive geoengineering projects (and perhaps a reinvestment in nuclear energy, which is closely connected to the fossil fuel industry). "We think most people on the Left," they go on, "don't fully realize that the phenomena of science denialism, emissions trading and geoengineering are not in fact unrelated or rival panaceas but rather constitute together the full neoliberal response to global warming."

Mirowski argues that the right has developed a strategy for managing discourse about climate change. If a critic is not silenced via denialism, they will be steered toward carbon credits. If this fails, then geoengineering becomes the solution. This kind of discourse management is purposely leaky and not everyone will agree with any of it, let alone all of it. The point is that the three nodes attract so much public discourse that the few voices who reject all the arguments will remain diffuse, minor, and unlikely to attract many adherents.

Further, the potentially obvious alternatives are implicitly discredited: they simply become unthinkable for most people. Nevertheless, "rather than allowing ourselves to be enrolled pragmatically in the neoliberal script, we need to remind ourselves there are other policy options. For example, fixed high or rising carbon taxes applied universally to wholesale coal, oil and gas transactions deserve our serious consideration, as they might actually accomplish the effect of a 'price signal' and spur disinvestment in the ever-expanding fossil-fuel sector. It is not surprising that the Right has so vilified this strategy." Cyberlibertarian framing does not rely on an exactly parallel spectrum of "allowable" discursive positions. Instead, it uses a variety of tropes and apparently obvious "truths" that lurk in the background of their arguments. These are relatively vague when applied to actual policies but can serve as ready alternatives no matter the issue at hand. This is especially obvious with regard to the promotion of privacy, on the one hand, and free expression and internet freedom on the other. Whichever of these two concerns might be most salient in any given political nexus will be invoked, regardless of whether the position contradicts the other (see chapter 6).

The main policy goal for U.S. cyberlibertarianism is to maintain Section 230 of the Communications Decency Act of 1996, as detailed in the next chapter. However, the law's form and function are deeply ambiguous, with an inherently dual function to promote content moderation and limit liability for companies that engage in it. As a result, the loudest voices among the digital commentariat have often used contradictory arguments to sustain the statute. This is compounded by the propensity of those who most strongly align themselves with the law to obfuscate its function, partly by accusing critics of failing to understand the law itself, which leads to a discursive field muddied to the point of opacity. The only certainty is that the internet could not exist without Section 230, and that democracies risk great (if unclear) dangers should they risk any modification to the law. As a result, the notion of altering the fundamental operation of digital technology companies is taken off the table.

Although cyberlibertarian framing is less clearly determined than climate change denialism, we can identify several persistent gestures. First, a series of rhetorical moves are used to put critical remarks beyond the pale of reasonable discussion: a critic is said to be fueled by "moral panic" or "technopanic," or to be engaged in "techlash." Each comes down to a kind of ad hominem attack on critics' motivations that makes it unnecessary to engage with the substance of their arguments. Second, technology is said to be inevitable and outside the control of democratic polities, but at the same time to be very good for democracy. Third, digital technology is compared to the printing press, and critiques of it are thereby said to be opposed to the entire development of knowledge and science. Fourth, regulation or law is said to destroy the "internet as we know it," which is taken for granted to be a thing that must be "saved." Finally, democracies are said to be on the verge of outlawing specific, widely loved phenomena such as memes, even if the policy under question makes no mention of those phenomena. In the world of Bitcoin and cryptocurrency these strategies have become so well-known that they are often joked about, even by those who aren't fully immersed in the discourse. HODL, laser-eyes, "to the moon," "have fun staying poor," and other phrases have entered the public imagination as tactics used by cryptocurrency enthusiasts to encourage people to buy into whatever token a promoter might be selling.

One of my main goals in this book is to provide a means to keep track of the rhetorical moves used by digital advocates. Once one becomes sensitive to these tactics, they become easier to dismiss, even if they exert a certain power in public discussions of important topics. The other strategies digital advocates use to frame discussions are more subtle. They fall into at least three additional groups:

- *Carefully framing descriptions of legitimate policy alternatives (along with the tacit identification of illegitimate ones).* For example, breaking up Facebook or Google is considered the "ultimate" form of regulation for them, while more radical solutions such as nationalizing their services or even criminalizing them fall off the table entirely.
- *The presentation of global narratives about the purpose and function of digital technologies.* This includes nostrums on the order of "the internet was meant to bring peace and democracy."
- *The shifting of debate in a circular fashion.* When privacy concerns are raised, digital advocates express great concerns about being constrained; however, if concerns about "openness" become prominent, those same advocates express great concerns about "privacy." Both "privacy" and "openness" are construed in highly specialized, digital-specific ways that often sit very uneasily with other understandings of these terms.

To illustrate framing and discourse management, consider responses to Shoshana Zuboff's 2019 book, *The Age of Surveillance Capitalism.* She is clear that "foundational values of democratic communities" (522), "human dignity" (522), and "the human expectation of sovereignty over one's own life and authorship of one's own experience" (521) are threatened by digital technologies. The only solution is for democracies to assert care and sovereignty over the political sphere via law and regulation (480–88). Zuboff has gone further since publishing the book, suggesting that democracies should "criminalize" (Zuboff 2021, 00:22:35) data extraction and behavioral manipulation, which are the literal stuff of surveillance capitalism.

These are new proposals that some members of the U.S. Congress are taking seriously, and that I believe should be considered by all democracies. They raise fundamental questions about the legitimacy of not just the business models but the modi operandi of companies like Google, Facebook, Reddit, and Amazon, as well as for putative not-for-profit or "decentralized" versions of similar technology (see chapter 5). Despite the presence of her book as arguably the central and most pointed argument made about digital technology in recent years, especially since the Trump and Brexit elections of 2016, the reception for Zuboff's ideas has been lukewarm, even muted, among most of those in cyberlibertarian punditry. Few comment on her proposals, despite her unusually specific and fundamental proposals for legal remedies to the digital hijacking of democracy.

Yet the phrase "surveillance capitalism" has entered the vocabulary of digital pundits and "digital rights" organizations who have avoided Zuboff's proposals. The term is taken as an unalloyed negative, as Zuboff intended. Digital rights organizations seem to realize this. However, in their spin, something subtle and remarkable happens. The solution to surveillance capitalism is not the kinds of laws and regulations Zuboff calls for but instead a reiteration of the same constitutively vague principles of "democratization," "decentralization," and "internet freedom" that *produced* surveillance capitalism.

Cory Doctorow's *How to Destroy Surveillance Capitalism* (2020) is the most sustained response to Zuboff's work from one of the many pundits most associated with digital "activism." His online "book" appears to accept Zuboff's critique but systematically redefines and disputes her facts and arguments. He reorients her proposals so that her work ends up supporting only the "backstop" argument digital rights organizations have long offered as their version of the "long-term solution" (similar to the way climate change denialists offer "geoengineering")—namely, breaking up Big Tech via antitrust actions. Doctorow proposes that a (moderately regulated) free market is the best agent to solve the problems Zuboff defines, despite Zuboff's explicit arguments that the free market, along with Section 230 and other forces, is exactly what has created the problem.

Doctorow's work is a master class in reframing the discussion and setting the boundaries for reasonable discourse. His left-leaning politics only help to establish the idea that he is providing a "progressive" interpretation of Zuboff's critique, though on any typical analysis of the political spectrum Zuboff's solutions are actually far to the left of Doctorow's.

It has been remarkable to see various factions among digital advocates appear to take up Zuboff's critique, no doubt due to the widespread adoption of the notion of surveillance capitalism as a way to understand the effects of digital technology. While Doctorow's treatment is the most extensive, the cryptocurrency and blockchain communities, which are themselves partly constituted in opposition to the government along the lines established by the cypherpunk community, began to talk about their favored technologies as solutions to the surveillance capitalism problem after the publication of Zuboff's book. She is abundantly clear that the kind of cyberlibertarian thinking that produced blockchain is the same thinking that produced surveillance capitalism (connections I detail in Golumbia

2016). Michael Casey—a *Wall Street Journal* journalist who is also chair of the advisory board for cryptocurrency industry publication *CoinDesk* and also a senior advisor for MIT's Digital Currency Initiative—expressly acknowledged the power of Zuboff's argument: "This book, which eviscerates the 'applied utopianism' and 'technological inevitably' of data-gobbling Silicon Valley titans such as Google and Facebook, will become a defining text of our age. Read it. It is of vital importance" (2019). However, Casey ultimately rejects most of Zuboff's analysis, claiming that the problems lie not with the specific features of digital technology Zuboff describes—such as data extraction and behavioral modification—but instead with "the real centralizing power-mongers of our digital economy [that] have been pillaging our data and reshaping humanity into an instrument of their domination."

Cyberlibertarian critics alter Zuboff's focus on the effects of technology into the idea that the real problem is *who* is using it, and that if the right people come along, they can use it and the politics on which it is built to do "good." According to Casey, Zuboff's critiques threaten to bolster an "anti-technology" position that is both unreasonable and a mark of mental or characterological weakness. Casey believes that "many of Zuboff's anti-technology positions [are] too extreme," and "if blockchain technology is to play an integral role in the evolution of the digital global economy and be a force for good, rather than a vehicle of computerized subjugation, its advocates will have to contend with the angry backlash against digital technologies that this book will help fuel." Readers influenced by this analysis will merely see an unjustified anger at technologies and need not confront Zuboff's idea that the cyberlibertarian belief that blockchain (or any technology) *can* be a "force for good" might actually lie at the root of the problem.

Zuboff believes that democracy provides the solution to the problems of surveillance capitalism, while Casey dismisses democracy as "the levers of government." However, blockchain promoters along with Casey know that "a blockchain solution for breaking down surveillance capitalism would naturally be a technological one, embracing the power of math and cryptography to design a new digital topography of trust that disempowers the centralized middleman and creates human agency within a decentralized system." Despite the fact that the notion of "centralized middlemen" and "decentralized systems" (see chapter 5) are vague technological anti-government sentiments that have characterized cyberlibertarianism from the beginning, Casey thinks "it's possible to envisage an information technology-enriched world in which truly autonomous, free-thinking humans more easily come together and collaboratively innovate," and asserts that "the open-source inventiveness of global blockchain development communities speaks directly to this." This means that "those building zero-knowledge-proof systems and other privacy-protection layers can talk to a vision of decentralized protocols that both empower individuals to control their own data and prevent the public ledger from becoming a new behavior extraction tool. That's one potential answer to surveillance capitalism." Thus, in the cyberlibertarian critique, the problem Zuboff spends hundreds of pages defining becomes the solution to that same problem.

Even though Casey is one of the more reasonable and responsible of blockchain promoters, he engages in discourse management that effectively takes strong critiques of technology off the table. Other cryptocurrency commentators have gone even further in appearing to accept Zuboff's critique while insisting, in a predictable trolling register, that she misunderstands the field so badly that she fails to see that existing technology is the obvious and only solution to the problems she describes. One of the less reasonable cryptocurrency commentators, Jamie Redman, self-described anarcho-capitalist and "news lead" at industry publication Bitcoin.com, commented in March 2020, as the Covid-19 pandemic was starting to affect the economy in general and the earning capacity of the economically disenfranchised in particular, and turned the rhetoric of surveillance capitalism on its head, insisting that $1,200 payments to citizens amounted to "$2 trillion for surveillance capitalism."

Never mind that Zuboff specifically describes surveillance capitalism as a threat to democratic governance. To Redman, because Bitcoin "is the very opposite of the concepts being pushed by politicians and central bank governors," it is not "privacy-invasive, crammed with KYC/AML protocols, and extremely centralized." KYC (Know Your Customer) and AML (Anti-Money Laundering) regulatory regimes that exist to protect citizens and democratic governance have been a major target of cryptocurrency promoters worldwide. Such discourse might lead someone concerned about surveillance capitalism to presume that cryptocurrency—among the most wildly unregulated and scam-filled instances of capitalism in a hundred years—is the answer to lack of regulation, oversight, and rapacious free marketeers. Indeed, Redman goes so far as to quote Zuboff criticizing technology that "claims human experience as free raw material for translation into behavioral data" and "surveillance capitalists [who] have grown immensely wealthy from these trading operations," yet then claims that what Zuboff means is that "free services and cash injections are the perfect onramps to monitor people's behaviors and financial transactions without consent." He provides no argumentation, let alone evidence, that this is what the stimulus package was designed to do (and of course there has been little to suggest that those were the effects of the package). And he conveniently overlooks the massive and obvious ways the Bitcoin trading market does exactly this, even if it is to some extent different from the core kinds of behavioral manipulation Zuboff writes about.

An even more remarkable example of this discursive management occurred in late summer 2021 when the U.S. Congress considered adding provisions to infrastructure legislation designed to collect taxes from cryptocurrency transactions. Alexis Goldstein, director of financial policy at the Open Markets Institute, described the opposition to this provision as "seeking to create the impression that this innovative technology is somehow ill-suited to meeting the tax-reporting requirements that apply to traditional banks and brokerages" (2021). However, "the lack of tax information from major cryptocurrency platforms," she writes, "isn't related to any technological limitation. It's a design decision."

> Stock brokerages such as Charles Schwab and TD Ameritrade regularly produce 1099-B forms, which summarize taxable gains for customers and help the Internal Revenue Service ensure that all taxes are paid. Not so in crypto—and particularly in the world of decentralized finance, where nebulously governed platforms execute transactions through automatic market makers. Consider the decentralized finance ("DeFi") exchange Uniswap, which gave away 150 million UNI coins to users last September—a taxable windfall worth at least half a billion dollars, and possibly as much as a few billion dollars total, depending on when people claimed their "airdropped" tokens. Uniswap didn't send out any forms to help users understand their tax liability, leaving them to figure it out for themselves. Many might simply ignore it, or turn to one of the third-party services that in some cases charge up to hundreds of dollars to generate tax forms.

The infrastructure bill proposal sought "to address this problem by extending 1099-type reporting requirements to crypto intermediaries, part of a broader effort to counter the vast underreporting of taxable cryptocurrency gains. The Joint Committee on Taxation estimates that the reporting change alone would bring in $28 billion over the next decade." Despite cryptocurrency advocates using a variety of arguments to try to defeat the initiative, which was not even a full-fledged proposed law yet as it had not yet gone through reconciliation, the most interesting line of attack was the claim that ordinary tax reporting, as required for essentially all financial transactions in world democracies, constitutes a kind of illicit surveillance. The world truly seemed to have turned upside-down.

Many in the crypto industry portrayed the tax reporting required by the infrastructure bill as nothing less than an existential threat. The CEO of crypto exchange Kraken, Jesse Powell, tweeted a "Join, or Die" graphic, urging followers and "cryptohornets" to "publicly shame" members of Congress. And Messari Crypto CEO Ryan Selkis (who recently closed on $21 million in funding from investors including Steve Cohen) described Treasury Secretary Janet Yellen as a "white collar criminal" and called on the industry to "destroy crypto's enemies before they destroy us."

There's no such threat. As Omri Marian, a law professor at the University of California, Irvine, put it, the industry is merely seeking to preserve an "unwarranted, accidental tax preference" that "enables tax cheats to, well, cheat."

Of course it has been part of cypherpunk dogma from the beginning that government is "criminal," despite that word having very little meaning beyond "violating criminal laws as enacted by a government." Therefore, the idea of government being criminal is essentially self-contradictory by definition.

Not only cryptocurrency promoters but digital rights organizations have also joined the bandwagon, claiming not only that attempts to require cryptocurrency traders to report taxable trades in the same way that all other traders must constitutes not just "surveillance" and a "disaster for digital privacy," as EFF put it (Reitman 2021), but that cryptocurrency constitutes our best way to combat "surveillance capitalism." Evan Greer—musician, longtime digital rights activist, director of the problematic digital rights organization Fight for the Future, and creator of a song called "Surveil-lance Capitalism" (2021a) that purports to be inspired by and about the same issues outlined by Zuboff—urged followers to contact their congressional representatives by stating that "decentralization is our best bet for having a future internet that's not based on surveillance capitalism and where people have basic rights. Cryptocurrencies are just sort of the tip of the iceberg, messy (and often scammy) proofs of concept for something much more important" (Greer 2021b). Zuboff's argument is turned upside-down and played against itself, so that the specific ideology, practices, technologies, and even entities that brought us to where we are today, we are told, are the solutions to the problem they have created.

Greer misstates the stakes of the bill, contending that compelling wealthy people who profit from cryptocurrency trading to pay taxes would interfere with "an internet that's not based on surveillance capitalism." Some commentators pushed back on Greer and asked for detailed explanations for why we should accept any of the propositions offered, but no explanations were forthcoming. For many of those who follow Greer, Fight for the Future, EFF, and other cyberlibertarian activists, the discourse had been successfully managed and reframed, and the very problems Zuboff analyzes had now been reframed as their own solutions. The Senate was inundated with demands to undo this provision, and only the tangled process of lawmaking saw proffered revisions of the offending part fail to make it into the bill. Nevertheless, the view that "decentralized technology" is the vital force that will redress the problems of surveillance capitalism, whereas law and regulation enacted by elected officials stands in the way of this "solution," gains even more strength as a form of response to criticisms of digital technology—criticism that digital rights organizations *appear* to take on board, only to deploy against themselves when push comes to shove.

"DIGITAL RIGHTS"

Among the most concerning aspects of digital politics is the rise of NGOs, think tanks, and academic and quasi-academic centers that present themselves as defenders of "digital rights." Some of the most influential U.S. organizations include EFF, CDT, and Fight for the Future, but there are many others active throughout the world. In contrast to NGOs whose remits are at least somewhat clear, digital rights organizations promote vague doctrines that frustrate independent academic inquiry. They often appear to act more like lobbying organizations for technology in general, and at times for digital technology companies in particular, than as protectors of civil rights in a way suggested by their names and self-descriptions. An exception to this is the Electronic Privacy Information Center, which often takes pro-citizen and pro–civil rights positions that put it at odds with EFF and the others. Notably, the American Civil Liberties Union, whose commitment to civil rights in specific forms is largely beyond question, has recently taken up causes related to digital rights. Its practices and doctrine in this arena are in stark contrast to the kinds of work it does elsewhere, so much so that some constitutional scholars and legal experts have come to doubt whether its digital rights arm has the same mission as the parts of the organization with which the public is more familiar (more on that below).

As a term of art, "digital rights" enters the discourse around technological progress and regulation in a curious way. Even in the early 2010s, works such as Herman (2013) and Postigo (2012) detail how distrust of copyright spread through digital activism, fueled by revisionist accounts of the history of copyright that were more informed by right-wing propaganda than some promoters understood. (Vaidhyanathan 2004 is a clear example of this, with its author's commitment to left politics clashing sharply with his adoption of rightist language about "hacking the real world" and schematic battles between "control" and "freedom.") Democratic procedures and values were given limited consideration.

One would be forgiven for hearing the term as a parallel construction to "civil rights" or "human rights," referring specifically to those rights as they are affected by digital technology. However, it is difficult to see how this is supposed to work. Digital rights are said to occupy a distinct category from the rights encoded in the Universal Declaration of Human Rights (UDHR) and world constitutions, and the organizations centered on them talk as if they are. But when pressed these collapse into existing civil rights distorted by cyberlibertarian dogma. "Freedom of speech" and "censorship" (see chapter 6) have new interpretations necessitated by digital technology, but these consistently expand civil rights into the "rights" of economic actors. There is no thick political philosophy to explain why such fundamental rights should change due to new communications technology. This is most visible in the promotion of "internet freedom," which even

Secretary of State Hillary Clinton once considered adding to the UDHR, though it seemed impossible to provide clear language that would indicate how it relates to the rich panoply of rights listed in that document.

The causes that cyberlibertarians of all political stripes congregate around, and the ones toward which their efforts have historically been most effective, are those that insist the government must keep its hands off digital technology. The emotions that accompany these sentiments are often quite strong, as if something precious and important will be lost if, for example, SOPA and PIPA were to have passed, or governments try to regulate Bitcoin, 3D printing, encryption, or drone technology. Cyberlibertarians rarely criticize corporations when they exercise powers or implement practices that mimic governmental regulatory practices. Their animus is reserved for government. Indeed, one of the only criticisms cyberlibertarians level at corporations is that they interfere with the "digital rights" the movement considers so crucial.

Examples of such corporate interference include digital technology companies complying with democratically enacted laws and regulations, such as X or Facebook "censoring" certain kinds of speech practices or internet service providers "throttling" certain forms of content. In fact, this is one of the only areas where cyberlibertarians actually tend to support regulation, under the name of "net neutrality" (see chapter 5), which is supposed to guarantee some kind of equal right of access to internet resources. Yet these regulations are not, in general, directed at restricting or providing guardrails for corporate development of technology, but rather to prevent corporations from restricting what are claimed to be user freedoms—though exactly what the relationship is of these freedoms to other, better-understood freedoms remains to be seen. Such a position works, of course, toward expanding corporate power and limiting democratic sovereignty.

Today there are hundreds of organizations worldwide whose charter includes some kind of commitment to "internet freedom." The Electronic Frontier Foundation is the most famous and long-standing, part of whose mission statement reads, "When our freedoms in the networked world come under attack, the EFF is the first line of defense" ("About the EFF" 2022). Other organizations include the Technology Liberation Front, the Internet Freedom Coalition, the Freedom2Connect Foundation, Richard Stallman's Free Software Foundation, the Open Knowledge Foundation, Public Knowledge, the Free Culture Foundation, the Open Technology

Institute, Fight for the Future, and the Center for Democracy and Technology. The charters of most of these foundations read remarkably similarly. They make heavy use of the terms "open" and "free"; associate both "democracy" and "innovation" with a "free internet"; focus on topics like digital rights management and the resistance of some countries to unregulated internet access in the name of democracy; and presume the beneficial effects of unregulated internet technology around the world. They often assert as fact the notion that social media is responsible for destabilizing or altogether dismantling authoritarian regimes.

What they typically do not feature is any sustained attempt to discuss the meaning of words like "open," "free," and "democracy" outside of the digital context, or their historical significance in the United States; the work of writers and thinkers on which democracies are based; or critical topics such as the nature of sovereignty, the rule of law, the interpretation of the U.S. Constitution, or other constitutional forms of government. The relationship of the "internet rights" they pursue so vigorously to other existing rights is also not addressed, nor is there any effort to invite discussion of what these terms might mean and how they might be used. Despite the fact that a glance at world history shows that the meanings of these terms are anything but clear, they are presumed to be so by these organizations. This is nowhere more apparent than in the discussion about the potential for internet technology to unseat authoritarian regimes. It is completely assumed that the United States can correctly identify which regimes are authoritarian and that, once they are so labeled, has the right to unseat them by implementing communication regimes that directly contravene the laws and regulations of those other countries. These advocates frequently recommend and even implement foreign policy directives that violate our own democratic procedures and the sovereignty of other nations in the name of democracy and freedom.

These organizations share more than a commitment to a narrow and oddly defined set of principles. While it is easy to assume that nonprofit organizations with words like "freedom" in their names and .org web addresses would be independent of corporate interests, in fact most of these institutions, like the World Wide Web Consortium itself, are the product of partnerships and funders either partly or wholly formed by corporations directly involved in the production of digital technology. Additionally, many of their board members and advisers are employees of these corporations.

EFF is a notable organization founded by Mitch Kapor, former president of Lotus Corp; John Perry Barlow, a noted cyberlibertarian who lacks expertise in law; and John Gilmore, an early employee of Sun Microsystems and an avowed political libertarian. Many EFF affiliates identify as or have close ties with the cypherpunk movement (see below). Despite being largely U.S.-based, EFF pursues "digital rights," a concept not articulated, even by implication, in the U.S. Constitution or the UDHR and without a rich history of law and jurisprudence to explain what it means. While EFF often uses this term to cover what copyright means in the digital context, the organization's remit is plainly larger than this.

The principles recommended by EFF are difficult to express in ordinary political terms. In practice, it targets the same things cyberlibertarianism usually does. One of its recent targets has been the Digital Millennium Copyright Act. EFF found itself frequently siding with major corporations, especially Google, that have a distinct financial interest in denying the rights of copyright holders. Indeed, the "entertainment industry" is seen as one of the signal villains in EFF's narratives, as it is for most cyberlibertarians. It is as if this sector dwarfs others in size, capital, and power when in fact, for the most part, this power relationship is reversed: behemoths like Google who oppose copyright hold much more power on the world stage. Thus EFF advertises its success with language such as this: "EFF fought against the Anti-Counterfeiting Trade Agreement (ACTA), a secretly-negotiated international treaty ostensibly designed to reduce the flow of fake physical goods across borders. In reality, ACTA would set up a global framework to give the entertainment industry its wishlist of copyright regulations and enforcement power" (2011, 9). These initiatives are framed to portray the interest of creators in being compensated for their own work as opposed to "freedom." This supposed "freedom" should, according to cyberlibertarians, be enforced in the same way as freedom of speech.

Yasha Levine explains that the origins of EFF are closely tied to the political libertarian culture around *Wired* magazine, set by George Gilder, Newt Gingrich, and *Wired*'s founding publisher Louis Rosetto and editor Kevin Kelly. EFF has made no secret of its pro-business, rightist political leanings. There is also significant traffic between participants in the cypherpunk mailing lists and community and EFF's advisers and staff. Levine also notes that software magnate Mitch Kapor "wrote an article for *Wired* ['Where Is the Digital Highway Really Heading?'] that laid out his and

EFF's position on the future internet: 'private, not public . . . life in cyber-space seems to be shaping up exactly like Thomas Jefferson would have wanted: founded on the primacy of individual liberty and a commitment to pluralism, diversity, and community'" (2018b, 138). While the final clause gives a mild nod toward liberal values, there is no mention of democracy, and even the invocation of Jefferson seems designed in anarcho-capitalist fashion to endorse property ownership as the core of citizenship.

EFF has cultivated a reputation as a civil rights organization, sometimes nodding toward democratic and non-rightist values, occasionally advocating for user privacy, but more frequently promoting the interests of business and "technology" while attacking critics using all the tools of cyberlibertari-anism. Its focus on "innovation" (see below) and the novel, digital-based notions of "free expression" and "privacy" (see chapter 6) do not align well with the actions of organizations with more explicit commitments to civil rights. As Levine wrote in a separate piece reflecting on an EFF "privacy" campaign that aligned precisely with Apple's marketing strategy, "The truth is that EFF is a corporate front. It is America's oldest and most influ-ential internet business lobby—an organization that has played a pivotal role in shaping the commercial internet as we know it and, increasingly, hate it. That shitty internet we all inhabit today? That system dominated by giant monopolies, powered by for-profit surveillance and influence, and lacking any democratic oversight? EFF is directly responsible for bringing it into being" (2018a).

EFF's mission all along was "privatization." After it cooperated too closely with the government in helping shepherd the Communications Law Enforcement Assistance Act (CALEA) through Congress in 1994, EFF policy director Jerry Berman went on to found CDT. EFF's constituents were not concerned about surveillance per se when it came to CALEA. Rather, the issue was that the government was allowed to participate. When EFF reconstituted itself after Berman's departure, it shifted its focus from internet service providers to the major technology companies like Google. In 2004, when Google announced the launch of Gmail, internet users raised serious concerns about privacy and surveillance from corporate power. EFF remained quiet and "took an optimistic wait-and-see attitude" (Levine 2018a).

What spurred EFF into action was not Gmail but the threat of legisla-tors regulating it:

California State Senator Liz Figueroa, whose district spanned a chunk of Silicon Valley, drafted a law aimed directly at Google's emerging surveillance-based advertising business. Figueroa's bill would have prohibited email providers like Google from reading or otherwise analyzing people's emails for targeted ads unless they received affirmative opt-in consent from all parties involved in the conversation—a difficult-to-impossible requirement that would have effectively nipped Gmail's business model in the bud.

Levine explains EFF's response:

Here's where EFF showed its true colors. The group published a string of blog posts and communiqués that attacked Figueroa and her bill, painting her staff as ignorant and out of their depth. Leading the publicity charge was [EFF staffer Donna] Wentworth, who, as it turned out, would jump ship the following year for a "strategic communications" position at Google. She called the proposed legislation "poorly conceived" and "anti-Gmail" (apparently already a self-evident epithet in EFF circles). She also trotted out an influential roster of EFF experts who argued that regulating Google wouldn't remedy privacy issues online. What was really needed, these tech savants insisted, was a renewed initiative to strengthen and pass laws that restricted the government from spying on us. In other words, EFF had no problem with corporate surveillance: companies like Google were our friends and protectors. The government—*that* was the bad hombre here. Focus on it. (2018a)

This is a perfect example of cyberlibertarianism. One can arrive at this position by sincerely believing a libertarian nostrum like "only government can do violence" or by cynically promoting concentrated commercial and technical power against all comers. EFF has pushed for privacy legislation in recent years, but mostly when the clear target of such regulation is government surveillance.

EFF has played central roles in the "grassroots" campaigns against SOPA/PIPA, the Allow States and Victims to Fight Online Sex Trafficking Act and the Stop Enabling Sex Traffickers Act, and any number of other proposed government regulations of digital technology. It is quick to spin out nightmarish scenarios depicting what will certainly happen if such legislation passes. However, it is slow to the point of being frozen when it comes to honestly examining whether such predictions have ever come true. When the relevant legislation has passed, the effects have been not just less than EFF and others suggest, but largely nonexistent. Yet when real threats to democracy and citizens emerge directly from companies, often with proven harms or at least strong evidence of them, EFF demurs. This was especially clear during the fallout of the Cambridge Analytica scandal:

> On paper, this controversy looked to be a dream organizing opportunity for EFF and its allies. Here was a Silicon Valley giant using its platform to spy on Americans and subvert the workings of our democracy. EFF should have been leading the charge. And yet in what was arguably the greatest public dispute concerning the planet's largest social networking platform, EFF was AWOL—nowhere to be found. As I continued scanning the privacy group's website in the weeks after Mark Zuckerberg's appearance on Capitol Hill, all the advice it offered to irate and concerned Netizens seeking to preserve their privacy on Facebook were pro forma notifications telling them to opt out of platform API sharing and download EFF's Privacy Badger ad blocker extension for Chrome—a browser made by Google, a Silicon Valley surveillance giant. (Levine 2018a)

Given its hyperbolic responses to what are typically marginal "threats" to sharing of copyrighted material, EFF's silence on such a dramatic and well-documented attack on democracy is deafening. It is hard not to wonder whether some inside EFF cheer them on.

April Glaser, a former EFF and New America staffer who has since become an important independent journalist, wrote about EFF's silence around the same time Levine did. She used her own contacts to ask EFF, CDT, and New America

> if they have campaigns related to Facebook, or have proposals for any kind of legislation that would address the ways Facebook and other companies surveil and monetize your every move. Not one does—the most they've done is write blog posts and start initial conversations. And Fight for the Future, a powerful and fierce grass-roots group that championed the winning fight to pass net neutrality protections in 2014, only just launched an online petition and set of broad demands that puts the onus on tech companies to reform themselves. Compare this level of engagement with these issues to the media, which has treated the weeks since the Cambridge Analytica

scandal broke as a public referendum on Facebook's entire business model, or the growing outcry from academics who have long studied and warned of the deleterious effects of broad corporate data collection. But this is clearly not enough. If the people whose job it is to care about digital privacy can't be bothered to push for laws to regulate how Facebook treats the data we give it, why should Congress? (2018)

Glaser also draws attention to the murky funding relationships between EFF and major tech corporations: "If these groups had focused more on protecting communities and their needs from the beginning, would they have been more likely to notice that people are not only harmed by government data collection but by corporate data collection, as well?" Yet as Levine writes, "That's what EFF is all about: it's a Silicon Valley corporate front group, no different than the rest. The only thing unique about it is how successful it's been in positioning itself as a defender of the people—so successful, in fact, that even the people who work for it believe it. The fact that EFF has been able to pull it off for so long shows the kind of immense power that Silicon Valley wields over our political culture" (2018a).

Legal scholar and activist Mary Anne Franks in her book *Cult of the Constitution* highlights the parts of ACLU that, building on its free expression advocacy, have turned to "digital privacy" and "free expression" much like EFF. While ACLU is a celebrated organization for its advocacy of causes such as freedom of religion, the rights to privacy (including abortion rights), due process, and many others, it is also understood as a civil rights organization. However, its relationship with free expression is more complicated. Franks notes ACLU's long experience protecting the speech rights of heavily capitalized sectors, including the pornography and tobacco industries (2019a, 125). She also points out the organization's unusual alignment with Koch Foundation money on issues relating to criminal justice reform (126). In recent policy and Supreme Court decisions, ACLU has sided with an extreme interpretation of the First Amendment according to which corporate action should be shielded from government oversight because action (especially, in the well-known *Citizens United* case, economic action) is speech. (See chapter 6 for a fuller discussion of free speech as a cyberlibertarian issue.)

The ACLU has consistently opposed citizen and governmental initiatives that threaten privacy and civil rights in the digital realm. Franks has long been an activist working to combat nonconsensual pornography, also known as "revenge porn." She has worked with both state and federal legislators and regulators to stop it from spreading online. Her efforts, aided by the Cyber Civil Rights Initiative, have been surprisingly successful in recent years. Yet ACLU and EFF, among others, have fought Franks and her associates at every step. About nonconsensual pornography, she writes: "Despite the devastating impact of these abuses on the speech and privacy rights of vulnerable groups, the ACLU has framed such abuses as exercises of free speech and efforts to combat them as censorship. The ACLU's fight to protect revenge porn in particular is reflective of a larger, disturbing tendency to treat women's constitutional and civil rights as secondary and subordinate to men's and has artificially constrained reflection and reform on these issues" (128).

"When the issue of nonconsensual pornography first began receiving extensive public attention," Franks writes, "the ACLU took the position that *no* criminal law prohibiting the nonconsensual distribution of sexually explicit images was permissible within the bounds of the First Amendment." Later, "for reasons that have never been made clear, the organization soon quietly backed away from this view and attempted a different approach, which was to insist on an arbitrarily narrow definition of the crime," requiring "that perpetrators be current or former intimate partners and be motivated by the intent to harass their victims." In May 2014, when the Arizona state legislature passed a law criminalizing nonconsensual pornography, "the ACLU initiated a lawsuit challenging the law on behalf of itself and a group of booksellers." Franks notes that "the ACLU's position on nonconsensual pornography laws directly conflicts with its own advocacy on privacy rights," and quotes from the ACLU's Technology and Privacy Project page, which states: "The ACLU works to expand the right to privacy, increase the control individuals have over their personal information, and ensure civil liberties are enhanced rather than compromised by technological innovation" (131).

ACLU is a large organization consisting of regional, state, and national offices with many staff members who disagree on fundamental issues. It is not unusual for its policy on one aspect of technology to conflict with another. However, it is notable that like EFF, even the Technology and Privacy Project page mentions "enhancing" the right to privacy via "technological innovation." "Innovation," as detailed below, is a critical piece of

the cyberlibertarian rhetorical toolkit, and it almost always refers to valu-
ing economic activity, especially unregulated economic activity, as a good
in and of itself. It became clear at a surprising moment that ACLU might
have at least some staff members who follow this "gospel of innovation"
despite its public reception as a left-leaning civil rights organization:

> Following the election of Donald Trump, the ACLU was flooded with dona-
> tions. The organization received a record-breaking $24 million in donations
> in a single weekend in January 2017 and raised more than $80 million total
> between November 8, 2016, and March 2017. In January 2017, it was an-
> nounced that the ACLU would be partnering with the powerful Silicon
> Valley startup accelerator Y Combinator, a relationship that would include
> funding and mentoring from the startup. ACLU Executive Director Anthony
> Romero said in a statement that "[b]eyond financial contributions, the Silicon
> Valley community can help organizations like ours harness recent member-
> ship surges and spread the word about what the ACLU is doing to protect
> people's rights from violations by the Trump administration." Some critics
> observed that one member of Trump's administration and major Trump
> donor, billionaire Peter Thiel, is a part-time partner in Y Combinator. (Franks
> 2019a, 126)

Without other corporate ties, this use of excess cash would not be noteworthy. But given the pattern Franks and other critics have noted, this looks
like people giving money to the very cause they believe they are opposing.
Given Silicon Valley's role in aiding the Trump campaign and other antidemocratic efforts in recent years, and Y Combinator's notoriously right-
wing-friendly politics (see chapter 7), it seems ludicrous that people would
give money to technology startups in the name of protecting civil rights.
Cyberlibertarian dogma and political action have the power and influence
to turn genuine concern for minorities' civil rights into something like its
opposite.

Academic and quasi-academic bodies such as Stanford University's Internet Observatory, the MIT Media Lab, the Berkman Klein Center at Harvard
University, and quasi-independent organizations such as Data and Society
are nearly as concerning as NGOs like EFF and ACLU. These organizations
dominate discussions of digital technology and exert a remarkable amount
of influence over public discourse. Their affiliates frequently exchange roles

with one another and with the digital rights NGOs, and they all have significant relationships with the most powerful elements of the digital technology industry. The centers' model is similar to those used decades ago for tobacco science and fossil fuel research, which have only been disrupted after years of concentrated work by politicians, faculty, and some university administrators. What these organizations share is a commitment to cyberlibertarian principles and a resistance to analyses that land on abolitionist conclusions.

The MIT Media Lab is the most telling of these institutes. While it is now known as a resource for digital experimentation and an authority on political and ethical issues raised by digital technology, its history and operations suggest something very different. The Media Lab provides a fundamental link between the military–industrial origins of Silicon Valley and its reinvention as cyberlibertarian populist "counterculture." It is also a major link between what Fred Turner calls the "new communalist" vision of Stewart Brand and other "apolitical" 1960s counterculture agitators and more recent digital activism. Brand heard founding director Nicholas Negroponte's plans for the Media Lab before it opened, and in 1986 "he taught at the Lab, met with its various scientists, attended classes and briefings, and ultimately began to draft a book about" it (Turner 2006a, 177), which was published in 1987 as *The Media Lab: Inventing the Future at MIT* (Brand 1987). Yet as Brand explained, the Media Lab "was a direct descendant of the Rad Lab" at MIT through its "postwar incarnation, the Research Laboratory of Electronics (RLE)" (Turner 2006a, 177). The Rad Lab (short for Radiation Laboratory) was devoted to military uses of technology, especially radar. As the RLE's own history journal puts it, "To protect the secrecy of its sensitive work, it was called the Radiation Laboratory. The name conjured thoughts of atomic and nuclear physics, a safe and acceptable field of scientific investigation at that time. It also served as a decoy for the laboratory's real work on sophisticated microwave radar" (Fleischer 1991).

Nicholas Negroponte is a key figure for cyberlibertarian politics. Negroponte "was a longtime ARPA contractor and had worked on a variety of military computer initiatives at MIT" (Levine 2018b, 130). Negroponte's work at MIT was concentrated in the Architecture Machine Group, which took for granted a cybernetic approach to computer development that, while describing itself as humanist, "constantly invokes an imagined future human that doesn't really exist partly because it's part of an ever-receding future but also because this imagined future human is only ever a privileged, highly individualized, boundary-policing, disembodied, white, western male human" (Emerson 2016). Negroponte's spearheading of the One Laptop per Child program has been widely criticized for its neocolonial attitude toward non-Western peoples and its wholesale embrace of messianic digital utopianism sans any thick account of the lives and experiences of the people he purported to help (Fouché 2012; Golumbia 2009, 124–25; Selwyn 2013, 127–46).

Of course this "humanism" was funded and produced for corporate and military power, even if that power was held at arm's length: "With an annual budget of $6 million a year, the Lab had almost one hundred sponsors at the time of Brand's visit, each of whom had paid a minimum of two hundred thousand dollars to join. The sponsors were not allowed to demand that any particular research be done on their behalf. Rather, they were buying permission to watch as the eleven different subdivisions of the Lab went about exploring the possibilities of human–machine interaction and multimedia convergence; a sponsor could later act on any insights that emerged" (Turner 2006a, 178).

It is hard to see how such an institution, despite its virtues, can be considered an independent academic center dedicated to the dispassionate analysis of core issues. Further, "the Media Lab was actively building real digital artifacts and networks. Like the products Brand had once reviewed in the Catalog, the Media Lab's digital newspapers and Lego robots could be bought and used, so to speak, at least by corporate clients. And like the Catalog itself, the lab served to link representatives of relatively disconnected groups—in this case, corporate, academic, and technical—into a single functioning network" (Turner 2006a, 178). Despite its overt commitment to a commercial and even defense-oriented mission starkly at odds with nonconservative political beliefs, the Media Lab was able to fuse its multifarious interests into a technological vanguard that successfully obscured its politics. By the late 2010s the Media Lab was widely understood to be a leader not just in building demos that corporations and the military might use but in analyzing the culture and politics of digital technology, despite having no particular disciplinary expertise related to those issues.

Joi Ito, an entrepreneur and venture capitalist with a long association with digital utopianism, succeeded Negroponte as director of the Media Lab. Oddly, despite the fact that it is ostensibly an academic center, its new leader had never completed a college degree (Markoff 2011). When Ito took over in 2011, there was no hint of the Media Lab being a center for policy analysis or critical thinking. MIT provost L. Rafael Reif, who hired him, described Ito as "an innovative thinker who understands the tremendous potential of technology and, in particular, the Internet, to influence education, business, and society in general" (Markoff 2011). Cyberlibertarianism has several executive seats at the table; abolition is not invited.

Yet, with an entrepreneur's eye toward market demands, by the mid-2010s Ito had become increasingly aware of the general public's growing concern about the impact of digital technology on people, culture, and politics. The Media Lab has pivoted; in addition to its proto-commercial activities, it now positions itself as the leader on "ethics," particularly what many call "AI ethics." No less a figure than Barack Obama (whose administration was already very deeply enmeshed with digital technology providers, especially Google; see Morozov 2011a) lauded Ito as an "expert" in AI and ethics in 2016. Yet Rodrigo Ochigame, an academic who worked at the Media Lab as a graduate student in 2018 and 2019, writes that "the discourse of 'ethical AI,' championed substantially by Ito, was aligned strategically with a Silicon Valley effort seeking to avoid legally enforceable restrictions of controversial technologies. A key group behind this effort, with the lab as a member, made policy recommendations in California that contradicted the conclusions of research I conducted with several lab colleagues, research that led us to oppose the use of computer algorithms in deciding whether to jail people pending trial" (2019).

Ochigame was one of several Media Lab associates who went public with this characterization of the organization in 2019, in the wake of discoveries that Ito had not only taken donations from disgraced and convicted sex offender Jeffrey Epstein, but "had a deeper fund-raising relationship with Epstein than it has previously acknowledged, and it attempted to conceal the extent of its contacts with him." Epstein made several donations to the Media Lab after his 2008 conviction for soliciting prostitution from a minor: "Although Epstein was listed as 'disqualified' in MIT's official donor database, the Media Lab continued to accept gifts from him, consulted him about the use of the funds, and, by marking his contributions as anonymous, avoided disclosing their full extent, both publicly and within the university." Further, "Ito disclosed that he had separately received $1.2 million from Epstein for investment funds under his control, in addition to five hundred and twenty-five thousand dollars that he acknowledged Epstein had donated to the lab" (Farrow 2019).

Ito resigned under pressure in the wake of these disclosures, which deservedly attracted the lion's share of public attention. However, the scandal may have drawn attention away from the rest of the story that the scandal itself helped to expose. The Media Lab's shift from an explicitly defense–industrial–commercial R&D center to being a leader in "ethics" should have raised serious concerns about the political and cultural consequences of digital technology. This shift made little sense given the Media Lab's history, function, staffing, and institutional position. Furthermore, this problem extends far beyond the Media Lab itself, but to all other centers with similar structure and funding, often staffed by people directly connected to the same circles.

As Ochigame explains, "Big tech money and direction proved incompatible with an honest exploration of ethics, at least judging from my experience with the 'Partnership on AI to Benefit People and Society,' a group founded by Microsoft, Google/DeepMind, Facebook, IBM, and Amazon in 2016. PAI, of which the Media Lab is a member, defines itself as a 'multistakeholder body' and claims it is 'not a lobbying organization'" (Ochigame 2019). He goes on: "In December 2018, three Media Lab colleagues and I raised serious objections to the Partnership's efforts to influence legislation. We observed that the Partnership's policy recommendations aligned consistently with the corporate agenda." It is especially revealing and relevant to the study of cyberlibertarianism that Ochigame feels "Ito did acknowledge the problem" and quotes an email from him expressing "concerns with [industry] self-regulation." Yet "the corporate–academic alliances were too robust and convenient. The Media Lab remained in the Partnership, and Ito continued to fraternize with Silicon Valley and Wall Street executives and investors." Ochigame then describes a meeting

with Mustafa Suleyman, founding co-chair of the Partnership and co-founder of DeepMind, an AI startup acquired by Google for about $500 million in 2014. In the meeting, Ito and Suleyman discussed how the promotion of "AI ethics" had become a "whitewashing" effort, although they claimed their initial intentions had been nobler. In a message to plan the meeting, Ito wrote to my colleagues and me, "I do know, however, from speaking to Mustafa when he was setting up PAI that he was meaning for the group to be much more substantive and not just 'white washing.' I think it's just taking the trajectory that these things take."

There is little reason to doubt the sincerity of this naivete, which is shared by many who consider themselves defenders of digital rights but lack the knowledge or wisdom to understand how industry capture works. However, those who have the political and economic power to drive that capture and build these relationships can hardly use this excuse. They are part of two of Mirowski's shells: an inner, more private funding shell, strongly allied with the "dark money" described by Mayer (2017), which is fully aware of its goals and strategies; and an outer, more public comment and policy shell, whose members may well believe they are empowered to act independently, only to realize far too late, if at all, that "the trajectory that these things take" is inscribed from the outset.

Although the Media Lab and its Epstein scandal serve as public reminders of how technology promoters and their supporting industries can dominate public and political discourse, this is only the tip of the iceberg. Focusing exclusively on the domain of "AI ethics," Ochigame explains that in addition to MIT and Harvard,

> many other universities and new institutes received money from the tech industry to work on AI ethics. Most such organizations are also headed by current or former executives of tech firms. For example, the Data & Society Research Institute is directed by a Microsoft researcher and initially funded by a Microsoft grant; New York University's AI Now Institute was co-founded by another Microsoft researcher and partially funded by Microsoft, Google, and DeepMind; the Stanford Institute for Human-Centered AI is co-directed by a former vice president of Google; University of California, Berkeley's Division of Data Sciences is headed by a Microsoft veteran; and the MIT Schwarzman College of Computing is headed by a board member of Amazon. During my time at the Media Lab, Ito maintained frequent contact with the executives and planners of all these organizations. (2019)

One noteworthy individual in this mix is danah boyd, founder and president of Data & Society and a partner researcher at Microsoft. For many years boyd was a fellow of the Berkman Klein Center at Harvard, another center for digital advocacy. In a speech she gave in accepting a 2019 "Trailblazing

Technology Scholar" award from EFF, and in the wake of the Epstein scandal, boyd noted that she got her start at the Media Lab, called for "a Great Reckoning in the tech industry," and noted that she "benefited from men whose actions have helped uphold a patriarchal system that has hurt so many people" (2019).

While boyd admits that at the Media Lab she "did some things that still bother me in order to make it all work" and "grew numb to the worst parts of the 'Demo or Die' culture," she notes that the Epstein scandal requires a response that verges on abolitionism: "How we respond to the calls for justice will shape the future of technology and society. We must hold accountable all who perpetuate, amplify, and enable hate, harm, and cruelty. But accountability without transformation is simply spectacle. We owe it to ourselves and to all of those who have been hurt to focus on the root of the problem. We also owe it to them to actively seek to not build certain technologies because the human cost is too great" (2019).

Even though she encourages her audience to take account of "your own contributions to the current state of affairs. No one in tech—not you, not me—is an innocent bystander. We have all enabled this current state of affairs in one way or another," she is curiously silent on what that means and what her own role may have been. After all, boyd's own work can be seen as opposing abolitionist approaches. In fact, her 2014 book *It's Complicated* is a signal work that helped social media to spread among especially vulnerable young people in a largely unregulated fashion. The publisher's blurb reads, "Ultimately, boyd argues that society fails young people when paternalism and protectionism hinder teenagers' ability to become informed, thoughtful, and engaged citizens through their online interactions. Yet despite an environment of rampant fear-mongering, boyd finds that teens often find ways to engage and to develop a sense of identity" (boyd 2014).

Characterizing the concerns of those not directly connected to the technology industry as "an environment of rampant fear-mongering" is a cyberlibertarian agitation for which boyd might be seen as taking responsibility in 2019. It is questionable whether an individual with long-standing ties to technology companies (Microsoft and Google), and individuals and institutes with problematic industry relationships (the Media Lab and Berkman Klein Center) should continue to direct an industry-funded research center that positions its work as independent. Data & Society is a frequent source for ameliorative "scholarship" like boyd's book, which is welcome to technology promoters. Such work has the effect of pulling attention away from ordinary scholars who lack the connections and financial power to publicize themselves the way boyd and Data & Society can.

These matters became more pointed in 2022, when activists and scholars uncovered exactly the kind of problematic relationship at Data & Society itself, directly associated with boyd, that she seemed to be taking responsibility for in 2019. This involved a text-based suicide intervention service called Crisis Text Line (CTL), founded in 2013 by Nancy Lublin, who describes herself on her personal website as "innovator, advisor, investor, and entrepreneur." In early 2022, *Politico* reporter Alexandra S. Levine wrote an investigative piece on CTL, drawing attention to its relationship with a "for-profit spinoff" called Loris.ai that "uses a sliced and repackaged version of that information to create and market customer service software." CTL, as Lublin described it, was a "tech startup." Ethicists and former CTL volunteers questioned the service's ability to obtain "informed consent" from individuals who were considering suicide as a precondition for using the service. CTL and Loris.ai executives claimed that the relationship between the two services was "ethically sound," as they were separated by "a necessary and important church and state boundary."

Levine noted that "Crisis Text Line also has a data, ethics and research advisory board that includes Reddit's vice president of data, Jack Hanlon, and medical experts affiliated with Harvard, Yale, Brown, and other health-focused institutions. (None are volunteer crisis counselors.) Until recently, the chief data scientist in charge of that committee was Crisis Text Line co-founder Bob Filbin, who left for Meta last fall" (2022). Soon after, technology writer Joanne McNeil wrote a detailed piece for *Motherboard* about CTL's relationship with the industry. Following the publication of Levine's story, the FCC requested information from CTL about its connections, and CTL "announced that it has ended its 'data-sharing relationship' with the for-profit subsidiary." McNeil noted that CTL "also took a page from the Silicon Valley playbook in its attack on existing public services," because the FCC itself had been developing a plan to offer text-based suicide prevention services, which went into effect in mid-2022. In 2020, during its deliberations about starting the service, the FCC received a letter urging it not to do so because "a duplicative government-run text line could confuse those who are in crises." An existing service, CTL, was already providing a version of the work and was able to leverage the "awesome power of technology—

including machine learning and data analytics—for good in innovative new ways."

The author of those words, of course, was danah boyd, who had been a CTL board member since 2012. She seemed less concerned with the question of providing suicide prevention services themselves, and more concerned with the survival of CTL and its relationship with Loris.ai. She appeared to be worried that the FCC service might make their business model obsolete. "Based on my experience as an academic researcher, professor, social advocate, and a board member of Crisis Text Line, I recommend that the government leverages Crisis Text Line to help support texters in crisis, rather than trying to duplicate their efforts," she wrote. boyd carefully avoided mention of her extensive collaborations with industry, while recommending that CTL collaborate with FCC "to save lives via text message in a safe, smart, and cost-efficient way, with the innovation and speed of a private tech company acting in the public interest" (McNeil 2022). As McNeil goes on, "boyd's letter to the FCC reveals similar incentives and aspirations to Uber as it supplants mass transit: once Crisis Text Line filled a gap in public resources, it claimed the gap as its turf. Meanwhile the organization incited user dependency and unintended consequences behind the smoke and mirrors that is the 'awesome power of technology.'"

McNeil and others called for boyd to resign from CTL and from Data & Society. She did not. Instead boyd remarked on Twitter that she "was wrong when [she] agreed to this relationship" (between CTL and Loris.ai) (McNeil 2022), and authored a long blog post in which she vowed to "continue to push up against the persistent and endemic question that plagues all non-profits: How can we build a financially sustainable service organization that is able to scale to meet people's needs?" (boyd 2022). She acknowledged that "having spent my career thinking about and grappling with tech ethics and privacy issues, I knew that—had I not been privy to the details and context that I know—I would be outraged by what folks heard this weekend." She points out that she was not just a board member of CTL but a "director," and that she "made a judgment call early on that not only was using texter data to strengthen training of counselors without their explicit consent ethical, but that to not do this would be unethical."

Seen in isolation, people of good faith might agree or disagree with boyd's decision and response. However, in context, her actions are part of a disturbing pattern to excuse and even justify the operations of not only predatory and extractive data providers, but also the murky relationship between seemingly independent academic (or partly academic, in boyd's case) and research centers and public discourse about technology ethics. Furthermore, when viewed in the context of boyd's relationship with MIT Media Lab and her own remarks in 2019 about holding "accountable all who perpetuate, amplify, and enable hate, harm, and cruelty" and the "great reckoning" the tech industry must experience, the fact that she wrote the next year to the FCC attempting to get them to forestall releasing a public service in favor of one with for-profit ties is profoundly disturbing. These events must raise real questions for anyone who takes at face value the claims to independence and impartiality one ordinarily expects of academic commentary on technology. Someone concerned with the *appearance* of impropriety would surely consider whether they are the right person to lead a major "independent" research organization with corporate ties whose substantial budget gives it remarkable influence over public discussion. But this solution does not seem to be one boyd is willing to consider.

Today, we are familiar with the tactics used by many in industry to twist independent research and activism, especially academic research, to serve the interests of for-profit entities. Research on this subject has focused most closely on tobacco science and climate change (Oreskes and Conway 2010), two cases where academia has had some limited success in distancing itself from industry, often under legislative and other political pressure. Research has also focused on pharmaceuticals and other parts of the for-profit medical industry, a problem whose scope researchers have only begun to map (Fabbri et al. 2018; Forsyth et al. 2014). However, due to the diffuse nature of the impact of digital technology, we have not even begun to map the myriad ways personal, political, and corporate interests manifest themselves in digital advocacy. It is not even clear that we have anything close to a robust way of accounting for what those interests might be. Writers like Turner and Yasha Levine, and more recently Jill Lepore (2020) and Evan Goldstein (2020), have only begun to scratch the surface.

So have public advocacy efforts like the Tech Transparency Project and Tech Inquiry, along with more general organizations like Source Watch, which attempt to trace the influence of corporate money and dark money on both politics and independent/academic research. However, the influence of these investigators is limited due, in part, to the public's disinclination to ask questions about the most prominent voices who assign themselves the roles of protectors of digital rights and digital ethics. Even many journalists and those who work in technology are reluctant to investigate. As we have seen with examples like SOPA/PIPA, the question of whether industry might be driving public discussion seems nearly off the table for many, no matter how thoroughly industry's involvement may be proved. Similarly, when the Tech Transparency Project (2017b) documented how much influence Google had over the minor amendment to the Communications Decency Act Section 230 to combat sex trafficking (see chapter 3), this had virtually no effect on public understanding of the law.

The Stanford University Internet Observatory, which positions itself as "a cross-disciplinary program of research, teaching and policy engagement for the study of abuse in current information technologies, with a focus on social media" ("About the Internet Observatory" 2024), is headquartered at the research institution with the most direct responsibility for incubating Silicon Valley. Its director is Alex Stamos, former Facebook chief security officer, and its big data architect and chief technology officer is David Thiel, another former Facebook employee. Despite this, it is consulted as an authority on privacy abuses by technology companies. When it comes to the press and public attention, the relationships between EFF, CDT, Fight for the Future, and ACLU and these companies seem to have little impact. In fact, these organizations are often turned to first, rarely with any attention paid to these conflicts of interest. These institutions have defined the ethics and politics of technology, often with an express eye toward protecting corporate interests and economic "innovation" first and foremost.

CYPHERPUNKS: THE ANARCHO-CAPITALIST HEART OF DIGITAL ACTIVISM

Everywhere in digital culture we see the remarkable influence of the so-called cypherpunks and crypto-anarchists. These self-described "activists" promote strong cryptography as an ineliminable human right. From the "Crypto-Anarchist Manifesto" (May 1992) and its subsequent incarnation as the "Cyphernomicon" (May 1994), to WikiLeaks, Bitcoin, absolute free speech, anonymity, "assassination markets," and many debates over encryption itself, the cypherpunks have been integral and often at the center. Most of their actions are centered in the Cypherpunks email list, although some members of the movement can be found at in-person activities around

Silicon Valley and worldwide conferences like the annual Chaos Communication Congress in Germany. For years, Julian Assange was a major presence, discussing the philosophy that led to WikiLeaks. Jim Bell, proponent of "assassination markets" (see chapter 7), one of the most obviously destructive ideas in the digital world, may well be its longest-standing member. Timothy C. May, often referred to as the founder of the movement, is thought by many to have played a major role in the development of Bitcoin; his writings on the need for "untraceable" money "outside the state" can be found even in the earliest versions of the group's manifestos.

And when they have not been the primary drivers, they have been at the ready to defend positions that line up with those of the more moderate actors whose statements we have been examining. The list of figures prominent in digital activism from the early 1990s to today (see, e.g., "Cypherpunk" 2022) is saturated with members of the Cypherpunks mailing list and self-identified crypto-anarchists. They figure, even today, as senior personnel in a surprisingly large number of "digital rights" organizations.

The cypherpunks are more than happy if the world perceives them as politically "neutral," which they mean in the same illegible sense that technology is said to be "neutral." But their putative neutrality is not just *tilted* toward the far right. To the contrary, the cypherpunks have from the beginning been *saturated* in far-right philosophy. The "Cyphernomicon" explicitly identifies the philosophy as a "form of anarcho-capitalist system" (May 1994, 2.3.4). Anarcho-capitalism—a far-right philosophy associated with figures like Murray Rothbard, David Friedman (son of Milton Friedman, and considerably more extreme than him), Patri Friedman (David's son, and even farther to the right than his father), and Hans-Hermann Hoppe—is one of the most obvious sites where a version of "radical libertarianism" bleeds without friction into outright fascism.

Crypto-anarchism is largely based on computer technology, rather than political theory, which means that its politics, as with all forms of cyberlibertarianism, can be vague and incoherent at times. It is no doubt true, as May himself says, that the cypherpunk community is composed of "a lot of radical libertarians, some anarcho-capitalists, and even a few socialists" (1994, 1.1). Proportionally those numbers seem constant, as does May's evident surprise that socialists would find themselves among what is overtly a far-right crowd. Yet there is a persistent effort in digital evangelism to portray this movement as either politically neutral or somehow compatible with whatever politics a particular activist brings to bear on it. No doubt, leftists can use encrypted messaging services to organize just as much as Nazis can. But does it follow from this that the tools have no politics?

May's breakdown of the community and its productions reveals a political spectrum that ranges from "moderate" rightist political libertarianism to Nazism. The cypherpunk community's active promotion of Nazism and white supremacy indicates a natural affinity between its view of technology and its politics. This can't be a surprise, as it's exactly what May and other founding cypherpunks like Eric Hughes put forward, although their advocacy for extreme right-wing positions was largely muted.

A significant number of the most prominent cypherpunk voices have expressed fascist opinions. And it is no surprise that the current version of the mailing list, resistant as it is to censorship of any sort, routinely features Holocaust denial; themes from *The Protocols of the Elders of Zion;* garishly racist depictions of Black people, Muslims, Asians, and other nonwhites; hatred of women; and support for many other controversial online figures and causes. (The list archives are available at https://lists.cpunks.org/piper mail/cypherpunks/; they are not for the faint of heart.)

The "Cyphernomicon" is named after H. P. Lovecraft's *Necronomicon* or *Book of the Dead,* which is an explicitly evil text that provides means for summoning the "Old Ones." In fact, May's manifesto includes any number of acknowledgments of the far-right foundations of crypto-anarchy. These foundations might be said to transcend good and evil, but only in a terrible and apocalyptic sense. The only book May recommends that is not a science fiction narrative about a fully surveilled future is Ayn Rand's notorious libertarian novel *Atlas Shrugged* (May 1994, 2.4.5). Although he acknowledges that "not everyone will agree with all of these points," May includes among the "core values" of the movement "technological solutions over legal solutions, avoiding taxation," and "bypassing laws." The last two are overt talking points among the far right, while the first is a core piece of cyberlibertarian dogma.

Unsurprisingly, the "Cyphernomicon" devotes much space to the same absolutist conception of free speech we see increasingly associated with the far right today (Franks 2019b). Perhaps somewhat surprisingly, the tools and the philosophy of cypherpunks were known to enable white supremacy, even in their early incarnations. This is evident in section 2.5.17 of the "Cyphernomicon," which asks, "Will strong crypto help racists?" May answers without hesitation, "Yes, this is a consequence of having secure virtual communities. Free speech tends to work that way!" He continues, "The Aryan Nation can use crypto to collect and disseminate information, even into 'controlled' nations like Germany that ban groups like Aryan Nation." That May considers this a positive can't help but be inferred from his final statement that "strong crypto will enable and empower groups who have different beliefs than the local majority, and will allow them to bypass regional laws"—where Nazism is explicitly characterized as "different beliefs than the local majority" as if that is a reasonable description. Later May writes that "many of us are explicitly anti-democratic, and hope to use encryption to undermine the so-called democratic governments of the world" (2.13.6) where it certainly sounds like May includes himself among the "us." In a much later section, May makes it clear that organized crime "will naturally take an interest" in crypto-anarchy (16.13.6) and crypto-anarchists may "make a deal with the devil" (i.e., "the Mafia"). It is a typical criticism of non-followers that the anarcho-capitalism gives permission to organized (and often authoritarian) crime syndicates to conduct their business without any legal or civil oversight.

As with so many other movements of the far right, accurate descriptions of the politics of cypherpunks are met not just with disagreement, but with ad hominem denunciations of those who point out what the movement's founders have themselves said publicly. The ideas of the cypherpunks have become more prominent, leading to a burgeoning industry of commentators who reinterpret the story of its origins and purpose.

A notable example was published in 2021 in the *Internet Histories: Digital Technology, Culture and Society,* a peer-reviewed journal that boasts many leading digital studies scholars on its editorial board. Yet in "Against Technocratic Authoritarianism. A Short Intellectual History of the Cypherpunk Movement," Enrico Beltramini studiously avoids engaging with almost any of the scholarship on the development of digital culture and history. Instead, he retells parts of the history of computer development in its intersections with the San Francisco counterculture covered in great detail by Markoff (2005) and Turner (2006a, 2006b), rejecting their analyses without even nodding toward them. To Beltramini, although "a libertarian ethos is an unmistakable thread in some of the most celebrated cypherpunk activists' ideology (think at Timothy C. May, for example)" (102), and "most of the self-produced cypherpunk literature is in fact the brainchild of a single mind—that of Tim May," May's own attestations of the right-wing nature of cypherpunk philosophy both are and are not dispositive.

May "recognized his debts to thinkers such as libertarian Ayn Rand and Murray Rothbard," Beltramini correctly notes, but he then adds that May also credited "the non-libertarian Michel Foucault." This "fact" is meant to convince us that there is something outside of political libertarianism in the cypherpunk ethos. However, Beltramini glosses over important details. Even if we grant the somewhat questionable notion that Foucault is an adequate left foil, in this specific context, to Rand and Rothbard, May never *publicly* referred to Foucault in his work. The sole source Beltramini provides is a private exchange he had with May in 2017, whose details and context the author does not provide us (116n2). Toward the end of the essay, he writes that "on several occasions he paid tribute to Foucault and his work, and eventually admitted that in drafting his own theory of crypto-anarchy, he was under several influences, including that of Foucault." Yet the only evidence for this is the same private conversation (116, 117n12). Beltramini's entire analysis acknowledges some affinities between the concerns about authoritarian aspects of digital technology developed by writers like Foucault and Roszak. However, it makes no effort to show whether these concerns are the same ones, play out the same way, or lead to the same conclusions as those routinely expressed among cypherpunks. It also obscures the syncretic nature of fascism, suggesting that the "Cyphernomicon" should not be understood as an obviously protofascist document because it contains implicit nods toward some non-right-wing thinking. To the contrary, such moves are characteristic of fascism and protofascism.

Beltramini quotes May in the "Cyphernomicon" writing that "many of us are explicitly antidemocratic and hope to use encryption to undermine the so-called democratic governments of the world." However, Beltramini argues that "if democratic government is no longer the liberal government of modernity, rather the illiberal government of late modernity, the expression 'democratic governments' takes on an entirely different meaning" (115). Even if we accept this highly unlikely and contextually unmotivated interpretation, the phrase "explicitly antidemocratic" is subject to no such restatement. Beltramini quotes the section of the "Crypto-Anarchist's Manifesto" that targets "government interference in economic transactions" as a specific affront to freedom. This is one of the main precepts of the right-wing libertarianism Beltramini thinks does *not* characterize crypto-anarchy. Beltramini overlooks the power and influence of antidemocratic movements in the decades since May wrote, the role played by digital technology in them, or the historical dangers in explaining away protofascist propaganda and activism.

There is an enormous volume of public information showing that cryptocurrency, Bitcoin, and blockchain software embody explicit design goals of the cypherpunk movement (Golumbia 2016b). Furthermore, Bitcoin's developers almost certainly were cypherpunks. Therefore, it is no surprise that attention to the movement's politics has increased as cryptocurrencies have attracted more and more public attention. Work by Beltramini and others is an unfortunate embodiment of the desire to redescribe the movement's politics to obscure its right-wing nature. Of course, this is the main point of the critique of cyberlibertarianism: that in the name of some vague form of technological liberation, involving both the use of technology and the resistance to it, we should understand right-wing politics as something other than what they are. This is simply a way to interfere with the concentration of power that is typical of right-wing politics. It is in favor of "technocratic authoritarianism," as long as the authority in question is the self. Extreme political libertarians like the sovereign citizens claim to oppose tyranny, but mostly do so to justify acting in a far more tyrannical way than the democratic governments they oppose (see chapter 7 for discussion of the proximity of crypto-anarchism to fascism).

THE SNOWDEN LEAKS AND WIKILEAKS

In 2014, at the height of Edward Snowden's media fame in exposing secrets of the NSA and the Five Eyes partnership, historian Sean Wilentz published a piece in the *New Republic* that provoked immense outrage among digital pundits across the political spectrum. In "Would You Feel Differently about Snowden, Greenwald, and Assange If You Knew What They Really Thought?" Wilentz explained:

> Snowden, Greenwald, and Assange hardly subscribe to identical beliefs, and differ in their levels of sophistication. They have held, at one time or another, a crazy-quilt assortment of views, some of them blatantly contradictory. But from an incoherent swirl of ideas, a common outlook emerges. The outlook is neither a clear-cut doctrine nor a philosophy, but something closer to a

political impulse that might be described, to borrow from the historian Richard Hofstadter, as paranoid libertarianism. Where liberals, let alone right-wingers, have portrayed the leakers as truth-telling comrades intent on protecting the state and the Constitution from authoritarian malefactors, that's hardly their goal. In fact, the leakers despise the modern liberal state, and they want to wound it.

Wilentz's critique followed a form that should be familiar to thinkers who follow the trajectories of cyberlibertarian dogma. In the case of all three figures he discusses, it is specifically the power of digital technology that licenses the syncretic blurring of left and right, which blocks attempts by clear political thinkers to delimit efforts that support left politics or right ones. Indeed, one of Greenwald's most persistent trolling tactics is to attack those who point out the right-wing foundations of many of his ideas (Potter 2021; Robinson 2021). This is in addition to his overt alignment with the political right (Grove and Baragona 2021; Harwell 2021; Higgins 2022), which was long clear to some like Wilentz. Nevertheless, even an august institution like the *New Yorker* referred to Greenwald as a "leftist journalist" in 2018 in a piece broadly documenting his many rightist positions (Parker 2018). These positions include very aggressively attacking Democratic critics of the Trump administration, appearing regularly and approvingly on Tucker Carlson's TV show, and following Trump's rhetoric in referring to the ongoing Mueller investigation as "the Russia hoax" only attended to by "deranged" liberals.

In fact, despite the blowback he got from many quarters, the main problem with Wilentz's analysis is that it didn't go far enough. Snowden, Assange, and Greenwald are not "truth tellers" doing useful work whose personal right-wing politics should give those on the left pause. The problem is deeper: they are *fundamentally* committed to advancing right-wing politics, using whatever truths they disclose as platforms to sow the untruths and conspiracy theories on which such politics depend. To this end, it is vital to realize that much of what the three actors distribute in public is simply not true. As in all right-wing conspiratorial thought, they deliberately misinterpret kernels of facts to build a false narrative.

Assange, notorious for his continual distortions of the "facts" exposed by WikiLeaks documents, is the most obvious example. Although his critics are aware of this (Poulsen 2018), it is surprising that his strong resemblance to conspiracy theorists like Alex Jones and David Icke does not register with much of the public. Assange directly intervened in a U.S. election through cooperation with Roger Stone, who himself used Jones and other conspiracy theorists for just that purpose (LaFraniere 2020). This is not an exaggeration: Assange is a proto-Nazi political provocateur whose overt anti-Semitism, anti-Black racism, climate change denial, misogyny, hatred for democracy, and support for authoritarian political regimes (see chapter 7 for discussion of Assange's career-long leanings toward fascism), including his effort to distort public opinion in the 2016 U.S. presidential election, routinely fail to penetrate the minds of observers who see as dispositive his use of digital tools and antiestablishment affect. Assange is one of the key figures for the syncretic politics of cyberlibertarianism. His identification with digital freedom allows his supporters to overlook his behavior and statements that contradict his overt politics.

Something similar is true of Glenn Greenwald. As Wilentz explains, Greenwald gained prominence as a civil rights lawyer who defended Nazis based on free speech absolutism. Although this position has a respectable history in U.S. politics, it must raise questions for further exploration and has been questioned by political commentators on the left (Delgado and Stefancic 2018; Columbia 2021). He supported the Iraq War in the early 2000s, despite the falsehoods promulgated by the U.S. intelligence establishment to advance the operation. Later, he used these same falsehoods to bolster his own political program. When he became one of the designated spokespeople for Edward Snowden's cache of documents about the capabilities of the U.S. National Security Agency and other parts of the intelligence apparatus, Greenwald completed a rebranding that had been underway for a while. Whereas his alignment with the political right had been overt prior to this, now he described himself as an "activist journalist." However, unlike almost any other activist in public life, he refuses to state on which side of the political aisle he sits. Unlike any other figure on the left, Greenwald routinely appears in right-wing media but does not challenge its politics. Indeed, he frequently appeared on *Tucker Carlson Tonight*, which many considered to be the leading broadcast media source for fascist and white supremacist politics in the United States (Blow 2021). Greenwald rarely challenged Carlson, and certainly not about his use of racist conspiracy theories. In fact, Greenwald gave the impression of indulging them (Higgins 2022; Lemieux 2021; Loomis 2018; Robinson 2021), perhaps even supporting them outright.

Snowden is the least overtly partisan of the three, although that may be more appearance than fact. Snowden's supporters rarely acknowledge that he was not an employee of the NSA at the time he began leaking documents to Greenwald, Assange, Laura Poitras, Barton Gellman, and others, but of Booz Allen Hamilton, a powerful defense contractor (Eichenwald 2013; Shaw 2018). Snowden's animus for the U.S. government and his conspiratorial dismissal of its claims to oversee intelligence programs through democratic means stops short of what many not on the right have long criticized: the outsourcing of governmental functions to private actors who are less fully accountable to the public than are government employees. Snowden worked for Booz Allen precisely because the lack of strong oversight over private contractors gave him the freedom to access information he already planned to release. Booz Allen CEO Ralph Shrader stated that "the only reason he became an employee of Booz Allen was to gain access to information. There was nothing about Booz Allen that was attractive other than we were a vehicle. That's his [Snowden's] words" (Aitoro 2014). In fact, Snowden was in contact with Greenwald prior to taking the job at Booz Allen (U.S. House Intelligence Committee 2016, 14). As even sympathetic portraits of Snowden emphasize, "since 9/11 and the enormous influx of intelligence money, much of the NSA's work had been outsourced to defense contractors, including Dell and Booz Allen Hamilton" (Bamford 2014).

These facts might seem irrelevant were it not for the explicit and implicit political analyses Snowden offers. They are explicit because Snowden has always identified as a right-leaning libertarian, with all the syncretism and incoherence attached to that position. They are implicit because Snowden accepts (and has expressed publicly) the right–libertarian belief that governmental power is particularly noxious and violent, so that corporate power is an entirely different thing on which we need not dwell. According to this familiar right-wing trope, "tyranny" is only ever attached to government and particularly *democracies*. As the philosopher Tamsin Shaw put it in a critical analysis of Snowden:

Cynicism about the rule of law exists on a spectrum. At one end, exposing government hypocrisy is motivated by a demand that a liberal–democratic state live up to its own ideals, that accountability be reinforced by increasing public awareness, establishing oversight committees, electing proactive politicians, and employing all the other mechanisms that have evolved in liberal democracies to prevent arbitrary or unchecked rule. These include popular protests, the civil disobedience that won civil rights battles, and, indeed, whis-tleblowing. At the other end of the spectrum is the idea that the law is always really politics in a different guise; it can provide a broad set of abstract norms but fails to specify how these should be applied in particular cases. Human beings make those decisions. And the decision-makers will ultimately be those with the most power. (2018)

This is not just haggling over the niceties of broadly opposed political frameworks. Shaw points out the political foundations for this second kind of antidemocratic cynicism:

On this view, the liberal notions of legality and legitimacy are always hypo-critical. This was the view promulgated by one of the most influential legal theorists of the twentieth century, Carl Schmitt. He was a Nazi, who joined the party in 1933 and became known as the "crown jurist" of the Third Reich. But at the turn of the millennium, as Bush took America to war, Schmitt's criticisms of liberalism were undergoing a renaissance on both the far right and the far left, especially in the academy. This set of attitudes has not been limited to high theory or confined to universities, but its congru-ence with authoritarianism has often been overlooked.

"Congruence with authoritarianism" may be too generous. As in Schmitt's case, charges of hypocrisy against democratic governance are cynically used by those who desire authoritarian power or will do nothing to stop it. It is no surprise to find these three figures either having supported Trump or doing little to stop him, and allying themselves with Vladimir Putin, who is never framed as authoritarian.

Shaw continues:

The cynicism of the figures around Snowden derives not from a meta-view about the nature of law, like Schmitt's, but from the view that America, the most powerful exponent of the rule of law, merely uses this ideal as a mask to disguise the unchecked power of the "deep state." Snowden, a dissenting agent of the national security state brandishing his pocket Constitution, was seen by [*Guardian* editor Alan] Rusbridger as an American patriot, but by his chosen allies as the most authoritative revealer of the irremediable depth of American hypocrisy.

In the WikiLeaks universe, the liberal ideal of the rule of law, both domestic and international, has been the lie that allows unaccountable power to grow into a world-dominating force. (2018)

This transition is one of the key problems posed by cyberlibertarianism. It uses the language of rights and freedoms to challenge real issues in both democracy as a system and particular instances of democratic governance. However, it sometimes embraces explicitly antidemocratic and even authoritarian politics, as if these are more freedom-preserving than democracies. The hypocrisy demonstrated in this stance is more serious and obvious than the one such actors lob at democracies. It is typically due to the existing freedoms in democratic polities that critics like Snowden have the liberty to act as they do in the first place. Snowden, Assange, and Greenwald demonstrate no willingness to be held accountable for their actions within a democratic infrastructure, unlike some other whistleblowers who sometimes ally themselves with Snowden (most famously Pentagon Papers leaker Daniel Ellsberg) and WikiLeaks associate Chelsea Manning. That is, they have decided ahead of time that democracy is an entirely illegitimate excuse for authoritarianism, and that therefore authoritarianism is preferable. Thus, even though in both Assange's and Snowden's cases, they enjoy whatever freedoms they have due only to special dispensations that are not granted to other citizens of the states that have chosen to shelter them.

In the years since he has been living in Russia, Snowden has turned even more clearly toward far-right politics. Although he appears to criticize Vladimir Putin, his rebukes are mild and seem to be designed solely to give the appearance of dissent without offering any substance. Rather than focusing on Russia's digital surveillance infrastructure or its role in promoting many global digital disinformation campaigns, to say nothing of the nation's manifest human rights abuses, Snowden has become a witting or unwitting participant in Russia's own expressly antidemocratic propaganda campaigns:

Putin has benefited from the appearance of being Snowden's protector, presenting himself as a greater champion of freedom than the United States. In their book *Red Web: The Kremlin's War on the Internet*, the Russian investigative journalists Andrei Soldatov and Irina Borogan [2015] recounted the experiences of human rights activists who were summoned via an email purportedly from Snowden himself, to a meeting with him at Moscow airport when he surfaced there with Sarah Harrison, to find they were joining the heads of various pro-Kremlin "human rights" groups, Vladimir Lukin, the Putin-appointed Human Rights Commissioner of Russia, and the lawyers Anatoly Kucherena and Henri Reznik. It was clear to the independent activists that Kucherena had organized the meeting. Kucherena is a member of the FSB's Public Council, an organization that Soldatov and Borogan say was established to promote the image of the Russian security service; he is also the chairman of an organization called the Institute for Democracy and Cooperation, which has branches in New York and Paris and was set up at Putin's personal instigation, the authors tell us, for the purposes of criticizing human rights violations in the United States. This institute publishes an annual report on the state of human rights in the United States. Using misleading moral equivalences to attack American hypocrisy is one of the most common tactics in Putin's propaganda war. (Shaw 2018)

Shaw goes on to talk about the rare occasions when Snowden does appear to criticize Putin. Snowden

barely deviat[es] from Putin's information agenda even as Putin has instigated extraordinarily repressive measures to rein in Internet freedoms in Russia. When Snowden agreed, for instance, to appear as a guest questioner on a televised question-and-answer session with Putin, he posed the Russian president a question that heavily criticized surveillance practices in the US and asked Putin if Russia did the same, which gave Putin an opening to assert, completely falsely, that no such indiscriminate surveillance takes place in Russia. Earlier this year, Snowden's supporters trumpeted a tweet in which he accused the Russian regime of being full of corruption, but Putin himself will use such accusations when he wishes to eliminate undesirable government actors. To be sure, Snowden is in a vulnerable position: he is notably cautious in his wording whenever he speaks publicly, as someone reliant on the protection of Putin might be.

When it comes to Russia, Snowden appears uninterested in the digital freedoms he nominally puts front and center in all his activism. This is not mere hypocrisy or simple anarchism. Snowden does not oppose "the state"; he opposes the United States for what he claims are hypocritical positions about human rights from a location in which he enjoys far fewer of those rights than he did back home, precisely because he is in a privileged position to benefit from authoritarian power.

Nassim Nicholas Taleb (2022) draws unexpected attention to Snowden's de facto political theory in a wide-ranging discussion prompted by Russia's invasion of Ukraine, focusing on the broad differences between states formed around nationalism and those formed around democracy. "A system seems all the more dysfunctional when it is transparent," he writes. "Hence my attacks on someone like Edward Snowden and his acolytes, who exploit this paradox to attack the West for the benefit of Russian plotters." Snowden, he says, is an "impostor" who "wants to destroy the system rather than improve it"; he is therefore among those who "do not realize that the alternative to our messy system is tyranny: a mafia-don like state (Libya today, Lebanon during the civil war) or an autocracy." As Taleb notes, Snowden recently claimed regarding governmental measures to deal with Covid-19 that "as authoritarianism spreads, as emergency laws proliferate, as we sacrifice our rights, we also sacrifice our capability to arrest the slide into a less liberal and less free world" and that "what is being built is the architecture of oppression" (Dowd 2020). Of course we should be concerned about all abuses of democratic governance powers, but little of substance has turned up regarding overreach related to Covid-19. Meanwhile, conspiracy theories, many of which have originated in Russia, have played a central role in exacerbating the problem and in the resulting large number of unnecessary deaths worldwide. Notably, Snowden has made few comments about Russia's invasion of Ukraine, claiming that people outside the region are "being made to feel [the way they feel] by the information bubbles that they consume" ("Edward Snowden" 2022) without any reflection from him on who is generating those bubbles and why.

Taleb, Shaw, and earlier critics like Wilentz are right that Snowden's critiques of democracy and democratic uses of technology are similar to right-wing conspiracy theories that claim to target authoritarianism but instead support authoritarians. Unlike Alex Jones, though, Snowden is taken seriously by many who think he supports democracy. It is no surprise that Snowden's speeches feature in many right-wing, apocalyptic conspiracy theories and even proliferate in videos made by the promoters of those theories (e.g., Destination Hub 2022a, 2022b, 2022c; Eye Opener 2022). However,

Snowden's politics are often misunderstood by progressives and others who sympathize with his hostility toward the United States. This is due, in part, to the syncretic politics of cyberlibertarianism. As a result, his near-identity and almost identical function with right-wing figures is effectively obscured.

It is crucial to realize that Snowden's status as a whistleblower is profoundly unclear. It is undeniable that some of the documents he released exposed abuses in the intelligence apparatus. However, many of these abuses referred to powers the government can use rather than instances of the government using them. This is critical to remember, since we are familiar with democratic accountability for such powers in other contexts. When landline phones were the only widely used person-to-person electronic communications technology, most U.S. citizens were aware that the government was *capable* of wiretapping any conversation. That fact has been fodder for conspiracy theory and spy fictions since we have had phones. But the fact remains that for the most part, these capabilities are used within lawful bounds, and there are very few examples of them being used otherwise.

We know from the Church Committee hearings and other sources that the government sometimes used these powers in violation of the law. In the 1950s and 1960s J. Edgar Hoover's FBI undoubtedly tracked political dissidents and took extralegal actions to disrupt what should be entirely legal dissent. However, in a democratic system of laws, the first remedy to such abuses is for the individual or group on whom information has been improperly gathered to challenge legal actions taken against it based on that information. Phone conversations that have been wiretapped without a warrant should be prohibited as evidence at trial. Although there were revelations of intelligence community overreach in the 1970s, there have been remarkably few actual instances of ongoing abuse. This is one of the reasons why critics of government surveillance are so quick to invoke the COINTELPRO set of covert and illegal FBI initiatives. COINTELPRO was a terrible program, but if it was the tip of the iceberg of ongoing, similar actions, then it is concerning that they have not been exposed yet and have not had much of an impact on the public. That is, it is notable how few individuals and groups who have been criminally indicted allege in their own defense, let alone prove, that the evidence against them was generated via illegal, large-scale surveillance systems of the kind described in Snowden's leaks.

It is true that every government *must* have the power to surveil all tele-communications (and to some extent, even physical, nonelectronic communications) in which its citizens engage. Snowden's leaks demonstrate that the U.S. government has these capabilities, as do some of its allies. This is an important fact for individuals and politicians to know and understand, although it seems odd to present it as a revelation or suggest it is unique to the United States. The one case that seems to identify abuse, although identified not by Snowden but by defendants in a terrorism conspiracy trial, *United States v. Moalin,* illustrates the problems raised by Snowden's disclosures.

Moalin concerned "four U.S. residents convicted of conspiring to provide material support to a foreign terrorist organization and conspiring to launder money from 2007 to 2008. On appeal, the defendants argued that evidence used against them at trial was derived from an allegedly unlawful electronic surveillance program run by the National Security Agency (NSA) at the time of the investigation and should have been suppressed" (Hanna 2020). The case became well-known in 2020 due to the Ninth Circuit Court of Appeals ruling that the "bulk phone records program violated FISA and acknowledging that it also was likely unconstitutional." But less noticed in the coverage was the fact that the Court "affirmed the defendants' convictions after determining that evidence used against the defendants at trial had not been tainted by information the NSA had collected through the program." The NSA discontinued the bulk collection program in the wake of Snowden's disclosures, which is one of the parts of those disclosures that most genuinely seems to qualify as whistleblowing. Yet even in a case where the defendants were convicted of just the sort of crime intelligence agencies are supposed to be looking for, the Court did eventually rule that their communications were not used this way. Had they been procured illegally, the resulting intelligence would have been inadmissible.

While the *Moalin* decision was celebrated as a vindication of Snowden, its consequences suggest that Snowden's actions are not as obviously understandable as whistleblowing as his supporters seem to believe. In another case, *Hepting v. AT&T,* originally brought in 2008, a wide group of plaintiffs, backed by EFF, claimed "the government enacted a massive domestic spying dragnet," in part when the "federal government conspired with telecommunications companies like AT&T to reroute internet traffic to a secret room in San Francisco where communications were reviewed and stored by the National Security Agency" (Renda 2021). Part of the Ninth Circuit's ruling had to do with the constitutionality of the data collection under the Foreign Intelligence Surveillance Act (FISA), a particular hobbyhorse of the conspiratorial subset of Snowden supporters. Regardless of whether FISA gave the intelligence agencies too much power, the courts have been satisfied that it is (or was, in some cases) constitutional. Further, and even worse for those who see Snowden as a whistleblower, the plaintiffs in *Hepting*, attempting to constitute a class for purposes of challenging the constitutionality of any governmental data collection program, were unable to establish standing in the case. That is, they were unable to show how the program in question had harmed them, or even that they had been targeted by it. The program may well sound bad, provided one rejects out of hand the notion that democratic governments can surveil everything but should only do so with proper warrant.

Despite Snowden's revelations regarding his ostensible main interest being the invasive overreach of intelligence surveillance programs, it is notable that much of what he released is not about that topic at all. In one of the most detailed listings of Snowden's disclosures, the nonprofit legal publication *Lawfare* identifies "tools and methods, overseas USG locations from which operations are undertaken, foreign officials and systems that NSA has targeted, encryption that NSA has broken, ISPs or platforms that NSA has penetrated or attempted to penetrate, and identities of cooperating companies and governments" ("Snowden Revelations" 2014). Most of the listed items describe capabilities one would be surprised to learn major world governments lack: "a 'Google-like' search engine that accesses phone calls, emails, and other forms of online communication of foreigners and US citizens"; the fact that "NSA has developed technology to compare satellite imagery with a photograph taken outdoors to determine where the photograph was taken"; that "NSA penetrated the network of Mexico's Secretariat of Public Security to collect information about drug and human trafficking along the US–Mexico border"; that "NSA and GCHQ have monitored the communications of several Israeli officials, including the Prime Minister and Defense Minister"; that "NSA has collected draft email messages written by leaders of the Islamic State of Iraq." The revelations do not indicate if the data collected were used or stored for later analysis. We can object to states acting in this manner, but it is hoped that we do so from a position of understanding what governments must do, rather than horror directed only at democratic governments spying.

Add to the question of whether Snowden's revelations really add up to what he claims they do the more complicated question of the documents he took and what he did with them. Here the 2016 U.S. House Intelligence Committee report on Snowden raises troubling questions. Estimates vary, but that report cites intelligence service sources claiming that Snowden copied or removed nearly 1.5 million documents, of which it is likely even he "does not know the full contents" (20). "Less than one-tenth of one percent" of them had been published by 2016 (few have been published since then, so presumably the number has remained about the same). Snowden, Greenwald, and others have told multiple stories about the total number of documents and their fate, so we will likely never know exactly what he took. But he and his supporters quickly published those with the most publicity value. It is also clear that in the opinion of the House committee and the intelligence services, Snowden "has had, and continues to have, contact with Russian intelligence services." Other parts of the report that deal with "foreign influence" are redacted, which suggests that there are additional concerns about the documents he copied.

The report notes that the "vast majority . . . were unrelated to electronic surveillance or any issues associated with privacy and civil liberties." Snowden claims he did not share any information with foreign intelligence agencies, but the report notes that "all of the documents that have been publicly disclosed . . . can be accessed by foreign militaries and intelligence services as well as the public" (22). The report accepts the claim of intelligence services that "Snowden's disclosures caused massive damage to national security" (24). The remaining portions of the report, including the damages and discussions of the documents Snowden has not released, are heavily redacted. However, the import is clear: Snowden took information from one major world power and handed it to others who almost certainly engage in near-identical surveillance or worse. Snowden refused to use any of the methods available to him to raise concerns about these programs through appropriate channels, including designated protocols for whistle-blowers, while later falsely claiming to have used them or that whistleblower protections did not apply to him (18–19). It is hard to credit the claim that the main thing he was interested in was addressing civil liberties concerns.

Rather, in keeping with his underlying cyberlibertarian political philosophy, Snowden was trying to do as much damage to democratic governance as possible. That he did so in the name of "hypocrisy" and "liberty" that so easily slides into direct authoritarianism should be no surprise, as this is the exact shape the most virulent strain of contemporary right-wing propaganda takes. Here Snowden's early history as an anarcho-capitalist online troll is relevant. Prior to becoming an international celebrity whistleblower, Snowden attacked social security; wrote in favor of the second amendment and gun ownership and against Barack Obama's suggestion that his administration might revive an assault weapons ban; and supported Ron Paul and a return to the gold standard (Wilentz 2014). "Contrary to his claims," writes Sean Wilentz, "he seems to have become an anti-secrecy activist only after the White House was won by a liberal Democrat who, in most ways, represented everything that a right-wing Ron Paul admirer would have detested."

In the wake of his relocation to Moscow and the apparent exhaustion of his cache of documents about the U.S. intelligence apparatus, Snowden has stayed true to that right-wing libertarian ethos. He believes that democratic government is inherently illegitimate but that authoritarian government somehow promotes "liberty"—although this latter prong of his belief system, as in all anarcho-capitalism, need never be addressed. As George Packer put it:

> Above all, Snowden is a soldier of the internet, "the most important invention in all human history." He has said that he grew up not just using it but in it, and that he learned the heroic power of moral action from playing video games. "Basically, the internet allowed me to experience freedom and explore my full capacity as a human being," Snowden told Greenwald when they met in Hong Kong. "I do not want to live in a world where we have no privacy and no freedom, where the unique value of the internet is snuffed out." (2014)

This leads almost directly to alignment with antidemocratic power:

> His more recent disclosures have nothing to do with the constitutional rights of US citizens. Many of them deal with surveillance of foreign governments, including Germany and Brazil, but also Iran, Russia, and China. These are activities that, wise or unwise, fall well within the NSA's mandate and the normal ways of espionage. Snowden has attached himself to Wikileaks and to Assange, who has become a tool of Russian foreign policy and has no interest in reforming American democracy—his goal is to embarrass it. Assange and Snowden are not the first radical individualists to end up in thrall to strongmen.

To Snowden, no democratic government can ever protect, let alone inhabit, the distributed sovereignty to which it is formally committed. Instead, the only way to protect the most fundamental human rights is to build technologies that make democracies impossible, but at the same time maximize the power of individuals to do whatever they please. This perspective, which some have referred to as "techno-feudalism," aligns with the tendency among cyberlibertarians to move toward fascism and recommend monarchy and other forms of absolute rule. From this perspective, the only politics that matter are those realized through technology: "Snowden's leaks can be seen, in part, as a determined effort to restore the web to its original purity—a project of technology rather than law. 'Let us speak no more of faith in man, but bind him down from mischief by the chains of cryptography,' wrote Snowden, in an early message to his collaborators" (Pack 2014). His speeches, while syncretic and inchoate, do sometimes refer to positive government actions and corporate abuses of privacy. Yet his core message does not deviate. "Our choices are being limited, guided. I think all our activities are being 'permissioned,'" he said, via virtual visit from Russia at a speech hosted by Bucknell University. "Liberty is freedom from permission. That ability to act without asking" (Benson 2022). These sentiments are very much the stuff of conspiracy theory and the alt-right. They are also near-direct quotes of anarcho-capitalist position papers about "permissionless innovation" (see below).

Snowden's concerns about the invasiveness of digital technology may seem to align with Mumfordian critique or tech abolition, but his use of "permission" and "privacy" as key terms indicates otherwise. While Facebook and invasiveness may be problematic, the solution is not government oversight, regulation, licensure, or outright bans of such companies and the underlying technologies they use. Instead, the proliferation of ever more technology, which accrues power to individuals, corporations, and governments, will somehow lead to more freedom.

According to Snowden's political theory, "privacy is the fountainhead of all other rights": "[It] is baked into our language, our core concepts of government and self in every way. It's why we call it 'private property.' Without privacy you don't have anything for yourself" (Schrodt 2016). It is revealing that Snowden associates what we today call privacy with private property, since that is literally the classical liberal conception of rights on which all anarcho-capitalist and neoliberal political theory depends—in *opposition* to which the entire discourse of civil rights developed around the world. Civil rights certainly do not depend on property. Nor do other civil rights flow from this Austrian-inflected notion of privacy as private property (a theme that would fit neatly into the theories of arch-right-wing theorist Hans-Hermann Hoppe; see chapter 7). But as most of us know, the United States does not even have a right to privacy formalized in the Bill of Rights. Clearly the framers of the Constitution did not think the freedoms of speech, press, assembly, and so on proceeded from the right to privacy—unless they are taken to mean that rights only attach to those who own private property, as Snowden seems to suggest.

Further, what Snowden means by "privacy" diverges from the understanding of most ordinary people, legislators, and legal scholars (see chapter 6 for full discussion of privacy in this context). Snowden's concept of privacy, like that of the cypherpunks and today's digital rights activists, is best understood as the absence of government or governance. Between his advocacy for unbreakable encryption and fully anonymizing technologies (see chapter 5), Snowden writes and talks about privacy much as it's described in the "Crypto-Anarchist Manifesto"—as a weapon that should be deployed by the most technologically sophisticated among us to increase our own personal power (and wealth), making oversight and regulation of our activities impossible. Indeed, while Snowden has criticized Bitcoin in the past in part for its lack of privacy features (Riley 2015), he has spoken out strongly in favor of cryptocurrency tokens that incorporate "privacy by design" (Chipolina 2021) such as zcash (Brockwell 2022) and Monero (Prasanna 2022). George Packer writes that "Snowden looked to the internet for liberation, but it turns out that there is no such thing as an entirely free individual. Cryptography can never offer the absolute privacy and liberty that Snowden seeks online" (2014). While in the strictest political sense this is true, the fact is that technology can be used to obviate significant functions of governmental oversight. To right-wing political actors this can look like "privacy and liberty," though to anyone committed to democracy it looks like authoritarian, quasi-feudal, and organized crime–like institutions.

Marcy Wheeler is an independent journalist and adviser to academic and legislative projects on cybersecurity. A fierce opponent of illegitimate government surveillance and critic of intelligence agencies, she originally welcomed the Snowden disclosures and celebrated him as a whistleblower (Levy 2013). She was similarly enthusiastic about WikiLeaks. For a brief time in 2014, at the height of the Snowden story, she was senior policy analyst at *The Intercept,* the publication founded around Snowden's documents by Greenwald along with Laura Poitras and Jeremy Scahill. After just a few months, she stepped down (Bhuiyan 2014), and soon after became more critical of Snowden, Assange, and Greenwald. In recent years, she has become an outspoken critic of all three, calling Snowden and Assange and their supporters people who "champion sociopathic liars and sloppy thinking" (Wheeler 2021c). She is especially critical of the idea that Assange should be treated by the legal system as a journalist, even if some of his activities are genuinely journalistic (Wheeler 2021b, 2021c). As Greenwald and Assange, in particular, have emerged more publicly as active partisans for Trump, the far right, and Putin's dictatorship in Russia, Wheeler has come more publicly to the view that Snowden and those around him were trying to encourage more leaks of more classified intelligence information to harm the United States and empower its opponents. One possibility is that "Vladimir Putin agreed to protect Snowden in hopes that he would inspire more leakers to release files that help Russia evade US spying" (Wheeler 2021a). "That Greenwald spends most of his days deliberately inciting Twitter mobs," she continues, "is just an added benefit, to those who want to weaken America, to Greenwald's defense of fascists."

Wilentz, Packer, and others who scrutinized the political sentiments of Assange, Greenwald, and Snowden were right to do so. These figures' emphasis on government surveillance, "privacy," freedom of speech, and computer-enabled "liberty" enable the same politics advanced by the political right all over the world. Despite their rhetoric of freedom, they agitate for autocratic rule and a move away from popular sovereignty. In short, they are antidemocracy activists strongly allied with the political right. They use their technical knowledge and the public's perception of their association with digital freedom to draw people further toward the right and away from progressive values.

STRATEGIC DIGITAL DENIAL

Digital rights promoters and activists devote much of their energy to developing an ever-changing set of strategies to deny, deflect, and defuse criticism of digital technology. Some of these are clustered around specific legislative proposals, such as SOPA and PIPA as discussed in the previous chapter, and Section 230 of the Communications Decency Act in the next;

others involve major ideas or terms (democratization, encryption, open) discussed in later chapters. Some are most profitably seen as pure rhetorical strategy: slogans and pseudo-arguments designed and used to end conversations and prevent reasoned, rigorous examination. These strategies are immensely useful and effective, especially due to the affordances of social media, whose very existence they are being used to demand. However, they also pick up on tactics used by industry-based denialists going as far back as the promotion of cigarette smoking once the tobacco industry had reasonable data about its health consequences. In much the same way the tobacco industry was (and still is) able to marshal the advocacy of "ordinary people" in the name of their "freedoms" to oppose legislation and regulation, digital denialism appears to champion the empowering aspects of digital technology per se. Some people who use these strategies, like many cigarette smokers, believe that democratic regulation is offensive to their own freedom. However, the strategic nature of these moves is clear in a society-wide sense, even without forensic work about digital technology advocacy undertaken by scholars like Oreskes and Conway (2010): for cyberlibertarians, nothing can be allowed to interfere with the largely unregulated proliferation of digital technology.

The Digital Denialists' Deck of Cards

In a classic 2007 article, legal scholar Chris Hoofnagle described the "denialists' deck of cards" as the "rhetorical techniques and predictable tactics to erect barriers to debate and consideration of any type of reform, regardless of the facts."[1] Although denialism is often associated with tobacco "science" and climate change, Hoofnagle's work is valuable because he describes his experience as a consumer protection lawyer, covering issues that range much more widely than these two fields. The desired policy result is remarkably similar across industries, and if anything, has grown more pointed in digital technology. He describes "public policy groups that spread doubt about the need for any type of reform. Chief among these groups are the American Enterprise Institute, the Competitive Enterprise Institute, the Manhattan Institute, and the Cato Institute, but many other similar groups exist that focus on specific issues" (1). Hoofnagle writes that

---

1. I thank Frank Pasquale who long ago brought this remarkable essay to my attention, specifically for its relevance to digital technology advocacy.

"whether the topic is tobacco, food and drug safety, or privacy legislation, these groups employ the same rhetorical devices to delay and stop consumer reform."

Hoofnagle explains that those who use denialist tactics, as Mirowski argues regarding climate denialists, "are not seeking a dialogue but rather an outcome" (1). That outcome is remarkably robust: to block "almost any form of consumer reform" (2). Hoofnagle lists an array of tactics, starting with "no problem": "Whatever consumer reform being debated is unnecessary. This is because there is no problem" (3). Next, industry attributes any problems it is forced to acknowledge to "bad apples" (4); demands that the public "wait and see" whether actual problems result (5); insists that "consumer freedom" is at stake, which is inherently a value more important than safety or efficacy of a given product (6); and reverts to delay when other methods fail (7).

All these tactics should be familiar to observers of digital rights advocacy, to say nothing of technology companies and other technology providers. Yet some cards in the denialists' deck have been perfected by technology advocates: that "competition," which is to say the free market, "solves all problems" (8); and that regulation of technology is always unwelcome because it "stifles innovation," which alternates with the contrary assertion that technology "can't be regulated." As Hoofnagle notes, the fact that these two assertions are incompatible only makes clear that "this exercise isn't about being cogent, it's about stopping whatever intervention the denialist opposes."

We frequently see the majority of Hoofnagle's deck strategies in digital denialism. Yet there is a host of new, more specifically digital tactics being developed to stave off whatever the new technology scandal might be. We could fill a substantial volume just documenting and explaining each of these rhetorical devices. But to make way for a focus on the key pseudo-political issues on which cyberlibertarian agitation rests, we will survey these tactics briefly, pausing only to examine in detail a few of the more interesting ones as illustrations of the general denialist moves.

Ad Hominems: "Techlash," "Moral Panic," "Technopanic," "Luddites," "Technophobes"

A popular move in recent technology advocacy is a subtle form of ad hominem attack that may appear to be a reasonable critique. The critic is accused

132 The Forms and Functions of Cyberlibertarianism

of having an emotional attachment to a critical position that invalidates any intellectual content their argument might claim to have. The most recent efflorescence of this device is the idea of "techlash," a portmanteau of "technology" and "backlash." Many digital advocates use it to explain the rising tide of criticism against Facebook, Google, and other large technology companies. The point seems to be almost physical: the power of these technologies and platforms inherently produces an automatic response, perhaps out of personal jealousy. The Information Technology and Innovation Foundation (ITIF)—a self-described "nonprofit, nonpartisan research and educational institute" that is nevertheless heavily funded by technology companies (see Watson 2017 in addition to the foundation's own lists of donors at https://itif.org/our-supporters/)—issued a report in 2019 titled "A Policymaker's Guide to the 'Techlash': What It Is and Why It's a Threat to Growth and Progress" (Atkinson et al. 2019). The report explains:

> As Microsoft President Brad Smith has asked in his new book, is technology a tool or a weapon? Until quite recently, the answer for most people would have been the former—that it is a valuable tool that makes our lives and society better. But in the last several years, views have shifted, particularly among opinion-leading elites who now finger "Big Tech" as the culprit responsible for a vast array of economic and social harms. Termed the "techlash," this phenomenon refers to a general animus and fear, not just of large technology companies, but of innovations grounded in IT.

The report goes on: "Techlash manifests not just as antipathy toward continued technological innovation, but also as active support for policies that are expressly designed to inhibit it. This trend, which appears to be gaining momentum in Europe and some U.S. cities and states, risks seriously undermining economic growth, competitiveness, and societal progress. Its policies are not rational, but the techlash has created a mob mentality, and the mob is coming for innovation." Phrases such as "opinion-leading elites," "general animus and fear," "not rational," and "mob mentality" all point at the sub rosa ad hominem nature of the "techlash" tactic. The idea that democracies and critics are irrationally pursuing regulation of technology companies due to "fear" of "innovation" obviates any need to evaluate or respond to specific criticisms. Terms like "moral panic" (a favorite of Jeff Jarvis; see Jarvis 2019) and "technopanic" (another of his favorites; see Jarvis 2013a) are virtual synonyms for "techlash" when used this way.

When she described it in an article in the *Financial Times* "Year in a Word" series in December 2018, journalist Rana Foroohar rightly noted that the term emerged because "Silicon Valley was for years the Teflon industry—beloved by equity markets, politicians and the public alike." But "at January's World Economic Forum in Davos, investor George Soros questioned the economic and political power of tech companies and their ability to manipulate public opinion in ways that challenge what John Stuart Mill would have called 'the freedom of mind.'" Facebook, Google, Amazon, Apple, and others came under public scrutiny for their roles in the Cambridge Analytica scandal and their steadfast refusal to participate in ordinary governmental oversight of their operations. Foroohar notes that Facebook in particular had "come under fire for revelations that its chief operating officer, Sheryl Sandberg, had signed off on the use of a rightwing PR firm to defame critics such as Mr Soros who called for more regulation."

Just before Soros spoke about the growing concern of technology in politics, Tom Donohue, president and CEO of the U.S. Chamber of Commerce, delivered his annual "State of American Business" address. (The organization is the largest U.S. industry lobby ranked by budget.) His address is often cited as the first use of "techlash" in recent discourse. He characterized techlash as the "backlash against major tech companies [that] is gaining strength . . . both at home and abroad, and among consumers and governments alike." As if quoting from Hoofnagle's deck of cards, he insisted that the techlash consisted inherently of "broad regulatory overreach that stifles innovation and stops positive advancements in their tracks" (Allen 2018). It's hardly surprising that the ITIF uses the passive voice to describe the rhetorical trope its own allies have developed to disqualify criticism—"termed the 'techlash'"—but in this case there is little doubt about where the term comes from and how and why it is used. Yet many mainstream publications have adopted the language uncritically, as if it is a neutral description of the world, rather than a deliberate and interested technique deployed to suggest from the beginning that critics and governments are irrational in calling for regulation.

Although "techlash" is the favored term used to label critics as being driven not by reason but emotion, there are many cognates that have served similar purposes. For many years Jarvis (2013a) and others used "technopanic," which was resurrected by the redoubtable Mercatus Center libertarian Adam Thierer (2019) to attack critics of biometric surveillance. Similarly, Robby Soave, senior editor for the libertarian publication *Reason,* in 2021 published *Tech Panic: Why We Shouldn't Fear Facebook and the Future*, which accused critics of being motivated by irrational "fear" and thus unworthy of serious attention. When all else fails, such fearful, tech-hating commentators can always be dismissed as "Luddites." However, it is ironic that the historical Luddites were not "technophobes" but thoughtful critics of technology concerned with core matters of civil and human rights (Loeb 2018b, 2021b; Mueller 2021).

"Four Horsemen of the Infocalypse"

Like so much else in cyberlibertarian discourse, "four horsemen of the infocalypse" comes from Timothy May in the "Crypto-Anarchist Manifesto" (1992) and its expansion into the "Cyphernomicon" (1994). In the "Manifesto" May writes, "The use of encryption by 'evil' groups, such as child pornographers, terrorists, abortionists, abortion protestors, etc., is cited by those who wish to limit civilian access to crypto tools. We call these the 'Four Horsemen of the Infocalypse,' as they are so often cited as the reason why ordinary citizen–units of the nation–state are not to have access to crypto." In section 8.3.4 of the "Cyphernomicon" May asks, "How will privacy and anonymity be attacked?"; in section 17.5.7 he asks, "What limits on the Net are being proposed?" In both cases one of the responses reads as follows: "Like so many other 'computer hacker' items, as a tool for the 'Four Horsemen': drug-dealers, money-launderers, terrorists, and pedophiles."

The far-right leanings of May and the cypherpunks are evident, as "abortion providers" are shockingly listed as something akin to child terrorists, as are "abortion protestors"—with no statement as to whether they are for or against choice—perhaps offered as a feint against the extremism of his position being too obvious (see Carey and Burkell 2007 for a survey of the actual occurrences of trope material in the Canadian press). May's clear intent, consistent with his position as a conspiratorial anarcho-capitalist, is to suggest that these tropes will be dishonestly used as a means for "the state" to deprive "ordinary citizen–units" of the privacy and anonymity that is their (natural) right. Of course May feels no obligation to ground these assertions in research or even robust anecdotal observation, and the full import of the assertion is not stated outright. That import is clear though: when authorities or critics mention one of the "four horsemen," they are lying to deprive you of your rights.

It is not surprising that the four horsemen trope occurs repeatedly in technology promotion about encryption and anonymity technology, often with the presumption that its existence proves that the concerns it mentions are absurd. Cory Doctorow responded to a statement by U.S. attorney general Eric Holder in 2014 that the FBI needs some kind of access to encrypted systems: "The arguments then are the arguments now. Governments invoke the Four Horsemen of the Infocalypse (software pirates, organised crime, child pornographers, and terrorists) and say that unless they can decrypt bad guys' hard drives and listen in on their conversations, law and order is a dead letter." By labeling these concerns—notice that they are not the same as either of May's lists: drug dealers and money launderers have been replaced by software pirates and organized crime, although plausibly the latter category includes both of the omitted ones—as the four horsemen, Doctorow writes as if he has demonstrated they are invented. This has two important effects: it provides encryptionists with a rhetorical tool that avoids engaging with the facts and arguments being offered; and it gives weight to the conspiratorial view that democratic governments lie to justify expansive powers they want for unstated reasons. In the age of people characterizing Covid-19 vaccine mandates as "like the Holocaust," we can see many examples of the natural endpoint of this kind of antigovernment agitprop.

Cyberlibertarianism uses tropes to prevent rational discussion of constraints on digital technology. In this case, the trope is a kind of criticism, much like I am offering throughout this book. Yet there is a vital difference. Cyberlibertarian tropes demand that we disregard the opinions of dedicated researchers and commentators, particularly those associated with democratic governments. As with all conspiracy theorists, their occasional suggestions that we "do our own research" are conditioned by pointing only to sources that reinforce their agnotological views. Further, they license the total rejection of evidence that supports assertions that they disagree with.

Forget software piracy, a phenomenon that only exists in the networked digital age and is therefore without question a real thing. Look at some of the other horsemen: money laundering, drug dealing, and child pornography. Advocates and experts report dramatic increases in these spheres, largely fueled by anonymized and encrypted digital technology. To take only the most glaring example, child protection advocates continue to see explosions in the creation and distribution of child sexual exploitation materials online (Dance and Keller 2020; Solon 2020). This is almost always associated with the "Dark Web" (i.e., the network made available through the use of Tor; more on that below) and encrypted messaging apps like

WhatsApp, which EFF and others argue should be made entirely impenetrable to law enforcement. One searches in vain for serious acknowledgment from digital rights advocates that this is a real problem, let alone one that follows naturally from the technology itself. There is no discussion among "four horsemen" promoters that maybe this one trope can't be dismissed out of hand. In fact, it continues to turn up with regularity on the Cypherpunks mailing list.

Even worse, the encryptionists have developed a political theory that considers absolute opacity to government oversight as the most fundamental human right. They can spin any concern about harms done to ordinary persons as inconsequential compared to what would happen if governments were allowed to enforce laws. This leads ideologues like Doctorow to make grandiose counterfactual statements like "the police have never had the power to listen in on every conversation, to spy upon every interaction" (2014). On the contrary, properly warranted, governments have had that power over every form of electronic communication, especially telephony, since they went into wide use.

When Andrew Lewman stepped down as executive director of the Tor organization, he stated that "95 percent of what we see on the onion sites and other dark net sites is just criminal activity. It varies in severity from copyright piracy to drug markets to horrendous trafficking of humans and exploitation of women and children" (O'Neill 2017). Clearly Lewman was in a unique position to know what he was talking about. Nevertheless, armed with the four horsemen trope, digital rights promoters attacked Lewman, claiming *he* was the one threatening human rights by daring to point out that the main use for these tools, especially if they are beyond democratic oversight, is to enable the worst kinds of antisocial behavior in our world. It is hard not to connect the dots and suggest that some of those promoting these tools as fundamental to human rights intend to use them for just the purposes mentioned in the four horsemen trope—and that they are able to use the strategy to forestall oversight of these activities by the authorities we entrust to prevent and prosecute them.

"Saving the Internet"

Internet pundits on both sides of the political spectrum agree that we must "save" something called the "internet as we know it." Almost always, this injunction comes in the form of a legal proposal that might constrain the power of technology in one way or another. So Tim Berners-Lee, the computer scientist credited with "inventing" the World Wide Web (Berners-Lee 1999), implored us that we must "act now to save the internet as we know it" in the face of FCC commissioner Ajit Pai's intention to repeal the 2015 net neutrality rules (see chapter 6), which would "upend the internet as we know it" (Berners-Lee 2017). Apple cofounder Steve Wozniak and former FCC member Michael Copps offered the same warning: "Ending net neutrality will end the internet as we know it" (2017). New York attorney general Eric Schneiderman said the same thing on the MSNBC program *All In with Chris Hayes* (Hayes 2017). AccessNow, another "digital rights" organization that takes substantial funding from major digital technology companies like Google, Reddit, and X, declares in a more anodyne tone only that "the internet as we know it is at risk" (White 2017). Well before this, Democratic senator Al Franken warned in 2010 that the FCC needed to implement net neutrality rules to "save the internet"; without them, "the internet as we know it is still at risk."

The related phrase "save the internet" is no less flexible, invoked to promote various pieces of net neutrality legislation and related policies. The Free Press organization, which claims to not "take a single cent from business, government or political parties" ("About Free Press" 2024), has maintained the SavetheInternet.com domain since at least 2007 and conducts campaigns under that name. Although the current incarnation of Free Press has a solidly left political orientation, it is worth noting that in its earliest and most public appearances, it was a coalition that included many figures whose political commitments are much less clear (e.g., Lawrence Lessig, Craig Newmark, Glenn Reynolds, the Christian Coalition of America, Susan Crawford, and Tim Wu; see "Save the Internet: Join Us" 2007). Despite its admirable work on many fronts, Free Press repeats many of the same tropes that we find across the political spectrum when it comes to digital technology. I am arguing that these tactics gather their primary force not from a literal interpretation of the words found in them, but rather as political organizing tools used by many of digital technology's most powerful entities (especially Google, Facebook, Amazon, and X) to distort policy and regulation in their name.

As David Newhoff (2012) notes, this time regarding identical rhetoric used in the SOPA and PIPA battles (recounted in chapter 1), these campaigns resemble the carefully engineered right-wing opposition to Obamacare organized around the idea of "death panels." If opposition to "death panels" were a serious belief, it would entail concern about the life and health of Americans who might be affected by the policy in question. Yet as the waves of Covid-19 disinformation have shown repeatedly, the same people who claimed to be concerned about "government" choosing who lives and who dies now side with death, mocking governmental efforts to protect life (via vaccinations and mask wearing).

Of course, net neutrality is not the only threat to "end the internet as we know it." SOPA and PIPA were similarly seen as threats as well. Despite the FCC repealing its 2015 Open Internet rules in 2017, "ending the internet as we know it," in 2018 the passage of bills to combat sex trafficking known as SESTA and FOSTA presented the same challenge (Romano 2018). The law passed, and so the internet as we know it had ended once again. In 2020, President Trump and other right-wing agitators began to question Section 230 of the Communications Decency Act. However, they did so along different lines from progressive activists who had long questioned it (see chapter 3). Berin Szóka, of the self-described "nonpartisan" but in fact right-oriented TechFreedom think tank, declared that Attorney General Bill Barr had "declare[d] war on the internet as we know it" (Szóka 2020). And of course the reliably derisive Mike Masnick of the nominally independent blog *TechDirt* frequently worries that "the internet as we know it" is not long for this world (e.g., Masnick 2011b, 2020a); a search for the phrase on the site produces nearly one hundred hits in articles alone, to say nothing of the voluminous and typically cyberlibertarian comment boards.

It is no accident that I have not even attempted to pull from these numerous articles exactly what the "internet as we know it" is supposed to be. It is obvious that this thing is of great value and it would be terrible to harm it. However, in each case, the campaign in which the phrase is used signals a *different* piece of legislation or policy proposal that would "destroy" this thing. This is odd given that the policy proposals do not always deal with the same aspect of digital technology. SOPA and PIPA are largely concerned with copyright, while the FCC Open Internet rules cover net neutrality, which is a doctrine about the provision of raw connectivity by internet service providers. Others deal with Section 230, a doctrine about liability and content moderation. The "internet as we know it" spans all these issues yet has some solid core that is so precious (and fragile) that touching any of them would somehow destroy its other aspects.

Further, while it depicts the "internet" as a fragile thing that could be "destroyed" by the simple act of regulation by democratic governments, the "internet as we know it" is a remarkably robust phrase, impervious to examination. Whatever the favored or disfavored legislative outcome around which any campaign is organized, we never need go back and ask if the "internet as we know it" was destroyed. It may not be possible to ask this question in the case of laws like SOPA and PIPA that have been defeated by these campaigns, but in others—such as the repeal of the FCC's Open Internet rules of 2015 and the passage of SESTA/FOSTA in 2018—it is very much possible to check these assertions against the facts. Yet this is rarely done, and certainly not with the vigor the apocalyptic warnings would seem to demand. The expansive claims made in these two instances were not realized, despite some very specific changes that occurred. Almost nothing about the "internet as we know it" changed due to the passage of SESTA/FOSTA or the repeal of the FCC's 2015 Open Internet Rules. However, internet pundits were able to repurpose this exact rhetoric in two subsequent campaigns, without pausing to ask whether their claims were remotely credible.

False Nostalgia: The "Dream," the "Web We Lost"

The idea of "saving the internet" is related to the idea that the internet and mass computerization were developed with the express intent of producing a more democratic and freer world. It is believed that freedom or democracy—though what these words mean is rarely made clear—would naturally follow from the widespread distribution of digital technology. These statements almost always fall into a few categories: they either breathlessly detail why the dream must come true or lament that it has not been realized *yet*, but needs redoubled effort to be achieved.

Thus in a paean to "decentralization," peer-to-peer technology, and cryptocurrency in the left-leaning *New Republic,* Paul Ford claims that the web was "a wonderfully autonomous, independent, and decentralized arrangement" and that "there's an obvious connection between a decentralized internet, in which individuals create and oversee their own digital identities, and a functioning democracy" (2016). Ford or his editors included in the piece's subtitle the phrase "the internet was supposed to be democratic and open to all." Ford seems not to notice the irony when he points out that "the people most excited about peer-to-peer technologies" are "bankers."

Similarly, *Washington Post* columnist David Ignatius, in an editorial rightly critical of Facebook's deforming effects on politics, writes, "The Internet was created with an idealistic dream: The global propagation of open information would expand human freedom and democracy. As the world became flat and citizens were empowered, authoritarian rulers would become weaker. Alas, it hasn't worked out that way. The paradox of the Internet is that it has enabled greater control by authoritarians and fueled greater disorder in open democracies" (Ignatius 2021a). This would be a "paradox" if that "idealistic dream" had actually existed. But whose dream was it, and where and by whom was it expressed, and with what authority? The most obvious subjects are people who explicitly rejected democracy and *embraced* authoritarianism, and said so.

Ignatius published another editorial the next day, in which he summarizes the views of Chris Inglis, President Biden's new "national cyber director": "His idea is that through new technology and better security, cyberspace can again become a zone of enrichment and freedom, rather than of risk and authoritarian control" (2021b). In both pieces Ignatius repeats the same homilies about "internet freedom" (see chapter 6) while relying on the words of the same experts (including Stanford Internet Observatory director and ex-Facebook CSO Alex Stamos) most responsible for spreading cyberlibertarian denialism.

In an essay in *The Verge* called "We Have Abandoned Every Principle of the Free and Open Internet," Russell Brandom declares that he "feels sad writing all of this down. These were important, world-shaping ideas. They gave us a specific vision of how networks could make society better—a vision I still believe did more good than harm" (2017). The world-shaping ideas he mentions are all familiar. In addition to "free" and "open," he declares that anonymity and free speech are being lost. He also believes that the values of "decentralized ownership" and "permissionless innovation" are at stake. Brandom cites the work of computer scientist and personal computing pioneer J. C. R. Licklider and internet pioneer Tim Berners-Lee. However, we have no reason to think that either Licklider or Berners-Lee had a credible vision of "making society better." Instead, their visions were focused on making computer networks better, and any ideas they had about society proceeded from their understandings of machines. If one believes, as do most non-right-wing critics, that the inherent tendency of technocratic reason is toward the right, then any political consequences of these inventors' views remain unclear. However, such inclinations will only point toward a better society if one accepts the political right's understanding of society.

Berners-Lee has been one of the signal promoters of false nostalgia. In a 2018 profile, he walks a fascinating fine line between declaring that the democratic dream was built into digital technology to begin with, and suggesting the opposite: "'We demonstrated that the Web had failed instead of served humanity, as it was supposed to have done, and failed in many places,' he told me. The increasing centralization of the Web, he says, has 'ended up producing—with no deliberate action of the people who designed the platform—a large-scale emergent phenomenon which is anti-human'" (Brooker 2018). "As it was supposed to have done" according to whom, and why? It is conceivable he is referring to himself as among the "people who designed the platform," and it may be true that he dreamed of a network that could produce democracy. Berners-Lee invented HTTP while working as a computer scientist at CERN. The idea that political transformations should come from computer science is already deeply troubling. Equally troubling is the influence of far-right ideas on the development of computer technology to that point, along with critical positions developed by progressive critics. Berners-Lee had an idiosyncratic dream that the web would make the world more democratic, informed by syncretic and inchoate ideas, many of which had their origins on the far right. Perhaps he took "no deliberate action" to create a tool that would "fail humanity," but that does not excuse willful ignorance of the tool's politics.

"Innovation"

When all else fails, one of the primary strategies that moves beyond rhetoric and into actual policy is to claim that innovation is at risk. EFF has long placed innovation alongside "digital privacy" and "free speech" as one of its three primary values. This makes EFF stand out among nonprofits that claim to be focused on civil and human rights, but fit right in with far-right organizations associated with political libertarianism. Most of the major digital technology companies demand that legislators think carefully about "interfering" with innovation. However, these claims are often expressed xenophobically or nationalistically. In the digital age, this has been most frequently seen in claims by U.S. tech companies that Congress must not regulate technology for fear that China will surpass them on one score of innovation or another. Hoofnagle already pointed to the reliance on "stifling innovation" as a key tool of denialism. "The denialist will argue that the intervention will stifle innovation," he writes; "arguments include 'this is just a tool,' and 'you're banning technology'" (2007, 8).

Innovation is particularly pernicious because, unlike other denialist strategies that may give regulators, legislators, and other observers pause because the arguments have an air of special pleading, opposing innovation in countries dominated by free market capitalism is tantamount to declaring oneself a communist. Like many other denialist tropes, "innovation" becomes a proxy term for economic deregulation.

Scholars have long noted that despite the near-universal acceptance of innovation as a good, it is difficult to identify any specific features that define "innovation" over and above "economic growth," at least at a society-wide level. In their 2020 book *The Innovation Delusion: How Our Obsession with the New Has Disrupted the Work That Matters Most,* science studies scholars Lee Vinsel and Andrew Russell describe "a culture that seeks to apply the wrong lessons from the digital world to the physical world, a culture whose conception of technology reflects an unholy marriage of Silicon Valley's conceit with the worst of Wall Street's sociopathy." They continue, "There is *actual innovation,* the profitable combination of new or existing knowledge, resources, and/or technologies. . . . But genuine innovation is quite distinct from *innovation-speak,* a breathless dialect of word salad that trumpets the importance of innovation while turning that term into an overused buzzword" (13). They go on:

Because innovation is such a flexible term—and because its success is followed by profit—its promoters have wrapped the concept in promises about its future impact. "The Segway will change the world!" "We're entering the era of the paperless office!" "The telegraph/airplane/Internet will usher in a new era of world peace!" And so on. We call this hype innovation-speak. Unlike actual innovation, which is tangible, measurable, and much less common, innovation-speak is a sales pitch about a future that doesn't yet exist.

Innovation-speak is fundamentally dishonest. While it is often cast in terms of optimism, talking of opportunity and creativity and a boundless future, it is in fact the rhetoric of fear. It plays on our worry that we will be left behind: Our nation will not be able to compete in the global economy; our businesses will be disrupted; our children will fail to find good jobs because they don't know how to code. (14)

A Marxist might quibble about whether profit is the best measure of real innovation, but Vinsel and Russell are right to draw attention to Joseph Schumpeter's theory of "creative destruction"—itself derived from Karl Marx's theories about the foundations of capitalist production—as a guiding feature of Silicon Valley thinking (see also Godin and Vinck 2017).

These theories rose to prominence in the digital age, especially after Harvard Business School advocated for them. The school's slight modification of Schumpeter's terminology into "disruptive innovation" gave Silicon Valley and its venture capitalists a powerful rhetorical device. As historian Jill Lepore wrote in her exhaustive critique of Christensen and his influence (for a more formal critique see King and Baatartogtokh 2015), "It's readily apparent that, in a democracy, the important business interests of institutions like the press might at times conflict with what became known as the 'public interest.' That's why, a very long time ago, newspapers like the *Times* and magazines like this one established a wall of separation between the editorial side of affairs and the business side" (2014). She documents how these business interests, usually allied with digital technology, target these "walls of separation" for "disruption," disregarding that those walls were put there to protect democratic values.

The dogma of innovation is often used to raise capital for investors and business owners, but it also serves a critical function in preventing democratic oversight of technological development. This is because it is one of the bright lines that even critical legislators and regulators are often unwilling or unable to cross. "Innovation" is closely aligned with "economic growth," and economic growth is something government should be careful about interfering with too much. The claim that regulations will "stifle innovation" is extremely effective in blocking a great deal of government action. Those who benefit from that preemption are aware of this and therefore work hard to describe everything they do as "innovation," without that word meaning much except for a different or new product in contrast to what already exists. This stretches the meaning of "innovation" past its breaking point. We might all agree that the smartphone and social media platforms represent new things in the world that enable us to do things we could not do before, and thus count as "genuine innovations" in Vinsel and Russell's terms. However, we will have more trouble agreeing whether new iterations of the smartphone or new social media platforms represent "innovation," if we mean by that "important new products or technologies that society would be worse off for not having."

Further, in the case of smartphones and social media platforms, the dogma of *genuine* innovation can serve unfortunate purposes. The discourse about innovation assumes that genuine innovations are good for society and democracy. However, many may have negative consequences that outweigh their positive ones. Schumpeter's use of the phrase "creative destruction" and Christensen's "disruptive innovation" suggest that drastic innovations will often hurt. Both authors focus on existing business practices and institutions they call "incumbents," which deserve to be displaced even when democracies or other societies have determined that an institution exists for good reason. If a commercial interest can profit from disruption, that disruption must tend to the good.

One of the first lines of defense from digital technology advocates, including companies, venture capitalists, lobbyists, digital rights organizations, and independent technologists, is that any and all regulations will "stifle innovation." As Yaël Eisenstat, former head of elections integrity operations for Facebook, and Nils Gilman, vice president of programs at the Berggruen Institute, put it in a 2022 article, "Silicon Valley came to maturity and dominance during this anti-regulation era and imbibed the swelling libertarian ethos that predominated from the 1980s onward. In this context, regulation became the enemy of 'innovation,' which soon emerged as the byword for 'tech' as a whole. As more recently described in a *Forbes* article on Tesla, 'We all generally perceive the government and regulations as a hurdle to progress and innovation.' For a whole generation of entrepreneurs, abetted by market fundamentalists, the central dogma became the right to 'permissionless innovation.'" What is so confounding about cyberlibertarianism is that this "swelling libertarian ethos" is accepted and promoted by so many who do not think of themselves as libertarians, and may even see themselves as progressive.

Eisenstat and Gilman link the phrase "permissionless innovation" to a paper by Adam Thierer for the Cato Institute, "Embracing a Culture of Permissionless Innovation" (2014), later expanded into a book titled *Permissionless Innovation* (2016). Thierer, recall, is part of the far-right thought collective centered at the Mercatus Center at George Mason University, former director of telecommunications at the Cato Institute, president of the Progress and Freedom Foundation, and a senior fellow at the Heritage Foundation. A synonym for "permission" as it is used in this instance is "democratic governance." Regardless of whether it is best for business to have democratic government looking over the shoulders of business, such oversight is necessary for democratic governance to mean anything (see Golumbia 2014a). Libertarians had to come up with a new term for what they want, because using "laws and regulations don't apply to us" might tip off ordinary citizens to what is really going on.

In 2013, the FAA proposed rules to create "test sites" for the use of commercial drones in commercial airspace. Given the dangers associated with air traffic and the heavily regulated nature of commercial airspace, it is not hard to see why the FAA would be concerned about the potential for danger. Rather than prohibiting drones from commercial airspace altogether, the regulator proposed a series of test sites where drone developers and proponents could experiment with the technology and how it interacts with commercial aircraft. This already seems a significant concession to industry, since the potential for problems are manifest. Yet the Mercatus Center–funded Technology Liberation Front (TLF) would have none of it. In a filing with the FAA, the TLF noted that Google's chief internet evangelist and digital technology pioneer Vint Cerf had recently equated "permissionless innovation" with the "open internet," worrying about "policies that enable government controls but greatly diminish the 'permissionless innovation' that underlies extraordinary Internet-based economic growth to say nothing of trampling human rights" (Cerf 2012). The TLF authors wrote, "Like the Internet, airspace is a platform for commercial and social innovation. We cannot accurately predict to what uses it will be put when restrictions on commercial use of UASs [Unmanned Aircraft Systems] are lifted. Nevertheless, experience shows that it is vital that innovation and entrepreneurship be allowed to proceed without *ex ante* barriers imposed by regulators" (Dourado 2013). Such sentiments from both Cerf and the TLF could not be clearer: the only values that matter are "innovation" and "entrepreneurship." Despite Cerf's rhetorical nod toward them, the only "human rights" that matter are those of technology itself, as realized in "innovation and entrepreneurship." Never mind that what is at stake in the FAA's remit is the safety of everyone who travels by air, not the success of venture capitalists or commercial startups. Reasonable regulation that allows for economic development is anathema to technology, and the logic undergirding that comes straight from beliefs about the nature of the "internet"—that is, from cyberlibertarianism.

CHAPTER 3

Deregulation and Multistakeholderism
A Case Study of Section 230

The rightward tendency of cyberlibertarianism is accompanied by a specific legislative and regulatory (more properly, deregulatory) program that has been highly effective for almost two decades. Climate denial, for example, relies on "scientists" who are not considered experts on climate science by anyone but themselves. Discussions of digital ethics and politics, on the other hand, tend to be dominated by authority figures seen as having "real" expertise, even by technicians working in the field (including engineers and computer scientists who openly espouse cyberlibertarian ideas). Their authority in the political sphere derives more from working with computers than from representing easily definable political positions. Their expertise is repurposed for activism, and the beneficiary of that activism is the computer as the locus of rights. Although these authority figures publicly portray themselves as defenders of civil rights, they actually promote specific deregulatory governmental programs.

In the United States, cyberlibertarian advocacy is galvanized around Section 230 of the Communications Decency Act of 1996. Section 230 advocacy is one of the places where industry influence is most visible. One of the most prominent speakers in the field is Daphne Keller, director of the Program on Platform Regulation at Stanford's Cyber Policy Center. A former longtime Google employee, until 2015 she was the company's associate general counsel for intermediary liability and free speech. She has also taken money from the Koch Foundation to address "free expression in a digital world" (Charles Koch Foundation 2020). Though Eric Goldman, professor of law at Santa Clara University, has fewer direct industry connections than Keller, the pair often play tag-team in defending Section 230 against all comers, turning it into a blanket ban on regulation that must be preserved no matter the cost.

Along with Mike Masnick of *TechDirt,* Goldman and Keller are among the most reliable media talking heads and congressional testifiers. Their positions, while sometimes nuanced, typically align with whatever Google happens to be promoting at that moment. The Tech Transparency Project noted in 2017 that when the SESTA/FOSTA bills, which offered only slight revisions to Section 230, were proposed, "almost all the nonprofits, academics and policy groups that have adopted a public stance against the bill have received financial support from Google" (2017b). Keller, Goldman, and Masnick are all included in this list. (Masnick is funded by the "innovation"-focused Copia Foundation he founded, which has taken money from Google and the VC film Andreessen Horowitz; the piece notes that Goldman is a faculty scholar at a center in Santa Clara that "received $500,000 from Google in 2011 as part of a *cy près* legal settlement the company made over privacy violation.") Listed as well are EFF, CDT, ACLU, "right-of-center groups such as the Heritage Foundation and R Street Institute; left-of-center and free speech groups such as the New America Foundation; and even academics at some of the leading institutions in America such as Harvard's Berkman Klein Center."

Section 230 is only the tip of the iceberg here. The TTP "identified 330 research papers published between 2005 and 2017 on public policy matters of interest to Google that were in some way funded by the company" (2017a). The report noted that even though academics received support from Google in more than half of the cases, a quarter of those authors did not disclose their funding relationship. In cases where the funding was indirect even fewer disclosed appropriately. This is an operation of immense sophistication and influence. The TTP rightly notes that "Google has paid scholars millions to produce hundreds of papers supporting its policy interests, following in the footsteps of the oil and tobacco industries." Of course this only talks about Google; Facebook, Amazon, X, and all other digital tech corporations employ similar strategies for shaping public discourse.

Outside the United States the situation is even more difficult to assess. The question of how the world should govern and regulate digital technology internationally, of great interest to technology companies, is addressed by the same actors who dominate the Section 230 discussion. They are joined by a group of "internet governance" experts who come from engineering and other computer-related fields and routinely work to undermine the fragile political structures that mediate international relations. They claim to act in the name of human rights but in fact promote a specific right-wing, free-market absolutist position that openly attacks democratic sovereignty, under the general heading of "multistakeholderism." One area this is especially visible is in the way both the internet governance and U.S. internet freedom caucuses respond to the nuanced, detailed, and potentially effective regulatory actions of the European Union.

THE HISTORY OF SECTION 230

Until the late 2010s, few Americans had heard of Section 230 of the Communications Decency Act (CDA) of 1996. In the later years of the Trump administration, that changed for many reasons, and Section 230 became a lynchpin of domestic cyberlibertarian political strategy. In the early 2020s, both Republicans and Democrats in Congress expressed significant concerns about the law, suggesting that it required revision but disagreeing about what changes should be made. Legal scholar Danielle Keats Citron explains the genesis of the CDA in 1995 congressional deliberations and how Section 230 came to be added to the law:

At the time, online pornography was considered the scourge of the age. Senators James Exon and Slade Gorton introduced the CDA to make the internet safe for kids. Besides proposing criminal penalties for the distribution of sexually explicit material online, the Senators underscored the need for private sector help in reducing the volume of noxious material online. In that vein, Representatives Christopher Cox and Ron Wyden offered an amendment to the CDA entitled "Protection for Private Blocking and Screening of Offensive Material." The Cox–Wyden amendment, codified in Section 230, provided immunity from liability for "Good Samaritan" online service providers that either over- or under-filtered objectionable content. (2018)

Yet this immunity from liability for attempting to remove pornography morphed into something much broader: "Granting immunity to platforms that deliberately host, encourage, or facilitate illegal activity would have seemed absurd to the CDA's drafters. The law's overbroad interpretation means that platforms have no reason to take down illicit material and that victims have no leverage to insist that they do so. Rebecca Tushnet put it well a decade ago: Section 230 ensures that platforms enjoy 'power without responsibility.'" She goes on:

> Twenty years ago, federal lawmakers could not have imagined how essential to modern life the internet would become. The internet was still largely a tool for hobbyists. Nonetheless, Section 230's authors believed that "if this amazing new thing—the Internet—[was] going to blossom," companies should not be 'punished for trying to keep things clean.' Cox recently noted that "the original purpose of [Section 230] was to help clean up the Internet, not to facilitate people doing bad things on the Internet." The key to Section 230, explained Wyden, was "making sure that companies in return for that protection—that they wouldn't be sued indiscriminately—were being responsible in terms of policing their platforms."

Section 230 was added to the CDA in part due to

> a single court ruling in May of that year [that] threatened to smother the internet in its crib. Prodigy, an early provider of online services, was found to be legally liable for a defamatory anonymous posting on one of its message boards. The ruling had chilling implications: If websites could be sued over every piece of content that someone didn't like, the internet's growth might come to a halt. Cox read about the Prodigy ruling on a flight from California to Washington and had one thought: I can fix this!
>
> "A light bulb went off," he told me recently. "So I took out my yellow legal pad and sketched a statute. Then I shared it with Ron."
>
> That statute eventually became Section 230. In hindsight, the concept is ridiculously simple: Websites aren't publishers. They're intermediaries. To sue an online platform over an obscene blog post would be like suing the New York Public Library for carrying a copy of *Lolita*. For a young internet facing a potential avalanche of speech-squelching lawsuits, Cox and Wyden's provision was a creative workaround—a hack—that allowed this new form of communication to grow into the thriving network of commercial enterprises we know today. (Zara 2017)

The notion of websites as "intermediaries," and intermediaries as a suitable name for services as varied as Google, Amazon, dating apps, Twitter, and so on, has hung on to this day. As a result, debates about Section 230 frequently refer to it as a matter of "intermediary liability." However, the question whether this accurately describes platforms remains open.

Cox and Wyden developed their "hack" for digital technology without going into too much depth on the fundamental question. The dilemma they saw was solved by giving platforms what many refer to as "two immunities." This interpretation was largely due to the 1997 Fourth Circuit *Zeran v. America Online* decision, which quickly established the terms under which Section 230 would be interpreted in the decades that followed. As Section 230 proponents Berin Szóka and Ashkhen Kazaryan put it recently:

> Section 230(c)(1) protects "interactive computer service" (ICS) providers and users from civil actions or state (but not federal) criminal prosecution based on decisions they make as "publishers" with respect to third-party content they are in no way responsible for developing. In its 1997 *Zeran* decision, the Fourth Circuit became the first appellate court to interpret this provision, concluding that "lawsuits seeking to hold a service provider liable for its exercise of a publisher's traditional editorial functions—such as deciding whether to publish, withdraw, postpone or alter content—are barred." A second immunity, Section 230(c)(2)(A) protects (in different ways) decisions to "restrict access to or availability of material that the provider or user considers to be . . . objectionable," even if the provider is partly responsible for developing it. (2020, 1061)

The language of the law and the interpretation of the Fourth Circuit court in *Zeran* were both determinative factors in what Section 230 means for the contemporary internet. Contrary to the opinions of dogmatists like Malcolm, most scholars and lawyers (Jain 2020; Kosseff 2020, 2019, 92–96; Sylvain 2020) believe that the *Zeran* interpretation was not inevitable and is itself critical to the functions of Section 230 under U.S. law. Describing Wilkinson's disagreement with the arguments offered by Zeran's attorney Leo Kayser, Jeff Kosseff writes:

> It is difficult to overstate the significance of Wilkinson's ruling. Had Wilkinson agreed with Kayser that Section 230 merely immunized online services until they received complaints or other notice about third-party content, then the legal landscape for platforms in the United States would look like

the laws in much of the rest of the Western world. This would allow any person or company who is unhappy with user content to bully a service provider into taking down the content, lest the provider face significant legal exposure. But Wilkinson disagreed with Kayser. He concluded that Section 230 immunizes online platforms from virtually all suits arising from third-party content. This would forever change the course of Internet law in the United States. (2019, 94–95)

Kayser then asked for further review, and his request was denied:

Zeran requested that all the judges on the Fourth Circuit—rather than just a panel of three—rehear the case, but the Fourth Circuit denied the request. He then asked the United States Supreme Court to rehear the case, but in June 1998 it refused to do so. He was stuck with Judge Wilkinson's ruling that he could not sue America Online over the anonymous user's posts. Wilkinson's interpretation of Section 230 was so broad that it exceeded the standard First Amendment protections afforded to publishers. *Zeran* turned Section 230 into a nearly impenetrable super–First Amendment for online companies. (95)

Kosseff and others argue that Wilkinson's ruling plays a key role in the Section 230 doctrine that followed. However, Kosseff also finds that one of Section 230's cosponsors, Ron Wyden, expected that outcome: "When Congress passed Section 230, did it intend to create the sweeping immunity that Wilkinson provided in *Zeran*? Absolutely, Wyden told me in 2017. 'We said very bluntly that we thought it would freeze innovation if somebody who owned a website could be personally liable,' Wyden said. 'There was not a lot of rocket science there.'" The claim is that Cox, Wyden, and other members of Congress, along with President Clinton, passed Section 230 into law as part of the Communications Decency Act of 1996 with the expectation that courts would rule as Wilkinson did. They intended to protect "innovation" as a matter of free expression. Section 230, like many other cyberlibertarian tenets, turns out to be primarily about protecting business interests, and only secondarily, if at all, about citizen or political interests.

While some commentators feel that the *Zeran* interpretation of Section 230 was inevitable and even intended by the law's authors, others, especially analysts with a left-leaning perspective, disagree. Legal scholar Olivier Sylvain analyzes the *Zeran* decision this way:

The immunity under the CDA, codified at 47 U.S.C. § 230, gives such intermediaries cover largely because courts have read the protection broadly. And they have had good reason to. The first operative provision of the statute states that "[n]o provider or user of an interactive computer service shall be treated as the publisher or speaker of any information provided by another information content provider." Congress's reference here to "publisher or speaker" draws from defamation law doctrine, where a defendant publisher is as liable for republishing reputation-damaging material as its author. When enacted in 1996, Section 230(c) was intended to bar courts from holding providers liable for publishing information that could harm users' reputation.

This was and remains an idiosyncratic and exceptional treatment under law. Newspapers and book imprints, for example, remain as liable for publishing unlawful classified advertisements or opinion editorials as the original authors are. Legislators in 1996 expressed the view that providers of online services and applications were different—that they should not be held to account for the massive amounts of third-party user content that they host and publish. Parroting the emergent ethos among technologists and internet free-speech activists, legislators in this period found that imposing liability on online intermediaries for failing to screen or remove all offending content would exact a "chilling" toll on all users that is far greater than it would be for traditional publishers. In such a world, providers would censor any content that they rightly or wrongly believe exposes them to liability. Section 230 relieves intermediaries of that heavy burden in the interest of promoting entrepreneurship and freedom of expression online.

Most legislators in 1996, however, could not have anticipated that the internet would permeate public life or that intermediaries would engineer practically all our online conduct. They did appreciate, however, that the protection could not be absolute. Section 230 specifically provides that the immunity recedes when the provider in question "is responsible, in whole or in part, for the creation or development" of the offending information. Congress also wrote in a "Good Samaritan" safe harbor to incentivize providers to mind their users' "objectionable" content. (2018, 210–11)

Sylvain goes on to explain that "courts read Section 230 extremely broadly in spite of how it is written. They hold that the provision immunizes networked services and online applications from liability for publishing the illegal content of their users. So, under current law, a social media company cannot be held responsible for allowing a user to post compromising private photographs of his ex-girlfriend publicly. A search engine cannot be called to task under law for displaying the advertisements of third parties that sell copyrighted ringtones" (215). Legal scholars Danielle Keats Citron and Benjamin Wittes echo these concerns: "The broad construction of the CDA's immunity provision adopted by the courts has produced an immunity from liability that is far more sweeping than anything the law's words, context, and history support. Platforms have been protected from liability even though they republished content knowing it might violate the law, encouraged users to post illegal content, changed their design and policies for the purpose of enabling illegal activity, or sold dangerous products. As a result, hundreds of decisions have extended § 230 immunity, with comparatively few denying or restricting it" (2017).

While *Zeran* in particular stresses that Section 230 appears to grant digital platforms immunity from laws that might otherwise apply to them, the law was intended to have two related effects that are at cross-purposes. One was to *encourage* platforms to moderate problematic content. Congress "hoped to encourage the companies to feel free to adopt basic conduct codes and delete material that the companies believe is inappropriate" (Kosseff 2019, 2). But it was also intended, Kosseff says, to "allow technology companies to freely innovate and create open platforms for user content. Shielding Internet companies from regulation and lawsuits would encourage investment and growth, they thought" (2–3).

INTERPRETING SECTION 230

One of the most fascinating aspects of Section 230 is that even the most well informed commentators do not agree about what it means. This confusion, while typical of the popular understanding of many laws and technical issues, is so magnified that one wonders whether it is part of the law's central function. These twenty-six words that "create the internet" in that they create a fog around questions of the legality of digital technologies nearly impenetrable for anyone, including judges and legislators, so that their effects are felt in ways that obscure their specific legal consequences. In 2020, the digital tech trade organization Internet Association surveyed more than five hundred cases spanning two decades. Their report claimed that "far from acting as a 'blanket immunity'—Section 230 only served as the primary basis for a ruling in 42 percent of the decisions we reviewed" and that "the law continues to perform as Congress intended, quietly protecting soccer parents from defamation claims, discussion boards for nurses and police from nuisance suits, and local newspapers from liability for comment trolls" (Banker 2020, 2). The need for the survey implies the confusion surrounding Section 230.

In Jamie Bartlett's 2017 BBC documentary *Secrets of Silicon Valley*, Jeremy Malcolm, a senior policy analyst at EFF, is featured in a segment where he advocates for both "internet freedom" and "multistakeholderism." Malcolm explains the importance of the legislation to EFF's worldview; when asked by Bartlett to read the "key line" in Section 230, Malcolm replies:

> It literally just says, "No provider or user of an interactive computer service shall be treated as the publisher or speaker of any information provided by another information content provider." That's it. So what that basically means is, if you're an internet platform, you don't get treated as the publisher or speaker of something that your users say using your platform. If the user says something online that is, say, defamatory, the platform that they communicate on isn't going to be held responsible for it. And the user, of course, can be held directly responsible.

Malcolm goes on:

> "I think if we didn't have this, we probably wouldn't have the same kind of social media companies that we have today. They wouldn't be willing to take on the risk of having so much unfettered discussion."
> BARTLETT: "It's the key to the internet's freedom, really?"
> MALCOLM: "We wouldn't have the internet of today without this. And so, if we are going to make any changes to it, we have to be really, really careful."

Given EFF's overtly activist positioning—Bartlett, a respected investigative journalist, describes EFF in the segment "a civil liberties group for the digital age"—it is striking that Malcolm so openly notes that the benefits of Section 230 have accrued to "social media" in general, and "social media companies" in particular. That is, to machines and to companies—but not to people, the clear focus of almost all civil rights (see Winn 2012 on assigning rights and freedoms to machines and not to people). Surprisingly, those doing the real legal work in these cases, despite being depicted as "civil liberties" NGOs, reflect this attitude in their defenses of Section 230.

Even more telling is Malcolm's injunction to "be really, really careful" if we want "to make any changes to" Section 230. This is a typically cyberlibertarian injunction to democratic governments to be cautious in regulating an industry that has grown *because* it has placed itself beyond ordinary government oversight—that is, outside the view of the mechanisms with which we express *caution*. This cyberlibertarian credo takes another particularly perverse form: we *should be* cautious about interfering with unfettered corporate growth using our democratic powers and responsibilities, but we *should not* be cautious about deregulated corporate growth that relies on largely untested technology that, whatever its benefits and however much we enjoy using it, has already been shown to have negative effects on society at large.

Bartlett doesn't tell us the date of the interview, but it appears to have been recorded in mid-2017—well after Trump had been elected, well after so many scandals over corporate misuse of data that it is no longer possible to keep track. One of the documentary's main subjects is how digital technologies are helping to enable not the *popular* uprisings pundits keep promising, but largely right-wing *populist* upsurges worldwide. This is the predictable outcome of such policies, as many of us involved in the critical study of the digital have long suggested. According to a leading "civil rights" group in the sector, despite the fact that these technology companies have been implicated in some of the most disastrous political events in decades, society's concern should be to avoid constraining their growth.

Of course terms like *popular* and *populist* should be examined carefully, but digital evangelists like Malcolm and EFF argue that we don't have time for *care*. The cyberlibertarian program aims to use Section 230 to create a deregulatory sphere for U.S.-based digital technology companies because they have taken advantage of local deregulation to overwhelm the regulatory capacities of other countries—most flagrantly and obviously in Uber under Travis Kalanick. We are only beginning to learn the extent of this problem (see Davies et al. 2022), but it is not limited to Uber. The political right looks for ways to engineer deregulation through legal and illegal means. They develop and find places where regulation may apply, but the letter of the law, legal precedent, or other factors put it beyond reach.

The title of Jeff Kosseff's 2019 book, *The Twenty-Six Words That Created the Internet* repeats and expands on Malcolm's claim in ways very typical among the law's most ardent supporters: that not just social media companies (most of which did not exist in 1996 when Section 230 was passed), and not just the World Wide Web, but the internet itself could not function without it. Appearing to endorse the claim that the law is necessary, Kosseff writes that "YouTube, Facebook, Reddit, Wikipedia, Twitter, and eBay . . . simply could not exist without Section 230" (4). Yet in the same paragraph Kosseff rightly notes that those companies operate in many (indeed, almost all) countries, few of which have anything like Section 230 protections, and yet the platforms do not come crashing to the ground. In none of them does the internet "break." We rarely hear stories of internet companies facing the kinds of consequences we are told would be omnipresent in the law's absence. Even if Section 230 "created" the internet, the internet persists quite robustly where the law does not exist.

It is not particularly notable that a law with many consequences is vague and confusing. Yet it is hard to overlook that those who most credit Section 230 with having "created the internet" are also those who most frequently chastise academics, activists, lawyers, politicians, and ordinary citizens for being "ignorant" about the legislation. This kind of agitation is especially odd given how digital rights activists insist we need the internet due to vague ideals such as the "democratization" of information or knowledge (see chapter 6). It is curious to claim that digital technology is fundamentally necessary for democracy because of its ability to create a better-informed citizenry, and yet in the same breath claim that the citizenry and politicians are too poorly informed about the "law that created the internet" to speak credibly about it.

Rep. Christopher Cox (R-Calif.), who cowrote Section 230 with Rep. Ron Wyden (D-Ore.), testified before the Senate in 2020 that "notwithstanding that Section 230 has become a household name, a complete understanding of how the law functions in practice, and what it actually does, is harder to come by" (Cox 2020, 10). The law exists in a penumbra of uncertainty. Cox's account of the history and function of Section 230 is detailed and consistent with those of most scholars and activists. He explains the reasoning that spurred him and Wyden to put forth their amendment:

Before the enactment of Section 230, internet platforms faced a terrible dilemma. If they sought to enforce even minimal rules of the road in order to maintain civility and keep their sites free from obscenity and obnoxious behavior, they became unlimitedly liable for all of the user-created content on their site. On the other hand, if the website followed an "anything goes" business model, with no content moderation whatsoever, then it could completely avoid that liability. From the perspective of any internet platform that attempted to maintain a family-friendly site, it was a classic case of "no good deed goes unpunished."

Section 230 eliminated the perverse incentive for "anything goes." By imposing liability on criminals and tortfeasors for their own wrongful communications and conduct, rather than shifting that liability to a website that did not in any way participate in the wrongdoing, it freed each website to clean up its corner of the internet. No longer would being a "Good Samaritan" buy trouble. (3)

Cox's dilemma presented a problem for a specific digital platform and business models. Another way of framing the problem is to say that purely unmoderated, absolute free speech platforms would inevitably and quickly emerge as sites for many kinds of behavior that laws exist to curtail and even prohibit. One might have hoped that legislators and jurists would have given more thought to this fundamental observation. Unmoderated platforms would allow not only speech like defamation that would be legally actionable under civil statutes, but a far wider set of speech and actions than the immediate issue suggested. Even though these kinds of speech and actions were already readily visible on the internet and World Wide Web (e.g., Usenet newsgroups, email mailing lists, private BBSs, and other services largely forgotten today), unmoderated platforms would allow for even more forms of speech and action.

Cox rightly notes that "another misconception about the coverage of Section 230, often heard, is that it created one rule for online activity and a different rule for the same activity conducted offline. To the contrary, Section 230 operates to ensure that like activities are always treated alike under the law" (2020, 12). This is correct, but it sidesteps the crux of the issue, which is whether the "activities" governed by Section 230 in the online context are "like activities" to those conducted offline. If so, what are they? Here, significant analytical work is needed. It is true that in non-digital speech platforms, the "platform" enabler is rarely held liable for the content of the speech presented or for moderating that speech. In some technological contexts, this is so obvious as to be unquestioned by almost everyone. For example, telephone companies are rarely held liable for activities conducted over the phone system, even if those activities go well past the typical speech torts of slander or libel, up to criminal activities that inherently involve speech but gain no speech protections (e.g., arranging murders or other violent crimes). Similarly, the owner of a performance hall is rarely held accountable for speeches made by event participants. Even if there may be outlier cases where the owner or event organizer has been held partly responsible for the actions of a speaker or performer, such parties have rarely been held responsible for the actions of the audience to a performance or speech. This appears to be reasonable parallel to digital platforms.

But that parallel may be misleading. Other platforms primarily organized around expression have considered the regulation and governance of content important for the flourishing of the medium and its fit into democratic principles. Radio and television are the most obvious examples, which required the provision of frequencies for their analog histories and needed ownership rights to function. As a condition of licensing channel 2 in the New York metropolitan area or AM band 760 in the Detroit metropolitan area, say, the providers of content and technical services pledged to moderate their output and were thus liable for any breaches.

Meanwhile, the vagueness surrounding Section 230 may serve more important functions than are immediately obvious. The claim that nobody understands the law is particularly common among the law's most ardent supporters, such as Keller, Goldman, and Masnick. Masnick in particular has made a career of mocking any and all presentations on the law, especially those by legislators and legal scholars. He suggests that "you just read the law, because it seems that many people who are making these mistakes seem to have never read it" (2020b). But he fails to note that understanding the law's effects requires at least a review of its complex jurisprudential history, especially *Zeran vs AOL,* whose application of the law some thought inevitable and others continue to think overbroad. While Masnick is right to point out some widespread misunderstandings (e.g., "Because of Section 230, websites have no incentive to moderate" or "A site that has political bias is not neutral, and thus loses its Section 230 protections"), most of his "corrections" are similar to those made by legal scholars like Citron, Franks, Wittes, and Sylvain (e.g., "Section 230 is a massive gift to big tech!" "Section 230 means these companies can never be sued!" "Section 230 is a get out of jail card for websites!" or "Section 230 gives websites blanket immunity!"), all of which suggest that the largest internet companies experience significant benefits from Section 230 that law cannot or should not regulate.

Despite Masnick and others insisting that critics of Section 230 simply need to "read the law," the fact remains that Section 230 plays several roles in the propagandistic framing of digital technology and its power, which the cyberlibertarian frame helps us to unpack. Section 230 provides legal protections in some cases but not in others; even courts disagree about when and how it should apply. However, the larger effect is to create the appearance that these companies should be outside the purview of law. Despite the fact that law is law and is largely understood to function via judicial and regulatory action, law also has other cultural and political functions. Masnick and others promote a "veil of ignorance" around Section 230, which has resulted in everyone from judges to legislators to litigants being hesitant to do anything that might touch on the apparent untouchability of internet companies. The repetitive nature of these attacks on critics for being "ignorant" is itself a mark of the power of Section 230 and the way cyberlibertarianism functions to preserve and expand the power of digital technology and its platforms.

Mary Ann Franks, who has studied the law closely both as a legal scholar and practitioner, writes that Section 230 "dramatically ramps up" a "morally hazardous conception of the First Amendment—allowing giant corporations to risk the safety, security, and wellbeing of billions of people in the pursuit of profit" (2019a, 181). Carrie Goldberg, a victims' rights litigator in New York, writes that "until 2018, the courts' application of Section 230 of the CDA was so broad that even websites facilitating online child sex trafficking and exploitation were able to do business with impunity" (2019, 47). She details her experience suing the makers of the dating app Grindr on behalf of Matthew Herrick, an actor–model who was targeted for ongoing and horrifying abuse by an ex-partner, Oscar Juan Carlos Gutierrez. After the couple broke up, Herrick discovered that Gutierrez was posing fake profiles for him on Grindr and other dating apps, where he "eagerly invited men for fisting, orgies, and aggressive sex. Fake Matt instructed strangers not to take no for an answer. If he resisted, Fake Matt assured prospective sex partners, it was part of the fantasy. They should just play along" (36).

Herrick sued Grindr after numerous attempts to get the company to take down fake profiles. He feared for his personal and bodily safety. During the court proceedings, Grindr representatives relied on Section 230 to protect themselves and to argue that "they couldn't control their product or disable Gutierrez's phony accounts" (49). Despite Herrick and his lawyers filing an amended complaint in March 2021 and more than a thousand men coming to Herrick's door due to the fake profiles since October 2016, a federal district court judge dismissed all but one of his claims in January 2018. The judge "agreed with Grindr that Section 230 of the CDA 'immunizes Grindr for content created by other users'" (52). Herrick and his attorneys appealed the ruling to the Supreme Court but were unsuccessful. *Herrick v. Grindr* is one of the most high-profile cases to directly address Section 230 immunity. It demonstrates that Section 230 enables and protects abuse and harassment, and empowers large technology corporations at the expense of individuals and their rights.

SECTION 230 IN A GLOBAL FRAME

Promoters of internet freedom have performed global surveys (Kaye 2017; Morar and dos Santos 2020) without recognizing that the global frame disproves the apocalyptic claims often made about the "internet" without Section 230. Yes, the internet and social media operate differently in each country. But no, the internet does not "break." And even free expression on the internet, if not identical with the U.S. regime, persists in forms that are relatively predictable given a country's overall approach to such matters. Activists nevertheless insist with remarkable vehemence that a form of Section 230–like rules should be implemented worldwide. A noteworthy example is the "Manila Principles" (2015), coordinated largely by EFF. This report takes as given the urgent necessity of installing these principles at the level of global civil society (and perhaps even the UN, where David Kaye has been the most notable agitator for the expansive cyberlibertarian notion of "free speech"; see Kaye 2017) without even considering the many reasonable objections mooted to this idea. Moreover, the report does not mention that the call for these changes comes almost exclusively from technology companies and cyberlibertarian promoters of technology for its own sake. Activists who worry about the huge array of human rights other than free expression have offered little encouragement.

Given the apparent bipartisan support for revising Section 230 in the United States in the early 2020s, it is not surprising that some advocates have started to explore the question of Section 230 protections abroad. Even the strongly pro-business and pro-technology Information Technology and Innovation Foundation (ITIF) notes that approaches to intermediary liability vary. Setting aside the fact that many internet companies openly operate in authoritarian and otherwise nondemocratic regimes, where the legal architecture does not provide the kinds of protections Section 230 does in the United States, the authors of the ITIF report note that even in other democratic countries Section 230–like statutes are far from the norm:

> Outside the United States, approaches to online intermediary liability in democratic countries generally fall in between a broadly permissive approach that shields online services from any and all liability for third-party content and a restrictive approach that holds online services fully responsible for the content on their platforms. When finding a compromise between the two extremes, democracies need to balance many different factors, including free speech, innovation, competition, transparency, accountability, and reducing online harms.
>
> There are many options beyond the binary of preserving Section 230 as it is and repealing it altogether. As U.S. policymakers consider a variety of proposals to reform Section 230, they should use other countries' approaches as a guideline, evaluating what has and has not worked and predicting some of the side effects different reforms would have for businesses, consumers, and the economy. (Johnson and Castro 2021)

One would be hard-pressed to find any such admissions, let alone surveys of facts on the ground, in the debates between Section 230 supporters and critics. However, even brief reflection shows that there are options available beyond the binary Johnson and Castro identify.

In late 2019, despite controversies over Section 230, technology firms, not human rights activists, pressed Congress to include Section 230–like provisions in the U.S.–Mexico–Canada Agreement (USMCA) on trade. By this point in the Trump presidency, those on the left were concerned about how Section 230 protections seemed to aid the right in attacking democracy, while the right had the opposite concern—that Section 230, through its "encouragement" for various forms of content moderation, was "censoring conservative speech." President Trump was trying to repeal Section 230 entirely during the USMCA deliberations. These efforts continued until the end of his term in late 2020, when he vetoed the annual National Defense Authorization Act because it failed to repeal Section 230 (Hatmaker 2020). The bill had such bipartisan support that both houses of Congress and representatives of both parties were able to overturn his veto with healthy margins (Mazmanian and Williams 2021).

On the surface, this development would indicate bipartisan support for Section 230. However, the USMCA negotiations showed the opposite. Technology companies and their representatives, including figures familiar from Section 230 advocacy, were the main voices demanding an inclusion of Section 230–like provisions in the USMCA. Yet independent critics—including legal scholar Danielle Citron, computer scientist Hany Farid (developer of the main algorithm used to moderate child abuse imagery), and Gretchen S. Peters, executive director of the Alliance to Counter Crime Online—were represented at the October 2019 hearings on the trade agreement (U.S. House Committee on Energy and Commerce 2019). These critics had little good to say about the proposed international expansion of Section 230 protections and much to say about how and why the provision might be revised in the United States. Further, industry representatives—including Google's global head of intellectual property Katherine Oyama, Reddit cofounder and CEO Steve Huffman, and EFF's legal director Corynne McSherry—were unable to provide cogent explanations for the new doctrine or its expected outcomes.

Prominent congressional members of both parties voiced opposition to the inclusion of Section 230 protections in the USMCA: "The Democratic chairman and ranking Republican on the House Energy and Commerce Committee—which oversees tech companies—complained that it was wrong to include the legal shield in the trade agreement at a time when some lawmakers were still debating the U.S. version. 'We find it inappropriate for the United States to export language mirroring Section 230 while such serious policy discussions are ongoing,' said the letter from Chairman Frank Pallone (D-NJ) and Rep. Greg Walden (R-OR)." Speaker Nancy Pelosi (through a spokesperson) indicated that there were "concerns in the

House about enshrining the increasingly controversial . . . liability shield in our trade agreements" (McKinnon and Mullins 2019; see also Feiner 2019). No less a business-friendly publication as the *Wall Street Journal* reported that "internet firms lobbied hard to include the immunity language in the trade agreement," and that Michael Beckerman, president of the industry lobby Internet Association, said: "The inclusion of these provisions [in the trade deal] represents a victory for the entire American economy" (McKinnon and Mullins 2019). Once again, "digital rights" organizations including EFF were lobbying on the side of tech corporations, and against independent scholars, activists, and politicians who saw the proposed expansion of Section 230 protections as interfering with the promotion of human rights.

Despite widespread opposition to including Section 230 protections in the USMCA as a carve-out specifically to benefit tech companies—so much so that Pelosi herself called it "a real gift to Big Tech" (DeChiaro 2019)—and President Trump's public demands for repeal of Section 230, Congress followed the guidance of U.S. trade representative Robert Lighthizer (even though he refused to testify at the October 2019 hearings). The USMCA was passed and signed by President Trump on July 1, 2020 (Swanson and Tankersley 2020), with the Section 230 provisions included intact.

GLOBAL POLICY AND GOVERNANCE:
MULTISTAKEHOLDERISM

The cyberlibertarian policy agenda has had a significant impact on global governance. The digital technology industry has been successful in reshaping world governance practices and theory, both at the United Nations and in NGOs. While corporate and private money have always influenced these spaces, cyberlibertarianism has successfully branded the purposeful warping of world governance toward companies, capital, and markets and away from democracy and shared sovereignty, as being about "civil liberties."

The main name for this campaign is "multistakeholderism," a word that seems designed to confuse those who are not familiar with it. The term suggests that anyone with a "stake" in a given decision or policy should be involved in its development. This is a common phrase in the current corporate lexicon. Anyone who has worked within or beside any institution that serves a wide constituency is familiar with the idea that "stakeholders" should be included in policymaking processes. Even here, one wonders why this language needs to supplant the language of democracy. After all, democracy is predicated on the idea that everyone—even those without a specific stake in a given policy—has some say in any policy of any governing body. In the corporate and institutional worlds where "stakeholder" has become a commonplace term, one wonders whether it is invoked to bypass any suggestion that the sphere is governed democratically. While this may be appropriate, at least in formal terms, for corporations and other bodies that are not required to be democratic, using "stakeholder" to supplant democratic engagement in normative contexts is more concerning.

Multistakeholderism did not originate from digital technology, but from the United Nations and others involved in international affairs. This idea, which has entrenched itself in cyberlibertarian dogma, has surprising origins on the left. Activists in the early 1990s were worried that international discussions about climate change did not adequately represent those affected by it. Global sustainability advocate and multistakeholderism consultant Minu Hemmati wrote in 2002:

> The term multi-stakeholder processes describes processes which aim to bring together all major stakeholders in a new form of communication, decision-finding (and possibly decision-making) on a particular issue. They are also based on recognition of the importance of achieving equity and accountability in communication between stakeholders, involving equitable representation of three or more stakeholder groups and their views. They are based on democratic principles of transparency and participation, and aim to develop partnerships and strengthen networks among stakeholders. MSPs [multi-stakeholder processes] cover a wide spectrum of structures and levels of engagement. They can comprise dialogues on policy or grow to include consensus-building, decision-making and implementation of practical solutions. The exact nature of any such process will depend on the issues, its objectives, participants, scope and time lines, among other factors. (2)

The point of multistakeholderism, on Hemmati's account, is to expand input into democratic or partly democratic processes. Their

> objectives are to promote better decisions by means of wider input; to integrate diverse viewpoints; to bring together the principal actors; to create trust

through honouring each participant for contributing a necessary component of the bigger picture; to create mutual benefits (win–win rather than win–lose situations); to develop shared power with a partnership approach; to reduce the waste of time and other scare resources that are associated with processes that generate recommendations lacking broad support; to create commitment through participants identifying with the outcome and thus increasing the likelihood of successful implementation. They are designed to put people at the centre of decision-finding, decision-making and imple-mentation. (9)

As these quotations make clear, multistakeholderism in its original formu-lation was intended to strengthen democratic processes and broaden their bases of support. Thus, to Hemmati, "participation is also not only a citizen's right. It also involves duties and responsibilities. For all stakeholder groups in MSPs, requirements such as representativeness, democratic structures, transparency and accountability are required. They are key elements of a stakeholder's legitimacy" (45).

Hemmati's vision of multistakeholderism is explicitly subordinated to the overall structure of democratic sovereignty. This framing is meant to account for the challenges posed by the fact that the UN itself is only partly democratic and includes member states that are not democratic at all. While Hemmati and other global sustainability advocates were sug-gesting augmentations to global governance with significant attention to democratic means and ends, ad hoc processes were underway in the inter-net governance space that saw this new language in a different way. Many technology advocates may have earnestly believed that their "stakes" in building out the global digital infrastructure meant they needed special status outside of formal democratic governance. However, when these prac-tices met the language of multistakeholderism, something new was born. The resulting approach followed the corporate precepts of "stakeholder theory" to suggest not augmenting democracy, but replacing it.

Multistakeholderism's digital roots can be traced back to the Internet Corporation for Assigned Names and Numbers (ICANN), which was formed in 1998 from the Internet Assigned Numbers Authority (IANA) by core ARPANET computer network scientists Jon Postel and Joyce K. Reynolds. This team had defined and performed the IANA function when it was still isolated inside ARPANET in the early 1970s. ICANN's main role is registering domain names (e.g., google.com, amazon.com) and managing associated activities like the provision of top-level domains like .com and .net. Since early internet activities, including ARPANET, occurred largely in the United States and were at first thought to be narrow in scope, the provision of domain names emerged organically among the community of technologists. However, as the power and influence of the internet and later the World Wide Web increased, the service became increasingly important, and the political consequences of the IANA and ICANN structure became topics of significant debate.

As Milton Mueller, one of the most prominent voices in internet governance, puts it: *"ICANN was one of the most prominent and important manifestations of the way the Internet was transforming the relationship between people and their governments.* ICANN's original institutional design marked a revolutionary departure from traditional approaches to global governance. It significantly reduced the power of national governments and existing intergovernmental organizations over communication and information policy" (2010, 60–61; emphasis in original). Mueller offers four "structural facts about ICANN" that made it groundbreaking: it was "set up to meet the need for *global* coordination of unique Internet names and addresses"; it "was one of the few *globally centralized points of control over the Internet*"; it "represented a *privatization* of significant aspects of the global governance function"; and it "was supervised by and accountable to a single sovereign and the world's only remaining superpower, the United States" (61; emphasis in original).

It is easy to see how this latter fact, in particular, can generate significant critique from any number of quarters and from those of different political orientations. Mueller is one of many to point out that if ICANN were to serve a global purpose, then there was an evident contradiction in its doing so as a U.S.-based NGO by virtue of exclusive contracts with the U.S. federal government, in partnership with a U.S.-based corporation (Verisign). Mueller is right to note that "sovereigns outside the United States perceived [ICANN] as a threat to their authority." At the same time, Mueller writes that "ICANN could be, and has been, criticized from a cyberlibertarian perspective as a new form of centralized control over the Internet and a sharp departure from the earlier Internet's freer, self-governing, and technically neutral administration" (64). Unlike the rest of his analysis, here Mueller acknowledges that the challenge to national sovereignty suggested by ICANN was salutary not merely because it pushed back on U.S. domination of the digital space, but because it highlighted how digital technologies would inevitably challenge national sovereignty itself.

Multistakeholderism is at times offered as a prescriptive and at other times a descriptive term for internet governance. As with many other topics at the intersection of digital technology and politics, the meaning of multistakeholderism is subject to continual shifts. Some of these shifts appear more or less deliberate on the part of interested participants, which can make clear reasoning about its role difficult. Laura DeNardis, director of the Internet Governance Lab at American University, rather than advocating for multistakeholderism, argues that "the very definition of Internet governance is that it is distributed and networked multistakeholder governance, involving traditional public authorities and international agreements, new institutions, and information governance functions enacted via private ordering and arrangements of technical architecture" (2015, 23).

A report from the nonprofit Institute for Multi-stakeholder Initiative Integrity, which engaged with multistakeholder processes and the institutions and individuals they intersect with, found that multistakeholder initiatives (MSIs) are "tools for corporate-engagement rather than instruments of human rights protection" (MSI Integrity 2020, 6). The report also states that they "should not be a substitute for public regulation" (7).

Between 2010 and 2017, MSI Integrity developed an evaluation tool for MSIs along with an associated research methodology. The tool was developed hand in hand with more than forty international standard-setting MSIs. Many of these organizations appear to have commitments to global civil society and democratic principles that are less questionable than those of digital technology advocates. The Rainforest Alliance, Forest Stewardship Council, Global Sustainable Tourism Council, and Infrastructure Transparency Initiative, among others, look like organizations that exist to empower citizens and raise concerns about rights violations: "Many MSIs were formed in response to the exposure of major industry-wide human rights abuses, which prompted demands to address the underlying governance gap that enabled the abuse" (26). In general, MSIs "evolved into a default response to business-related human rights crises as a compromise between non-regulation and mandatory regulation" (33).

EXPLICIT ANTIDEMOCRACY IN
GLOBAL (DIGITAL) GOVERNANCE

Mueller's invocation of "cyber-libertarian" critique only hints at the politics he and other multistakeholderism advocates put forward. In the specific context he provides, it may even sound reasonable. However, as Mueller's analysis continues, it becomes increasingly clear that he is relying on a rightist political framework. By the end of the 2010 volume *Networks and States,* he states bluntly that "the nation–state axis has at the rightmost extreme a complete subjection of the Internet to national sovereignty, and at the leftmost extreme a fully globalized domain, with the dissolution of national borders or sovereignty as a relevant factor in governing the Internet. The right favors relying on existing, national political institutions; the left favors creating or evolving new, transnational institutions around the global space for human interaction the network creates" (255). He offers a second "axis" to understand global politics: the "networking-hierarchy axis reflects the degree to which one believes the problems associated with Internet governance should be solved using hierarchical mechanisms, or left to the peaceful forms of association and disassociation we have defined as *networking*" (257; emphasis in original).

Despite perhaps sounding good to the uninitiated, almost none of the substantial words Mueller uses stand up under scrutiny. "Hierarchical mechanisms" are contrasted with "peaceful forms," as if organizations relying on hierarchies are inherently violent, and as if organizations can exist without any hierarchies whatsoever, itself a central cyberlibertarian trope that turns much of democratic theory on its head (that is to say, democratic organizations are both typically hierarchical and typically exist specifically to provide alternatives to physical violence as a means of governance). Despite the scope of his argument at this point, Mueller sees no need to tie it to any existing theory; unlike the other chapters of *Networks and States,* which refer abundantly to theories of technical networks and specific governance matters like copyright, in this final chapter of the book, "Ideologies and Visions," that offers a near-complete rewrite of both international and national governance, almost no reference is made to any recognizable political theory that is taken seriously by supporters of democracy whether from left or right orientations.

In fact, one must read carefully to note the many ways that Mueller incorporates far-right ideas into his thinking, often as if they are obvious or even in some sense "neutral." Thus "nation–states—including the United States of America, not just undemocratic ones—constitute some of the biggest threats to the global character and freedom of networked communications." Meanwhile, "the communication–information sector may need state-like powers to prosecute and incarcerate criminals, ensure due process of law, counter harmful private aggregations of power, or formalize individual rights and sanction violations of them by states or other actors." In other words, corporations should have state-like powers while actual democratic state powers should be minimized. A typical right–libertarian or even anarcho-capitalist political philosophy subtends Mueller's thinking, though he tries to present his view as disinterested. As a chief example, Mueller uses the term "liberalism" frequently. Since he does this within the context of political theory, one would be forgiven for imagining that he means something like democratic governance. Only in the margins does the reader come to realize that Mueller does not mean political liberalism at all, but *economic* liberalism, which is to say the view that "free" markets are the only political entities of note. Thus Mueller indicates in a footnote that he is "using the terms *liberal* and *liberalism* the way Europeans use them (i.e., in their correct, historical sense). *Liberalism* means policies and philosophies that favor individual liberty and choice" (262n7; emphasis in original).

Muller, like only those farthest to the right, identifies the "left" with national sovereignty. He posits an anarcho-capitalist, "anti-globalist," international, market-based system as the only acceptable political entity, even though this resembles the very "globalism" Mueller claims to oppose. Thus, "even the rightwing libertarians of the Ron Paul variety, while more consistent in their liberalism, are completely stuck in the nationalistic rut. They lack any conception of the Internet community as a distinctive polity" (263). Lest this sound in some way consonant with left critiques of globalization, Mueller is quick to criticize "the extreme leftist tendency . . . to criticize as domineering, exploitative, and a tool of the United States any political tendencies that embrace market liberalism." Mueller adds in a note that the conservative British journalist Nick Cohen offers "a dissection of the way leftists have embraced Islamic theocrats and fascists."

Mueller claims to criticize multistakeholderism by recognizing that it "addresses issues of representation and process; it does not provide any guidance on the substantive policy issues of Internet governance" (264).

However, he also argues that it "evades the key axes of national sovereignty and hierarchical power"—where "national" and "hierarchical" become synonymous and unacceptable, versus a networked form of power insulated from hierarchy and abuse. Mueller, echoing Carl Schmitt, descries this basic form of multistakeholderism advocated for by sustainability advocates like Hemmati, as it tends toward "a simple-minded communitarianism that implies that all political, economic, and social conflicts can be resolved if everyone involved just sits down and talks about them together. By focusing almost exclusively on the interaction or dialogue among stakeholders, it tends to evade or ignore issues of rights, access, power, and related issues of institutional design. It invites private sector and civil society actors to 'participate' in decision-making process, leaving their precise role or authority over the process indeterminate" (264–65). Mueller contradicts himself by demanding hierarchy, despite his belief that it should be avoided at all costs. He also suggests that multistakeholderism did not originally subordinate itself to democratic forms, which is incorrect. To the contrary, democracy is "all talk," just as Schmitt famously stated. The new anti-hierarchy "network" is a thing of action, which is ironic given that Mueller views digital technology as primarily a *communications* medium, therefore enabling talk in the broadest sense. For this reason, it should be put beyond the reach of democratic polities.

Rather than multistakeholderism or another paradigm he calls "access to knowledge," Mueller recommends "denationalized liberalism." Recall that in Mueller's terminology, liberalism is always *economic:*

At its core, a denationalized liberalism favors a universal right to receive and impart information regardless of frontiers, and sees freedom to communicate and exchange information as fundamental and primary elements of human choice and political and social activity. Political institutions should seek to build upon, not undermine or reverse, the limitless possibilities for forming new social aggregations around global communications. In line with its commitment to freedom, this ideology holds a presumption in favor of networked, associative relations over hierarchical relations as a mode of transnational governance. Governance should emerge primarily as a byproduct of many unilateral and bilateral decisions by its members to exchange or negotiate with other members (or to refuse to do so). This networked liberalism thus moves decisively away from the dangerous, conflict-prone tendency of other ideologies to build political institutions around linguistic, religious, and ethnic communities. Instead of rigid, bounded communities that conceal domination with the pretense of homogeneity and a "collective will," it offers governance of communication and information through more flexible and shifting social aggregations. (269)

Mueller, in his most caricatured forms of anarcho-capitalism, explicitly posits "states" as the agents of violence rather than (or in addition to being) the protectors of polities against violence. He also claims "free markets" to be the only meaningful arbiter of violence. It can be no surprise that Mueller expands Barlow's vision far beyond what he ever imagined: the "denationalized liberalism" Mueller advocates seeks "to detach the transnational operations of Internet infrastructure and the governance of services and content from those limited jurisdictions as much as possible, and to prevent states from ensnaring global communications in interstate rivalries and politico-military games." While at other times extolling the fact that "services and content" from internet platforms will encompass more and more of the everyday activities of citizens, this explicitly antidemocratic vision pretends that somehow the "internet" can be carved out from the rest of society when it comes to governance principles most citizens expect. Lastly, it should be noted, virtually no ordinary people believe that internet technology now requires democratic dissolution.

Mueller's denationalized liberalism, like most forms of libertarian pseudo-reason, often prevaricates over which powers belong to an informed citizenry. His

denationalized liberalism strives to make Internet users and suppliers an autonomous, global polity. It favors what might be called *neodemocratic* rights to representation and participation in these new global governance institutions. The concept of democracy is qualified by the realization that the specific form of democratic governance associated with the territorial nation–state cannot and should not be directly translated into the global level. However, it does maintain the basic objectives of traditional democracy—to give all individuals the same formal rights and representational status within the institutions that govern them so that they can preserve and protect their rights as individuals. Such a liberalism is not interested, however, in using global governance institutions to redistribute wealth. (270)

Thus "individual rights," a traditional hobgoblin of the far right's reinterpretation of democratic values, are said to be "the same" under this global market regime. But individuals lack the powers not just to regulate technology (whatever the reaches of that term might indicate), but to "redistribute wealth" (i.e., to tax).

Somewhat surprisingly, Mueller concedes that "if multistakeholderism means only that people who are strongly impacted by policies should be actively heard from, then it is nothing but normal pluralist politics. In any democratic policy-making process, there are numerous opportunities for public hearings and comment and decision makers are open to legitimate forms of persuasion from various interest groups" (266). Despite Mueller's pointed critiques, multistakeholderism has become the catchall word for an approach to "internet governance" that stands outside of nation–states and the United Nations. Mueller and other advocates portray that outsider status as advocating "for the internet," as if it names a separate entity from the people and polities that make up the globe. They suggest there is a force called "technology" or "digital technology" that is so independent of existing powers and structures as to require new forms to manage it. Mueller is resistant to discussing corporate power and at the same time points at an unregulated free market as the only meaningful arbiter of conflict and provider of human and civil rights.

As Colombian political scientist and internet governance critic Jean-Marie Chenou put it in 2014: "The principles of Internet exceptionalism and multi-stakeholderism are part of a hegemonic discourse that emerged in the 1990s. This discourse was instrumental in the formation of a power elite and in generating support from non-dominant groups. It relied heavily on neoliberal visions of Internet governance, but it also drew from the concept of the global public good and the cyber-libertarian discourse. Sovereigntist and anti-marketization perspectives on Internet governance were excluded from the debates, as were their advocates" (206). Multi-stakeholderism appears to be based on the democratic principle that anyone affected should be included in debate and policymaking. However, in practice, the discourse has come to mean the opposite. Those with the most power and influence should have all the say. There should be no accountability to polities that have formal governance powers over the domain in question. Indeed, Chenou uses the term "cyber-libertarianism" specifically to identify this trend: "The basic premise of cyber-libertarianism is Internet exceptionalism: the Internet creates a new world and changes social relations, which renders existing regulations obsolete. Cyberspace is, by definition, a world of freedom and equality, and any intervention might threaten these characteristics" (213). He goes on: "Although the principles of Internet exceptionalism and multi-stakeholderism were not genuinely implemented in the institutionalization of Internet governance in the 1990s, they acquired a status of doxa, or 'common sense,' in the field of Internet governance. Few actors question their application today, and the instrumental role that they played in the unification and institutionalization of a transnational power elite within Internet governance is generally obscured" (219).

For many years, multistakeholderism and other studied assaults on democratic governance as an international paradigm went relatively unnoticed. This continues today, in part due to the remarkable topic-shifting practiced by digital promoters. At times, "internet governance" refers to highly technical and specific matters, while at other times it refers to broad political issues on which the internet invariably touches. Few commentators and activists have noticed the remarkably studied and forceful attack on institutions that were already fragile and often ill-suited for the tasks they face.

The UN, for instance is a flawed institution based on a mix of solid and questionable ideas. However, it is the only global organization that even pays lip service to democratic values and seeks to encourage all countries and persons to exercise sovereignty over the planet. In the name of a technological revolution, multistakeholder advocates and more extreme thinkers like Mueller seek to shift any political power the UN does have to "technology" per se and technology companies in particular. They have no interest in improving this deeply flawed global organization and do not criticize in order to reform or even replace it with a more democratic and robust institution that protects the full panoply of human rights. As Mueller himself said in a shocking admission to the digital studies scholar Geert Lovink, "Governments participate in Internet governance to further their own power and pursue their own organizational aggrandizement. The emergence of countervailing power centers such as the tech community and ICANN is a good thing" (Lovink 2006, 207–8). Using the typical far-right framing, he contends that democratic governments are not political representatives of citizen sovereignty, but instead the "elite" representatives of a self-interest that somehow trumps the self-interest of technology promoters and wealthy corporations. Later in the same interview, appearing to speak in the broadest possible terms, he states that "the UN is in no position to control anything" (217).

Michael Gurstein, a Canadian activist and academic, was one of the few observers who paid careful attention to the multiple ways in which digital technology and its promoters have worked to de-legitimize democracy at a global level. He was the originator of an approach to technology governance called "community informatics." Up until his death in 2017, Gurstein was one of the world's foremost critics of the effects of cyberlibertarian agitation on global governance, especially the promoters of multistakeholderism and more extreme figures like Milton Mueller. In the early 2010s, Gurstein wrote a series of pointed blog posts and articles detailing his exasperating encounters with the international internet governance community. Despite their claims of "inclusion" and the suggestion that all "stakeholders" would be involved in crucial decision-making processes, he noted that the multistakeholder community was overtly hostile toward the representation of anyone who did not meet its own self-determined criteria for "technical knowledge" and authority, regardless of the generality of the issue over which a governance body might have power. That is, they were explicitly "technicist" (Stanley 1978), "technocratic" (Mumford [1934] 2010, 1971, 1974), and even "producerist," suggesting that only people with requisite technical expertise should be permitted to contribute to discussions of issues that have political consequences, while also suggesting that those with political expertise (or formal representative responsibilities) should be excluded. (See chapter 2 for this claim regarding government officials, and chapter 7 for a discussion of producerism as a political theme.)

In 2012–13 Gurstein sought to participate in the UN Commission on Science and Technology for Development, a formal body created in part by the processes that had brought multistakeholderism to the fore as a method for international internet governance. Appropriate for his background and expertise, Gurstein tried to join the Technical and Academic (T/A) stakeholder group. Remember that the focus of these groups was not just the provision of domain names, but the much larger issue of development, which includes the ways that technology affects some of the world's most marginalized and vulnerable people. The T/A nominating committee rejected his application because, according to the committee itself, the body was intended to comprise "the scientists who developed the Internet and the technical organizations/people who run it, and not to social scientists and the like" (Gurstein 2013). Perhaps so, but given the wide remit of the committee, it seems unfair to limit the input of those not specifically invested in building technology. Most troubling, Gurstein asked "to be pointed to the specific document and authoritative reference where this definition was presented (as for example by the UN itself)." He received no reply. Upon further inquiry, he was told that the rejection was due to conversation with "many individuals from Civil Society and the Business community (including their focal points)"—with presumably much stress on the latter (and its incursions into the former), since the less technically focused parts of civil society were among Gurstein's supporters. It is no surprise that the criteria for membership in the T/A group was able to further restrict itself to "individuals who have technically built the Internet" and "the community of organizations and individuals who are involved in the day-to-day operational management of the Internet and who work within this community." Although this group would seem to include individuals like Gurstein and organizations like the ones in which he participated, it could now be redefined to include only a small set of technicians.

Gurstein goes on to provide his own interpretation of this set of events:

What this means I think is that the prevailing and self-determined definition of the T/A stakeholder group includes probably no more than 3–400 people in the entire world, all of whom have some professional association with the technical management of the Internet (the alphabet soup of technical Internet governance organizations—ICANN, the Internet Registries and a few others in standards organizations), perhaps at least 80% of whom are from developed countries and at least 80% of those being US based, at least 80% being male (it is probably much higher given the absence of women in these kinds of technical roles) and from sad experience having essentially no knowledge or interest in matters that stretch beyond their narrow highly technical realm.

It further means that the group representing the T/A stakeholder "community" is able to design its own "restrictive covenant" (define who is a member and who is not), exclude whomever it wishes on whatever basis suits it and moreover is not accountable or required to have any degree of transparency in its internal operations, decision making procedures, internal governance structures and so on. Notably, this group functions in an area of

considerable and increasing public responsibility and as peers with an equivalent group representing all of the governments of the world, a second group
(CS) representing all of the citizens of the world and a third group representing all of the businesses of the world.

Thus a body was created and designed to represent all "stakeholders" regarding how technology would impact lives, livelihoods, and rights all over
the world, convened by the single institution with the most responsibility
for such tasks. Yet instead of increasing participation and representation as
intended by the original calls for multistakeholderism, the process is turned
on its head. The most powerful get seats at the table, the least powerful get
no seat at all, and there is no transparency. What had been at best a flawed
approach to democratic representation becomes "a fundamental challenge
to what we understand as democratic governance and governing processes."

Gurstein was never shy in describing the real point of multistakeholderism and its function, which he saw as undermining democracy. It is no
accident that the post from which the foregoing quotations are taken was
titled "Multistakeholderism vs. Democracy." In a subsequent post he elab-
orates on the explicitly antidemocratic character of multistakeholderism,
at least as applied in the digital technology space:

> The difficulty with creating or even conceptualizing a "democratic multi-
> stakeholderism" is that at its core multistakeholderism is not "democratic."
> Thus the governance notion implicit in multistakeholderism is one where
> governance is by and for those with a "stake" in the governance decision thus
> shifting the basis of governance from one based on people and (at least indi-
> rectly) citizenship or participation in the broad community of the governed
> to one based on "stakes" i.e. an "interest" in the domain to which the gover-
> nance apparatus is being applied. The historical notion of "stake" in a con-
> text such as this one generally refers to a financial or ownership interest in
> the area under discussion but in the evolving Internet Governance sphere
> (and others) this has been extended to include a "technical stake" (as in a
> professional interest) or even a "normative stake" as in ensuring an outcome
> which is consistent with one's values or norms.
>
>   What is not included in any of the conventional approaches to multi-
> stakeholderism however, are broad notions of democratic participation (or
> accountability) i.e. where the governance is structured so as to include for

example, those without a "direct" stake in the outcomes but who neverthe-less might as a consequence of their simple humanity be understood to be impacted by the decisions being taken.

To me it is quite clear that "democratic governance" and "multi-stakeholder governance" are internally in contradiction with each other. At their core, democracy as in the "rule of the people" is one form of government and multi-stakeholderism as in "the rule of 'stakeholders'" is another and com-peting form. I don't think that they can be reconciled. (Gurstein 2014b)

In a manner familiar to those who pay attention to the rhetoric of techno-logical politics, Gurstein wrote that the multistakeholder "model is being presented as the model which would replace the now 'outmoded' and 'obso-lete' processes of democratic decision-making in these spheres—in the ter-minology of some proponents, providing an 'enhanced post-democratic' model for global (Internet) policy making" (2014a). As in most cyberliber-tarian agitation, the global program for international governance promotes "privatization of public services such as education and health care in Less Developed (and Developed) Countries," undermines "the social contract and social safety nets in Developed Countries with the associated increases in child poverty, homelessness, and hunger," and provides "the ideological drivers (and models) for a significant social and economic attack globally on the poor and vulnerable."

A startling instance of the global internet governance community's contempt for human rights, framed in typically rightist terms as the *protec-tion* of those principles, occurred in 2019 after the brutal, Islamophobic, social media–fueled mass murders of fifty-one people at two mosques in New Zealand by white supremacist Brenton Tarrant (Hendrix and Miller 2019). Live-streaming the massacre on Facebook, Tarrant appeared to derive part of his philosophy from alt-right extremists in the United States, who openly celebrated the attack (Purtill 2019). Such celebration even extended to another "ecofascist" murder in El Paso, Texas (Achenbach 2019).

In May 2019, following the horrific and virtually unprecedented violence in New Zealand, Prime Minister Jacinda Ardern held a summit in Paris called the "Christchurch Call to Action Summit," which resulted in the Christchurch Call to Eliminate Terrorist and Violent Extremist Content Online, "a community of over 130 governments, online service providers, and civil society organisations acting together to eliminate terrorist and violent extremist content online" (New Zealand Ministry of Foreign Affairs and Trade 2019). The Christchurch massacre and the specific role played by digital technology were taken seriously by the New Zealand government and many other democratic countries across the world. However, the U.S. government, led at that point by President Donald Trump, did not join the effort (though in mid-2021, under President Joe Biden, the United States finally took part; see U.S. White House 2021).

Internet advocates in the global governance space took the issue even more seriously, but in the opposite direction. There was nearly universal outcry about the massacres from citizens, such that technology companies including Facebook, Microsoft, Twitter, and Google (via YouTube) joined in the effort. However, the Call was diluted to the point that the document itself reads like a restatement of Barlow's "Declaration." "A free, open and secure internet is a powerful tool to promote connectivity, enhance social inclusiveness and foster economic growth," the Call begins, in a paragraph set in larger type than the rest. "The internet is, however, not immune from abuse by terrorist and violent extremist actors," it goes on. And thus the opinion of critics that the internet is an especially powerful tool for fueling extremism, spreading economic growth at the cost of civil rights and democratic values, was taken off the table.

Despite the Ardern government's bravery and initiative in issuing the Christchurch Call, its effects have largely been invisible. This is likely due to the influence of internet companies that have defused the powers of democratic governments to take action against the antidemocratic power of technology. Yet despite its muted power, this has not been enough. Prominent voices in the internet governance community, including Milton Mueller, leaped into action the very moment the Christchurch Call was issued. They acted not to address the problem of violent extremism online, but to protect the "internet" from the "threat" Ardern's action posed.

In their lexicon, the Christchurch Call was no longer one to address the threats of violent antidemocracy and terrorism using online tools. Instead, it was a call to protect digital technology from the threat of democratic regulation. Today, virtually the only people who use "Christchurch Call" are internet governance insiders. The clearest of these messages came from Farzaneh Badii, cochair of the Christchurch Call Advisory Network. In a remarkable piece published in late 2021 titled "The Christchurch Call: Are We Multistakeholder Yet?" Badii never mentions the terror attacks following Christchurch, but concerns herself mainly with whether the decision process used for the Christchurch Call qualifies as "multistakeholder." She claims that "the Christchurch Call commitments were drafted and signed with no participation from civil society," implicitly suggesting there are bodies outside of democratic governments that must be included in decision making. In her view, the failure to include this amorphous group, which includes many actors with corporate ties they do not need to disclose when providing "advice," "is a way to differentiate a democratic mindset from an authoritarian mindset." One notes no specific recommendations made by Badii about the actual Christchurch Call, but instead a series of procedural imperatives that seem designed to blunt the Call's impact.

In an editorial written after a racially motivated mass murder in Buffalo, New York, in May 2022, Center for Countering Digital Hate (CCDH) CEO Imran Ahmed notes that the shooter mentioned the Christchurch terrorist by name in his manifesto. However, "despite pledges made in the wake of the Christchurch terrorist attack and subsequent, ideologically driven extremism attacks," the most recent CCDH report "found that the big social media companies were collectively failing to act on 89% of posts that advocated the great replacement theory," a cornerstone of far-right and white supremacist ideology. Given the apparent agreement among corporations and governments to take actions that seem not to have been taken, it is hard to avoid guessing that the multistakeholder civil society groups represent the part of the digital–industrial alliance determined to subvert democratic regulation of technology.

INTERNET GOVERNANCE IN THE EUROPEAN UNION

In recent years, the European Union (EU) has been the global governance body most attentive to the destructive and antidemocratic aspects of digital technology. Many of their efforts have been effective. And because internet companies with global reach want to continue to operate there, EU regulations have frequently been adopted worldwide.

At every stage, with every proposal, the global internet community, including its apparently nonprofit exponents, has used every trick in the digital denialist book to forestall these measures. In nearly every case, technology promoters have distorted, exaggerated, and outright lied about the intent and likely effects of such laws. And as in the SOPA/PIPA debate and so many other campaigns, they have rarely been held to account for their deceptive practices.

Some of these conflicts show how digital promoters use a U.S.-centric conception of human rights law to manipulate and negate such laws in other democracies. The EU and its member nations have long had much stronger privacy and reputation protections enshrined in human rights law. In the digital age, the right to manage one's public profile and protect one's reputation has been severely challenged. This is due to the persistence and availability of misinformation, as well as derogatory yet correct information that may be unduly influential despite having occurred long ago. Thus, in the EU, as well as some other nations, there exists a formal or de facto "right to be forgotten" (RTBF) that allows individuals, especially private citizens, to have some control over how widely information about themselves is disseminated (Mantelero 2013; Da Baets 2016). It is not clear that all accurate information should be made perpetually available. Some countries have laws that prohibit employers from considering certain kinds of criminal convictions in employment decisions after set time periods. However, persistent digital information about such convictions can in practice obviate such legislation.

In the early 2010s, a variety of laws and court cases brought preexisting reputation rights into focus. These questions were not focused on the direct provision of information, but instead on the role played by search engines in providing links to information. Such services publicize data about which an individual may have privacy or reputation rights. Frank Pasquale provides an anonymized example of the problem:

> Consider Google's "autocomplete" associations regarding a former first lady
> of Germany, Jane Doe. Users typing "Jane Doe" into the search engine in 2012
> would be likely to see the suggested searches "Jane Doe *prostituierte*" and "Jane
> Doe escort" underneath their search box. The suggestions reflect numerous
> rumors about Jane Doe, who obtained over thirty cease-and-desist orders in
> Germany against bloggers and journalists who raised the possibility of sex
> work in her past. Jane Doe feared that all those legal victories could be for
> naught if users interpreted the autocomplete suggestions as a judgment on
> her character, rather than an artifact of repeated legal battles. (2015, 521)

The German legal system had already determined that Jane Doe had a cause for action against anyone who spread apparently false information about her. However, Google's search engine continued to spread it. The company, which is neither a publisher nor distributor of data, was not necessarily reachable by the same laws she was able to successfully use against those who originally posted the information.

Predictably, Google and its many defenders attacked both the judicial decisions and the EU legislation as gross abrogations of what they called "human rights." Although RTBF refers only to the question of *linking to* information, not deleting it, opponents continued to portray the law as an attack on the ability to publish information in the first place. Many public opponents accepted this misleading framing. Google asserted that its own "free speech" rights (see chapter 6) trump the explicit, legally established rights of privacy and reputation ascribed to private individuals by the EU and its member states (Powles and Chaparro 2015). Jimmy Wales and the Wikimedia Foundation both claimed that RTBF would attack both the real human right to free speech and the important values (but not enumerated human rights) to "history" and "truth." They did not note that RTBF protects specific rights enshrined in law and constitutions (Jones 2016; Powles 2014).

EFF published a position paper opposing the EU's attempts to make Google delink certain entries from its search engine because it "threatens rights in the United States to publish and receive information, including information about government activities" (Greene et al. 2016, 2). EFF's jab at "government activities" displays its typical hostility toward democratic governance, misleadingly deployed in an inapplicable context to promote antigovernment conspiracism. EFF also insists that its version of U.S. free speech absolutism should apply to democratic polities, especially the EU, that have other ways of protecting speech. Just as predictably, *TechDirt* has continued to remind readers of its opposition to RTBF because it "stifles a free press and free expression" (Masnick 2019). The site publishes on average ten stories each year attacking the EU and other countries that attempt to manage individual privacy and reputation rights.

Despite this outsize coverage of the issue, in general the actual effects of RTBF have been neither disastrous nor widespread. In response to both the court cases and EU law, in 2014 Google created an advisory council to take requests from citizens who wanted their search listings delisted. The body included Google CEO Eric Schmidt, Google's chief legal counsel, and Wikipedia cofounder and RTBF opponent Jimmy Wales (Sullivan 2014). Notably, analysis of the results of the advisory council showed that "delisting is already contingent on personal data *not* being in the public interest" (Powles 2015, quoting van Alsenoy and Koekkoek 2015; emphasis added). Examples of RTBF requests Google accepted included the following: "A victim of physical assault asked for results describing the assault to be removed for queries against her name" and "Links to the fact that someone was infected with HIV a decade ago." Meanwhile, rejected requests included these examples: "A public official asked to remove a link to a student organization's petition demanding his removal" and "Elected politician requesting removal of links to news articles about a political scandal he was associated with" (examples from Powles 2015, quoting van Alsenoy and Koekkoek 2015).

While reasonable people will disagree about specific cases, it is clear RTBF was not being used to prevent linking to (let alone publication of) information in the public interest. Instead, it was being used to realize rights that are established in EU law. Rather than accepting the fact that EU states have used their democratic powers to recognize these rights, digital advocates change the terms of argument, issue misleading statements about the nexus of rights in the conflict, and use a variety of other dishonest tactics to defeat democratic oversight.

To be sure, RTBF is part of a wider rights regime, which includes a broader "right to erasure" that targets not only search engines but also "data collectors" such as Facebook, Google, Uber, Apple, data brokers, and "security" companies such as Palantir. As a recent survey of these efforts by legal scholar Jef Ausloos documents, the EU's efforts "are emblematic of a broader issue in today's information society: the lack of (meaningful) control over the collection and use of one's personal data. This absence of control becomes particularly evident in an online environment dominated by a handful of private companies that find themselves at the central nerve points through which most (personal) data flows online" (2020, 3). Despite the fact that the extent of their practices is not well understood by the public (Zuboff 2019), internet companies and their apparently independent advocates consistently frame EU attempts to regulate technology—so as to secure rights to privacy, reputation, and control of one's own data—as instead being about the denial of human rights.

Whenever the EU considers new regulations for technology and technology companies, the same people emerge to offer the same arguments against them. They often rely on central denialist and cyberlibertarian tropes while using clear disinformation tactics to gain public support. Building in part on the RTBF and related issues, in 2016 the EU developed the Generalized Data Protection Regulation (GDPR), which passed into law in 2018. Adam Thierer of the Mercatus Center's Technology Liberation Front, the Center for Data Innovation's Daniel Castro, and longtime Koch associate and right-wing economist Will Rinehart launched a wide-ranging public attack on the legislation, all using similar talking points. In a forum conducted by the Federalist Society, Thierer laid them out: "compliance is very costly"; "GDPR will hurt competition & innovation"; "the EU is surrendering on the idea of competition being possible going forward"; "GDPR hurts global flow of information"; "GDPR doesn't solve bigger problem of government access to data"; and "GDPR doesn't really move the needle much in terms of real privacy protection" because "what consumers need is new competitive options and privacy innovations" (Thierer 2018). An interesting twist on the "innovation" card suggests that legislation like GDPR will "strengthen" (whatever this means) internet giants like Facebook and Google, because GDPR compliance is "costly": "The law will actually benefit the same big companies that the EU has been going after on antitrust grounds."

These talking points from avowedly right-wing actors get picked up by others whose political commitments remain less clear. EFF in particular expressed cautious support for the regulations, though tempered with its characteristic skepticism of governmental regulation: "The GDPR increases fines and the ability of regulators to intervene on behalf of potential privacy violations—but with great power can come great irresponsibility. If you've seen how copyright law can be twisted to turn into an engine for censorship and surveillance, it will have come as no surprise when Romanian authorities attempted to use the GDPR's wide powers to threaten journalists investigating corruption in the country" (O'Brien 2018). EFF is not as vocal in its support for GDPR and other privacy legislation like the 2018 California Privacy Protection Act as it is about fundamental issues like copyright, free expression, and "innovation." And even with that support, EFF finds reasons to express "concern" and "caution." Similarly, when the EU proposed its Digital Markets Act (DMA) and Digital Services Act (DSA) in 2020, which took effect in 2020, EFF rarely expressed open enthusiasm. Instead, it pointed out "room for improvement," especially around another cyberlibertarian frame issue, "interoperability" (Doctorow and Schmon 2020). It also expressed concern for a key cyberlibertarian antigovernment technological value, encrypted messaging systems (see chapter 5), fearing that legislation like DMA might have "unintended consequences, such as creating incentives for companies to compromise on the security of users' communications" (Stoltz, Crocker, and Schmon 2022). As always, EFF frets about the unintended consequences of legislation and governmental action while overlooking the same issue with regard to unregulated technological development.

Mike Masnick and *TechDirt,* characteristically, went even further, helping to seed a great deal of online commentary with talking points that echoed and in some cases surpassed those of the Mercatus Center. They referred to GDPR as a "ghastly, dumb, paralyzing regulation" that "poorly advances the important policy goals purportedly prompting it" due to the "enormous costs of compliance," pointing for support to the work of Daphne Keller (Gellis 2018). Even though "there's no quarrel that user privacy is important" and that the GDPR has a "noble mission," it is only "something to praise" in that GDPR encourages "privacy by design," which is to say industry and technological self-regulation. Despite the many actions taken under GDPR, including many large fines and notices to change practices directed at service providers large and small in the years since it became law, in 2022 Mike Masnick doubled down on these criticisms and virtually replicated the Federalist Society talking points from Thierer four years earlier. "Multiple studies have shown that it hasn't lived up to any of its promises," he writes, citing only one study from 2018 that focused exclusively on GDPR's short-term effects on venture capital investment in technology (Jia, Jin, and Wagman 2018), while claiming that GDPR has "actually harmed innovation." "And don't get me started," he goes on, "on how the GDPR has done massive harm to free speech and journalism." Focusing solely on a set of real concerns raised by European Data Protection supervisor Wojciech Wiewiórowski about enforcement of GDPR not being strong enough (Manancourt 2022), Masnick concludes that the law has "failed" and now the EU "wants to make it worse."

Digital rights and technology advocates have consistently misrepresented EU legislation and regulatory efforts, typically walking a fine rhetorical line according to which they seem to support the goals of regulation but sowing doubts about the actual effects and implementation. They play fast and loose with facts and pretend to champion core human rights values while subtly (and not so subtly) undermining them in the same breath. Even when they endorse the legislation, they rarely create internet-wide campaigns to promote it, unlike the campaigns they create to oppose legislation that they find offensive to their core values, especially innovation and anti-copyright (see chapter 5). They also rarely reflect on the nationalistic orientation of their advocacy, which frequently supports the power of U.S.-based technology giants like Facebook, Google, and Apple, against the economic interests of other countries. Cyberlibertarian dogma is characterized by such advocates' ability to speak out of both sides of their mouths, emphasizing real interests while scolding democratic polities for protecting the enumerated rights of their citizens.

PART II

MYTHS OF CYBERLIBERTARIANISM

CHAPTER 4

Digital Technology and the Printing Press

No sentiment is more universally relied on in cyberlibertarian discourse than the belief that networked digital technology is the second coming of the printing revolution. According to this story, the printing revolution was responsible for producing democracy, science, and other central virtues of modern civilization. The second printing revolution, then, will produce these again—or perhaps more or better versions of them, and new virtues besides. Because it will offer such benefits, any opposition to the development of digital technology must be rejected out of hand.

The printing revolution metaphor is central to cyberlibertarian dogma, most frequently used as a demand and warning. We must view digital technology as having overwhelmingly positive effects on society. Computers are as world-shattering as the printing revolution was, so we must be cautious about managing technology, lest we interfere with the good that is coming for us.

In this chapter and the next two, I refer to the rhetorical strategies and metaphors found in cyberlibertarian dogma as "myths," much as critical theorist and activist Per Strömbäck does in his pamphlet *21 Digital Myths: Reality Distortion Antidote* (2016). Some of the myths discussed below are the same as, or part of, the ones Strömbäck identifies. Myths are generally understood to be false, which is why the term is appropriate. But the general falsehood of myths does not imply there is *nothing* accurate about these strategies and tropes. To the contrary, it is often the case that stories surrounding comparisons, such as the printing press myth, so overwhelm the relevant facts that it becomes difficult to reason about the topic in question.

HOW CYBERLIBERTARIANISM USES THE
PRINTING PRESS ANALOGY

Cyberlibertarian claims about the printing revolution rewrite history in fundamental ways. In the name of its beneficence, they paradoxically disparage many of the benefits that scholars of the printing revolution actually attribute to the press. They justify a destructive disinformation campaign directed at the institutions and practices they claim to be championing. The strongest advocates of this point of view misrepresent almost every aspect of the printing revolution described by the scholarship on which the claim itself depends.

Until the 1960s, the printing revolution had been almost exclusively a matter of narrow scholarly interest. Elizabeth Eisenstein's groundbreaking work—which most cyberlibertarian dogmatists refer to in their use of the printing press metaphor—is predicated on the observation that "there was not even a small literature available for consultation" (1979, xi). However, some scholars (e.g., Dane 2004, esp. 11–21) have criticized Eisenstein for appearing to ignore in this statement a great deal of prior work on the printing press, research she does in fact acknowledge elsewhere. In the scholarly world the meaning of the printing revolution has been a topic of intense debate. Few, including Eisenstein herself, point to it as a simply interpreted and demarcated historical event whose causes and consequences are obvious.

The printing revolution trope, following the pattern of other cyberlibertarian dogma, is promoted by actors who appear to cross the political spectrum, and who may well differ when it comes to topics other than digital technology. In the "Crypto-Anarchist Manifesto," founding cypherpunk Tim May claims that "the technology of printing altered and reduced the power of medieval guilds and the social power structure" and so the encryption technology for which he has long advocated will "fundamentally alter the nature of corporations and of government interference in economic transactions" (1992, 62). Other cypherpunk and crypto-anarchist discussions refer to the printing press frequently. Right-wing libertarian economist and full-throated cyberlibertarian Tyler Cowen tweeted in 2017, in transparent defense of Facebook's destructive business practices, "If you read a criticism of Facebook, try subbing in the word 'printing press' and see if it still makes sense."

In his characteristically populist volume *An Army of Davids,* right-wing law professor Glenn Reynolds writes that "what is going on with journalism today is akin to what happened to the Church during the Reformation. Thanks to a technological revolution (movable type then, the Internet and talk radio now), power once concentrated in the hands of a professional few has been redistributed into the hands of the amateur many" (2006, 91–92). 3D gun printing advocate, avowed crypto-anarchist, and later convicted felon (for paying for sex with a minor) Cody Wilson writes in *Come and Take It: The Gun Printer's Guide to Thinking Free* that the printing press "drove the complete inversion of the incumbent, Catholic order. What could we expect with self-replicating, networked, material printers?" (2016, 39), he asked, using the typical libertarian business term "incumbent" to drive the point home. Another urtext of right-wing computer-fueled conspiracy theory, Jimmy Dale Davidson and Lord William Rees-Mogg's 1997 *The Sovereign Individual,* makes ongoing reference to the print revolution, tossing off half truths like "printing rapidly undermined the Church's monopoly on the word of God, even as it created a new market for heresy" (110).

The printing press metaphor even confounds pundits who end up making it toward ends not obviously compatible with their apparent politics. Jeff Jarvis, while advocating for digital technology, frequently used the printing press for metaphors and arguments, especially in the early 2010s (see Jarvis 2011a, 2011b, 2011c, 2011d), as discussed below. And Clay Shirky, in his bestselling 2008 book *Here Comes Everybody* (ironically named, without notice, after words from a signal printed work, James Joyce's *Finnegans Wake*), occasionally invokes the printing press with accuracy and nuance, but also intertwines it with business-school nostrums lacking historical grounding or applicability to our world. "In 1492, almost half a century after movable type appeared," Shirky writes, "Johannes Trithemius, the Abbot of Sponheim, was moved to launch an impassioned defense of the scribal tradition" (68). "The Abbot's position would have been mere reactionary cant ('We must preserve the old order at any cost') but for one detail," he goes on: the Abbot's book "was not itself copied by scribes; it was set in movable type, in order to get a lot of copies out cheaply and quickly." Shirky calls this "instructive hypocrisy," failing to mention the reasons Trithemius gave for the importance of scribal culture, which had nothing to do with cheap or quick distribution. Meanwhile Shirky, like Jarvis a few years later, does not remark on the more significant and relevant hypocrisy of his presenting in printed book the argument that digital publishing is superior to print precisely because it can be distributed more cheaply and quickly. The use of the metaphor flattens the complexity of the actual history in order to make easy points that end up confusing rather than illuminating the current situation.

Like Clayton Christensen and other advocates for "disruptive innovation" who draw their inspiration from public choice theory and other rightist economic doctrines, Shirky can only conceive of the relationship between books and the public in market terms. Trithemius, for example, can only have written of the virtues of scribal culture due to "gatekeeping" and "professional self-conception and self-defense, so valuable in ordinary times, [which] become[s] a disadvantage in revolutionary ones, because professionals are always concerned with threats to the profession" (69). Like "reactionary," Shirky's use of "revolutionary" suggests politics without ever making clear what politics he is advancing, nor why we should accept that analysis. "In most cases, those threats are also threats to society," he rightly notes; but "in some cases the change that threatens the profession benefits society, as did the spread of the printing press." No diagnostic is required to determine which change is which, and the implication, often stated outright, is that our "printing revolution" is the second kind, and this is so obvious that supporting argument and evidence are unnecessary.

Some scholars who strongly identify with digital technology, along with full-throated evangelists, routinely gesture at print culture scholarship as if it supports their triumphalist account of computerization. They also suggest that subsequent scholarship has given credence to communications theorist Marshall McLuhan's most oracular pronouncements, even though these prognostications were not uniformly positive. In the early 2000s in particular, a raft of books framed themselves around the metaphor, including Borgman's *From Gutenberg to the Global Information Infrastructure* (2000), Goldstein's *Copyright's Highway: From Gutenberg to the Celestial Jukebox* (2003), and Shillingsburg's *From Gutenberg to Google* (2006). It is rare for such books to have been written by experts in technology and media change, let alone the printing press or Reformation Europe. More were written by technology and legal scholars with little historical background.

One of the most striking of these revisionist reinterpretations comes in the form of the "Gutenberg Parenthesis" (Sauerberg 2009; Pettit 2012). This thesis, developed by Danish scholar Lars Ole Sauerberg in the late mid-1990s (Pettit 2012, 95), claims that "the period from the late Renaissance to the beginning of the twenty-first century will be seen as dominated and even defined by the cultural significance of print"; that the printing revolution "affected not merely the material appearance of information and knowledge dissemination but also, in the process, the very nature of cognition"; and that today, in an "analogous but inverse manner," "the book" is being reduced to "just another option in a wealth of different media modes and permutations." The printing revolution is thus framed as "opening" a historical epoch that is now "closing": "The opening of the Gutenberg Parenthesis meant the closing of privileged production and consumption of textually communicated knowledge, statement and information, the closing of the Gutenberg Parenthesis symmetrically implies the opening up to a completely new and so far only partially glimpsed—let alone understood—cognitive situation" (Sauerberg 2009, 2).

Although Sauerberg is a literature professor, he focuses his remarks on canned and epochal generalizations rather than more sober and scholarly descriptions of the phenomena in question. Among the most glaring of these are his assertions about "the book" being the primary and privileged mode of information sharing due to the printing press. However, most scholarship, including Eisenstein's, notes that *non*-book printed materials were at least as influential, if not more so, than books during much of the post-Gutenberg history. Additionally, there is a scarcely noticed elision of all other forms of media, so as to claim that the rise of the internet-connected computer marks a particularly significant change in the media environment of most ordinary people. Rather, it is one in an extended sequence of changes that extends as far back in history as one looks. It is hard not to notice that the "closing" of the Gutenberg Parenthesis seems to imply that some, perhaps most, of the benefits of the printing revolution will end as well.

Business leaders, too, are among those who repeatedly draw attention to what was until recently an esoteric academic subject. Venture capitalist Jennifer Carolan, offering a typical sales pitch for virtual reality, relies on a chance remark by cognitive psychologist Steven Pinker to assert that "the first major empathy technology was Guttenberg's printing press, invented in 1440. With the mass production of books came widespread literacy and the ability to inhabit the minds of others" (Carolan 2018). From this it follows that the technologies in which she invests can also increase "empathy." Mike Masnick of *TechDirt* consistently brings up all the cyberlibertarian points, referring to the same Trithemius discussed by Clay Shirky as "a near perfect 15th century version of Nick Carr." He argues that Trithemius's objections to print technology are only the familiar "technopanic" that is exclusively a product of being "someone who hates some new technology because it somehow 'undermines' the good 'way things were'" (2011a). Therefore, Masnick believes that Trithemius's objections can be dismissed. In their 2013 *Radical Openness,* business consultants Don Tapscott and Alex Williams praise "communications technologies like the printing press" that aid "the spread of democratic norms." Unsurprisingly, the "radical openness" represented by the web and Wikipedia will "accelerate the long-term process of devolution from authoritarian governance to an increasingly flat society where power and authority are much more decentralized," meaning that market forces will take the place of the democracy now recast within the span of just a few sentences as authoritarianism.

It is unsurprising that cryptocurrency promoters have also used the printing press myth to their own ends. Despite more than a decade of repeated failures to find any real-world use cases for blockchain technology other than financial speculation or evading appropriate regulation, thousands of articles portray Satoshi Nakamoto, the technology's pseudonymous creator, as a reincarnation of Gutenberg. Self-described "guerilla capitalist" Mark Jeftovic repeats central bank conspiracy theories while claiming that Satoshi's Bitcoin whitepaper "set off a chain of events as sure as Martin Luther's '95 Theses' set in motion the secular decline of another hitherto undisputed hegemonic central power: The Catholic Church," which "never regained its central power position" (2017). Another cryptocurrency promoter, Stephen J. Green, offers an even more sustained comparison. He writes that both Martin Luther and Satoshi started "revolutions." In Satoshi's case, instead of the Catholic Church, "the orthodoxy being challenged was that of the International Financiers and the Federal Reserve."

Admittedly these examples skip the Gutenberg step and move straight to Martin Luther and the Reformation as obvious consequences of the printing revolution, but others are more straightforward. Major cryptocurrency promoter Jon Matonis puts the invention of blockchain "on the level of the Gutenberg printing press" (O'Hagan 2016). *Bitcoin Magazine,* arguably the leading industry-funded publication, has mentioned Gutenberg and the printing press in at least a dozen pieces over the years. Most writers claim that Protestantism "decentralizes" faith in comparison to the

Catholic Church. Protestant congregants "truly had 'skin in the game' and were participants in their faith because of the Reformation, rather than subjects to the rulers of their faith" (Pattillo 2021), describing Protestant denominations very different from those we see in today's world. Another doubles down on revisionism, making the economic base of the analysis more explicit: what "Johannes Gutenberg and Satoshi Nakamoto gave us were new methods to permissionlessly transport information across time and space, outside the purview of the establishment" (Anil 2022).

Finally, the long-standing, Koch-funded libertarian think tank Foundation for Economic Education embeds its encomium to Satoshi and Bitcoin in a long-form discussion based in Murray Rothbard and Friedrich Hayek. Commentator Wendy McElroy praises Bitcoin for being "profoundly revolutionary" because it "does not directly confront governments or corrupt institutions; it sidesteps and obsoletes them" (2017). She writes that "few things short of Gutenberg's printing press have offered such freedom and opportunity to the individual," before invoking Voltaire to insist that "financial self-interest" is the core of an "extreme religious toleration" with which democratic governance is inherently at odds.

As in so much cyberlibertarian discourse, scholarly research is repurposed and reanalyzed so that the scholars who did the research become *disqualified* as experts in their own areas of specialization, in favor of industry apologists with commercial interests in the specific interpretation of the scholarship that benefits them. Facts and expertise are trusted only insofar as they support the pro-technology agenda on offer. This simultaneous reliance on and disparagement of knowledge and inquiry should be a serious cause for concern among anyone thinking about the fate of inquiry in the digital age.

THE VARIETIES OF MEDIA REVOLUTION

It has become so natural to compare the advent of digital technology with the rise of the printing press that obvious questions about the parallel are rarely asked. One question that should arise during any dispassionate inquiry is whether the printing press is the only radical change in media technology and communications, or even the most relevant one, that we can compare to digital technology.

It takes little reflection or knowledge to see that the answer to this question, unlike the question itself, is not obvious at all. Even if we accept the

questionable proposition that the "printing revolution" names a discrete historical event, it is clear that many other media technologies were developed
in the wake of the printing press, and that all have been accompanied by
significant advocacy for and theorizing about their roles. Electrical telegra-
phy enabled messages to be transmitted over long distances in real time
around the 1830s, but depended on rapidly changing technologies to expand
its influence through the late nineteenth and early twentieth centuries. The
telephone, which allowed instantaneous transmission of audio content over
ever-expanding networks, began in the late nineteenth century and experienced several serious technological upheavals during its history. Radio broadcasting began in the 1920s and 1930s, making audio content widely available
to individuals without a physical network connection to the sender. Cellu-
loid film allowed the distribution of visual and audiovisual content through
physical media and became widely available during the 1910s. It underwent
revisions even more major than the others, encompassing the very different
technology for television that emerged in the 1950s.

Digital technology is prized because it replicates and expands on the
capacities of all these media forms, and many others. Any fair-minded discussion of the impact of digital technology requires careful attention to each
of these changes, especially when the particular capacity replicates one that
existed in another medium. Once we subtract from the "digital revolution"
all the parts that build on these major media changes, it becomes difficult
to determine what is left over that we might characterize as an epoch-
making change comparable to the transformative impact of print.

Of course, nuanced and detailed historical analysis rarely makes for good
headlines, whether in journalism or scholarship. It certainly does not make
for good corporate storytelling: "incremental improvement over CB radio"
is a sales pitch unlikely to win much venture capital. But it is worth noting that the story evangelists want to tell about the printing press—that
it developed outside of and in opposition to governmental control and
regulation—is easier to sustain in that context, despite being false, than it
is with regard to the more recent media technologies, all of which developed
directly through complex networks of cooperation and encouragement of
governments. In some recent cases, such as the repeal or relaxation of the
U.S. fairness doctrine (Pickard 2014), and concentration regulations for
broadcast media (Leeper 2000), which had a particular impact on radio,
many informed commentators outside the industry have been aware that

media regulation worked well, and that deregulation weakened the ability to serve democracy. Deregulation was undertaken as an industry-based effort, often funded by dark money, to turn media toward the interests of wealth and power. This leaves the printing press as the historical event far enough back in time that can justify the story that deregulation is the *most* democratic approach to media change. However, few people are familiar enough with that history to see that the story is false even in that case.

The advent of computing is different from more recent media revolutions in that some scholars have described it as *epochal*. This means it is a change that causes a rupture or break in human history of a dramatic sort, so that it makes sense to talk of history before and after the change. The best-known of these figures is Marshall McLuhan, a wide-ranging synthetic thinker whose popular persona exceeds his scholarly reputation, especially in recent years. McLuhan developed many concepts that remain touchstones for digital culture, such as the "global village" and the idea that "the medium is the message." His reputation in academia has suffered in no small part because of his propensity for hyperbolic statements. In *Understanding Media* ([1964] 1994), the book of his that has maintained the strongest scholarly reputation in recent years, epochal changes proliferate. He catalogs inventions as various as the electric lightbulb, roads, clocks, bicycles, housing, clothing, and comics as forms of media, and in each case ascribes world-changing effects to their development. It would be hard to argue against the general proposition that such developments change us. It is easier to take issue with McLuhan's relentless pronouncements of dramatic historical ruptures to accompany not merely each invention, but the variety of changes that elements like clothing, housing, and roads have undergone. It becomes hard to avoid the sense that dramatic change is a part of life, and that by emphasizing profound difference McLuhan significantly downplays the remarkable continuities in human experience.

The book of McLuhan's that directly preceded *Understanding Media* was called *The Gutenberg Galaxy: The Making of Typographic Man* (1962). Like *Understanding Media,* it describes ruptures and epochs wherever it looks. Unlike the later book, it confines its focus to two historical breaks caused by a relatively limited number of technological changes. The first is the "abstracting or opening of closed societies" that resulted in the development of "the phonetic alphabet, and not of any other form of writing or technology" (8). But as the title suggests, McLuhan's main interest is in the early European Renaissance and the development of the printing press. The printing press produces (or at least solicits) mass literacy, and literate cultures and oral cultures are fundamentally different, a theme with many echoes in writers who followed McLuhan. "The marginal man is a centre-without-a-margin, an integral independent type. That is, he is feudal, 'aris-tocratic,' and oral," he writes, whereas "the new urban or bourgeois man is centre–margin oriented. That is, he is visual, concerned about appearances and conformity or respectability. As he becomes individual or uniform, he becomes homogeneous. He belongs. And he creates and craves large centralist groupings, starting with nationalism" (213). "The school system," he goes on, "custodian of print culture, has no place for the rugged individual. It is, indeed, the homogenizing hopper into which we toss our integral tots for processing" (215).

Pronouncements like these are hard to resist on first reading. There must be a grain of truth to them. But there is much more to marshal against them. If we could analytically determine what the "rugged individual" refers to as opposed to some other kind of individual, it is hard to know how we could look at various phrases of world cultures and not see them as over-invested in the promotion of such individuals. Others are more interested in communal values. How might we account for the striking differences in these societies if they all have print? Further, McLuhan's analysis is peppered with references to artists and writers who escape the constraints he claims print puts on the individual, often expressing their dissidence in print itself. Perhaps most pointedly, on what accounts is McLuhan depending to determine that "oral cultures" are without the same proclivities he assigns to print culture? Not only was McLuhan in no way an anthropologist, but his reading in anthropology was quite limited, as was his awareness of the persistence of Indigenous people in the present. The concept of a distinct "modern human" apart from Indigenous communities is widely rejected by Indigenous commentators, particularly those within these communities.

McLuhan is a patron saint to many vocal enthusiasts of the digital revo-lution, and was given this title by *Wired* magazine when it launched in 1993 (Levinson 1999, 14). This is due in no small part to his apparent technologi-cal determinism, a term of art used to designate thinkers who believe there are clear lines to be drawn between the development of certain technolo-gies and the social changes that follow in their wake. McLuhan is not only an example of such figures but also their apotheosis. The number of tech-nologies that produce the range of remarkable changes he describes seems overwhelming, especially when his work is read cumulatively. McLuhan's views on digital technology appear prescient, which is why he is often cited in discussions about the digital. However, his influence is disproportionate to that of Lewis Mumford, a more grounded thinker whose cautions about computerization have been largely overlooked (Loeb 2018a, 2021a).

McLuhan's concept of the "global village," found both in *The Gutenberg Galaxy* and *Understanding Media,* is central to his influence. In the first, he writes that "the electro-magnetic discoveries have recreated the simultaneous 'field' in all human affairs so that the human family now exists under conditions of a 'global village.' We live in a single constricted space resonant with tribal drums" and that "the new electronic interdependence recreates the world in the image of a global village" (31). In the latter he offers the curious opinion that "as we begin to react in depth to the social life and problems of our global village, we become reactionaries. Involvement that goes with our instant technologies transforms the most 'socially conscious' people into conservatives" (34). Even more curiously, he writes:

> The speed-up of the electronic age is as disrupting for literate, lineal, and Western man as the Roman paper routes were for tribal villagers. Our speed-up today is not a slow explosion outward from center to margins but an instant implosion and an interfusion of space and functions. Our specialist and fragmented civilization of center–margin structure is suddenly experiencing an instantaneous reassembling of all its mechanized bits into an organic whole. This is the new world of the global village. The village, as Mumford explains in *The City in History,* had achieved a social and institutional extension of all human faculties. Speed-up and city aggregates only served to separate these from one another in more specialist forms. The electronic age cannot sustain the very low gear of a center–margin structure such as we associate with the past two thousand years of the Western world. Nor is this a question of values. If we understood our older media, such as roads and the written word, and if we valued their human effects sufficiently, we could reduce or even eliminate the electronic factor from our lives. (92–93)

Even on its own terms, none of this sounds like a recipe for global harmony or what most of us understand as peaceful democratic rule.

McLuhan remains critical to those who proclaim the beneficence of the digital revolution because he is the closest thing to a serious thinker who sees human history as determined by waves of technological change. Unlike even Lewis Mumford, McLuhan seems to ascribe to technology a mysterious determining power, one that humans can only direct imperfectly. To a greater degree than the other epochal philosophers of communications technology—like Harold Innis or Walter Ong—McLuhan's pronouncements express a kind of cultural–technological progressivism, where technological changes lead inexorably to the improvement of the "human condition." (That progressivism, of course, is highly biased toward what the West sees as its own historical development, let alone the tendentious connections it presumes between historical change and political change.) Of course even these syntheses misstate or mischaracterize some of McLuhan's writings, for he is by no means as uniformly enthusiastic about technological changes as are digital evangelists like Jarvis, Shirky, and Brand.

Elizabeth Eisenstein's relationship to McLuhan himself is instructive, despite the way her work has been repurposed by these figures. While in the early stages of thinking about the project that became *The Printing Press as an Agent of Change,* she writes that she "ran across a copy of Marshall McLuhan's *The Gutenberg Galaxy*" (2005, xiv). "McLuhan's book," she writes, "seemed to testify to the special problems posed by print culture rather than those produced by newer media. It provided additional evidence of how overload could lead to incoherence" (xiv–xv). She notes that despite McLuhan's pronouncements—many based on readings of Shakespeare and other major literary texts—"no one had yet attempted to survey the consequences of the fifteenth-century communications shift" (xv). That is, McLuhan drew his conclusions without much evidence to support them. It is not a surprise to find her suggesting that "it is difficult to imagine just what figure Marshall McLuhan had in mind when he wrote about the 'making of typographical man,'" "given the religious, linguistic, and socioeconomic diversity of European readers" (102) even during Gutenberg's time.

Eisenstein, despite originally being inspired by McLuhan's work, has explicitly rejected his approach. This is partly because Eisenstein herself has sometimes been taken to be a technological determinist on the order of McLuhan, despite going to significant lengths to point out the many differences between them. In an afterword to the 2005 edition of the one-volume condensation of her major work, Eisenstein specifically objects to a critic calling her view of history "McLuhanesque." She notes that this scholar, Joseph Dane (2004, 13), bases the appellation on his own misreading of

Eisenstein's clear critique of McLuhan and praise for the historical scholarship Dane also recommends (Eisenstein 2005, 316). Two of the major works of print culture studies to have emerged in wake of Eisenstein's book—Michael Warner's *The Letters of the Republic* (1990) and Adrian Johns's *The Nature of the Book* (2000)—more directly accuse Eisenstein of being a technological determinist in the mold of McLuhan. In both cases, Eisenstein had detailed exchanges with her critics regarding these allegations, in which she reiterated her rejection of technological determinism (Baron, Lundquist, and Shevlin 2007). Indeed, toward the very beginning of *The Printing Press as an Agent of Change* she stresses the use of the indefinite article in the book's title: "As *an* agent of change, printing altered methods of data collection, storage and retrieval systems and communications networks used by learned communities throughout Europe. It warrants special attention because it had special effects. In this book I am trying to describe these effects and to suggest how they may be related to other concurrent developments. The notion that these other developments could ever be *reduced* to *nothing but* a communications shift strikes me as absurd" (1979, xvi). The critical fact that emerges from these exchanges for the study of digital media is that *none* of these scholars accepts the notion that technological change leads to specific, identifiable social changes— *even in retrospect*. Thus the desire of evangelists like Jarvis and Shirky to turn Eisenstein's work so that it makes not just predictions but descriptions of what *inevitably* will happen thanks to digital technology beggars the imagination.

Jarvis articulates these themes exclusively through reference to Elizabeth Eisenstein's work. In *Public Parts* (2011d), he repeatedly references the printing revolution, Johannes Gutenberg's invention of the printing press, and Eisenstein's work as the principal underpinnings for his claims about the beneficial and transformational nature of the digital revolution. The new form of publicness entailed by digital technology "is at the heart of a reordering of society and the economy that I believe will prove to be as profound as the one brought on by Johannes Gutenberg and his press"; "Gutenberg empowered Martin Luther to smash society apart into atoms, until those elements re-formed into new societies defined by new religions and shifting political boundaries" (10); "today, with our new tools for making publics, the people can again become proprietors of media (see: blogs) and the public sphere (see: revolutions in the Middle East). We all have our Gutenberg presses and the privileges they accord" (79). The significant ambiguities in this last sentence seem strategic.

The reference to the so-called Twitter revolutions suggests that the second Gutenberg age is celebrated specifically for its political and social effects, which are understood as directly parallel with effects of the first printing revolution. Thanks to Gutenberg, "books made it possible to gather, compare, analyze, and spread new information"; this "made the scientific revolution possible" (83, citing Dewar and Ang 2007); printed books "disturbed the elite" (83); they "enabled Thomas Jefferson to collect all the laws of Virginia"; books "took knowledge that had been diffuse and easily lost in a few handmade copies and made it permanent, consistent, and accessible to many" (84).

Claims like these have been widely promulgated since the early days of computing and especially the internet. In a famous 1998 report, RAND Corporation prognosticator James Dewar wrote, "Changes in the information age will be as dramatic as those in the Middle Ages in Europe. The printing press has been implicated in the Reformation, the Renaissance and the Scientific Revolution, all of which had profound effects on their eras; similarly profound changes may already be underway in the information age" (2). There are at least three problems with assessments like these that deserve attention. First, they demonstrably misrepresent most scholarship on the printing revolution and its consequences. Second, they make unjustified assumptions about the societies into which digital technology is being introduced. Finally, they make inferences about alterations to our own global cultures that pretend both that the past has happened (e.g., since the printing revolution "created democracy") and that it hasn't (since the digital revolution will "create democracy," even though we already have democracy).

In turn, the supposed parallel between the printing press and the internet is used to defuse any criticisms of digital technology by those who do not buy into cyberlibertarian narratives. In keeping with cyberlibertarian denialism, Jarvis talks about the printing revolution in almost exclusively positive terms, even though much of print culture scholarship rejects, or at least resists or complicates, this triumphalist narrative. Some, most famously McLuhan's student Walter Ong (1982) and his teacher Harold Innis (1950, 1951), who raised real questions about the social and political consequences of the printing revolution, are not mentioned by Jarvis or other digital utopians.

Instead, Jarvis uses a single word repeatedly in *Public Parts* to character-ize anyone who worries about the lightning-fast spread of digital technol-ogy: *fear*. The word appears over seventy times in the book, almost always used to describe anyone who questions the benefits of digital technology. This is true even when the fear is not in response to the abstract question of the societal consequences of computerization, but rather the exposure of vast amounts of private information without the subject's consent: "Pri-vacy advocates worry for our young people, who they fear are saying too much. Bad things could happen, they warn. But then, bad things always could" (2011d, 3); technology "breeds fear"; "the invention of the printing press did that five centuries ago, as did the invention of the camera a cen-tury ago and countless other technologies since" (10). Like his later terms of art, "technopanic" and "techlash" (see chapter 2), Jarvis uses these ad hominems to disparage anyone who raises concerns about digitization, try-ing to disempower democratic sovereignty while claiming that technology is obviously beneficial because it benefits democracy.

THE WORLD BEFORE PRINT AND
THE WORLD BEFORE DIGITAL TECHNOLOGY

Perhaps the most serious problem with the analogy between the printing revolution and the development of digital technology is that it requires an inaccurate parallel between European societies prior to the advent of the printing press and world culture prior to the advent of the computer. What-ever they were or were not, the enormous changes wrought by the printing press took place in part because printing and all other mass media and media reproduction and distribution technologies *did not exist yet*. Prior to the printing press, books were rare and available to a select few. Moreover, their form and content differed from what we have come to think of as books (Diringer 1982). The Christian Bible existed, but mainly in Latin, and only priests and some aristocrats had copies. Scientific and philosophical texts existed in extremely small numbers, but tended not to have tables, charts, maps, and graphic images that were identical from copy to copy, as the print-ing revolution allowed. According to advocates of the printing revolution as a model for digital technology, the ability of masses of people to access knowledge that was previously unavailable to them led to a series of explo-sions in various forms of knowledge and the practices used to produce them.

It is hard to see how we might draw any useful parallel between Europe in the 1400s, 1500s, or even 1600s and the twentieth century. Despite the cant of internet promoters, it is hard to look at our world even in the 1950s and declare credibly that it was suffering from a lack of *information*. The availability of knowledge in 1950 or 1990 (depending on where one declares that the information age begins) is nothing like what it was in Europe in the 1500s. The availability of printed matter, radio, television, films, telephones, and other technologies have dramatically changed the world since the early twentieth century. However, the impact of these changes, at least in metropolitan centers, cannot compare to the shattering effect of the printing revolution, which occurred in a world where almost nobody, even the small number of wealthy and powerful people who would be able to read books, had access to media beyond the spoken word. As Eisenstein writes, "Several studies . . . have illuminated the difference between mentalities shaped by reliance on the spoken as opposed to the written word. The gulf that separates our experience from that of literate elites who relied exclusively on hand-copied texts is much more difficult to fathom. There is nothing analogous in our experience or that of any living creature within the Western world at present" (1979, 9). Technology promoters seem to have forgotten that almost all the benefits they claim for the printing press depended on its introduction into *a world that did not have anything like it.* Less obviously, they implicitly compare the world before the printing press to our own time, which removes the printing press from its historical and geographical context.

Most scholars attribute the rise of the printing press to Martin Luther's use of movable type during the Protestant Reformation. This historical development could only have happened because the Catholic Church unilaterally controlled access to information for many of its congregants. More generally, it depended on the relative *unavailability* of reading material to the ordinary person prior to the printing revolution, which was due to a complex and interlocking set of rules, technologies, and social practices. The critical fracture between Catholicism and Protestantism in this regard is said to be that Protestants, including Luther, wanted everyone to have access to the text of the Bible. To democratize belief and knowledge, they used the printing press and translations of the Bible from Latin into the languages spoken by Europeans in the sixteenth century.

Those who advocate the printing press metaphor as a rule never explain what it is about our day that resembles that of Europe—let alone the rest of the world—prior to Gutenberg, so that we can understand just what dramatic changes we should expect thanks to digitization. This argument, at its crudest, is based on a crypto-libertarian conspiracy theory. It implies that our polities are equivalent to monarchical regimes ruled over by a unitary Catholic Church, and that we have yet to experience democratic governance or have access to information. Although these counterfactual assumptions are often only implied by arguments rather than stated explicitly, they still influence a great deal of digital advocacy. This advocacy, in turn licenses the destructive animus that is so pervasive in cyberlibertarian discourse. This discourse aligns uncomfortably with many aspects of extreme capitalist and even fascistic politics. After all, it is no exaggeration to say that the most vocal proponents of the printing–internet parallel argue for the elimination of many of the most salient features of the printing revolution even as they try to convince us of print's unalloyed beneficial effects.

WHAT DID THE PRINTING REVOLUTION DO, AND WHAT DID IT NOT DO?

It's ironic that Jarvis explicitly relies on Elizabeth Eisenstein's scholarship, which often lurks in the background of these invocations, to support his assertions about the nature of the digital revolution. Although Eisenstein is a renowned scholar of the development of print and is famously enthusiastic about the printing press, the fact is that most of the beneficial historical changes attributed to the development of print by Jarvis, Shirky, and others are specifically ones *that Eisenstein says did not happen.* Indeed, it is hard not to notice that when Jarvis directly asks Eisenstein "how she compares the era she studied with that of the internet," Eisenstein "says she's not sure what to make of this new society that [internet users] are creating." In a characteristic manner, after turning to a scholar for authority, Jarvis disqualifies her, although in a complimentary manner: "the professor is too modest," for she "is in a unique position to inform our grasp of the internet age" (2011d, 79–80), he writes, not seeming to notice that he has dismissed her expertise in the same paragraph. While Evgeny Morozov (2013b) has rightly drawn attention to strands of scholarship that take different

positions from Eisenstein's—especially the highly regarded work of literary scholar Michael Warner (1990; see also Dane 2004; Johns 2000; and
the essays in Baron, Lundquist, and Shevlin 2007)—he seems not to have
noticed that even the scholarship on which Jarvis and others claim to rely
rejects the conclusions they draw from it.

Jarvis asserts that the printing revolution includes the following events,
which are separated by centuries. Of course he includes Gutenberg's invention of the printing press in Mainz (in what is now Germany) in the
1450s. The Renaissance in southern Europe began in the mid-1300s, up
to one hundred years before Gutenberg, and continued for several hundred more years. In northern Europe, including England, the Renaissance
is generally said to extend from the mid-1500s through the seventeenth
century. There are broader accounts that insist that renaissances occurred
all over Europe starting as early as the ninth century. The scientific revolution, which spanned from the fifteenth or sixteenth centuries through to
the eighteenth or even nineteenth, is also included. The Protestant Reformation (early 1500s), the Age of Enlightenment (typically attributed to the
long eighteenth century, extending from the late seventeenth to early nineteenth centuries), and the American and French Revolutions (late 1700s)
are also part of the printing revolution.

Although all these developments and events are sometimes attributed to
the printing press, it is unlikely that a single technology could cause such
a wide range of occurrences across different places and times without also
causing them in other places and times where it was available. If the "printing press" produced the scientific revolution, why did some parts of that
revolution not occur until the nineteenth century? If it produced both
the Renaissance and the Enlightenment, what accounts for the differences
between them and the fact that they occurred at such different periods in
time? Did government overreach prevent the printing press from shifting
Italy, France, and Spain from Catholicism to Protestantism, despite this
change happening in other Catholic areas with the printing press? Further,
how are we to draw parallels between each of these developments and
changes in our own society?

Eisenstein makes it clear that the printing press did not cause most of
these events, even if we give "cause" the nuance that Eisenstein, unlike
digital utopians, does. Eisenstein has been known as a deterministic thinker
about technologies, but from the beginning she has worked hard to draw

a much more complex picture. That the wide range of historical changes sometimes attributed to the printing revolution "could ever be *reduced* to *nothing but* a communications shift," she writes, "strikes me as absurd" (1979, xvi; emphasis in original). Many promoters of digital technology make exactly the kind of "absurd" mistake Eisenstein cautions against, and this despite not having anything like the historical knowledge she did on which to ground an analysis. Jarvis insists that *before* social and cultural developments, parallel to those caused by the printing press, even occur, we know that they *will*. We also know that these changes will happen very soon, despite the changes we point to happened over many hundreds of years. Worse still, we know that the changes will be largely or even overwhelmingly *positive,* despite having no agreement about what positive change might be. This knowledge of the generally positive nature of change permits us to ignore or dismiss evidence of negative changes occurring. While the printing revolution is now understood and praised specifically because of the roles print played in changes of world-historical proportions, we need not—must not—wait for such events to occur when understanding and regulating digital technology.

Eisenstein was initially inspired by McLuhan. However, she eventually criticized him for presenting arguments similar to those offered by today's cyberlibertarians: "Developments that have been unfolding over the course of five hundred years, affecting different regions and penetrating to different social strata at different intervals, are randomly intermingled and treated as a single event" (1979, 40). To the contrary, Eisenstein takes it as proven that the "Italian cultural revival" that we now call the Renaissance was "already under way" when the printing press was introduced (170); "not at all did printing make the Petrarchan revival [part of the Northern Renaissance] 'possible'; Gutenberg came too late for that" (178); and a more reasonable thesis is that the "preservative powers" of print may be "related to the emergence of a so-called permanent Renaissance" (181), that is, a series of cultural changes that were less transitory than other "medieval classical revivals" (182) in Europe, of which the "Italian Renaissance" is one among many. That is, arriving at the tail end of one revival (itself caused by a host of factors, most of them solidly cultural and economic; 173–74), printing helped make that one more lasting. But note how remote that is from the claims of Jarvis (and others) about digital media producing a "new Renaissance."

The only change left standing is the Protestant Reformation, itself a com-plex set of historical events (Cameron 2012). It is routinely portrayed as an unambiguous good. One particular aspect of the Reformation is typically highlighted for praise: the idea that the Catholic Church maintained a "monopoly on knowledge" through the Latin liturgy and its tight control over the availability of books, especially the Bible, well past the period when Latin was widely spoken in Europe; and that Martin Luther disrupted this monopoly by using Gutenberg's press to distribute copies of the Bible and other religious texts translated into vernacular languages. This in turn licenses a metaphor that may be too seductive in its reach: those who publish or produce information are cast as monopolists like the Catholic Church, and everyone who uses disruptive information technology is cast on the side of "democratization of knowledge" and "anti-monopoly." A little of this story goes a long way. It may be true in broad outlines, but the details make the metaphorical lessons much harder to parse.

It is certainly not the case, for example, that the Reformation was a global change that everyone agrees, in retrospect, was welcome. The Catholic Church did not go away. In many countries it persists quite strongly to the present day, and the vast numbers of Catholics then and now may well not see the Reformation as a positive event at all. Perhaps more pointedly, the Catholic Church is often viewed as a deeply problematic institution today due to its role in promoting colonialism and violence, suppressing dissent, and demanding conformity.

It is truly difficult to look at the history of the various sects of Protes-tantism and see them as notably different in this regard. Colonial history is almost equally divided between Protestants and Catholics, with many of the bloodiest wars fought between powers whose rivalry was fueled in part by this religious clash. The later history of these two branches of Christian-ity is not much different, at least in terms of ascribing to one or the other tendencies toward the worst aspects of human conduct. Both Catholics and Protestants have colonized and enslaved; both have also protested and re-sisted each practice. Antidemocratic politics, including Fascism and Nazism, are found among congregants in both branches. Martin Luther himself was a notorious anti-Semite and used Gutenberg's press to distribute a wide variety of hateful material about Jews (see "Martin Luther and Anti-semitism"). This pattern might be taken more seriously by those who rec-ommend the print–digital parallel—Protestant attitudes toward Catholics have typically been no less vicious. Looking at the Reformation as an opening and welcoming "democratization" of power and politics in world history is easy. However, upon closer inspection, it becomes much harder to discern what that statement is supposed to mean, except for those whose commitment to Protestantism itself is somewhat militant.

DIGITAL CULTURE AS THE (CREATIVE) DESTRUCTION OF PRINT CULTURE

One of the most striking aspects of the deployment of the print/digital parallel is that computer enthusiasts often value the dismantling of exactly those things for which they celebrate the printing revolution. This contradiction is not limited to the background. Jarvis, while overemphasizing the importance of the printing revolution to much of European and world civilization, simultaneously disparages it in a remarkably blunt way. "Print is where words go to die," he writes. "Print is far too one-way for this two-way world" (Jarvis 2005). "Print is not dead," he writes, "it just needs a savior" (2011a, perhaps referring to himself or Google, to whom he assigns an explicitly messianic role in the title of his first book, 2009's *What Would Google Do?*).

"The means of production and distribution of print are what mandated the invention of the [newspaper] article," he writes (2011a). But today—at most thirty years into a revolution apparently as transformative as one that informed world cultures for three or four hundred years—we should no longer let print "dictate the form and rhythm of news." Instead, we should put "digital first," a change we should "aggressively implement," letting it "drive all decisions," because it is a "vestige of the old culture" that "held that we should know everything" about a story before we are "prepared to share it with the public." The news reporter today must "mimic the architecture of the internet, end-to-end," because we are "driving the strategy to a digital future, no longer dependent on the print crutch." Jarvis insists that he is not saying we should dispense with not just the technology but the social conventions of print altogether. Rather, he is saying print comes "last," not that print "is dead. Print, at least for a time, still has a place in serving content and advertising."

Jarvis's encomia to print is more focused on burying than praising. It is more than a little odd then that Jarvis wants to derive so many lessons for the digital age from a revolutionary technology he in the same breath tells us is outmoded, old-fashioned, and on its last legs, despite the fact that it continues to do what it has long done. The internet revolution is the antithesis of the printing revolution but also its apotheosis: "Gutenberg empowered Martin Luther to smash society apart into atoms, until those elements reformed into new societies defined by new religions and shifting political boundaries. With the Industrial Revolution—of which Gutenberg himself was a first faint but volatile spark—the atoms flew apart again and re-formed once more, now in cities, trades, economies, and nations" (2011b, 10).

This is wildly different from the way scholars of print culture, including Eisenstein, frame the benefits of the printing revolution. In fact it is hardly praises the printing revolution at all, but rather deflects the advent of print into the kind of "creative destruction" described by Joseph Schumpeter and the "disruptive innovation" championed by Clayton Christensen. What is actually being lauded is not anything about human life benefiting from technological change, but more the ability of waves of technological changes to generate profits for their inventors. Typically, this is done by putting other companies out of business. In Christensen's most classic cases, the disruptor can undercut the prices of existing businesses without necessarily providing equal, let alone better, products and services. Print is not celebrated for "smashing apart" what preceded it; the digital revolution now functions not as an intensified version of the book, but instead as an atom smasher, tearing apart the social order just because it can.

The internet is frequently celebrated as the second coming of print, even as the same speakers dismiss the very qualities that make print so celebrated by its true admirers. Jarvis is repeating "print is dead" because it is so widely used today. It is hard not to notice the stark incompatibility of this phrase with the notion that the internet is terrific because it is *like* print. It is not just "print" in the abstract that cyberlibertarians like Jarvis proclaim as now passé. Books are too long (Shirky 2008b wrongly claims that "no one reads *War and Peace*. It's too long, and not so interesting"; see also the Juskalian 2008 interview with Shirky), reading and writing in long form are burdensome, and publishers and libraries exist to *deny* access to information.

Jarvis offers an extremely thin explanation for why he has chosen to write, publish, and sell books if all the infrastructure of print and publishing, which themselves incorporate huge amounts of digital technology, is so outmoded. "I have put my content behind the pay wall known as a book," he writes. It is "hypocrisy" that he does not release the material as "a free, searchable, linkable online-only thing" (2011b, 181). His excuse for not doing this is that "Simon & Schuster paid [him] and gave [him] distribution in bookstores, not to mention considerable and valuable help from [his] editor." It is hard not to notice that there is no actual explanation offered here that does not then contradict most of the rest of Jarvis's advice, up to and including his disparagement of the book as a "pay wall," a phrase familiar from the realm of so-called free culture and open access (see chapter 5). Surely if publishers were in the business of *denying* readers access to material—which is a central pillar of his thought, evidenced among other places in his use of the term "pay wall"—Jarvis should have bypassed them entirely. Even though today "we all have our Gutenberg presses and the privileges they accord" (79), Jarvis has failed to use his own Gutenberg press in what should be the single most obvious action one can carry out using the personal version of "God's gift." This is not the minor hypocrisy of climate change scientists attending scientific meetings via pollution-emitting airplanes, which propagandists often blow up to discredit the researchers' findings. It is outright self-contradiction, wherein Jarvis's actions offer direct contrary evidence to his conclusions.

Jarvis claims to celebrate the printing revolution, but he disparages not only the form of the book but also the activities of publishers. He rejects Nicholas Carr's (2010) assertion that digital technology can interfere with our "deep reading" of books, based on Carr's introspections on his own experience. However, Jarvis admits that he reads "fewer books" today than he did prior to the advent of digital technology. He then denies that books "are necessarily the only or best way to stimulate thought"—thus reducing print to the single benefit of "stimulating thought," contrary to Eisenstein's work and Jarvis's earlier triumphalist account of the printing press. He asserts that he is "more curious thanks to the net," and that "writing in books can be deep or shallow—as ideas can be deep or shallow online" (2011b, 90). In characteristic fashion, Jarvis ends up admitting that Carr is correct in his assessments, that Jarvis's own experiences provide an example of the phenomenon Carr describes—and that Carr is still wrong, despite Jarvis having abandoned all the counterarguments he claimed to have. Meanwhile, if any of Jarvis's claims are true, then his writing and publishing of a book is not only hypocritical, but also incomprehensible. This is because every bit of the "deep thinking" contained in the book should have already been made much more widely available than a book ever could. Why did Simon & Schuster waste so much money on publicizing a useless product, and pay Jarvis himself to write it? Why did Jarvis write and publish it if books are useless?

This is not mere hairsplitting. Jarvis relies on Eisenstein more than any other thinker to describe and define the printing revolution, whose benefits are so notable that we should welcome a second transformation that somehow intensifies and makes more available those advances. Yet Eisenstein is careful in detailing what those benefits were, and many of them are incompatible with, or outright dismantled by, the digital revolution. One of her chief breakthroughs was enumerating and examining these changes at a specific level. It is curious that those who champion computers and the internet as the heir to print rarely consider Eisenstein's central achievement and her principal thesis about the printing revolution.

Some of the changes she attributes to the printing press certainly seem to be magnified or intensified by aspects of the digital environment. Since the cultural conditions necessary for large-scale developments like the Renaissance, the Reformation, the scientific revolution, democratic revolutions, and Enlightenment are complex, ascribing them to discrete technological factors is difficult even for Eisenstein. Thus, specific qualitative shifts engendered by the press may be more relevant than inevitable historical transformations when assessing the potential effects of digital media. The effects she describes as most directly attributable to the printing press include "wide dissemination: increased output and altered intake" (1979, 74); standardization, the development and reinforcement of more-or-less identical typefaces, copies of books, images of various kinds, spelling, and many other cultural phenomena, including entire languages (80); the "rationalizing, codifying, and cataloging" of data in ways that had not before been possible (88); a related "new process of data collection" (107) thanks to which the sequence of "corrupted copies [characteristic of scribal book culture] was replaced by a sequence of improved editions" (109); the "preservative power of print," which Eisenstein declares is possibly its "most important" feature (113); the "amplification and reinforcement" of "stereotypes and sociolinguistic divisions," a consequence in part of standardization, and in general a more negative than positive effect (126); largely operational and "unevenly phased" shifts, with "social and psychological" consequences, from "hearing" to "reading" publics (129), with effects realized in religious, public, and family life; and the rise of what many have called the "republic of letters" (136), said to have especially pronounced consequences for the Enlightenment and the political revolutions of the late eighteenth century.

It is remarkable how difficult it is to map these specifically described changes onto the apparent and even potential effects of digital technology, even on the accounts of enthusiasts like Jarvis and Shirky. On first glance, it is arguable that digital technology significantly increases dissemination, both in terms of output and intake. Therefore, it could be said that digital technology offers benefits similar to those of print. Similarly, the surface-level argument supports the view that digital technology expands on the rationalization of data and the process of data collection.

It is hard to see why we would want to embrace digital technology so wholeheartedly if it also intensifies standardization, stereotypes, and socio-linguistic division. If digital technology has social and psychological effects analogous to print, those are by no means obviously positive. Even Eisenstein is extremely careful to point out the destructive as well as constructive effects of implications of changes to social structure, and others go further. As noted, scholars believe that the printing press helped to produce a "republic of letters" vital to democracy. Therefore, it is necessary to argue that in the spirit of democracy, the technology in question should be dismantled or replaced in order to produce "more" democracy. It would be as if the printing press suddenly turned out to be insufficient for the exact effects it is said to have had. Finally, if a great many of the effects of print have to do with its permanence and preservative power—remembering that these are the effects Eisenstein considers its "most important"—we must reckon with the relatively strange way in which the digital is and is not permanent. While some things are difficult to erase, many other aspects of what we have understood as "permanence," including ones vital to political culture, have been jettisoned almost entirely. Jarvis even reports Eisenstein herself worrying about this question before he dismisses it (2011d, 57–48).

The most vocal supporters of the print–digital parallel argue that the printing revolution was so transformative for good that democratic governments should not attempt to regulate or watch over it. Two ironies stand out in particular regarding this viewpoint. One, the controls imposed on the printing press, including those given by digital promoters, were typically enacted by authoritarian regimes such as the Catholic Church and the various monarchs of Europe. These rules are often criticized for hindering the transfer of political power to citizens. It is extremely paradoxical to say that *democratic* citizens should not exercise the democratic power that earlier communicative technologies enabled. Far-right thinkers like Rothbard characterize representative democratic governance as authoritarian tyranny. This formulation only makes sense if we accept it as a foundation. But once we accept that equivalence, it is not clear why we should want another "revolution" that will just produce more democratic "tyranny."

Second, it is ironic that print technology underwent significant changes *despite* the fact that printing presses were subject to more stringent controls in the past than they are today. This is because political control did not prevent print's positive effects in the past, although laws, controls, and effects varied depending on the location and time period. In contrast, we are expected to believe that political management of new technologies can only *prevent* the positive transformations that technology has to offer us, despite living in a politically advanced era. Rather than arguments to support that view, though, we are presented with revisionist histories of the printing revolution with which few scholars would agree but offered as if most scholars support them.

THE PRINTING PRESS METAPHOR
AS AN AGENT OF CHANGE

In the wake of the Snowden revelations, free software advocate Eben Moglen developed an especially elaborate and symptomatic version of the printing press myth:

> For the last half-thousand years, ever since there has been a press, the press has had a tendency to marry itself to power, willingly or otherwise. The existence of the printing press in Western Europe destroyed the unity of Christendom, in the intellectual, political and moral revolution we call the Reformation. But the European states learned as the primary lesson of the Reformation the necessity of censorship: power controlled the press almost everywhere for hundreds of years.
>
> In the few places where the European press was not so controlled, it fueled the intellectual, political and moral revolution we call the Enlightenment

and the French Revolution, which taught us to believe, as Thomas Jefferson said, "When the press is free and every man able to read, all is safe."

But in the world liberal capitalism made, as A. J. Liebling declared, freedom of the press belonged to him who owned one. Venality, vanity, fear, lust for profit and other forces brought the owner, slowly or rapidly as character determined, into power's embrace. In the twentieth century, the press—and its progeny, broadcast—became industrial enterprises, which married power and money far more incestuously than any megalomaniac press lord ever could, which is why the few remaining corporeal examples, nor matter how semi-corporate their vileness, retained a certain quaint, freebooting flavor.

Now, the vast interconnection of humanity we call the internet promises to divorce the press and power forever, by dissolving the press. Now, every mobile phone, every document scanner, every camera, every laptop, are part of an immense network in which everything we see, we think, we know, can be transmitted to everyone else, everywhere, immediately. Democracy in its deepest sense follows. Ignorance ceases to be the inevitable lot of the vast majority of humanity.

The great promise of the Enlightenment is finally fulfilled: the greatest intellectual, political and moral revolution in the history of humanity. (2011)

While this rhetoric may sound persuasive, it is remarkable how contradictory, self-serving, and at odds with the facts it is—to say nothing of how pervasive some version of this revisionist history is in digital advocacy.

Note that one of Moglen's main targets is the fact that "the press has a tendency to marry itself to power," including commercial power. No doubt this is true. But where does the faith come from that the press *also* produces "democracy in its deepest sense"? How can we as a democratic polity distinguish the difference, especially if we, as Moglen insists, disempower democratic governments in their attempt to regulate the concentration of power? Further, what if, as many political libertarians do, one believes that the marriage of commercial power and the press is an *embodiment* of democracy? We are no longer talking about the "press" if we distinguish between *some* forms of the press and others, let alone if we admit that "the European states learned as the primary lesson of the Reformation the necessity of censorship." Are capital and business and "states" less influential in our world than they were in the past, and what evidence is there to suggest this? Given the overwhelming and obvious evidence that multinational corporations, including the very multinationals that exert most dominance over the internet itself, are not only not going away, but are in fact strengthened by the proliferation of digital technology, how can we imagine that the "more democratic" internet will reverse this trend?

Moglen's sweeping judgments are incoherent, and his specifics are often demonstrably at odds with the facts. Indeed, they often point in the opposite direction from the one he appears to intend. Moglen tells us that the printing press "destroyed the unity of Christendom." It is unclear from which political orientation one needs to sit to see the replacement or supplementation of the Catholic Church with a variety of Christian sects as a metaphorically meaningful cultural advance for our own age, especially as time went on. Moglen says that "in the few places where the European press was not so controlled . . . it fueled the Enlightenment and the French Revolution." This is truly a bizarre rereading of history.

Although many of the authors whose works we typically consider part of the Enlightenment emerged from England, the specific target of the American Revolution, they were not suppressed in England by censorship (which was a common practice in that country at the time). If it is merely the *availability* of printed material that fuels democratic revolutions, why is it that Locke's writings were unable to generate the same revolution in England they did in the Americas, despite being widely distributed in both places? France, which Moglen mentions specifically, remained a Catholic country up to and through the French Revolution. It was somehow vulnerable to political enlightenment but not religious reformation. France continued to enforce as much if not more state censorship than did other European countries. Despite the inclusion of press freedom in the Declaration of the Rights of Man in 1789, the proclamation was issued after the French Revolution had already begun. The press in France remained censored until well into the nineteenth century. Sweden was the first European nation to declare and enact anti-censorship principles in 1766. Although Sweden remains a monarchy, it experienced a series of relatively peaceful reforms that led to a constitutional–parliamentary democratic system that is very similar to the UK system. The monarch became largely a figurehead in Sweden in 1974.

Moglen omits Gutenberg's home country, Germany, which had an explosive press from the seventeenth century onward. Germany, like Sweden, experienced the most obvious effects of the Reformation firsthand, but did not experience political reforms associated with the American or French Revolutions. Like England and heavily censored France, Germany was home to some of the authors most associated with Enlightenment thought, especially Immanuel Kant. His works were widely distributed around the entire European continent soon after they were published in German. Clearly, the relationship between political change, censorship, and a "free press"— all of which mean something far different today than they did in the seventeenth and eighteenth centuries—is more complex and multifarious than Moglen credits.

It is also notable that Moglen picks out the Enlightenment and the French Revolution (along with the Protestant Reformation) as exemplary, because these two are linked in a very disturbing way. Few French people today, of whatever political party, look on the French Revolution as an unambiguously positive development. And although they promoted and were even involved in the early stages of the French Revolution, most American supporters, including Thomas Jefferson and Thomas Paine, were appalled by the waves of violence and terror that characterized the Revolution in its later phases. These events were associated by the Revolution's critics— most famously and presciently, Edmund Burke, who wrote in 1790—directly with its roots in the Enlightenment's contempt, at least at its extremes, for all existing systems and social institutions, and its belief that an enlightened and self-appointed group of elite leaders could remake society from top to bottom in a "rational" way. Many of us who are not sympathetic with Burke's politics will still admit that developments like the Terror and the rise of Napoleon Bonaparte are inextricably part of the French Revolution. If this is the best advocates can do in explaining that the internet is like the printing press and that this similarity tells us anything at all about the likely effects of the internet on our political formations and about how governments change as a result of information technology, then the parallel is as troubling as it is promising. We may already be experiencing the internet equivalent of the Terror in the early twenty-first century, with the crashing waves of antidemocratic sentiment and violence all over the world.

Yet Moglen is clear—although also, apparently, confused—about the lessons we must draw from the print–digital parallel. First, he promotes his personal hobby horse of free software as the antidote to the stranglehold of concentrated capital on culture, despite the movement's slogan of "free as in speech, not as in beer" (see chapter 5). He paradoxically (and without apparent irony) notes that free software "runs Google and Facebook" and "performs flawlessly every day in every bank, insurance company, engineering firm, supermarket and pretty much everywhere else," while noting that "every government and every deep pit of misbegotten wealth on earth is trying to centralize and thus control the net that is humanity's future" (2011). Free software is designed to offer no impediment to commercial usage of its products and in general gives away both the products and the labor associated with them to corporations. Companies, including the very "centralized services for social networking and publication," that "are operated by businesses that can be coerced, bought or bribed" are given access to free software. Why should we expect that free software will at some point in the future lead *away* from commercial development or otherwise destabilize concentrated private capital? There is already a great deal of evidence that this does not work. Capital and concentrated business power are already using free and open-source software maximally in their for-profit environments. If it is this bad after only a few decades, what is going to cause a turnabout, producing the logically and empirically improbable outcome in which the widespread availability of software anyone can use and inspect is going to provide resistance to corporate power?

Relying on the same fallacious equation of software with speech that informs a great deal of the rhetoric of digital enthusiasts (see chapter 6), Moglen paradoxically tells us that the promise of the printing press can be realized "by dissolving the press" itself. Dismissing as unimportant the many parts of the printing apparatus that have to do with promotion, distribution, and editorial interaction, Moglen repeats the canard familiar from Shirky and Jarvis that having the "power" to post items to a blog is equivalent to having a major publisher issue a book. He also suggests that major publishers themselves are equivalent to government censorship, which would come as a surprise to authors as prominent as Toni Morrison or Stephen King. Intent on promoting the wonders of the "digital" and particularly its (apparent) isolation from corporate influence, Moglen offers pronouncements contrary to the facts he cites in the same essay: "Tiny computer systems will be scattered around every home and office in almost all societies, ubiquitous as mobile phones, and much more powerful. With free software inside, they can become 'FreedomBoxes': devices that assure each individual user, each still-human being, of the right to communicate safely, freely, without monitoring or control" (2011). Bizarrely, Moglen seems to forget that he just told us that the manufacturers of the current commercial versions of these devices rely heavily on free software *already*. They have "free software inside," and from a certain political–economic perspective they are already "FreedomBoxes," but that is only if one discounts the very practices Moglen critiques.

Moglen accurately assesses corporate power in the digital age. However, he offers only one solution to connect his political goals with the current policy and legal architecture, and that is a familiar one: *government should not regulate hardware, software, and computer networks*. This is coupled with the now-familiar hatred of the U.S. government couched in the language of surveillance, the NSA, and Edward Snowden, in which the level of emotion far overwhelms the provision of facts. In more recent work, Moglen's antipathy for the U.S. government has only become more pronounced. For instance, in a 2013 lecture series he frequently refers to the current system as "totalitarian" while offering no explanations for how the "Freedom-Boxes" he recommends can exist outside the government's capability to enforce the law by surveilling them. Nor does he explain how the freedom he invokes so often is to be realized when he promotes a thorough distrust of what the government says it is doing and what the evidence indicates.

Moglen uses the print–digital parallel to advance a revisionist, contradictory, and self-serving interpretation of history. He turns this interpretation toward the promotion of his own vision of technological change, via his ideal solution of free software. This promotion entails the widespread distribution of ever more digital devices, even if that "free software" is inherently open to inspection and therefore human redirection and misdirection. Therefore, his own solution results in the very problem he claims to solve. Despite the anti-corporate nature of much of Moglen's rhetoric, he ends up holding a position almost identical to that of RAND analyst James Dewar: "The above factors combine to argue for: a) keeping the Internet unregulated, and b) taking a much more experimental approach to information policy. Societies who regulated the printing press suffered and continue to suffer today in comparison with those who didn't. With the future to be dominated by unintended consequences and a long time in emerging, a more experimental approach to policy change (with special attention to unintended consequences) is soundest" (1998, 3). Do not regulate. The democratic polity should act only through market forces, and market forces are the only legitimate means of democratic governance. Do not consider digital tools and devices as even potentially harmful. Do not consider surveillance an inherent feature of the network, but instead encourage the network to proliferate even as we decry the effects of that proliferation and blame "government" rather than the manufacturers and distributors of surveillance technology. We must not examine the proposition that proliferation *itself* is the problem, as that would interfere with a nebulous new "democratization" and "Enlightenment" that both go far beyond the ideals of the past and dismantle the institutions we had, until recently, understood as the embodiments of those ideals.

At worst, the print–digital parallel tells us that we *must not resist the digital,* even if that injunction must be surrounded with the most mind-numbing contradictions imaginable: "I believe the internet could prove to be as momentous an invention, as profound a platform. This is why we must protect the net from the control of governments and corporations—especially because they are the objects of the disruption technology enables. Only if it remains as open as the printing press for anyone—no, everyone—to use can the net realize its potential and can we realize ours" (Jarvis 2011c, loc. 298–301). How exactly do we "protect the net from the control of corporations" without government, which in this respect is the name for the power of citizens to structure society outside of capital (and, make no mistake, *by* capital as well)? Which political philosophy offers any concrete recommendations for achieving that goal? How do we reconcile the fact that for the "net" to "realize its potential" is, in the minds of Sergey Brin, Jimmy Wales, Eric Schmidt, Mark Zuckerberg, and many others—even Jeff Jarvis, one suspects, when he is speaking to corporate clients—to do exactly what it is doing, to foster "disruptive innovation" of the very institutions of democracy, education, and information we have spent centuries creating? The answer is clear: the disruption will put more of our lives in the hands of neoliberal commercial–political control, which can be exploited by the most concentrated forms of power. The pursuit of "freedom" through mass digitization aims only in the direction of economic freedom, negative freedom, and not the kinds of political and personal freedom and equality that most of us not on the extreme right associate with the word.

THE PRINTING PRESS MYTH MAKES IT
HARDER TO EVALUATE DIGITAL TECHNOLOGY

Why worry about the parallel with the printing press? Is it not true that, even if it does not exactly parallel the printing press, and even if it eliminates some of the specific benefits the printing press is supposed to have produced, the "internet" is a revolution in human communication? Which means it is a revolution in how our most important political and social institutions function, and for this reason it is unobjectionable to celebrate it, right?

While there is some truth to these sentiments, they are deeply misguided and misleading. The most strident claims made about the printing press–internet analogy insist that our most fundamental practices and institutions "are being radically transformed." These claims, as with many commercially backed technological transformations since the nineteenth century, emerge *prior to* significant evidence of their veracity. In a fundamental way, they put the cart before the horse. Rather than having the Protestant Reformation occur and then looking back and seeing the role of the printing press in that event, it's as if we are staring at the printing press itself and declaring "The Reformation is coming any day now, and it will definitely be a good thing."

The view that our global society is in a parallel position to that of Europe prior to the printing press is not merely contentious but much more likely wrong than right. Attending to the rhetoric of the parallel and the specific arguments it licenses is important, as it allows us to be more specific about why we believe that our world has insufficient communication media that are no longer capable of supporting democracy, among other things. Especially if we believe that print "produced" democracy in some sense, what happened to reverse that, and why does the advent of the internet fix whatever "broke" print in the first place? What is the character of democratic cultures worldwide—but especially in those regions where print is already widespread—such that they no longer experience the benefits of print culture, or that digital culture will reintroduce these benefits? Why should we accept this strange "second coming" of the printing press when it often overtly expresses a desire to destroy many of the features of print that are deemed politically necessary?

Related to, but conceptually distinct from this concern, is the deep question of whether the "printing revolution" should be viewed as a *technological* or *social* change. Of course it is both, but almost all advocates of the print–digital analogy take it for granted that the most important effects of the transition to print were technological, thus aligning these interests with the general technological determinism that informs cyberlibertarian dogma. It is not that society *wanted* to become "more democratic" or that intellectual conditions and developments were such that the "scientific revolution" occurred in specific times and places; rather, it is the technology of print that is largely responsible for a social change that, speaking counterfactually, would not have occurred without print and would have occurred with print, regardless of the social conditions into which print was introduced. At their worst, these thinkers write as if nobody ever *wanted* the changes associated with democracy or science to occur. Instead, they emerged as inevitable consequences of implacable, unregulated technological change. Here, the digital utopian literature stands in stark contrast to most of the excellent print culture scholarship following Eisenstein's work, such as Michael Warner's, which argues that social forces played critical and, in many cases, determinative roles in political developments sometimes attributed to printing.

Such a deterministic view of history is inherently dismissive of human efforts and agency. It does not even want to ask whether there were social changes taking place that worked with print—or maybe even *regardless of* print—that produced these social changes. Further, when do we stop attributing social developments to technological causes and instead ascribe them to the social forces that were also part of their histories? This line of thinking has been among the most powerful responses to Eisenstein's original work, even though she is less committed to the transformative power of technology than are many digital utopians.

Some of the deepest investigations of these questions have been undertaken by Michael Warner. Tellingly, Jarvis in *Public Parts* refers several times to *Publics and Counterpublics* (2002), a book by Warner about the history of the public–private distinction. However, he does not mention an earlier book by Warner that is arguably more relevant. *Letters of the Republic* (1990) engages with the nature of the interaction between print and politics, and specifically the creation of a democratic republic, during and after the American Revolution. Warner addresses the relationship between printing technologies and political regimes and cultures, more specifically than many analysts of the printing revolution. He asks what made democratic revolution possible in the emerging United States, and what set the conditions for the specific printed forms used then to do the work they did. Even though printed works and access to the press were famously available in eighteenth-century Britain, it was the New World, not England, that rebelled against monarchy. The monarchy had been weakened by the English Civil Wars in the mid-1600s. Was this the effect of printing, or was it not, since the colonies eventually rebelled against British rule as well? Is that because print was less effective, less meaningful, and less well distributed in Britain than in the colonies? Or was there something other than print technology at work, or at least *also* at work, in what we now see as one of history's most profound instances of democratization? For example, was it in part the remoteness of America from the levers of political control available in Great Britain itself, a kind of remoteness that the "internet" has done a great deal to eradicate?

Warner notes that despite Eisenstein's frequent nods toward the multiple causes of major historical events, even for her "politics and human agency disappear . . . whether the agency be individual or collective, and culture receives an impact generated outside itself" (1990, 6). Such a view "must suppose, therefore, that a technology could come about, already equipped with its 'logic,' *before* it impinged on human consciousness and *before* it became a symbolic action" (6–7). As Warner demonstrates, even changes that we now understand as technological can be seen as shaped by inarguably social factors. For example, "although printing was initially another way of reproducing in quantity books that were already being reproduced in quantity, at a certain point printing came to be specially defined as publication, now *in opposition* to manuscript circulation" (8). This was less of a technological change and more of a social one. The same physical objects were now viewed in a different light. This is why the worldwide distribution of printing does not produce uniform effects, why "among the Chinese or the Uighur Turks, printing took on different defining features and had different 'consequences,'" a fact that mitigates against the view of print-revolution historians that "the technology of printing, once 'discovered,' yielded the result of standardized mass production, with its cultural symptoms" (9). Scholars have long understood that even what we refer to as "printing" is a collection of disparate technologies and social forms. The emergence of these technologies in world culture is far more diffuse and complicated than the Gutenberg story suggests (see esp. Innis 1950, 1951).

Thus the "printing" that played an important role in the development of the American republic was a social production, resulting from particular thoughts and cultural attitudes about printing, society, politics, and forms of government that were both independent of and intertwined with the technical features of the print and publication apparatus. "The republican ideology of print," Warner writes, "elevated the values of generality over those of the personal. . . . The social diffusion of printed artifacts took on the investment of the disinterested virtue of the public orientation, as opposed to the corrupting interests and passions of particular and local persons" (1990, 108). This "republican ideology of print" was not inevitable, even with the "printing press" a permanent part of political culture in the emerging United States; and its sources are readily traced to specific figures, texts, events, discourses, and movements, ones that an overweening commitment to the "effects" of the "printing revolution" downplays, as if by design.

The dangers of promoting such views are obvious and immediate. They fail to address the *character* of the political changes that "we" hope will occur. It is clear that different factions see different political changes as welcome. These views also fail to address how power will be wielded, the historical and intellectual bases of the changes to be implemented, and the culture and politics of the society in which "liberation" is to take place. Rather than inspiring people to make political changes—although they may inspire short-term protests and social media–based "activism"—such views promote *quietism* and *discourage* political engagement in any direct sense. They explicitly express the political message that technology is liberating the people, and therefore the people do not need to take any particular action or form any particular political consensus or culture to realize the political ends they appear to embody. Such "revolutions" would be different in character from those we typically celebrate as political emancipation.

Even if we grant that media revolutions have social power of various kinds, it is disturbing that cyberlibertarian dogma looks almost exclusively for the *positive* changes caused or aided by technological developments. This triumphalist history cannot account for the true power of either technology or society and fails to consider the ways totalitarian regimes have been adept at using communications technologies to magnify and make permanent their power. We tend to look at the "suppression" and "censorship" of print and writing in Soviet Russia or Communist China and push aside the tremendous amount of printed matter generated by and supporting these regimes, as if they somehow "betray" the essentially democratic nature of print. Instead, we should see that print has a range of uses and affordances, which are in many ways not merely conditioned by but products of the societies and polities in which they are used. We may well obscure these negative effects in our understandable desire to write histories of progress and positive change.

The idea that print had widespread negative effects, *even as* it had positive ones, is visible in the work of Walter Ong (1982) and Harold Innis (1950, 1951), among others. That the "internet" may have a wide range of negative effects, including the dismantling of the positive changes of the printing revolution, could not be clearer. Warner, for example, notes that print was praised in early America for engendering a culture of "politeness," and that "there was a tension between the civic humanist paradigm of print as a public and general sphere of action and a proto-liberal paradigm of print as an arena for managed esteem and distinction" (1990, 138). The kinds of esteem and distinction print may have helped to promote among the American founders look very different from the kinds of "politeness" promoted today on Reddit, 4chan, and the apparent digital equivalent of eighteenth-century coffeehouses, the comments sections of newspapers and other online publications. Indeed, the incivility of such environments reflects, in part, the danger of presuming that technology is "democratizing" in the robust political sense of the term. By relying on that mechanical democratization, we demonstrate little interest in promoting the kinds of deep and at least partly civil political discussions out of which our own democracy was built. The proceedings of the constitutional conventions appear scabrous to us, but they are hotbeds of enlightened civility when lined up next to today's political discourse.

Cyberlibertarian discourse claims to engage with scholarship about important historical developments, but it shows its ideological nature by not understanding what that scholarship actually says. The historical scholarship on print culture—and indeed on literacy in general—is deeply ambivalent about the developments it charts. Some, like Eisenstein, tend to credit technology with changing a great deal, and to cast those effects as positive, although in a more muted way than pundits like Jarvis suggest. Other scholarship is more critical, suggesting that it is a mistake to look to technology for direct social and political effects. It is suggested that whatever their cause, those effects might be negative as well as positive, something Eisenstein agrees with. Some historians even suggest that the negative may outweigh the positive. It is another bitter irony that one of the virtues for which the printing revolution is almost universally celebrated—the development of a well-informed public that can fully debate all sides of a given issue—is one the cyberlibertarian discourse about the printing revolution militates strongly *against*. Pundits like Shirky and Jarvis do not want people to read widely on this subject (which is again ironic for people celebrating the benefits of the printing press) or to think carefully about how print has worked and what that might mean for digital technology. Thus they reduce a complex and highly contentious series of historical changes into clear and settled truths, always pointing in the direction that happens to serve their worldview.

It is worth taking a moment to reflect on the overt embrace of destruction that accompanies paeans to the power of the printing revolution. As we have seen, that love of destruction can seem counterintuitive at first, but within cyberlibertarian discourse it becomes normalized. "Creative destruction" is a key feature of the libertarian economic program, and along with "innovation" it is a central topic in cyberlibertarian discourse (see chapter 2). We are told to focus on the "creative" part and less on the "destruction," but when looking at the print–digital parallel the destructive aspects emerge with real prominence. Given digital enthusiasts' superficial understanding of the relationship of media technology to political structures (among other important relationships), we should be cautious in heeding the exhortations of technology promoters who tell us that print is one of the most important developments in five hundred years of human history, and that the few decades of internet history mean we should be eager to dismantle the results of that history. The long history of print should teach us that massive transformations take time. As such, it would seem wise to embrace a more careful view of the parts of the world that digital technology— especially those parts directly aligned with business interests—seems eager to jettison. Humility suggests that we are in no position to know what these changes will mean. The burden of proof must be on those who tell us that, in the name of the revolutionary powers of print, print itself should be destroyed.

CHAPTER 5

The Myth of "Free Culture"

Cyberlibertarianism manifests as rhetorical tropes and strategies that shape discussions of digital technology, government, politics, and social issues. It is also a form of advocacy for a set of issues. These issues are both less and more than what they seem. They are less because they often distort the political contexts into which they are said to be critical. They are more because the political and social work they do is often obscured by digital advocacy itself. These issues are best understood in the way "greenwashing" and "astroturfing" are understood: as carefully crafted strategies that do a great deal of political work for their advocates, but appear to do something very different to those not in the know. Greenwashing in the case of plastics recycling, for example, advances the power of the fossil fuels industry and its associates, while giving the impression of advocating for environmental protections.

Clear threads emerge when the issues are grouped together. The most obvious thread is that advocates take for granted the beneficial and pro-democracy nature of digital technology, as seen in the promotion of Section 230, and work to advance its power. This is primarily in the form of corporate power but also, in some disturbing cases, outside of corporations, at least on the surface and for the moment. This embrace of technological power is underpinned by a discourse about democracy and democratic governance that is less obvious, but according to which, essentially, democracy is impossible. The discourse suggests that all government is authoritarian and all nongovernmental power is more or less welcome. The only exception is the core neoliberal use of governmental power to write preemptive law, which appears to restrict governmental power to regulate technology even as it licenses the nearly unchecked growth of that technology. Section 230 is a particularly strong example of this, as we have seen (see Schriever 2018 for Uber and Lyft explicitly deploying this strategy to advance their corporate interests).

This chapter and the next survey the issues that digital advocates, technologists, and digital rights organizations tell us are central not just to technology but to politics in general. The two chapters are loosely organized into issues that appear to be primarily about technology in this chapter and about politics in the next. This distinction is offered purely for convenience; all the issues covered here are social, technological, and political at once. The way these issues manifest in politics is of particular concern to anyone interested in the health of democracy. In each case, they work to limit the power of democracy to regulate itself, while promoting the power of technology to do whatever its advocates and users choose. This is true even when words like "open," "free," and even "democracy" are used to describe that power.

"OPEN" AND "FREE"

The terms "open" and "free" are primary marketing labels for cyberlibertarianism as a movement. Many in the public take these terms as being directly connected to core political notions of freedom and democracy, often almost completely uncritically. Once one side of a debate or a particular way of looking at an issue has been labeled "open" it becomes almost impossible to have reasoned debate about the issue at hand. The overwhelming assumption is that anyone arguing against "open" is therefore arguing in favor of "closed." Among all the terms used in cyberlibertarian discourse, these two are among the most likely to be subject to the constant shifting of meaning described in chapter 2 as a key method used in strategic digital denial.

Of course these rhetorical moves have long been noted by critics. "Open" does not have a firm political definition, and the relationship of its relatively clearer technical applications to politics is never obvious. Like many other cyberlibertarian keywords, it often comes down to nothing more than "absence of government." As paradoxical as it may seem, the absence of democratic oversight is often used as a synonym for "open" (or "democracy" for that matter). Evgeny Morozov has been particularly clear about the travails of "open": "'They want to be "open," they want to be "disruptive," they want to "innovate,"' Morozov told me. 'The open agenda is, in many ways, the opposite of equality and justice. They think anything that helps you to bypass institutions is, by default, empowering or liberating. You might not be able to pay for health care or your insurance, but if you have an app on your phone that alerts you to the fact that you need to exercise more, or you aren't eating healthily enough, they think they are solving the problem'" (Packer 2013). "The opposite of equality and justice" may seem hard to reconcile with the tacit equivalence between "open" and "democracy." But this is exactly how cyberlibertarian rhetoric works. It hollows out the substantive values of key terms and subtly (and then, less subtly) replaces them with hard-right values like "innovation," deregulation, and markets.

The education technology critic Audrey Watters, reflecting on a tweet in which she coined the term "openwashing" to refer to "having an appearance of open-source and open-licensing for marketing purposes, while continuing proprietary practices," expands her observation to ask what "open" is meant to suggest in the various technological spheres in which it is used: "Does 'open' mean openly licensed content or code? And, again, which license is really 'open'? Does 'open' mean 'made public'? Does 'open' mean shared? Does 'open' mean 'accessible'? Accessible how? To whom? Does 'open' mean editable? Negotiable? Does 'open' mean 'free'? Does 'open' mean 'open-ended'? Does 'open' mean transparent? Does 'open' mean 'open-minded'? 'Open' to new ideas and to intellectual exchange? Open to interpretation? Does 'open' mean open to participation—by everyone equally? Open doors? Open opportunity? Open to suggestion? Or does it mean 'open for business'?" She goes on: "We act—at our peril—as if 'open' is politically neutral, let alone politically good or progressive. Indeed, we sometimes use the word to stand in place of a politics of participatory democracy. We presume that, because something is 'open' that it necessarily contains all the conditions for equality or freedom or justice. We use 'open' as though it is free of ideology, ignoring how much 'openness,' particularly as it's used by technologists, is closely intertwined with 'meritocracy'—this notion, a false one, that 'open' wipes away inequalities, institutions, biases, history, that 'open' 'levels the playing field'" (Watters 2014). "We sometimes use the word to stand in place of a politics of participatory democracy," while also using it "as though it is free of ideology." This is cyberlibertarian politics in a nutshell:

antidemocracy portraying itself as both democracy and "above" politics, when it is anything but.

The primary usage of "open" in digital discourse is of course "open source," discussed more fully below. It is worth noting that open source, as defined by the Open Source Initiative and in standard texts such as St. Laurent's *Understanding Open Source and Free Software Licensing* (2004) and Weber's *Success of Open Source* (2004), refers to a broad set of methods for software development as well as a type of software licensing. That licensing program, which its proponents stress more often than the development methodology, embodies a critique of what they call "property." Yet in their critique, open-source advocates follow a typical cyberlibertarian two-step. They offer revisionist accounts of existing political categories, which they believe are no longer fit for purpose. They then assert that their novel categories justify the revisionist derogation of the existing categories. St. Laurent, for example, writes that "under the American copyright system an effective monopoly is vested in the creator of each work," but that "rights held under copyright are rarely enforced by the work's creator" (2004, 4). He has elided the fact that publishers and other distributors typically enforce creators' copyright through contract, and that every important work produced today with one or more creators is issued under copyright with significant benefit to the individuals or companies that produce and help to distribute the work. St. Laurent undermines copyright as a useful category at the start of the analysis, and then uses the resulting conclusions to dismiss copyright itself. He does not provide empirical evidence to support his assertions.

Like so much else in digital culture, open source is an idea developed by engineers and computer enthusiasts with little interest in, and sometimes outright contempt for, democratic politics. This is only one of the reasons the digital environment is so conducive to right-wing positions. Open source advocates developed a reactionary "gotcha" that they baked into their development models. They believe that non-techies are wrong about the importance of democracy. Even if non-techies were right, they claim that open is a better version of democracy than democracy itself. Never mind that no reasonable reading of democracy or political alignments would support such a game of turnabout. After all, politics and power go hand in hand, and the point was always that computer enthusiasts were finally going to get theirs. This was inherently democratic and "open"—open to *them*.

The Open Government and Open Data movements make it clear that they entail *political* values, specifically that governmental operations should be transparent or open to inspection by the public. However, they also almost universally entail the value that governmental resources should be made available for *free,* without any sort of remuneration. Often, these resources are used by private corporations who neither return profit to the source of the data nor make their own operations open or transparent in the sense required of governmental programs. The matter is further complicated by the fact that "open source" existed prior to its use in the digital milieu. It meant information that is not proprietary to military or intelligence services. Typically, it was used within that context to distinguish information published in public sources (such as newspapers and encyclopedias) from that collected by intelligence agents. Thus some of the most vociferous advocates of "open source" include writers like Robert David Steele, whose *Open-Source Everything Manifesto* takes it as given that "open" used in each of these instances is the same, so that "Open-Source Everything is our path to peace, power, and prosperity . . . [it] reconnects us all to the root power of the cosmic universe, restores our harmony, and unleashes our inherent gifts of innovation, entrepreneurship, and generosity" (xix).

With his breathless claims of revolution and social transformation and his exhortations to open source "everything," Steele's animus is reserved for government and his positive doctrine is oriented toward efficient and unimpeded flows of capital. Like so many others chronicled here, Steele begins his analysis by invoking the usual cyberlibertarian suspects from both the moderate political left and political right, and their promotion of what he calls "collective intelligence": Alvin Toffler, Matt Drudge (who is praised for breaking the Monica Lewinsky story "when corporate media was holding back because of its incestuous relationship with the two-party tyranny that strives to control what We the People can learn"; xiv), Glenn Reynolds, Howard Rheingold, Pierre Levy, Lawrence Lessig, James Surowiecki, and Clay Shirky. Steele sees these writers as all expressing the same point of view, according to which "top–down governance has become corrupt and does not work . . . [and] the nanny state attempts to micro-manage what it does not understand" (xv). As Morozov has written, "'Open government'— a term once reserved for discussing accountability—today is used mostly to describe how easy it is to access, manipulate and 'remix' chunks of government information. 'Openness' here doesn't measure whether such data increase accountability, only how many apps can be built on top of it, even if those apps pursue trivial goals" (2013c). Even more pointedly, in the same piece he rightly notes that "a victory for 'openness' might also signify defeat for democratic politics, ambitious policy reform and much else." We must add: when "open" defeats democratic politics, it tells us that it is a victory for democracy.

Part of my brief here is to show how often this cluster of ideas is taken up by figures on the right, even if that is not what their authors intend. While authors are not liable for controlling what others do with their ideas, they do have a responsibility to note how their ideas are being received, especially in the broad strokes. The few left-leaning writers mentioned above seem to be either unaware or uninterested in the degree to which their work is continually referred to as authoritative by those whose politics they disagree with. It is possible to make one's political views clear and demonstrate that one's analysis should not lead to results that are strongly favored by one's political opponents, especially when those opponents are as virulent and powerful as today's political right. These figures are unwilling to change their views because they are conceptually *unable* to do so. The theory they promote was designed to advance the cause of the political right in general and neoliberalism in particular.

Nathaniel Tkacz (2012) provides a trenchant critique of the use of "open" in digital rhetoric, demonstrating how its lineage can be traced from rightwing thinkers to today's digital theorists. He shows that the intellectual frameworks applied by these writers are remarkably consistent, tracing the preeminence of "open" in today's discourse to the work of Karl Popper. Noting that "Popper was not the first to write about the concept of openness, nor even of the open society," Tkacz observes that it was nevertheless Popper's two-volume *Open Society and Its Enemies* (1945) that drew popular attention to these concepts. The achievement of these volumes, authored while Popper was in exile during World War II, is to rewrite the history of Western philosophy:

> The summation of Popper's thought is a re-articulation of existing political concepts (democracy, fascism, communism), of the writings of key historical figures of political philosophy (Plato, Aristotle, Hegel, Marx and others) and of lived conflict (the Peloponnesian War, WW2) around the new master categories of open and closed. In this new politics of the open/closed, the

fate of a nation and its people, or alternatively the class inequalities produced by capitalism, are no longer the primary concern. The question is no longer about identity, race or class, but whether or not a social programme, that is, a set of knowledges and related practices, is able to change. Social programmes based on unchallengeable truths—the so-called laws of history or of destiny—emerge as the fundamental enemy, and what might be considered radically different political programmes in a different frame of analysis—communism and fascism—are made equivalent. The positive side of this political equation, the open society, is one where totalising knowledge is necessarily impossible. Openness is necessary because nobody can know for certain what the best course for society might be from the outset, and at the same time it is assumed that openness provides the best possible conditions for producing knowledge and, therefore, making better decisions. (Tkacz 2012, 389)

To say Popper's philosophical readings are unorthodox would be a significant understatement.

A reader who notices a conceptual harmony between Popper's position and some of those associated with the Neoliberal Thought Collective, particularly Hayek's in "The Use of Knowledge in Society" (1945), would be onto something. In fact, Popper was a member of the NTC, a close associate and friend of Hayek, and one of the original Mont Pelerin Society (MPS) members. While there would seem to be tension between Popper's avowed promotion of "open" societies and the closed nature of the MPS, and "Popper continued to argue at early MPS meetings against the idea that fruitful discussions of politics required prescreening for ideological homogeneity" (Mirowski 2013, 71), Mirowski argues that this tension is responsible for "the birth of one of the trademark 'double truth' doctrines of neoliberalism at the MPS": "a liberalism for the twenty-first century could be incubated and sustained only by an irredeemably illiberal organization" (72):

Popper himself at least glimpsed that his youthful exaltation of tolerance for unlimited criticism was unavailing in many circumstances that resembled those the MPS was constructed to counter. For instance, in a long footnote in *Open Society* he grants the plausibility of paradoxes of tolerance ("Unlimited tolerance must lead to the disappearance of tolerance") and democracy ("the majority may decide that a tyrant should rule"), but had little to offer concerning how those paradoxes should be defanged. Yet around the same time, Popper was already flirting with the Hayekian "solution": membership in the Open Society had to be prescreened to conform to a "minimum philosophy": but the principles of selection for that philosophy were never made as explicit as they were by Hayek in practice. (71)

Popper was not fully on board with what later became the esoteric and exoteric doctrines of the NTC. However, the theory and practice of those closest to the theory's development contain the paradoxical question of "open." Additionally, there are close conceptual connections between "open" as what Tkacz rightly calls a "master category" and Hayek's rewriting of world political and intellectual history. In Hayek's view, any hint of collectivist values is assigned automatically to a totalitarian system. Therefore, only unregulated capitalism and concentrations of wealth and power can be construed as freedom. Even the relative powers of these are irrelevant, much like Aristotelian democracy is indistinguishable from the antidemocratic political systems recommended by Plato (at least in some of his dialogues).

Mirowski draws attention to the curious symbiosis between "openness" and the most rapacious commercial interests of our time. In *Never Let a Serious Crisis Go to Waste* Mirowski discusses the concept of "murketing," a term he uses to point to techniques used by advertisers and other "modern hidden persuaders [who] have gladly nurtured the conviction of the average person that he is more clever than those who seek to manipulate him in order to render him all the more open to that manipulation" (2013, 140). "One of the most fascinating technologies of faux rebellion in the modern neoliberal murketing toolkit," he writes, is "the construction of situations in which the mark is led to believe she has opted out of the market system altogether" (141). He mentions as exemplary "a new breed of ad agency recruited unpaid volunteers to talk up products with which they were unfamiliar among their friends and acquaintances," noting that "it helps if the initiating guerrilla cadres sport an edgy character, mime disdain for their clients, and wax ironic about their faux rebelliousness, with names like BzzAgent, the Ministry of Information, Bold Mouth, and Girls Intelligence Agency" (142).

In Mirowski's sense, murketing is almost a term for how individuals identify cyberlibertarianism as a political, countercultural movement, while in fact promoting the dominant, exploitative culture. He draws this connection himself, pointing specifically at "open" and "free":

> What is striking is the resemblance of such promotional techniques to those of the open-source movement. There also, people are recruited to provide the fruits of their labor gratis in the guise of a rebellion against the market system, which is then reprocessed by other parties into fungible commodities. Although promoted under the banner of "freedom" the process is much more attuned to fostering the self-image of the insolent anarchic hacker culture, while averting participants' gaze from the sheer amount of hierarchical coordination that is required to invest any such project with a modicum of persistence and continuity. Their work is cherished as direct expression of their individuality, but assumes significance only when folded into a well-integrated scheme of insiders and outsiders. The consciousness of participants is so thoroughly socialized that many of them voluntarily become avid acolytes of Hayek and his notions of spontaneous organization, without detecting the possibility of their own personal collapse of kosmos into taxis. (142–43)

It is a sign of the corporate–technological capture of academia that most digital scholarship discussing hackers and hacking adopts exactly the perspective Mirowski describes, praising the self-image of hackers as rebellious outsiders rather than the nearly perfect embodiments of neoliberal subjectivity they are. This is only reinforced by the ease of movement between "outsider" hacker collectives and "insider" corporations. Some of the largest digital "insiders," especially Facebook (whose corporate headquarters have from the beginning been located at 1 Hacker Way, Menlo Park, California, on a private street Facebook named), pride themselves on hiring hackers (But 2012), all the while claiming to be rebelling against—something.

Worse, too much of the scholarship that is critical of capital digital power takes these sites of manufactured rebellion as authentic. We are told that the problems with Facebook, X, and so on would be ameliorated if they were made fully open-source and nonprofit. However, this is not the case. These "solutions," even if they were tenable, offer no resistance to capital continuing to use the data they generate to its own ends. This is despite the fact that platforms like Facebook already run on open-source and free software, in just the labor-exploitative manner Mirowski suggests.

Few conversations are more frustrating than trying to get such open-source social media advocates to explain what kinds of protections their imagined utopian platform would have against the hundreds of data brokers that Pasquale (2014, 2016; Citron and Pasquale 2014), Angwin (2014), and others point to in their work. Instead, demonstrating how profoundly cyberlibertarian dogma emerges from reactionary principles, these conversations degenerate into vituperation, "aggrieved entitlement," and repetition of the term "open source" as if it were a utopia-generating magic word.

In many ways, even more than "open"—and fitting with the vaguely libertarian commitments out of which it is born—"freedom" is the concept most directly at issue in cyberlibertarianism. Cyberlibertarianism's most profound and disturbing effect is to promote a highly specialized conception of freedom that has little in common with most people's understanding of the term. This is not exclusive to cyberlibertarianism, but is part of both the libertarian and neoliberal programs at many levels. The most influential central figures within the innermost "shells" of this movement seem to be aware that promoting alternative notions of freedom is one of the most effective ways to gain widespread popular support for views that benefit only a small minority. The advent of digital technology has given these ideologues essential new tools. However, these tools are ideological rather than technological. They provide metaphors, narratives, and ways of speaking that inspire significant numbers of people to take a wide range of actions. Unfortunately, this support is then used to counter almost directly their interests.

In the hands of the far right, "freedom" is often treated as nearly synonymous with "liberty." When the right wing uses it, this word is set apart from its more general meanings and attached to holistic bodies of political thought, so that it can sound reasonable to oppose Social Security or Medicare on the grounds that they offend liberty, despite the lack of mainstream political thought that would make such assessments coherent. Mark Levin, a right-wing ideologue and talk show host, titled one of his best-selling books *Liberty and Tyranny: A Conservative Manifesto* (2009). He misleadingly claims that social programs enacted under the New Deal (6–7) are a threat; in another discussion, he claims that "the Founders understood that the greatest threat to liberty is an all-powerful central government" (4). The right uses the term "liberty" to mobilize populist energy against the very same democratically enacted structures and programs that are designed to limit the *abuse* of individual liberty by concentrated economic power. The effect is to make such concentrations of power even more possible and even less subject to oversight (which is very much the direction Bitcoin has taken).

Few invocations of "free" are more famous in digital culture than Richard Stallman's advocacy for free software, which is often seen as the "real" or left alternative to the capital-friendly (and labor-hostile) practice of open source. The argument goes that if open source is a rightist or market-oriented movement, then free software is firmly oriented toward the left. Although Stallman's personal politics seem to lean left, the content of the Free Software project is not easy to harmonize with what we usually identify as left perspectives on economics, rights, or labor. His perspectives on freedom may even be more in line with libertarian ideas than with non-libertarian frameworks of rights and responsibilities.

Stallman presents his work with such moral force that no less relevant a commentator than Eric Scott Raymond has termed his orientation a "moral crusade" (see Raymond 2012; the word also occurs in the title of Stallman's semiofficial biography, Williams 2002). Stallman's essays are collected in a volume titled *Free Software, Free Society* (2002). Stallman and many of his followers believe that the model of software distribution he recommends is connected to the fundamental notion of freedom at the heart of much political philosophy. But what is that connection?

Despite Stallman's moral fervor and frequent animadversions toward some fundamental values, there is little in Stallman's work that indicates the connection between freedom as written about by Locke or Mill, or as described in the Universal Declaration of Human Rights, and free software (FS). According to Stallman himself, the concept of free software is widely misunderstood, leading to a distinction that is widely repeated throughout the free and open-source software (FOSS) development world. This distinction uses the partly obsolete words "gratis" and "libre" to resolve an ambiguity in our usage of the word "free." In perhaps the most famous statement of the FS movement, Stallman (n.d.) writes, "'Free software' is a matter of liberty, not price. To understand the concept, you should think of 'free' as in 'free speech,' not as in 'free beer.'" In this equation, gratis equals free beer, and libre equals free speech. Stallman writes in this way because of the understandable confusion. I will argue that this confusion haunts the project almost irrevocably, despite his protestations. It stems from the fact that the term "free software" in modern usage *sounds* a lot more like it means free beer than it does free speech. While "free speech" now refers exclusively to *libre*-style freedom, "speech" and "software" are not analogous nouns, since "speech" refers to an activity and "software" to a product.

"Free" is a keyword in many cyberlibertarian formulations, not just "free software" but also "freedom of speech," "free culture," and "internet freedom." It is also, of course, part of our ordinary political discourse, where not just freedom across the board but freedom of speech, freedom of religion, and free markets are highly contested concepts. Today, "freedom" is often used to refer to "a relative absence of law and regulation," as in Berlin's concept of negative freedom. Even the core political concept of "freedom of speech" is easily accommodated to "free as in free markets." Stallman's free software is curiously silent about markets, despite his own expressed hostility toward markets as a solution to social problems. This is especially odd given that FOSS has turned out, perhaps paradoxically on first glance, to be one of the greatest boons to concentrated financial and political power in recent history.

FREE AND "OPEN SOURCE"

The term "open source" has one of the oddest and most telling patterns of development and usage of any in the cyberlibertarian lexicon. It has a specific, pro-capitalist, pro-business history: it was designed by far-right computer advocates as a way to ensure that certain forms of apparently selfless behavior by software developers could be harnessed for the extraction of profit. Despite this, "open source" is often described as a kind of "communist" movement. However, the genealogy of this claim is difficult, perhaps impossible, to ascertain. Additionally, its general outline is hard, maybe impossible, to reconcile with left-leaning political or economic imperatives.

One of the first writers to make this claim, oddly, is the same Richard Barbrook whose "Californian Ideology" offers one of the most trenchant critiques of cyberlibertarianism. In a paean published in 2000 to American pragmatism as opposed to European "theoretical obsessions," Barbrook declares that "the same right-wing Americans" who "still virulently oppose the public provision of welfare services considered indispensable in other developed countries" nevertheless "are happily participating in the construction of cyber-communism" (2000, 31). The basis for this assessment is the willingness of these "right-wing Americans" to participate in what Barbrook (like many others) calls the "hi-tech gift economy." To Barbrook, open-source founder Eric Raymond can be "simultaneously a passionate advocate of the decommodization of software" and "a self-described right-wing libertarian" (31) who fails to admit his devotion to "cyber-communism" because it "sin[s] against the national myth" of the free market.

To Barbrook, "as information is incessantly reproduced, the quantity of collective labour embodied in each copy is soon reduced to almost nothing. Under these social and technical conditions, circulating information as gifts can be not only more enjoyable, but also more efficient than commodity exchange. Although appreciating the benefits of e-commerce, Americans are enthusiastically participating within an alternative form of collective labour: cyber-communism" (2000, 32). He writes that "circulating information as gifts" is pushing America toward "the abolition of capitalism" without "revolutionary uprisings, mass mobilizations and modernizing dictatorships": "Instead of destroying the market economy, Americans are now engaged in the slow process of *superseding* capitalism." Barbrook sees this development as a clash between "contradictory visions of the Net," pitting "hi-tech neo-liberals [who] perfect the existing relations of production by developing e-commerce: work-as-commodity" against "left-wing activists [who] destroy information property within the on-line potlatch: waste-as-gift." Beneficiaries of this gift economy will sometimes "look for monetary rewards," but "on many occasions, they will prefer the freedom of autonomous labour" (33).

Barbrook's essay is the most detailed exposition of the possible conceptual connections between open-source and left economic imperatives. It includes fairly thoughtful if brief discussions of central writings by Marx along with brief nods to Lenin and Stalin. However, the essay's descriptions of free software remain extremely abstract. Barbrook does not try to find passages in these authors' works that discuss ideas, intellectual labor, intellectual property, or even scarcity, all of which were well-known issues to them. He asserts that "all users of the Net enthusiastically participate in [a] left-wing revival" and that "each of them desires the digital transcendence of capitalism" (5). Of course, they desire it without realizing they desire it, let alone actively promoting it.

In a later work, Barbrook notes that while his late 1990s work can't be understood "without remembering the bizarre moment in the late-1990s

when so many pundits believed that the Net had almost magical powers"
(2005), he insists that it remains "hardly controversial" that "the sharing of
information over the Net disproved the neo-liberal fantasies of *Wired*. The
leading role of capitalist businesses within the open source movement was
incompatible with the anarcho-communist utopia." In the late 1990s, "the
open source movement was the iconic example of non-commercial production over the Net."

Writing in a slightly more skeptical vein, literature and education scholar
Christopher Newfield shared that he "began to worry about open source
when the corporate world stopped worrying and learned to love open source"
(2013, 6). Newfield's worry was triggered by the observation that Microsoft,
along with other major corporations, was shifting its attitude toward open
source, "acknowledging real overlap between the open and proprietary forms
of intellectual property that had been seen as polar opposites throughout
the 1980s and most of the 1990s" (7). Newfield describes a "coexistence and
stand-off between open source and corporate open source, between my right
to create and use, and your right to own and charge through the platform"
(11). He notes that in contrast to what he calls "corporate open source,"
"much of the current interest in open source borrows from Marxian and
autonomist traditions in Italy, France, and elsewhere that have been working for years on post-industrial labour systems, focusing in particular on
cognitive capitalism and immaterial labour" (10).

It is possible that "autonomous Marxism" is the part of the contemporary
left most interested in open source and most likely to see the movement
as compatible with its left (or progressive, or in Barbrook's terminology
"communist") goals. But this is a strange association that requires us to overlook or reinterpret the words, beliefs, and practices of overtly right-wing
figures to make them compatible with left politics. Furthermore, the assessment requires us to toss out the explicit, public justification for the creation of open source. It offers a novel interpretation of left economics of
labor whose justification within that economic system is hard, perhaps impossible, to provide.

Barbrook, Newfield, and many others seem to have confused the work
of Richard Stallman's Free Software Foundation (Stallman 2002) with open
source, which has led to their mistaken understanding of history. FS, as
discussed below, *sounds like* an effort to take software outside the capitalist

circuit altogether. Thus, on the surface, it appears to present an alternative to the capitalist economy in the form of a gift economy or "supersession" of capitalism, among other possibilities. But this feature of FS made it inhospitable and unmarketable to corporations. The Open Source Initiative, begun in 1998 by Eric Raymond and self-described "open-source evangelist" Bruce Perens, was *explicitly* intended as an alternative to FS meant to make noncommercial software development *attractive to business*. Perens has made it clear that the main difference between FS and open-source software is that the latter "can be explained entirely within the context of conventional open-market economics" (2005). While they were not attracted to Stallman's apparently anti-capitalist philosophical orientation, "business people are pragmatists and are more impressed by economic benefit"— and open source provides just that.

Raymond himself, in *The Cathedral and the Bazaar* and elsewhere, used terms like "gift economy" to promote open source. But there is no doubt that Raymond, Perens, and O'Reilly understood that the open-source project and the freest of free-market capitalism were compatible. The roots of open source do not emerge from Marx. Instead, they are more in line with anarcho-capitalists like Murray Rothbard and David Friedman. This means they are directly opposed to left political understandings of markets and labor. As Philip Mirowski writes about Wikipedia, it is only through the "masquerade" of neoliberalism as a "radically populist philosophy" that the site's writers and editors "think they are squirreling away for the betterment of humankind, while Google positions itself to be the premier portal for information on the web and the biggest corporate success story of the 'New Information Economy'" (2009, 425). From the perspective of the individual, which neoliberalism and right-wing political philosophy endlessly promote, it may look as if there is a "gift economy." Within this framework, individuals exchange their work without regard to the vicissitudes of capitalism. Yet viewed from the vantage point of capital—in Wikipedia's case, from Google—another view entirely emerges. The "cyber-communism" of open source reappears as one of the baldest forms of Marx's singular capitalist fault: the devaluation, disempowerment, exploitation, and alienation of labor. Further, despite the interesting division between Stallman's free software project and the capital-friendly idea of open source, both are equally incompatible with most non-libertarian approaches to labor and value.

COPYRIGHT AND "FREE CULTURE"

Copyright may well be the signal cyberlibertarian issue. Mentioned in all the founding documents, hallowed in slogans and battle cries, few causes have rallied universal outrage so long as has copyright. However, its ubiquity also points backward, as many of the characteristic rhetorical and political moves occur here in great abundance. Almost everyone who identifies with digital technology thinks that copyright is an unadorned evil. This is so much the case that, with very few and only very recent exceptions, surveys of the topic that are supposed to be neutral do not examine it from all sides. Copyright defenders are often dismissed as self-interested, while attacks on copyright are understood as democratic and selfless. Attacks on copyright are "beyond left and right," and attempts to situate them politically are pushed aside.

Meanwhile, both the left and right demonize copyright without considering how they might agree on the legal doctrine surrounding intellectual property. This occurs without any need for further elaboration or reflection on the doctrine's esoteric nature. Even worse, consideration of the cui bono question regarding copyright is rarely found. Copyright is aligned with entertainment companies and the "copyright lobby" (Falkvinge 2015; Khanna 2014; Masnick 2013a; Shapiro 2011), and this somehow prevents people from asking whether there might not be any kind of "lobby" that benefits from anti-copyright agitation. However, it has long been clear that many of the most important technology companies benefit from intellectual property being available to them without needing to pay creators for it. Much as with free and open-source software, the anti-copyright discourse can be read as a sustained discussion of the value of labor, with the bottom line that labor should be entirely unpaid.

Much anti-copyright discourse positions itself as labor *advocacy*, even when it comes from right-wing thinkers. This is similar to other rightist propaganda campaigns, not least the decision to call legislation that makes forming labor unions nearly impossible "right to work." In hindsight, it is strange that works by authors who are ostensibly left-leaning—such as Siva Vaidhyanathan (2004), Cory Doctorow (2015), James Boyle (2008), and Lawrence Lessig (2004, 2008), whose politics are so thoroughly drenched in cyberlibertarianism as to be difficult to place on any conventional left–right axis (see Mayer-Schönberger 2008; Mirowski 2017)—could present nearly identical arguments as works by political libertarian Stephen Kinsella (2008) and the strongly pro-business *Wired* editor Chris Anderson (2009), to say nothing of syncretic figures like Eben Moglen and the members of the various "e-democracy" Pirate Parties.

One of the strongest voices in the movement to radically devalue all "content" and end "copyright monopolies" is Mike Masnick, founder and lead writer of *TechDirt* (whom I also discussed in chapter 3). His site functions as a terrific platform for cyberlibertarian dogma, because it is often taken as a project primarily devoted to "internet freedom" and the "stranglehold" of copyright. However, it discreetly maintains an even deeper focus on enlarging the profit potential for a specific set of business strategies and against others. Often understood as anti-corporate in nature, *TechDirt* is explicitly as well as tacitly pro-corporate while happily accepting the attention of those who do not grasp the full nature of its project.

TechDirt consistently criticizes the entertainment industry for copyrighting its works and charging people to access them. Arguments against copyright often focus on the most extreme cases, such as the seventy-plus year hold that the Walt Disney Company has on its cartoon characters and the intensity of its legal proceedings against any possible breach of that copyright. Yet *TechDirt*'s targets are typically media producers such as cable networks, musicians, film producers, and game makers, and the copyright under which they release their current works.

TechDirt advances a fairly novel economic theory that underwrites this perspective. The relationship between this argument and other forms of economics (even libertarian economics) remains unclear. However, the theory is similar to others widely endorsed by the Pirate Parties, FOSS advocates, Doctorow (2015), and others. In one of the most enduringly popular pieces on the site, titled "The Grand Unified Theory on the Economics of Free," Masnick (2007b) writes that content creators "should *encourage* people to get their content for free." His reasoning is remarkably general and supported with only a few specific cases, and its applicability to most situations is somewhere between opaque and altogether occluded. Masnick's analysis builds on a favorite canard among cyberlibertarians, especially those who focus on economics: the putative distinction between "scarce" and "non-scarce" goods.

This position is based on the observation that computer technology has made the copying and storage of files cost-free. More accurately, the cost per file has been reduced to such a low amount that it is unlikely to be noticed. However, there are still a variety of "sunk" costs involved with having the basic equipment required to copy, store, and use these files. Masnick and others like him argue that "scarcity doesn't exist. Instead, you have abundance. You can have as much content as you need—and in that world, it makes perfect sense that there's no costs, because without scarcity there need not be a cost. Supply is infinite, and price is zero" (Masnick 2006). The entertainment industry is the persistent target of this analysis. What riles Masnick and his supporters, extending up to the Pirate Parties who often cross-cite Masnick and *TechDirt,* is that they see copies of electronic files that they could download and copy themselves for free, but are prevented from doing so by the content creators.

In every forum, we repeatedly read the complaint that "copying isn't stealing because the original thing still remains." The implication is that if anyone has created a "copyable" product, they have no right to charge for it and must expect and tolerate that it will be widely copied without charge. One thing they hate with particular fury is digital rights management (DRM) technologies, technical means for ensuring that the only copies made are authorized by creators. In this one area, cyberlibertarians oppose a technical fix to a legal and social problem, which is interesting because they usually champion such solutions. As always, the dominant principle is me-first: *I* can protect my own machine by encrypting *my* communications, so nobody should stop me from doing it; but *I* can see that new game or music file and can't use it due to DRM, so DRM should be outlawed. (DRM creates an interesting conceptual conundrum for the vague first principle of freedom in Stallman's description of free software, since it's unclear why the use of such software would not be a freedom that developers should enjoy even though it ends up violating some of the other freedoms.)

TechDirt and the Pirate Parties are fascinating because they receive little to no support from the industries they claim to help. Masnick argues that giving content away for free will provide more income to creators. He believes that the availability of "free" content itself requires content providers to give away their own content for free, since "saying you can't compete with free is saying you can't compete period" (Masnick 2007a). Masnick also believes that if content creators knew what was good for them, they would be giving away their content at no cost. *TechDirt* has long targeted the hit HBO show *Game of Thrones,* which was widely regarded to be the most-pirated property during 2012 and 2013. The site promotes the bizarre view that "HBO-style shows owe a lot to piracy for their cultural dominance, because, if they were actually as exclusive as HBO wants to pretend they are, they would have had a much harder time gathering fans" (Beadon 2012). Site writers even claim that "piracy is at least partially responsible for the success of the show" or even "helps [the] show survive" (Geigner 2013). One wonders how it is that any movies or television programs were "culturally dominant" or "gathered fans" prior to the internet, when piracy at scale was virtually impossible.

In fact HBO had wildly successful shows (*The Wire, The Sopranos*) before online piracy became as easy as it is today. Huge amounts of content are available freely online both legitimately and illegitimately and do not achieve the level of popularity that *Game of Thrones* has. And perhaps most critically, despite the condescending tone *TechDirt's* writers take regarding HBO, the company has a fiduciary duty to maximize its profits, legal and contractual requirements to pay the many workers who create the show, and a host of web-savvy developers who understand distribution technology. The free content advocates assume that HBO does not know its own business and fails to explore every avenue for maximizing its profits, which seems absurd given HBO's success. It is counterintuitive that an HBO executive would suggest abandoning their subscription model and making the entire show available for free. However, from the consumer-first, anti-labor perspective associated with political libertarians, such a decision would make a strange kind of sense.

There is no doubt that some downloads have publicity value and that illegal pirating has led to people signing up for HBO subscriptions. This is because the show itself has been deemed of significant enough entertainment value that many people want to watch it, and in far greater numbers than other shows. The only legitimate cause for the show's success is that it is a great product. The notion that it would not succeed without piracy or that it would be more successful if it were even more freely available stands in stark contrast to common sense, business practice, and the evidence of real experience.

In this sense, HBO can be said already to be implementing the policy Masnick claims to promote: allowing some people to get copies of the material for free but requiring those who want the entire package to pay. If HBO could earn more money by giving the show away more freely, it would be required by its shareholders and fiduciary obligations to do so. The idea that it is refusing to do so, knowing that it could increase profits from this new strategy, solely to hold onto the power of "copyright monopoly" and to demonstrate its arrogance over the fans who just want to appreciate the show, challenges reason. It also verges on conspiracy theory of a particularly ugly sort, since it accuses "media elites" of hoarding for themselves something of culture or economic value just because they can. At the same time it does not challenge the self-oriented, me-first, adolescent attitude of cyberlibertarianism: I see it, it's mine, not yours, no matter who made it or how hard they worked on it.

It is remarkable to anyone thinking about the problem that the constituencies not represented in significant numbers among the pirate and free content communities, including *TechDirt,* are the producers and distributors of content. *TechDirt* writers and commentators often speculate on the arrogance of industrial and personal power they believe comes together in the content industry's refusal to give away its wares. They often see these industries as working together in some conspiratorial fashion, significantly or even primarily to prevent people who deserve (free) access to that content from getting it, even knowing that it would (in unspecified ways) ultimately improve their profits. The apparent lack of knowledge displayed (or pretended to be displayed, given *TechDirt's* generally sophisticated engagement with business practices) about the competitiveness of corporate practices is startling. The idea that there is a hugely profitable business model out there that nobody is willing to try because refusing to do it makes illegal downloaders angry, is absurd. It is suggested that upsetting the illegal downloaders is more important to these businesses than making money. In the United States, if a wildly successful business model exists in an established industry that nobody has yet tried, one can rest assured that somebody will try it, and it will work. The fact that it is not working is prima facie proof that the free content supporters are wrong in their basic assertions.

Covid-19 provided a particularly telling illustration of how cyberlibertarian anticopyright agitation works. In early 2020, the Internet Archive (IA) announced the creation of a program under which it would "suspend waitlists for the 1.4 million (and growing) books in our lending library by creating a National Emergency Library (NEL) to serve the nation's displaced learners" (Freeland 2020). The IA did not mention that many works in its lending library are still under copyright. The licenses under which it and other libraries allow access to those works were negotiated with publishers and authors who deserve compensation for the use of those materials. Rather than approaching any of those publishers and authors about permission to use those works in this manner, the IA simply asserted that the emergency allowed it to distribute unlimited numbers of the works free of charge and free of restriction. As is typical of cyberlibertarian activism, the stripping away of ordinary rights (which largely accrue to individual authors, not megacorporations like Disney) was presented as a social good. Brewster Kahle, founder of the IA, stated that "the library system, because of our national emergency, is coming to aid those that are forced to learn at home. This was our dream for the original Internet coming to life: the Library at everyone's fingertips." The project claimed support "from over 100 individuals, libraries and universities across the world, including the Massachusetts Institute of Technology."

Kahle's decision to create the resource without first consulting publishers and authors speaks directly to the real investments of cyberlibertarian anticopyright activism. The user comes first; the worker comes last, if at all. The free provision of content benefits major corporations, especially Google, which has itself been the target of litigation surrounding its distribution of unauthorized copyrighted material, especially on YouTube (Kafka 2014), which caused it to change its practices and provide mechanisms for copyright holders to request the removal of material to which they have rights. Even librarians (see, e.g., Madigan 2016) and others whose job would seem to be in part the preservation and support of the producers of cultural materials can become the opponents of that very work. They claim in truly counterfactual fashion that not just authors and publishers but libraries are "gatekeepers" interested not in providing but in preventing access to those materials.

Publishers and authors reached out to Kahle, offering several suggestions for how the NEL might move forward while still respecting copyright interests. Rather than working with them, Kahle rebuffed their attempts and doubled down on what most authors and publishers considered a novel and "invented" (so far as statutory or case law is considered) theory of copyright, according to which a library "scans a print copy of a book they have legally acquired, then makes the scan available to be borrowed in lieu of the print book" (Albanese 2020). The faults in this "theory" are obvious.

Libraries could photocopy endless copies of paper books and then distribute them without paying the publisher or author, rather than purchasing as many copies as they would like to have in their collections. Libraries constitute a long-standing and critical feature of book distribution, allowing hundreds or thousands of people to gain access to books, typically for free in most public libraries. Authors and publishers are compensated in a small fraction of the income they would receive for selling a copy for every reader. Libraries' role in the current publishing ecosystem reflects real generosity and openness, which is also seen in newer policies that allow a limited number of readers to access digital books based on the number of licenses the library purchases. Both the long-standing and newer digital policies evolved from close and largely cooperative connections among creators, publishers, libraries, and readers.

Kahle had to assert that these authors and publishers did not understand their own interests in their own work. When authors such as Colson Whitehead, Neil Gaiman, Chuck Wendig, and Alexander Chee, whose works were included in the NEL, along with organizations like the Authors Guild objected to the project, Kahle accused them of just retweeting "what they see on social media" (Dwyer 2020). Kahle refused to back down or modify his position, resulting in a lawsuit filed by Hachette Book Group, HarperCollins, John Wiley & Sons, and Penguin Random House, in coordination with the Association of American Publishers, who called the NEL an "opportunistic attack on the rights of authors and publishers" (Albanese 2020). As copyright activist David Newhoff wrote, "What is most galling about the IA in this regard is the pretense to public service and largesse against the backdrop of a real emergency. One cannot be 'generous' with the labor and property of others, particularly those who are, themselves, vulnerable to the economic hardship caused by crisis" (2020). Yet, not only do agitators like Kahle somehow manage to make this "generosity" with other people's labor seem reasonable, they also make it appear as if it benefits the very people being harmed.

In his 2016 novel *I Hate the Internet,* Jarett Kobek claims that Jack Kirby is "the central personage of" his book "despite never appearing as a character within its pages" (21). Kirby is the comic book writer and artist who created most of the characters now world famous due to the blockbuster Marvel films. Kirby was famously denied participation in the profits on account of the work-for-hire agreements he was made to accept in his early years in publishing. Kobek describes Kirby as "the individual most screwed by the American comic book industry, and the American comic book industry is the perfect distillation of all the corrupt and venal behavior inherent in unregulated capitalism." "The Internet," continues Kobek, "and the multinational conglomerates which rule it, have reduced everyone to the worst possible fate. We have become nothing more than comic book artists, churning out content for enormous monoliths that refuse to pay us the value of our work." There are few more apt descriptions of the world anti-copyright activists want.

ENCRYPTION AND ANONYMIZATION

Encryption is at the heart of a surprising amount of talk about digital politics. Both the "cypher" and "crypto" prefixes in the cypherpunk/crypto-anarchy movements derive from it ("cypher" is an alternative spelling of "cipher," which refers to the method by which a message has been obscured, and "crypto" comes from "cryptography," the study of ciphers). The early writings of this group focus on encryption to the point of obsession. Many of the purported successes of digital activist movements, especially the fight over the Clipper chip in the mid-1990s (Levy 1994), center on the practice. Many of the cypherpunks' early ideas about encryption seem more popular today than when they were first set down. The technical ideas and rights rhetoric that cypherpunks used to promote issues in digital culture have disseminated into popular, academic, and legal culture. However, they have been uncritically stripped of the political extremism that their originators saw as essential.

This move may seem surprising because the ties between "encryptionism"—a term I use to designate all those who promote encryption as a special and fundamental right, regardless of whether they explicitly endorse cypherpunk politics—and direct opposition to democracy and civil rights have been clear from the beginning. As early as 1996, leading computer scientist and network security expert Dorothy Denning noted how closely entwined these ideas were:

A few years ago, the phrase *crypto anarchy* was coined to suggest the impending arrival of a Brave New World in which governments, as we know them, have crumbled, disappeared, and been replaced by virtual communities of individuals doing as they wish without interference. Proponents argue that crypto anarchy is the inevitable—and highly desirable—outcome of the release of public key cryptography into the world. With this technology, they say, it will be impossible for governments to control information, compile dossiers, conduct wiretaps, regulate economic arrangements, and even collect taxes. Individuals will be liberated from coercion by their physical neighbors and by governments. This view has been argued recently by Tim May.

Behind the anarchists' vision is a belief that a guarantee of absolute privacy and anonymous transactions would make for a civil society based on a libertarian free market. (85)

Denning's essay was posted to the Cypherpunks mailing list and reprinted in Ludlow's volume of essays, *Crypto Anarchy, Cyberstates, and Pirate Utopias* (2001). However, despite (or perhaps because of) Denning's role as a professional in the computer science and information security communities, her voice has been relatively silenced in ongoing discussions of encryption. Although the views of ideologues like Tim May and Eric Hughes have been taken as authoritative, they are separated from the political architecture that underlies their ideas.

In this, encryption resembles the debates around the politics of cryptocurrency (Golumbia 2016). Cryptocurrency uses encryption in the blockchain software, but its name and origins in the cypherpunk community explain why it has become the default meaning of the stand-alone term "crypto," which used to refer to encryption. Both were developed by far-right thinkers as means to bypass or invalidate democracy. However, both cryptocurrency and encryption promoters who claim not to be part of the extreme right, assert that these technologies can be used to promote the political values of groups who are often diametrically opposed to those of cypherpunks. It is a mark of the strength of cyberlibertarianism that most of these non-far-right actors seem unaware of the political origins of these technologies.

It is not hard to understand why encryption and antidemocratic politics are so hospitable to each other. In 1997, encryption advocates described the importance of encryption technology as follows: "Encryption is an essential tool in providing security in the information age. Encryption is based on the use of mathematical procedures to scramble data so that it is extremely difficult—if not virtually impossible—for anyone other than authorized recipients to recover the original 'plaintext.' Properly implemented encryption allows sensitive information to be stored on insecure computers or transmitted across insecure networks. Only parties with the correct decryption 'key' (or keys) are able to recover the plaintext information" (Abelson et al. 1997, 5). Stated so plainly, it is clear how important encryption is to the operation of digital technology. We could not hope to conduct secure financial transactions, communicate about our health care, talk with family and friends about personal matters, or do much of anything electronically without some assurance that our communications cannot easily be observed and recorded without authorization.

But already this puts us in a situation unlike anything we've dealt with before at a society-wide level: the worry is that bad actors could obtain a wide range of data on many people, simultaneously, and deploy that data toward ends we do not want. We are used to our communications being private due to network designs that most of us have rarely considered. It is possible to open a person's postal box or use audio technology to "bug" their home or office, but such behavior is both unusual and requires a specific interest in targeting an individual or group of people. Moreover, the person doing the surveillance has been at risk of being caught themselves. The advent of digital technology has virtually reversed the situation. So much communications data are passed constantly over public networks and are observable at many points along the way. It is now easy for people who wish to do so to observe and even record a vast array of transactions without necessarily wanting to target specific individuals.

Yet this reversal in the availability of personal information has created an affective context that society was not prepared for. In earlier decades, it was generally understood that believing all of our communications were being surveilled was a form of paranoia. However, in the age of digital technology, this understanding must be reversed. Without significant protection, our communications *will certainly* be surveilled. Arguably we have yet to deal adequately with the psychological consequences of this shift. When we can no longer say it is the exception for us to be observed, but rather the rule, and that measures must be taken to avoid being seen by unwanted actors, we alter something fundamental about our social relations.

The diffuse paranoia that must haunt all of us is all too easily taken up by those for whom paranoia is not just an article of faith, but a particularly alluring entryway into conspiracy theory. Conspiratorial paranoia is characterized by the search for persecutory figures. They are seen as illicit authorities who exist to persecute us, regardless of their stated motivations.

Given the U.S. government's documented history of abusing its surveillance powers, it is understandable that this search for a persecutory figure lands on "the government." It is true that distrust of government is found across the political spectrum. However, in recent years, we have seen with uncanny and disturbing force how much antigovernment and antidemocratic rhetoric serves the right in particular.

Given this trend, it is notable that nearly all the encryptionist discourse is opposed to the government rather than other individuals and entities with an interest in compiling information about us. The state is posited as either entirely criminal or unavoidably engaged in malfeasance. Corporate power is often ignored in encryptionist discourse. In fact, encryptionists often explicitly invoke the freedom of corporations to operate outside of governmental regulation, a familiar theme in libertarian politics, under the heading of "innovation." Further, at the cypherpunk heart of encryptionism, we should not simply maintain a healthy distrust of government statements. Rather, we should understand that government is a malign force, and that being associated with government renders one incapable of making factual statements. This a priori judgment makes reasonable discussion impossible: any statement in favor of democratic oversight of technology is automatically false, and any opposition to it is likely true.

In 2015, a group of experts, including contributors to the 1997 report on encryption, produced a revised and updated document, "Keys under Doormats: Mandating Insecurity by Requiring Government Access to All Data and Communications" (Abelson et al. 2015). Speaking broadly, the document takes to have *proven* that it is impossible to build encrypted systems that allow for authorized access by legitimate actors. The reasoning is remarkably a priori. In the earlier document, which is more strident than the later version, the authors note that "many have suggested that the very notion of a pervasive government key recovery infrastructure runs counter to the basic principles of freedom and privacy in a democracy and that that alone is reason enough to avoid deploying such systems" (Abelson et al. 1997, 4). The "many" here can only refer to cypherpunks and others like them, as it is remarkably hard to find anyone else arguing that democratic governments should be unable to recover encrypted communications even with properly warranted access. Further, the view that digital communications should be beyond government access is a technological means for attacking the core of democracy.

While some of the signatories have overt cypherpunk associations, most portray themselves as politically moderate and have chosen not to engage in the kinds of far-right agitation familiar among cypherpunks. As such, both Abelson documents are particularly important artifacts for tracking cyber-libertarian politics. Despite their trappings, both documents are relentlessly political. They encode analysis of the shape and function of government within the language of network security. They hypostatize an invasive entity called "government" that will always misuse its powers, from which citizens will have no recourse, such as due process in the courts in the case of improperly gathered evidence. While magnifying the dangers of government, they fail to recognize the powers they are granting to other actors, including governments that refuse to follow the law.

Without going into great detail, it is important to understand what is a priori about the arguments made in both documents. The authors repeatedly emphasize the importance of encryption for user privacy, but fail to acknowledge that it comprises a set of real technologies that can be deployed in the world, tested, examined, and improved through iteration. They argue that "an exceptional access requirement overlaid on the traditional content surveillance will put the security of the content at risk. To the extent that capabilities exist to provide law enforcement exceptional access, they can be abused by others" (Abelson et al. 2015, 18). The substance of this argument is repeated endlessly in agitation campaigns by EFF, CDT, and others: that "weakening" encryption in any way, by providing a "key" makes the whole encrypted system impossibly insecure, rendering encryption virtually useless.

This is a curious argument on many levels. It pretends that the danger to users comes only from unwanted surveillance of our activities, and therefore we must have "perfect" encryption to block surveillance from everyone. Yet this overlooks the dangers posed by actors *not* interested in surveillance—such as the many scams and frauds perpetuated every day on the internet. That is before we get to the question of people taking advantage of unbreakable encryption to break the law, a problem that has exploded in digital technology, mitigated only by the fact that most encryption is not entirely unbreakable. On the contrary, bad actors are often able to gain unauthorized access to encrypted data through a variety of "social hacking" techniques that put them in the position of a user.

This "user" position is the obvious a priori aspect of the "Keys under Doormats" argument. To be useful to ordinary people, encrypted systems must be decoded at some point. This decryption is a constant process and a required feature of all widely used encryption systems, including those that Abelson's team use to justify calling attention to this issue. Banks and financial institutions provide users with unencrypted access to their own account information, typically through a password which, like all entry points into a system, can be hacked. Further, banks are expected to be able to recover the password or account information for users who lock themselves out. In fact, any regulated company in the United States is *required* to provide complete access to user account information and its own internal communications when faced with regulatory overview, such as during audits and SEC reviews, as well as civil and criminal proceedings. That is, the systems we use every day are *full* of keys. Whether through statute or technical operation, most of us rarely if ever find our data hacked. And when this does happen, laws typically require the provider to make users whole.

The authors of "Keys under Doormats," who are security experts, recognize this fact despite it often being overlooked by readers of the documents:

> Many corporations *already insist on escrowing keys* used to protect corporate data at rest (such as BitLocker on corporate laptops). So this is one field with an already deployed escrow "solution": a fraud investigator wanting access to a London rogue trader's laptop can simply get a law enforcement officer to serve a decryption notice on the bank's CEO. But still, many of the same problems arise. Suspects may use encryption software that does not have escrow capability, or may fail to escrow the key properly, or may claim they have forgotten the password, or may actually have forgotten it. The escrow authority may be in another jurisdiction, or may be a counterparty in litigation. In other words, what works tolerably well for corporate purposes or in a reasonably well-regulated industry in a single jurisdiction simply does not scale to a global ecosystem of highly diverse technologies, services, and legal systems. (Abelson et al. 2015, 20; emphasis added)

Whatever disaster will supposedly happen were "governments" provided with access to encrypted systems *should already be happening*. Yet it is not, at least not at scale. It is hard to imagine that if stories of such key escrow systems creating massive vulnerabilities were available, the authors would not have used them to support their argument. Thus their argument is abstract, despite it being about a real-world technology widely in use.

The authors propose a single global solution to the encryption problem as the approach governments demand, which is a strange approach. This may have been a reasonable way to understand what the controversial NSA Clipper chip might have been at an earlier stage of digital technological development. But it is notable that the authors provide no citations to show that this is in fact a demand of "global" law enforcement and democratic governments. To the contrary, they give an example of one such system working perfectly. The London bank's system already has an internal key escrow system. Therefore, when the fraud investigator has a warrant to see certain communications, the bank uses its own decryption abilities to respond to law enforcement. This is one way to satisfy the needs of the legal system. Yet the authors are so caught in their vision of an overarching "big government" that they overlook the real-world examples of corporations using encryption, just as democracies require. Their argument, taken to the extreme as advocates typically do, would reverse the situation and allow the corporation to conceal the fraudulent activities of the hypothetical broker in question.

Both Abelson documents are reasonable and thoughtful, putting forward a series of questions about balancing interests that should be at the forefront of all encryption systems and their legal oversight. They even acknowledge that these are the questions *already* being asked by governments, software vendors, and customers; and that by feeding the perception that there is some monumental "government" that wants uniform and ongoing access to all communications (not incidentally, of the sort whose plans Edward Snowden presented to the world; see chapter 2) they may be feeding the antigovernment and antidemocratic activism that lurk everywhere in digital discourse. Despite the relative nuance of these documents, public reception and reliance on them has been almost unanimous in establishing that "backdoors make us less secure." This has led to the belief that the proper state toward which technology should tend is complete governmental opacity of communications, which is essentially the same as having no government at all.

Although absolutely impenetrable encryption might seem to be enough to accomplish this goal, cypherpunks have long had a second tool in their arsenal: anonymization. The ability to be anonymous is another cherished value of digital evangelists. Here, too, they have an arsenal of pseudo-arguments used to bolster their position. The most common and disingenuous is to point at the pseudonymous *Federalist Papers*. The argument goes that because John Jay, James Madison, and Alexander Hamilton chose to publish their commentaries on the U.S. Constitution under assumed names, everyone in a democracy has an absolute right to act with some level of significant anonymity in an arbitrarily large number of social contexts. This is an example of "completely different and exactly the same" (Golumbia 2013), where the manifest differences between digital technology and earlier forms of media are at once embraced and denied.

Anonymity and encryption come together in the shape of Tor, the well-known tool originally developed by the U.S. Naval Research Laboratory. While the Tor system makes use of encryption technologies, it is primarily a system for anonymization. Here that means something more robust than making up a fake name for a social media account. As the Tor Project explains the technology:

> In the 1990s, the lack of security on the internet and its ability to be used for tracking and surveillance was becoming clear, and in 1995, David Goldschlag, Mike Reed, and Paul Syverson at the U.S. Naval Research Lab (NRL) asked themselves if there was a way to create internet connections that don't reveal who is talking to whom, even to someone monitoring the network. Their answer was to create and deploy the first research designs and prototypes of onion routing.
>
> The goal of onion routing was to have a way to use the internet with as much privacy as possible, and the idea was to route traffic through multiple servers and encrypt it each step of the way. This is still a simple explanation for how Tor works today. ("About Tor" n.d.)

Note that what the developers refer to as "privacy" here, as in most digital discourse (see chapter 6), goes well beyond privacy as that right has been defined in most human rights and legal regimes.

The Tor network is often misunderstood because it has at least two faces. This is obscured by the fact that in recent years, most users download a single package to use Tor, which enables both functions. The first function is the Tor network itself, the feature that hides the origins of network traffic. The second function, "Hidden Services" (which technically requires the first function), refers to websites hosted through the Tor network, so that the actual host and hosting location are not accessible on the open web. Although estimates vary, it is claimed that Hidden Services make up only a small part of Tor network traffic. To be clear: you can use Tor without using Hidden Services, but you can't use Hidden Services without using Tor.

Most people who use digital technology have heard of Tor because it provides access to the Dark Web, best-known for black markets in commodities like drugs and weapons. These Dark Web sites use Tor Hidden Services. The most famous of them was the original Silk Road, run by now-convicted drug trafficker Ross Ulbricht. The Silk Road's URL was something like silkroad7rn2puhj.onion, an address that did not use the ordinary Domain Name System used by regular websites and therefore would only resolve if a user were running Tor.

Most of the troubling activity on the Tor network takes place on the Hidden Services, at least according to critics, including Tor's ex-director Andrew Lewman (O'Neill 2017). Yet when advocates describe the benefits of Tor, they almost always fail to mention Hidden Services. The Tor Project describes itself as "an effective censorship circumvention tool, allowing its users to reach otherwise blocked destinations or content. Tor can also be used as a building block for software developers to create new communication tools with built-in privacy features," that "individuals use Tor to keep websites from tracking them and their family members, or to connect to news sites, instant messaging services, or the like when these are blocked by their local Internet providers," "for socially sensitive communication: chat rooms and web forums for rape and abuse survivors, or people with illnesses," and that "journalists use Tor to communicate more safely with whistleblowers and dissidents. Non-governmental organizations (NGOs) use Tor to allow their workers to connect to their home website while they're in a foreign country, without notifying everybody nearby that they're working with that organization" ("Tor Project").

All these uses of Tor involve the Tor network, but not Hidden Services. Although these methods anonymize network traffic, they do not inherently anonymize the user. If I use an encrypted messaging app over Tor, both the sender and receiver of the message know who I am, regardless of whether my identity is made clear in the technological infrastructure. When a user accesses a newspaper website that is censored in their country, anonymity refers to the ability of the government to determine that the access came from within their country, rather than the identity of the person viewing the website. It is less about the identity of the person taking any kind of deliberate action beyond reading that paper. Whatever we think of Tor's utility or politics for the above apparently positive uses, none of them requires the creation or maintenance of a separate, "dark" web. Yet when former Tor director Andrew Lewman stated that "95 percent of what we see on the onion sites and other dark net sites is just criminal activity" (O'Neill 2017), he was referring to Hidden Services, not the Tor network .

The maintenance of the Hidden Services network, much more than the network itself, is what gives the Tor Project the appearance of a deliberate, antigovernment political project. It certainly seems that Hidden Services exist largely to promote antigovernment and antidemocratic politics as well as the interests of organized crime. The Tor Project has never adequately explained why the Hidden Services are necessary. When defending them, the organization typically cites statistics about what a small percentage of Tor traffic goes to Hidden Services compared to the rest of the network. As such, it is hard to understand why they are being offered at all. The sites that Hidden Services offer beyond what is available on the open web are often criminal in nature. It is hard to shake the impression that the promoters of the Tor Project actively encourage such services. In some cases, it may certainly be that such sites are offered as "honeypots" in cooperation with law enforcement. More than a few prosecutions of child sexual abuse materials have proceeded this way.

Yet it is hard to imagine, given the prominence of antigovernment rhetoric in Tor's promotional material and among its community members, that it is a clandestine pro-government project. To the contrary, Tor manifests an uneasy and troubling relationship with governance. Tor is perhaps the purest expression in technology of internet freedom, rejecting out of hand the right of governments to oversee technology. The community around Tor particularly loves to mock and excoriate governments who try to regulate it. Since the Tor Project follows cyberlibertarian dogma in its fullest form, it construes all activity by individuals conducted with computers as "speech." Therefore, any regulation of technology can be understood as "censorship." It then asserts that everyone in the world has a "right" to use technology in any way they see fit, which transcends whatever legal infrastructure that person might live under, even by acknowledged consent. Although digital advocates are doing their best to advocate, there is no such right found in the Universal Declaration of Human Rights or in most world constitutions—and for good reason.

The Tor Project's developers, promoters, and supporters insist on the need for and acceptability of the technology by explicitly referencing human rights discourse. In response to a wave of negative press reports in 2014, Tor Project lead developer Roger Dingledine echoed the general paranoia of the Tor community in a piece called "Possible Upcoming Attempts to Disable the Tor Network." Dingledine uses the typical cyberlibertarian strategy of describing the most sympathetic, albeit hypothetical, user to legitimize the technology's existence: "The Tor network provides a safe haven from surveillance, censorship, and computer network exploitation for millions of people who live in repressive regimes, including human rights activists in countries such as Iran, Syria, and Russia. People use the Tor network every day to conduct their daily business without fear that their online activities and speech (Facebook posts, email, Twitter feeds) will be tracked and used against them later." This is expert rhetoric, but it is much less skilled in terms of providing hard data, conforming to logic, or exhibiting clear thinking. The cases for criminal and harmful uses of Tor are as evident as those of "human rights activists." Even easier to overlook is the fact that Dingledine positions the Tor organization, itself closely tied to the U.S. intelligence and diplomatic apparatus, as an entity that can accrue to itself the power to intervene in the affairs of sovereign governments as it sees fit. If we replace the ideologically loaded framing Dingledine uses with others less favorable—"Tor enables fascist networks to coordinate attacks on democratic governments without fear of detection"—which is no less logically plausible than Dingledine's version—we see the problems with private actors deciding for themselves when and if laws apply. This is no exaggeration: as is detailed in chapter 7, far-right terror networks are among the most persistent and innovative users of encrypted and anonymizing tools, specifically to organize antidemocratic violence.

Yet Dingledine and other Tor advocates insist that Tor must exist specifically *because* of core democratic values:

Every person has the right to privacy. This right is a foundation of a democratic society. For example, if Members of the British Parliament or US Congress cannot share ideas and opinions free of government spying, then they cannot remain independent from other branches of government. If journalists are unable to keep their sources confidential, then the ability of the press to check the power of the government is compromised. If human rights workers can't report evidence of possible crimes against humanity, it is impossible for other bodies to examine this evidence and to react. In the service of justice, we believe that the answer is to open up communication lines for everyone, securely and anonymously.

The Tor network provides online anonymity and privacy that allow freedom for everyone. Like freedom of speech, online privacy is a right for all. (2014)

This high-minded rhetoric sounds good, but it is turning the practice and theory of democracy on their heads. "Privacy" as Dingledine describes it has almost nothing in common with the right as it is understood in democratic polities. We need look no further than the attempted insurrection against the U.S. government on January 6, 2021, to see how the British Parliament and U.S. Congress cannot operate in the face of systems that make it impossible for them to track threats. If what he means by "government spying" is meant to indicate that Members of Parliament or members of Congress should be using Tor for their ordinary communications among themselves and their constituents, they would in many cases be violating open records laws that exist precisely because democracy is based not on "privacy" of governmental operations, but on their openness to examination by citizens.

I was involved in some of the press coverage of Tor at this time and asked Dingledine on the Tor Project blog what he meant by "privacy" in the above quote. I noted that despite his reference to its fundamental importance to democracy, "the 'right to privacy' does not mean what you assert it means here, at all, even in those jurisdictions that (unlike the US) have that right enshrined in law or constitution." Rather than answering the question directly, Dingledine replied:

Live in the world you want to live in. (Think of it as a corollary to "be the change you want to see in the world.")

We're not talking about any particular legal regime here. We're talking about basic human rights that humans worldwide have, regardless of particular laws or interpretations of laws.

I guess other people can say that it isn't true—that privacy isn't a universal human right—but we're going to keep saying that it is. (Dingledine 2014)

Thus, in a single exchange, Dingledine goes from saying that the very existence of a democracy depends on the "privacy" Tor provides, to stating that he does not care about or intend to refer to the legal infrastructure of the United States or any other country. Instead, he refers to a right outside the law, whose exercise can and does vitiate the law, and so much the worse for the law (and democracy) if it does. This is not democratic theory: it is "natural rights" political philosophy, one of the most common elements of far-right antidemocratic agitation, especially in our online age. While it is no surprise to see such politics cloak themselves in the language of democracy, it remains wholly antidemocratic.

NET NEUTRALITY

Routinely depicted as one of the most important civil rights issues of our age, "network neutrality" is an obvious site for cyberlibertarian activism in the United States. To call it bizarre would be a radical understatement. While some of the principles advanced by net neutrality activists may make sense and be preferable to alternatives, the fact remains that the vision articulated by those activists is almost entirely at odds with the facts on the ground. Net neutrality activism is best understood as tilting at windmills, inventing fictitious enemies and nightmare scenarios that have little to do with anything we can observe or that is even likely to happen. Further, the basic principle advanced by net neutrality activists is difficult to reconcile with the actual operation of digital technology. Like many cyberlibertarian causes, such as SOPA and PIPA, net neutrality posits a clear and morally righteous principle against a range of nefarious actors who want to "destroy freedom." However, the debate is hard to determine; to the extent that it can be, it is out of step with obvious facts. As early as 2011, the digital studies scholar Kevin Driscoll was already documenting the wide range of topics various actors described as NN (net neutrality), yet this remarkable polysemy has rarely been noted by the concept's advocates. The energy expended on net neutrality is disproportionate to any legible cause its advocates claim to pursue. Therefore, one of its main effects is to galvanize political support away from far clearer causes. It brings together a wide range of political actors as a kind of "digital bloc" whose outrage is all too easily channeled in other directions.

The term was coined by legal scholar and digital technology expert Tim Wu in two papers, "A Proposal for Network Neutrality" (2002) and "Network Neutrality, Broadband Discrimination" (2003). Wu's original concern, which has remained constant across twenty years of activism, was that home broadband operators—providers of physical internet access, typically referred to as internet service providers (ISPs)—might "restrict the use of their broadband networks in ways that distort the market for internet applications, home networking equipment and other markets of public value" (2002, 1). Written in conversation with others in the libertarian-leaning world of internet law at the time, including Lawrence Lessig and Mark Lemley (see Wu 2003, 141), both of Wu's early papers are explicit that their major concern is business competition: "the danger of harm to new application markets" (2002, 1) and "the public's interest in a competitive innovation environment centered on the Internet" (2003, 141); "the argument for network neutrality must be understood as a concrete expression of a system of belief about innovation" (2003, 145). Despite the rapid adoption of net neutrality as a principle to protect freedom of expression and democracy, Wu argues that the doctrine's primary purpose was to protect *businesses*. This highlights the strange political bedfellows characteristic of cyberlibertarian activism.

Wu's papers from the early 2000s largely distinguish among three categories of participants in digital networks: content providers (such as the *New York Times,* CNN, or individual bloggers), ISPs (such as Comcast or Verizon), and users (typically understood to be individuals). Wu proposes a "rule" that would "forbid broadband operators, absent a showing of harm, from restricting what users do with their Internet connection, while giving the operator general freedom to manage bandwidth consumption and other matters of local concern" (2003, 168). He introduces the term "discrimination" to describe how ISPs might manage content they provide to users. This arguably salts the discussion with a social justice flavor that Wu himself admits might be misleading: "discrimination among Internet applications is a different context" from discrimination according to criteria "such as race, sex, or national origin" (152).

While Wu may have had innocent reasons for introducing this terminology, it is hard not to see it as having had massively deforming effects on the entire discussion. It is not the case that choosing to provide better service to one content provider over another is a "different context" from race or gender discrimination: it is more accurate to say it is an entirely different meaning of the word "discrimination." This is not to say that it is welcome or unwelcome, but only that the question of whether Comcast slows down *World of Warcraft* users is a different question entirely from whether Black people are denied bank loans. While the two concepts can be related, such as in the hypothetical scenario where an ISP blocks access to sites promoting Black people's voting rights, on the surface they are distinct. Given the intensity of political discussions about racial and gender discrimination, another term might well have set us on a different course entirely.

Wu's papers lay out some of the complexities in network topology that existed even in his day, but these typically get lost in the discussion. For example, a user need not be an individual: it can be and often is a commercial entity. A content provider might also be a user and even an ISP. Indeed, one of the real fears that has motivated the whole network neutrality discussion is the fact that ISPs might themselves take more of an active role as content providers, and therefore favor their own content over those from other providers. In the following years, this complexity has only become more serious, as the notion that ISPs have direct influence over how users experience digital technology has been shown to be false. If anything, the discussion has not only doubled down on the simplistic characterizations of the network found in Wu's papers but also expanded or shifted the domain of his arguments to be far wider and far less clearly focused on competition and business innovation than he was originally. This is despite the fact that his arguments are problematic even at the level he places them, and become far more so when expanded in the direction of politics and civil rights.

Among the most troubling aspects of the NN "debate" is that it is disconnected from the facts. Few who have looked closely at the matter agree that there is much to be worried about regarding ISPs throttling or blocking user access to content. Indeed, and surprisingly given the heat of the debate, advocates have provided few concrete examples of such behavior, let alone practices that amounted to anything like a challenge to democracy. Even self-described NN activist Russell Newman, who provides a more-or-less comprehensive set of examples drawing on an earlier version of Karr (2021), cites as his most wide-ranging instance "Netflix or video conferencing aboard AT&T, Time Warner Cable, and Verizon . . . 'failing to provide enough capacity for this traffic to make it on to their networks in the first place'" (2019, 335). Yet providing enough bandwidth for video-heavy services clearly falls under the forms of "discrimination" that even the 2015 FCC Open Internet rules, to say nothing of 2010 UK Ofcom rules, explicitly *allow* if justified by usage considerations. Indeed, it is difficult to find a civil or human rights issue in the question of whether Netflix, ISPs, or consumers should pay for a data-heavy service, especially since the costs will likely be passed on to consumers regardless.

In a typical piece of NN agitation, the *Wall Street Journal* argued against the rollback of the 2015 Open Internet rules by noting that in the early 2010s, cell phone providers routinely offered tiered data service plans that sometimes included "zero rating" provisions for content from its own providers: for example, "AT&T Inc. gave paying customers unlimited usage of its own online video service DirecTV Now" (McKinnon and Knutson 2017). (The relationship of NN to internet provided over cellular networks is already complicated, and it has not always been clear that NN rules designed for ISPs also apply to cell service.) Plans like this "drew criticism from some net-neutrality advocates," and the "practice became so wide-spread that Obama administration regulators, in one of their final actions, sought to declare several plans illegal, including those offered by AT&T and Verizon." Yet the proposed regulation did not take hold, and such plans dwindled in popularity regardless. The reasoning is not hard to grasp: most people prefer plans that treat data equally, and the marketing language and facts about the plans became well-known. Provision of data over these networks is of course closely monitored by users and advocacy groups, and yet we hear few complaints about the kinds of internet-ending service-blocking NN advocates routinely scream about.

Sometimes, critics who are more familiar with the history of NN make claims that are closer to the facts in terms of what NN has actually meant as government regulation. In so doing, they have perhaps unintentionally demonstrated how distant these concerns are from what we typically understand as civil rights. For instance, *New York Times* reporter Keith Collins writes, "Many consumer advocates argued that once the rules were scrapped, broadband providers would begin selling the internet in bundles, not un-like cable television packages" (2018). But he fails to note that whether consumers like the way cable companies package their services is hardly an important civil rights cause. The American Library Association offers a similar assessment: "In a worst-case scenario, the internet could degrade into something similar to cable TV where you get priority access via the more expensive 'gold' subscriber plan vs. a lower level of access from the less expensive 'bronze' plan" (Bocher 2018). Again, such plans are the norm across many kinds of products and services and are rarely understood as matters of civil rights.

Activists across the country became incensed by the Trump administration FCC commissioner Ajit Pai's reversal of the 2015 FCC Open Internet order, which they *knew* would have a negative impact. Consider this sample of the many "news" and opinion pieces that explained exactly what would happen. A piece in *TechCrunch* declares that NN rules contain the "hunger these companies [ISPs] have had for the destruction of your right to a neutral internet"; "America may not have a dictatorship, but it now, if net neutrality is repealed, will have an oligopoly," explicitly confusing political sovereignty with corporate size and market sector dominance; "the future is darker than you think" because we may pay "$20 more for 'unlimited' access," which will lead to the United States becoming "less attractive to talent" from abroad (Gorodyansky 2017). Similarly, New York attorney general Eric T. Schneiderman said in a statement:

> The FCC's vote to rip apart net neutrality is a blow to New York consumers, and to everyone who cares about a free and open internet. The FCC just gave Big Telecom an early Christmas present, by giving internet service providers yet another way to put corporate profits over consumers. Today's rollback will give ISPs new ways to control what we see, what we do, and what we say online. That's a threat to the free exchange of ideas that's made the Internet a valuable asset in our democratic process.
>
> Today's new rule would enable ISPs to charge consumers more to access sites like Facebook and Twitter and give them the leverage to degrade high quality of video streaming until and unless somebody pays them more money. Even worse, today's vote would enable ISPs to favor certain viewpoints over others. (2017)

In an email to a *New York Times* reporter written after the formal repeal of the Open Internet rules, Democratic FCC member Jessica Rosenworcel stated that "internet service providers now have the power to block websites, throttle services and censor online content. They will have the right to discriminate and favor the internet traffic of those companies with whom they have pay-for-play arrangements and the right to consign all others to a slow and bumpy road" (Collins 2018). Two years later but still projecting into the future, a piece in the tech publication *OneZero* argued that "with no net neutrality rules, ISPs can also use their power as internet access gatekeepers to disadvantage companies they compete with. AT&T, for example, only hits users with costly and unnecessary bandwidth usage caps and overage fees if they use a competing service like Netflix—but not if they use AT&T's own streaming services" (Bode 2019).

All these statements use the language of civil rights in a general way, but then refer to specific economic concerns about costs for tiers of service that are not civil rights concerns. These concerns exist in many other sectors of media and communications, where they are rarely, if ever, framed as having anything to do with civil rights. Again, this is not to suggest that the repeal of the 2015 Open Internet order was correct. It is to note only the surprising disconnect between the language used to rally support for NN versus the concrete impact of the policies themselves.

Despite the enormous number of statements to this effect, the number of stories following up on what would seem an incredibly important question was surprisingly thin. Surprising, that is, unless one is attuned to this typical pattern in cyberlibertarian rhetoric and press coverage, where claims of doom and destruction are routinely issued yet retrospective fact-checking is virtually anathema. One telling exception was a piece by Zachary Mack (2019) in the tech magazine *The Verge,* in which he interviewed former FCC commissioner, law professor, and Public Knowledge cofounder Gigi Sohn, a reliable repeater of cyberlibertarian dogma.

Mack notes that even the conservative *National Review* stated that "the internet apocalypse didn't happen" but still asserts that "there's a lot of little things that did happen that aren't great." Sohn disagrees: "I don't think these are little things. I actually think they're very big things." She then offers three examples of changes due to the repeal of the FCC's Open Internet order: "Verizon throttling the Santa Clara Fire Department's broadband"; "T-Mobile, Sprint and AT&T were found to have sold the precise geolocation data of their customers"; and "a customer bought his own router for two hundred dollars and Frontier kept charging him ten dollars a month to rent it." Neither Mack nor Sohn notices that none of these things has anything to do with what the public understands NN to be, even though Sohn somehow attributes the selling of geolocation data to NN. The power to regulate such practices may well be present in the FCC's Open Internet order, but it isn't NN as typically defined. Not only that, these reflect broad industry practices that should be monitored or even abolished for other reasons. Worse, if Sohn's point is that the FCC regulates ISPs while nobody regulates the many platforms and data brokers that traffic in personal data, she is contributing to an interindustry battle between ISPs and platforms that has little to do with civil rights.

Nevertheless, claims about NN as a vital civil rights cause turn up again and again. In July 2021, the ACLU praised President Biden's request that FCC restore the 2015 Open Internet order, but then insisted that "net neutrality can't wait" because "the internet's anti-corporate censorship rules known as net neutrality" ensure that ISPs "cannot block or slow down users' access to internet content it disapproves of for business or political reasons" (Marlow 2021). The insertion of "political reasons" is especially telling. ACLU claims that "powerful ISPs like Verizon and Comcast have been free to do just that—and they have," but "do just that" refers not to restrictions of access to content for political reasons. Rather, the typically threadbare examples they offer refer to favoring or disfavoring content from Microsoft, Netflix, YouTube (aka Google), and the ISPs themselves. Like the other few post-hoc analyses, many of their examples are practices that the Open Internet order does not cover. None involves the blocking access to political information at all. The remaining examples come down to the same issue we have seen repeatedly: consumers may have to pay a little extra for unlimited access to video streaming platforms or certain audiovisual real-time communications services. As always, the strange implication is that by setting up shop as an ISP, a company should be compelled to provide all its customers with unlimited bandwidth at the highest available speed for an identical price.

While this may well be one reasonable approach to service pricing, it is not obviously more or less in line with civil rights than many other pricing plans, nor are such pricing plans in other media such as cable and specific platform offerings typically discussed as civil rights issues. Further, the bottom line always implies that some very large corporations, especially Google, Facebook, and Netflix, should be able to demand any amount of bandwidth from ISPs and pass along the costs of that usage to either ISPs or consumers. While consumers will surely pay that price in the end, it is odd to look at this complex network diagram and decide that civil or human rights depend on where those costs are explicitly borne. It is a perverse incentive for Netflix to have the power to issue video in ever higher definition while being able to force Verizon to pay for it, according to the law.

Despite the fact that numerous agencies and analysts, including Wu himself, have long clarified that NN is fundamentally about markets and "innovation," many of the digital rights organizations and others allied with them continue to insist that NN is about the phantom problem that agitators have insisted on from the beginning. A *Wired* guide published in 2020 reads, "Net neutrality is the idea that internet service providers like Comcast and Verizon should treat all content flowing through their cables and cell towers equally. That means they shouldn't be able to slide some data into 'fast lanes' while blocking or otherwise discriminating against other material. In other words, these companies shouldn't be able to block you from accessing a service like Skype, or slow down Netflix or Hulu, in order to encourage you to keep your cable package or buy a different video-streaming service" (Finley). As of 2022, EFF continues to use the following as the first paragraph of its information on NN: "Network neutrality—the idea that Internet service providers (ISPs) should treat all data that travels over their networks fairly, without improper discrimination in favor of particular apps, sites or services—is a principle that must be upheld to protect the future of our open Internet. It's a principle that's faced many threats over the years, such as ISPs forging packets to tamper with certain kinds of traffic or slowing down or even outright blocking protocols or applications" (Electronic Frontier Foundation n.d.). ACLU's most recent update, dated December 2017, offers a similar description on its "What Is Net Neutrality?" page: "What you can see on the internet, along with the quality of your connection, are at risk of falling victim to the profit-seeking whims of powerful telecommunications giants. If the FCC has its way, those companies could disfavor controversial viewpoints or smaller websites and favor the content providers who have the money to pay for better access." Unsurprisingly, Fight for the Future, one of the main agitators in NN activism, continues to write on its main page that "NN is the basic principle that ensures no one can block our access to websites, throttle our internet speeds, or impose unfair fees" (n.d.).

It is not surprising that charities and lobbying organizations that rely on member contributions reduce their activist causes to slogans that are easily grasped by the public. This pattern is by no means exclusive to digital activism. However, given the putative relationship of the internet as a provider of information and the explicit attachment of organizations like ACLU, EFF, and Fight for the Future to what they construe as "rights," it is disconcerting to have them continue to promulgate a story about both law and the nature of the network itself that has long been proven false. This narrative serves as a placard for causes very different from what the label suggests, and has effects that do not in any obvious ways relate to the values these organizations say they stand for. Further, the reluctance of these organizations to reflect on the basic facts that many specialists in the area repeatedly expose—that NN names essentially one side of an industry-internal debate about who should bear the costs of providing various services—suggests that they recognize and benefit from the general public misinformation about the nature of the NN debate "proper."

Russell A. Newman (2019) describes with great frustration his own participation in NN policy development during the 2010s and how NN itself became a "wrecking ball" in which a "debate not rooted in facts or modern liberal discourse even while referring to their existence and terms; [and] the long-constructed supporting institutions of liberalism itself were turned against themselves with a ferocity that took even the most world-weary observers by surprise" (2019, 405). Newman (at least in his earlier phases) and other left-leaning activists like Robert McChesney and others at the Free Press Foundation believed the NN debate to be about what media scholars Victor Pickard and David Elliot Berman call "a more democratic internet" (2019, 105). Pickard and Berman tie this idea to public policy notions that are directly linked to political considerations, especially the fairness doctrine (120). Newman refers throughout his book to "open access" and the "open internet" as better names for the policy he recommends, which he suggests entails "a reversal of the commercial operation of the internet itself" (2019, 448). Of course, both "open access" and "open internet" as phrases are subject to the same terminological diversions that haunt the NN debate. Newman claims that with "open access" it "was not the case" that the "hypercommercialism" of the internet was "swept under the rug" (26). While "open access" was certainly used by some activists in this regard, it was also employed by others in various ways. Even if the term were more widely used, it is not at all clear how that would avoid the same problem.

As Newman notes, the rules we currently refer to as net neutrality are formally called Open Internet rules by the FCC (see FCC 2015).

None of them takes on the more problematic original move: how is it that "net neutrality," a term coined to increase "innovation and competition" and whose entire ethical–political charge might at best be put on the same order as antitrust actions, can have captured the popular imagination to mean something entirely different, to which the public and activists cling as if something incredibly important hangs on it, and indeed where vast numbers of agitators can be harnessed to "save the internet" from a danger it does not face, in the name of a policy that will not be mooted, let alone realized?

Net neutrality is an especially interesting issue in digital politics. In contrast to many other questions addressed in this book, opponents of NN tend to come from the political right (and ISPs) and its supporters come from the progressive or centrist left and major technology corporations. But NN does not provide an exception to cyberlibertarian principles. Instead, it shows the especially troubling "liberal" face, in which not just the language but the passion and energy of people genuinely devoted to civil rights are turned toward advocating for something that, in the words of two especially thoughtful journalists, "isn't necessarily even about neutrality, at least not in the way it sometimes seems. Instead, we're sussing out where innovation begins and what government should do to encourage it" (Madrigal and LaFrance 2014). That is, NN becomes a kind of deregulatory regulation whose main purpose is to ensure "innovation," which is not at all what well-meaning civil rights activists appear to think it's about, but is exactly the reconstruction of civil rights promoted by right-wing free market ideologues.

CHAPTER 6

Political Myths

ew sites are more obvious for observing cyberlibertarianism in action than the political sphere, broadly defined. This includes the nature and form of government, as well as popular participation in government. Cyberlibertarian discourse is characterized by the remarkable certainty of digital utopians that digital technology not only has political effects, but also radically reforms existing governmental structures in democratic directions and realizes the vision of those existing structures. Digital democracy is said to seek the same goals as our democratic systems, but in ways both unavailable to and unforeseeable by prior generations. When reading the most strident of these writers, it is difficult to understand how democracy ever emerged as a political form without the liberating power of the technology we have today.

Politics is one area where the interestedness of digital utopians is most evident. The loudest voices who advocate for the beneficial effects of digitization on politics often speak passionately, directly, and stridently about matters in which they have never before expressed any interest. When Clay Shirky, Jeff Jarvis, and others first wrote about social media's role played in political uprisings in Iran (then called the "Twitter Revolution") and later in the Arab Spring (see Guesmi 2021 for a retrospective view of these claims), it appeared to be the first time they had ever written anywhere about the Middle East. The area became interesting because there was now something to say about the "digital" in it. After the Twitter Revolution failed to result in a change in the political leadership and structure of the state, Iran ceased to be of interest to digital utopians. As a result, these writers have rarely, if ever, written about it again. Nevertheless, among the digerati, cyberlibertarian pronouncements about Twitter revolutions and the like are taken as seriously, perhaps more so, than area and political experts who are actually paying attention to Iran.

The same can be said of much of the propaganda about the role of the digital in the so-called Arab Spring. The area is not well understood by the most vocal advocates for the transformative effects of the digital. To the contrary, they pay careful attention to what they see as the inevitable effects of digitization. Their knowledge of the details of the political events they celebrate is limited, perhaps even nonexistent. Many continue to refer to the effects of social media on the Arab Spring in countries where the results of the events are almost as bad as, and possibly worse than, the authoritarian regimes that were displaced by protests. Thus the cyberlibertarian position emerges as a bizarre form of special pleading. If something "we" deem to be "good" happens, then we should look for the ways social media may have caused the "good" event to happen. If something "bad" happens, not only do we not look for social media's causal roles—in general, "we" aren't interested in those events at all, or at best we see them as a "failure" that followed the "success" made possible by digitization.

Cyberlibertarian rhetoric about the effects of the digital on politics is misleading, premature, and interested; this would be reason enough for concern. But it is also implicated in larger political movements of which participants seem almost entirely unaware. In the name of abstract notions of "freedom" and "democracy," the most ardent cyberlibertarian writings on politics both local and domestic work to blind populations to the free-market fundamentalism that quietly accompanies almost all promotion of digital technology. In the name of offering democracy and freedom to "developing nations," digital utopians demand that "we" recognize their "human right" to computers, cell phones, and a "free and open" internet. This is done without considering the meaning of these instruments on the ground and the impact they will have on people whose economic status or cultural norms are not suited to the affordances and consequences of such tools. The close ties between "freedom of speech" tools and organizations, on the one hand, and relatively conservative, Western-based organizations and Western governments—for example, the U.S. State Department is one of the chief advocates for "internet freedom"—points at how such developments make other countries "more democratic" by making their resources (human, natural, and industrial) available for exploitation by capital.

DEMOCRATIZATION

The fundamental political claim made for digital technology is that it *democratizes*. Few truths seem so unassailable. Yet as with so much else in cyberlibertarian discourse, few slogans are harder to translate into sensible ideas that can withstand ordinary levels of scrutiny. In pre-internet usage, especially in the mid-twentieth century, the word "democratization" had a fairly specific meaning: the movement of political regimes toward more democratic forms (pace the obvious nuance needed to define "democracy" as a political system to begin with). The word was especially prominent in development discourse; it is easy to find documents from the United Nations and global development bodies discussing the desirability of "democratization" of states in Africa and South America, for example (Whitehead 2002; "Democratization"). These documents looked at fundamental issues of political organization, such as the availability and fairness of voting procedures, the stability of institutions, access to education, and various civil rights. Such discourses have been the subject of much criticism and analysis, across the political spectrum. This is due to the complexities of development and the question of what democracy means, particularly in countries that do not have long traditions of discussion and debate on the subject.

As used in digital discourse, though, "democratization" has taken on an entirely different set of meanings, whose relationship with this earlier meaning is both tenuous and problematic. We are told with little hesitation that it would be desirable and socially productive to "democratize" almost every institution and civil society sector we might name, including information, knowledge, finance, the professions, money, energy, and commerce of all sorts. The meaning of "democratize" in these discourses may seem relatively clear, and by stipulation not overtly political. The idea is that the benefits of these parts of society have exclusively been enjoyed by segments of the population limited by geography or access to political or economic power. This group is often disparaged as an "elite," a blurry amalgam of unearned social status, such as legacy admissions to universities, and directly earned accomplishments, such as medical or legal licensure. So the internet, and especially the web, is said to "democratize" knowledge. Providers like Google and Wikipedia make information easily available to people who would have otherwise had to seek it out in piecemeal and often haphazard fashion, if they could access it at all.

For example, consider the claims of François Chollet, a Google senior staff engineer who specializes in artificial intelligence (AI). Asked in 2016 "Why is it important to democratize machine learning?" Chollet answers, in part: "If we believe that AI has a high return on investment, then democratizing AI is simply the rational strategy. AI is about to create a fantastic amount of opportunities, and these opportunities should not be reserved to Ivy League grads, or to people born in the US. They should be open to all." So here "democratize" appears to mean "distribute widely across many members of society." Yet beyond that, "democratize machine learning" remains opaque. It is a powerful slogan, but what is it describing? It sounds as if Chollet simply means "market availability." If we substitute a consumer product like "smartphones" for machine learning (ML) in this case, it becomes difficult to understand why the word "democratize" has any other meaning than that; it seems nearly synonymous with "affordability."

Chollet goes on to provide a second reason that "democratizing machine learning" is desirable:

> The other reason I see is perhaps more subtle: we should make AI accessible for the sake of social and economic stability. In the near future, ML and AI will automate many jobs, and much of the value created by AI will accrue to those who develop it (though overall the dynamics of the free market will ensure that everyone will end up benefiting to some extent). One way to counter-balance this is to make value creation through AI as broadly available as possible, thus making economic control more distributed and preventing a potentially dangerous centralization of power. If everyone can use AI to solve the problems that they have, then AI becomes a tool that empowers individuals. If using AI requires contracting a specialized company (that will most likely own your data), then AI becomes a tool for the centralization and consolidation of power.

Here we find a full flowering of cyberlibertarian rhetoric, which lacks almost any substance. Even if it is true that AI and ML will "automate many jobs," a proposition that haunts digital discourse and that many have raised serious doubts about (e.g., Pasquale 2020), it is not clear how making ML "as broadly available as possible" could have any impact on "centralization of power." Even in 2016, consumers had access to ML and other AI techniques, which were widely available in Google's search algorithms, many smartphone apps, and beyond. While it is true that consumers may not be able to manipulate these algorithms directly, it is unclear what benefit there would be in doing so to "empower" anyone, especially if major technology players like Google have the economic power to gather any real loci of power that threaten their own. It is important to note that Chollet is by no means a right-wing actor. He seems genuinely to believe that "democratizing AI" is a good political thing. Yet he falls into the typical pattern of deploying boilerplate cyberlibertarian rhetoric, in the nominal interests of individual freedom, to support the interest of one of the world's most powerful companies. As Dorothea Baur, an AI tech ethicist, writes, any "link between 'making AI accessible to as many people as possible' and democracy" simply "doesn't exist" (2020).

A slightly narrower instance of "democratization" is found in "democratizing journalism": the idea of "a radically 'democratized' media, decentralized, participative, and personally emancipating" (Carr 2018); or put differently, a "decentralized, multimedia communication network that would encourage the development of a 'democratic personality'" (Carr 2018, quoting Turner 2018). Given the long-standing tie between journalism and democratic theory, the stakes of "democratizing" discourse should be clearer. Surely we would only want to "democratize journalism" if it was no worse than what it replaces or augments. Indeed it is hard to imagine a reason for "democratizing journalism" other than improving democracy and journalism's well-understood functions within it. Again from Carr: "The founders of companies like Google and Facebook, Twitter and Reddit, promoted their networks as tools for overthrowing mass-media 'gatekeepers' and giving individuals control over the exchange of information. They promised, as Turner writes, that social media would 'allow us to present our authentic selves to one another' and connect those diverse selves into a more harmonious, pluralistic, and democratic society" (2018, quoting Turner 2018).

Yet, Carr continues, "the democratization of media produced not harmony and pluralism but fractiousness and propaganda, and the political energies it unleashed felt more autocratic than democratic." That is, in a familiar pattern, the promotion of technological "democratization" not only has, as Baur (2020) rightly says, "nothing to do with equality in a democratic sense"—that is, democracy—but also uses the language of democracy to oppose democracy. The assumption—far too closely echoing the sentiments of right-wing propagandists like Alex Jones—that the "mainstream media" is a "gatekeeper" that wants to keep the truth from citizens, while participatory "journalism" is somehow free from self-interest and bias, turns hundreds of years of institution-building on their heads.

It is no accident that the internet is typically held responsible for some of the most destructive practical effects on journalism worldwide. This is partly due to conspiratorial disparagement of institutions of journalism as "elites" and "gatekeepeers," which in part distracts from considering technology providers themselves as massively powerful "gatekeepers" (Hindman 2009, 38–57). The internet has also diverted the revenue streams that once made newspapers and magazines sound businesses in the United States (Stoller 2019; United Nations 2022; Weber 2014). During this series of crushing blows to journalism, digital promoters—frequently with significant self-interest, but just as often full of their own ignorance and ego— told us that burning journalism to the ground would produce better and more "democratic" journalism. Those who pushed back on this unlikely and fact-resistant narrative were dismissed with the kind of bullying tactics familiar across cyberlibertarian promotion. As Carr writes, again echoing Turner, "Just as we failed to see that democratization could subvert democracy, we may have overlooked the strengths of the mass-media news organization in protecting democracy. Professional gatekeepers have their flaws— they can narrow the range of views presented to the public, and they can stifle voices that should be heard—yet through the exercise of their professionalism they also temper the uglier tendencies of human nature." Yet Carr also observes that Turner's is one of the few voices in the 2018 collection he is reviewing, *Trump and the Media* (Boczkowski and Papacharissi 2018), to derive the obvious lesson: "What democracy needs first and foremost is not more personalized modes of mediated expression [but rather] a renewed engagement with the rule of law and with the institutions that embody it" (Turner 2018).

As a rule, "democratization" appears to mean tearing apart institutions, regardless of their nominal functions, including institutions whose purpose is to promote or even embody democracy. Thus the "democratization of knowledge" slips readily into questioning the idea of knowledge and the institutions established to develop and promote it, particularly the idea that one needs to study and work in a given area for a sustained period of time to speak about it with authority. It is hard to see how democracy is promoted when Wikipedia, which is rapidly becoming the world's most important information repository, actively resists subject-area experts who provide what they consider to be accurate information about their subjects. Instead, this desire is derided as "elitism" and "gatekeeping," typical terms of cyberlibertarian derision.

In a familiar dynamic, Wikipedians' claims of "democratized" expertise fall flat when it comes to the one area over which they feel power and dominance: Wikipedia itself. Some of the most vicious battles on Wikipedia have occurred historically when subject-area experts have run into Wikipedia's complex and arcane editing rules. The vicious condescension these editors frequently display toward experts reveals the authoritarian heart pumping behind internet faux democratization. What is at stake is not the radical distribution of expertise but the negation of *some* people's expertise, at the expense of those who identify with the digital revolution, who have appointed themselves the "real" experts over the "elite" experts who got there via institutional and social accomplishment.

The closer one gets to direct political engagement, the more discourses of "democratization" reveal themselves to be the inverse of what they seem. Internet pundits envision a "democratized" world where central social actors like doctors, lawyers, and teachers will be replaced by a "wisdom of crowds," which repeatedly turns into a technocratic elite with even thinner claims to authority than the experts they have displaced. These problems were fully on display during the Covid-19 pandemic, when wave after wave of digital evangelists—notably including tech investor Balaji Srinivasan—offered contrary "wisdom" that veered between "reasonable" if overstated skepticism about public health issues to outright conspiracy theory. "One story of a suspected Covid-19 opportunist," writes a journalist in *Wired*, "involves Aaron Ginn, a Silicon Valley technologist whose five minutes of fame arrived in March after he wrote a contrarian essay proposing that evidence didn't support the 'hysteria' over the consequences of the pandemic, that the problem might be sorta bad, but not really, really bad. Ginn flaunted some unusual credentials in support of his authority on the matter: a talent for making products go viral. 'I'm quite experienced at understanding virality, how things grow, and data,' he wrote" (Ogbunu 2020). The view that expertise in digital technology is not only equivalent to expertise in public health, but trumps it, proceeds directly from the cyberlibertarian perspective that expertise must be "democratized." However, "democratization" does not mean that anyone can become a public health expert through education and professional accreditation, but rather that such expertise is the problem itself.

When we turn to cryptocurrency and blockchain, the absurdity of democratization reaches its apotheosis and, along the way, reveals its deepest commitments. Blockchain discourse is replete with claims of "democratization." This is odd given the remarkable hostility toward democratic governance that features prominently in that discourse, often from the same people (Golumbia 2016). Cryptocurrency and Bitcoin promoters insist that their products will "democratize money," "democratize finance," and "democratize capital." These ideas are ludicrous when examined for coherence (Golumbia 2020a, 2020b), with "democratize" implying exemption from government regulations, especially those of democratic governments.

It should be no surprise that a common trope in blockchain discourse is that the technology "democratizes democracy"—sometimes through blockchain voting technology (yet another of blockchain's purported use cases that fails conceptually and has never been made to work in practice; see Gerard 2017; Madore 2017), and sometimes for "government transparency" that is guaranteed by the "trust" proponents say will be created by blockchain applications (Ogundeji 2017). Sometimes the claims become even more florid, as when a lawyer and self-described "cryptocurrency millionaire" Jeffrey Berns, CEO of Blockchains, "a company with no history," purchased "an enormous plot of land in the Nevada desert—bigger than nearby Reno . . . for $170 million in cash" (Popper 2018). "Drawn to Nevada by its tax benefits, including its lack of income tax," Berns claims he bought the land in Storey County to build "what he calls a 'distributed collective entity'" that would "operate on a blockchain where everyone's ownership rights and voting powers will be recorded on a digital wallet"—though he "acknowledged that all this is way beyond what blockchains have actually accomplished." Replete with artists' renderings of futuristic-looking cities, the plan depends on the Nevada governor to help create "innovation zones" where, despite Berns's declaration that he is "not anti-government," he aims to "democratize democracy" (Nevett 2021). In these zones, "residents would manage most of their affairs on blockchain applications," although "many of the applications needed for the city have not been developed." Even in business-friendly Nevada, "the elected leaders of Storey County voted to oppose the formation of a 'separatist' government on land owned by Blockchains." That is, on the ground, members of a democratic government saw technology promoters promising "more democracy" but meaning something closer to no democracy at all.

Matters get even worse when we look into digital discourse about democracy as a form of government. Despite talk of "democratization," many use the language of democracy against itself and reject democracy as a form of government. It is a paradoxical element in libertarian discourse that democracies are undemocratic, and that some other form of anti-governance would be democratic in some sense of individual freedom and absence of rules. WikiLeaks comes to mind. Julian Assange claims to want to improve governance via transparency, but over time his profound animus for democracy has become clearer and clearer. This is evident in his own organization, which is run in a profoundly autocratic fashion, as well as in his attitudes toward existing world democracies, which he typically describes only with loathing. Additionally, Assange supports authoritarian regimes such as Russia (see chapter 7).

When taken to its extreme, the discourse of democratization is not only premature or misguided but also actively deceptive. This becomes clear when we remember that the central tenet of cyberlibertarianism is that governments must not regulate the internet. According to most extant definitions of "democracy," democratic institutions, including governmental institutions, are instruments for the realization of democratic politics. The damaging and paradoxical result of these discourses is that for many proponents of "democratization," digital technology has made democracy itself, as ordinarily understood, anathema. When they refer to "democratization," they are advocating for bypassing or eliminating democracy, as most of us would understand the term.

The discourse of digital democratization is troubling in another critical way: it helps to frame discussions around the question "How much does the internet help to spread democracy?" This keeps off the table another serious and related question: "Does digital technology *hurt* democracy?" Of course, if we could collect and enumerate all of the effects of digital technology on politics, we would find many ways in which it both helps and hurts democracy. But if we want to ask on balance whether digital technology is good for democracy, and then more nuanced questions about which aspects of technology are good or bad for democracy, we find ourselves outside the "democratization" framing promoted so heavily by digital advocates.

Reasonable commentators have long understood that the promises of digital technology to democratize were both self-interested and often directly hostile to democracy itself (see, e.g., Ferdinand 2000; Jenkins and Thorburn 2003; Dahlberg and Siapera 2007). Despite being widely varied in methodology and overall political orientation, as a group they provide profound reason to be at best skeptical of claims that digital technology has or will contribute positively to democracy. There are many reasons to worry that its corrosive effects are significant. These analyses precede the worldwide rise in authoritarianism and protofascism that became evident in the mid-to-late 2010s. It is hard to see them as anything but too cautious. Even studies sympathetic to democratization claims (e.g., Grofman, Treschel, and Franklin 2014) note that positive effects on democratic engagement (itself a more narrowly tailored claim than democratization full stop) are at best small in size. Such works also argue that positive effects appear most legible in phenomena like online and offline protest, without carefully interrogating the question of whether the antidemocratic nature of so much social media–fueled protest should count as democratization in any sense that democracy advocates would welcome.

The editors, all political scientists, of the 2021 volume *Digital Technology and Democratic Theory* (Bernholz, Landemore, and Reich 2021) rightly note that "what is needed is an avoidance of digital utopianism and dystopianism, and a more sober, long-term, assessment" (3). Yet this casting of exploration of negative effects as "dystopian" suggests that the game has already been given up to cyberlibertarian framing. So does their offhand but characteristic assertion that the Arab Spring "would not have been possible without social media" (1). Local experts now generally reject this claim, or even see it in reverse, meaning that social media benefited authoritarian power more than it did democratic movements (Guesmi 2021). While many of its essays are strong, it is hard to overlook the fact that the collection almost entirely avoids discussion of fascism, white supremacy, anti-Semitism, anti-Black racism, or any of the other profoundly antidemocratic political formations whose contemporary proliferation seem directly tied to digital technology. Instead, the book typically favors more ameliorative terms like "polarization" and "disinformation" that are frequently favored by the loudest voices in digital rights spaces.

Despite the clarity with which Lincoln Dahlberg (2001, 2007) has noted the details of various proposals and the kinds of evidence necessary to show that digital technology is an important contributor to democracy, and not-withstanding the shocking evidence in recent years of technology's close entanglement with far-right politics, discussion of digital politics cling to the notion of democracy proceeding as if algorithmically from the pro-liferation of computing technology. Matthew Hindman, in *The Myth of Digital Democracy* (2009), demonstrated that "online audience concentra-tion equals or exceeds that found in most traditional media" (17), that "normative debates about the Internet have gotten ahead of the evidence" (18), and that focus is needed on the influence of "powerful hierarchies shaping a medium that continues to be celebrated for its openness." Yet the myth of "democratization" continues to hold as much, perhaps more, sway than it has for decades.

DECENTRALIZATION

Like its close kin, democratization, "decentralization" is a core term of art in cyberlibertarian discourse. Unlike democratization, decentralization lacks a clear political referent to anchor it. Instead, decentralization relies on a spatial metaphor whose overall import is not immediately apparent. While anyone who prefers democracy will likely think democratization is a good thing, it is not clear who should inherently prefer decentralization over centralization. Yet preference is almost uniformly taken as given. As Nathan Schneider puts it, "The promise to decentralize *x*—or everything—is as ubiquitous in the heady realm of blockchain-based technology as the prom-ise to 'disrupt' has been among those seeking venture-capital investment in Silicon Valley," despite the fact that "this decentralizing enthusiasm has rarely heeded the most cogent methodological proposals" (2019, 266).

Langdon Winner devotes a short chapter to decentralization in his 1986 volume *The Whale and the Reactor,* under the hopeful title "Decentralization Clarified." Despite Winner's hopes to have clarified the discussion around what was already a widely deployed term in the 1980s, few writers on the topic appear to have consulted, much less followed, his wise inquiry. Despite the ease with which antidemocratic actors have paradoxically repurposed "democratization" into support for their own efforts, decentralization begins from a syncretic political base that may be even more troubling. As Winner notes, "The call for decentralization has been a crucial theme among activ-ists seeking an appropriate technology. Similar notions are prominently

featured in recent attempts to advance the cause of participatory democracy"
(85), where the activists he mentions are explicitly on the left. Yet "spokes-
men of both the far Left and the far Right include plans for decentralization
in their lists of desirable political goals, although they have much different
institutional targets in mind." Decentralization, more than democratization, frames a discursive field where the overall politics of our goals may be
entirely opaque. This is especially true when we simply assume they are
what we want because they are "decentralized."

As Winner rightly notes, decentralization "is one of the foggiest, most
often abused concepts in political language," a point echoed and expanded
on by other commentators in more recent literature (e.g., Schneider 2019).
The word seems to rely on space or place for its literal meaning, yet "geo-
metrical centers as such, the centers of circles or parcels of land, are not at
issue. The meaning of 'center' in question is usually that of a geographical
or institutional place in which a particular kind of activity or influence is
concentrated" (Winner 1986, 86). Looking across a variety of institutions,
Winner suggests that we ask questions like "How many centers are there?
Where are they located? How much power do they possess? How much
cultural diversity and vitality do they exhibit?" With regard to political and
social power, Winner writes, "Disputes about centralization and decentralization frequently hinge on the issue of who has how much social, economic,
or political power and whether or not the exercise of such power is legitimate. Advocates of centralization often point to advantages of efficiency
and superior control that may come from placing power in relatively few
hands. In contrast, decentralists argue that from a practical and moral point
of view, power is best used when it is widely dispersed" (87). Even in Winner's dedicated leftist approach to the politics of technology, we can see the
marks of anarchism. This relationship to other politics is never as easily
specifiable as its advocates would like it to be, as demonstrated by the explosion in varieties of rightist anarchism (especially crypto-anarchism and
the closely allied anarcho-capitalism).

Winner is largely right that "historically speaking, those who have chosen
to use the term 'decentralization' to represent a positive social goal, rather
than as a neutral descriptive term, have been partisans of certain factions
within the political Left" (89), citing the anarchists Murray Bookchin and
Peter Kropotkin. However, it is worth considering whether these discourses
themselves play a role in opening the self-described left to the right. This

is especially true since virtually all the gains made by progressive actors in the past two centuries, along axes like "civil rights" and "human rights," have been those implemented and, more important, made long-standing by democratically elected governments. Thus, the anarchist insistence that government be entirely or largely abolished cannot help but at least ask the question of how ending Social Security, Medicare, and Medicaid in the United States or the National Health Service in Great Britain might *better* realize the goals of those programs than we would by leaving them intact.

It should be no surprise that decentralization has been taken up as a keyword that realizes the goals of antigovernment activists on the right and far right. Many invocations of the neutral value of "open" in the context of digital technology hark back to the writings of both Hayek (see chapter 2), for whom "centralized planning" referred to communism, socialism, and even fascism; and Hayek's contemporary and in some ways rival Karl Popper, whose promulgation of an "open society" mirrors Hayek's disdain for "centralization" (Tkacz 2015). Although Winner is correct to note the prevalence of decentralization in left political discourse, the pervasive influence of neoliberal theory, especially through its rightist exemplars, requires particular attention. (For more on the history of right-wing neoliberalism, see Mirowski 2013; Mirowski and Plehwe 2009. For more on the function of neoliberalism in right and left politics, see Golumbia 2016.)

As Nathaniel Tkacz explains in detail, much of the foundational theory of digital technology is derived from a relatively decontextualized reading of Hayek. For example, Wikipedia founder Jimmy Wales relied on Hayek's "Use of Knowledge in Society" (1945) in his plans for the open encyclopedia. While Hayek's explicit targets in *The Road to Serfdom* are the totalitarianisms of communism and fascism, nascent in that work is the idea that government itself is "centralized" and that "any attempt at centralized planning (i.e., socialism, communism, fascism) which is founded on exactly the assumption that what is best for all society is directly knowable, is likely to produce bad decisions that only satisfy a small group. For Hayek, giving one group the ability to make decisions for the whole results in the overall reduction of liberty and the advent of totalitarianism" (Tkacz 2012, 389–90). Tkacz rightly quotes from Hayek's *Road to Serfdom:* "It is only as the factors which have to be taken into account become so numerous that it is impossible to gain a synoptic view of them, that decentralisation becomes imperative. . . . Decentralisation has become necessary because nobody can consciously balance all the considerations bearing on the decisions of so many individuals, the co-ordination can clearly not be affected by 'conscious control,' but only by arrangements which convey to each agent the information he must possess in order effectively to adjust his decisions to those of others" ([1944] 2001, 51). Thus, as Tkacz, Mirowski, and others have noted, the only non-centralized form of political power becomes the market.

In its deployment as a cyberlibertarian keyword, "decentralized" functions so well because it is vague and almost entirely metaphorical. Decentralization is symptomatic in that it combines political discourses with technical ones. While people may reasonably disagree about whether governmental power and corporate power are correctly viewed as "centralized" or "decentralized," or on how to measure degrees of centralization so that we can come to rational agreement about a given institution, computer scientists have developed a notion of decentralization around which the internet itself is said to be built.

The intertwining of technical thinking about the internet and its protocols along with sometimes inchoate and vague political aspirations makes for a heady and frequently impenetrable mix of claims. In the early-to-mid 1960s, computer network scientist Paul Baran of the RAND Corporation (1962), interested in developing an electronic communications technology of which parts would be able to survive nuclear war, iterated on existing ideas to suggest that "it was possible to build a message switching network with fast end-to-end transmission of messages and small, inexpensive switches [which] was a radical challenge to the existing understanding of such systems" (Abbate 1999, 14). While message switching systems, "the concept of 'distributed communications,'" and "a variety of systems based on a network of decentralized nodes linked by multiple connections" (14) all had been suggested prior to Baran, his proposals moved more power to process messages onto network nodes, so that they "would have to have enough 'intelligence' to perform their own routing—they would have to be computers, not just telephone switches" (16).

At this level, the internet appears to be a system that lacks a single authority, and thus seems to be an apt metaphor for a core value of democracy: political power that is shared widely among citizens, and that in some sense *cannot* be reconcentrated into a small number of actors. Yet this is at best a metaphor, and one with troubling implications. For at least in its foundational depictions, the decentralized network of the internet comprises physical nodes that can be seen and diagrammed. Once they have been diagrammed, their contribution to the political whole is clear. Political power shared among people, though, is not easily described in this sense, as it is affected by shifting alliances, votes for policy and representation, and so on. We might look at a network and say that it is more or less decentralized, but it is much more difficult to look at a polity and determine that it is *structurally* decentralized. It is not clear what such a description might mean, especially when it is compared to democracy itself.

The idea that the "network" is decentralized is more metaphorical and observer-dependent than the description suggests. If the point is that what we see as "hierarchical control"—in political terms, totalitarian, dictatorial, or monarchical authority—is *impossible* in a decentralized technical system, we have to do a lot of work to determine what we mean by "control." One of the foundational texts in digital studies, Alexander Galloway's 2004 *Protocol: How Control Exists after Decentralization,* makes this problem clear: despite the fact that digital networks appear resistant to what we think we recognize as "control," which here means both political and technical power, the internet "has a different, more horizontal system of command and control" (69). Galloway describes protocol itself—including "technical standards (such as the OSI Reference Model), network technologies (HTTP), [and] institutional histories (IEEE)"—as "a technology able to establish real-world control when it lacks certain fundamental tools such as hierarchy, centralization, and violence," a "massive control apparatus that guides distributed networks, creates cultural objects, and engenders life forms" (243).

This is abstract, yet there are concrete aspects to the critique as well. Galloway and others suggest that a distributed network pushes more of its processing functions out to nodes, especially toward nodes controlled by end users. This is in contrast to Baran's packet-switching model, which depends more on some nodes with special privileges and powers. These nodes can be compared to cloud services and routing systems such as DNS. In a "decentralized" network, power is widely shared, but not all nodes are equal. In a distributed network, the nodes are more or less equal. But due to the context-dependent nature of what is being measured when we ask whether a system is decentralized, it is not clear which criteria should be used to determine what to call it.

Consider Facebook. The social network is a singular corporate entity with remarkable power and a remarkably powerful platform. Thus in casual

discussions of digital politics, it is routinely described as "centralized." Yet
Facebook's resources are distributed across its main server farms and content delivery networks all over the world. If the nuclear war that Baran and
other RAND Corporation planners feared were to happen, it seems likely
that much of Facebook would survive. This is due to the decentralized
network itself, as well as Facebook's use of it. Depending on the context
and the questions we ask, we might say that Facebook is also decentralized.
From some angles it is; from others it is not.

It is not clear that supposedly decentralized or fully distributed social
networking platforms like Discord or Mastodon are more decentralized in
the narrow networking sense than Facebook. While we extend the political
metaphor "up the chain," insisting that there is no "central authority" determining what happens on those networks, we skip the networking facts on
which the metaphor is built to erect yet another metaphor. Is Facebook less
decentralized than Mastodon, despite the fact that Facebook employs tens
or hundreds of thousands of people to order its content and write its programs, and billions of people generate and share content for it? Mastodon
boasts far smaller user bases, and its administrators arguably have relatively
more power over at least some aspects of the platform than do individual
Facebook employees or contractors. Does working for Facebook make a
person "part of" a central authority in a way that being part of Mastodon,
a nominally nonprofit entity, does not?

These questions do not have easy answers, and it could be argued they
do not have empirical or factual answers at all. They rely on technical–
political metaphors that were vague when they were introduced and have
only become more so since they were widely deployed in digital discourse.
Further, Ashwin Matthews argues in a detailed analysis of claims that "the
internet cannot be controlled by any centralized or territorial authority"
(2016, 1), and the tendency for "the most enduring responses to attempts
to control the internet involve designing new technologies which are ever
more decentralized, capable of evading control" (1–2), that when we look
from the perspectives of some of the internet's most important technical
pieces, these claims are false. Looking at the routing protocol that "integrates
diverse networks . . . into the global whole of the internet" (6), the Border
Gateway Protocol (BGP), Matthews finds that "the practice of operating
BGP is anchored by the centralized resource allocation functions of the
RIRs [Regional Internet Registries], and the centralized standardization

function of the IETF [Internet Engineering Task Force]; and regulated by national and international telecommunications bodies and law" (11). To Matthews, though BGP is "invisible to internet users under normal conditions" (4), "since the routing of data on the internet is managed through BGP, the analysis of the internet as decentralized or distributed is in many ways defined by the characteristics of BGP" (2). Yet "decentralisation was not a design goal, nor the actual outcome, in the creation and subsequent operation of BGP, and by extension, of the internet."

Whether BGP is the right place to ask the question of the internet's degree of centralization is a matter of reasonable debate. Yet Matthews shows that despite the metaphors and rhetoric applied to the network, alternative metaphors and rhetorical frames exist that allow us to see things in ways that contradict their current depiction. This problem not only haunts discussions of decentralization as a political goal in digital technology, it also essentially structures them. Determinations as to whether a technology or institution is centralized are almost entirely dependent on the frame with which we approach the question.

In contrast to democratization, where NGOs and scholars have developed clear assessments that make their analytic frames explicit and can still do empirical work, assessing whether a technology is centralized becomes buried in rhetorical murk, especially in its intersections with society and politics. Indeed, outside the specifically digital space, political scientists have developed at least twenty-five competing indexes to measure decentralization, but study of the problem "has not yet produced a standard methodology." This "lack of consensus [is] mainly due to the different theoretical and methodological approaches followed by researchers" (Harguindéguy, Cole, and Pasquier 2021, 188), despite the fact that such standardized measures are one of the most notable accomplishments of political science. Researchers familiar with producing standardized data sets with consistent definitions face difficulty in developing robust measurements for decentralization. Therefore, it is unsurprising that within digital discourse, which is not renowned for its ability to produce such measurements of nontechnical phenomena, decentralization is only spoken about in vague and frequently misleading terms.

In an article that openly declares its support for Marxist and socialist politics, Melanie Dulong de Rosnay and Francesca Musiani fall into many of the cyberlibertarian rhetorical traps haunting not just "decentralization"

but many other core notions, such as "peer production" and "open." Along
the way they cite the work of thinkers and projects that emerge directly
from right-wing thought without noting, let alone reflecting, on their re-
purposing of these concepts for left-wing purposes. Indeed it is hard to
read the article without concluding that the authors are unaware of the political histories of the concepts they deploy. Their overall reliance on decentralization as an inherently better value extends from "ownership of the
platform (understood as a means of production)" (2016, 194) to "technical
infrastructure" to "governance model" to "copyright regimes" to the "value
generated by peer production" (195). Although they rightly note that "governance in peer production may actually, and counter-intuitively, tend
towards concentration ('oligarchy') as projects grow"—citing the work of
Shaw (2012) and Shaw and Hill (2014), and stating that they "do not wish
to suggest that there is a mix of 'ideal' levels of decentralisation that these
five features can achieve in order to build, in turn, an 'ideal' peer-production
platform" (203)—they conclude by arguing that the typology they develop
serves the purpose of "breaking down and exposing the political benefits of
decentralisation for specific peer production dynamics."

Yet decentralization remains almost entirely a metaphor throughout their
typology, without any attempt to drill down into the specifics either political scientists or network scientists have applied to understand whether systems are decentralized and in what respect. Decentralization, as analyzed
by the authors, follows the typical pattern of cyberlibertarian discourse,
and roughly corresponds to "good." The authors' interpretation of Marxist
or socialist desiderata aligns with a notion of decentralization, but they have
not shown why the reader should accept these attestations. Furthermore,
the authors have not explained how to square their endorsement of values
for their political purposes with the frequent endorsement of the same
formal values for exactly the opposite political purposes when deployed by
their opponents.

In recent years, decentralization has gained attention due to its critical
importance to Bitcoin and the blockchain software that other cryptocurrencies are built on. Even more than the Bitcoin blockchain, the Ethereum
blockchain, created to host applications other than cryptocurrencies, fore-
grounds decentralization as a core virtue. In fact, one of the first efforts
to realize the advertised potential of the Ethereum blockchain, so-called

decentralized autonomous organizations (DAOs), puts the term first in its acronym.

Despite the intense focus on decentralization, the term is highly variable in practice: "In the discourses surrounding blockchain-based crypto-networks, decentralization has come to assume a heightened heft and significance; rather than regarding it merely as a technical characteristic, they treat decentralization as a way of life" (Schneider 2019, 266). Even blockchain supporters, including Balaji Srinivasan and Ethereum cofounder Vitalik Buterin, acknowledge that the term must be used with care in specific domains and subdomains. But these two relatively aligned supporters differ on what those domains are. Srinivasan is disappointed that "despite the widely acknowledged importance of [decentralization], most discussion on the topic lacks quantification" (Srinivasan and Lee 2017). He then develops a nonce statistic, the "minimum Nakamoto coefficient, as a simple, quantitative measure of a system's decentralization." The statistic examines several aspects of the Bitcoin and Ethereum blockchains, including mining, exchanges, and software developers. In each case, a huge amount of interpretation is silently incorporated into the measurements, but at least Srinivasan's approach demands we look at the facts on the ground to determine how decentralized a system is, rather than relying on the theory that is said to inform it.

Buterin (2017), by contrast, uses only three domains—architecture, politics, and logic—and relies on qualitative and philosophical analysis. He takes for granted that, all things being equal, a decentralized system is superior to a centralized one, although he admits that "tradeoffs are unavoidable" in building centralized versus decentralized systems, like Srinivasan and so many others. Given the variable meaning of the term, it's uncertain where this inclination comes from, as it seems to precede political or philosophical analysis. Analyzing whether any particular frame or approach allows for a meaningful determination remains challenging, even with the quantification proposed by Srinivasan.

St. Mary's University law professor Angela Walch has long noted that in addition to "decentralized," terms like "immutable," "permissioned," and "permissionless," "tamper-proof," and even "truth" are applied in ways "inconsistent, confusing, and sometimes misleading" (2017, 11), and that this "confused language . . . increases the potential for regulatory capture, as well as the potential for inconsistent regulation across jurisdictions." Some of the terms echo "the lingo of the cypherpunk and crypto-anarchist groups that Bitcoin emerged from, and is bizarrely political and out-of-place in a statute" (10, written partly as a comment on a 2017 Arizona state statute heralded as a "groundbreaking blockchain and smart contract" law).

In a 2019 essay confronting the widespread use of the term "decentralized" in not just cryptocurrency promotion but in the language of regulators and legislators, Walch rightly notes that "virtually every description of cryptoassets or blockchain technologies includes the adjective 'decentralized.' Indeed, 'decentralization' is viewed as a core feature of blockchain systems, and one of the magic ingredients that is said to enable these systems to generate a record that is very difficult to alter, reliably reflects transactions in the system's native digital token, and does not require trust in a single, central party" (41). "In mainstream discourse, the words 'decentralized' and 'decentralization' are inescapable in discussions about the technology," she writes, yet it "has been rare to see clear explanations" of them when they are used. Despite the vigorous discussions of the term in academic and blockchain/cryptocurrency circles themselves, it is difficult to see any consensus emerging over what it means. Rather, "to be fully decentralized (whatever that means) is viewed as one of the ultimate goals of a permissionless blockchain system, a utopian summit to be scaled" (43).

Unlike Buterin and Srinivasan, but in line with the preceding analysis, Walch distinguishes only two domains in which decentralization might apply. On the one hand, the term is used to refer to "the network of computers . . . that comprise a permissionless blockchain" and, on the other, "to describe how power or agency works within permissionless blockchain systems" (42). "In picking up the terms from the crypto space, and using them uncritically (or at least with insufficient critical inquiry), the conflations and overstatements embedded in the terms have helped to establish people's beliefs about the characteristics of permissionless blockchain systems," she writes, despite the fact that in the second, political usage, "decentralization, or power diffusion, has more political or ideological undertones to it, and seems tied to the cypher-punk, crypto-anarchist roots of Bitcoin (the first blockchain)" (42–43). This is one of the most characteristic dynamics of cyberlibertarian discourse: terms developed from an explicit rightist politics get applied within the digital infrastructure, and then reemerge into popular and political discussions, where their ostensive technical referent obscures their political valence.

Walch notes several structural defects in both popular and technical discussions of decentralization, including that "no one knows what 'decentralization' means" (47), that even within specific domains there must be a spectrum of centralization versus decentralization rather than a "simple binary property" (49), and that even when we can carefully define it the property is "dynamic" (i.e., systems can and do change in their degree of decentralization). Moreover, the quality is often "aspirational rather than actual"—which is another way of saying that a system may well be described as decentralized in theory, but this does not mean that when running it maintains the qualities the theory claims for it.

Given the notable agreement between cyberlibertarian discourse in general and its specific instance around blockchain and cryptocurrency, Walch's observation that "decentralization enables groups of people to obscure power and escape consequences for breaking rules," including criminal laws, is especially important, as is her statement that "the term 'decentralized' is being used to hide actions by participants in the system in a fog of supposedly 'freely floating authority'" (51). Within digital activism, "decentralization" is a synonym for "absence of oversight." Therefore, even more than "freedom of speech," "decentralization" is taken up as a cause because it functions as "a veil over the critical actions of certain parties within the system, effectively shielding them from liability" (58). It is no surprise that "decentralization" functions in a similar way to Section 230 of the CDA: as a kind of political–technical claim about the nature of the system that is advocated as if it points to an important social and political value; however, it is most vigorously promoted by those who intend to abuse others for profit, power, or both.

It has become clear from the history of decentralization in blockchain that abstract or theoretical decentralization may have little or nothing to do with decentralization in practice. This should not be controversial, but it points to fundamental problems in decentralization discourse. The network map diagrams typically used to illustrate types or degrees of centralization do not provide much information about the qualities of the nodes that are said to be centered or decentered. Additionally, they present information as if it exists in a single state forever, from beginning to end. For instance, in the original Bitcoin paper Satoshi Nakamoto speaks of "peer-to-peer" and "distributed" systems, and more frequently of "nodes," though they use "trusted central authority" (2009, 2) to name the thing the system wants to avoid. Talk of "nodes" and "peers" suggests that participants in the network are in some way equal. Indeed that it is the connotation of "peer" in some of its most widespread digital uses, such as "peer production" and "peer-to-peer collaboration."

Like other terms of cyberlibertarian art, "peer" admits of multiple definitions whose simultaneous usage serves to obscure the nature of the claims made for it. Consider the opening of the Wikipedia entry for "Peer-to-Peer" (2021):

> Peer-to-peer (P2P) computing or networking is a distributed application architecture that partitions tasks or workloads between peers. Peers are equally privileged, equipotent participants in the application. They are said to form a peer-to-peer network of nodes. . . .
>
> The concept has inspired new structures and philosophies in many areas of human interaction. In such social contexts, peer-to-peer as a meme refers to the egalitarian social networking that has emerged throughout society, enabled by Internet technologies in general.

In the first paragraph, an assertion is made about the abstract nature of the network, according to which peers are "equally privileged" and "equipotent." This is then metaphorized to "egalitarian social networking" in "social contexts," with the heavy implication being that peers in society are also equally privileged and equally potent. Much of the internet-driven social theory surrounding peer-to-peer takes for granted this fundamental equivalence, as if it is imposed on system participants by virtue of participation itself.

While some network topologies insist that nodes contribute only a specific amount to a network, and participate only if they can contribute that amount (of processing power, disk storage, etc.), in practice this is rare. Although we can see some angles from which every X account is equally privileged and potent, there are many others from which that is not the case. Even though each account starts with zero followers, once time has passed and some have grown to include hundreds of thousands or millions of followers, the egalitarianism they started from is less clear. At first, it might have seemed that only individuals would run X accounts, but corporations, nonprofits, government agencies, and other institutions also run them. Many considerations outside those confined to the network come into play, including the celebrity of the user, their appearance in other media outlets, or their possible roles in business or politics. So we might look at

X and call it a "peer-to-peer" network, because each account has the theoretical ability to "speak to" any other account. But over time, massive power imbalances come to exist. Even if we think that "peer-to-peer" names a virtue in social interactions, we make a mistake in looking at a system's initial state—in which there is a theoretical description of "nodes" or "peers" as fundamentally equal—and assume that this carries through to its later history.

Claims that "decentralized social media" might address the manifest problems miss this point entirely. Although X, to take the most obvious example, is certainly a centralized provider, once we are inside the ecosystem there are many angles from which it appears to be highly decentralized. Save for the use of features like blocking and muting, anyone can speak to anyone else. Even if someone has zero followers, there is a theoretical chance of their tweet being read by anyone. However, the MIT Media Lab report on decentralized social media by Barabas, Narula, and Zuckerman found that despite overall support for decentralization, there are still limitations: "Protecting the future of speech online involves not only these ambitious experiments in decentralization, but the cultivation of an ecosystem of competing publishing platforms, diverse in governance strategies, interoperable and connected by a diversity of federated clients. We hope that those most concerned with the potential of the network public sphere will support not only experiments with decentralization, but the legal, normative and technical work necessary for these types of projects to thrive" (2017, 112). Throughout the report it's evident that the crucial factor isn't the platform's decentralization but rather the presence of laws, regulations, and norms determining its aggregate effects on democracy as a whole and individual citizens.

This mistaking of an abstract or initial state for a later set of facts is particularly pronounced in blockchain and cryptocurrency. Theoretically, in Nakamoto's vision, full nodes (those that process all Bitcoin transactions and are occasionally rewarded with cryptocurrency tokens as a reward) are described abstractly, as if they are "equally privileged" and "equipotent" participants in the blockchain network. They might well be described that way. However, because any computer can run the Bitcoin software, the contribution of any one node is affected by a number of factors, especially processing power. Therefore, the more powerful the processor is, the more tokens it can generate. As the Bitcoin and Ethereum networks have grown, the processing power (and electricity) required to produce a reasonable return on investment has skyrocketed. While some cryptocurrency promoters dispute these facts, the generally accepted wisdom is that, as a writer for *Investopedia* put it in 2020, "old timers (say, way back in 2009) mining bitcoins using just their personal computers were able to make a profit" (Zucchi). Yet by 2013, application-specific integrated circuit chips (ASICs) "offered up to 100 billion times the capability of older personal machines, rendering the use of personal computing to mine bitcoins inefficient and obsolete." Typical ASICs cost over $5,000, which makes the cost of entry prohibitive. In addition, today's state-of-the-art systems devote many machines solely to Bitcoin, rather than only devoting extra processing cycles to the network as early participants did.

In practice, while it is theoretically possible for any machine on the network to achieve profitability by receiving a Bitcoin token as a reward, the tokens are distributed randomly. Therefore, the more processing power a miner can devote to mining, the more likely it is that the miner will receive any specific randomly awarded token. At a gross level, the situation might be compared to lottery tickets. Everyone is free to purchase as many dollar tickets as they choose. But then each ticket purchaser is "equally privileged" and "equipotent" only in an abstract sense. A person who can afford to purchase a thousand tickets has a thousand more chances to win than someone who can only afford a single ticket. (Indeed, this is a reason some criticize state lotteries as regressive taxes; see Wyett 1991.) In a formal sense the system looks egalitarian, but in a practical sense it is anything but.

Despite its claims to decentralization, Bitcoin is far more centralized than the systems run by "central authorities" it claims to supplant. Walch cites several well-known events that have highlighted the concentration of power in blockchain development. These include the bug in Bitcoin software discovered in September 2018, found by a small community of Bitcoin software developers, "fewer than a dozen people," which if it "hadn't [been] fixed . . . immediately" would have threatened the Bitcoin system with "potentially catastrophic failure" (54); the March 2013 hard fork of the Bitcoin software; and a hard fork of the Ethereum blockchain software in July 2016 coordinated by an even smaller group of developers to manage problems with an early decentralized autonomous organization (56–57). Even Srinivasan's pro-blockchain quantitative examination of the development communities admits that "a relatively small number of engineers have done most of the work on Bitcoin Core, and that for the reference client of Ethereum, development is even more concentrated, with two developers doing the lion's share of commits" (Srinivasan and Lee 2017).

While many have commented on the irony that the development of Bitcoin and other blockchain software is highly centralized, and that even governance decisions about that software appear to use mechanisms few would consider decentralized, these do not point to the main operations of blockchain or cryptocurrency, namely the mining of tokens itself. Overhanging the question of decentralized token mining is the implication that everyone can get rich by mining their own tokens, although we have seen how this flies in the face of the capital investment mining requires. The rhetoric skips over facts, so that the cryptocurrency press is flooded with claims that owning or trading cryptocurrency tokens is decentralized in some fundamental sense, and that this decentralization of finance is welcome for the ordinary investor. Leaving aside the serious concerns anyone should have about what it means to "invest" in cryptocurrency, the veil of decentralization hides the massive and troubling ways in which cryptocurrency markets are at least as "centralized" as well-established trading venues such as stock and bond markets.

Reports vary depending on many factors, including the number of Bitcoin that remain in circulation and are available for trading, the correspondence of Bitcoin wallet addresses with individuals and institutions, and more. However, a commonly cited statistic is that "about 40 percent of Bitcoin is held by perhaps 1,000 users" (Kharif 2017). Contrast this with statistics developed by NYU economist Edward Wolff that "as of 2013, the top 1 percent of households by wealth owned nearly 38 percent of all stock shares," and "the 10 percent of households with the highest wealth owned more than 80 percent of all stock shares" (Kurtzleben 2017). While there is room to quibble over specifics, including the comparison of global holdings of the single token Bitcoin with the entirety of the U.S. stock market, it is worth noting that according to the Census Bureau, there were over 125 million U.S. households as of 2023 ("Quick Facts" n.d.), of which 10 percent is approximately 12.5 million, and 1 percent is 1.25 million. Despite the massive inequality these numbers disclose, it would be next to impossible to use them to argue that cryptocurrency ownership is less centralized or concentrated than stock ownership: a thousand "households" worldwide own 40 percent of Bitcoin, whereas even in one of the world's richest countries 1.25 *million* households own 40 percent of stock market wealth. Speaking crudely, and without trying to create sympathy for the wealthiest 1 percent of U.S. households, one could say with confidence that Bitcoin ownership is at least a *thousand times* more centralized than stock ownership (and likely much higher).

The oscillation between theoretical or abstract decentralization, on the one hand, and de facto centralization, on the other, is a characteristic feature of cyberlibertarian discourse (and indeed of many libertarian-inflected political formations). This is why political scientists have worried about the promotion of abstract decentralization in governmental and development contexts (see Prud'homme 1995 for the argument in principle; and Lewis 2014 for a specific example). What is claimed to promote freedom, and is cloaked in the rhetoric of egalitarianism and human rights, promotes the opposite: the freedom of a few (typically but not always "bad") actors to skirt laws, regulations, rules, and institutional norms that were put in place to protect people as individuals and as groups. Even "a centralized, quasi-democratic institution as flawed as the US Federal Reserve System, which Satoshi Nakamoto sought to replace, has features arguably more accountable to the common good than the ad-hocracy of Bitcoin miners" (Schneider 2019, 262). Because *decentralization,* more clearly than *democratization,* posits some force other than democratic governments as the agencies of egalitarianism, the concept is too easily yoked to the antigovernment and antiliberal agitation that characterizes right-wing political power. It is surely right to argue that "critical use of the decentralization frame should also avoid demonizing anything with a center." Decentralization as a concept can obscure the purpose and effects of policy prescriptions. Instead, it is better to use specific descriptions of why a certain form of power is wielded improperly or in too concentrated a fashion. Additionally, it is also important to describe how power can be spread out more widely among relevant constituencies without reliance on an abstract sense of "decentralization."

PRIVACY AND SURVEILLANCE

Like freedom of speech, "privacy" names one of the fundamental human and civil rights to which all democracies must, by law and theory, commit themselves. Although not formally enshrined in the U.S. Constitution, some form of a right to privacy has been inferred by many courts, based on wording in the Bill of Rights and the Fourteenth Amendment. Privacy has been formally enshrined in many constitutions written more recently than the late eighteenth century as well as Article 12 of the 1948 Universal Declaration of Human Rights.

Legal scholar Ronald J. Krotoszynski Jr. examines the "highly protean nature of the concept of 'privacy'" (2016, 1), a concept that "seems to mean everything—and nothing—at the same time" (2). He suggests that rather than resolving this inherent polysemy, we "learn to live with the privacy hydra" (3) while seeking greater definitional clarity. Privacy issues cross transnational borders and thus cannot be adjudicated solely in national terms, even if "local culture strongly informs and shapes the articulation and protection of privacy interests within particular legal systems" (4). Krotoszynski offers three rough conceptual glosses on privacy: (1) "nondisclosure" or "informational privacy," "the ability to control the gathering and dissemination of personal information, whether by the government or other persons" (191n24); (2) "dignity," according to which "everyone has inherent dignity and the right to have their dignity respected and protected" (xiii, quoting the Constitution of South Africa); and (3) "autonomy," "the right of the individual to be self-regulating in matters of central importance to happiness and identity" (6).

Privacy, even more than freedom of speech, is of signal interest to nearly everyone concerned with the intersection of human and civil rights with digital technology. While independent thinkers, activists, scholars, and technology users tend to embrace thick conceptions of privacy that relate in a variety of ways to the polysemy of the word "privacy" that Krotoszynski notes, digital rights activists and technology promoters tend to use the word in a different way. They consider privacy to mean absolute opacity to democratic regulation, regardless of whether democracies have legitimate interests and have used legitimate means to exercise their oversight responsibilities. In the previous chapter we explored much of this when discussing encryption and anonymization technologies. The advocates of these technologies believe that democracy is a sham and that all governments are inherently authoritarian. Therefore, ordinary people must take advantage of all available technology to block everyone from observing everything they do.

Many of the most prominent digital rights organizations have seized on privacy as a value on which they can capitalize to garner public support. This is in part because freedom of speech is more readily recognized now as a value that has been distorted so fully that its current form seems to serve those who want to eradicate democracy more than those who support it. As legal scholar Woodrow Hartzog puts it, "It turns out that a broad and singular conceptualization of privacy is unhelpful for legal purposes. It guides lawmakers toward vague, overinclusive, and underinclusive rules. It allows industry to appear to serve a limited notion of privacy while leaving people vulnerable when companies and people threaten notions of privacy that fall outside the narrow definition. And it often causes people who discuss privacy in social and political settings to talk past each other because they don't share the same notion of privacy" (2021, 1679).

As with net neutrality, what internet freedom activists and mainstream civil rights activists (including lawyers and legal scholars in both camps) mean by privacy is almost entirely different. Krotoszynski and other legal scholars' subtle shadings of meaning attached to privacy do not survive in cyberlibertarian discourse. Instead, government is put on one side and privacy is put on the other, effectively turning privacy into anti-government dogma, as in the "Cyphernomicon" (introduced in chapter 2). The initial item in the opening section of the "Cyphernomicon" is labeled "The Basic Issues," and the first of these is "Great Divide: privacy vs. compliance with laws" (May 1994), which could not make clearer how digital rights advocates construe the issue. It is worth noting that none of the meanings of world constitutions, as detailed by Krotoszynski and others, casts privacy in these terms. Privacy and surveillance are critical issues for all users of digital technology, especially for members of racial, ethnic, and other minorities (Benjamin 2019; Browne 2015). But what these words mean in the hands of critics and activists authentically concerned with civil rights is very different from what they mean in cyberlibertarian discourse.

One of the most troubling ways cyberlibertarianism influences discussions of privacy is that most activism around privacy is directed at government surveillance. Reading the position papers of EFF, Fight for the Future, and all the others, one would be forgiven for thinking surveillance is a priori an activity that only governments perform. For institutions that prioritize "innovation," the solution to privacy problems is to give more control over to corporations and technology, while disempowering governments. Nowhere is this clearer than in public discussions of facial recognition and other forms of biometric surveillance. Fight for the Future sponsors a project called "Ban Facial Recognition," which rightly describes the problem

with this technology: "Like nuclear or biological weapons, facial recognition poses a threat to human society and basic liberty that far outweighs
any potential benefits. Silicon Valley lobbyists are disingenuously calling
for light 'regulation' of facial recognition so they can continue to profit by
rapidly spreading this surveillance dragnet. They're trying to avoid the real
debate: whether technology this dangerous should even exist" ("Ban Facial
Recognition" 2020). This sounds like a call for abolition. Indeed it uses the
language of abolition. The naive reader may not notice that the remaining
sentence of the paragraph reads, "Industry-friendly and government-friendly
oversight will not fix the dangers inherent in *law enforcement's use* of facial
recognition: we need an all-out ban" (emphasis added).

To make the point clearer, even though it uses the phrase "ban facial
recognition" at several points, the project offers a bill that it asks supporters to promote with their congressional representatives. HR 7235, offered
to the House of Representatives by seven members in June 2020, is titled
the Stop Biometric Surveillance by Law Enforcement Act. The bill's main
provision reads, "A State or unit of local government may not use facial
recognition technology or other biometric surveillance systems on any
image acquired by body-worn cameras of law enforcement officers." That
is, the bill contains no hint of an "all-out ban." It would ban *only* governments from using the technology.

While the proposal might make sense on its own, it arrives in the context of a decades-long attack on democratic sovereignty, which has largely
been engineered by corporate power, with digital technology front and center. Advocates will argue that disempowering governments and law enforcement is a "first step" toward total abolition. However, there is little evidence
to support this claim, and there is little historical precedent for politics working in this way. To the contrary, deregulatory use of governmental power is
at the heart of neoliberal and right-wing political action.

On the surface, too, this proposed prohibition turns ordinary democratic
politics on their heads. Democratic governance is formally accountable to
citizens, which is why we permit it to have powers that ordinary citizens
do not have. Indeed, this is the grain of truth lodged within Max Weber's
talk of a governmental "monopoly on legitimate violence." Most dangerous technologies are *only* available to the government to use, and then only
in specific circumstances prescribed by law. When private citizens and corporations are allowed to use deadly weapons and toxic chemicals, it is only

under strict regulation or licensure. Yet somehow when it comes to digital biometric surveillance, activists have made it sound reasonable that corporations and individuals should have access to this destructive technology, largely outside regulation, but that government should not. While advocates may disagree about whether governments should be able to use biometrics, it seems clear that if we are even asking whether governments should be able to use them at all, it stands to reason that corporations and individuals should be unable to use them before we even get to the government question. While it may be understandable to think that government and law enforcement use of biometric surveillance is especially egregious, examination of the facts suggests that corporations use these technologies at least as invasively as governments do, and with considerably less oversight.

In 2021 the U.S. Congress deliberated over and then passed HR 3684, the Infrastructure Investment and Jobs Act," which President Biden signed on November 15. A minor provision of the bill concerned reporting of cryptocurrency transactions for tax purposes. David Kamin, deputy director of the National Economic Council, said that "the tax enforcement agenda the president has put forward is focused on—and this is basic—having people pay the taxes that are owed under current law" and noted that "disproportionately, there is evasion when it comes to those at the top, often because their sources of income are more opaque." The passage of HR 3684 "would be followed by a multiyear rule-making process, where the crypto industry would have plenty of say," according to journalist Ezra Klein. The language of the provision "was expansive not because the Treasury Department wants to force everyone who touches a blockchain to produce a 1099 but because it doesn't want to prejudge how the crypto networks were structured" (Klein 2021).

It should be no surprise that the cryptocurrency industry reacted negatively to the inclusion of these provisions in the bill. What may be surprising is the rhetoric the industry used to oppose it: cryptocurrency promoters claimed the bill's stipulations amounted to illegitimate government surveillance and a violation of user privacy. As Alexis Goldstein, former director of financial policy at the progressive Open Markets Institute, put it, "Cryptocurrency advocates are waging a battle against legislation—part of the infrastructure package now in Congress—aimed at curbing tax evasion in the rapidly growing market. Crypto enthusiasts such as Twitter CEO Jack Dorsey, employing a combination of jargon and threats to move overseas, are seeking to create the impression that this innovative technology is somehow ill-suited to meeting the tax-reporting requirements that apply to traditional banks and brokerages" (2021). Goldstein's analysis is exactly correct, not least in her pointing out that what Congress set out to do is to hold cryptocurrency traders and trading platforms responsible for paying taxes, the same way they are when trading more established instruments, and using the same methods for doing so. Goldstein is also right that the only reason to object to a leveling of the playing field is that cryptocurrency is taking advantage of gaps in existing regulation to profit off what is essentially cheating on taxes.

Even more, she is right that industry used a "combination of jargon and threats" to stave off the regulations. At the core of these threats was the language of privacy and surveillance. One of the most extreme examples could be found in the crypto industry publication *CoinDesk,* which published an opinion piece by Marta Belcher as part of its "Privacy Week" that declared the tax provisions "unconstitutional" (2022). She called the bill "warrantless surveillance of sensitive financial information" that "violates the Fourth Amendment of the US Constitution" while declaring that "financial privacy is not bad or illegal. To the contrary, it is essential for civil liberties." She also suggested that the U.S. Supreme Court needs to reexamine its 1974 *Burrows v. Superior Court* decision about bank secrecy—without mentioning that, were the Court to do as she suggests, *all* reporting of financial transactions to the IRS would be declared unconstitutional, a result that would fulfill the decades-old dreams of right-wing anti-tax conspiracy theorists.

Similarly, Fight for the Future responded to the infrastructure bill with a social media campaign and a website called DontKillCrypto.com. The group declared that crypto exists "to create alternatives to Big Tech" and the infrastructure bill would "undermine human rights and free expression, and create harmful surveillance requirements for artists & creators" (Fight for the Future 2021). The bill "mandates mass surveillance of the crypto-economy in the name of reducing tax avoidance. This puts many fundamental cryptocurrency participants in an impossible position," the group claims. Therefore, resisting the bill is about "the United States' ability to participate in cryptocurrencies and a decentralized future that puts the rights of people above the exploitative and manipulative business models of Big Tech." It is scarcely possible to measure the dishonesty in these statements, which defend the practices of one of the most exploitative and rapacious industries in recent memory, operating above and beyond the law, while claiming to do just the opposite. It is worth noting that groups like EFF and Fight for the Future can advocate for the industry's rapacious practices while simultaneously appearing to criticize Big Tech.

FREE SPEECH AND CENSORSHIP

One of the main rallying cries for both digital technology promoters and digital technology companies is "free speech," even though these interests are sometimes portrayed as different from each other. The idea that digital technology does not merely promote free speech, but *is* free speech, remains fundamental to the cyberlibertarian construction of technology as liberatory. This is despite the fact that free speech and "censorship" must be reframed so that they mean different things from the reasoning put forward by the major thinkers who put freedom of speech at the center of democracy. This framing, as with so many other matters of cyberlibertarian ideology, does most of the argumentative work before the discussion even begins. As one of the legal scholars who has worked most closely on this issue, Mary Anne Franks, puts it in a 2019 essay, "In a 2019 survey conducted by the First Amendment Center of the Freedom Forum Institute, 65 percent of respondents agreed with the statement that '[s]ocial media companies violate users' First Amendment rights when they ban users based on the content of their posts.' That is, a majority of respondents believe that the First Amendment applies to private actors. This belief animates the multiple lawsuits that have been filed against companies such as Twitter and Google for alleged free speech violations and fuels the increasingly common claim that social media platforms are censoring conservative viewpoints." She goes on:

> But as the text of the First Amendment itself makes clear, this belief is wrong as a matter of law. The First Amendment states that "Congress" shall make no law abridging the freedom of speech: the right to free speech, like all rights guaranteed in the Bill of Rights, is a right against the government. While the reference to Congress is now understood to include a wide range of government action, the "state action" doctrine maintains the fundamental distinction between governmental and private actors. Private actors are not subject to the restraints of the First Amendment except in the rare cases when they perform a "traditional, exclusive public function." (2019b)

This is not some arcane legal point with which only scholars should be concerned. Rather, the First Amendment is a remarkably "fundamental" statement of principle (see also Franks 2019a) around which democracy is said to be organized, despite the way that many of its most fervent promoters dismiss democratic governance as an important value. The First Amendment exerts a "gravitational pull" or "cultural magnetism" that even outside of digital technology, in legal scholar Daniel Greenwood's words, "threatens to swallow up all politics" (1999).

Ordinary citizens who accept this argument on its face may unwittingly grant even more power to nongovernmental actors, regardless of how much power those actors already possess. It is no accident that as early as 2012, Twitter described itself as "the free speech wing of the free speech party" (Halliday 2012), despite its product's tendentious relationship to freedom of speech as a legal concept. If tech companies' claims were taken seriously, newspapers would be unable to operate at all. This is because the simple decision to edit the paper, to print the work of some reporters and not others, to print some letters and not others, would be a violation of "freedom of speech." The only allowable speech platforms would be those that permitted everyone to speak, without regard for the means they were able to bring privately toward amplifying that message.

One of the fascinating fractures between "digital rights" promoters and the companies they generally represent is over freedom of speech. In a 2014 document that seems quite bizarre a decade later, EFF chastised Twitter for complying with court orders to take down content in countries "where they do not have significant assets or employees" (Galperin 2014). Twitter, EFF claimed, was "stepp[ing] down from the Free Speech Party." EFF's legal reasoning is quite strange, but its consequences are even stranger: Twitter, in EFF's opinion, *must* display any content its users choose to post, everywhere, regardless of government policies.

This policy can be understood in a different fashion when viewed from the perspective of popular sovereignty. EFF's view is that even if a government is fully democratic in form, its citizens should have no power whatsoever to regulate how Twitter operates. Further, unless Twitter has an office in that country, the country *must* accept Twitter's product and all communications that occur on it. Even though EFF is criticizing Twitter, it is difficult to miss the absolutist deregulatory impulse at work. EFF is using framing and pressure to prevent any company from complying with democratic laws.

The same piece calls "on users to remain vigilant, using resources such as The Chilling Effects Project to keep Twitter honest, specifically citing the need to watch out for Twitter caving to government pressure to censor overtly political speech." The EFF nods at the central concern of free speech juris-prudence, "overtly political speech," to temper the antidemocratic thrust of its position.

As Franks argues, while a general orientation toward less rather than more interference with user speech may be a welcome principle in content moderation, platforms are under no obligation to "allow" any specific per-son to use or not use their product. Indeed, this inversion of democratic principle—under which we now learn that it is implicit in the Constitu-tion that *only* platforms that allow unmoderated speech should be fully legal—is so absurd as to rarely be said out loud (not least to the extreme amounts of content moderation required to keep child abuse imagery and other fully illegal materials from swamping any such platform; see Gillespie 2018; Roberts 2019). Yet it remains the default conceptual argument that digital rights organizations claim to stand by.

The free speech framing is critical because it takes off the table the fun-damental question of who decides whether social media platforms like X are legitimate businesses to operate and/or legal technologies that can oper-ate without a license. Democratic governments highly regulate many forms of communications technology, and in fact, those with the most reach, such as television and radio, have often been the most subject to regulation and licensing. Given the tremendous power of social media, it is unclear whether it fits into a democratic polity, especially without oversight. Despite what advocates frequently say, First Amendment jurisprudence in the United States is not absolute, even though it is the closest to "absolute" free speech protection in the world. These include not just exceptions for private spaces, as Franks and others have noted. Although in general what we call "public spaces" are required to allow any legal speech across the board, govern-ments are permitted to, and frequently do, impose what are called content-neutral time, place, and manner restrictions on speech even in public forums. This is so central to First Amendment jurisprudence that the general prin-ciple is considered to be solid and generally untouchable law.

A report prepared for the U.S. Congress in 2014 made clear these and other principles of exception to the First Amendment. Kathleen Anne Ruane explains that "some public spaces, such as streets and parks, are known as 'traditional public forums,' which means that they generally are open to all people to express themselves by speech-making, demonstrating, or leafleting, and the like" (2014, 7). In these forums, she goes on, "the government may regulate speech as to its time, place, and manner of expression, so that, for example, two demonstrations do not occur at the same time and place" (8). Further:

> Even speech that enjoys the most extensive First Amendment protection may be subject to "regulations of the time, place, and manner of expression which are content-neutral, are narrowly tailored to serve a significant government interest, and leave open ample alternative channels of communication." In the case in which this language appears, the Supreme Court allowed a city ordinance that banned picketing "before or about" any residence to be enforced to prevent picketing outside the residence of a doctor who performed abortions, even though the picketing occurred on a public street. The Court noted that "[t]he First Amendment permits the government to prohibit offensive speech as intrusive when the 'captive' audience cannot avoid the objectionable speech." (9)

These rarely considered aspects of free speech jurisprudence are highly relevant to the debate about free speech and digital technology. Even though social media platforms like X and Facebook are wholly owned by private companies, the "spaces" they offer are taken by digital advocates to be functionally the same as "public forums" as defined by the Supreme Court. But neither case law nor statute supports this contention.

Further, even in the unlikely case that the noncommercial parts of the internet were to be declared "public forums," the question of content-neutral time, place, and manner restrictions should come into play. Digital rights promoters have tried to keep this line of reasoning off the table, but it deserves closer examination. U.S. public forum jurisprudence depends on the notion of physical property. In general, to be a public forum, the people must own a specific place or building, and it is the public ownership of the property that requires speech protections. The implicit cyberlibertarian doctrine is that there is an infinite supply of such space, that ownership does not matter, and that regardless of who sets up the space, who owns it, and so on, it must be kept free of (speech) regulation. Buried within this logic is the repudiation of the content-neutral time, place, and manner doctrine, due to the nonphysical, unowned nature of the "property" involved.

Suppose, prior to the advent of the internet, someone were to propose the creation of a massive, person-to-person, group-to-group public square in which all speech were to be allowed (although even here the specific exceptions to free speech would have to be respected). It would be up to the democracy to decide whether to create that space, how to create it, and when it would and would not operate, and so on. We see this all the time in more limited ways: local governments create "free speech walls," for example, but may choose to paint them over periodically, to add or remove space from them, and so on. This is up to the people to decide through their democratically elected representatives.

"Digital rights" advocates subtly turn this upside down. Their view is that *anyone* may erect "free speech walls" that float free of property ownership, and governments have no say over this, nor do they have any say over the speech conditions on these walls. In other words, governments have no control over the creation and designation of "public forums." This means that governments do not have the power to manage public spaces, which is one of the core functions of democratic governance. This is, at its heart, a resurgence of the anarcho-capitalist doctrine of "permissionless innovation" (see chapter 2).

Now imagine an alternative scenario. Suppose that, as with physical space, governments retained the power to decide whether particular online spaces are "public." In the case of X, Facebook, and the like, this scenario raises a profound question: *why* must governments allow these companies to run what are thought of as public forums, despite not having the power we associate with governmental ownership and oversight of such forums? Another way of asking this question is as follows: Are purportedly public forums like X and Facebook legal to begin with? And even if they are de facto legal because nobody thought to ask this question when the companies were started, should they remain legal?

Given the destructive and antidemocratic power of social media, it seems appropriate to ask whether Zuboff's (2019, 2021) suggestion that digital technology and social media constitute a form of behavioral management that democracies should consider outlawing is consistent with this question. An alternative approach would be to consider licensing (Pasquale 2021), which was done to great effect in the United States with regard to broadcasting. This seems to be the intent behind the support for net neutrality as described in the last chapter, although it has little to do with the specific policies that go by that name.

It is no accident that agitation over Section 230, "free speech," and "censorship" online keeps off the table the question of the legitimacy and legality of purportedly "public" speech forums, whatever their negative effects might be and no matter how fully they are documented. The free speech argument for digital technology is a fundamental backstop that makes it nearly impossible for democracies to consider the central question: To what extent do democratic polities need to allow to proliferate technologies whose function is to make democratic sovereignty difficult or even impossible?

It is also no accident that the most vociferous advocates for "free speech online" like EFF and the technology arm of ACLU refuse to reflect on recent U.S. Supreme Court doctrine that increasingly equates money and corporate action with speech. The ACLU has sided with corporations in this regard, which has raised profound questions for many longtime ACLU supporters about the organization's commitment to democratic values. For decades, Daniel Greenwood has noted the expansion of free speech jurisprudence in the United States, arguing that "the First Amendment principle of abstention has expanded beyond a program of making politics safe to become a primary vehicle in a post–New Deal attempt to reduce the scope of conscious collective control over the market" (1999, 661). "The First Amendment, understood in this way as a fundamental limitation on the scope of government, has become the locus of a new Lochnerism," Greenwood writes, "or rather, a revival of the old Lochnerism under a new doctrinal label." Indeed, "First Amendment Lochnerism" has entered the vocabulary of legal scholars, including some who work on digital technology issues, including Tim Wu: "Scholars and dissenting judges have critiqued parts of the Supreme Court's First Amendment jurisprudence as 'First Amendment Lochnerism.' The critique suggests that the protection of commercial speech has become a means for the judiciary to strike down economic regulation at will, creating a contemporary equivalent to the substantive due process theories relied upon by the Court in *New York v. Lochner*" (Wu 2019). No less a mainstream conservative than Supreme Court Justice William Rehnquist, when he was still an Associate Justice, referred to Lochnerism in a famous 1980 dissent in *Central Hudson v. Public Service Commission* as a "bygone era . . . in which it was common practice for this Court to strike down economic regulations adopted by a State based on the Court's own notions of the most appropriate means for the State to implement its considered policies." He also called it a "discredited doctrine" that labels "economic regulation of business conduct as a restraint on 'free speech.'"

Note that what is at issue in the idea of Lochnerism is using free speech as a way of describing economic activity, and then using that description to prevent regulation of economic activity. (Somewhat suggestively for the politics of cyberlibertarianism, *Central Hudson* was decided 8–1 by the generally liberal Court, who determined that restrictions on some commercial speech violated the First Amendment. Rehnquist's dissent is the only opinion to mention *Lochner*—perhaps because the case had long been a talking point in right-wing legal circles but was considered beyond the pale for most mainstream legal scholars.) This goes far beyond the famed "money is speech" doctrine that many feel the Supreme Court made into case law with its *Citizens United* decision, by entirely blurring the line between speech and action. Such a distinction is fundamental to free speech law. It is only by dint of being describable as speech that something gains First Amendment protections, which seriously restricts the way democratic governments can regulate it. Even though in a philosophical sense, the line between speech and action can be hard to formalize, it is only because the two can be distinguished in a rough sense that free speech doctrine exists at all. If all speech were action and all action were speech, democratic governance would be impossible.

Unfortunately, the power of digital technology has made it a vanguard site for reinterpreting action as speech. The most obvious place to see this is in the doctrine that "code is speech." This holds that because computer programs are made of code that looks something like human language, everything done with computer code deserves First Amendment protections— even though the whole point of computer programs is to *do* things (i.e., to take actions). EFF and other digital advocates routinely suggest that "code is speech" is an obvious and well-established legal principle. Apple made this claim in court filings in 2016, when it said it had a First Amendment right not to provide the FBI with a way of unlocking, under legal warrant, the iPhone of a suspect in the 2016 San Bernardino terror attack.

"Code is speech" is a remarkable and disingenuous interpretation of legal philosophy. EFF, arguably its most vibrant defender, claims that the case

Bernstein v. DOJ "established code as speech" (Dame-Boyle 2015; see also the EFF website for a full case archive). Before going into some of the details about that case, it's important to note that the ruling was vacated during the appeals process when the government decided not to enforce the relevant regulations due to changing facts. It is no longer considered valid precedent at all. Further, advocates tend to refer to a lower court ruling in *Bernstein* in 1996, but the later appellate rulings don't fully support the reasoning the lower court offers, raising serious questions about the core claims advocates extract from the cases. Citing this as settled law, or anything close to it, is nothing short of deceptive. Not only was the decision vacated, but due to its particular role in the string of cases it was never subject to higher court review. Even now, we have no idea whether the "code is speech" doctrine could survive legal challenge, though it continues to drive the cyberlibertarian worldview in significant ways.

The reasoning used in the 1996 *Bernstein* decision is also remarkable. *Bernstein* was nominally about the publication of some computer code in a magazine. Under the weight of a barrage of digital technology experts and their legal advocates, the court restricted its judgment to that question and refused to address the use of the code. So even in the maximal interpretation, what the court actually decided was that "code can be published the same way as other things can, and in that context, it gets First Amendment protections." But this does not address the ordinary context in which we think of "code," which is its execution on computers. In this context, it is clear that code is action. The court did not rule on this fundamental question, to some extent putting its head in the sand by ruling as if the point of code is to be read rather than to be run.

In fact, although the ruling to which EFF and other advocates love to refer sidestepped the question in just this fashion, other judges have not. The part of *Bernstein* most often cited by EFF and other advocates reads, "This court can find no meaningful difference between computer language, particularly high-level languages as defined above, and German or French. . . . Like music and mathematical equations, computer language is just that, language, and it communicates information either to a computer or to those who can read it." At first glance this might seem reasonable, but after any careful examination it is anything but. Patel relies on no expert sources to argue that not just "computer language" but also music and math are "just language," which is something few experts in law, language, music, or math would agree with. The more one thinks about it, the more curious it becomes that there is "no meaningful difference" between these phenomena. Things that are not meaningfully different can also be called "the same." If music, mathematical equations, and computer programming are the same thing as human languages like German and French, why do they occupy such different roles in our societies? German and French are functionally equivalent to English, Greek, Latin, Swahili, and Japanese, as they serve much the same roles and are taught and learned in very similar ways. Yet there are no human societies that speak music, mathematical equations, or C++ as their primary means of communication.

The ruling is worth dwelling on because it is the one that EFF and other advocates insist has "established" that "code is speech." Yet it does not even approximate a thoughtful or learned opinion on the complex relationships— especially in the sphere of law—between human languages and programming code. If that question were ever to be adjudicated in a court of law, unlike in the courts that heard *Bernstein* and the cases that followed it, it would be necessary to include a wide range of experts in hearings—not just the computer advocates who saw in *Bernstein* an opportunity to press for the anarchic anti-government politics to which many of them subscribed.

Consider this from the more limited appeals ruling by Betty Fletcher: "Cryptographers use source code to express their scientific ideas in much the same way that mathematicians use equations or economists use graphs. Of course, both mathematical equations and graphs are used in other fields for many purposes, not all of which are expressive. But mathematicians and economists have adopted these modes of expression in order to facilitate the precise and rigorous expression of complex scientific ideas. Similarly, the undisputed record here makes it clear that cryptographers utilize source code in the same fashion." Thomas Nelson's dissent is even stronger. He writes that he is "inevitably led to conclude that encryption source code is more like conduct than speech. Encryption source code is a building tool. Academics and computer programmers can convey this source code to each other in order to reveal the encryption machine they have built. But, the ultimate purpose of encryption code is, as its name suggests, to perform the function of encrypting messages. Thus, while encryption source code may occasionally be used in an expressive manner, it is inherently a functional device."

Considered dispassionately, as it is used, not printed, code is *action,* not speech. A huge amount of code is promulgated by corporations, not individuals. The effect of embracing "code is speech" is to say that governments cannot regulate what corporations do. That might seem like hyperbole, but it is completely in line with the Silicon Valley view of the world, the overt anarcho-capitalism that many of its leaders embrace, and the covert cyberlibertarianism that so many more accept without fully comprehending its consequences. It is profoundly antidemocratic. It is confounding that many see Apple as a civil rights actor, given that its mission is to sell products that block the serving of legal, targeted warrants. Furthermore, Apple has made outrageous statements regarding the corporate taxes it would owe if not for the existing successful capture of regulatory and legislative bodies that enable the kinds of corporate inversions it employs to dodge taxes (Cassidy 2013).

Daniel Greenwood has long argued that "nothing in the structure or language of the Bill of Rights suggests that the traditional rights of American citizens apply to corporations" (2013, 14). To most scholars who don't have a vested financial interest in the success of one company or another (e.g., those who don't work for corporations or corporate-funded think tanks), the encroachment of corporations into rights language has been one of the signal failures of U.S. democracy. This is not to say corporations never should have rights, or even that the notion of an "artificial person" is entirely bankrupt. (It seems to do important work, for example, in the rights of both corporations and natural persons to act as equal parties in contracts and to use the civil courts to adjudicate breaches of those agreements.) But that the general expansion of corporate personhood and identification of corporations as the locus of constitutional rights is among the most significant dangers facing democratic governance today.

Consider this truly jarring statement from EFF executive director Cindy Cohn: "The Supreme Court has rejected requirements that people put 'Live Free or Die' on their license plates or sign loyalty oaths, and it has said that the government cannot compel a private parade to include views that organizers disagree with. That the signature and code in the Apple case are implemented via technology and computer languages rather than English makes no difference. For nearly 20 years in cases pioneered by EFF, the courts have recognized that writing computer code is protected by the First

Amendment" (2016). EFF is mostly staffed by lawyers. Cohn is an attorney with a long history of working for civil and human rights. In fact, she worked on *Bernstein,* which EFF mischaracterizes in several critical ways. Yet here Cohn purposely blurs the lines between code as action and code as speech, as well as the line between individuals and corporations.

She writes that "the FBI should not force Apple to violate its beliefs," but the only case that the Supreme Court has ever decided that even suggests that corporations have "beliefs" is the horribly right-wing 2014 *Hobby Lobby* decision, which nobody outside of far-right ideologues should endorse. Furthermore, this decision depends on the fact that Hobby Lobby is a family-owned, private corporation, not a publicly traded company like Apple. It is fine to endorse this view, I suppose, but to frame it in terms of loyalty oaths is dirty pool. This is right-wing politicking of the highest order, demanding that corporations be extended the full panoply of rights which the framers and almost all non-technology and non-right-wing thinkers have always thought apply *only* to natural persons. That it can somehow be mounted in terms of "human rights" and "freedom" is shocking. As a principle, "code is speech" does not represent a natural extension of rights, but rather a significant curtailing of rights, by putting ordinary actions outside the penumbra of legal regulation.

Although digital rights activists do not acknowledge First Amendment Lochnerism as a problem, they are quick to use arguments that make sense only within that framework. They do this in part through a novel use of the concept of "censorship." To the ordinary person, censorship means something very specific: governments exercising prior restraint over the publication of information, whether in print or electronic and broadcast media. In this context, censorship is understood as the primary possible violation of freedom of speech.

Of course the term is sometimes used this way in digital advocacy, but from early on it has taken on another meaning. John Gilmore—cofounder of EFF and the Cypherpunks mailing list, wealthy early Sun Microsystems employee, and "lifelong Libertarian Party member" who considers "the two major parties in the US to both be morally bankrupt, and largely indistinguishable from each other" (2013)—famously stated in a 1993 *Time* article that "the Net interprets censorship as damage and routes around it." He explains the meaning of the phrase both when he first said it and in more recent years:

In its original form, it meant that the Usenet software (which moves messages around in discussion newsgroups) was resistant to censorship because, if a node drops certain messages because it doesn't like their subject, the messages find their way past that node anyway by some other route. This is also a reference to the packet-routing protocols that the Internet uses to direct packets around any broken wires or fiber connections or routers. (They don't redirect around selective censorship, but they do recover if an entire node is shut down to censor it.)

The meaning of the phrase has grown through the years. Internet users have proven it time after time, by personally and publicly replicating information that is threatened with destruction or censorship. If you now consider the Net to be not only the wires and machines, but the people and their social structures who use the machines, it is more true than ever. (Gilmore 2013)

One must read carefully to detect the subtle shift in meaning of "censorship" that happens here. Gilmore is discussing Usenet groups, which he helped create by inventing the widely used alt.* hierarchy. He is characterizing as censorship a wide range of activities that are nongovernmental in origin. These activities may be legitimate restrictions of speech, such as blocking child abuse imagery, which was widely available on earlier internet-based systems like Usenet but has exploded in volume in recent years. Other activities have nothing to do with speech per se, but instead with blocking the operation of software—which is to say, with blocking *actions*.

This elaboration of "censorship" into the opposite of its usual meaning becomes most evident when Gilmore talks about packet-routing protocols that direct traffic around broken connections. This is an inbuilt design feature of internet technology, which is typically attributed to the need for a communication network that could survive a nuclear attack. But the physical removal of nodes in a communication network that provides a software platform (or even an entire protocol, as Usenet was) has little to do with the legal concepts of free speech and censorship. Rather, it is better understood as technical means for preventing government regulation of technology by labeling it "censorship."

Recently, the claim has been amplified through its association with cryptocurrencies and blockchain technology. Public, permissionless blockchains are theoretically decentralized, so that the software can be run by anyone with sufficient computing power and network connectivity. Therefore, there is not necessarily one person or group responsible for running the software in a specific area. At first glance, it is not clear how a governmental authority might restrict its operation. Regulating or prohibiting blockchain software is difficult in practice, much like the protocols on which the internet and web operate. Digital evangelists have named this property "censorship resistance." They believe that any attempt to manage how the software runs would be censorship, regardless of whether it involves anything recognizable as what ordinary people and ordinary law call "speech." This in turns licenses typical antigovernment agitation and digital exceptionalism. Despite the avowed intention of many in the cryptocurrency and blockchain communities to bypass or even eliminate democratic governance, any attempt by democracies to limit technological and economic power can be understood as breaking a central formal rule said to be prohibited to democracies—censoring "free speech."

The notion of blockchain as "censorship resistant" is widespread among enthusiasts, and is also occasionally mentioned by more apparently neutral commentators. As early as 2011, EFF issued one of its typical cryptocurrency explainers that asserted Bitcoin was "a step toward censorship-resistant digital currency" (Reitman 2011), though it made no effort to explain why censorship or resistance to it is an appropriate vantage point from which to view financial transactions. In recent years, blockchain syncretists have become bolder, as seen in a 2021 piece in *CoinDesk* called "Bitcoin's Censorship-Resistance Was a Step Change in History" (Dale 2021). Drawing on Gilmore's chestnut and central theorists of free speech such as John Stuart Mill and John Milton, the wildly revisionist piece quotes early Bitcoin entrepreneur Adam Ludwin's statement that "nothing can stop me from sending bitcoin to anyone I please." It then explains that "censorship resistance is a jargony way of saying speech, or any other activity, that [*sic*] can't be vetoed or stopped. . . . Censorship resistance is also a step change in the history of political philosophy."

Dale's insertion of the phrase "or any other activity" into an otherwise reasonable definition of censorship might be overlooked by readers, making it easier to miss the fact that what is characterized as "censorship" here is the transmission of funds from one person to another. Thus the core action involved in economic activity is somehow assimilated to the core activity in political discourse (as in *Citizens United*), and the desirability of speech for the latter is used to prevent political speech itself from affecting the real world. As with so much cyberlibertarian dogma, core democratic values are invoked only to prevent democracies from exercising their powers in ways that all political actors, except for those on the far right, consider legitimate and necessary.

EFF continues to promote the view that governmental regulation of technology must be understood as "censorship." Established legal and human rights thinking about censorship is to be discarded in favor of the power of digital technology. In a remarkable prologue to the book *Silicon Values: The Future of Free Speech under Surveillance Capitalism,* EFF's director for international freedom of expression Jillian C. York complains that "even today, I am sometimes chastised, usually by law professors, for distorting the (US) legal definition of" (2021, xi) censorship. She goes on:

> On this point I stand strong: censorship is not a legal term, nor is it the sole domain of government actors or synonymous with the First Amendment. Throughout history, censorship has been enacted by royals, the Church, the postal service, the Inquisition, publishers, the state, and yes, corporations. Though the details differ, censorship exists in some form in every locale throughout the world. Throughout history, censorship has most often served those at the top, allowing them to consolidate power while silencing the voices of anyone who might engage in protest. But the struggle for freedom of expression is as old as the history of censorship, and it isn't over yet.

Unsurprisingly, York offers no alternative definition, let alone a rigorous one, of "censorship" that supports this sweeping description. While she dismisses censorship as a legal term of art, she fails to propose an alternative legal perspective, ignoring its significance in discussions of democracy and democratic governance. She offers no discussion of the Lochnerism problem. To the contrary, she frequently discusses what both technology companies and users do as "actions," the regulation or prevention of which she calls "censorship." All this might not matter at all, were York anything other than the top officer at the leading "digital rights" organization ostensibly dedicated to protecting "digital privacy" and "free speech."

Some independent academics and activists have realized that digital rights promoters use "free expression" as a cudgel with which to rebuff any attempts by democracies to regulate and constrain the power of digital technology. Academics working with the Canadian Centre for International Governance

Innovation noted that "in a liberal-democratic society, there's little room for debate once you've pulled the 'censorship' pin on the free-speech grenade. It's a conversation-ender in the same way calling someone a Communist was during the Cold War" (Haggart and Tusikov 2021). They describe a spring 2021 debate about a bill that "would have allowed, among other things, the government's arm's-length telecommunications regulator to require certain social media platforms to prioritize Canadian content posted to their platforms" (which it should be noted is already a licensing condition placed on other Canadian media companies):

> What could have been a nuanced argument over whether these specific regulations were appropriate, or how to amend the provision, quickly devolved into free-speech total war.
>
> The digital rights group Open Media called it a "dangerous censorship bill." The Internet Society, whose corporate members include Google and Facebook, published an open letter signed by some of Canada's leading internet scholars calling on Prime Minister Justin Trudeau "to stop harming the Internet, the freedoms and aspirations of every individual in this country, and our knowledge economy through overreaching regulatory policies that will have significant, yet unintended consequences for the free and open Internet in Canada."

EFF chimed in as well: "The prominent US digital rights group Electronic Frontier Foundation (EFF), for example, asserted that the government's proposed online harms plan was 'one of the most dangerous proposals' in the world, leaving little room for meaningful debate. Similarly, comparisons linking Canada's proposals to those of authoritarian governments effectively serve to delegitimize democratic efforts to regulate online speech and platforms."

It is hard to read this kind of studied, repeated, and strategic use of identical arguments as more than the application of industry-based disinformation to the "threat" of democratic power. In this context, we were repeatedly warned that the "free and open internet" was in grave danger. However, the nature of this danger and why it should be prioritized over the interests of properly elected democratic representatives and their constituencies is never made clear:

This idea of a free and open internet in which free speech is the guiding principle is evident in social media companies' self-portrayal. They sell themselves as mere technical, passive "intermediaries" facilitating interactions among users, thereby downplaying the extent to which they themselves create a heavily structured and content-curated environment, in pursuit of profit. Even though they are only companies that use the network of the internet—they're not the internet itself—and even though their algorithms, by definition, order and present content in a way that's just as "unnatural" as anything a government could propose, they've co-opted this ideology to the extent that regulation of their activities is seen as an attack on the internet itself.

And of course, the language of attacks on the "internet itself" are themselves disingenuous and flexible. Any regulation at all will "break" the internet, despite the inability of EFF and others to explain exactly what these harms will be, let alone why they trump the principles and powers of democratic sovereignty to decide what is best for their own citizens.

"INTERNET FREEDOM"

In July 2012 a group of internet activists drafted what they called the "Declaration of Internet Freedom." Like many other similar efforts, this declaration models itself on political forms of speech. Indeed, the Declaration was deliberately issued to coincide with the July 4 U.S. Independence Day holiday:

We believe that a free and open Internet can bring about a better world. To keep the Internet free and open, we call on communities, industries and countries to recognize these principles. We believe that they will help to bring about more creativity, more innovation and more open societies.

We are joining an international movement to defend our freedoms because we believe that they are worth fighting for.

Let's discuss these principles—agree or disagree with them, debate them, translate them, make them your own and broaden the discussion with your community—as only the Internet can make possible.

Join us in keeping the Internet free and open.

DECLARATION

We stand for a free and open Internet.

We support transparent and participatory processes for making Internet policy and the establishment of five basic principles:

- Expression: Don't censor the Internet.
- Access: Promote universal access to fast and affordable networks.
- Openness: Keep the Internet an open network where everyone is free to connect, communicate, write, read, watch, speak, listen, learn, create and innovate.
- Innovation: Protect the freedom to innovate and create without permission. Don't block new technologies, and don't punish innovators for their users' actions.
- Privacy: Protect privacy and defend everyone's ability to control how their data and devices are used. (Free Press and Free Action Fund 2012)

The Declaration, which is organized by the progressive Free Press foundation, is signed by a mix of NGOs, individuals, and media organizations, including all the major digital rights organizations we have been discussing: EFF, CDT, Fight for the Future, the Open Technology Institute of the New America Foundation, Public Knowledge, and *TechDirt*, as well as others that are no longer operating. The signing individuals read like a who's who of cyberlibertarian and cypherpunk activism: Google lawyer Marvin Ammori, Creative Commons activist and lawyer Renata Avila, Yochai Benkler, danah boyd, Cory Doctorow, Jeff Jarvis, Reddit cofounder Alexis Ohanian, Jillian C. York, and Jonathan Zittrain. Each of these individuals has multiple intersecting connections with one another, as well as with the NGOs and corporations, particularly Google, that promote "internet freedom." In most such statements of "internet freedom," there is little to no attempt to explain how the issues raised in the document relate to civil and human rights principles as described in fundamental documents like the Universal Declaration of Human Rights. No explanation is offered for why the various progressive signatories support a statement so opposed to government regulation and the democratic sovereignty on which it rests.

The document employs the "saving" rhetoric I am calling into question. The affirmations of faith articulated in the Declaration's Preamble—that the Internet "can bring about a better world" and foster "more creativity, more innovation and more open societies"—has no particular ground. In the third paragraph we are told that "only the Internet can make possible" something, but the preceding clauses of the sentence do not follow syntactically into this statement: it might mean that only the internet can make possible the discussion of principles, or that only the internet can allow us to agree, disagree, debate, and translate them. Whatever the intended meaning of the sentence, its triumphalist assignment of abilities that are unique to the internet fits into the rhetorical excess that characterizes cyberlibertarianism. This stance rests on a cursory examination of the shape of human cultures without networked computing.

More central to the mission of the Declaration is the confusion between free and open networks and free and open societies. Such blurring is not incidental to the intended impact of the Declaration, as the invocation of "more open societies" makes clear. This confusion is compounded by the apparent lack of any need to define terms. What is meant by "permission," "free to connect," "free and open," or "transparent and participatory" is thought to be beyond question. Even the economic ambiguity between "free of charge" and "free from regulation" is obscured, especially in the entries for "openness" and "innovation." It is also interesting to note the assertion that someone must "provide universal access," which may or may not include the provision of such access without charge.

Politically, however, the most salient fact about the Declaration as a rhetorical construction is its foundational assumption: those it represents and those who will sign it share our honest intent, goodwill, and—one senses, at least—self-perception as noncommercial actors in the internet ecology. This assumption is also present in arguments supporting hackers and universal computerization, which focus solely on the good intentions of those who possess the power and presume the network is magically immune to use by bad or powerful actors. Yet the very notion of the open internet radically militates against this. What criteria should determine the entities deserving of such rights? Should they be restricted only to well-intentioned persons and groups whose charter includes overt acknowledgment of various forms of rights and responsibilities? The document's signatories include such overtly rights-oriented bodies as EFF, ACLU, Center for Democracy and Technology, and *Daily Kos*, and others, along with a range of commercial entities whose commitment to such principles prior to profit is not at all clear. The list of rights organizations can be viewed as an expression of the

Declaration's wishful thinking, while the list of commercial entities may conceal the lack of critical thinking that informs the Declaration as a whole.

The rights called for by the Declaration are far less clear than the rhetoric suggests, as there is no mechanism to distinguish between "good actors" and "bad actors," between individuals with and without power, and especially between commercial, governmental, and noncommercial entities. This is most apparent in the clauses on "innovation" and "privacy." In the innovation clause we are told that we have a right to "innovate and create without permission," while in the privacy clause we are told that there is a right to "control how one's data and devices are used." Should an individual be allowed to determine the distribution and use of intellectual property they create, as the privacy clause states, or should they be required to allow others to repurpose and use that property without permission, as the innovation clause states? While many signatories to the Declaration come from the political left, many also come from the right. However, there is no explicit discussion of how or why the rights the document accords would not be available across the board, to bad actors as well as good. And if the rights apply to bad actors, it is not clear why the benefits advertised by the Declaration would actually obtain.

When we read the Declaration from the perspective of Amazon, Facebook, Google, or the U.S. government, we note that there is no language or argument that would exclude them from the rights proposed. However, it is unclear how such rights would be guaranteed and distributed. Does the Declaration intend on enforcing its implicit stance that all intellectual property should be outlawed, for all commercial entities? Do the commercial signatories intend to sacrifice the economic value embedded in their patents and copyrights as part of a general accession to *internet* rights? Such an assertion is beyond any socialist or communist scheme for redistribution of wealth. However, the Declaration does not provide any mechanism for this redistribution or why owners of such property should abandon ownership due to the existence of the internet or the Declaration. Furthermore, it does not explain how and why capital should be distributed under a regime in which intellectual property is outlawed.

Of course, on another reading, the Declaration does not suggest that intellectual property should be outlawed. In fact, even on charitable readings the Declaration is openly self-contradictory. It does not offer any specific mechanism by which "users" should be identified, and under most existing legal regimes the notion of a "user" of a technology, patent, or copyright is not constrained to biological individuals. Legally, it is beyond question that Amazon, Facebook, and Disney have the right to "control how their data is used." One of the names those corporations give to such control is "intellectual property." How is it possible for Disney or Facebook to control the use of their data while allowing creation without permission? Facebook openly praises a "free and open internet" while maintaining billions of dollars' worth of proprietary software and tools that are only available to paying commercial customers. Much of this software includes statistical data on users' activities that is poorly understood by the users themselves, who imagine their "privacy" is protected by Facebook's control settings. Such preferences do not protect users from a wide range of software aggregative and statistical data-sharing, to which all platform visitors are inherently subject. Facebook always claims that such sharing is in the users' interests.

Much of the Declaration is written from the perspective of an empowered individual. *Give me what I have and want, now,* he says. *What I see in front of me is mine, and if what I see appears to be yours, it should be mine as well. However, what is mine belongs to me, and it should be up to me whether you feel it should belong to you.* These values are not merely in conflict with each other; they are in direct contradiction. One cannot insist both that all data should be open and free, on the one hand, and that individuals should be able to choose whether to allow their own data to be open and free on the other.

The blindness of such efforts to the variant power and status of the actors in networks characterizes nearly all claims for internet freedom that do not ground themselves in careful considerations of *human* freedom—as Joss Winn (2012) has put it, in "freedom of people" rather than "freedom of things." Unlike the Universal Declaration of Human Rights, which carefully outlines the freedoms to be accorded to "all members of the human family" and advocates "a world in which human beings shall enjoy freedom of speech and belief and freedom from fear and want," the Declaration of Internet Freedom substitutes wishful projections about "openness and freedom" that, due to lack of precision, extend rights to corporate and governmental actors whose interests will often conflict with individual human beings. Further, very little in the Declaration of Internet Freedom adds to the Universal Declaration of Human Rights. As such, it is not clear what is added to the original, nor how the authors of the new Declaration intend for conflicts between the two charters to be resolved.

Comparing the two Declarations reveals the intellectual thinness that underlies the more recent of them. Almost all nations of the world are signatories to the Universal Declaration, so any right it guarantees need not be restated by new documents. Yet Article 12 of the Universal Declaration (whose full text is available on the UN website), reads: "No one shall be subjected to arbitrary interference with his privacy, family, home or correspondence, nor to attacks upon his honour and reputation. Everyone has the right to the protection of the law against such interference or attacks." This is more extensive than the privacy section in the new Declaration, and affords legal protections not mentioned by the later document.

Similarly, Article 19 reads, "Everyone has the right to freedom of opinion and expression; this right includes freedom to hold opinions without interference and to seek, receive and impart information and ideas through any media and regardless of frontiers." The inclusion of "any media" in the new Declaration raises the question of what is being added to the old. It certainly makes one wonder how many signatories to the new Declaration have read the existing, ratified, and still active Universal Declaration. Regardless, one wonders whose interests are being served by the new Declaration, what needs prompt them, and what legal bodies are intended as the guarantors of the rights enumerated.

Like so much cyberlibertarian discourse, the Declaration seems like a harmless enough and even valiant exercise, until one presses a bit on the surface. What if the energy devoted to the Declaration were instead devoted to investigating and enforcing the many human rights accorded under the Universal Declaration that are not upheld in practice for many human beings? What is the level of familiarity of the signatories of the new Declaration with the earlier and more comprehensive UN document, and how many of them imagine that there is some reciprocity or equivalence between the internet Declaration and a true Declaration of human rights? The new document lacks care and detail, which inadvertently—or purposely, in the minds of some signatories?—grants conflicting rights to corporate and governmental bodies. Due to their greater power relative to individuals, these entities are likely to end up serving the powerful more than the powerless. Should Disney sign the new Declaration, it's doubtful the company would give up its vigorous protection of its legal intellectual property rights worldwide. The belief that signing such a document supports human freedoms, like much computer utopian action and rhetoric, might ultimately do more harm than good, except to corporations intent on using such rhetoric for their own profit.

Shawn Powers and Michael Jablonski have written the most thorough analysis of the discourse of internet freedom available so far, *The Real Cyber War: The Political Economy of Internet Freedom* (2015). As they explain, "Efforts to create a singular, universal internet built upon Western legal, political, and social preferences alongside the 'freedom to connect' is [*sic*] driven primarily by economic and geopolitical motivations rather than the humanitarian and democratic ideals that typically accompany related policy discourse" (3). They note that at the height of the Obama administration— which was nearly a partnership with Google (as exemplified in *The New Digital Age*, the 2013 volume cowritten by former Google CEO Eric Schmidt and former Google executive and State Department adviser Jared Cohen)— Secretary of State Hillary Clinton maintained an "evolving doctrine of internet freedom." Despite being "veiled in ideological language," this was in fact "the realization of a broader strategy promoting a particular conception of networked communication that depends on American companies (for example, Amazon, AT&T, Facebook, Google, and Level 3), supports Western norms (such as copyright, advertising-based consumerism, and the like), and promotes Western products" (6). Clinton even proposed an "expanded interpretation of the UDHR" (7), which includes that vaguely defined "freedom to connect."

While the intersection between political sovereignty and this "proposed new freedom" remained vague, the Obama internet freedom agenda as realized by Clinton "also focused on the economic logic of allowing for greater transnational flows of information" (8). The authors argue that "Clinton's articulation of the benefits of free and open communication on international peace, espousing the democratizing power of the internet and the economic benefits of being online—'A connection to global information networks is like an onramp to modernity'—obfuscates geopolitical motivations driving trends toward global connectivity" (9). This nod toward "modernization theory" carries overtones of white-man's-burden paternalism toward non-Western countries and realpolitik toward Western democracies. It follows in the tradition of neoliberal economics so ably analyzed by Mirowski (2013) and others, substituting economics for politics using a rhetorical tool developed by cyberlibertarianism dogmatists.

In some ways the discourse of internet freedom cuts against the usual functions of cyberlibertarianism by advancing the interests of "open" democracies against authoritarian non-democracies. Yet at a more subtle level, it fits perfectly by substituting for both national and international politics the economic power of communications technologies, including the companies that build, deploy, and maintain them, as well as the technologists who operate them. Some of these technologists appear to be separate from commercial interests. But it has remained next to impossible to articulate "internet freedom" as a clear, abstract principle such that its inclusion in a document like the UDHR makes any sense. Copyright activist and digital rights critic Neil Turkewitz drew attention in 2018 to a report generated by Freedom House, a nonpartisan organization founded in 1941 "to encourage popular support for American involvement in World War II at a time when isolationist sentiments were running high in the United States" (Turkewitz 2018). Freedom House is a problematic organization that has at times shifted between promoting democratic values and promoting U.S. power in an overt and jingoistic manner. Even granting this, upon reading the report, Turkewitz "found [it] to be shocking in its bias and its oversimplification of extremely complex issues."

Turkewitz focuses on the vagueness in Freedom House's attempts to define internet freedom "as the absence of government restraints on internet-based conduct, thereby channeling the cyber-Utopianism of John Perry Barlow. But while the absence of government oversight is what provides freedom to Google and other Silicon Valley companies, the public's freedom may be found elsewhere." The report authors "repeatedly warn about 'digital authoritarianism,' but then seem to define it as the very application of national laws to the internet which isn't authoritarianism, but governance and the rule of law." The report's pronouncements are shaped to sound good—"The health of the world's democracies depends" on "global internet freedom," they write—but the report is directed against democracies having any power to manage the growth of digital technology, even when that technology produces and supports real authoritarianism around the world. "Freedom House, after having correctly identified the toxicity of the present internet environment, then designates efforts to address such toxicity as a threat to internet freedom." The report focuses on typical cyberlibertarian myths and causes such as Section 230, net neutrality, and "censorship" (of U.S.-based technology companies) rather than being concerned about obvious and crucial threats to democratic rule. It also exhibits a troubling strain of America First propaganda. Unsurprisingly, Google and the Internet Society, a digital rights organization, funded the work. Rather than promoting democracy or civil rights in any legible fashion, this leading report on "internet freedom" turns out to be a "lobbying tool" notable "for the absence of anything that would strengthen the authority to defend the rule of law, or hold platforms to a higher level of accountability for their conduct." Yet again, the apparent promotion of democracy turns out to be anything but.

"CODE IS LAW"

Lawrence Lessig introduced the concept that "code is law" in the 1999 book *Code: And Other Laws of Cyberspace* (subsequently revised and reissued in 2006), one of the earliest scholarly works to argue that the modern technical environment poses significant challenges for constitutional and representative governance. Lessig is widely known as one of the academic and legal world's internet advocates who is not overtly a member of the right wing. He frequently opines on issues of intellectual property, copyright, and politics in ways that many on the left consider hospitable to their politics. In many ways they are correct.

Yet Lessig is an odd candidate for the position of *non*-rightist proponent of rights in the digital era. Evgeny Morozov describes the model Lessig advances in *Code:* "Lessig's model assumes four forces—market, norms, laws, and code—and, to many, it looks innocent and objective enough" (2013d). But Morozov goes on:

> To make full sense of this model, one needs to know where Lessig comes from intellectually. His framework packs many assumptions about human behavior, regulation, knowledge, and political economy. That Lessig matured at the University of Chicago Law School, that he was profoundly influenced by the legal theorist and judge Richard Posner (Lessig clerked for him), that the code framework is rooted in the law and economics tradition of legal theory—a tradition that is very friendly to neoliberalism—all of this matters. Just like there's nothing natural about the discourse of law and economics,

there's nothing natural about the discourse of "code" or the discourse of "cyberspace" that Lessig did so much to shape in the 1990s.

The "law and economics tradition" mentioned by Morozov is not simply one tradition among many "very friendly to neoliberalism." It is a central part of the tradition that gives rise to the practices of the Neoliberal Thought Collective and the Austrian school of economics typically associated with Friedrich von Hayek and Ludwig von Mises. This is done via the closely allied Chicago School of Economics most famously associated with Chicago economists Milton Friedman, Gary Becker (both presidents of the Mont Pelerin Society), digital patron saint economist and MPS member Ronald Coase, and MPS member Richard Posner.

Philip Mirowski notes that the work of a computationally driven project originally part of the World War II military apparatus, the Columbia University Statistical Research Group (SRG), underwrote the development of the NTC: "The SRG was responsible in many ways for the peccadilloes of the postwar 'Chicago school' of political economy" (2002, 201). Along with a few other U.S. working groups, the Chicago School developed what has come to be called "Neoclassical Price Theory" or sometimes just "neoclassical economics." Mirowski describes this theory as follows: "Briefly, to risk caricature of this position, its first commandment is that the market always 'works,' in the sense that its unimpeded operation maximizes welfare. Its second commandment is that the government is always part of the problem, rather than part of the solution. The third commandment is that the demand curve is the rock-bottom fundamental entity in price theory, and that attempts to 'go behind' the demand curve in order to locate its foundations in the laws of utility or 'indifference' . . . were primarily a waste of time and effort" (203–4).

These "commandments," especially the first two, form the core of neoliberal thought and practice to this day. The second in particular is the element of neoliberal and libertarian doctrine that has filtered down into cyberlibertarianism—with the proviso added later, in the mid-1980s, that the way to ameliorate government being "always part of the problem" is to take for oneself the levers of governmental power, in part by advancing in public the view that government is the problem. Yet even the third "commandment," which appears to be a technical thesis about economic analysis, turns out to ground theory in an extremely political point of view.

In this case, although we may know that human beings in real markets are not purely rational agents, they still pursue what most right-wing thinkers term "maximal utility." This refers to the pursuit of the greatest good for oneself, or for us, the greatest wealth for oneself, following more or less in the footsteps of John Stuart Mill and Jeremy Bentham.

Lessig's claim that "code is law" is built on his belief, mentioned by Morozov, that there are four modalities for regulating human behavior: norms, markets, laws, and architecture. As the legal scholar Viktor Mayer-Schönberger writes in a thoughtful critical analysis of this claim, "Lessig is less interested in norms, laws, and markets, and more in what he sees as an overlooked fourth mode of regulation: architecture. Following in the footsteps of a long line of theorists, he suggests that the tools we use to interact constrain us" (2008, 716–17). Among these tools, digital media (aka "cyberspace") is special: "Because cyberspace is plastic—a space that we can shape like no other place—and it constrains human behavior, designing cyberspace is a very powerful regulating activity. It produces what Lessig calls 'West Coast Code,' software code that regulates human behavior" (717). Lessig contrasts "West Coast Code" with "East Coast Code," which is to say "laws," which, in Mayer-Schönberger's words,

> are created through a highly formalized and complex mechanism in democracies. For the most part, passing laws is difficult, expensive and time-consuming. Most importantly, before laws are enacted, they will be made public and can be scrutinized. We as a society can discuss them. This is, Lessig suggests, how we want it to be. West Coast Code on the other hand is much cheaper and faster to create. It is built into software that we use. It does not need to be made transparent, and no legislative body representing us, the sovereign, has to cast a vote. All that is necessary is for engineers in a corporation producing software to code it. (717–18)

In many ways this analysis is hard to disagree with. It comes down to the view that engineers are creating de facto regulatory architectures that constrain and even determine human behavior outside the channels we as a society have decided appropriate for this activity: that is, governments. (Lessig's emphasis on computer code notwithstanding, many corporate practices serve as de facto regulations and laws in many spheres of conduct, even in democracies.)

This argument deserves closer scrutiny. In ordinary usage, the word "code" has a wide range of meanings. Relevant to this discussion, both the contents of computer programs and bodies of law are referred to as "code." It is also used to refer to regulations and guidelines that are not the same thing as laws enacted by the government—building codes and codes of conduct, for example. Further, even with respect to laws, our government like many others distinguishes between two fundamentally distinct kinds of code: civil and criminal. In addition, "regulation" typically refers to a specific and interesting subset of laws that are propagated by regulatory agencies (such as the DOE, EPA, HUD, or NRC). These rules are specifically meant to govern the behavior of targeted entities (such as nuclear power plants or vulnerable parts of the environment) that legislators have determined require specialized oversight.

In a technical sense, such "regulations" themselves are not even laws. This is notable because Lessig refers almost exclusively to the regulatory, rather than legal, functions of the code he claims functions as law. He must be aware of this, and the mere fact that what he calls "West Coast Code" has the potential to regulate human behavior does not justify the terminological equivalence between computer programs and legislation. Not only do they (usually) inhabit distinct parts of our social structure, they function very differently. All things being equal, laws can only be changed by formal and overt acts of elected representatives. Computer code, on the contrary, can be changed at the whim of whoever wrote or maintains that software. While citizens are expected to know the laws regulating their behavior in a given region, there is no parallel expectation for users to understand the kinds of embedded "regulatory" computing code behavior, which need not be made visible to them.

While "terms of service" agreements are familiar to anyone who uses web-based tools, they cover only a fraction of the actual "behavior regulating" features of those software products. Further, the world is full of "regulatory" structures that are not commonly referred to as "code" but function just as Lessig alleges "West Coast Code" does. When we enter a supermarket, the architecture and design guide us to walk down the aisles and not through them. Our behavior is subtly (or not so subtly) regulated to direct us toward appealing items we may not have intended to purchase. While it is useful to think about such practices as exerting control over human behavior, equating them with laws is not helpful.

In the first 1999 version of *Code* Lessig writes:

> Cyberspace presents something new for those who think about regulation
> and freedom. It demands a new understanding of how regulation works and
> of what regulates life there. It compels us to look beyond the traditional
> lawyer's scope—beyond laws, regulations, and norms. It requires an account
> of a newly salient regulator.
>
> That regulator is the obscurity in the book's title—*Code*. In real space we
> recognize how laws regulate—through constitutions, statues, and other legal
> codes. In cyberspace we must understand how code regulates—how the soft-
> ware and hardware that make cyberspace what it is regulate cyberspace as it
> is. As William Mitchell puts it, this code is cyberspace's "law." *Code is law.* (6)

There is a trivial sense in which Lessig's first paragraph is certainly true, but
no truer than it has been since the Constitution was ratified. Law must
adapt to changing circumstances, whether by metaphorical application of
existing law, enacting of new law, or both. (See Wallace and Green 1997 for
an account of this process with specific reference to digital media.) Beyond
that, there is an obvious way that Lessig's point is refuted by widely known
facts. It is bizarre to suggest that because an activity takes place on the internet has much, if any, bearing on its relationship to law, as existing laws and
regulations already cover activities that take place on the internet. This is not
mere technicality. Laws and regulations against false advertising apply to
internet advertisements the same way they do to any other advertisements.
The same is true for laws against libel and slander. Communications used
in furtherance of criminal acts or criminal conspiracies are searchable by
warrant just like any other communications. Buying something illegal over
the internet is exactly as illegal as it is in person. Tax laws apply to corporations regardless of the modality in which they conduct business. So the
boldest strokes of Lessig's rhetoric are seriously misleading: "the software
and hardware that make cyberspace what it is" do not "regulate" the internet to the exclusion of the same laws that regulate all our other activities.

In the 2006 version of *Code*, this critical passage is replaced with a more
nuanced discussion:

> Lawyers and legal theorists get bothered, however, when I echo this slogan
> [that "code is law"]. There are differences, they insist, between the regulatory

effects produced by code and the regulatory effects produced by law, not the least of which is the difference in the "internal perspective" that runs with each kind of regulation. We understand the internal perspective of legal regulation—for example, that the restrictions the law might impose on a company's freedom to pollute are a product of self-conscious regulation, reflecting values of the society imposing that regulation. That perspective is harder to recognize with code. It could be there, but it need not. And no doubt this is just one of many important differences between "code" and "law."

I don't deny these differences. I only assert that we learn something useful from ignoring them for a bit. Justice Holmes famously focused the regulator on the "bad man." He offered a theory of regulation that assumed that "bad man" at its core. His point was not that everyone was a "bad man"; the point instead was about how we could best construct systems of regulation.

My point is the same. I suggest we learn something if we think about the "bot man" theory of regulation—one focused on the regulation of code. We will learn something important, in other words, if we imagine the target of regulation as a maximizing entity, and consider the range of tools the regulator has to control that machine. (5–6)

Lessig offers no counterargument to the points his interlocutors make. Despite his position as perhaps the pre-eminent legal theorist of cyberspace, he acknowledges that "lawyers and legal theorists" find his identification of "code" with "law" inaccurate. Even though this chapter is still titled "Code Is Law" in the 2006 edition, Lessig backs off that assertion almost entirely. Indeed, he deletes its occurrence as the summary point of the paragraph in which it originally occurred. Instead of insisting that code is law, Lessig posits only that "we learn something" if we *look at* code as a kind of regulation. Further, his emphasis has shifted, subtly but critically, from viewing code *as* regulation to the "regulation *of* code." Yet cyberlibertarian rhetoric demands that the "digital" remains a space of exception, beyond the reach of governmental power or democratic oversight, where "Governments of the Industrial World . . . have no sovereignty," as Barlow (1996, 28) put it. So it comes as no surprise that despite Lessig's retraction of the "code is law" formula, it remains a prominent part of cyberlibertarian rhetoric.

What concerns Lessig, at least in the *Code* volumes, is not the direct intervention of unelected representatives ("West Coast" coders) in social spaces most of us understand as the proper domains of government ("East Coast" coders), but instead the impact of these practices on digital media itself: "Lessig is worried about this shift from East Coast Code to West Coast Code. He fears that it will cause cyberspace to lose much of the quality that it initially had as a place of open, robust discussion. He is troubled by the prospect that the values that underlie how cyberspace is designed will change" (Mayer-Schönberger 2008, 718). Thus the major target of Lessig's critique is what he sees as the ability of certain corporations—the media industries, as opposed to computer-centered organizations like Google— to take unfair advantage of government's copyright power, and the alleged new opacity of government made possible by computerization. Governments, in Lessig's view (according to Mayer-Schönberger), have a "general tendency . . . to desire control over society" (718). As a result of the new capabilities made available by West Coast Code,

> governments will move from directly constraining behavior with East Coast Code to indirectly constraining behavior with laws that regulate West Coast Code. Such indirect regulation is much less transparent and thus less likely to face the stiff public opposition that has kept the government within our society's system of checks and balances. Lessig is also worried that the plasticity of software allows governments to constrain behavior more easily and to a greater extent than they could through law alone. Corporations will work with government to change the architecture of cyberspace because they, too, profit from a more controllable space. Intellectual property rights can thus be better enforced, advertisements more precisely targeted, and some of the harsh wind of competition can be more easily avoided through a more regulable space. (718)

What this describes, speaking politically, is fascism (or what is called in contemporary euphemism "corporate capitalism"): the corporate capture of government. This assessment captures the most worrisome tendency in contemporary society and offers an accurate assessment of the problems we face.

Although Lessig is concerned with this problem, in the *Code* volumes he focuses on the specific, artificially nostalgic, and sentimental martyrdom of an "internet" that should have been but now is lost, or in danger of being lost: "Lessig's central fear is that this coalition of producers of East Coast Code and producers of West Coast Code will replace the values embedded in the original Internet with ones that reflect their own—values that may not comport with the preferences of the citizens. Lessig uses intellectual property, privacy, and free speech as three examples of this potential shift in values" (718–19). Instead of being concerned with the internet as an attack on the system of constitutional and representative democracy itself, he worries that this attack might be muted or constrained *by* government. This concern is bolstered by the typical cyberlibertarian idea that there are "values embedded in the original internet" that we are on the verge of losing. Such a view requires an extremely narrow and self-interested reading of both social and technological history. If there is such a thing as the "original internet," the only value that can be ascribed to it with some degree of confidence is "partial survivability after world nuclear war," a value not really touched by any of the considerations Lessig raises.

Not surprisingly, Lessig offers a familiar remedy for this problem: "There may be an antidote, Lessig suggests, in the form of 'open code': West Coast Code that is open and thus not controllable by corporate coders. Such open code may be less vulnerable to indirect regulation through laws, and it is certainly less susceptible to corporate desires for control" (719). Yet nothing of the sort is true. Open source code is widely used by corporations in the service of control. The fact that it is available for inspection does not tell most of us—perhaps any of us—much about *how it is being used* or give us the power to do much about it.

Underneath this analysis is one grounded firmly in the law and economics tradition and even the specific analyses of the Neoliberal Thought Collective, even if Lessig does not always frame things this way: "Lessig wants users to choose. The choice he envisions, however, is a specific one. It is the choice of consumers selecting goods in the marketplace. Lessig does not hide this preference; his argument often reflects a strong presumption for the market. Choice for him is the ability to select from two or more options. As long as there are options for users, there is competition. Competitive markets ensure that users remain empowered. Choice is the first foundational value of Lessig's theory" (721). This is the fundamental precept of Chicago School neoclassical economics, the law and economics movement, and contemporary neoliberalism. In the guise of providing "choice" and equating "choice" with "freedom," many social spaces not previously made available to the market are reconfigured as markets. According to Mayer-Schönberger:

> Fundamentally, therefore, Lessig's argument rests on the omnipresence and beneficial power of the market. This must not surprise us. In a way, Lessig's foundations may reveal a personal path-dependence. He is, after all, a creature of the University of Chicago Law School, where he spent his early years as a legal academic and a clerk of Judge Richard Posner. Consequently, it is likely he is well-attuned to the law and economics movement, spearheaded by Posner. His politics may have changed over the years (he started out as a Republican, only to turn into a liberal later in life), but the political theory that undergirds his thinking has not. (723)

Thus again, the language of freedom, individual revolution, and openness that characterizes much of Lessig's rhetoric conceals a commitment to neoliberal concepts that mesh poorly with politics that do not come from the right. That overt anarcho-capitalists like Adam Thierer and Berin Szóka can characterize Lessig as "cyber-collectivist" (2009, 5) shows only that the spectrum of political thought available regarding digital technology extends from moderate right to far right.

Lessig's changing position on the phrase "code is law" might have caused it to become another dead letter in the cyberlibertarian lexicon, but its recurrence in the worlds of Bitcoin and blockchain has kept it alive. In part, this is due to the ill-named bits of computer code that Ethereum cofounder Vitalik Buterin referred to as "smart contracts" (although he has since come to regret the terminology; see Scott 2018). Smart contracts are said by advocates to fix the problems with ordinary contracts, which are apparently too uncertain and ambiguous for engineers who want to rewrite fundamental parts of the social world. However, they fail to function the way actual contracts do for just those reasons (Gerard 2017; Levy 2017).

Cryptocurrency ideologues continue to promote the idea, mostly to disparage the messy system of human politics and offer their own "clean," "untainted," "unbiased" algorithmic systems as replacements. They demonstrate that they are not fit for that purpose. Even some of those who admit that as currently constituted code does not seem to function the way laws are supposed to, they continue to hold out "hope" that someday computer programs will replace legal infrastructure (Abegg 2016). Others offer industry-friendly ameliorations suggesting that there is something of substance to the idea (De Filippi and Wright 2018; Hassan and De Filippi 2017). Forgetting that the point of law, at some level, is to ensure democracy and even justice, which are human social phenomena that require human participation for their very substance; even at the most basic level, as a cryptocurrency industry publication somewhat surprisingly put it with appropriate skepticism, "the Silicon Valley 'geeks' are wrong": "code isn't law—law is law" (Rozen 2021).

PART III

CYBERFASCISM

CHAPTER 7

Cyberlibertarianism and the Far Right

The inchoate and syncretic politics of cyberlibertarianism make it a potent vector through which right-wing thought spreads. The rhetorical devices and strategies it uses solicit the support of many who do not actively identify with the right. Understanding this ability to garner political assent from beyond its nominally proper base is one of the main reasons for developing the cyberlibertarian analytical framework. Cyberlibertarianism has been one of the primary forces helping to shift global politics to the right, though it would be a mistake to see it as the only force propelling that shift. Analysis of cyberlibertarianism has not so far left examined a highly pointed question: what role does cyberlibertarianism play in encouraging overt fascism and Nazism?

ANARCHO-CAPITALISM
AND THE FAR RIGHT

There are important historical and philosophical ties between nominally libertarian politics and the far right. Commentators from both the moderate right and across the left have pointed repeatedly to what one writer called the "libertarian-to-fascism pipeline" (Dougherty 2017; see also Anderson 2011; Fenwick 2019; Slobodian 2019). Some have gone so far as to see political libertarianism as the "friendly" or public face of fascism, attracting those who may not be consciously ready to embrace the hateful core of fascism (UnKoch My Campus n.d.). Others draw attention to the ways that almost all anarchist and libertarian philosophies cannot help but create openings for the far right—what Ross (2017) calls the "fascist creep."

Even granting these general principles, digital technology (and its promotion) has specific and notable effects in the promotion of far-right politics. As I discuss in *The Cultural Logic of Computation* (2009), there are "natural" affinities between digital technology and the foundations of political reaction, especially with the conviction that might makes right: that the dominant salient political factor in the world is how much power a person or group can accrue to itself, and that any action is licensed in the pursuit of that power and its maintenance once achieved: and ultimately that "might makes right." The widespread belief that technological *empowerment* is inherently positive is almost indistinguishable in social terms from the belief that technological change is inherently politically progressive, or at least politically welcome. Although this empowerment is said to be attached to minority or otherwise vulnerable populations, it is not always easy to find it credibly embedded within larger politics that resist the might-makes-right perspective.

The Cultural Logic of Computation focused more narrowly on something like political psychology, the underlying ideas about self and society that tend to be endorsed by those who strongly identify with computers and the digital revolution. The connections of this analysis to general questions of political philosophy are to some extent obvious. A political philosophy that is based solely on the empowerment of the self or the group with which the self identifies does not align with the values associated with core democratic politics. These values include sovereignty that is widely dispersed across all people. The psychological appeal of digital technology to the least rational parts of our brains and bodies has pushed populations toward the promotion of more or less authoritarian power and away from democratic and dissensus-based political theories. Here again the irony must be noted of the claim that digital technology "democratizes," despite the manifest ways it presses so firmly against core democratic values.

It is not surprising that at the rightward extreme of digital technology proponents there is an overrepresentation of far-right actors, whether they overtly identify with the far right or simply express far-right ideas without declaiming their political identities (or, in some important cases, explicitly disavowing them). For many, perhaps most, digital evangelists, this creates a political paradox with which they strenuously avoid engaging: if the digital promotes democracy, how is it that the spread of digital technology has been nearly coterminous with, and in most cases directly implicated in, the worldwide resurgence of fascism and a corresponding weakening of commitment to democratic values?

Cyberfascism overlaps in significant ways with formations such as the alt-right and QAnon. The point here is not to describe a discrete group of fascist ideologies. Rather it is to show that fascism is profoundly active in online communities, that these communities frequently draw direct connections between their experiences with digital technology and their involvement with far-right politics, and that the online far right are among the most persistent and loudest promoters of cyberlibertarian politics. That is, digital fascists are adept at championing causes like open source, decentralization, and encryption, drawing meaningful connections between these causes and their extremist politics. Many thinkers have long raised the question whether ACLU's now-proverbial support for "Nazis at Skokie" was protecting principles or "just supporting Nazis" (Delgado and Stefancic 2018). At least in that case, ACLU can point to a fully articulated set of foundational political commitments it claims require it to support Nazis if it supports anyone. In the case of cyberlibertarian propaganda and the defense of "digital rights" and "internet freedom," there is no robust body of principled foundations. Therefore, the fact that defense of these principles keeps empowering fascism raises even more serious questions about the overall shape of the underlying political project. In the case of digital technology, we are not simply defending the right of the "worst among us" to speak, but rather we are defending everyone's right to speak. We are talking about defending technologies designed by fascists and intended to promote fascism, all in the name of protecting a set of vague, principle-like slogans that fascists themselves helped articulate.

There is no doubt that a clear line of division can be drawn between non-fascist and fascist promotion of cyberlibertarian dogma. Some of the figures whose statements have been most concerning will move backstage, while others will come forward. Many digital rights organizations, activists, journalists, and scholars deplore fascism, and many make their opposition to fascism well-known. Yet however welcome it is, such vocal opposition can ring hollow.

Despite the clear utility of digital tools for the spread of fascist propaganda and the coordination of fascist direct action, many digital rights organizations downplay or dismiss this fact entirely. They insist on the usefulness of these tools for non- or anti-fascist movements, which does not disprove their utility for fascism. This can even double down on the original problem by failing to explain how and why tools intended to connect everyone and magnify their voices will not differentially magnify the voices of those who already have the most power and the most ability to manipulate these tools and networks. (See Schradie 2019 on the usefulness of digital tools for the right and far right; and Eubanks 2011 on the relatively impotence of digital activism for progressive causes.)

They also deflect attention from digital tools by pointing out that other forms of media, especially right-wing talk radio and cable networks as well as evangelical broadcasting, all play roles in the spread of fascist propaganda (Neiwert 2009, 2018). There is no doubt this is true, but that does not absolve digital media of its role in growth of worldwide fascism. Indeed, most of these other media forms predate the World Wide Web, so in raw historical terms it is the rise of digital media that occurs simultaneously with the move toward the right. Further, these same lines of denialist argument are often advanced by those who elsewhere celebrate the power of digital media to connect, coordinate, and do political work. It is only when critics point out how useful these tools are for the far right that denialists downplay their influence. Finally, and perhaps most damning of all, most of these activists and organizations steadfastly resist every call to examine how their policy positions, themes, ideas, and issues—all those we have examined so far—magnify the power of the far right.

As we have seen in previous chapters, all libertarian pseudo-philosophies are largely inchoate groups of apologies for concentrated power. They leave significant openings for authoritarian politics and have often been described as a kind of human face for those politics. In our world, most but not all authoritarian politics emerge from the far right, and much more so since the rise of digital technology than prior to it. This is in line with what early critics of digital technology, such as Mumford and Ellul, anticipated. The explosion of libertarian pseudo-philosophy is directly complicit with the rise of fascism.

Murray Rothbard, Ayn Rand, Ron Paul, and other leading anarcho-capitalists, whose works are often cited for support by cypherpunks and digital activists, have been accused of being sympathetic to fascist politics by some of their fellow travelers and critics. This became especially apparent during and after the 2016 election of Donald Trump and with the rise of the "alt-right." As moderate libertarian and proprietor of the *Bleeding Heart Libertarians* blog Steve Horwitz wrote in 2017:

> The paleo-libertarian seed that Ron Paul, Murray Rothbard, and Lew Rockwell planted in the 1990s has come to bear some really ugly fruit in the last couple of years as elements of the alt-right have made appearances in various libertarian organizations and venues. Back in February, alt-right hero Richard Spencer stirred up a fuss at the International Students for Liberty Conference in DC after being invited to hang out by a group of students calling themselves the "Hoppe Caucus." Hans-Hermann Hoppe, long associated with the Ludwig von Mises Institute as well as a panoply of racists and anti-Semites, is perhaps the most popular gateway drug for the alt-right incursion into libertarianism.

Horwitz rightly names Hoppe as a particular locus of concern for those who accept the idea of a strong connection between libertarianism and fascism. Yet to some extent, like many of those sympathetic to libertarianism, Horwitz underplays the evidence necessary to make the connection clear. Hoppe, who was once a student of Murray Rothbard and later taught alongside him at UNLV, is best known for his controversial book *Democracy: The God That Failed* (2001). Hoppe's readers tend to focus on passages in which he makes troubling remarks about "an anarcho-capitalist society," which he considers "the only social order that can be defended as just." In such a society

> all land is privately owned, including all streets, rivers, airports, harbors, and so on. With respect to some pieces of land, the property title may be unrestricted; that is, the owner is permitted to do with his property whatever he pleases as long as he does not physically damage the property owned by others. With respect to other territories, the property title may be more or less severely restricted. As is currently the case in some housing developments, the owner may be bound by contractual limitations on what he can do with his property (voluntary zoning), which might include residential versus commercial use, no buildings more than four stories high, no sale or rent to Jews, Germans, Catholics, homosexuals, Haitians, families with or without children, or smokers, for example.

342 Cyberlibertarianism and the Far Right

Hoppe justifies his remarks by noting that discriminatory property title policies, including all those he mentions, are currently found "in some housing
developments." If such notices were merely occasional they might be overlooked. Instead, throughout the book, Hoppe consistently makes remarks
that seem to target LGBTQ people, Black people, and other historically
discriminated minorities as unfit to be included in his ideal communities.
He also relies on the same highly questionable assertions about race, ethnicity, and "intelligence" that are found frequently among far-right extremists. "Civilization and culture do have a genetic (biological) basis" (184), he
writes. "However, as the result of statism—of forced integration, egalitarianism, welfare policies, and family destruction—the genetic quality of the
population has most certainly declined. Indeed, how could it not when
success is systematically punished and failure rewarded? Whether intended
or not, the welfare state promotes the proliferation of intellectually and
morally inferior people and the results would be even worse were it not
for the fact that crime rates are particularly high among these people, and
that they tend to eliminate each other more frequently" (184–85). Defenders of Hoppe justify this kind of remark as truth-telling that is free of bias.
However, thinkers more attuned to the patterns and practices of fascism
and white supremacy will disagree.

Hoppe's advocates (e.g., Kinsella 2010) argue that he is not personally
biased, racist, or homophobic. His demands for fascist political programs
are deflected as a matter of personal feeling, and we are expected to ignore
the obvious contexts of those political programs in the face of purportedly
good-faith attestations of personal belief. Of course, many fascists insist
that they are "good people" who love their neighbors (Baker 2016), but even
this misses the forest for the trees. Fascism is not just about constructing
and oppressing hated "others." It is also about replacing democratic sovereignty, equal rights, and universal enfranchisement with the economic philosophy of absolutely free markets. This is the heart of fascist philosophy
for both Mussolini's Italy and Hitler's Germany, as articulated by Landa
(2010). On these points Hoppe is unambiguous.

FASCISM AND DIGITAL TECHNOLOGY

"Fascism" is a challenging term to use and to define. In its most specific historical formation, the word refers to the political regime of Benito Mussolini
in Italy in the period leading up to and including World War II. While the

movement certainly had some exponents outside of Italy, especially in Spain and France, some argue that fascism proper should not even be applied to Germany. This is because "'fascism' was an Italian term, which Nazis, being German nationalists, did not want to borrow" (Mann 2004, 9), and that "only Nazi racism perpetrated genocide," according to those who see Nazism and fascism as distinct. Yet Michael Mann, a sociologist and contemporary expert on fascism, echoes most other scholars in concluding that "the two movements shared similar core values" and that "Hitler and Mussolini thought they belonged to the same movement."

The definition of fascism is further muddied by the far right's deliberate propaganda to obscure its function and meaning. From the outset of the movement as a world political force, Mussolini and other European fascists placed themselves on the far right of the political spectrum. In contrast, the right in the United States has attempted to turn the term against itself, labeling those who oppose fascism as fascists themselves, sometimes even the "real" fascists. This typical rightist anti-logic is particularly potent with regard to the term "fascism." Its purpose is abundantly clear: to prevent any analysis that acknowledges there can be extreme right-wing political formations.

Fascism scholar Roger Griffin has developed a synthetic definition of the core of fascism, or what he calls the "fascist minimum," that has wide currency among scholars today: "Fascism is a genus of political ideology whose mythic core in its various permutations is a palingenetic form of populist ultranationalism" (1991, 26). His definition is echoed at major points by scholars such as Mann (2004), Robert Paxton (2004), and Jason Stanley (2018). (See "Definitions of Fascism" (2022) for a full range of perspectives.) In Griffin's definition, "palingenetic" refers to "the myth of renewal, of rebirth" (1991, 32), along with "the sense of a new start or of regeneration after a phase of crisis or decline which can be associated just as much with mystical (for example the Second Coming) as secular realities (for example the New Germany)" (33).

It is important to keep these definitions in mind when identifying fascist currents in digital culture. At the same time, it is important to pull back toward wider perspectives that identify fascist tendencies regardless of whether they have developed into full-fledged fascism. Umberto Eco's 1995 description of "Ur-Fascism," is one of the most influential, in which Eco embraces the oft-noted fact that historical fascism was a *fuzzy* totalitarianism, a collage of different philosophical and political ideas, a beehive of contradictions." Fascism is "a rigid discombobulation, a structured confusion. Fascism was philosophically out of joint, but emotionally it was firmly fastened to some archetypal foundations." Today we most often refer to this collection of features as protofascism.

The features of protofascism include, in Eco's terms, "irrationalism"; the "cult of action for action's sake"; nationalism that offers "to people who have been deprived of one a clear social identity"; a "popular elitism" that implies "contempt for the weak"; a "selective populism"; and a transference of the fascist's "will to power to sexual matters." Although one or two of these features might not be enough to kindle the flame of fascism when taken in isolation, the fact that we think of such formations in terms we understand from history may make their translation into the digital more obscure than they should be. To the contrary, we might profitably think of ways the digital environment offers troubling parallel formations to the already-contradictory features of existing fascism.

In a recent study conducted under the auspices of the University of California–Berkeley Center for Right Wing Studies, Maik Fielitz and Holger Marcks begin to develop an analysis of digital fascism. They note that while classical or historical fascism is organized in a "highly centralist way," digital fascism exhibits "a historically uncommon extent of decentralization. Most prominently, this is expressed by the swarm-like penetration of online discussion boards that undermines the openness of debate, equal access to it and finally the accessibility of public opinion. This kind of leaderless swarm activity spreads messages and contributes to dynamics that are neither centrally controlled nor in any way controllable or governable. In particular, the growing subcultural collectives that act out in discussion boards and chat forums follow their own trolling logic of *schadenfreude* that may cause repercussions differing from the strategic logic of formal far-right parties and groups" (2019, 15). While classic fascist formations have historically structured themselves around dictatorial leadership and have been focused on particular geographical areas, digital fascism may exist despite eschewing both of these features. It may be distributed, appear leaderless or with varied and conflicting leadership, and may not coalesce into specific political parties that agitate directly to take power over individual localities.

As Fielitz and Marcks suggest, "digital fascism differs significantly from classical fascism in organizational terms" (2), instead functioning through a kind of tribalism that "is bound together by fears produced and shared in virtual networks and less guided by formal and hierarchical organizations."

This makes "digital fascism a more fluid and ambivalent movement [compared to its non-digital forms], which cannot be fully grasped with actor- or ideology-centered approaches." They argue that the most useful frame for understanding digital fascism is Paxton's (2004, 218) view of fascism as characterized by "obsessive preoccupation with community decline, humiliation, or victimhood and by compensatory cults of unity, energy, and purity." Of course the conceptual resemblance of Paxton's formulation to Griffin's should not be overlooked, nor should their resemblances in practice. "Narratives of victimhood and imperilment are key to understanding" (Fielitz and Marcks 2019, 9) fascism in both its digital and non-digital manifestations. Yet digital media, and social media in particular, "does not simply offer opportunities for far-right actors to spread their worldviews, but offers opportunity structures that are particularly beneficial for far-right agency. Moreover, social media itself (re-)produces orders of perception that are prone to the fascist rationale" (14).

It is no accident that the most obvious instances of fascism in digital media appear organized around such narratives of victimhood and imperilment. GamerGate, QAnon, the pickup artists and men's rights movements, and much of the alt-right in general (Lyons 2017; Neiwert 2018) all begin from a position of aggrievement that has long concerned researchers about the imminence of resurgent fascism in digital contexts. Further, the manifest ways in which social media is designed (both deliberately and organically) to engage our "hottest" affective centers and coordinately to suppress the cooler parts of our minds makes it an especially potent vector for both the development and dissemination of this new kind of fascism. It is not surprising to find that incidents of violence in the physical world are increasingly tied to inspiration from materials disseminated in social media. Digital media forms are used to stoke those fires in ways that are hard to replicate with other forms of media. Older forms of media technology, such as radio and film, may have played a role in shaping historical forms of fascism, particularly in the rise of the Nazis and the Italian fascists. This is because broadcast (radio) or one-to-many distribution (film) can be largely contained within specific geographical environments, and thus contain the spread of fascism's inchoate lust for violence within typically national borders.

Cyberfascism only secondarily recognizes many of historical fascism's traditional categories. Although there is no shortage of hate and "othering" directed at familiar categories of race, gender, and ethnicity, some of the primary vectors of cyberfascism fall along new lines. Consider one of the best-known popularizations of fascist thinking: the fascist expresses quasi-religious beliefs in "blood and soil." These are taken to point at two fictions: the idea that there is such a thing as "a people" connected by inheritance that far exceeds what we today understand as genetic heritability, so that some ineffable "spirit" of the "German people" inheres in the physical bodies of people with correct parentage; and that this spirit is similarly tied to specific places in Germany that are properly inhabited only by those with German blood.

While many members of the alt-right and other neofascist groups certainly embrace overtly racialized notions of "blood," the physically distributed nature of digital technology causes even more incoherence along the lines of "soil" than we had already seen. This leads to remarkable alignments between U.S. fascists who loudly proclaim American superiority over all other world polities, and yet proudly ally themselves with fascists from Eastern Europe and Russia, typically along an axis of white supremacy that seems to have forgotten its commitment to geographical place.

Even more interesting is the line of thought we have already seen legible in Barlow's "Declaration of the Independence of Cyberspace," which suggests a digitally empowered innovation in the meaning of "blood." We have already seen how the "Declaration" crafts a troubling political distinction between "government," which is to say "democracy," and the "civilization of the Mind in Cyberspace" (1996, 30), an aspect of the document that at least a few critics have gestured at over the years (e.g., Morrison 2009; Franks 2019a). Yet what has escaped attention is more remarkable for the frequency with which it occurs in the document: an explicit distinction between an "us" who is identified with "cyberspace," and a "them" who is somehow outside of or alien to it: "*You* are not welcome among *us*" (emphasis added), Barlow writes, where the nominal addressee is the "government," which I have argued must be taken as synonymous with "democracy." Membership in the group is said to be due to an "act of nature," one that has been cultivated by its "natives," in which the exercise of democratic power can only be carried out by those who "will always be immigrants." "*We* are creating a world," Barlow repeatedly proclaims: "*You* . . . invade our precincts." "*We* are forming our own Social Contract. This governance will arise according to the conditions of *our* world, not *yours*. *Our* world is different." Indeed, given the brevity of the "Declaration," it is remarkable how much of the text is devoted to defining a group of "natives" who "belong," and a group of "tyrants" who do not.

No less troubling is the fact that no criteria are offered for determining who is a member of each group. This is not to say that true membership in a fascistic nationality like Fascist Italy or Nazi Germany was a stable and incontestable quality. As we have seen by watching Donald Trump's constantly shifting alliances, fascist nationalism is characterized by changing definitions of consanguinity that ultimately have more to do with personal loyalty than actual ancestry. But in "cyberspace," nativism has an even more ephemeral and free-floating nature. Rather than primarily being characterized by kinship, cyberspace nativism depends on an ephemeral quality of belonging, a group membership that does not even have the bare supports in material reality one might expect. Becoming a "member" of the digital "us" seems more a matter of affect and personality than anything else, although that membership may be qualified in important ways by other ephemeral qualities, especially one's ability to code.

In its most anodyne forms, "learn to code" is a common slogan of the digital age that encourages people to acquire a certain set of skills. But it morphs quickly into a less savory judgment: that proficiency in coding is superior to other knowledge sets. Part of the reason for this superiority is the belief that coding is a natural or necessary skill for dealing with digital technology, suggesting that "knowing how to code" provides a better way of engaging digital media compared to those of us who are mere users.

Like all protofascist ideological formations, this one is blurry and mobile. What constitutes "knowing how to code" changes widely from context to context; proof of one's knowledge is almost always subject to challenge. Further, those challenges are frequent tools in social contests over the right to belong or the right to participate in digital spaces, and therefore in society at all (to those most identified with the digital). Claiming that one's interlocutor does not know how to code, lacks the requisite "hacking" skills, or is dishonest about their coding accomplishments, are among the first means used by the participants in protofascist digital spaces to deauthorize anyone with whom they disagree. In such forums, arguments often arise over whose coding skills are truly sufficient to allow debaters to speak with authority or to belong at all in digital space.

This substitution of coding skill for blood belonging is not as big a leap as it may seem. One of the minor themes in contemporary U.S. fascism is so-called producerism, which is "the idea that the real Americans are hardworking people who create goods and wealth while fighting against parasites at the top and bottom of society" (Berlet 2009, 26; see also Berlet and

Lyons 2000; Mudde and Rovira Kaltwasser 2017). These "parasites at the top and bottom of society" (typically referring to Jewish people, though by no means exclusively to them) occupy a structural or role-based type that appears to only secondarily entail race. Yet as Berlet argues, they almost inevitably assume that "proper citizenship is defined by white males" (Berlet 2009, 26). Thus the apparently deracialized distinction between "producer" and "person who does not produce" is loaded with the same affective energy usually reserved for the racial "us" and the racial "them." The fact that specific, concrete racial identities seem to be overlooked in this formation belies the fictive nature of race itself. This is especially true as it occurs in fascist and protofascist discourse. As a result, nonracial categories can easily be transferred back into racial ones when necessary or useful. They provide a kind of "cover" for the protofascist, allowing him to claim he never had race or ethnicity in mind at all. Instead, he only had the innocent question of whether a person has the "skill" required to contribute to a discussion. In other words, whether that person truly is "one of us."

Producerism is not just one theme among many in the digital fascist bag of rhetorical tricks. Instead, along with the putative "placelessness" of cyberspace, it serves as a cornerstone for establishing "digital media" as a place that is dominated by and organic only to a certain class of people, those who take their place in digital space by dint of their special, insider status, which can only be granted by the same people who use producerism as a criterion for carving up the world into "us" and "them." One of the most obvious points of connection between cyberlibertarian dogma and protofascism is found in the ways technology promoters, frequently allied with the most concerted centers of money and power in digital technology, insist that journalists, researchers, and ordinary citizens have no right to speak about the effects of digital technology unless they meet some arbitrary level of technical facility.

Andreessen Horowitz is a well-known venture capital firm in the technology world. Both its founders, Marc Andreessen and Ben Horowitz, have histories with the far-right that are concerning. The firm's best-known dip into right-wing waters, though, comes from former general partner Balaji Srinivasan. He frequently takes up tropes from right-wing thought while, in a manner familiar across much of the contemporary right, simultaneously disavows its right-wing content. Srinivasan, along with other right-adjacent figures like Andreessen himself, former Facebook executive Antonio García-Martínez, Y Combinator founder Paul Graham and its president Sam Altman, is among the Silicon Valley voices who most frequently criticize individuals who speak about technology without actually "making anything." So when the generally tech-friendly *New York Times* journalist Kevin Roose criticized venture capitalists including Marc Andreessen for their promotion of "critical infrastructure" despite their general lack of interest in and knowledge about the topic, Srinivasan (2020a) tweeted in response "guy who has built nothing thinks he can critique guy who invented the web browser." When Roose responded with a barbed comment about Srinivasan's crypto startup, Srinivasan (2020b) replied, "You don't even understand the industry you think you're qualified to cover. Quick, Kevin: what's the difference between merge sort and quicksort?"

The buried implication that Andreessen's having been the leader of the team that developed the Mosaic web browser at the National Center for Supercomputing Applications in 1992–93 constitutes "building something," whereas writing articles for the *New York Times* is not "building something," shows the in-built prejudice and pronounced anti-intellectualism of much pro-digital discourse. It also fits directly into the main producerist construction, in which no matter how much "work" people may do, some forms of work, especially those associated with finance or ideas, are "parasitic," while other work, always characterized as "building," is "productive." Like all protofascist formations, what seems a clear enough distinction on the surface becomes much vaguer when examined closely. Srinivasan's taunt of Roose regarding his knowledge of the difference between two different algorithmic methods for sorting data shows his commitment to a fundamental distinction between the deserving "us" and the undeserving and parasitic "them," which is characteristic of protofascism.

Some works that advocates of digital politics refer to as articulations of their principles are, in fact, invitations to fascism. *The Sovereign Individual* (Davidson and Rees-Mogg 1997)—which in many ways is indistinguishable from the business-focused technology promotion of figures like Alex and Don Tapscott, George Gilder, and Kevin Kelly—stands out for persistent invoking far-right rhetoric, not least its contempt for and dismissal of democracy as "the fraternal twin of communism" (328); endorsement of public choice theory (332), which Nancy MacLean (2017) puts at the heart of the radical right's attack on democratic governance; its continual nods to the power of "machinery" as superior to democratic sovereignty; its nods to "exit"; its description of democracy as the "nanny state" (95–126); and its description of our era as similar to what the authors call "the last days of politics" in the fifteenth century. The book reads much like it was written by a modern-day Carl Schmitt, the Nazi jurist whose antipolitical theories of raw power have surprisingly experienced a resurgence in the digital age.

This seems not at all coincidental. Although (or even because) Rees-Mogg is reported not to have authored much of the book, which was largely written by "American investment guru and conservative propagandist" James Dale Davidson (Beckett 2018), he serves as a remarkable embodiment of the protofascist ideology that informs much technology promotion. "Born in Bristol into a family of Somerset gentry—Moggs have lived in the county for centuries" (Bates 2012) reads an obituary. Despite being widely known now by the title "Lord," Rees-Mogg spent much of his life working as an editor at *The Times* of London, where "he was regularly derided as 'Mystic Mogg'—a parody of a tabloid astrologer—for his occasionally perverse or wrong-headed assumptions, but none could deny that his columns were serious, if often pompous, or—a term he would have relished—influential in circles that mattered."

Both Davidson and Rees-Mogg fit snugly into the characterization of fascism advanced by Landa (2019) and other major thinkers on the topic: a movement directed by those with the most wealth and power and who are expert at developing support among the citizenry with whom they have only an exploitative relationship. In keeping with many other fascist and protofascist statements of position, *The Sovereign Individual* seems to argue that democracy is an impossible and ludicrous form of political organization, but does so exclusively via dismissive adjectives. Democracy is repeatedly characterized as a "civic myth," and existing democracies characterized as "nanny states." The work follows the typical shape of anarcho-capitalist propaganda, focusing on two particular issues as being all that one needs to know of politics. The first is the canard that nation–states have a "monopoly on violence," a bastardized reinterpretation of thinking from the sociologist Max Weber, and that this "protection" is all a democracy has to offer, making democratic states functionally the same thing as organized crime. "Government is not only a protection service; it is also a protection racket," they write. "Government often operates like organized crime, extracting resources from people within its sphere of operations as tribute or plunder" (130).

The second prong of the authors' anarcho-capitalism is the familiar far-right complaint that democratic regulation of economic activity is inherently illegitimate and the most important restriction on "freedom" imaginable.

According to them, the "deepening of markets" caused by digital technology will "erode the capacity of politicians to impose their will arbitrarily upon the owners of resources by regulation" (274). One can only call the will of politicians "arbitrary" if one rejects the idea that elected representatives (or even political majorities via referenda) have any legitimate claim to authority. This is the core argument of sophisticated fascist propaganda since its early days, exactly what Landa (2010) identifies as the fascist promotion of economic "liberty" as the apotheosis of the political "liberty" that, on non-fascist accounts, requires popular sovereignty for its realization. In recent U.S. right-wing agitation, this line of argument has its clearest exemplar in so-called public choice theory, a quasi-economic doctrine developed by those Chicago School and Mont Pelerin Society thinkers who sit at the core of contemporary protofascism. According to this viewpoint, we can disregard all claims to democratic representation, voting rights, or the ability of politicians to act honestly to realize the will of the people who elected them. Public officials are in fact maximally greedy and self-interested, and all claims to responsible citizenship should be rejected, mostly because they are somehow dishonest. Corporate and inherited wealth, on the other hand, can and should be overlooked, presumably because it does not claim to be democratic.

Nancy MacLean explains in her 2017 book *Democracy in Chains: The Deep History of the Radical Right's Stealth Plan for America* that public choice theory was (and remains) an elaborate fiction designed by right-wing academics to promote deregulation of markets. This theory was devised specifically in opposition not to the power of government to tax per se, but instead to the advancing cause of U.S. civil rights, particularly for Black people in the wake of the *Brown v Board of Education* decision of 1954. As MacLean puts it, "*Brown* so enraged" (50) conservatives in the 1950s that it energized a redoubling of the right's efforts to dismantle the New Deal that was already in motion via the Mont Pelerin Society and other avatars of economic liberalism. These thinkers toyed with several names for their movement, all of which resonate today: "conservative," but also "neoliberal," "libertarian," and even "radical right." "Classical liberal," one of the favored terms of some of the movement's more intellectually minded figures, sounded good, but "had problems as well because they parted with classical liberals such as Adam Smith and John Stuart Mill on so much—not least, enthusiasm for public education. One thing all advocates of economic liberty agreed on, at least, was that they were 'the right,' or the 'right wing,' and against 'the left' and anything 'left wing'" (51).

It is unsurprising that Davidson and Rees-Mogg have incorporated these lines of thought into their work, while disguising their political valence at least rhetorically, and instead framing them as inevitable consequences of the shift to digital technology. In the book's penultimate chapter, "The Twilight of Democracy," the authors declare democracy to be "the fraternal twin of communism" (1997, 328), before declaring that "analysis by Public Choice economists" leads to the inexorable conclusion that digital technology enables "the more creative participants in the new economy [to be] geographically distributed. Therefore, they are unlikely to form a sufficient concentration to gain the attention of legislators" (332). The attentive reader notes that Davidson and Rees-Mogg have earlier cited John C. Calhoun— the influential congressional defender of chattel slavery and a signal architect of some of its most influential evasions such as "states' rights"—as an ur–public choice theorist, who "shrewdly sketched the arithmetic of modern politics. Calhoun's formula divides the entire population of the nation-state into two classes: *taxpayers,* who contribute more to the cost of government services than they consume; and *tax consumers,* who receive benefits from government in excess of their contribution to the cost" (266). In this archetypal and quasi-Schmittian revisionist interpretation of the democratic polity, Davidson and Rees-Mogg follow nearly to the letter the arguments made by other right-wing advocates of "economic liberty," including the clutch of economists at wildly conservative institutions like the University of Chicago and George Mason University.

MacLean shows repeatedly that despite their claims to be interested only in economics, which is at once deeply political and supposedly apolitical, these thinkers repeatedly dip into the most noxious strain of American politics, the part that tried to develop pro-slavery politics prior to the Civil War. They tried to articulate a coherent position in terms of a Constitution that accommodated the slaveholding South but also contained much that pointed toward its eventual dissolution. "Calhoun had no rival," she writes, in developing methods "to construct the operations of democratic government" (2017, 3). Calhoun's "ideas about government broke sharply from the vision of the nation's founders and the Constitution's drafters, and even from that of his own party. He wanted one class—his own class of plantation owners—to overpower the others, despite its obvious numerical minority."

Writers like Davidson and Rees-Mogg, and some of their more recent
epigones like George Mason economists Tyler Cowen and Alex Tabarrok,
refer to Calhoun's economic theories as precursors of their own, and specifically in Cowen and Tabarrok's case as a public choice theorist. However,
they also acknowledge Calhoun's advocacy for slavery as revealing a "lack
of ethical foundations which continues to hurt his reputation and draw
attention from his more valid and interesting contributions" (Tabarrok and
Cowen 1992, 671–72). These writers lack a sophisticated understanding
of race and racial politics, and as such they are uninterested in or outright
dismissive of cultural analysis that seeks to identify tropes, narratives, and
connections between the various expressions of politics, economics, and
culture. While a cultural critic may wonder why a purely economic theory
would choose to ground itself in the thought of the most prominent pro-
slavery politician in U.S. history—and how that theory could emerge in the
wake of arguably the most significant pro–civil rights decision in Supreme
Court history while claiming to have nothing to do with race—few thinkers
of non-right-wing political orientations will find such an argument persuasive. This is particularly true since the nod toward Calhoun is unnecessary
in theoretical terms.

The Sovereign Individual follows the shape of protofascist theorizing as
articulated by Landa and others. It claims to be a theory of political freedom,
but it rapidly reinterprets freedom to mean exclusively economic liberty.
This interpretation excludes and outright rejects the democratic values
that motivated the theory of political freedom to begin with. The theory
of economic liberty is not a story about how everyone can achieve greater
freedom or rights. Instead, it is a theory explicitly directed at those with
extreme wealth. The book makes clear that the "sovereign individual" of
the title is only a person who has the economic power to buy escape from
the reach of the democratic polity, which will still exist but be deprived
of the resources once provided by the very wealthy. Much like the "theory"
of ur-cyberlibertarian George Gilder, to which Davidson and Rees-Mogg
refer throughout their own book, The Sovereign Individual was explicitly,
if somewhat quietly, an advertisement for the investment newsletter the
authors published, Strategic Investment (Davidson and Rees-Mogg 1997,
401–3), along with "an investment club for accredited individuals, Strategic
Opportunities" (402), whose $995 annual subscription price clearly identi-
fies who is and is not accredited. The authors recommend that individuals

who have "investment of sums in excess of $100,000" open offshore accounts in tax havens, and those with even more means partake of their own private investment services, "secure your own tax-free zone," and "carve out your minisovereignty."

"Citizenship is obsolete" (398), write the authors; therefore, somehow, "the argument of this book clearly informs the decision to redeploy your capital, if you have any." But, they continue, "suppose you agree with the premises of this book and are excited by the prospect of the Information Age, but lack the ready capital to deploy in order to take advantage of opportunities to benefit from commercialized sovereignty," prior to advertising their investment services targeted at high-net worth individuals. "Any recipe for success," they argue, "is bound to disappoint" (399). So "you should make it one of your priorities to study and evaluate the works of the various gurus who attempt to teach useful hints about how to succeed," no doubt including Davidson and Rees-Mogg themselves, despite their explicit bias toward those who already do have substantial capital. No wonder the book repeatedly nods, often in a muted voice, at the purported needs of those with substantial inherited wealth, framing them as more important than the rest of us. No wonder, too, that these individuals, capable of exploiting world financial systems make themselves nigh-unto feudal lords, are those the authors' protofascism identifies as candidates for sovereign individual status.

The Sovereign Individual devotes much of its first half to a revisionist account of European history, lauding the advent of the printing press for destroying the bureaucratic authority of the Catholic Church—as if it were the sole political authority of its day, and as if its political authority were its only function. The secular political authorities of the first 1,500 years of Western history, as well as the Protestant Reformation, are mostly celebrated around the edges. The authors do not explain why these forms of political and cultural authority are not like bad Catholic authority. The authors say nothing about the similar role played by Protestant denominations, for example, in colonizing the parts of the world that Catholics did not. They also say little about the Anglican Church, for example, or the role of Protestants in colonizing what became the United States; nothing about Orthodox Christianity; and nothing about other religious systems. Indeed, Christianity in particular turns out to be a force for good in much of the book. And since the authors are uninterested in addressing the kinds of power used by right-wing political authorities and their cultural avatars, their rhetoric sounds like the typical anti-Catholic propaganda generated by right-wing agitators in the Protestant-dominated world from the KKK to the John Birch Society.

This moderate homophony is only magnified when the book veers toward its conclusion. We have seen that what is recommended for the world's wealthiest people is to hold democracies hostage and extort them for reduced taxation as a price for some modified form of citizenship. In typical protofascist fashion, ardent and largely inchoate dismissals of the very idea of democratic sovereignty as having anything at all to do with human freedom are countered by claims that absolute economic freedom is all there is to political freedom, and that the rest of it is irrelevant. Here, the authors' long-standing promotion of conspiracy theories about Bill and Hillary Clinton (368–73) emerge, as do ambivalent statements about drug cartels and organized crime. Since the authors assume that democratic governments themselves are nothing but organized crime, and that the "natural economy" is responsible for the trade of commodities such as drugs and weapons, their disregard for law and regulation and their opposition to economic power limits make it unclear whether they are in favor of crime syndicates. Despite occasionally acknowledging the destructive and violent nature of organized crime, they appear to be promoting the creation of crime fiefdoms or endorsing the numerous such organizations that already exist—except for democratic governments, which are disqualified from the legitimate power of the sovereign individual due to their claim of being governed by law.

These recommendations of absolute power unencumbered by laws or rights unsurprisingly give way to more-or-less explicit attacks on the claims of minorities and the economically disenfranchised. "Social morality and economic success are insolubly linked" (375), they write. "For human beings it is the struggle rather than the achievement that matters" (376)—this despite their archetypical sovereign individual being a person of inherited wealth who struggles not at all to gain political and economic power. Here the language of social Darwinism intrudes. "The survival of human societies depends," they tell us, "on cultural choices that are based on human intelligence." As with so many other rightist thinkers, the Darwinian principle of "survival of the fittest" is turned into metaphor, and economic competition via free markets becomes its apotheosis. Not only that: economic competition becomes "moral" competition, and a "successful social morality . . .

must be strong" (381). The first example of a "strong social morality," fittingly enough with the Nietzschean tinges of the sovereign individual idea itself, is Hitler, who "had a strong morality for survival, but its destructive quality nearly destroyed his own society." Even granting Hitler the credibility that Nazism promoted the "survival" of some group (Aryans, presumably), describing that as "morality" of any kind, is to misunderstand fascism.

In just a few pages scattered throughout the book, the authors come close to admitting the real shape of their political program. Reflecting for a moment on political liberty—that is, democracy—as it was understood by its major theorists, the authors note that

> a shared morality in a tolerant society was the ideal of John Locke and of early philosophers of liberty. They did not at all believe that a society, of any kind, can be maintained without rules, but they thought that the rules ought to be subject to the best of reason, and that people should be coerced to accept only the essential rules. They did recognize that coercion was inevitable in social morality, particularly in the protection of life or of property, because they considered that no society can survive if there is no security. They applied an almost absolute tolerance to variations in personal choices that did not affect the welfare of others. (382)

Yet the authors quickly back away from this apparent endorsement of democratic theory. "The original phrase of John Locke had it right" (383), they write: "Everyone has a right to life, liberty, and estate." Thomas Jefferson's alteration to "life, liberty and the pursuit of happiness" was a mistake, despite being a "very fine phrase": "Society depends absolutely on the right to life and the right to property." Thus as Landa's (2010) analysis shows, the language of liberalism is twisted against itself, and freedom for economic activity replaces the rest of the values theorists like Locke, whatever their faults, actually recommended.

Despite the sometimes obvious, sometimes occluded protofascism, especially their full-throated support for unregulated markets as the only proper forces for justice and rights, Davidson and Rees-Mogg's work is frequently mentioned in contemporary digital advocacy. As Wendy Chun has written, the book's "vision has fueled and still fuels the development of seasteading, cryptocurrencies and other plans for escape that dominate today. That it gets many things wrong is no comfort, however, for closing the distance between its predictions and reality drives many Silicon Valley business plans" (2021, 12). It does not merely drive them to develop a similar or sympathetic viewpoint. Its foundational observations come directly from digital technology propagandists. One of the figures whom the book quotes most frequently is George Gilder, patron saint of *Wired* magazine, arch anti-feminist (Borsook 2000), and coauthor of the "Magna Carta for the Knowledge Age" (Dyson et al. 1994), which served as the basis for Winner's original analysis of cyberlibertarianism (1997). Even more significant, the book is routinely invoked by Silicon Valley leaders, especially those whose sympathies tend toward far-right politics.

Among core cyberlibertarian texts, *The Sovereign Individual* has special status. It is routinely invoked, especially by venture capitalists and promoters of cryptocurrency and blockchain, to convey a bizarre mix of protofascist politics and technological utopianism. Notably, Peter Thiel considers it one of his "six favorite books that predict the future" (*The Week Staff* 2016) because it "breaks the taboo on prophecy: We're not supposed to talk about a future that doesn't include the powerful states that rule over us today. Rees-Mogg and Davidson argue that national governments could soon become as antiquated as 19th-century empires."

Cryptocurrency advocates have taken the book and run with it, and in their hands its overtones become explicit. As even cryptocurrency and technology promoter E. Glen Weyl, who is himself given to technology-driven syncretism, has stated in a recent review of the book that there is very little new in it. Rather, it "takes as a starting point a roughly Thomas Friedman–esque 'the internet flattens the world' and a set of predictions about technology that were prevalent in the 1990s" (2022). Then "it layers on top of this an Objectivist (viz. the philosophy of Ayn Rand) worldview." "Aspiring 'sovereign Individuals,'" he writes, "have become the closest of political allies to and business funders of precisely the sort of movements and businesses that the book would see as epitomizing contemptible reaction." The book's readers and promoters, he argues, "are deliberately sowing reaction and discord to accelerate the collapse of the societies that allowed them to reach their positions of power to be liberated from the remaining constraints those societies impose, a course of action explicitly advocated by thinkers Thiel has funded such as Curtis Yarvin (aka Mencius Moldbug)." Weyl concludes:

In short, *Sovereign Individual* is roughly the *Das Kapital* of the Ayn Rand worldview. It is a profoundly inaccurate statement of fact and set of projections intended to create a self-fulfilling dystopia. It has had a powerful influence on many of those shaping our digital future, particularly in the crypto space. Those subscribing to it should be persuaded where possible but resisted at every turn where not. Anyone considering allying with them politically or taking funding from them should be thinking of it in similar terms to how they would consider doing the same with an open adherent of a totalitarian ideology. The world that has captured their imaginations is not one we must or should want to live in.

Of course this exhortation makes sense only if those promoting these ideas do not mean to be advancing a totalitarian ideology. Yet there is significant evidence that they do, and it has been in plain view from the earliest days of digital advocacy. It is not merely that the crypto-anarchist/cypherpunk movement (see chapter 2), to take only the most important example, advances the anarcho-capitalist economic philosophy that subtends fascism. As we have seen, it persistently crosses the line into overt fascism. Although Tim May publicly expresses his far-right political philosophy through his contributions to the cypherpunk movement, his statements about encrypted communications helping the Aryan Nations appear to align with even more explicitly fascist sympathies. In a 2010 interview with May, journalist Andy Greenberg describes him, with May's apparent approval, as a "hard-core libertarian looking out for his own Randian self-interest" (Greenberg [2012] 2013, 91): "Let the Africans kill each other." Greenberg follows up with ex-Tor, ex-WikiLeaks personality Jacob Appelbaum, who tells Greenberg that "Tim May is a fucking racist." Greenberg relays this to May, who replies, "I call 'em as I see 'em. If I see blacks driving themselves into the gutter, I call it as it is." No wonder that in an infamous 2004 posting to a local Santa Cruz newsgroup, May referred to Martin Luther King Jr. as a "house n****r," says that "it was GOOD that this commie promoter of derelict/n****r causes was whacked-out by a CIA SPECOPS team" (May 2005). May concludes his post by declaring that "forty million Americans need a trip up the chimneys, 3 million of them the facilitators, 35 million of them the Jew/n****r/s****k recipients of what the first group stole." In the ensuing discussion of his post, May opines that "we are not 'required' to honor this n****r" and that "these n****rs and s****s get paid to do nothing, I am taxed. Ergo, my money is being given to n****rs and s****s," providing yet another example of the close ties between political libertarianism and far-right white supremacy.

While May is probably the most public cypherpunk member with fascist leanings, many of his peers and colleagues come very close to crossing that line. The Cypherpunks mailing list has always been full of explicit invocations of fascism, racism, antisemitism, anti-left propaganda, producerism, nativism about the digital space, and more. (The group's archives are publicly visible at lists.cpunks.org.) Some of the most prominent members promote conspiracy theories that would make Alex Jones blush. They suggest that the Holocaust was actually a psyop engineered by Jewish people themselves to consolidate world power. Additionally, they claim that all civil rights activism is organized by Jewish people to keep down the "people." Mixed in with this overt fascist discourse is a constant stream of promotion of all the familiar cyberlibertarian causes: anti-copyright, decentralization, free and open source, the lionization of Assange and Snowden, and so on. However, many people in the digital world still draw inspiration from the cypherpunk movement and even associate with the label, trying to pretend the community is something other than what it is.

CYBERFASCISM, SOCIAL MEDIA, AND "FREE SPEECH": THE CHANS

Although cypherpunk anarcho-capitalism provides a detailed theory that binds cyberlibertarianism to fascism and protofascism, and the contributors to the Cypherpunks mailing list often express this theory in practice, there are clearer examples of cyberfascism emerging from cyberlibertarian dogma. The most obvious of these are the chans, the most famous of which is 4chan, a site that turns up with uncanny frequency in news stories about hate, Nazism, and even mass murder. (To be more accurate, 4chan is a *kind* of site, although the succession of sites that have appeared under that are best-known examples.)

As the writer Dale Beran describes it in his excellent history and analysis of the phenomena, *It Came from Something Awful* (2019), the site we today call 4chan builds on a Japanese social networking model centered on otaku culture (i.e., fans of anime and manga). As Beran writes, even in the early 1990s, "a weird spiral of unhappiness that began in films and TV was drawn directly onto the internet. The new communities that dominated the web largely derived their habits, style, and culture from otaku culture. People interacted on the web as collectives of isolated individuals, immersed in fantasy products, cruel-minded gore, and self-obsession, all a means of escape from the multiplying anxieties and dissatisfactions of real life. And at the center of this, the quivering, vulnerable, and pale underbelly of the internet that would digest it all, would be the chans" (36). A succession of bulletin boards of this sort proliferated in Japan, "collectively referred to as *Nanashii Warudo* ('The Nameless World')" (37). In the Nameless World, otaku could "discard not only the hierarchy, but the sad fact of themselves, and roam not simply without their bodies but without their souls in a ghostly Saturnalia where all laws, prohibitions, and even human identity dematerialized into a catalog of interests, desires, and self-gratification." The overlap between this "ghostly Saturnalia" and the philosophy of anarcho-capitalists, which is nominally rule-free but also profoundly authoritarian and destruction-friendly, is fundamental, not incidental.

Many of the specifics of chan culture, including its near-obsessive focus on anime and manga, ported over to versions of the Nameless World that traveled outside Japan. The embrace of cyberlibertarian principles as foundational also followed suit. From the *Amezou* (First channel) service that introduced an algorithm that pushed popular content to the top, to its successor *Ni channeru* (2channel)—developed by a student named Hiroyuki Nishimura who in 2015 took over as administrator of 4chan itself from its creator, Christopher Poole—the chans prize absolute free speech and anonymity as the core values of digital culture. They also embrace a culture of destruction and hate but seem uninterested in reflecting on how this relates to their other principles. As Beran points out, Japanese users of 2channel found "relief in escaping Japan's strict hierarchy of polite deference. Unlike the hyper-polite real world, people found they could be rude to one another with impunity" (38). Regardless of whether such social conventions are welcome or constricting, the 2channel rejoinder to them embraces a different politics altogether: "2channel's most popular replies were '*omae mo na!*' ('you too, asshole') and '*itteyoshi*' (meaning either 'please leave' or 'please die')."

Beran explains that 4chan's development in the United States was not initially modeled after Japan's, but was instead influenced by the deep engagement with digital technology, *Wired* magazine, and the video game

Quake II of an engineering school dropout and system administrator named
Richard "Lowtax" Kyanka (40). Lowtax, unlike some other cyberlibertarians, openly embraced the nihilism and hate (of self and others) that grounds
all fascism. In the late 1990s he "founded a site he called Something Awful
(SA). It was a name he plucked out of nothing, specifically the nothing of
the fast food–littered suburbs, a phrase he uttered all the time, as in 'that
Del Taco burrito sure is something awful'" (41).

SA embraced, rather than attempted to tamp down, "the same systemic
problems since the days of Usenet: flame wars, obsessive users, and rude
comments" (43). Its forums "encouraged exactly what moderators elsewhere
took great care to eradicate: bile, cynicism, cruelty, mockery, and vulgar-
ity." There had been places like SA prior to it, but this was an intensifica-
tion and acceleration of what had come before. This was fueled in no small
part by the culture of absolute free speech and the power of unaccountable
online anonymity. The site was dominated by an affect of adolescent rebellion and anger, full of bile and hate directed at everyone, but particularly
minorities of all kinds. One user, "a fifteen-year-old kid who lived with his
mother in Westchester, New York, named Christopher Poole" (50)—who
in his own words "spent a good 6–12 hours per day playing video games
in a bedroom with blacked-out windows, and rarely went outdoors or
socialized"—"on his favorite message board, SA, chose a name of bleak
negation, 'moot.'" After discovering the Japanese site 2channel, Poole decided that the most extreme parts of SA were not extreme enough for him.
He secured the domain 4chan.net and ported 2chan's PHP code over to
the new site.

It would be hard to convey to the uninitiated just how extreme 4chan
quickly became, to say nothing of its many spinoffs. Some scholars and
journalists, some of whom are associated with 4chan, have written about
the site's "transgressive" and "controversial" nature, while acknowledging
that its racism and misogyny are unpleasant. Few, though, have made the
association that should be obvious: these sites are hotbeds for fascist and
protofascist politics. Whether this emerges "organically" from the obsessive
interests of those drawn to the platform's cultural transgressions, or through
a variety of manipulative practices conducted by actors who intend to
exacerbate fascist politics, makes little difference. As powerful as hate radio,
evangelical broadcasting, and conspiracy theorists like Alex Jones are, it is

hard to imagine more influential tools for promoting fascism than the chans and similar sites. In short, promoting fascism is arguably one of the main reasons sites like 4chan exist.

4chan and its offshoots are at the heart of nearly every fascist and pro-tofascist movement in the countries where they are widely used. The chans spread movements like GamerGate, which served as a precursor and model for subsequent right-wing conspiracies such as Pizzagate and QAnon. An entirely manufactured controversy ostensibly concerned with "ethics in games journalism," Gamergate was an "anti-feminist, anti-identity politics, anti–social justice warrior, and in some cases, just plain anti-women" (Beran 2019, 145) fascist cultural uprising whose promoters insisted that "it was they, young white men, who were the marginalized outcasts." Despite the clear similarities to reactionary protofascist movements in areas where white supremacy is dominant, many in the media and even some scholars (see Mueller 2015) were divided on the issue, giving GamerGate supporters the benefit of the doubt they did not deserve and paving the way for new movements that use the same model. Despite some commentators recognizing that GamerGate was a protofascist hate campaign, and that "the myth of the Wild West of tech and the 'be yourself' freedom of microblogging platforms leads to belief that online harassment is the disconnected work of individuals, when really strategic organizing is taking place" (Harry 2014), far too many in online advocacy, especially the digital rights communities, were at best vocal about the abhorrence of the actions of individuals and groups, while maintaining that the underlying technology and the politics surrounding it were somehow the solution to the problems they had created.

Reddit's management acted with at least some haste to shut down sub-reddits like r/The_Donald (Peck 2020) that had been at the heart of hate campaigns and conspiracy theories used by Donald Trump to target his enemies and spread lies. They also added much stricter moderation rules to the entire site. It is unsurprising that these measures were largely effective (Coldeway 2017). However, it is difficult to say whether the wider internet community has absorbed the lesson.

In a telling event that presaged what was to come, in 2009 4chan was the subject of a denial of service attack (i.e., a flood of traffic likely intended to bring down the site). Trying to manage the situation, AT&T shut off access to 4chan, a typical response to managing such floods. Yet the prospect of AT&T shutting off access to the site was met with horror and outrage across the internet. "The threats to the freedom and freedom of speech on the internet are legion, and AT&T is the evil empire that netizens love to hate," as a journalist for *The Guardian* characterized the response (Anderson 2009). Even though moot, the 4chan founder, stated that "this wasn't a sinister act of censorship, but rather a bit of a mistake and a poorly executed, disproportionate response on AT&T's part," cries of suppression of free speech, "censorship," and violations of net neutrality were widespread. Rather than raising questions about the politics embodied in these dogmatic calls, they were instead often taken at face value. This was echoed by moot's statement that AT&T's response was "disproportionate," despite the fact that only the network service provider, not the website manager, was in a position to understand the nature of the attack and the best strategies to address it.

4chan and its offshoots are not simply "unfortunate" and "unforeseen" consequences of cyberlibertarian dogma: they are among its most direct and pure expressions. 4chan users regularly invoke most of the major points of that dogma and organize harassment campaigns against anyone who questions them. They particularly focus on free speech, encryption, and anonymity, which is unsurprising given the platforms' anonymous nature. Indeed, the promotion of absolute free speech is a notable overlap between the far right and digital rights advocates, and this is especially visible on sites like 4chan, along with far-right social media sites like Gab and Truth Social. Mass murders around the world regularly emerge from 4chan, and antigovernment insurrectionists routinely post there.

JULIAN ASSANGE AND WIKILEAKS

The politics represented by Julian Assange and WikiLeaks are some of the most divisive and controversial in the digital technology space. As discussed in chapter 2, the cluster of individuals surrounding WikiLeaks all display significant investments in right-wing libertarianism, despite their remarkable ability to solicit support, and even political defense, from those whose politics are very different. It is difficult to discuss the political libertarianism of Assange, Greenwald, and Snowden among the digerati. All three have consistently associated their own digital politics with libertarian or even more extremist right-wing principles. It is important to ask how and why people with other politics should sign on to their campaigns.

Yet simply gesturing at their politics as libertarian risks giving them too much credit. Not only does the right-wing libertarianism these figures advocate, even in its syncretic variety seen with special force in the case of Glenn Greenwald, tend toward and constantly create openings for overt fascism. To the contrary, especially in Assange's case, fascism has always been out in the open. Yet even here, the political force of cyberlibertarianism is such that he has many supporters, even on the progressive left, who refuse to acknowledge the basic facts, let alone what they say about the digital politics Assange advances. Assange's supporters continue to portray his politics as something different from what they are, despite repeated and explicit demonstrations. They present him and his cause as anything other than fascist. Assange exemplifies syncretism or fascist entryism—a figure who continues to draw figures from the left toward the far right, precisely because he uses cyberlibertarian pseudo-causes to obscure his own clear political commitments.

While hagiographic accounts of Assange's life and work portray him as a heroic whistleblower and journalist focused on a just society, more neutral and objective accounts paint a different picture, even when those accounts come from Assange's close associates who believe (or at one time believed) in his apparent mission. One need not go even that far, though, to see the syncretism in Assange's political views. One of his clearest statements of purpose is found in the coauthored book *Cypherpunks: Freedom and the Future of the Internet* (Assange et al. 2012), published by OR Books, which itself is a persistent source of syncretic fascist propaganda. Assange is sometimes seen as something other than a technological utopian, due to statements like "the internet is a threat to human civilization" (1), which is prominently featured on the book's back cover. Yet that obscures the more familiar cyberlibertarian sentiments offered on the same page as well as throughout the book: the internet is "our greatest tool of emancipation" (1); and the only reason it is not fulfilling that role is that "states are systems through which coercive force flows" (2)—a tenet of anarchism, not democracy. Although the relationship between anarchism and the left-right distinction is complex, Assange makes clear that he is firmly on the right-wing side of the divide: "Land ownership, property, rents, dividends, taxation, court fines, censorship, copyrights and trademarks are all enforced by the threatened application of state violence" (2–3).

None of this should be surprising. The book is explicitly titled after the cypherpunks, the overtly anarcho-capitalist encryption advocates from whom so much of the right-wing nature of internet advocacy stems. This is no accident: Assange developed his outlook from his own participation in the Cypherpunks mailing list, and most of his ideas about digital technology and politics are slogans that could have been copied and pasted from "The Cyphernomicon" or the "Declaration of Independence of Cyberspace":

> Recall that states are the systems which determine where and how coercive force is consistently applied.
>
> The question of how much coercive force can seep into the platonic realm of the internet from the physical world is answered by cryptography and the cypherpunks' ideals.
>
> As states merge with the internet and the future of our civilization becomes the future of the internet, we must redefine force relations.
>
> If we do not, the universality of the internet will merge global humanity into one giant grid of mass surveillance and mass control. (6)

It is difficult to ignore the general avoidance of discussion of economic relations or problems of social welfare in most of the propaganda spread by the cypherpunks. The propaganda only mentions "states" and "violence." Anyone who opposes "state violence," regardless of their methods, is on the side of justice.

In his early days, and in the early days of WikiLeaks, Assange may have embraced a right-anarchist opposition to "authority" and a suspicion of all claims to political power. The characteristic openness of this position toward far-right politics was already visible in his case, as described above in chapter 2. It is not surprising that distrust of "governmental power" quickly turned into opposition to democratic governments, even if that meant embracing overt authoritarianism. Here quite a few of Assange's followers broke with him, as they embraced his sloganeering about "radical transparency" as an aid toward fuller democracy, not its destruction. Yet these tendencies in Assange's thinking and practice had long been visible. In the late 2000s, he began to purge WikiLeaks of members who seemed most devoted to its principles. The organization's spokesperson, Daniel Domscheit-Berg, who had been with WikiLeaks almost since its inception, left the organization in 2010 (Rosenbach and Stark 2010). Domscheit-Berg claims he quit; Assange claims he was fired.

Domscheit-Berg's narrative clearly shows how the cyberlibertarian ideas and slogans that led him to join WikiLeaks were easily turned into their opposites. The project was "devoted above all to one goal: subjecting the power that was exercised behind closed doors to global scrutiny" (Domscheit-Berg 2011, ix). Most world democracies already believe that government operations should be exposed to public scrutiny, so there is a conspiratorial edge to this statement, even if it is also true. But then Domscheit-Berg asserts that what most convinced him the sentiment is correct was Assange's own conduct: "Over the course of my time with Julian Assange at Wiki-Leaks, I would experience firsthand how power and secrecy corrupt people." He hoped that the "almost reticent criticism" he expressed about Assange's conduct "would cause people to question the power of WikiLeaks and the chief figure behind it," but "in fact, the opposite happened." Despite Wiki-Leaks' professed commitment to "transparency" and revealing the false-hoods of the powerful, "Julian also had a rather casual attitude toward the truth" (65), reflecting the typical fascist and protofascist stance of mistrust-ing "power," yet harboring a strong desire to seize it. Perhaps especially revealing of this dynamic is Domscheit-Berg's observation that "in early 2010 his tone toward me changed radically. 'If you fuck up, I'll hunt you down and kill you,' he once told me" (70–71).

By 2016, it was becoming clear to many others that Assange was not pur-suing transparency or accountability per se, but instead trying to realize an agenda that was distinctly political and strongly aligned with the far right. Even in early 2016, *Die Zeit* editor Jochen Bittner, in a *New York Times* opin-ion piece called "How Julian Assange Is Destroying WikiLeaks," affirmed that the site "has been a boon for global civil liberties" but "the problem is that the project is inseparable from the man. Mr. Assange has made little secret about his skepticism toward Western democracy and his willingness to work with autocratic governments like Vladimir V. Putin's Russia. His personal politics undermines WikiLeaks' neutrality—and the noble cause for which WikiLeaks used to stand. What we need is a WikiLeaks without the founder of WikiLeaks." Despite referring to WikiLeaks as embodying a "noble cause," Bittner raises important questions about its basic mission:

> One element of Assange-think has been clear from early on: There is no such thing as a legitimate secret. The public is entitled to share any knowl-edge governments hold. Only complete transparency can stop and prevent conspiracy. . . .
>
> This is not only nonsense, it is dangerous radicalism.

He goes on: "In his simplistic reading, the West is hypocritical because it stands for civil liberties, and all secrets are antithetical to liberty. No wonder he got a show on Russian television—his viewpoint puts him nicely in line with Mr. Putin's ideological agenda." Despite the nod toward civil liberties, the ideological agenda Assange and Putin share is nothing like democracy—it is fascism.

At the core of fascism is the belief that people are divided into kinds. Ideologues use all kinds of descriptive terms to divide people into groups, sometimes stressing the superiority of themselves (Aryans, *Übermenschen*, white supremacists) and sometimes the inferiority of others (racial and ethnic slurs, "sheeple," "muggles"). Assange's case shows how easily that belief emerges in contexts that seem oppositional to them. In a recent full-throated defense of Assange precisely because he "adopted the principles of cypherpunk ethics, but he placed them into a distinctively cosmopolitan context. By combining cypherpunk ethics with antiwar values and Enlightenment ideals," Patrick Anderson (2021, 307) avoids all discussion of either cypherpunk or Assange's personal politics. At the center of those cypherpunk ethics and Assange's own is the slogan "transparency for the powerful, privacy for the weak." Anderson and most other supporters of Assange do not seem to notice that the slogan splits the human world into two groups— "weak" and "powerful"—and grants only certain, self-elected persons the right and power to decide who belongs in each group.

It is important to remember that historical fascists, including those in Italy and Germany before and during World War II, typically cast themselves as both the "weak" and the "powerful" depending on need. From Nazis claiming Jews actually control the world to KKK members attacking Black Americans for their alleged physical or sexual prowess, the key is always a denial of the core commitment of democracy—that we are all the same. Fascists decide on their own how society should be arranged, without regard for the rights or interests of people in general. As we have seen, this antidemocratic splitting is evident all over cypherpunk propaganda and is frequently made explicit in the anarcho-capitalist literature on which cypherpunk is based.

It is unsurprising that Assange, despite his rise to immense cultural and social power worldwide, continued to assert his absolute right to categorize himself as "weak," and thus entitled to "privacy." Meanwhile, he continued to expose and attack civil servants and others, who were not implicated in any sort of wrongdoing whatsoever, solely because they were "powerful," working for or with democratic governments. As the mid-2010s approached, he began to target those who worked with liberal and left parties in demo-cratic countries. While he released emails that were intended to damage or even physically endanger diplomats whose only alleged "crime" was work-ing for the State Department or the Democratic National Committee, he simultaneously worked with members of the Trump campaign, who rep-resented the apex of global political and economic power. He worked with them because apparently they were "weak." Given the many neo-Nazi and fascist associations between the GOP (especially under Trump), it is no stretch to see Assange here replicating the fascist division of the world into the good self and the bad other.

Further, this alignment with powerful authoritarianism in the service of a supposedly victimized or embattled "self" is familiar from Assange's history. This is arguably the main point of Domscheit-Berg's history of WikiLeaks: that Assange "was engaged in a constant battle for dominance" (Domscheit-Berg 2011, 73), that Assange saw himself as "untouchable" (264), that he is "so paranoid, so power-hungry, so megalomaniac" (3), and what's needed is to subject WikiLeaks itself to the kind of transparency it pre-scribes for others, including its finances—"who decides how money is allo-cated" (277)—its "organizational and decision making structure" (ibid., 278), Assange's personal "financial interest in how and when the diplomatic cables were published," and whether Assange and his associates profit from the activities of WikiLeaks. In other words, Assange's personal and organi-zational politics align with those of Trump, Roger Stone, Nigel Farage, and other far-right actors with whom he worked closely in 2016.

Assange's supporters on the left took his professed commitment to "trans-parency" as evidence of his skepticism toward what many consider to be the sole, uniquely abusive global power in the modern age: the U.S. govern-ment and its democratic allies. Yet when this commitment shifted to exclude the party that has historically been most allied with that hegemonic power, many of Assange's supporters seemed not to notice. Organizations with far better-established commitments to government transparency as a fun-damental value in democracies than WikiLeaks, including the Sunlight Foundation, raised real questions about whether Assange was interested in government transparency, or instead was engaged in "weaponizing" transparency for partisan gain (Howard and Wonderlich 2017). Supporting

Trump for president in secret, lying repeatedly about his connections to Trump's campaign, never releasing "leaks" about Trump's intensive secrecy regarding his personal and business operations—all this could still be construed as "transparency for the powerful," because somehow Trump, like Assange, was now "weak." To critics, this shows the flexible and adaptive nature of fascism: anything that helps the self and its allies to gain and exercise power while damaging the enemy is good. It should be more shocking that, thanks in large part to cyberlibertarian discourse about "free speech," "censorship," and "openness," many around the world can laud Assange as a champion of democratic values as he overtly rebukes them.

It is not even clear that Assange supports anything resembling democratic values, despite his sometimes using the language of democracy to justify his actions. Assange's close associates have long noted his promotion of anti-Semitism (Ball 2011; Feldman 2016), misogyny (Rozsa 2017; Schrager 2017), and dallying with Holocaust denial (Feldman 2016). They have also noted his critical role in spreading disinformation about climate change (Keating 2012) and his dissembling about the nature of the material he himself leaks. In 2013, Assange founded the WikiLeaks Party in Australia and ran for the Senate. However, the party collapsed due to its association with far-right parties, including the neo-Nazi Australia First party, and Assange's refusal to disavow the association (Matthews 2013). Despite his protestations about "transparency," the figure Assange most resembles in world media is Alex Jones. However, Assange has frequently obtained access to actual classified material, though he frequently twists its contents to spread Jones-like conspiracy theories. Assange repeatedly spread the same conspiracy theories as Jones—including stories about Vince Foster's death—before, during, and after the 2016 U.S. presidential election. He also helped to generate and continued to promulgate a WikiLeaks-specific conspiracy theory that DNC staffer Seth Rich had leaked data that almost certainly came from Russian intelligence, after its obvious falsehood was repeatedly demonstrated (Poulsen 2019).

Assange receives support from across the political spectrum, with many taking his claim to be a journalist at face value. There may well be genuine differences of opinion as to whether collecting, curating, and posting large collections of leaked material constitutes "journalism." Alex Jones, too, claims to be engaged in absolute freedom of speech and opposition to censorship, and even to "leak" secret information. Assange deserves a robust defense of his claims in court like any defendant. However, claiming to be a journalist does not exempt him from possible prosecution for espionage if he engaged in it. In fact, there is robust evidence to suggest he did (Poulsen 2019). The principle that would be endorsed by such a defense—that as long as someone can claim to be a journalist, they are free to engage in espionage—is ludicrous under any democratic rule of law.

Despite the fact that Assange had long indicated that his political preferences in the United States aligned, unsurprisingly, with right-wing libertarians like Ron Paul and Rand Paul (Good 2013; Wilentz 2014), many of his supporters seemed unable to grasp that he had identified himself with some of the most powerful antidemocratic forces in the world. They often make hyperbolic slippery slope claims about the threats to "freedom of the press" posed by Assange's prosecution. However, they seem unwilling to look at the far greater evidence that the only people who have been prosecuted in the WikiLeaks orbit have had serious charges of espionage levied against them. Furthermore, only when courts and juries have been satisfied have those prosecutions resulted in convictions. Even journalists like Glenn Greenwald and Laura Poitras, journalists associated with Assange, Snowden, and others, have not faced legal action for reporting on Assange's leaks. This provides prima facie evidence that it is espionage, not journalism, that is under fire.

Despite Alex Jones's *InfoWars* being fueled by the same principles as WikiLeaks, and despite their political alignment and cooperation with Roger Stone and other members of Donald Trump's election team, many who see Jones for what he is still support Assange as if he stands for principles of freedom and openness that underpin democratic societies. Yet all the evidence points the other way: Assange, like Jones, supports white supremacist fascist power, and uses the language of principle to sell that fascism as if it is something else. That language of "principle" is typical of cyberlibertarianism. The fact that Assange is seen by many non-fascists as a hero shows the deceptive power of cyberlibertarian rhetoric and its disturbing propensity to gather the energies and passion of democracy supporters to agitate against it.

THE ALT-RIGHT, RATIONALISM, AND NEOREACTION

The rise of the alt-right in the early 2010s brought with it a host of new, online-based political movements characterized by neologisms and frantic revisionist rewriting of history, philosophy, and political theory. Birthed out of a heady mixture of transhumanism (especially via the extropians; see Carrico 2005, 2013; Pein 2016), cypherpunk anarcho-capitalism, science-fictional thoughts about "artificial intelligence" (by which they really mean something closer to "computer consciousness") and conspiracy theory, movements with names like rationalism, neoreaction (NRx), and Dark Enlightenment all display heavy investment in the reduction of biological and social phenomena to computational ones. In this sense they are remarkable examples of computationalism taken to its logical extreme, with all the attendant right-wing politics I have described in prior work (2009). Most of the strongest critical commentary on these movements ("Armistead" 2016; Frank 2015; Haider 2017; Pein 2014, 2017, 2018; Ratcliffe 2020; Sandifer 2017; Smith and Burrows 2021; Turner 2019) dwells on the profound synergies among the digital technology industry, the programmer/engineer mindset, the basic assumptions behind conservative and far-right politics, the affordances of computers and digital platforms, and the emergence of these new fascist and protofascist movements. Less noticed have been the points of significant continuity between, and often explicit embrace of, cyberlibertarian principles and political programs, and the alt-right as both cultural and political force.

Rationalism and NRx (and to a lesser extent the Dark Enlightenment) are known best through the writings of a number of thinkers, all of them white men, and all of them with greater or lesser investments in digital technology and many of the ideological positions that define cyberlibertarianism. Eliezer Yudkowsky, a self-identified "AI researcher," is a leading figure of rationalism. He produces massive, largely unedited books and blog posts. Curtis Yarvin, known under the pen name Mencius Moldbug, is a computer science PhD dropout and entrepreneur of sorts. He also writes massive, largely unedited blog posts. Nick Land is a former academic and early theorist of digital technology with outsize influence across many fields. His turn toward overt fascism in the 2010s has sadly dented his popularity only slightly. Michael Anissimov is a self-identified futurist, transhumanist, and technologist.

As the pseudonymous "Josephine Armistead" recounts the beginnings of these movements:

In 2006, Eliezer Yudkowsky began collaborating with George Mason University (funded by ExxonMobil, the Koch brothers, and the Cato Institute)

economist Robin Hanson on the blog Overcoming Bias. This would later
be the basis for LessWrong, a community blog for Overcoming Bias and run
under the umbrella of SIAI, now known as MIRI (Machine Intelligence
Research Institute). The initial audience for LessWrong were fellow transhu-
manists, including the Extropians and SL4 mailing lists. In 2007, Curtis
Yarvin started the first neo-reactionary blog, Unqualified Reservations under
the pseudonym Mencius Moldbug, though he did not call himself, initially, "neo-reactionary": he preferred to call himself a "formalist" or a "neo-
cameralist" (after his hero, Frederick the Great). This, however, was not the
beginning of his blogging career. Prior to founding his own blog, Moldbug
commented on 2Blowhards and GNXP (a racist site) as 'Mencius'–and then
on Overcoming Bias. (2016, 15)

As journalist Corey Pein put it, speaking just of Yarvin but in a pithy phrase
that could be applied to the writings of all these figures, "Moldbug reads
like an overconfident autodidact's imitation of a Lewis Lapham essay—if
Lewis Lapham were a fascist teenage Dungeon Master" (2014).

Populist derogation of expertise and the use of blogs and social media
sites as primary sources of information are only two of the points of harmony between neoreaction and cyberlibertarianism. They also come together around core issues such as decentralization, internet freedom/freedom
of speech, anonymization, and encryption. Additionally, they incorporate
fundamentally right-wing political precepts as if they flow naturally from
purportedly immutable facts about the world, such as technological development or human nature. As Pein wrote with real prescience in 2014,
"Moldbuggism, for now, remains mostly an Internet phenomenon. Which
is not to say it is 'merely' an Internet phenomenon. This is, after all, a technological age. Last November, Yarvin claimed that his blog had received
500,000 views. It is not quantity of his audience that matters so much
as the nature of it, however. And the neoreactionaries do seem to be influencing the drift of Silicon Valley libertarianism, which is no small force
today. This is why I have concluded, sadly, that Yarvin needs answering."
He goes on:

In a widely covered secessionist speech at a Silicon Valley "startup school"
last year, there was more than a hint of Moldbug . . . The speech, by former
Stanford professor and Andreessen Horowitz partner Balaji Srinivasan, never

mentioned Moldbug or the Dark Enlightenment, but it was suffused with neoreactionary rhetoric and ideas. Srinivasan used the phrase "the paper belt" to describe his enemies, namely the government, the publishing industries, and universities. The formulation mirrored Moldbug's "Cathedral" [an amalgam of universities and the mainstream press]. Srinivasan's central theme was the notion of "exit"—as in, exit from democratic society, and entry into any number of corporate mini-states whose arrival will leave the world looking like a patchwork map of feudal Europe.

The interpenetration of NRx and all the flavors of libertarianism (political, cyber) could not be more thorough. Pein draws attention to what is arguably the most notorious passage in Srinivasan's 2013 speech:

> We want to show what a society run by Silicon Valley would look like. That's where "exit" comes in. . . . It basically means: build an opt-in society, ultimately outside the US, run by technology. And this is actually where the Valley is going. This is where we're going over the next ten years. . . . [Google cofounder] Larry Page, for example, wants to set aside a part of the world for unregulated experimentation. That's carefully phrased. He's not saying, "take away the laws in the US." If you like your country, you can keep it. Same with Marc Andreessen: "The world is going to see an explosion of countries in the years ahead—doubled, tripled, quadrupled countries." (Srinivasan 2013)

In addition to Moldbug, Srinivasan seems to be lifting material directly from *The Sovereign Individual,* which should be no surprise. Srinivasan is a former partner at Andreessen Horowitz, a venture capital firm known for promoting far-right ideas through digital technology, including cryptocurrency, Web3, and the metaverse. He delivered his speech at Startup School, an online program run by Y Combinator, another influential Silicon Valley venture capital firm that has significant ties to the far right, notably through its cofounder Paul Graham and former president Sam Altman. The program is designed to help new venture capitalists. Peter Thiel was also a part-time partner at Y Combinator, a position he left in 2017. Altman refused to comply with "some members of the tech community [who] began to question Y Combinator's connections to Thiel" (Mac 2017) when Thiel formally aligned himself with Donald Trump after he won the 2016 U.S. presidential election. Although Altman "vocally opposed the Republican nominee," he claimed that separating the firm from Thiel would be an example of what actually causes fascism: "Cutting off opposing viewpoints leads to extremism and will not get us the country we want."

Everywhere in NRx and rationalism, we find similar prescriptions that seem to have been influenced by Ayn Rand and Robert Heinlein novels, as well as anarcho-capitalist and protofascist political writings. These prescriptions place a special emphasis on the freedom-producing character of digital technology and internet connectivity, which has the inherent power to destabilize democracy. Thiel is one of the figures who keeps turning up at the center of these prescriptions. Pein is right to state that like Srinivasan, Thiel was also echoing Moldbug (along with many other anarcho-capitalists like Rothbard, Patri and David Friedman, and Hoppe) when in 2009 he infamously wrote in an essay for the far-right Cato Institute that he "no longer believe[s] that freedom and democracy are compatible." He also stated that "the fate of our world may depend on the effort of a single person who builds or propagates the machinery of freedom," quoting the title of David Friedman's libertarian manifesto *The Machinery of Freedom* (1989). Friedman is one of the anarcho-capitalists most invested in promoting digital technology as a wedge toward building his libertarian future. His most sustained treatment of the topic, *Future Imperfect: Technology and Freedom in an Uncertain World* (2008), includes four dedications, three of whom are among the farthest right of digital technology promoters: Eric Drexler, Tim May, and Eric S. Raymond. The fourth, science fiction author Vernor Vinge, is credited with inventing the concept of a "technological singularity" and has many associations with free market libertarianism (Carrico 2005; Godwin 2007).

Thiel's recommendation for an alternative to democracy is monarchy, which is in keeping with NRx and the inevitable outcome of anarcho-capitalism. This monarchy is formed on the specific model of Silicon Valley digital technology companies: "It is clear that Thiel sees corporations as the governments of the future and capitalists such as himself as the kings, and it is also clear that this is a shockingly common view in Thiel's cohort" (Pein 2014). Pein notes that it was the strange comments of Google engineer Justine Tunney, who explicitly referenced Moldbug, that drew his attention to the political influence of NRx. She created a petition to replace all democratic government with Google's corporate leadership:

1. Retire all government employees with full pensions.
2. Transfer administrative authority to the tech industry.
3. Appoint Eric Schmidt CEO of America. (Qtd. in Hall 2014)

Tunney is an especially interesting example of the syncretism that characterizes cyberlibertarianism and its openness to fascism. She gained public attention as "a leader in 'Tech Ops' for Occupy Wall Street" (Chu 2014), a protest movement that was partly fueled by online activity. Occupy's rejection of left-right politics, at least by some of its participants, made it vulnerable to incursions by the far right, including libertarians like Ron Paul (Budowsky 2011; McCormack 2011). While her earlier Occupy activism may have appeared aligned with the left, in 2014 "Tunney's rants shifted from being against the Occupy movement as a failure of left-wing activism to being against the Left itself. She posted a Storify claiming that the tech industry, as a whole, were 'the true progressives' and that the Left were actually 'reactionaries' because of negative news stories coming out criticizing the Bay Area tech elite" (Chu 2014). Soon after that, "in April, she tweeted 'Read Mencius Moldbug.'"

As journalist Arthur Chu writes, "Tunney is not just an isolated anomaly. She's the leading, crankish edge of a broad cultural trend" (2014). The leading edge is a common flaw in many inchoate activist movements, especially those that create a metaphysical barrier between "government" and the "people," with all the Schmittian overtones of "enemy" and "friend." The problem becomes not one of ineffective or irresponsible or immoral systems, but simply one of power: "Tunney was never against the one percent— she just thought that the one percent were the wrong people. The problem was they were tie-wearing investment banker fratboys and didn't deserve to be on top. Just like in her view government fat cats and Hollywood celebrities and snooty academics don't deserve to be on top. But tech geeks, with their superhuman ability to manipulate ones and zeroes, do." Tunney's revision of the language in "progressivism" and "reaction" is indicative of the cyberlibertarianism movement, which is characterized by a disregard for politics and a focus on technology. The most powerful technology executives and companies are seen as the former, while anti-capitalist activists are seen as the latter. This movement is marked by a synthesis of technology and politics, which is then turned back against politics itself. As Chu writes:

This is why, as one of those young millennial whippersnappers who nonetheless identifies with the Old Left more than my own generation, I distrust
the message we keep getting about the democratizing power of the Internet
and New Media, about how progressive the Millennial Generation is.
    I distrust my fellow young nerds. I distrust techies when they bear gifts.

The "gifts" referred to are all political and cultural. Such activists insist that
an emancipatory politics can only be realized by following rules that they
claim are built into the technology, which is above and beyond politics.
However, this sublates the politics that ordinary people understand into
their superior version.
    One of the areas where the far right and digital technology connect is
artificial intelligence and a seemingly unrelated philosophical doctrine called
"effective altruism." These come together in the so-called rationalist community, a widely distributed group of people with especially pronounced
influence online and troubling ties to many of the far right's leading figures.
RationalWiki—a project that has roots in some of the same intuitions and
ideas that ground the rationalist movement but embraces a far more varied
and evidence-based approach to argumentation—provides some sense of the
close interconnections among rationalism, AI, and the far right. The best-
known hub for rationalism is a blog and community discussion site called
LessWrong. As RationalWiki explains it, "LessWrong is a community blog
focused on 'refining the art of human rationality.' To this end, it focuses on
identifying and overcoming bias, improving judgment and problem-solving,
and speculating about the future. The blog is based on the ideas of Eliezer
Yudkowsky, a research fellow for the Machine Intelligence Research Institute (MIRI; previously known as the Singularity Institute for Artificial Intelligence, and then the Singularity Institute). Many members of LessWrong
share Yudkowsky's interests in transhumanism, artificial intelligence, the
Singularity, and cryonics" ("LessWrong"). The entry goes on to explain the
close ties between LessWrong and the particular conception of AI advanced
by Yudkowsky and others in his orbit:

> In July of 2000, Eliezer Yudkowsky founded the nonprofit Singularity Insti-
> tute for Artificial Intelligence (SIAI) to "create a friendly, self-improving arti-
> ficial intelligence." In 2006, Yudkowsky began contributing to Overcoming
> Bias along with GMU economist Robin Hanson. After several years and

increasing popularity, Yudkowsky started a collaborative blog/community to focus on some topics of particular interest to himself and SIAI, such as rationality, philosophy, AI, and transhumanism. Overcoming Bias remains as a "sister blog" to LessWrong, where Hanson and others discuss how human beings can compensate for natural biases (and ideas stemming from Hanson's speculations on economics).

MIRI, where Yudkowsky remains a research fellow, hosts and maintains LessWrong to provide "an introduction to issues of cognitive biases and rationality relevant for careful thinking about optimal philanthropy and many of the problems that must be solved in advance of the creation of provably human-friendly powerful artificial intelligence." Yudkowsky considers LessWrong useful insofar as it advances SIAI's work, and the site is a key venue for SIAI recruitment and fundraising. The most popular post of all time on LessWrong, for example, is an assessment of SIAI by charity evaluator GiveWell.

LessWrong originally attracted the bulk of its userbase from communities interested in transhumanism. In addition to Overcoming Bias, these communities include the SL4 mailing list and the Extropians mailing lists (dating back to the 1990s). Accordingly, LessWrong has long been an essentially transhumanist community, emphasizing a focus on rationality per se in order to attract those who might otherwise be skeptical of apocalyptic AI.

It may seem surprising that a community dedicated to rational thought would also be committed to transhumanism and "apocalyptic AI." However, these topics appear to be entirely different from "human rationality." Further, AI is an abstract, philosophical topic explored from many different angles in industry and academia, inviting a range of views. One might imagine that rationalists would be committed to reading and understanding the academic research and engineering accomplishments of AI in the real world. To the contrary, Yudkowsky, "a homeschooled individual with no college degree" ("Eliezer Yudkowsky"), describes himself as "an AI researcher." However, in addition to having "no training in his claimed field, Yudkowsky has pretty much no accomplishments of any sort to his credit beyond getting Peter Thiel to give him money." In addition to Thiel, Vitalik Buterin (founder of Ethereum and a recipient of Thiel Fellowship funds that explicitly eschew formal higher education) and Stanford University have provided support to Yudkowsky's MIRI ("Machine Intelligence Research Institute").

MIRI and Yudkowsky differ from most academic and commercial research on AI by taking advantage of a key ambiguity built into AI discourse from its inception. For several decades, academics, mostly engineers and less so experts in psychology or neuroscience, believed in AGI (artificial general intelligence), which is also known as "strong AI." These advocates seem to share the intuition that machines are one day going to "wake up" and "think," words that must be put in quotation marks because of the many background assumptions they import almost beyond the notice of many people. First, they equate "intelligence" with the kinds of algorithmic processing done by computers, which is already a tendentious proposal. Next, they equate that kind of intelligence with "thinking," even though few people who study the mind, whether human or animal, would agree that "intelligence" and "thought" refer to the same things. Next, they equate "thinking" of this highly algorithmic sort with "consciousness," although this is done almost entirely under the table.

What we today call computers were once called "thinking machines," and fiction is replete with what appear to be representations of machines that think, talk, and feel much like human beings do. These representations have led many to believe that such constructions are possible, without doing the necessary conceptual and empirical work to show that this is the case. The academic work that supports AGI typically makes a huge leap from the notion of a "generalized problem solver" that could theoretically answer any question—much like Siri and other voice assistants can now answer questions thanks to interfacing with search engines and encyclopedias—to a machine that is actually conscious. These thinkers, who tend to come from computer science and engineering, have at best threadbare accounts of core concepts like "feeling," "knowing," and "thinking." Instead, they assume that "processing rules algorithmically" is equivalent to all these other concepts. In some cases it seems right to see in this assumption a real hatred for the non-algorithmic parts of human beings (as well as other living beings that we guess possess some form of consciousness, especially the higher mammals). It is no accident that one of the positions in recent philosophy associated with this way of thinking is called "eliminative materialism," a program of reduction that suggests that in some future version of science, all the messy parts of human consciousness will be understood in mechanistic terms.

Despite their commitment to rational enquiry, the rationalists simply assert without evidence that there is a discrete quantity called "intelligence," which can be measured by IQ tests. They believe that this quantity is not just *related to,* or *part of,* the mind, but simply *is* the mind. Because their account of intelligence maps onto what computers can do, this somehow means that as computers become more powerful, humanlike minds will arise in them. This sub-rosa account of superior intelligence rooted in quantifiable measures like IQ is why I and others have suggested that the dream of AGI has much in common with white supremacy (Golumbia 2020b; Katz 2020). Further, AGI in this extended, nonacademic form has more than a suggestion of messianic religion. When AGI arises, it will not simply be another humanlike mind in the world. Instead, it will be vastly smarter than us, and therefore vastly superior. This will produce an epistemic and cultural crisis. For all intents and purposes, a god will have been created.

This is a bizarre assumption to find at the heart of a community that prides itself on rational thought. It is especially odd given that some of those at the edges of this community, like right-leaning provocateur Sam Harris, profess to a deep atheism that is not infrequently racist, especially toward Islam. They hold to a belief system about machines that demands we accept inexplicable miracles not just as possibilities but as realities from which we dare not turn away. This is where the story of Roko's basilisk comes in. As RationalWiki puts it:

> Roko's basilisk is a thought experiment about the potential risks involved in developing artificial intelligence. Its conclusion is that an all-powerful artificial intelligence from the future might retroactively punish those who did not help bring about its existence, including those who merely knew about the possible development of such a being. It is named after the member of the rationalist community LessWrong who first publicly described it, though he did not originate it or the underlying ideas.
>
> The basilisk resembles a futurist version of Pascal's wager, in that it suggests people should weigh possible punishment versus reward and as a result accept particular singularitarian ideas or financially support their development.
>
> Despite widespread incredulity, this argument is taken quite seriously by some people, primarily some denizens of LessWrong. While neither LessWrong nor its founder Eliezer Yudkowsky advocate the basilisk as true, they do advocate almost all of the premises that add up to it. ("Roko's Basilisk")

Unlike Pascal's wager, though, Roko's basilisk makes many assumptions that emerge not from hundreds of years of religious thought about the nature of the Christian God. Instead, it emerges from unstated propositions about the nature of consciousness and political power, in addition to tendentious accounts of intelligence, mind, and computers. The god that appears in Roko's basilisk is most notable for being a vindictive, authoritarian dictator that may be even more cruel than the God of the Old Testament. It will ruthlessly punish anyone who fails to believe in it before its existence. Pascal's wager suggests that we believe in God to gain eternal happiness as a reward. In Roko's basilisk, we must believe, and even work hard to invoke the god that is coming, because the nature of its power is ruthless, cruel, and ultimately hateful toward humankind and even life itself. In some versions of the story, the AI god is so vindictive that it "might make simulations of [those who didn't act to create AI], first to predict their behavior, then to punish the simulation for the predicted behavior so as to influence the original person" ("Roko's Basilisk"). The AI god will punish everyone who did not help bring it into being, even those who are already dead.

The AI god posited by Roko's basilisk displays many characteristics compatible with far-right and fascist belief systems. The principal feature is its assertion of an infinitely cruel and omnipotent ruler that has the power to control our behavior even when it does not exist. This ruler splits the world with binary clarity into "good" (people who helped build it) and "bad" (people who did not). It is worth recalling that much of the other thinking in and around the rationalist and alt-right communities posit similar forms of rule in terrestrial forms, including various forms of absolutist rule such as monarchy.

Despite their claims to rationality, followers of the Roko's basilisk story experienced a profound existential crisis as soon as the thought experiment hit LessWrong. As Elizabeth Sandifer explains:

> The result was a frankly hilarious community meltdown in which people lost their shit as ideas they'd studiously internalized threatened to torture them for all eternity if they didn't hand all of their money over to MIRI, culminating in Yudkowsky himself stepping in to ban all further discussion of the dread beast. This went more or less exactly how anyone who has ever used the Internet would guess. Those interested in the details can readily look them up, but suffice to say it was not the sort of incident from which one's school of thought recovers its intellectual respectability. (2017, 14)

Despite his near-total lack of standing in responsible AI research, Yud-kowsky and MIRI retain a real hold over the imaginations of many close to the space, including many technology developers who do not specialize in AI, and even some who do. While MIRI "has put out a couple of minor papers, there's a conspicuous lack of research on machine intelligence emerging from it. Aside from the problem that Yudkowsky is not actually a brilliant programmer capable of making headway on the persistently dif-ficult problems that have been facing artificial intelligence for decades, this is largely because the problem he identifies—how to make an AI friend-lier—is simply not one that artificial intelligence research is in a position to grapple with yet." Even this presumes that the notion of an AI being "friendly" (or not) is coherent, which few AI researchers would grant.

More notably, the amount of money and effort directed at creating and then managing this apocalyptic deity pass for "politics" and "civic good" in the rationalist world. As the writer Shuja Haider put it, "Roko's Basilisk isn't just a self-fulfilling prophecy. Rather than influencing events toward a particular result, the result is generated by its own prediction. The implica-tions blur the boundaries between science and fiction. The archives from which an artificial intelligence draws data will contain the work of both Ray Kurzweil and H. P. Lovecraft, and it may not distinguish between them the way we do. Instead of Kurzweil's world without death and disease, it may attempt to build Lovecraft's R'lyeh, a loathsome city in the sea that exists on a plane of non-Euclidian geometry" (2017). The fact that a brutal, authoritarian god that makes hard distinctions between "us" and "them" and murders all of the "them" who have failed, prior to its appearance, to work hard enough to create it, is a technofascist fantasy that would make historical fascists blush, even if its dreamers don't seem to understand that.

NICK LAND AND THE CYBERNETIC ROOTS OF CONTEMPORARY FASCISM

There may be no figure more central in joining belief in the transformative power of digital technology with an unexpectedly dramatic turn to the darkest aspects of right-wing thought than Nick Land. A British philoso-pher, Land along with Sadie Plant, a feminist theorist and philosopher, formed the Cybernetic Culture Research Unit (CCRU), which was loosely affiliated with the University of Warwick. Both Land and Plant taught in the philosophy department. The CCRU existed from 1995 to 1998, although its unofficial status makes it difficult to establish precise dates of its existence. Despite its brief tenure, the project continues to exert considerable influence over contemporary digital culture. Many prominent writers and theorists, especially those associated with digitally oriented movements such as speculative realism / object-oriented ontology and accelerationism, were either trained by or worked with Land and the CCRU.

The CCRU, like many of the early quasi-political digital theory movements, combined a philosophy directly constructed on foundations derived from digital technologies and the thinking surrounding them, with fringe, science-fictional, drug-oriented, and conspiracy material. The CCRU site has a page of links that includes information on topics such as alien abduction, UAP, the Anunnaki Invasion, astrology, the Cthulhu Mythos, theosophy, Atlantis, nanotechnology, and work from prominent computer scientists like AI researcher Marvin Minsky and roboticist Hans Moravec. Their theoretical work showed a taste for the most extreme elements of Continental thought, namely Gilles Deleuze, Félix Guattari, and in particular Georges Bataille, on whom Land did some of his earlier and more conventional work.

One of the CCRU's most telling early concepts was the notion of "cyberpositive." In their 1994 text "Cyberpositive," Plant and Land explicitly invoke the AIDS epidemic, which at that time seemed beyond the reach of medical science. "Cyberpositive" recalls the then-ubiquitous phrase "HIV positive," suggesting that one might embrace and even deliberately spread the fatal infection. The authors' tone already shows signs of craving an apocalypse whose near-term advent they seem certain about: "Catastrophe is the past coming apart. Anastrophe is the future coming together. Seen from within history, divergence is reaching critical proportions. From the matrix, crisis is convergence misinterpreted by mankind. The media are choked with stories about global warming and ozone depletion, HIV and AIDS, plagues of drugs and software viruses, nuclear proliferation, the planetary disintegration of economic management, breakdown of the family, waves of migrants and refugees, subsidence of the nation state into its terminal dementia, societies grated open by the underclass, urban cores in flames, suburbia under threat, fission, schizophrenia, loss of control."

Plant and Land directly connect their apocalyptic vision to digital technology and the politics they claim it embodies:

Rotted by digital contagions, modernity is falling to bits. Lenin, Mussolini, and Roosevelt concluded modern humanism by exhausting the possibilities of economic planning. Runaway capitalism has broken through all the social control mechanisms, accessing inconceivable alienations. Capital clones itself with increasing disregard for heredity, becoming abstract positive feedback, organizing itself. Turbular finance drifts across the global network.

[Norbert] Wiener is one of the great modernists, defining cybernetics as the science of communication and control; a tool for human dominion over nature and history, a defence against the cyberpathology of markets. His propaganda against positive feedback—quantizing it as amplification within an invariable metric—has been highly influential, establishing a cybernetics of stability fortified against the future. There is no space in such a theory for anything truly cyberpositive, subtle or intelligent beyond the objectivity required for human comprehension. Nevertheless, beyond the event horizon of human science, even the investigation of self-stabilizing or cybernegative objects is inevitably enveloped by exploratory or cyberpositive processes.

Cruelly mixing Lenin, Mussolini, and Roosevelt into a single "modern" edifice of "economic planning"—notably, an unacknowledged gesture at the totalizing antidemocratic extremism of Hayek, the Liberty League, and the John Birch Society—Plant and Land develop the idea that there are two strains of digital technological development. One aims toward "stability" and another that aims toward "contagion," with the latter now construed as "positive" in much the same way being infected with HIV can be archly reinterpreted as "positive": if, that is, one maintains a relentlessly negative, upside-down vision of society and its possibilities, in which one courts destruction and disease as desirable outcomes.

Plant and Land both worked in the then (and to some extent, still) prominent mode of European Continental philosophy, which has been taken to have primarily a left-oriented political orientation. In a 1998 interview and analysis (published online in 2005), journalist and CCRU participant Simon Reynolds sums up the CCRU program:

"Cyberpositive" was originally the title of an essay by Sadie Plant and Nick Land. First aired at the 1992 drug culture symposium Pharmakon, "Cyberpositive" was a gauntlet thrown down at the Left-wing orthodoxies that still dominate British academia. The term "cyberpositive" was a twist on Norbert

Wierner's ideas of "negative feedback" (homeostasis), and "positive feed-back" (runaway tendencies, vicious circles). Where the conservative Wiener valorized "negative feedback," Plant/Land re-positivized positive feedback— specifically the tendency of market forces to generate disorder and destabi-lize control structures.

"It was pretty obvious that a theoretically Left-leaning critique could be maintained quite happily but it wasn't ever going to get anywhere," says Plant. "If there was going to be scope for any kind of . . . not 'resistance,' but any kind of discrepancy in the global consensus, then it was going to have to come from somewhere else." As well as Deleuze & Guattari, another crucial influence was neo-Deleuzian theorist Manuel De Landa's idea of "capitalism as the system of antimarkets." Plant and the CCRU enthuse about bottom-up, grass-roots, self-organizing activity: street markets, "the frontier zones of capitalism," what De Landa calls "meshwork," as opposed to corporate, top-down capitalism. It all sounds quite jovial, the way CCRU describe it now— a bustling bazaar culture of trade and "cutting deals." But "Cyberpositive" actually reads like a nihilistic paean to the "cyberpathology of markets," cele-brating capitalism as "a viral contagion" and declaring "everything cyber-positive is an enemy of mankind." In Nick Land's essays like "Machinic Desire" and "Meltdown," the tone of morbid glee is intensified to an apoca-lyptic pitch. There seems to be a perverse and literally anti-humanist identi-fication with the "dark will" of capital and technology, as it "rips up political cultures, deletes traditions, dissolves subjectivities."

This gloating delight in capital's deterritorializing virulence is the CCRU's reaction to the stuffy complacency of Left-wing academic thought. "There's definitely a strong alliance in the academy between anti-market ideas and completely scleroticised, institutionalized thought," says CCRU's Mark Fisher. "It's obvious that capitalism isn't going to be brought down by its contradic-tions. Nothing ever died of contradictions!" Exulting in capitalism's perma-nent "crisis mode," CCRU believe in the strategic application of pressure to accelerate the tendencies towards chaos.

Land, who is remarkably central to many contemporary manifestations of fascism, locates the sources of his own thought in the same cyberliber-tarian worldview that informs much discourse about digital technology. As early as the mid-1990s, he was discussing digital technology policy in the popular science magazine *New Scientist*. His views were similar to the pro-encryption, anti-government views that appeared in *Wired* and the Cypherpunks mailing list. He also reviewed Ludlow's 1996 anthology *High Noon on the Electronic Frontier,* claiming that cryptographer Dorothy Denning is "itching for a declaration of martial law" (Land 1996). He praises John Perry Barlow and EFF because they aim to "guarantee freedom from government control and interference on the internet." More recently, Land has become a vocal advocate for Bitcoin and other cryptocurrencies. In 2018 he released a long and profoundly incoherent book called *Crypto-Current: Bitcoin and Philosophy* full of such pseudo-Deleuzianisms as "Economies are assembled from flows. Unsurprisingly, therefore, their native codes are currencies, or current-signs. As societies mobilize matter–energy resource streams, their monetary conventions register these flows by inversion, and strict reciprocity. Hole-flow in electronics is a close analog" (§0.02) and "At the level of maximum abstraction, money—already in its most primitive instantiation—enables the commercial disintegration of time. This is captured at the level of hominid ethology by the facilitation of delayed reciprocity" (§5.43).

As the scholar Robert Topinka, among others, explains, Land's writings intersect with those of other digitally-based fascist theorists, especially Moldbug:

Land's "Dark Enlightenment" text attempts to formalize Moldbug's prolific if rambling blogposts into a neoreactionary theory of capitalist acceleration grounded in a despotic sovereign political order. Moldbug and Land follow the form of a left and postcolonial critique of modernity, but turn the critique on its head: the modern promise of equality and democracy was not compromised (by slavery, colonialism, and capitalism); the promise is itself the compromise that prevents capitalism's flourishing. Modern notions of equality legitimate any grievance as oppression, and democracy compels the state to recompense any grievance claim. Democracy and equality therefore combine to promote personal failure. Neoreaction seeks to replace democratic voice with exit, or the right to leave any polity at any time, and to restore sovereignty in the figure of a CEO–King who seeks only to maximize value and therefore to accelerate capitalism. Race serves a crucial function in this theory: ministered to by the "Cathedral," race mediates between citizens and state, sanctioning grievance claims and incentivizing dysfunction. However, by properly reprogramming race through neo-eugenics rather than modern notions of equality, it could become the accelerationist motor capable of restoring the lost future of capitalist sovereignty before its corruption through enforced diversity. (Topinka 2019)

Both Land and Moldbug tell stories full of familiar fascist tropes, inflected with a "new" form of racial hatred updated for the digital age. Here again is Topinka:

> Land and Moldbug are profoundly lapsarian thinkers. For them, progressivism—the conspiracy the "Cathedral" sustains—is the fall that obscures and indeed encourages the degeneration of the races. Land . . . argues that the progressive Enlightenment follows the "logical perversity" of "Hegel's dialectic," enforcing the "egalitarian moral ideal" through progressivism's sustaining formula: "tolerance is tolerable" and "intolerance is intolerable." This formal structure guarantees a "positive *right to be tolerated,* defined ever more expansively as substantial entitlement." . . . If progressivism is the fall, tolerance is the juggernaut that tramples any attempt at ascent. For Land, the American Civil War is a moment of original sin that that "cross-coded the practical question of the Leviathan with (black/white) racial dialectics." (interpolated quotations are from Land 2013)

From the right angle, Land's thought reads like an uncanny squaring of a circle that began with William Shockley's dual promotion of semiconductors and racial eugenics at the heart of Silicon Valley. Topinka calls this, quoting Peter Thiel, a desire to return "back to a past that was futuristic," with all the technological trappings of futurity but the past's acceptance of racial hierarchy. The problem is still the "Cathedral":

> Land proposes as a formal fix "hyper-racism," his vision for accelerating the "explicitly superior" and already "genetically self-filtering elite" through a system of "assortative mating" that would offer a "class-structured mechanism for population diremption, on a vector toward neo-speciation." . . . This is eugenics as a program for exit, not only from the progressive Enlightenment but also from the limits of humanity. Despite its contemporary jargon, this hyper-racism is indistinguishable in its form from late Victorian eugenics, which also recommended a program of "assortative mating." Of course, now eugenics places us on a vector toward neo-speciation; so it's back to the past, but now it's futuristic. (quotation from Land 2014b)

In Land's thought in particular, the affordances of digital technology and the usefulness of digital platforms to spread memetic content that both is and is not directly expressive of racial hatred: "The alt-right has fully anticipated critical unmasking and absorbed it into the meme form, which refuses symbolic decoding and provides a formal interface for the participatory reappropriation and bricolage that characterize media practice in this age of communicative capitalism." The affordances of digital technology and the politics surrounding it constitute "a form, an interface between certain technical predicates (race as a gathering and sorting mechanism) and the social (the lost white future of the CEO–King)."

Despite his embrace and promotion of extremely toxic politics, Land continues to exert significant influence over many parts of contemporary culture, including an unexpectedly wide range of movements spanning the art world, creators and promoters of digital technology, and even those who see themselves as offering countercultural resistance to the hegemony of fascism and capitalism. However, some of these movements believe that the solution to the hegemony is to make it even worse. This idea has gained currency under the name "accelerationism." It is a particularly potent vector for red–brown syncretism, which has exponents on both the right and left. They first accept the same basic premises of burning down the world so that a new, better one emerges. However, they then claim to embody an altogether different politics from the fascism that inspired them. It is no surprise that Land, along with Moldbug, Yudkowsky, and many others in these various right-wing orbits, is found at the center of online antidemocratic agitation.

In a 2017 article exploring how the ideas of these demagogues proliferate online and influence formal politics, including the 2016 U.S. presidential and UK Brexit elections, *The Atlantic* editor Rosie Gray interviewed several far-right leaders, including Land, who praises the then-new Trump administration: "I think it's fair to say that early signs are surprisingly NRx-positive. That's to say, the libertarian themes of the administration (de-regulation, appointments that 'question the very existence of their own departments . . .') are far stronger than might have been expected from the Trump election platform." As Topinka writes, "Land's systematization of Moldbug sketches a program for fulfilling [Trump strategist Steve] Bannon's desire for sovereignty. This program relies on race as a formal explanatory category—a mode of immanent critique—and an interface that can reconfigure the political order, assigning a place for the lost future of the

CEO–King" (2019). Echoing almost precisely, and then expanding on, the fascist techno-utopianism of *The Sovereign Individual,* Land takes fascism to its endpoint, overtly embracing death and destruction as natural. Elizabeth Sandifer calls Land a "philosophical pessimist and a nihilist, meticulously keeping his potentially subvertable positive investments to a bare minimum" (2017, 106). She draws attention to Land's invoking of the "Great Filter" (Land 2014a), a force of near-Lovecraftian cosmic horror that exterminates nearly all civilizations before they can "rise" to intergalactic communication. This would explain what some call the Fermi paradox, according to which it is remarkable that we have not yet encountered extraterrestrial life. Perhaps unsurprisingly, the Great Filter was introduced by one of the major promoters of cyberlibertarian economic ideas, the George Mason University economist and ur-rationalist Robin Hanson, who also plays a critical role in developing some of the most troubling, overtly fascist technology proposals of our time.

DEATH TECHNOLOGIES

The case of Jim Bell is one of the most revealing offshoots of the cypherpunk movement, and it is not well-known outside critics of digital politics. Bell was an early member of the Cypherpunks mailing list (and continues to participate on it to this day). After graduating from MIT and working at Intel, in 1982 he formed SemiDisk Systems, which produced external RAM disks (McCullagh 2001). Bell was convicted on conspiracy and weapons charges in the late 1990s. During a 2001 federal prosecution, Bell declared that "he has been a member of the Libertarian Party and indicated his political beliefs were anarcho-libertarian, saying: 'I don't advocate chaos. I don't think there should be a lack of order. I think there should be a lack of orders.'" He was not simply a dabbler in right-wing libertarianism but an active supporter of some of its most extreme exponents, including the militia and sovereign citizens movements. The Vancouver, Washington, newspaper *The Columbian* reported in 1997 that Bell "frequented meetings of the Multnomah County Common Law Court, an anti-government group with no legal authority" (Branton 1997).

Bell distinguished himself in crypto-anarchist history by writing and releasing a ten-part essay in 1995 and 1996 called "Assassination Politics" (often referred to by the initials AP; Bell 1997. It is worth noting that political assassinations had already been mentioned approvingly in both the "Crypto-Anarchist Manifesto" [May 1992] and "Cyphernomicon" [May 1994]). McCullagh describes Bell's plan as "an unholy mix of encryption, anonymity, and digital cash to bring about the ultimate annihilation of all forms of government. The system, which Bell spent years talking up online, uses digital cash and anonymity to predict and confirm assassinations" (2000). McCullagh rightly notes that AP intends to end government, because, echoing a refrain familiar across the far right, government is itself automatically criminal. After all, "if tax collection constitutes aggression, then anyone doing it or assisting in the effort or benefiting from the proceeds thereof is a criminal," Bell (1997) writes, using the anarchist keyword "aggression" to refer to the so-called nonaggression principle (NAP), advocated by rightist libertarians/anarcho-capitalists like Murray Rothbard, according to which "taking someone else's property by use or threat of force is a violation of the NAP, and hence impermissible. So, too, is forcefully preventing people from doing whatever (nonaggressive) things they might want to do with their own bodies or property" (Zwolinski 2016, 63), all of which sounds fairly unexceptional.

But anarcho-capitalists "apply the principle not just to the personal behavior of private citizens, but to the state and its agents as well. And they hold that it establishes not merely a strong presumption against activities involving the initiation of physical force, but an absolute moral prohibition. Thus, if my taking your money without your consent is theft, so too is taxation" (Zwolinski 2016, 63). As the sympathetic but not libertarian political philosopher Matt Zwolinski puts it, "Follow this logic far enough, and pretty quickly almost all the activities of the modern regulatory/welfare state, if not the state itself, are seen as aggressive and hence, according to the NAP, absolutely impermissible" (63–64). The NAP thus provides yet another anarcho-capitalist master argument according to which governmental power is illegitimate. The power to murder those we dislike, though, is both legitimate and welcome.

Bell's essay refuses to consider the practical consequences of any system like the one he proposes. He claims, following the great majority of anarcho-capitalist dogma, that all democratic government, especially the kind that issues laws and regulations and collects taxes, is violent tyranny. But his solution to this problem of "violence" is to develop a mechanism that ensures ubiquitous, unstoppable targeted murder, carried out by anyone, against anyone. Bell refuses to acknowledge this problem because he adopts a fascist presumption that is characteristic of anarcho-capitalists and other far-right extremists. He simply declares by fiat that "government" names a different kind of power and human being than the rest of us. He believes that those who work in "government" are automatically and inherently evil from the moment they accept any position in it. Bell also believes that this obvious metaphysical evil is visible to all. The assassination marketplace will only be used by good people against evil people, where "evil" means *only* people who work in government.

AP is full of populist protofascist rhetoric that neatly divides the world into us and them, good and evil, never acknowledging that people will disagree about who falls into those two categories. This is particularly true in democratic countries, where most citizens do not see government service as inherently wrong, let alone transmuting the civil servant into an avatar of evil. Bell acknowledges a problem with his scheme, but only one that is identified from within his anarcho-capitalist frame. "With the adoption of libertarianism in one country, surrounded by non-libertarian states," he characterizes as "problematic" "the question of how a country would defend itself, if it had to raise its defenses by voluntary contribution" (1997). He does not explain why members of the military, who are governmental employees, would not be targeted by the assassination marketplace and thus either eliminated or scared away from serving. However, he does not see this as a problem because "large armies are only necessary to fight other large armies organized by the leadership of other, non-libertarian states, presumably against the will of their citizenry. Once the problem posed by *their* leadership is solved (as well as ours; either by their own citizenry by similar anonymous contributions, or by ours), there will be no large armies to oppose." The world is neatly divided into camps, and wars happen only because corrupt leaders coerce good citizens (which sounds plausible until one thinks about the many citizens who volunteer for military service when their country or an ally is being invaded).

Although AP claims to end violence, it is actually a recipe for a society riddled by murders. In this sense, it is a direct embodiment of the fascist endpoint, in which death and destruction rule every aspect of a society. It is characteristically framed as a defense of unfairly victimized (typically white, typically male) people who are made vulnerable by their inability to use force however they see fit against anyone they perceive as "other." In these constructions the "others" have no vulnerability and no personhood to speak of. Bell and other AP advocates do not seem to recognize the potential for the *Mad Max* future their ideas would create. This is because they make the analytically prior Schmittian decision that the world is divided into good and bad people. There are those who care for each other and those who just want to harm and hurt. They always project these destructive desires onto the other, even when, as in the case of AP, it is oneself who is actively recommending them. It is unsurprising that AP is discussed in the most extreme segments of the far right, including those associated with the sovereign citizens movement and at least flirting with neo-Nazism (e.g., Liberty under Attack Publications). This is due to the incoherent embrace of total destruction along with the unjustified presumption that oneself and one's "good" friends and family will be exempt from that destruction, which is characteristic of all such movements.

AP has not remained confined to these obscure political niches, however. Far-right hero Robin Hanson has long made "prediction markets" a signal area of his research. When the U.S. Defense Advanced Research Projects Agency (DARPA) put out an RFP in 2001 for the use of markets as prediction tools, Hanson teamed up with Net Exchange, a company cofounded by his Cal Tech dissertation adviser John Ledyard. Their proposal was awarded a million-dollar grant (Kahn 2003) to develop what they called the Policy Analysis Market. In typical libertarian fashion, Hanson and the project's other promoters claimed to be using financial interests as the only real measure of social action, following the Chicago School economics model according to which social equity can only be achieved by assigning monetary values to anything and everything. Hanson saw his goal as trying to use money bets to improve forecasting about important events, including wars, assassinations, and terrorism. "This seemingly toxic idea was what came to be known as the 'terrorism futures market,'" wrote a CNN journalist in 2003. "The exchange was assailed as immoral, a 'futures market in death,' and a ghoulish way for terrorists to profit from their evil acts. Less than 24 hours after Democratic Senators Byron Dorgan and Ron Wyden held a press conference to denounce it in July, the Defense Department scrapped the project" (Kahn). Unlike Bell, Hanson persistently disclaims the idea that the prediction markets could incent people to engage in behavior, which is a strange blind spot for a philosophy that puts financial incentives at the heart of nearly all decision-making. Despite the fact that

Hanson's projects have been criticized for incentivizing violence and murder, his own defenses (see esp. Hanson 2006) typically avoid addressing the issue directly.

Currently, assassination marketplaces seem technologically and practically infeasible, due in part to problems at the intersection of information and the physical world that technology promoters are unable to acknowledge. The "oracle problem" is a particularly vexing issue, as it is difficult to understand how an entity could provide *physical* proof of an assassination to a software program, but not provide that same proof to law enforcement or someone seeking revenge for the first killing. In addition most cryptocurrencies, although originally and erroneously understood by many to be anonymous, are very nearly the opposite. However, there have been projects that have a disturbing amount in common with the goals laid out by Bell. In 2018, a decentralized betting market called Augur was launched using the so-called smart contract features of the Ethereum blockchain. Almost immediately, "a single person used the Augur protocol to bet on whether President Donald Trump would survive 2018, and that person apparently placed the bet on a lark after a Twitter discussion" (McCullagh 2018). Declan McCullagh, the journalist who had previously covered Jim Bell's legal cases in the early 2000s with skepticism, dismissed concerns about the use of Augur to incentivize assassination as "panic" and "handwringing." However, this seemed to be more properly directed at the question of whether Augur could be used for AP, rather than whether AP itself is desirable or possible.

Bell, May, and other cypherpunks saw technology affordances that could make democratic governance impossible. They described a direct path from "uncensorable," encrypted, anonymous technologies including cryptocurrencies, to a distributed fascism. According to their vision, the greatest crime of all is to attempt to govern responsibly, and that crime would be punishable by death. Few visions of the human future are darker than this one, which embodies the distributed fascism that informs so much digital agitation, whether knowingly or unknowingly. Across the political spectrum, and especially among the racist right (Miller 2022), violence directed at our political opponents seems to be a more and more acceptable option. It is hard not to wonder how few technology "innovations" might be necessary for the *Mad Max* future to be realized. This vision is shared by anarcho-capitalists like Bell and May along with the armed members of right-wing militia movements and their only slightly more moderate allies in the gun rights movements. Many of them have accepted the rightist claim that fascism is ultimately about "big government," rather than the embrace of death and destruction no matter who the target. This leaves them open to falling into a fascist dystopia. A smaller group actively seeks to create it. The fact that these actors have placed digital technology at the center of their goals, often deriving their politics directly from what they consider to be core features of such developments, should give everyone who seeks to resist such dystopias serious pause about the technology's unchecked proliferation.

One of the most troubling and strange extensions of the logic underlying AP is the promotion of weapon printing using 3D printers and other off-the-shelf technology to circumvent governmental regulations on guns and other weapons. In the United States, where gun regulation is next to nonexistent, this is already a problematic issue. But this is even more true in other democracies that strictly limit the availability of guns and other weapons, and is framed as a direct affront to democratic governance. The most public figure to be associated with 3D printed guns is Cody Wilson (see chapter 4), whose bizarre syncretic manifesto *Come and Take It: The Gun Printer's Guide to Thinking Free* (2016) deserves special mention as a document of cyberlibertarianism becoming cyberfascism.

Wilson's project is so anti-government that the book reads like a technology-enhanced version of *The Turner Diaries*. He promotes the uncheckable, unregulated spread of deadly weapons with evident glee. His bravado and absolute lack of interest in the opinions of anyone who thinks otherwise is remarkable. Wilson draws inspiration from many of the cyberlibertarian touchstones: "peer-to-peer technology," free and open source, including the words of Richard Stallman; encryption; Tor; the cypherpunks including Tim May; wiki software; "makers" and "hackers"; cryptocurrency; and the reinterpretation of all governmental regulation of action, including economic activity, as "censorship." He coyly teases out the authoritarianism implicit in much cyberlibertarian dogma: "Obviously democratization is too important a task to let just *anyone* do it" (74).

Invoking both the syncretism in cyberlibertarian dogma and some of the most troubling syncretic figures in digital technology, Wilson is linked with Bitcoin promoter and self-described anarchist revolutionary Amir Taki (Bartlett 2014). Immersed in the extremes of libertarian, Second Amendment culture that characterize militia movements, Waco, the Oklahoma

City bombing, sovereign citizens, and so on, Wilson is convinced that all freedoms proceed exclusively from each citizen being armed to the teeth, without regard to the bloodshed and terror (a word Wilson uses throughout the book in a positive sense) that must ensue. He calls this regime "the highest ground of political realism" (9). Fueling that sentiment is the idea that the plans for 3D gun printing are "open source software" and "WikiLeaks for guns" (8)—that is, cyberlibertarianism made into fascist direct action.

WEEV'S DANGEROUS "WISDOM"

There may be no clearer example of the passage between cyberlibertarianism and cyberfascism than the one embodied in the person of Andrew Auernheimer, who styles his name as weev. A self-identified hacker who prided himself on berating others for their lack of skill, often focusing on minorities and women, weev had long been active in hacker, cryptography, and far-right social media sites like 4chan, especially the "unofficial 4chan wiki" (Read 2011) called Encyclopedia Dramatica (Schwarz 2008). Auernheimer is a lifelong white nationalist, neo-Nazi, and anti-Black racist (Southern Poverty Law Center n.d.) who has frequently associated with many of the most virulent figures, platforms, and publications associated with the far right. He used his influence with digital advocates to direct abuse toward those he disliked. The most notable example concerned Kathy Sierra, a programmer, author, and game developer who was driven from her career and home by a torrent of targeted harassment, much of which was organized by Auernheimer (Citron 2014, 35–39). In later years he became an outspoken leader of the global neo-Nazi movement, writing and speaking often about the need for "a global empire run by whites," "killing them all" (apparently in reference to all non-whites), and asking Donald Trump to "kill the Jews" (Southern Poverty Law Center n.d.). Auernheimer wrote frequently for the neo-Nazi website the *Daily Stormer* and served for a time as its webmaster (O'Brien 2017).

Although these inclinations became more public in the mid-2010s, Auernheimer's history as a neo-Nazi was already well known among his many friends and followers. He did little to hide it. To the contrary, he often made it very public: "While Auernheimer was gaining infamy as an internet troll in the late 2000s, he was producing online quasi-religious racist and antisemitic podcasts calling himself the 'iProphet,' under the auspices of his own 'Last Church of Christ,' which he registered as a business in West Hollywood in 2009. Among his iProphet rants: 'America is a f— nation! Jews are violent preobrate [*sic*] rebels against God's will! Thank God for IEDs! Israel's doom is coming. God's promises are sure! God bless Fred Phelps. God bless Shirley Phelps-Roper. God bless the Westboro Baptist Church!'" (Southern Poverty Law Center n.d.). He also gained notoriety in 2009 when he misused a reporting mechanism on Amazon to flag LGBTQ literature as "inappropriate": "A script of code Auernheimer wrote caused hundreds of LGBT books to be flagged as 'adult' material and excluded from Amazon's best-seller lists, resulting in the online retailer being accused of corporate homophobia until Auernheimer took credit on his LiveJournal blog." Again from the Southern Poverty Law Center: "'The hypocracy [*sic*] of the gay community disgusted me,' he wrote in a post about the hack. 'So I decided to get them back, and cause a few hundred thousand queers some outrage.'"

Despite its extremism, all this would be par for the course for cyberfascism and of interest only to those who track the operations of neo-Nazis and white supremacists. Auernheimer's story is noteworthy in the history of cyberlibertarianism because he was frequently taken seriously by publications and platforms that either refused to investigate his background or deliberately ignored it. In his heyday, he appeared regularly on major network news programs and in newspapers and magazines. He was sometimes characterized as a cybersecurity expert, sometimes as an "infamous hacker." At one point he was a guest on the business channel CNBC to promote what he called a hedge fund but observers took as an open threat to extort companies and individuals for profit (La Roche 2014). In virtually none of these cases was Auernheimer described as what he is—a worldwide leader of the neo-Nazi movement. The protective aura around him seemed to stem from his identification with digital technology and their politics, which could be described as emancipatory even as their fascist underpinnings were overlooked entirely.

In 2011 Auernheimer was arrested for violating the Computer Fraud and Abuse Act (CFAA). The following year he was convicted for accessing the email addresses of more than one hundred thousand iPad users through "a security loophole on AT&T's website" (Bilton and Wortham 2011). CFAA is an example of an attempt to regulate the use of digital technology that advocates from every direction criticize as a terrible offense to freedom, despite its being largely parallel with statutes for wire and mail fraud that are largely accepted. Such disingenuous attacks on the law—which tend to read statutes in a literal way that has little in common with how lawyers and judges actually interpret them—give rise to many social media posts that claim users may "go to jail for violating the Terms of Service of websites." This claim is clearly beyond the law's intended scope and has never happened. Nonetheless, such posts continue to generate significant anti-government, pro-technology sentiment among promoters of digital technology. Indeed, CFAA has rarely been used; when it has, it's almost always in a way that parallels long-standing wire and mail fraud regulations. Yet Mike Masnick and others are not writing heated jeremiads about "going to federal prison for putting the wrong address on a postcard" or lying over the telephone, despite such sentiments being functionally identical with those expressed about CFAA.

Auernheimer's prosecution under CFAA brought out defenders from across the range of digital advocacy, all of whom saw his prosecution as unjust and hurtful to freedom. None of them, however, noted his politics. These defenses reached their apotheosis in the *New York Times* in 2013 when philosopher Peter Ludlow—whose editing of the signal collections *High Noon on the Electronic Frontier* (1996) and *Crypto Anarchy, Cyberstates, and Pirate Utopias* (2001) displayed both knowledge of and some sympathy for the most extreme cypherpunk politics—wrote a piece called "Hacktivists as Gadflies" defending Auernheimer. The grounds for Ludlow's defense of Auernheimer were not simply that CFAA was bad law, a point on which experts can and do disagree, but that Auernheimer was a cultural hero comparable to Socrates. The piece begins by making the comparison explicit: "Around 400 BC, Socrates was brought to trial on charges of corrupting the youth of Athens and 'impiety.' Presumably, however, people believed then as we do now, that Socrates' real crime was being too clever and, not insignificantly, a royal pain to those in power or, as Plato put it, a gadfly. Just as a gadfly is an insect that could sting a horse and prod it into action, so too could Socrates sting the state." He goes on: "We have had gadflies among us ever since, but one contemporary breed in particular has come in for a rough time of late: the 'hacktivist.' While none have yet been forced to drink hemlock, the state has come down on them with remarkable force. This is in large measure evidence of how poignant, and troubling, their message has been." Auernheimer was convicted of stealing from people for his own gain, something he openly bragged about doing in other cases before and after. This had nothing to do with helping people or advancing some kind of "wisdom." To Ludlow, however, Auernheimer was an example of "individuals who redeploy and repurpose technology for social causes" who are "different from garden-variety hackers out to enrich only themselves." Not only is the latter exactly what Auernheimer was trying to do, but he had already demonstrated his commitment to hacking for the good of Nazism and against the good of anyone else—none of which Ludlow sees fit to mention.

It is difficult to determine what "Socratic wisdom" Ludlow and others believe Auernheimer has to offer the world:

> When the federal judge Susan Wigenton sentenced Weev on March 18, she described him with prose that could have been lifted from the prosecutor Meletus in Plato's *Apology*. "You consider yourself a hero of sorts," she said, and noted that Weev's "special skills" in computer coding called for a more draconian sentence. I was reminded of a line from an essay written in 1986 by a hacker called the Mentor: "My crime is that of outsmarting you, something that you will never forgive me for."
>
> When offered the chance to speak, Weev, like Socrates, did not back down: "I don't come here today to ask for forgiveness. I'm here to tell this court, if it has any foresight at all, that it should be thinking about what it can do to make amends to me for the harm and the violence that has been inflicted upon my life." (Ludlow 2013)

The sentences Ludlow quotes certainly do not parallel what Socrates says in Plato's dialogues. Contrarily, they echo the typical protofascist, white supremacist complaint that the person prosecuted for harming others is actually the victim. The cause for which Auernheimer is said to be advocating or even sacrificing himself is entirely unclear. Is CFAA an unjust law? Is it in fact being used to target people who don't deserve it? Are they unable to defend themselves in court? None of these questions is even open for discussion. CFAA has been used so infrequently that there have been few prosecutions, and even fewer convictions. This fact raises questions about the putative offense it must be to democracy and freedom.

Auernheimer's conviction was overturned after the hearing, but not because the CFAA was found to be an inherent violation of important rights.

In fact the CFAA issue wasn't part of the final adjudication, which turned instead on the question of whether Auernheimer had been prosecuted in the correct venue (Kravets 2014). Just as troubling, many individuals and groups associated with digital rights came to Auernheimer's defense. UC Berkeley law professor Orin Kerr, renowned technology lawyer Tor Ekeland (Kerr 2013), and EFF (Cushing 2013) all chose to represent Auernheimer; Kerr and EFF donated their services pro bono. They were all convinced that CFAA was not just an overbroad law but a deep offense to freedom and civil rights. None of them, to my knowledge, explained how CFAA differs from the parallel wire and mail fraud statues. None noted that Auernheimer's motive almost certainly was fraud, regardless of whether he committed a technical violation of CFAA as it was intended to function. Worst, none of them remarked on Auernheimer's politics, which in his own opinion drove both his specific actions in this case and his overall "activism." Unlike the infamous ACLU case defending a Nazi march in Skokie, Illinois, none of Auernheimer's defenders found it necessary to mention or explain their support for a Nazi defendant promoting Nazi ideas.

Before his sentencing in 2013, Auernheimer gave a public speech on the courthouse steps that raised even more questions about his serving as an avatar of suppressed, Socratic insight:

> So, I stand outside this courthouse today, and I feel like America is in a cultural decline. That, I look around the kind of pace, and the kind of people, that we've had in the past 50 years, and it doesn't match the 50 years previous. I feel like, I feel like [*laughs*], there's something wrong. And in my country there's a problem. And that problem is the Feds. They take everybody's freedom, and they never give it back. And if you go, if you go to Georgia, and you have a staph infection, they can have a bacteriophage that they genetically engineer [to] eat your staph. Like, no joke. Whereas here they're like, we're gonna cut your arm off, or flood you with antibiotics until you die. Like there, they can have a treatment that's known to be the best in the world, because their FDA doesn't define each individual bacteriophage as a new treatment that has to go through clinical trials. If you want to put a drone in the air, how many commercial applications of drones are there? There's a shit-ton. If you want to put a drone in the air and have it speak TCAS, the Traffic Collision Avoidance System, you just can't do that. There's no licensing path for the FDA, for the FAA, to do this. You're not allowed to innovate. Stop thinking outside the box, Western man.

I feel [*laughs*], I feel like, you know, we could have laptop batteries, that last a hundred fucking years. Fuckin . . . with betavoltaics. And we can't have this, because the NRC says no. (Crook 2013)

Auernheimer is here explicitly—and virtually exclusively—committed to that apparently most persecuted of beliefs, market fundamentalism and faith in "innovation." There is no concern with equal rights, civil rights, democracy, any of that. There is concern only with the ability of corporations and individuals to make as much money as possible, consequences be damned. The "betavoltaics" weev mentions, for instance, are radioactive batteries containing tritium with half-lives as long as the "hundred fucking years" for which weev says they will work. They have not been licensed out of a prudent concern for having laptops and cellphones carrying radioactive material inside of them widely among the general population. It is no stretch to say that society is freer because the Nuclear Regulatory Commission prohibits radioactive batteries, preventing "nuclear hackers" from playing with fire.

Auernheimer's statements are nothing more than explicitly libertarian pieties about the failure of U.S. innovation and the lack of (economic) freedom. This is an "unpopular" wisdom that has been uttered in detail, repeatedly, by Rand and Ron Paul, Grover Norquist, and anyone at the American Enterprise Institute. Unlike Socrates, none of these figures has been prosecuted or convicted. Their pieties are coupled with familiar fascist claims of "cultural decline." Only through the blinkered lens of cyberlibertarianism can we view someone who is stating obvious platitudes that are widely distributed in society, especially by some of its most powerful actors, and asserting his right to use a computer in ways for which we have perfectly adequate resources already allocated, as "persecuted" as a Socratic gadfly. Yet it is part of the core function of cyberlibertarian dogma that Auernheimer is understood by many as a freedom fighter for the liberating possibilities of technology, rather than as what he is: a neo-Nazi. This is especially unfortunate because Auernheimer's Nazism is not hidden. Rather, it is a core part of his character, one he openly advertises. In all its forms, cyberlibertarianism blinds us to its own far-right politics.

Epilogue

Computers without Cyberlibertarianism

t is conventional to include in any work critical of the computation
regime sentiments suggesting that the author is "not a Luddite,"
"does not hate computers," does not want to "stand in the way
of innovation," and so on. These demands are themselves marks of cyberlibertarianism, not least because they seem to require a kind of obeisance
to the purported beneficial social effects of digitization that must be open
to discussion and demonstration. The assertion that computers are obviously good for society and democracy is often used to shut down questions
about them, which is a species of the faux "democratization" that structures cyberlibertarianism.

Technology promoters use frames like "techlash" to disqualify criticism.
They insist that the world is full of unthinking rejection of digital technology. To even participate in the conversation, one must acknowledge that
even if there are flaws, digital technology is a force for good. Further, critical perspectives are always asked to talk about how we can resuscitate the
"dream" of an internet that benefits everyone.

All these perspectives put digital technology before the political, the social,
and the human. They ask us to care about digital technology as a primary
concern. This is the work of cyberlibertarianism. Neither democracies nor
human beings concerned with overall well-being need to make the proliferation of digital technology a fundamental priority. Sometimes media and
technology serve those fundamental priorities. Many times they don't. Acting as if they are indispensable is not just misguided, but can advance a very
different politics from those we hope for. Thinkers with wide experience
have understood from the beginning that computers, despite their benefits,

are unlikely to be emancipatory technologies. In fact, they are more likely to decrease democratic sovereignty and increase concentrations of power and "might makes right" politics. We have every reason to think that putting computers first, as so many do today, is not going to lead to strengthened democracies and widespread human flourishing. Absent strong evidence that sentiments like "if you want to democratize a people, give them the internet" are correct, those of us who care about equality, democracy, and human well-being should put those values first, and worry about how we get to them only in that context.

Could we develop versions of digital technology, particularly social media, that are not only compatible with but also beneficial for democracy? Those closest to social media work insist so strongly that their products are "democratizing." However, they are doing everything they can to prevent democracies from exercising their political sovereignty over the technology itself. This is strong evidence that they do not think so. The technology has been shown in study after study to correlate with the most striking retreat of democratic values in over a century. The technologies that advocates sometimes point to as democracy-friendly replacements for the platform giants frequently feature even more antidemocratic content. This suggests there is little reason to hope. Democracies must consider implementing robust and forceful regulatory regimes for these products, similar to the European Union's recent approach. The idea of setting up de facto "public squares" that are not owned or regulated by the people seems anathema to the very idea of democratic sovereignty.

Rejecting cyberlibertarianism as a valid philosophy is likely to arrive at a different perspective on digital technology and its relationship to democratic politics and values. Given the tremendously destructive and antidemocratic affordances of these technologies, democracies would be justified in adopting positions that might be called abolitionist or firmly regulated—via the very powers of democratic oversight that the rhetoric of "permissionless innovation" seeks to upend. As figures coming at the problem from angles as different as Ruha Benjamin (2019) and Shoshana Zuboff (2019, 2021) have argued, many parts of the current digital infrastructure need to be abolished altogether. For Benjamin, this would seem to extend to digital technologies that differentially harm minorities. For Zuboff, it is those technologies that make possible tracking, monitoring, and especially manipulating behavior, whether for profit or not. From another angle, Frank Pasquale (2021) rejects the arguments for "permissionless innovation," arguing that for some class of technologies licensure is the correct approach.

These orientations have a great deal in common. In general, they recommend that democracies have not only the right but also the responsibility to determine whether certain technologies (construed broadly) are compatible with healthy and democratic societies. Many modern democracies allow the advertisement of addictive products with negative health consequences, such as tobacco and alcohol. Despite the oft-noted failures of U.S. alcohol prohibition in the 1920s, more recent efforts to contain and minimize the damage caused by tobacco have proven successful and embody principles that many supporters of democracy see as central. Other technologies that are more immediately dangerous have been either outlawed altogether or restricted in use only to licensed professionals. The most obvious examples are technologies that involve radioactive materials, but many other technologies are restricted as well. In many cases, especially those of addictive substances, industry has been remarkably adroit at pushing back on every regulation democracies offer, changing aspects of their products to get around regulations, and knowingly engaging in activity that is nearly as harmful. For example, Big Tobacco shifted to vaping products when the number of smokers started to fall. These companies generate the appearance of popular support for deregulatory policies, and even genuine popular support by product users who may not think about, or at least may not care about, the fact that their "grassroots" support for destructive products is being solicited and manipulated by industrial actors whose bad faith and propensity to exploit have long been demonstrated beyond question.

The European Union is currently the world leader in standing up to digital technology companies and even nonindustrial digital technology promoters. It is able to make clear to the public when technology proponents' stories about the dangers of regulation fail to match reality. Despite the introduction of regulations, digital technology has not fallen into disuse in the EU and the democratic character of member nations has advanced higher in international rankings of democracy.

We remain at the beginning of an international regime of strict regulation of digital technology, which we hope will prioritize democracy. This regime should not only rule out certain particularly destructive practices but also lay out clear principles that products must adhere to before being introduced. Digital technologies should be made to adhere to clear principles that regulators, legislators, and jurists, along with citizens, determine are compatible with democracy, much as medical and food regulators have standards for safety and efficacy that must be met by all products. This may not mean they must meet the "do no harm" standard associated with medical services, although it is worth noting that medical standards in fact partake of a complex cost–benefit calculation that is likely to have analogues in digital technology regulation.

It seems clear that technologies that enable the collection and analysis of information about people and their actions must be high on the list of candidates for regulation. A question that must be addressed is whether nongovernmental actors should have the ability to create "public squares" without more detailed accounts of their relationship to democratic speech laws and human rights. Despite its manifest benefits and pleasures, this is one technology that strikes me as a likely candidate for abolition or something close to it. Most forms of biometric data collection, and the postprocessing of that data, seem like candidates for abolition as well. This would likely include, to the disappointment of their many fans, visual and auditory surveillance systems and voice-activated devices of many sorts. Regulators face the challenge of determining whether the contexts in which audio devices are the only safe or useful alternatives to attain certain goals (such as for people who cannot see or use a keyboard or in moving vehicles) can be effectively isolated from general use. Additionally, regulators must determine whether such contexts can still provide enough data for the products to function effectively. These are exactly the kinds of questions that regulators will have to face, as they do every day for many other points of law, consumer products, and technology.

Works Cited

Abbate, Janet. 1999. *Inventing the Internet*. Cambridge, Mass.: MIT Press.

Abegg, Lukas. 2016. "Code Is Law? Not Quite Yet." *CoinDesk*, Aug. 27. https://www.coindesk.com/markets/2016/08/27/code-is-law-not-quite-yet/.

Abella, Alex. 2008. *Soldiers of Reason: The RAND Corporation and the Rise of American Empire*. New York: Houghton Mifflin.

Abelson, Hal, Ross Anderson, Steven M. Bellovin, Josh Benaloh, Matt Blaze, Whitfield Diffie, John Gilmore, Peter G. Neumann, Ronald L. Rivest, Jeffrey I. Schiller, and Bruce Schneier. 1997. "The Risks of Key Recovery, Key Escrow, and Trusted Third-Party Encryption." Massachusetts Institute of Technology. https://academiccommons.columbia.edu/doi/10.7916/D8GM8F2W.

Abelson, Hal, Ross Anderson, Steven M. Bellovin, Josh Benaloh, Matt Blaze, Whitfield Diffie, John Gilmore, Matthew Green, Susan Landau, Peter G. Neumann, Ronald L. Rivest, Jeffrey I. Schiller, Bruce Schneier, Michael Spencer, and Daniel J. Weitzner. 2015. "Keys under Doormats: Mandating Insecurity by Requiring Government Access to All Data and Communications." MIT Computer Science and Artificial Intelligence Laboratory. https://dspace.mit.edu/handle/1721.1/97690.

"About the EFF." 2022. Electronic Frontier Foundation. Last modified Nov. 11. https://www.eff.org/about-eff.

"About Free Press." 2024. Free Press. Last modified Feb. 16. https://www.freepress.net/about.

"About the Internet Observatory." 2024. Stanford Internet Observatory Cyber Policy Research Center. Last modified Feb. 20. https://cyber.fsi.stanford.edu/io/about.

"About OTI." 2024. New America Foundation Open Technology Institute. Last modified Feb. 13. https://www.newamerica.org/oti/about/.

"About Tor: History." n.d. Tor Project. Last modified Mar. 19, 2024. https://www.torproject.org/about/history/.

Achenbach, Joel. 2019. "Two Mass Killings a World Apart Share a Common Theme: 'Ecofascism.'" *Washington Post*, Aug. 18. https://www.washingtonpost.com/science/two-mass-murders-a-world-apart-share-a-common-theme-ecofascism/2019/08/18/0079a676-bec4-11e9-b873-63ace636af08_story.html.

ACLU. 2017. "What Is Net Neutrality?" Dec. https://www.aclu.org/issues/free-speech/internet-speech/what-net-neutrality.

Agence France-Presse. 2020. "Facebook Says It Rejected 2.2m Ads for Breaking Political Campaigning Rules." *The Guardian*, Oct. 17. https://www.theguardian.com/technology/2020/oct/18/facebook-says-it-rejected-22m-ads-seeking-to-obstruct-voting-in-us-election.

Ahmed, Imran. 2022. "Buffalo Might Never Have Happened If Online Hate Had Been Tackled after Christchurch." *The Guardian*, May 16. https://www.theguardian.com/commentisfree/2022/may/16/racist-words-social-media-kill-buffalo-meta-twitter-google-radicalisation.

Aitoro, Jill R. 2014. "Edward Snowden on Booz Allen: Here's What We've Learned from His *Wired* Profile." *Washington Business Journal*, Aug. 14. https://www.bizjournals.com/washington/blog/fedbiz_daily/2014/08/edward-snowden-on-booz-allen-heres-what-weve.html.

Albanese, Andrew. 2020. "Internet Archive to End 'National Emergency Library' Initiative." *Publishers Weekly*, Jun. 12. https://www.publishersweekly.com/pw/by-topic/digital/copyright/article/83584-internet-archive-to-end-national-emergency-library-initiative.html.

Allen, Mike. 2018. "First Look: 'Techlash' Warning." *Axios*, Jan. 9. https://www.axios.com/2018/01/09/first-look-at-techlash-warning-1515534954.

Amadae, S. M. 2003. *Rationalizing Capitalist Democracy: The Cold War Origins of Rational Choice Liberalism*. Chicago: University of Chicago Press.

Anderson, Chris. 2009. *Free: The Future of a Radical Price*. New York: Hyperion.

Anderson, Gary. 2011. "Exposing the Racist History of Libertarianism and Murray Rothbard." *Business Insider*, Oct. 3. https://www.businessinsider.com/exposing-the-racist-history-of-libertarianism-and-murray-rothbard-2011-10.

Anderson, Kevin. 2009. "Fury at AT&T's Web 'Censorship.'" *The Guardian*, Jul. 29. https://www.theguardian.com/technology/2009/jul/29/web-forum-censorship.

Anderson, Patrick D. 2021. "Privacy for the Weak, Transparency for the Powerful: The Cypherpunk Ethics of Julian Assange." *Ethics and Information Technology* 23: 295–308. https://doi.org/10.1007/s10676-020-09571-x.

Angwin, Julia. 2014. *Dragnet Nation: A Quest for Privacy, Security, and Freedom in a World of Relentless Surveillance*. New York: Times Books.

Anil. 2021. "Bitcoin and the Printing Press." *Bitcoin Magazine*, Jan. 8. https://bitcoinmagazine.com/culture/bitcoin-and-the-printing-press.

Appelbaum, Anne. 2021. *Twilight of Democracy: The Seductive Lure of Authoritarianism*. New York: Knopf.

Arendt, Hannah. (1948) 1979. *The Origins of Totalitarianism*. Rev. ed. New York: Harcourt.

"Armistead, Josephine." 2016. "The Silicon Ideology." May 18. https://archive.org/details/the-silicon-ideology. [Paper posted to Archive.org.]

Assange, Julian, Jacob Appelbaum, Andy Müller-Maguhn, and Jérémie Zimmermann. 2012. *Cypherpunks: Freedom and the Future of the Internet*. New York: OR Books.

Atkinson, Robert D., Doug Brake, Daniel Castro, Colin Cunliff, Joe Kennedy, Michael McLaughlin, Alan McQuinn, and Joshua New. 2019. "A Policymaker's

Guide to the 'Techlash': What It Is and Why It's a Threat to Growth and Progress." Information Technology and Innovation Foundation, Oct. 28. https://itif.org/pub lications/2019/10/28/policymakers-guide-techlash/.

Ausloos, Jef. 2020. *The Right to Erasure in EU Data Protection Law.* New York: Oxford University Press.

Badii, Farzaneh. 2021. "The Christchurch Call: Are We Multistakeholder Yet?" *Digital Medusa,* Nov. 14. https://digitalmedusa.org/the-christchurch-call-are-we-multistake holder-yet/.

Baker, Kelly J. 2016. "Nice, Decent Folks." KellyJBaker.com, Nov. 17. https://www .kellyjbaker.com/nice-decent-folks/.

Ball, James. 2011. "Israel Shamir and Julian Assange's Cult of Machismo." *The Guard-ian,* Nov. 8. https://www.theguardian.com/commentisfree/cifamerica/2011/nov/08/ israel-shamir-julian-assange-cult-machismo.

Bamford, James. 2014. "Edward Snowden: The Untold Story." *Wired,* Aug. https:// www.wired.com/2014/08/edward-snowden/.

"Ban Facial Recognition." 2020. Fight for the Future project website. Last modified Mar. 20, 2024. https://www.banfacialrecognition.com/.

Banker, Elizabeth. 2020. "A Review of Section 230's Meaning and Application Based on More Than 500 Cases." Internet Association, Jul. https://web.archive.org/ web/20211217114027/https://internetassociation.org/wp-content/uploads/2020/07/ IA_Review-Of-Section-230.pdf.

Barabas, Chelsea, Neha Narula, and Ethan Zuckerman. 2017. "Defending Internet Freedom through Decentralization: Back to the Future?" MIT Media Lab, Aug. https://static1.squarespace.com/static/59aae5e9a803bb10bedeb03e/t/59ae908a46c3c 480db42326f/1504612494894/decentralized_web.pdf.

Baran, Paul. 1962. "On Distributed Communications Networks." RAND Corpora-tion. https://doi.org/10.7249/P2626.

Barbrook, Richard. 1998. "The Hi-Tech Gift Economy." *First Monday* 3:12 (Dec. 7). https://doi.org/10.5210/fm.v3i12.631.

Barbrook, Richard. 2000. "Cyber-Communism: How the Americans Are Superseding Capitalism in Cyberspace." *Science as Culture* 9:1 (Mar.): 5–40.

Barbrook, Richard. 2005. "The Hi-Tech Gift Economy: Special Issue Update." *First Monday* S3 (Dec. 5). https://firstmonday.org/ojs/index.php/fm/article/view/631/552.

Barbrook, Richard, and Andy Cameron. 1995. "The Californian Ideology." *Mute* 3 (Sep.) https://www.metamute.org/editorial/articles/californian-ideology.

Barbrook, Richard, and Andy Cameron. 1996. "The Californian Ideology." *Science as Culture* 6:1 (Jan.): 44–72. [Expanded version of Barbrook and Cameron 1995.]

Barlow, John Perry. 1996. "A Declaration of the Independence of Cyberspace." In Lud-low 2001, 27–30.

Baron, Sabrina Alcorn, Eric N. Lundquist, and Eleanor F. Shevlin, eds. 2007. *Agent of Change: Print Culture Studies after Elizabeth L. Eisenstein.* Amherst: University of Massachusetts Press.

Bartlett, Jamie. 2014. *The Dark Net: Inside the Digital Underworld.* London: William Heinemann.

Bartlett, Jamie, dir. 2017. *Secrets of Silicon Valley.* Two-part documentary film. London: BBC Two. https://www.bbc.co.uk/programmes/b0916ghq.

Bates, Stephen. 2012. "Lord Rees-Mogg Obituary." *The Guardian,* Dec. 29. https://www.theguardian.com/media/2012/dec/29/william-rees-mogg-obituary.

Baur, Dorothea. 2020. "No, We Don't Want to 'Democratize' AI." *Medium,* Dec. 4. https://dorotheabaur.medium.com/no-we-dont-want-to-democratize-ai-c5b481d b5afa.

Beadon, Leigh. 2012. "*Game of Thrones* on Track to Be Most Pirated Show of 2012; Pirates Still Asking HBO for Legitimate Options." *TechDirt,* May 11. https://www .techdirt.com/2012/05/11/game-thrones-track-to-be-most-pirated-show-2012-pirates -still-asking-hbo-legitimate-options/.

Beckett, Andy. 2018. "How to Explain Jacob Rees-Mogg? Start with His Father's Books." *The Guardian,* Nov. 9. https://www.theguardian.com/books/2018/nov/09/ mystic-mogg-jacob-rees-mogg-willam-predicts-brexit-plans.

Belcher, Marta. 2022. "Tucked Inside Biden Infrastructure Bill: Unconstitutional Crypto Surveillance." *CoinDesk,* Jan. 25. https://www.coindesk.com/layer2/2022/01/ 25/tucked-inside-biden-infrastructure-bill-unconstitutional-crypto-surveillance/.

Belew, Kathleen. 2019. *Bring the War Home: The White Power Movement and Paramilitary America.* Cambridge, Mass.: Harvard University Press.

Bell, Jim. 1997. "Assassination Politics." Self-pub., Apr. 3. http://jya.com/ap.htm.

Beltramini, Enrico. 2021. "Against Technocratic Authoritarianism. A Short Intellectual History of the Cypherpunk Movement." *Internet Histories* (2): 101–18. https://doi .org/10.1080/24701475.2020.1731249.

Benjamin, Ruha. 2019. *Race after Technology: Abolitions Tools for the New Jim Code.* Boston: Polity.

Benkler, Yochai. 2007. *The Wealth of Networks: How Social Production Transforms Markets and Freedom.* New Haven, Conn.: Yale University Press.

Benson, Chris. 2022. "Whistleblower Snowden Visits Bucknell Virtually." *Daily Item,* Feb. 23. https://www.dailyitem.com/news/update-whistleblower-snowden-visits-buck nell-virtually/article_1a6d0780-945a-11ec-80d5-efec40e5fc01.html.

Beran, Dale. 2019. *It Came from Something Awful: How a Toxic Troll Army Accidentally Memed Donald Trump into Office.* New York: All Points Books.

Berlet, Chip. (1990) 1999. "Right Woos Left." Political Research Associates. https:// politicalresearch.org/1999/02/27/right-woos-left.

Berlet, Chip. 2009. *Toxic to Democracy: Conspiracy Theories, Demonization and Scapegoating.* Rev. ed. Somerville, Mass.: Political Research Associates.

Berlet, Chip. 2016. "What Is the Third Position?" Political Research Associates, Dec. 19. https://politicalresearch.org/2016/12/19/what-third-position.

Berlet, Chip, and Matthew N. Lyons. 2000. *Right-Wing Populism in America: Too Close for Comfort.* New York: Guilford Press.

Berners-Lee, Tim. 1999. *Weaving the Web: The Original Design and Ultimate Destiny of the World Wide Web by Its Inventor.* New York: HarperCollins.

Berners-Lee, Tim. 2017. "Act Now to Save the Internet as We Know It." *Medium,* Dec. 12. https://medium.com/@timberners_lee/act-now-to-save-the-internet-as-we-know-it -ccf47ce8b39f.

Bernholz, Lucy, Hélène Landemore, and Rob Reich, eds. 2021. *Digital Technology and Democratic Theory.* Chicago: University of Chicago Press.

Bertrand, Natasha, and Daniel Lippman. 2019. "Inside Mark Zuckerberg's Private Meetings with Conservative Pundits." *Politico,* Oct. 14. https://www.politico.com/news/2019/10/14/facebook-zuckerberg-conservatives-private-meetings-046663.

Bhuiyan, Johana. 2014. "Marcy Wheeler Leaves *The Intercept.*" *Politico,* May 16. https://www.politico.com/media/story/2014/05/marcy-wheeler-leaves-the-intercept-002247/.

Bilton, Nick, and Jenna Wortham. 2011. "Two Are Charged with Fraud in iPad Security Breach." *New York Times,* Jan. 18. https://www.nytimes.com/2011/01/19/technology/19ipad.html.

Binder, Matt. 2021. "Zuckerberg Feared Facebook's Conservative Users, So They Received Special Treatment." *Mashable,* Feb. 22. https://mashable.com/article/facebook-mark-zuckerberg-conservative-pages.

Birkerts, Sven. 2006. *The Gutenberg Elegies: The Fate of Reading in an Electronic Age.* New York: Farrar, Straus and Giroux.

Bittner, Jochen. 2016. "How Julian Assange Is Destroying WikiLeaks." *New York Times,* Feb. 17. https://www.nytimes.com/2016/02/08/opinion/how-julian-assange-is-destroying-wikileaks.html.

Blow, Charles. 2021. "Tucker Carlson and White Replacement." *New York Times,* Apr. 11. https://www.nytimes.com/2021/04/11/opinion/tucker-carlson-white-replacement.html.

Blue, Violet. 2017. *How to Be a Digital Revolutionary.* San Francisco: Digita Publications.

Bocher, Robert. 2018. "ALA Net Neutrality FAQ." American Library Association, Apr. https://www.ala.org/advocacy/sites/ala.org.advocacy/files/content/telecom/netneutrality/ALA%20Network%20Neutrality%20FAQ.pdf.

Boczkowski, Pablo J., and Zizi Papacharissi, eds. 2018. *Trump and the Media.* Cambridge, Mass.: MIT Press.

Bode, Karl. 2019. "Killing Net Neutrality Was Even Worse Than You Think." *OneZero,* Nov. 20. https://onezero.medium.com/killing-net-neutrality-was-even-worse-than-you-think-132a21aab55a.

Bonilla-Silva, Eduardo. 2017. *Racism without Racists: Color-Blind Racism and the Persistence of Racial Inequality in America.* 5th ed. Lanham, Md.: Rowman & Littlefield.

Borgman, Christine. 2000. *From Gutenberg to the Global Information Infrastructure.* Cambridge, Mass.: MIT Press.

Borsook, Paulina. 2000. *Cyberselfish: A Critical Romp through the Terribly Libertarian Culture of High Tech.* New York: PublicAffairs.

boyd, danah. 2014. *It's Complicated: The Social Lives of Networked Teens.* New Haven, Conn.: Yale University Press.

boyd, danah. 2019. "Facing the Great Reckoning Head-On." *Medium,* Sep. 13. https://onezero.medium.com/facing-the-great-reckoning-head-on-8fe434e1063o.

boyd, danah. 2022. "Crisis Text Line, from My Perspective." *Apophenia,* Jan. 31. https://www.zephoria.org/thoughts/archives/2022/01/31/crisis-text-line-from-my-perspective.html.

Boyle, James. 2008. *The Public Domain: Enclosing the Commons of the Mind.* New Haven, Conn.: Yale University Press.

Bracha, Oren, and Frank Pasquale. 2008. "Federal Search Commission: Access, Fairness, and Accountability in the Law of Search." *Cornell Law Review* 93(6) (Sep.): 1149–1210. https://scholarship.law.cornell.edu/clr/vol93/iss6/11/.

Brand, Stewart. 1987. *The Media Lab: Inventing the Future at MIT.* New York: Viking Penguin.

Brandom, Russell. 2017. "We Have Abandoned Every Principle of the Free and Open Internet." *The Verge,* Dec. 19. https://www.theverge.com/2017/12/19/16792306/fcc-net-neutrality-open-internet-history-free-speech-anonymity.

Brandom, Russell, Alex Heath, and Adi Robertson. 2021. "Eight Things We Learned from the Facebook Papers." *The Verge,* Oct. 25. https://www.theverge.com/22740969/facebook-files-papers-frances-haugen-whistleblower-civic-integrity.

Branton, John. 1997. "Activist Bell Faces Sentencing Friday." *The Columbian* (Vancouver, Wash.), Nov. 20. https://cryptome.org/jdb/jimbell6.htm.

Brockwell, Naomi. 2022. "Edward Snowden Played Key Role in Zcash Privacy Coin's Creation." *CoinDesk,* Apr. 27. https://www.coindesk.com/tech/2022/04/27/edward-snowden-played-key-role-in-zcash-privacy-coins-creation/.

Brodwin, David. 2015. "The Chamber's Secrets." *U.S. News & World Report,* Oct. 22. https://www.usnews.com/opinion/economic-intelligence/2015/10/22/who-does-the-us-chamber-of-commerce-really-represent.

Brooke, Heather. 2011. *The Revolution Will Be Digitised.* London: William Heinemann / Windmill Books.

Brooker, Katrina. 2018. "'I Was Devastated': Tim Berners-Lee, the Man Who Created the World Wide Web, Has Some Regrets." *Vanity Fair,* Jul. 1. https://www.vanityfair.com/news/2018/07/the-man-who-created-the-world-wide-web-has-some-regrets.

Browne, Simone. 2015. *Dark Matters: On the Surveillance of Blackness.* Durham, N.C.: Duke University Press.

Budowsky, Brent. 2011. "Ron Paul and Occupy Wall Street Can Change the World Together." *The Hill,* Nov. 7. https://thehill.com/blogs/pundits-blog/economy-a-budget/177914-ron-paul-and-occupy-wall-street-can-change-the-world-together/.

Burns, Alexander, and Maggie Haberman. 2013. "2013: Year of the Liberal Billionaire." *Politico,* Nov. 1. https://www.politico.com/story/2013/11/liberal-billionaires-fundraising-2013-elections-tom-steyer-mark-zuckerberg-michael-bloomberg-099207.

But, Jason. 2012. "Facebook Welcomes Hackers, If They Wear a White Hat." *The Conversation,* May 9. https://theconversation.com/facebook-welcomes-hackers-if-they-wear-a-white-hat-6892.

Buterin, Vitalik. 2017. "The Meaning of Decentralization." *Medium,* Feb. 6. https://medium.com/@VitalikButerin/the-meaning-of-decentralization-a0c92b76a274.

Byers, Dylan, and Claire Atkinson. 2020. "'Same Old Defense': Civil Rights Groups Hammer Facebook after Meeting." *NBC News,* Jul. 7. https://www.nbcnews.com/tech/tech-news/same-old-defense-civil-rights-groups-hammer-facebook-after-meeting-n1233114.

Cadwalladr, Carole. 2017. "Robert Mercer: The Big Data Billionaire Waging War on Mainstream Media." *The Guardian,* Feb. 26. https://www.theguardian.com/politics/ 2017/feb/26/robert-mercer-breitbart-war-on-media-steve-bannon-donald-trump -nigel-farage.

Cadwalladr, Carole. 2019. "Facebook's Role in Brexit—and the Threat to Democracy." *TED,* Apr. https://www.ted.com/talks/carole_cadwalladr_facebook_s_role_in_brexit _and_the_threat_to_democracy.

Cameron, Euan. 2012. *The European Reformation.* 2nd ed. New York: Oxford University Press.

Carey, Robert F., and Jacquelyn A. Burkell. 2007. "Revisiting the Four Horsemen of the Infopocalypse: Representations of Anonymity and the Internet in Canadian Newspapers." *First Monday* 12:8 (Aug. 6). https://firstmonday.org/ojs/index.php/ fm/article/view/1999/1874.

Carolan, Jennifer. 2018. "Empathy Technologies Like VR, AR, and Social Media Can Transform Education." *TechCrunch,* Apr. 22. https://techcrunch.com/2018/04/22/ empathy-technologies-like-vr-ar-and-social-media-can-transform-education/.

Carr, Nicholas. 2010. *The Shallows: What the Internet Is Doing to Our Brains.* New York: Norton.

Carr, Nicholas. 2018. "Can Journalism Be Saved?" *Los Angeles Review of Books,* Mar. 27. https://lareviewofbooks.org/article/can-journalism-be-saved/.

Carrico, Dale. 2005. "Pancryptics: Technocultural Transformations of the Subject of the Privacy." PhD diss. University of California–Berkeley. https://amormundi.blog spot.com/2012/07/pancryptics-my-dissertation-online.html.

Carrico, Dale. 2013. "Futurological Discourses and Posthuman Terrains." *Existenz* 8(2) (Fall): 47–63. https://existenz.us/volumes/Vol.8-2Carrico.pdf.

Carusone, Angelo. 2020. "Facebook and Twitter Don't Censor Conservatives: They Hire and Promote Them." *NBC News,* Oct. 29. https://www.nbcnews.com/think/ opinion/facebook-twitter-don-t-censor-conservatives-they-hire-promote-them-ncna 1245308.

Casey, Michael J. 2019. "The Crypto-Surveillance Capitalism Connection." *CoinDesk,* Feb. 4. https://www.coindesk.com/markets/2019/02/04/the-crypto-surveillance-capi talism-connection/.

Cassidy, John. 2013. *"Apple's Tax Dodges: Where's the Public Outrage?" New Yorker,* May 21. https://www.newyorker.com/news/john-cassidy/apples-tax-dodges-wheres-the-pub lic-outrage.

Cerf, Vinton G. 2012. "Keep the Internet Open." *New York Times,* May 24. https:// www.nytimes.com/2012/05/25/opinion/keep-the-internet-open.html.

Charles Koch Foundation. 2020. "New Stanford Program Will Explore Implications of Making Companies Responsible for Users' Online Speech." Press release, Sep. 9. https://charleskochfoundation.org/news/new-stanford-program-will-explore-impli cations-of-making-companies-responsible-for-users-online-speech/.

Chenou, Jean-Marie. 2014. "From Cyber-Libertarianism to Neoliberalism: Internet Exceptionalism, Multi-Stakeholderism, and the Institutionalization of Internet Governance in the 1990s." *Globalizations* 11:2: 205–23. https://doi.org/10.1080/1474 7731.2014.887387.

Chipolina, Scott. 2021. "'Bitcoin Must Be Private by Design': Edward Snowden." *Decrypt,* May 6. https://decrypt.co/70049/bitcoin-must-be-private-by-design-edward -snowden.

Chollet, François. 2016. "Why Is It Important to Democratize Machine Learning?" Quora, Aug. 15. https://www.quora.com/Why-is-it-important-to-democratize-ma chine-learning.

Chozick, Amy. 2013. "Jimmy Wales Is Not an Internet Billionaire." *New York Times Magazine,* Jun. 30. https://www.nytimes.com/2013/06/30/magazine/jimmy-wales-is -not-an-internet-billionaire.html.

Chu, Arthur. 2014. "Occupying the Throne: Justine Tunney, Neoreactionaries, and the New 1%." *Daily Beast,* Aug. 1. https://www.thedailybeast.com/occupying-the-throne -justine-tunney-neoreactionaries-and-the-new-1.

Chun, Wendy Hui Kyong. 2021. *Discriminating Data: Correlation, Neighborhoods, and the New Politics of Recognition.* Cambridge, Mass.: MIT Press.

Citron, Danielle Keats. 2014. *Hate Crimes in Cyberspace.* Cambridge, Mass.: Harvard University Press.

Citron, Danielle Keats. 2018. "Section 230's Challenge to Civil Rights and Civil Liber- ties." In "Intermediary Immunity and Discriminatory Designs." Knight First Amend- ment Institute at Columbia University, Apr. 6. https://knightcolumbia.org/content/ section-230s-challenge-civil-rights-and-civil-liberties.

Citron, Danielle Keats, and Frank Pasquale. 2014. "The Scored Society: Due Process for Automated Predictions." *Washington Law Review* 89(1) (Mar.): 1–34. https://digital commons.law.uw.edu/wlr/vol89/iss1/2.

Citron, Danielle Keats, and Benjamin Wittes. 2017. "The Internet Will Not Break: Denying Bad Samaritans § 230 Immunity." *Fordham Law Review* 88(2): 401–23. https://ir.lawnet.fordham.edu/flr/vol86/iss2/3.

Clegg, Nick. 2020. "Facebook Does Not Benefit from Hate." *Ad Age,* Jul. 1. https:// adage.com/article/digital/facebooks-open-letter-ad-world-we-dont-profit-hate/226 5331.

Cohn, Cindy. 2016. "Code Is Free Speech." *Time,* Mar. 17. https://time.com/4248928/ code-is-free-speech/.

Coldeway, Devin. 2017. "Study Finds Reddit's Controversial Ban of Its Most Toxic Subreddits Actually Worked." *TechCrunch,* Sep. 11. https://techcrunch.com/2017/ 09/11/study-finds-reddits-controversial-ban-of-its-most-toxic-subreddits-actually -worked/.

Collins, Keith. 2018. "Net Neutrality Has Officially Been Repealed. Here's How That Could Affect You." *New York Times,* Jun. 11. https://www.nytimes.com/2018/06/11/ technology/net-neutrality-repeal.html.

Costley White, Khadijah. 2018. *The Branding of Right-Wing Activism: The News Media and the Tea Party.* New York: Oxford University Press.

Cowen, Tyler. 2017. "If you read a criticism of Facebook . . ." X, Oct. 30. https://twitter .com/tylercowen/status/925007745228648448.

Cox, Christopher. 2020. "The PACT Act and Section 230: The Impact of the Law that Helped Create the Internet and an Examination of Proposed Reforms for Today's Online World." Testimony before the U.S. Senate Committee on Commerce,

Science, and Transportation, Subcommittee on Communications, Technology, Innovation, and the Internet, Jul. 28. https://www.commerce.senate.gov/services/files/BD6A508B-E95C-4659-8E6D-106CDE546D71.

Crook, Jordan. 2013. "Watch Weev's Angry Pre-sentencing Speech about the Failure of Our Nation." *TechCrunch,* Mar. 19. https://techcrunch.com/2013/03/19/watch-weevs-angry-pre-sentencing-speech-about-the-failure-of-our-nation/.

Crowell & Moring. 2020. "Expansion of Section 230 of US Communications Decency Act with July 1 Implementation of US–Mexico–Canada Agreement (USMCA)." Jul. 1. https://www.crowell.com/en/insights/client-alerts/expansion-of-section-230-of-u-s-communications-decency-act-with-july-1-implementation-of-u-s-mexico-canada-agreement-usmca. [Client alert.]

Culp, Andrew. 2016. *Dark Deleuze.* Minneapolis: University of Minnesota Press.

Curtis, Adam, dir. 2007. *The Trap: What Happened to Our Dream of Freedom.* Three-part documentary film. London: BBC Productions.

Curtis, Adam, dir. 2011. *All Watched Over by Machines of Loving Grace.* Three-part documentary film. London: BBC Productions.

Cushing, Tim. 2013. "Orin Kerr and Members of the EFF Representing AT&T Hacker 'Weev' Pro Bono during His Appeal." *TechDirt,* Mar. 27. https://www.techdirt.com/2013/03/27/orin-kerr-members-eff-representing-att-hacker-weev-pro-bono-during-his-appeal/.

"Cypherpunk." 2022. Wikipedia. Last modified Aug. 25. https://en.wikipedia.org/w/index.php?title=Cypherpunk&oldid=1106626762.

Da Baets, Antoon. 2016. "A Historian's View on the Right to Be Forgotten." *International Review of Law, Computers, and Technology* 30(1-2): 57–66. https://doi.org/10.1080/13600869.2015.1125155.

Dahlberg, Lincoln. 2001. "Democracy via Cyberspace: Mapping the Rhetorics and Practices of Three Prominent Camps." *New Media and Society* 3(2): 157–77.

Dahlberg, Lincoln. 2007. "The Internet and Discursive Exclusion: From Deliberative to Agonistic Public Sphere Theory." In Dahlberg and Siapera 2007, 128–47.

Dahlberg, Lincoln. 2010. "Cyber-Libertarianism 2.0: A Discourse Theory / Critical Political Economy Examination." *Cultural Politics* 6(3) (Nov.): 331–36. https://doi.org/10.2752/175174310X12750685679753.

Dahlberg, Lincoln, and Eugenia Siapera, eds. 2007. *Radical Democracy and the Internet: Interrogating Theory and Practice.* New York: Palgrave Macmillan.

Dale, Brady. 2021. "Bitcoin's Censorship-Resistance Was a Step Change in History." *CoinDesk,* Jul. 22. https://www.coindesk.com/markets/2021/07/22/bitcoins-censorship-resistance-was-a-step-change-in-history/.

Dame-Boyle, Alison. 2015. "EFF at 25: Remembering the Case that Established Code as Speech." Electronic Frontier Foundation, Apr. 16. https://www.eff.org/deeplinks/2015/04/remembering-case-established-code-speech.

Dance, Gabriel J. X., and Michael H. Keller. 2020. "Tech Companies Detect a Surge in Online Videos of Child Sexual Abuse." *New York Times,* Feb. 7. https://www.nytimes.com/2020/02/07/us/online-child-sexual-abuse.html.

Dane, Joseph. 2004. *The Myth of Print Culture: Essays on Evidence, Textuality, and Bibliographic Method.* Toronto: University of Toronto Press.

Davidson, James Dale, and Lord William Rees-Mogg. 1997. *The Sovereign Individual: Mastering the Transition to the Information Age.* New York: Simon & Schuster.

Davies, Harry, Simon Goodley, Felicity Lawrence, Paul Lewis, and Lisa O'Carroll. 2022. "Uber Broke Laws, Duped Police and Secretly Lobbied Governments, Leak Reveals." *The Guardian,* Jul. 11. https://www.theguardian.com/news/2022/jul/10/uber-files-leak-reveals-global-lobbying-campaign.

DeChiaro, Dean. 2019. "'A Real Gift to Big Tech': Both Parties Object to Immunity Provision in USMCA." *Roll Call,* Dec. 17. https://rollcall.com/2019/12/17/a-real-gift-to-big-tech-both-parties-object-to-immunity-provision-in-usmca/.

De Filippi, Primavera, and Aaron Wright. 2018. *Blockchain and the Law: The Rule of Code.* Cambridge, Mass.: Harvard University Press.

"Definitions of Fascism." 2022. Wikipedia. Last modified Jul. 18. https://en.wikipedia.org/w/index.php?title=Definitions_of_fascism&oldid=1099091105.

Delgado, Richard, and Jean Stefancic. 2018. *Must We Defend Nazis? Why the First Amendment Should Not Protect Hate Speech and White Supremacy.* New York: NYU Press.

"Democratization." 2021. Wikipedia. Last modified Jul. 17. https://en.wikipedia.org/w/index.php?title=Democratization&oldid=1034086921.

DeNardis, Laura. 2015. *The Global War for Internet Governance.* New Haven, Conn.: Yale University Press.

Denning, Dorothy. 1996. "The Future of Cryptography." In Ludlow 2001, 85–101.

Destination Hub. 2022a. "'I Tried to Warn You' IT'S ALREADY HERE—Edward Snowden 2022." YouTube video, Feb. 9. https://youtube.com/watch?v=n1NEFwY9TiQ. [Video since deleted.]

Destination Hub. 2022b. "'IT'S TOO LATE!! 'This is the Secret They Are Hiding from You' | Edward Snowden 2022." YouTube video, Feb. 20. https://www.youtube.com/watch?v=rT6dS82kGuA. [Video since deleted.]

Destination Hub. 2022c. "This Is Getting Serious, Why Is Nobody Talking about This? Edward Snowden 2022." YouTube video, Apr. 23. https://www.youtube.com/watch?v=LQQeuocI1SY. [Video since deleted.]

Dewar, James A. 1998. *The Information Age and the Printing Press: Looking Backward to See Ahead.* Los Angeles: RAND Corporation.

Dewar, James A., and Peng Hwa Ang. 2007. "The Cultural Consequences of Printing and the Internet." In Baron, Lundquist, and Shevlin 2007, 365–77.

Dingledine, Roger [arma]. 2014. "Possible Upcoming Attempts to Disable the Tor Network." *Tor Blog,* Dec. 19. https://blog.torproject.org/possible-upcoming-attempts-disable-tor-network/.

Diringer, David. 1982. *The Book before Printing: Ancient, Medieval, and Oriental.* New York: Dover.

Doctorow, Cory. 2014. "Crypto Wars Redux: Why the FBI's Desire to Unlock Your Private Life Must Be Resisted." *The Guardian,* Oct. 9. https://www.theguardian.com/technology/2014/oct/09/crypto-wars-redux-why-the-fbis-desire-to-unlock-your-private-life-must-be-resisted.

Doctorow, Cory. 2015. *Information Doesn't Want to Be Free: Laws for the Internet Age.* New York: McSweeney's.

Doctorow, Cory. 2020. *How to Destroy Surveillance Capitalism.* San Francisco: Medium Editions. https://onezero.medium.com/how-to-destroy-surveillance-capitalism-8135 e6744d59.

Doctorow, Cory, and Christoph Schmon. 2020. "The EU's Digital Markets Act: There Is a Lot to Like, but Room for Improvement." Electronic Frontier Foundation, Dec. 15. https://www.eff.org/deeplinks/2020/12/eus-digital-markets-act-there-lot-room -improvement.

Domscheit-Berg, Daniel. 2011. *Inside WikiLeaks: My Time with Julian Assange at the World's Most Dangerous Website.* New York: Crown.

Dougherty, Michael Brendan. 2017. "The Libertarianism-to-Fascism Pipeline." *National Review,* Aug. 24. https://www.nationalreview.com/2017/08/libertarians-sometimes -become-fascists-heres-why/.

Dourado, Eli. 2013. "Making Airspace Available for 'Permissionless Innovation.'" Technology Liberation Front, Apr. 23. https://techliberation.com/2013/04/23/making -airspace-available-for-permissionless-innovation/.

Dowd, Trone. 2020. "Snowden Warns Governments Are Using Coronavirus to Build 'the Architecture of Oppression.'" *Vice,* Apr. 9. https://www.vice.com/en/article/ bvge5q/snowden-warns-governments-are-using-coronavirus-to-build-the-architec ture-of-oppression.

Driscoll, Kevin. 2011. "Net Neutrality Research Database, 0.1." Aug. 9. https://kevin driscoll.org/projects/netneutrality/nn.html.

Duffy, Clare. 2020. "Facebook VP on Ad Boycott: We Have 'No Incentive' to Allow Hate Speech." *CNN,* Jun. 28. https://www.cnn.com/2020/06/28/tech/nick-clegg -facebook-boycott-reliable/index.html.

Dulong de Rosnay, Melanie, and Francesca Musiani. 2016. "Towards a (De)centralization-Based Typology of Peer Production." *tripleC* 14(1): 189–207. https://doi.org/10.31269/ triplec.v14i1.728.

Dwyer, Colin. 2020. "Authors, Publishers Condemn the 'National Emergency Library' as 'Piracy.'" *National Public Radio,* Mar. 30. https://www.npr.org/2020/03/30/8237 97545/authors-publishers-condemn-the-national-emergency-library-as-piracy.

Dyson, Esther. 1997. *Release 2.0: A Design for Living in the Digital Age.* New York: Broadway.

Dyson, Esther, George Gilder, George Keyworth, and Alvin Toffler. 1994. "Cyberspace and the American Dream: A Magna Carta for the Knowledge Age." *Future Insight,* Aug. http://www.pff.org/issues-pubs/futureinsights/fi1.2magnacarta.html.

Eco, Umberto. 1995. "Ur-Fascism." *New York Review of Books,* Jun. 22. https://www .nybooks.com/articles/1995/06/22/ur-fascism/.

Edelson, Laura, Minh-Kha Nguyen, Ian Goldstein, Oana Goga, Tobias Lauinger, and Damon McCoy. 2021. "Far-Right News Sources on Facebook More Engaging." *Medium,* Mar. 3. https://medium.com/cybersecurity-for-democracy/far-right-news -sources-on-facebook-more-engaging-e04a01efae90.

"Edward Snowden Explains Why He Doesn't Talk about Ukraine Crisis." 2022. *Coin Desk,* Jun. 11. https://www.coindesk.com/video/edward-snowden-explains-why-he -doesnt-talk-about-ukraine-crisis/.

Edwards, Paul N. 1997. *The Closed World: Computers and the Politics of Discourse in Cold War America.* Cambridge, Mass.: MIT Press.

e-flux. 2018. "Why Is Nick Land Still Embraced by Segments of the British Art and Theory Scenes?" *e-flux Conversations,* Mar. https://conversations.e-flux.com/t/why-is-nick-land-still-embraced-by-segments-of-the-british-art-and-theory-scenes/6329.

Eichenwald, Kurt. 2013. "The Errors of Edward Snowden and His Global Hypocrisy Tour." *Vanity Fair,* Jun. 26. https://www.vanityfair.com/news/2013/06/errors-edward-snowden-global-hypocrisy-tour.

Eisenstat, Yaël, and Nils Gilman. 2022. "The Myth of Tech Exceptionalism." *Noēma,* Feb. 10. https://www.noemamag.com/the-myth-of-tech-exceptionalism/.

Eisenstein, Elizabeth L. 1979. *The Printing Press as an Agent of Change: Communications and Cultural Transformations in Early-Modern Europe.* New York: Cambridge University Press.

Eisenstein, Elizabeth L. 2005. *The Printing Revolution in Early Modern Europe.* 2nd ed. New York: Cambridge University Press.

Electronic Frontier Foundation. n.d. "Net Neutrality." Last modified Mar. 3, 2024. https://www.eff.org/issues/net-neutrality.

Electronic Frontier Foundation. 2011. *Annual Report, 2009–2010.* https://www.eff.org/files/eff-2009-2010-annual-report.pdf.

"Eliezer Yudkowsky." 2021. RationalWiki. Last modified Jun. 22. https://rationalwiki.org/w/index.php?title=LessWrong&oldid=2336968.

Emerson, Lori. 2016. "Selling the Future at the MIT Media Lab." LoriEmerson.net, Feb. 17. https://loriemerson.net/2016/02/17/selling-the-future-at-the-mit-media-lab/.

Enlund, Martin. 2022. "On Gutenberg, Satoshi and Polarization." *metaperspectiv,* Jan. 6. https://enlund.org/en/posts/gutenberg/.

Eubanks, Virginia. 2011. *Digital Dead End: Fighting for Social Justice in the Information Age.* Cambridge, Mass.: MIT Press.

Eye Opener. 2022. "'If You Knew What's Coming, You Would Get Prepared Now'— Edward Snowden (2022)." YouTube video, May 23. https://www.youtube.com/watch?v=Uj8Gwq-9dEo. [Video since deleted.]

Fabbri, Alice, Alexandra Lai, Quinn Grundy, and Lisa Anne Bero. 2018. "The Influence of Industry Sponsorship on the Research Agenda: A Scoping Review." *American Journal of Public Health* 108:11 (Nov. 1). https://doi.org/10.2105/AJPH.2018.304677.

Falkvinge, Rick. 2015. "Language Matters: All the Copyright Lobby's Subtleties." *TorrentFreak,* Oct. 18. https://torrentfreak.com/language-matters-all-the-copyright-lobbys-subtleties-151018/.

Farrow, Ronan. 2019. "How an Élite University Research Center Concealed Its Relationship with Jeffrey Epstein." *New Yorker,* Sep. 6. https://www.newyorker.com/news/news-desk/how-an-elite-university-research-center-concealed-its-relationship-with-jeffrey-epstein.

FCC. 2015. "FCC Releases Open Internet Order." Mar. 12. https://www.fcc.gov/document/fcc-releases-open-internet-order.

Feiner, Lauren. 2019. "Pelosi Pushes to Keep Tech's Legal Shield Out of Trade Agreement with Mexico and Canada." *CNBC,* Dec. 5. https://www.cnbc.com/2019/12/05/pelosi-pushes-to-keep-section-230-out-of-usmca-trade-agreement.html.

Feldman, Ari. 2016. "Why Does WikiLeaks Have a Reputation for Anti-Semitism?" *Forward,* Aug. 15. https://forward.com/news/347546/why-does-wikileaks-have-a-reputation-for-anti-semitism/.

Feldman, Brian. 2020. "Facebook Has Always Been Right-Wing Media." *Vice,* Oct. 29. https://www.vice.com/en/article/n7vvwq/facebook-has-always-been-right-wing-media.

Fenwick, Cody. 2019. "Here's Why Economist Brad Delong Believes Libertarianism Is Essentially a Form of White Supremacy." *Salon,* Jan. 4. https://www.salon.com/2019/01/04/heres-why-this-economist-believes-libertarianism-is-essentially-a-form-of-white-supremacy_partner/?fbclid=IwAR1FcoNjI-P4tCEsgI7i9rVM5UdCyTM8zAZxOXBhVsR_23UQvE7EXzDSYeE.

Ferdinand, Peter, ed. 2000. *The Internet, Democracy, and Democratization.* New York: Routledge.

Fielitz, Maik, and Holger Marcks. 2019. "Digital Fascism: Challenges for the Open Society in the Time of Social Media." University of California–Berkeley Center for Right-Wing Studies Working Paper, Jul. 16. https://escholarship.org/uc/item/87w5c5gp.

Fight for the Future. n.d. "Projects." Last modified Nov. 20, 2023. https://www.fightforthefuture.org/projects/.

Fight for the Future. 2021. "Don't Kill Crypto." Campaign website. Last modified Mar. 3, 2024. https://www.fightforthefuture.org/actions/stop-the-senate-from-sneaking-through-total-surveillance-of-the-crypto-economy/.

Finley, Klint. 2020. "The *Wired* Guide to Net Neutrality." *Wired,* May 5. https://www.wired.com/story/guide-net-neutrality/.

Fleischer, Dorothy A. 1991. "The MIT Radiation Laboratory: RLE's Microwave Heritage." *RLE Currents* 4:2 (Spring). https://web.archive.org/web/19990225094504/http:/rleweb.mit.edu/Publications/currents/4-2cov.htm.

Foroohar, Rana. 2018. "Year in a Word: Techlash." *Financial Times,* Dec. 16. https://www.ft.com/content/76578fba-fca1-11e8-ac00-57a2a826423e.

Fouché, Rayvon. 2012. "From Black Inventors to One Laptop per Child: Exporting a Racial Politics of Technology." In Lisa Nakamura and Peter A. Chow-White, eds., *Race after the Internet.* New York: Routledge, 61–84.

Ford, Paul. 2016. "Reboot the World." *New Republic,* Jun. 22. https://newrepublic.com/article/133889/reboot-world.

Forsyth, Susan R., Donna H. Odierna, David Krauth, and Lisa A. Bero. 2014. "Conflicts of Interest and Critiques of the Use of Systematic Reviews in Policymaking: An Analysis of Opinion Articles." *Systematic Reviews* 3:122. https://doi.org/10.1186/2046-4053-3-122.

Frank, Sam. 2015. "Come with Us If You Want to Live: Among the Apocalyptic Libertarians of Silicon Valley." *Harper's Magazine,* Jan. https://harpers.org/archive/2015/01/come-with-us-if-you-want-to-live/.

Frank, Thomas. 1997. *The Conquest of Cool: Business Culture, Counterculture, and the Rise of Hip Consumerism.* Chicago: University of Chicago Press.

Franken, Al. 2010. "The Internet as We Know It Is Still at Risk." *Huffington Post,* Dec. 22. https://www.huffpost.com/entry/the-internet-as-we-know-i_b_800159.

Franks, Mary Ann. 2013. "The Lawless Internet? Myths and Misconceptions about CDA Section 230." *Huffington Post,* Dec. 18. https://www.huffpost.com/entry/sec tion-230-the-lawless-internet_b_4455090.

Franks, Mary Anne. 2019a. *The Cult of the Constitution: Our Deadly Devotion to Guns and Free Speech.* Stanford, Calif.: Stanford University Press.

Franks, Mary Anne. 2019b. "The Free Speech Black Hole: Can the Internet Escape the Gravitational Pull of the First Amendment?" Knight First Amendment Institute at Columbia University, Aug. 21. https://knightcolumbia.org/content/the-free-speech -black-hole-can-the-internet-escape-the-gravitational-pull-of-the-first-amendment.

"The Free-Knowledge Fundamentalist." 2008. *The Economist,* Jun. 7. https://web.archive .org/web/20220301190721/https:/www.economist.com/technology-quarterly/2008 /06/07/the-free-knowledge-fundamentalist.

Freeland, Chris. 2020. "Announcing a National Emergency Library to Provide Digitized Books to Students and the Public." *Internet Archive Blogs,* Mar. 24. https://blog .archive.org/2020/03/24/announcing-a-national-emergency-library-to-provide -digitized-books-to-students-and-the-public/.

Free Press and Free Action Fund. 2012. "Declaration of Internet Freedom." Jul. 4. https://web.archive.org/web/20120920041723/http:/www.internetdeclaration.org/.

Frenkel, Sheera, and Cecilia Kang. 2021. *An Ugly Truth: Inside Facebook's Battle for Domination.* New York: HarperCollins.

Friedman, David. 1989. *The Machinery of Freedom: Guide to a Radical Capitalism.* 3rd ed. New York: Open Court.

Freidman, David. 2008. *Future Imperfect: Technology and Freedom in an Uncertain World.* New York: Cambridge University Press.

Galloway, Alexander. 2004. *Protocol: How Control Exists after Decentralization.* Cambridge, Mass.: MIT Press.

Galperin, Eve. 2014. "Twitter Steps Down from the Free Speech Party." Electronic Frontier Foundation, May 21. https://www.eff.org/deeplinks/2014/05/twitter-steps -down-free-speech-party.

"GDPR Fines and Notices." 2022. Wikipedia. Last modified Jul. 12. https://en.wikipe dia.org/w/index.php?title=GDPR_fines_and_notices&oldid=1097679934.

Geigner, Timothy. 2013. "*Game of Thrones* Director: I'm 100% Opposed to the Piracy I Just Said Helps My Show Survive." *TechDirt,* Feb. 28. https://www.techdirt.com/ 2013/02/28/game-thrones-director-im-100-opposed-to-piracy-i-just-said-helps-my -show-survive/.

Gellis, Cathy. 2018. "The GDPR: Ghastly, Dumb, Paralyzing Regulation It's Hard to Celebrate." *TechDirt,* May 25. https://www.techdirt.com/2018/05/25/gdpr-ghastly -dumb-paralyzing-regulation-hard-to-celebrate/.

Gerard, David. 2017. *Attack of the 50 Foot Blockchain: Bitcoin, Blockchain, Ethereum, and Smart Contracts.* Self-pub., CreateSpace.

Gerard, David. 2020. *Libra Shrugged: How Facebook Tried to Take Over the Money.* Self-pub.

Gerard, David. 2022. "Creationism on the Blockchain (Review of George Gilder, *Life After Google*)." *b2o Review,* Apr. 29. https://www.boundary2.org/2022/04/david-gerard -creationism-on-the-blockchain-review-of-george-gilder-life-after-google/.

Giddens, Anthony. 1985. *The Nation-State and Violence.* Cambridge: Polity Press.

Gillespie, Tarleton. 2018. *Custodians of the Internet: Platforms, Content Moderation, and the Hidden Decisions That Shape Social Media.* New Haven, Conn.: Yale University Press.

Gilmore, John. 2013. "John Gilmore, Entrepreneur and Civil Libertarian." Toad.com. Last modified Nov. 27. http://www.toad.com/gnu/.

Gitlin, Todd. 1993. *The Sixties: Years of Hope, Days of Rage.* Rev. ed. New York: Bantam.

Glaser, April. 2018. "The Watchdogs That Didn't Bark." *Slate,* Apr. 19. https://slate.com/technology/2018/04/why-arent-privacy-groups-fighting-to-regulate-facebook.html.

Glaser, April. 2019. "There Are at Least Five Reasons Why Mark Zuckerberg Would Have Tucker Carlson over for Dinner." *Slate,* Oct. 15. https://slate.com/technology/2019/10/mark-zuckerberg-tucker-carlson-ben-shapiro-facebook-conservatives.html.

Godin, Benoît, and Dominique Vinck, eds. 2017. *Critical Studies of Innovation: Alternative Approaches to the Pro-Innovation Bias.* Northampton, Mass.: Edward Elgar.

Godwin, Mike. 2007. "Superhuman Imagination: Vernor Vinge on Science Fiction, the Singularity, and the State." *Reason,* May. https://reason.com/2007/05/04/super human-imagination/.

Gogarty, Kayla. 2020. "Facebook Is Letting the Trump Campaign Publish at Least 529 Ads with False Claims of Voter Fraud." *Media Matters,* May 19. https://www.media matters.org/facebook/facebook-letting-trump-campaign-publish-least-529-ads -false-claims-voter-fraud.

Goldberg, Carrie. 2019. *Nobody's Victim: Fighting Psychos, Stalkers, Pervs, and Trolls.* New York: Plume.

Goldman, Eric, and Jeff Kosseff, eds. 2020. *Zeran v. America Online E-Resource.* Santa Clara University Legal Studies Research Paper. https://dx.doi.org/10.2139/ssrn.3663 839.

Goldstein, Alexis. 2021. "Crypto Doesn't Have to Enable Tax Cheats." *Bloomberg,* Aug. 27. https://www.bloomberg.com/opinion/articles/2021-08-26/crypto-doesn-t-have -to-enable-tax-cheats.

Goldstein, Evan. 2020. "Higher Ed Has a Silicon Valley Problem." *Chronicle of Higher Education* (Sep. 23). https://www.chronicle.com/article/higher-ed-has-a-silicon-valley -problem.

Goldstein, Paul. 2003. *Copyright's Highway: From Gutenberg to the Celestial Jukebox.* Stanford, Calif.: Stanford University Press.

Golumbia, David. 2009. *The Cultural Logic of Computation.* Cambridge, Mass.: Harvard University Press.

Golumbia, David. 2013. "Completely Different and Exactly the Same." *Uncomputing,* Mar. 6. Last modified Sep. 17, 2023. http://www.uncomputing.org/?p=22.

Golumbia, David. 2014a. "'Permissionless Innovation': Using Technology to Dismantle the Republic." *Uncomputing,* Jun. 11. Last modified Dec. 21, 2023. https://www .uncomputing.org/?p=1383.

Golumbia, David. 2014b. "Tor Is Not a 'Fundamental Law of the Universe.'" *Pando Daily,* Dec. 12. https://web.archive.org/web/20141218100032/https:/pando.com/2014/ 12/12/tor-is-not-a-fundamental-law-of-the-universe/.

Golumbia, David. 2015. "Tor, Technocracy, Democracy." *Uncomputing*, Apr. 23. Last modified Dec. 2, 2023. http://www.uncomputing.org/?p=1647.

Golumbia, David. 2016a. "Code Is Not Speech." SSRN, Apr. 13. https://dx.doi.org/10.2139/ssrn.2764214.

Golumbia, David. 2016b. "Marxism and Open Access in the Humanities: Turning Academic Labor against Itself." *Workplace: A Journal for Academic Labor* 28 (Sep. 16). https://doi.org/10.14288/workplace.v0i28.186213.

Golumbia, David. 2016c. "'Neoliberalism' Has Two Meanings." *Uncomputing*, Jul. 22. Last modified Oct. 5, 2023. http://www.uncomputing.org/?p=1803.

Golumbia, David. 2016d. *The Politics of Bitcoin: Software as Right-Wing Extremism.* Minneapolis: University of Minnesota Press.

Golumbia, David. 2017. "The Militarization of Language: Cryptographic Politics and the War of All against All." *boundary 2* 44:4 (Nov.). 95–112. https://doi.org/10.1215/01903659-4206337.

Golumbia, David. 2020a. "Blockchain: The White Man's Burden." *Medium*, Feb. 21. https://davidgolumbia.medium.com/blockchain-the-white-mans-burden-e3ef75c97830.

Golumbia, David. 2020b. "Cryptocurrency Is Garbage. So Is Blockchain." *Medium*, Jun. 27. https://davidgolumbia.medium.com/cryptocurrency-is-garbage-so-is-blockchain-3e80078e77fe.

Golumbia, David. 2021. "Trump's Twitter Ban Is a Step toward Ending the Hijacking of the First Amendment." *Boston Globe*, Jan. 10. https://www.bostonglobe.com/2021/01/10/opinion/stretching-first-amendment/?event=event25.

Good, Chris. 2013. "Julian Assange Backs Ron and Rand Paul." *ABC News*, Aug. 17. https://abcnews.go.com/blogs/politics/2013/08/julian-assange-backs-ron-and-rand-paul.

Gorbis, Marina. 2013. *The Nature of the Future: Dispatches from the Socialstructed World.* New York: Free Press.

Gorodyansky, David. 2017. "This Is the Future If Net Neutrality Is Repealed: The Creeping, Costly Death of Media Freedom." *TechCrunch*, Dec. 9. https://techcrunch.com/2017/12/09/this-is-the-future-if-net-neutrality-is-repealed-the-creeping-costly-death-of-media-freedom/.

Graham, Megan, and Salvador Rodriguez. 2020. "Facebook Meeting with Civil Rights Groups 'a Disappointment,' Ad Boycott Organizers Say." *CNBC*, Jul. 7. https://www.cnbc.com/2020/07/07/leaders-of-facebook-ad-boycott-no-commitment-to-action-from-execs.html.

Gray, Rosie. 2017. "Behind the Internet's Anti-Democracy Movement." *The Atlantic*, Feb. 10. https://www.theatlantic.com/politics/archive/2017/02/behind-the-internets-dark-anti-democracy-movement/516243/.

Greelish, David. 2013. "An Interview with Computing Pioneer Alan Kay." *Time*, Apr. 2. https://techland.time.com/2013/04/02/an-interview-with-computing-pioneer-alan-kay/.

Green, Stephen J. 2017. "The Cryptocurrency Reformation: Comparing Martin Luther and Satoshi Nakamoto." *Steemit*. https://steemit.com/cryptocurrency/@stevg/the-cryptocurrency-reformation-comparing-martin-luther-and-satoshi-nakamoto.

Greenberg, Andy. (2012) 2013. *This Machine Kills Secrets: How WikiLeakers, Cypherpunks, and Hacktivists Aim to Free the World's Information*. New York: Plume.

Greene, David, Corynne McSherry, Sophia Cope, and Adam Schwartz. 2016. "Rights at Odds: Europe's Right to Be Forgotten Clashes with U.S. Law." Electronic Frontier Foundation, Nov. https://www.eff.org/files/2016/11/29/rtbf-us_law_legal_back ground.pdf.

Greenwald, Glenn. 2010. "Palin and the Tea-Party 'Movement': Nothing New." *Salon*, Feb. 7. https://www.salon.com/2010/02/07/palin_64/.

Greenwald, Glenn. 2011. "The Tea Party and Civil Liberties." *Salon*, Feb. 9. https://www.salon.com/2011/02/09/tea_party_9/.

Greenwood, Daniel J. H. 1999. "First Amendment Imperialism." *Utah Law Review*, 657–99. https://dx.doi.org/10.2139/ssrn.794786.

Greenwood, Daniel J. H. 2013. "Do Corporations Have a Constitutional Right to Bear Arms? and Related Puzzles in Post-National Jurisprudence." Draft paper. Last modified Sep. 17, 2023. https://people.hofstra.edu/Daniel_J_Greenwood/pdf/2dA DRAFT.pdf.

Greer, Evan. 2021a. "Surveillance Capitalism." Get Better Records, Apr. 8. YouTube video, 00:03:31. https://youtu.be/NvBHFLFllJ8?.

Greer, Evan. 2021b. "Decentralization is our best bet . . ." X, Jul. 15. https://twitter.com/ evan_greer/status/1415640718299779077.

Griffin, Roger. 1991. *The Nature of Fascism*. New York: Routledge.

Griffin, Roger. 1995. *Fascism*. New York: Oxford University Press.

Grofman, Bernard, Alexander H. Treschel, and Mark Franklin, eds. 2014. *The Internet and Democracy in Global Perspective: Voters, Candidates, Parties, and Social Movements*. New York: Springer.

Grove, Lloyd, and Justin Baragona. 2021. "Is Glenn Greenwald the New Master of Right-Wing Media?" *Daily Beast*, Jun. 6. https://www.thedailybeast.com/is-glenn -greenwald-the-new-master-of-right-wing-media.

Guesmi, Haythem. 2021. "The Social Media Myth about the Arab Spring." *Al Jazeera*, Jan. 27. https://www.aljazeera.com/opinions/2021/1/27/the-social-media-myth-about -the-arab-spring.

Gurstein, Michael. 2013. "Multistakeholderism vs. Democracy: My Adventures in 'Stakeholderland.'" *Gurstein's Community Informatics*, Mar. 20. https://gurstein.word press.com/2013/03/20/multistakeholderism-vs-democracy-my-adventures-in-stake holderland/.

Gurstein, Michael. 2014a. "The Multistakeholder Model, Neoliberalism and Global (Internet) Governance." *Gurstein's Community Informatics*, Mar. 26. https://gurstein .wordpress.com/2014/03/26/the-multistakeholder-model-neo-liberalism-and-global -internet-governance/.

Gurstein, Michael. 2014b. "Democracy OR Multistakeholderism: Competing Models of Governance." *Gurstein's Community Informatics*, Oct. 19. https://gurstein.word press.com/2014/10/19/democracy-or-multi-stakeholderism-competing-models-of -governance/.

Hagey, Keach, and Jeff Horwitz. 2021. "Facebook's Internal Chat Boards Show Politics Often at Center of Decision Making." *Wall Street Journal*, Oct. 24. https://www.wsj .com/articles/facebook-politics-decision-making-documents-11635100195.

Haggart, Blayne, and Natasha Tusikov. 2021. "How 'Free Speech' Kills Internet Regulation Debates: Part Two." Centre for International Governance Innovation, Sep. 10. https://www.cigionline.org/articles/how-free-speech-kills-internet-regulation-debates/.

Haider, Shuja. 2017. "The Darkness at the End of the Tunnel: Artificial Intelligence and Neoreaction." *Viewpoint Magazine,* Mar. 28. https://viewpointmag.com/2017/03/28/the-darkness-at-the-end-of-the-tunnel-artificial-intelligence-and-neoreaction/.

Hall, Zac. 2014. "Occupy Wall Street Co-founder: Appoint Eric Schmidt CEO of America." *9to5Google,* Mar. 20. https://9to5google.com/2014/03/20/occupy-wall-street-co-founder-appoint-eric-schmidt-ceo-of-america/.

Halliday, Josh. 2012. "Twitter's Tony Wang: 'We Are the Free Speech Wing of the Free Speech Party.'" *The Guardian,* Mar. 22. https://www.theguardian.com/media/2012/mar/22/twitter-tony-wang-free-speech.

Halpern, Sue. 2018. "Cambridge Analytica, Facebook, and the Revelations of Open Secrets." *New Yorker,* Mar. 21. https://www.newyorker.com/news/news-desk/cambridge-analytica-facebook-and-the-revelations-of-open-secrets.

Hanna, Rachael. 2020. "Metadata Collection Violated FISA, Ninth Circuit Rules." *Lawfare Blog,* Sep. 14. https://www.lawfaremedia.org/article/metadata-collection-violated-fisa-ninth-circuit-rules.

Hanson, Robin. 2006. "Foul Play in Information Markets." In Bob Hahn and Paul Tetlock, eds., *Information Markets: A New Way of Making Decisions in the Public and Private Sectors.* Washington, D.C.: AEI Press, 126–41. https://mason.gmu.edu/~rhanson/foulplay.pdf.

Harguindéguy, Jean-Baptiste Paul, Alistair Cole, and Romain Pasquier. 2021. "The Variety of Decentralization Indexes: A Review of the Literature." *Regional and Federal Studies* 31(2): 185–208. https://doi.org/10.1080/13597566.2019.1566126.

Harry, Sydette. 2014. "Ouroboros Outtakes: The Circle Was Never Unbroken." *Model View Culture,* Dec. 8. https://modelviewculture.com/pieces/ouroboros-outtakes-the-circle-was-never-unbroken.

Hartzog, Woodrow. 2021. "What Is Privacy? That's the Wrong Question." *University of Chicago Law Review* 88:7 (Nov.): 1677–88. https://lawreview.uchicago.edu/print-archive/what-privacy-thats-wrong-question.

Harwell, Drew. 2021. "Rumble, a YouTube Rival Popular with Conservatives, Will Pay Creators Who 'Challenge the Status Quo.'" *Washington Post,* Aug. 12. https://www.washingtonpost.com/technology/2021/08/12/rumble-video-gabbard-greenwald/.

Hassan, Samer, and Primavera De Filippi. 2017. "The Expansion of Algorithmic Governance: From Code Is Law to Law Is Code." *Field Actions Science Reports* 17: 88–90. https://journals.openedition.org/factsreports/4518.

Hatmaker, Taylor. 2020. "Trump Vetoes Major Defense Bill, Citing Section 230." *TechCrunch,* Dec. 23. https://techcrunch.com/2020/12/23/trump-ndaa-veto-section-230/.

Haworth, Alan. 1994. *Anti-Libertarianism: Markets, Philosophy, and Myth.* New York: Routledge.

Hayek, Friedrich A. (1944) 2001. *The Road to Serfdom.* New York: Routledge.

Hayek, Friedrich A. 1945. "The Use of Knowledge in Society." *American Economic Review* 35(4) (Sep.): 519–30.

Hayes, Chris. 2017. "The End of the Internet as We Know It." *All In with Chris Hayes.* MSNBC, Dec. 14. https://www.msnbc.com/all-in/watch/net-neutrality-vote-the-end -of-the-internet-as-we-know-it-1117045315686.

Hemmati, Minu. 2002. *Multi-stakeholder Processes for Governance and Sustainability: Beyond Deadlock and Conflict.* London: Earthscan.

Hendrix, Steve, and Michael E. Miller. 2019. "'Let's Get This Party Started': New Zealand Shooting Suspect Narrated His Chilling Rampage." *Washington Post,* Mar. 15. https://www.washingtonpost.com/local/lets-get-this-party-started-new-zealand -gunman-narrated-his-chilling-rampage/2019/03/15/fb3db352-4748-11e9-90f0 -occfeec87a61_story.html.

Herman, Bill D. 2013. *The Fight over Digital Rights: The Politics of Copyright and Technology.* New York: Cambridge University Press.

Higgins, Eoin. 2022. "Apologist for Tucker Carlson's Racism: Glenn Greenwald." *Nation of Change,* May 27. https://www.nationofchange.org/2022/05/27/apologist -for-tucker-carlsons-racism-glenn-greenwald/.

Hindman, Matthew. 2009. *The Myth of Digital Democracy.* Princeton, N.J.: Princeton University Press.

Hitt, Tarpley. 2021. "Facebook a Hotbed of 'Child Sexual Abuse Material' with 20.3 Million Reports, Far More Than Pornhub." *Daily Beast,* Feb. 24. https://www.the dailybeast.com/facebook-a-hotbed-of-child-sexual-abuse-material-with-203-mil lion-reports-far-more-than-pornhub.

Hoffmann, Anna Lauren, Nicholas Proferes, and Michael Zimmer. 2018. "'Making the World More Open and Connected': Mark Zuckerberg and the Discursive Construction of Facebook and Its Users." *New Media and Society* 20(1) (Jan.): 199–218. https://doi.org/10.1177/1461444816660784.

Hoofnagle, Chris Jay. 2007. "Denialists' Deck of Cards: An Illustrated Taxonomy of Rhetoric Used to Frustrate Consumer Protection Efforts." SSRN, Feb. 9. https:// dx.doi.org/10.2139/ssrn.962462.

Hoppe, Hans-Hermann. 2001. *Democracy: The God That Failed: The Economics and Politics of Monarchy, Democracy and Natural Order.* New Brunswick, N.J.: Transaction.

Horwitz, Steve. 2017. "The Rhetoric of Libertarians and the Unfortunate Appeal to the Alt-Right." *Bleeding Heart Libertarians,* Aug. 4. https://bleedingheartlibertarians .com/2017/08/rhetoric-libertarians-unfortunate-appeal-alt-right/.

Howard, Alex, and John Wonderlich. 2016. "On Weaponized Transparency." Sunlight Foundation, Jul. 28. https://sunlightfoundation.com/2016/07/28/on-weaponized -transparency/.

Ifill, Sherrilyn. 2019. "Mark Zuckerberg Doesn't Know His Civil Rights History." *Washington Post,* Oct. 17. https://www.washingtonpost.com/opinions/2019/10/17/ mark-zuckerberg-doesnt-know-his-civil-rights-history/.

Ignatius, David. 2021a. "As the Anti-Facebook Frenzy Accelerates, Remember: The Problem Isn't Just a Single Platform." *Washington Post,* Oct. 26. https://www.wash ingtonpost.com/opinions/2021/10/26/facebook-papers-zuckerberg-misinformation/.

Ignatius, David. 2021b. "The State Department Gets Serious About the Global Technology Race." *Washington Post*, Oct. 27. https://www.washingtonpost.com/opinions/2021/10/27/state-department-gets-serious-about-global-technology-race/.

Innis, Harold. 1950. *Empire and Communications*. Toronto: University of Toronto Press.

Innis, Harold. 1951. *The Bias of Communication*. Toronto: University of Toronto Press.

Jain, Samir C. 2017. "The Non-inevitable Breadth of the 'Zeran' Decision." In Goldman and Kosseff 2020, 55–56.

Jarvis, Jeff. 2005. "About Me and Disclosures." *BuzzMachine*, Jul. 4. https://buzzmachine.com/about/.

Jarvis, Jeff. 2009. *What Would Google Do? Reverse-Engineering the Fastest-Growing Company in the History of the World*. New York: HarperCollins.

Jarvis, Jeff. 2011a. "The Article and the Future of Print." *BuzzMachine*, Jun. 18. https://buzzmachine.com/2011/06/18/the-article-and-the-future-of-print/.

Jarvis, Jeff. 2011b. "Gutenberg of Arabia." *BuzzMachine*, Feb. 13. https://buzzmachine.com/2011/02/13/gutenberg-of-arabia/.

Jarvis, Jeff. 2011c. *Gutenberg the Geek: History's First Technology Entrepreneur and Silicon Valley's Patron Saint*. Seattle: Amazon Digital Services. Kindle.

Jarvis, Jeff. 2011d. *Public Parts: How Sharing in the Digital Age Improves the Way We Work and Live*. New York: Simon & Schuster.

Jarvis, Jeff. 2013a. "Technopanic: The Movie." *BuzzMachine*, Apr. 12. https://buzzmachine.com/2013/04/12/technopanic-the-movie/.

Jarvis, Jeff. 2013b. "That's like investigating cameras . . ." X, Mar. 5. https://twitter.com/jeffjarvis/status/309123359772381184.

Jarvis, Jeff. 2019. "A Rising Moral Panic." *BuzzMachine*, Jan. 18. https://buzzmachine.com/2019/01/18/a-rising-moral-panic/.

Jeftovic, Mark E. 2017. "This Time Is Different Part 2: What Bitcoin Really Is." *HackerNoon*, Dec. 12. https://hackernoon.com/this-time-is-different-part-2-what-bitcoin-really-is-ae58c69b3bf0.

Jenkins, Henry, and David Thorburn, eds. 2003. *Democracy and New Media*. Cambridge, Mass.: MIT Press.

Jia, Jian, Ginger Zhe Jin, and Liad Wagman. 2018. "The Short-Run Effects of GDPR on Technology Venture Investment." National Bureau of Economic Research Working Paper, Nov. https://www.nber.org/papers/w25248.

Johns, Adrian. 2000. *The Nature of the Book: Print and Knowledge in the Making*. Chicago: University of Chicago Press.

Johnson, Ashley, and Daniel Castro. 2021. "How Other Countries Have Dealt with Intermediary Liability." Information Technology and Innovation Foundation, Feb. 22. https://itif.org/publications/2021/02/22/how-other-countries-have-dealt-intermediary-liability/.

Jones, Meg Leta. 2016. *Ctrl + Z: The Right to Be Forgotten*. New York: NYU Press.

Juskalian, Russ. 2008. "Interview with Clay Shirky, Part I: 'There's Always a New Luddism Whenever There's Change.'" *Columbia Journalism Review*, Dec. 19. https://archives.cjr.org/overload/interview_with_clay_shirky_par.php.

Kafka, Peter. 2014. "It's Over! Viacom and Google Settle YouTube Lawsuit." *Vox*, Mar. 18. https://www.vox.com/2014/3/18/11624656/its-over-viacom-and-google-settle-youtube-lawsuit.

Kahn, Jeremy. 2003. "The Man Who Would Have Us Bet on Terrorism—Not to Mention Discard Democracy and Cryogenically Freeze Our Heads—May Have a Point (About the Betting, We Mean)." *CNN Money,* Sep. 15. https://money.cnn.com/magazines/fortune/fortune_archive/2003/09/15/349149/index.htm.

Karr, Tim. 2021. "Net Neutrality Violations: A History of Abuse." *Free Press,* Jul. 9. https://www.freepress.net/blog/net-neutrality-violations-history-abuse.

Katz, Yarden. 2020. *Artificial Whiteness: Politics and Ideology in Artificial Intelligence.* New York: Columbia University Press.

Kaye, David. 2017. *Report of the Special Rapporteur on the Promotion and Protection of the Right to Freedom of Opinion and Expression.* United Nations Human Rights Council. https://digitallibrary.un.org/record/1304394?ln=en.

Keating, Joshua E. 2012. "How WikiLeaks Blew It." *Foreign Policy,* Aug. 16. https://foreignpolicy.com/2012/08/16/how-wikileaks-blew-it/.

Kerr, Orin. 2013. "*United States v. Auernheimer,* and Why I Am Representing Auernheimer Pro Bono on Appeal before the Third Circuit." *Volokh Conspiracy,* Mar. 21. https://volokh.com/2013/03/21/united-states-v-auernheimer-and-why-i-am-representing-auernheimer-pro-bono-on-appeal-before-the-third-circuit/.

Khanna, Derek. 2014. "The Conservative Case for Taking on the Copyright Lobby." *Business Insider,* Apr. 30. https://www.businessinsider.com/time-to-confront-the-copyright-lobby-2014-4.

Kharif, Olga. 2017. "The Bitcoin Whales: 1,000 People Who Own 40 Percent of the Market." *Bloomberg Businessweek,* Dec. 8. https://www.bloomberg.com/news/articles/2017-12-08/the-bitcoin-whales-1-000-people-who-own-40-percent-of-the-market.

King, Andrew A., and Baljir Baatartogtokh. 2015. "How Useful Is the Theory of Disruptive Innovation?" *MIT Sloan Management Review,* Sep. 15. https://sloanreview.mit.edu/article/how-useful-is-the-theory-of-disruptive-innovation/.

Kinsella, Stephen. 2008. *Against Intellectual Property.* Auburn, Ala.: Ludwig von Mises Institute.

Kinsella, Stephen. 2010. "Hoppe on Covenant Communities and Advocates of Alternative Lifestyles." StephenKinsella.com, May 26. https://www.stephankinsella.com/2010/05/hoppe-on-covenant-communities/.

Klein, Ezra. 2021. "The Way the Senate Melted Down over Crypto Is Very Revealing." *New York Times,* Aug. 12. https://www.nytimes.com/2021/08/12/opinion/senate-cryptocurrency.html.

Kobek, Jarret. 2016. *I Hate the Internet.* San Francisco: We Heard You Like Books.

Koenig, Bryan. 2013. "Facebook's Zuckerberg Gives Himself a Label." *CNN,* Sep. 18.

Kosseff, Jeff. 2017. "The Judge Who Shaped the Internet." In Goldman and Kosseff 2020, 57–60.

Kosseff, Jeff. 2019. *The Twenty-Six Words That Created the Internet.* Ithaca, N.Y.: Cornell University Press.

Kraus, Rachel. 2020. "Once Again, There Is No 'Anti-Conservative' Bias on Social Media." *Mashable,* Jul. 28. https://mashable.com/article/anti-conservative-bias-facebook.

Kravets, David. 2014. "Appeals Court Reverses Hacker/Troll 'Weev' Conviction and Sentence." *Ars Technica,* Apr. 11. https://arstechnica.com/tech-policy/2014/04/appeals -court-reverses-hackertroll-weev-conviction-and-sentence/.

Krotoszynski, Ronald J., Jr. 2016. *Privacy Revisited: A Global Perspective on the Right to Be Left Alone.* New York: Oxford University Press.

Kurtzleben, Danielle. 2017. "While Trump Touts Stock Market, Many Americans Are Left Out of the Conversation." *National Public Radio,* Mar. 1. https://www.npr.org/ 2017/03/01/517975766/while-trump-touts-stock-market-many-americans-left-out -of-the-conversation.

LaFraniere, Sharon. 2020. "Roger Stone Was in Contact with Julian Assange in 2017, Documents Show." *New York Times,* Apr. 29. https://www.nytimes.com/2020/04/29/ us/politics/roger-stone-julian-assange.html.

Land, Nick. 1996. "Shoot-Out at the Cyber Corral." *New Scientist,* Aug. 17: 41.

Land, Nick. 2013. "The Dark Enlightenment." Self-pub., n.p. https://web.archive.org/ web/20190928101326/http:/www.thedarkenlightenment.com/the-dark-enlighten ment-by-nick-land/.

Land, Nick. 2014a. "Exterminator." *Outside In,* Aug. 8. https://web.archive.org/web/20 141028044642/http:/www.xenosystems.net/exterminator/.

Land, Nick. 2014b. "Hyper-Racism." *Outside In,* Sep. 29. https://web.archive.org/ web/20190401033904/https:/www.xenosystems.net/hyper-racism/.

Land, Nick. 2018. *Crypto-Current: Bitcoin and Philosophy.* Self-pub., Oct. 31. https:// etscrivner.github.io/cryptocurrent/.

Landa, Ishay. 2010. *The Apprentice's Sorcerer: Liberal Tradition and Fascism.* Boston: Brill.

Landa, Ishay. 2019. *Fascism and the Masses: The Revolt against the Last Humans, 1848– 1945.* New York: Routledge.

La Roche, Julia. 2014. "Infamous Hacker 'Weev' Went on CNBC to Explain the Fas- cinating Hedge Fund He's about to Launch." *Business Insider,* Apr. 28. https://www .businessinsider.com/andrew-weev-auernheimer-hedge-fund-2014-4.

Larson, Max. Forthcoming. "Computer Center Sabotage: Luddism, Black Studies, and the Diversion of Technological Progress." *boundary 2.*

Leahy, Patrick. 2011. "Senate Judiciary Committee Unanimously Approves Bipartisan Bill to Crack Down on Rogue Websites." Press release, May 26. Last modified Dec. 2022. https://www.leahy.senate.gov/press/senate-judiciary-committee-unanimously -approves-bipartisan-bill-to-crack-down-on-rogue-websites.

Leahy, Patrick. 2012. "Senate Should Focus on Stopping Online Theft That Undercuts Economic Recovery." Press release, Jan. 23. Last modified Dec. 26, 2022. https:// www.leahy.senate.gov/press/leahy-senate-should-focus-on-stopping-online-theft -that-undercuts-economic-recovery.

Lee, Seung. 2016. "Is Facebook—and Zuckerberg—Liberal or Conservative? It's Com- plicated, Data Shows." *Newsweek,* May 11. https://www.newsweek.com/facebook -and-zuckerberg-liberal-or-conservative-its-complicated-data-shows-458823.

Leeper, Sarah Elizabeth. 2000. "The Game of Radiopoly: An Antitrust Perspective of Consolidation in the Radio Industry." *Federal Communications Law Journal* 52(2): 473–96. https://www.repository.law.indiana.edu/fclj/vol52/iss2/9.

Lemieux, Scott. 2021. "Glenn Greenwald Excited by Tucker Carlson's National Socialism." *Lawyers, Guns, and Money,* Mar. 4. https://www.lawyersgunsmoneyblog.com/2021/03/glenn-greenwald-excited-by-tucker-carlsons-national-socialism.

Lepore, Jill. 2010. *The Whites of Their Eyes: The Tea Party's Revolution and the Battle over American History.* Princeton, N.J.: Princeton University Press.

Lepore, Jill. 2014. "The Disruption Machine." *New Yorker,* Jun. 23. https://www.newyorker.com/magazine/2014/06/23/the-disruption-machine.

Lepore, Jill. 2020. *If Then: How the Simulmatics Corporation Invented the Future.* New York: Liveright.

Leslie, Stuart W. 1993. *The Cold War and American Science: The Military–Industrial–Academic Complex at MIT and Stanford.* New York: Columbia University Press.

"LessWrong." 2021. RationalWiki. Last modified Jun. 22. https://rationalwiki.org/w/index.php?title=LessWrong&oldid=2336968.

Lessig, Lawrence. 1999. *Code: And Other Laws of Cyberspace.* New York: Basic Books.

Lessig, Lawrence. 2004. *Free Culture: How Big Media Uses Technology and the Law to Lock Down Culture and Control Creativity.* New York: Penguin.

Lessig, Lawrence. 2006. *Code: And Other Laws of Cyberspace, Version 2.0.* New York: Basic Books.

Lessig, Lawrence. 2008. *Remix: Making Art and Commerce Thrive in the Hybrid Economy.* New York: Penguin.

Levin, Mark R. 2009. *Liberty and Tyranny: A Conservative Manifesto.* New York: Simon & Schuster.

Levine, Alexandra S. 2022. "Suicide Hotline Shares Data with For-Profit Spinoff, Raising Ethical Questions." *Politico,* Jan. 28. https://www.politico.com/news/2022/01/28/suicide-hotline-silicon-valley-privacy-debates-00002617.

Levine, Yasha. 2018a. "All EFF'd Up." *The Baffler,* Jul. https://thebaffler.com/salvos/all-effd-up-levine.

Levine, Yasha. 2018b. *Surveillance Valley: The Secret Military History of the Internet.* New York: PublicAffairs.

Levinson, Paul. 1999. *Digital McLuhan: A Guide to the Information Millennium.* New York: Routledge.

Levy, Karen E. C. 2017. "Book-Smart, Not Street-Smart: Blockchain-Based Smart Contracts and the Social Workings of Law." *Engaging Science, Technology, and Society* 3: 1–15. https://doi.org/10.17351/ests2017.107.

Levy, Pema. 2013. "The Woman Who Knows the NSA's Secrets." *Newsweek,* Oct. 4. https://www.newsweek.com/2013/10/04/woman-who-knows-nsas-secrets-238050.html.

Levy, Steven. 1994. "Battle of the Clipper Chip." *New York Times,* Jun. 12. https://www.nytimes.com/1994/06/12/magazine/battle-of-the-clipper-chip.html.

Levy, Steven. 2002. *Crypto: How the Code Rebels Beat the Government—Saving Privacy in the Digital Age.* New York: Penguin.

Levy, Steven. 2010. *Hackers: Heroes of the Computer Revolution.* 25th anniversary ed. Sebastopol, Calif.: O'Reilly Media.

Lewis, Janet I. 2014. "When Decentralization Leads to Recentralization: Subnational State Transformation in Uganda." *Regional and Federal Studies* 24(5): 571–88. https://doi.org/10.1080/13597566.2014.971771.

Liu, Alan. 2004. *The Laws of Cool: Knowledge Work and the Culture of Information.* Chicago: University of Chicago Press.

Loeb, Zachary. 2018a. "From Megatechnic Bribe to Megatechnic Blackmail: Mumford's 'Megamachine' after the Digital Turn." *b2o: An Online Journal,* 3(3) (Aug.). https://www.boundary2.org/2018/07/loeb/.

Loeb, Zachary [Librarian Shipwreck]. 2018b. "Why the Luddites Matter." *Librarian Shipwreck,* Jan. 18. https://librarianshipwreck.wordpress.com/2018/01/18/why-the-luddites-matter/.

Loeb, Zachary. 2021a. "The Magnificent Bribe." *Real Life,* Oct. 25. https://reallifemag.com/the-magnificent-bribe/.

Loeb, Zachary. 2021b. "Specters of Ludd (Review of Gavin Mueller, *Breaking Things at Work*)." *b2o Review,* Sep. 28. https://www.boundary2.org/2021/09/zachary-loeb-specters-of-ludd-review-of-gavin-mueller-breaking-things-at-work/.

Loomis, Erik. 2018. "Today on Tucker's White Power Hour. . . . Mr. Glenn Greenwald, Again!" *Lawyers, Guns, and Money,* Jun. 14. https://www.lawyersgunsmoneyblog.com/2018/06/today-tuckers-white-power-hour-mr-glenn-greenwald.

Lovink, Geert. 2006. "Trial and Error in Internet Governance: ICANN, the WSIS, and the Making of a Global Civil Society." In Jodi Dean, Jon W. Anderson, and Geert Lovink, eds., *Reformatting Politics: Information Technology and Global Civil Society.* New York: Routledge, 205–19.

Ludlow, Peter, ed. 1996. *High Noon on the Electronic Frontier: Conceptual Issues in Cyberspace.* Cambridge, Mass.: MIT Press.

Ludlow, Peter, ed. 2001. *Crypto Anarchy, Cyberstates, and Pirate Utopias.* Cambridge, Mass.: MIT Press.

Ludlow, Peter. 2013. "Hacktivists as Gadflies." *New York Times,* Apr. 13. https://archive.nytimes.com/opinionator.blogs.nytimes.com/2013/04/13/hacktivists-as-gadflies/.

Lyons, Matthew. 2017. *Ctrl-Alt-Delete: The Origins and Ideology of the Alternative Right.* Somerville, Mass.: Political Research Associates. https://politicalresearch.org/2017/01/20/ctrl-alt-delete-report-on-the-alternative-right.

Lytvynenko, Jane, Craig Silverman, and Alex Boutilier. 2019. "White Nationalist Groups Banned by Facebook Are Still on the Platform." *BuzzFeed News,* May 30. https://www.buzzfeednews.com/article/janelytvynenko/facebook-white-nationalist-ban-evaded.

Mac, Ryan. 2017. "Y Combinator Cuts Ties with Peter Thiel after Ending Part-Time Partner Program." *BuzzFeed News,* Nov. 17. https://www.buzzfeednews.com/article/ryanmac/y-combinator-cuts-ties-with-peter-thiel-ends-part-time.

Mac, Ryan, and Craig Silverman. 2021. "'Mark Changed the Rules': How Facebook Went Easy on Alex Jones and Other Right-Wing Figures." *BuzzFeed News,* Feb. 22. https://www.buzzfeednews.com/article/ryanmac/mark-zuckerberg-joel-kaplan-facebook-alex-jones.

"Machine Intelligence Research Institute." 2021. Wikipedia. Last modified Jun. 28. https://en.wikipedia.org/w/index.php?title=Machine_Intelligence_Research_Institute&oldid=1030850724.

Mack, Zachary. 2019. "Net Neutrality Was Repealed a Year Ago—What's Happened Since?" *The Verge,* Jul. 9. https://www.theverge.com/2019/7/9/20687903/net-neutrality-was-repealed-a-year-ago-whats-happened-since.

MacLean, Nancy. 2017. *Democracy in Chains: The Deep History of the Radical Right's Stealth Plan for America*. New York: Random House.

Madigan, Kevin. 2016. "Librarians' Contradictory Letter Reveals an Alarming Ignorance of the Copyright System." George Mason University Center for Intellectual Property x Innovation, Dec. 19. https://cip2.gmu.edu/2016/12/19/librarians-contradictory-letter-reveals-an-alarming-ignorance-of-the-copyright-system/.

Madore, P. H. 2017. "How Votem Intends to Democratize Democracy through Blockchain Technology." *CryptoCoins News*, Dec. 2. https://web.archive.org/web/201702 12204949/https:/www.cryptocoinsnews.com/votem-blockchain-democracy-voting/.

Madrigal, Alexis C. 2017. "The Dumb Fact of Google Money." *The Atlantic*, Aug. 30. https://www.theatlantic.com/technology/archive/2017/08/the-dumb-fact-of -google-money/538458/.

Madrigal, Alexis C., and Adrienne LaFrance. 2014. "Net Neutrality: A Guide to (and History of) a Contested Idea." *The Atlantic*, Apr. 25. https://www.theatlantic.com/ technology/archive/2014/04/the-best-writing-on-net-neutrality/361237/.

Malcolm, Jeremy. 2008. *Multi-Stakeholder Governance and the Internet Governance Forum*. Perth, Aust.: Terminus Press.

Manancourt, Vincent. 2022. "What's Wrong with the GDPR?" *Politico*, Jun. 15. https:// www.politico.eu/article/wojciech-wiewiorowski-gdpr-brussels-eu-data-protection -regulation-privacy/.

"Manila Principles on Intermediary Liability." 2015. Electronic Frontier Foundation, Mar. 24. https://www.eff.org/files/2015/10/31/manila_principles_1.0.pdf.

Mann, Michael. 2004. *Fascists*. New York: Cambridge University Press.

Mantelero, Alessandro. 2013. "The EU Proposal for a General Data Protection Regulation and the Roots of the 'Right to Be Forgotten.'" *Computer Law and Security Report* 29(3): 229–35. https://dx.doi.org/10.1016/j.clsr.2013.03.010.

Marantz, Andrew. 2019a. *Antisocial: Online Extremists, Techno-Utopians, and the Hijacking of the American Conversation*. New York: Viking.

Marantz, Andrew. 2019b. "The Dark Side of Techno-Utopianism." *New Yorker*, Sep. 23. https://www.newyorker.com/magazine/2019/09/30/the-dark-side-of-techno-utopianism.

Markoff, John. 2005. *What the Dormouse Said: How the Sixties Counterculture Shaped the Personal Computing Industry*. New York: Penguin.

Markoff, John. 2011. "MIT Media Lab Names New Director." *New York Times*, Apr. 25. https://www.nytimes.com/2011/04/26/science/26lab.html.

Marlow, Chad. 2021. "Why Net Neutrality Can't Wait." *ACLU News and Commentary*, Jul. 9. https://www.aclu.org/news/free-speech/why-net-neutrality-cant-wait.

"Martin Luther and Antisemitism." 2022. Wikipedia. Last modified Jul. 8. https://en .wikipedia.org/w/index.php?title=Martin_Luther_and_antisemitism&oldid=1097 006280.

Masnick, Mike. 2006. "The Importance of Zero in Destroying the Scarcity Myth of Economics." *TechDirt*, Nov. 8. https://www.techdirt.com/2006/11/08/the-importance -of-zero-in-destroying-the-scarcity-myth-of-economics/.

Masnick, Mike. 2007a. "Saying You Can't Compete with Free Is Saying You Can't Compete Period." *TechDirt,* Feb. 15. https://www.techdirt.com/2007/02/15/saying -you-cant-compete-with-free-is-saying-you-cant-compete-period/.

Masnick, Mike. 2007b. "The Grand Unified Theory on the Economics of Free." *Tech-Dirt,* May 3. https://www.techdirt.com/2007/05/03/grand-unified-theory-econom ics-free/.

Masnick, Mike. 2011a. "A Fifteenth Century Technopanic about the Horrors of the Printing Press." *TechDirt,* Feb. 25. https://www.techdirt.com/2011/02/25/fifteenth -century-technopanic-about-horrors-printing-press/.

Masnick, Mike. 2011b. "E-PARASITE Bill: 'The End of the Internet as We Know It.'" *TechDirt,* Oct. 27. https://www.techdirt.com/2011/10/27/e-parasites-bill-end-internet -as-we-know-it/.

Masnick, Mike. 2011c. "Yes, SOPA Breaks the Internet: By Breaking the Belief in Trust and Sharing That Is the Internet." *TechDirt,* Nov. 13. https://www.techdirt.com/2011/ 11/16/yes-sopa-breaks-internet-breaking-belief-trust-sharing-that-is-internet/.

Masnick, Mike. 2013a. "Copyright Lobby: The Public Has 'No Place in Policy Dis-cussions.'" *TechDirt,* Mar. 25. https://www.techdirt.com/2013/03/25/copyright-lobby -public-has-no-place-policy-discussions/.

Masnick, Mike. 2013b. "HBO: The Key to Combating Piracy Is to Make *Game of Thrones* More Available . . . Except Here." *TechDirt,* Mar. 7. https://www.techdirt .com/2013/03/07/hbo-key-to-combating-piracy-is-to-make-game-thrones-more-avail able-except-here/.

Masnick, Mike. 2013c. "Mike Masnick's Favorite *TechDirt* Posts of the Week." *Tech-Dirt,* May 4. https://www.techdirt.com/2013/05/04/mike-masnicks-favorite-techdirt -posts-week-2/.

Masnick, Mike. 2013d. "NSA Gave Employees Ridiculous 'Talking Points' to Spread among Friends and Family over the Holidays." *TechDirt,* Dec. 3. https://www.tech dirt.com/2013/12/03/nsa-gave-employees-ridiculous-talking-points-to-spread-among -friends-family-over-holidays/.

Masnick, Mike. 2013e. "The War on Computing: What Happens When Authorities Don't Understand Technology." *TechDirt,* Jan. 23. https://www.techdirt.com/2013/01/ 23/war-computing-what-happens-when-authorities-dont-understand-technology/.

Masnick, Mike. 2019. "How a Right to Be Forgotten Stifles a Free Press and Free Ex-pression." *TechDirt,* Oct. 11. https://www.techdirt.com/2019/10/11/how-right-to-be -forgotten-stifles-free-press-free-expression/.

Masnick, Mike. 2020a. "20 Years Ago Today: The Most Important Law on the Inter-net Was Signed, Almost by Accident." *TechDirt,* Feb. 8. https://www.techdirt.com/ 2016/02/08/20-years-ago-today-most-important-law-internet-was-signed-almost -accident/.

Masnick, Mike. 2020b. "Hello! You've Been Referred Here Because You're Wrong about Section 230 of the Communications Decency Act." *TechDirt,* Jun. 23. https:// www.techdirt.com/2020/06/23/hello-youve-been-referred-here-because-youre-wrong -about-section-230-communications-decency-act/.

Masnick, Mike. 2022. "EU Officials Finally Coming to Terms with the Fact That the GDPR Failed; but Now They Want to Make It Worse." *TechDirt,* Jun. 28. https://

www.techdirt.com/2022/06/28/eu-officials-finally-coming-to-terms-with-the-fact
-that-the-gdpr-failed-but-now-they-want-to-make-it-worse/.

Mason, Paul. 2012. *Why It's Kicking Off Everywhere: The New Global Revolutions.* New York: Verso.

Mathew, Ashwin J. 2016. "The Myth of the Decentralized Internet." *Internet Policy Review* 5(3) (Sep.). https://doi.org/10.14763/2016.3.425.

Matthews, Dylan. 2013. "Why I Resigned from the WikiLeaks Party." *The Guardian,* Aug. 21. https://www.theguardian.com/commentisfree/2013/aug/22/wikileaks-julian
-assange.

May, Timothy C. 1992. "The Crypto Anarchist Manifesto." Activism.net, Nov. 22. http://www.activism.net/cypherpunk/crypto-anarchy.html. Reprinted in Ludlow 2001, 61–63. [Talk written in 1988 and read at hacker and cypherpunk conferences in 1988, 1989, 1990, and 1992, and distributed to Cypherpunk mailing list.]

May, Timothy C. 1994. "The Cyphernomicon: Cypherpunks FAQ and More, Version 0.666." https://web.archive.org/web/20110922120111/http:/www.cypherpunks.to/faq/cyphernomicron/cyphernomicon.txt. [Post to Cypherpunk mailing list.]

May, Timothy C. 2005. "Commie Rag Praises MLK." Jan. 18. https://scruz.general.nar kive.com/29QgNUds/commie-rag-praises-mlk. [Post to scruz.general Usenet mailing list.]

Mayer, Jane. 2017. *Dark Money: The Hidden History of the Billionaires behind the Rise of the Radical Right.* New York: Anchor.

Mayer-Schönberger, Viktor. 2008. "Demystifying Lessig." *Wisconsin Law Review* 4, 713–46.

Mazmanian, Adam, and Lauren C. Williams. 2021. "The US Senate Joined the House of Representatives in Overturning President Trump's Veto of the Annual Defense Policy Bill in a Rare New Year's Day Vote." *Business of Federal Technology,* Jan. 1. https://www.defenseone.com/defense-systems/2021/01/defense-bill-prevails-over
-trump-veto/195098/.

McCarthy, Ryan. 2020. "'Outright Lies': Voting Misinformation Flourishes on Facebook." *ProPublica,* Jul. 16. https://www.propublica.org/article/outright-lies-voting
-misinformation-flourishes-on-facebook.

McCormack, John. 2011. "Ron Paul Praises Occupy Wall Street." *Washington Examiner,* Dec. 29. https://www.washingtonexaminer.com/?p=1254933.

McCullagh, Declan. 2000. "Crypto-Convict Won't Recant." *Wired,* Apr. 14. https://nettime.org/Lists-Archives/nettime-l-0004/msg00109.html.

McCullagh, Declan. 2001. "Cypherpunk's Free Speech Defense." *Wired,* Apr. 9. https://www.wired.com/2001/04/cypherpunks-free-speech-defense/.

McCullagh, Declan. 2018. "Markets in Assassination? Everybody Panic!" *Reason,* Jul. 27. https://reason.com/2018/07/27/markets-in-assassination-everybody-panic/.

McCulloch, Craig. 2019. "Christchurch Call: Tech Companies Overhaul Organization to Stop Terrorists Online." *Radio New Zealand,* Sep. 24. https://www.rnz.co.nz/news/political/399468/christchurch-call-tech-companies-overhaul-organisation-to-stop
-terrorists-online.

McElroy, Wendy. 2017. "An Introduction to 'The Satoshi Revolution.'" *FEE Stories,* Oct. 12. https://fee.org/articles/an-introduction-to-the-satoshi-revolution/.

McGonigal, Jane. 2011. *Reality Is Broken: Why Games Make Us Better and How They Can Change the World*. New York: Penguin.

McKinnon, John D., and Ryan Knutson. 2017. "Want to See a World Without Net Neutrality? Look at These Old Cellphone Plans." *Wall Street Journal*, Dec. 11. https://www.wsj.com/articles/mobile-wireless-market-might-be-our-post-net-neutrality-world-1512988200.

McKinnon, John D., and Brody Mullins. 2019. "Nancy Pelosi Pushes to Remove Legal Protections for Online Content in Trade Pact." *Wall Street Journal*, Dec. 4. https://www.wsj.com/articles/nancy-pelosi-pushes-to-remove-legal-protections-for-online-content-in-trade-pact-11575503157?.

McLuhan, Marshall. 1962. *The Gutenberg Galaxy: The Making of Typographic Man*. Toronto: University of Toronto Press.

McLuhan, Marshall. (1964) 1994. *Understanding Media: The Extensions of Man*. Cambridge, Mass.: MIT Press.

McNeil, Joanne. 2022. "Crisis Text Line and the Silicon Valleyfication of Everything." *Motherboard*, Feb. 10. https://www.vice.com/en/article/wxdpym/crisis-text-line-and-the-silicon-valleyfication-of-everything.

Miller, Cassie. 2022. "SPLC Poll Finds Substantial Support for 'Great Replacement' Theory and Other Hard-Right Ideas." Southern Poverty Law Center, Jun. 1. https://www.splcenter.org/news/2022/06/01/poll-finds-support-great-replacement-hard-right-ideas.

Mirowski, Philip. 2002. *Machine Dreams: Economics Becomes a Cyborg Science*. New York: Cambridge University Press.

Mirowski, Philip. 2009. "Defining Neoliberalism." In Mirowski and Plehwe 2009, 417–55.

Mirowski, Philip. 2013. *Never Let a Serious Crisis Go to Waste: How Neoliberalism Survived the Financial Meltdown*. New York: Verso.

Mirowski, Philip. 2017. "What Is Science Critique? Lessig, Latour." In David Tyfield, Rebecca Lave, Samuel Randalls, and Charles Thorpe, eds., *The Routledge Handbook of the Political Economy of Science*. New York, Routledge, 429–50.

Mirowski, Philip. 2018. "The Future(s) of Open Science." *Social Studies of Science* 48(2): 171–203. https://doi.org/10.1177/0306312718772086.

Mirowski, Philip. 2019. "Hell Is Truth Seen Too Late." *boundary 2* 46(1) (Feb.): 1–53. https://doi.org/10.1215/01903659-7271327.

Mirowski, Philip, and Dieter Plehwe, eds. 2009. *The Road from Mont Pèlerin: The Making of the Neoliberal Thought Collective*. Cambridge, Mass.: Harvard University Press.

Mirowski, Philip, Jeremy Walker, and Antoinette Abboud. 2013. "Beyond Denial." *Overland Literary Journal* 213 (Autumn). https://overland.org.au/previous-issues/issue-210/feature-philip-mirowski-jeremy-walker-antoinette-abboud/.

Moffitt, Mike. 2018. "How a Racist Genius Created Silicon Valley by Being a Terrible Boss." *SFGate*, Aug. 21. https://www.sfgate.com/tech/article/Silicon-Valley-Shockley-racist-semiconductor-lab-13164228.php.

Moglen, Eben. 2011. "Liberation by Software." *The Guardian*, Feb. 24. https://www.theguardian.com/commentisfree/cifamerica/2011/feb/24/internet-freedomofinformation.

Moglen, Eben. 2013. "Snowden and the Future." Four-part lecture series delivered at Columbia Law School, Oct.–Dec. http://snowdenandthefuture.info/index.html.

Moon, David, Patrick Ruffini, and David Segal, eds. 2013. *Hacking Politics: How Geeks, Progressives, the Tea Party, Gamers, Anarchists and Suits Teamed Up to Defeat SOPA and Save the Internet.* New York: OR Books.

Morar, David, and Bruna Martins dos Santos. 2020. "Online Content Moderation Lessons from Outside the US." Brookings Institution, Jun. 17. https://www.brookings.edu/articles/online-content-moderation-lessons-from-outside-the-u-s/.

Morozov, Evgeny. 2011a. "Don't Be Evil." *New Republic,* Jul. 13. https://newrepublic.com/article/91916/google-schmidt-obama-gates-technocrats.

Morozov, Evgeny. 2011b. *The Net Delusion: The Dark Side of Internet Freedom.* New York: PublicAffairs.

Morozov, Evgeny. 2013a. "Ghosts in the Machine." *Der Feuilleton* (blog), Oct. 10. Last modified Sep. 21, 2023. https://blogs.sueddeutsche.de/feuilletonist/2013/10/10/ghosts-in-the-machines/.

Morozov, Evgeny. 2013b. "How to Stop a Sharknado." *Die Zeit,* Oct. 2. https://www.zeit.de/digital/internet/2013-10/morozov-sharknado-chomsky-foucault.

Morozov, Evgeny. 2013c. "Open and Closed." *New York Times,* Mar. 16. https://www.nytimes.com/2013/03/17/opinion/sunday/morozov-open-and-closed.html.

Morozov, Evgeny. 2013d. *To Save Everything, Click Here: The Folly of Technological Solutionism.* New York: PublicAffairs.

Morrison, Aimée Hope. 2009. "An Impossible Future: John Perry Barlow's 'Declaration of the Independence of Cyberspace.'" *New Media and Society* 11(1–2): 53–72.

MSI Integrity. 2020. *Not Fit-for-Purpose: The Grand Experiment of Multi-stakeholder Initiatives in Corporate Accountability, Human Rights and Global Governance.* Berkeley, Calif.: Institute for Multi-Stakeholder Initiative Integrity. https://www.msi-integrity.org/wp-content/uploads/2020/07/MSI_Not_Fit_For_Purpose_FORWEBSITE.FINAL_.pdf.

Mudde, Cas, and Cristóbal Rovira Kaltwasser. 2017. *Populism: A Very Short Introduction.* New York: Oxford University Press.

Mueller, Gavin. 2015. "Trickster Makes This Web: The Ambiguous Politics of Anonymous." *b2o Review,* Feb. 11. https://www.boundary2.org/2015/02/trickster-makes-this-web-the-ambiguous-politics-of-anonymous/.

Mueller, Gavin. 2019. *Media Piracy in the Cultural Economy: Intellectual Property and Labor under Neoliberal Restructuring.* New York: Routledge.

Mueller, Gavin. 2021. *Breaking Things at Work: The Luddites Are Right about Why You Hate Your Job.* New York: Verso.

Mueller, Milton. 2010. *Networks and States: The Global Politics of Internet Governance.* Cambridge, Mass.: MIT Press.

Mumford, Lewis. (1934) 2010. *Technics and Civilization.* Chicago: University of Chicago Press.

Mumford, Lewis. 1971. *Technics and Human Development: The Myth of the Machine, Vol. I.* New York: Harcourt Brace Jovanovich.

Mumford, Lewis. 1974. *Pentagon of Power: The Myth of the Machine, Vol. II.* New York: Harcourt Brace Jovanovich.

Murphy, Laura W., et al. 2020. "Facebook Civil Rights Audit." Facebook, Jul. 8. https://about.fb.com/wp-content/uploads/2020/07/Civil-Rights-Audit-Final-Report.pdf.

Murse, Tom. 2020. "Is Mark Zuckerberg a Democrat or a Republican?" *ThoughtCo,* Jul. 4. https://www.thoughtco.com/members-of-congress-supported-by-facebook-33 67615.

Nakamoto, Satoshi. 2009. "Bitcoin: A Peer-to-Peer Electronic Cash System." Bitcoin.org, May 24. https://bitcoin.org/bitcoin.pdf.

Negroponte, Nicholas. 1996. *Being Digital.* New York: Vintage.

Neiwert, David. 2009. *The Eliminationists: How Hate Talk Radicalized the American Right.* New York: Routledge.

Neiwert, David. 2018. *Alt-America: The Rise of the Radical Right in the Age of Trump.* New York: Verso.

"Net Neutrality." 2022. Wikipedia. Last modified Aug. 8. https://en.wikipedia.org/w/index.php?title=Net_neutrality&oldid=1103227281.

Nevett, Joshua. 2021. "Nevada Smart City: A Millionaire's Plan to Create a Local Government." *BBC News,* Mar. 18. https://www.bbc.com/news/world-us-canada-56409 924.

Newfield, Christopher. 2013. "Corporate Open Source: Intellectual Property and the Struggle over Value." *Radical Philosophy* 181 (Sep./Oct.): 6–11.

Newhoff, David. 2012. "Anti-Piracy Battle Reveals Dysfunctional Thinking." *The Hill,* Jan. 18. https://thehill.com/blogs/congress-blog/technology/103104-anti-piracy-battle-reveals-dysfunctional-thinking/.

Newhoff, David. 2020. "Internet Archive Uses Pandemic to Justify Looting." *Illusion of More,* Mar. 29. https://illusionofmore.com/internet-archive-uses-pandemic-to-justify-looting/.

Newhoff, David. 2021. "Why Is the Press So Bumfuzzled about Copyright Issues?" *Illusion of More,* Dec. 27. https://illusionofmore.com/why-is-the-press-so-bumfuzzled-about-copyright-issues/.

Newman, Russell A. 2019. *The Paradoxes of Network Neutralities.* Cambridge, Mass.: MIT Press.

Newton, Casey. 2020. "Mark in the Middle." *The Verge,* Sep. 23. https://www.theverge.com/c/21444203/facebook-leaked-audio-zuckerberg-trump-pandemic-blm.

New Zealand Ministry of Foreign Affairs and Trade. 2019. "Christchurch Call to Eliminate Terrorist and Violent Extremist Content Online." https://www.christchurchcall.com/.

Noys, Benjamin. 2014. *Malign Velocities: Accelerationism and Capitalism.* Winchester, UK: Zero Books.

O'Brien, Danny. 2018. "The Year of the GDPR: 2018's Most Famous Privacy Regulation in Review." Electronic Frontier Foundation, Dec. 28. https://www.eff.org/es/deeplinks/2018/12/year-gdpr-2018s-most-famous-privacy-regulation-review.

O'Brien, Luke. 2017. "The Making of an American Nazi." *The Atlantic,* Dec. https://www.theatlantic.com/magazine/archive/2017/12/the-making-of-an-american-nazi/544119/.

O'Hagan, Andrew. 2016. "The Satoshi Affair." *London Review of Books* 38(13) (Jun. 30). https://www.lrb.co.uk/the-paper/v38/n13/andrew-o-hagan/the-satoshi-affair.

O'Neill, Patrick Howell. 2017. "Tor's Ex-Director: 'The Criminal Use of Tor Has Become Overwhelming.'" *CyberScoop,* May 22. https://cyberscoop.com/tor-dark-web-andrew-lewman-securedrop/.

Oberhaus, Daniel. 2017. "Nearly All of Wikipedia Is Written by Just 1 Percent of Its Editors." *Vice,* Nov. 7. https://www.vice.com/en/article/7x47bb/wikipedia-editors-elite-diversity-foundation.

Ochigame, Rodrigo. 2019. "The Invention of 'Ethical AI': How Big Tech Manipulates Academia to Avoid Regulation." *The Intercept,* Dec. 20. https://theintercept.com/2019/12/20/mit-ethical-ai-artificial-intelligence/.

Ogbunu, C. Brandon. 2020. "Don't Be Fooled by Covid-19 Carpetbaggers." *Wired,* Apr. 5. https://www.wired.com/story/opinion-dont-be-fooled-by-covid-19-carpetbaggers/.

Ogundeji, Olusegun. 2017. "ETH Proponents: Ethereum Will Democratize, Build Trust, and Make Governments Transparent." *Cointelegraph,* Jan. 20. Last modified May 28, 2023. https://cointelegraph.com/news/eth-proponents-ethereum-will-democratize-build-trust-and-make-governments-transparent.

Ong, Walter S. J. 1982. *Orality and Literacy: The Technologizing of the Word.* New York: Routledge.

Oreskes, Naomi, and Erik M. Conway. 2010. *Merchants of Doubt: How a Handful of Scientists Obscured the Truth on Issues from Tobacco Smoke to Global Warming.* New York: Bloomsbury.

Oreskovic, Alexei. 2019. "Martin Luther King's Daughter Slams Mark Zuckerberg for Invoking the Civil Rights Movement and Said 'Disinformation Campaigns' Led to MLK's Killing." *Business Insider,* Oct. 17. https://www.businessinsider.com/bernice-king-daughter-mlk-criticizes-mark-zuckerberg-2019-10.

Packer, George. 2013. "Change the World." *New Yorker,* May 20. https://www.newyorker.com/magazine/2013/05/27/change-the-world.

Packer, George. 2014. "The Errors of Edward Snowden and Glenn Greenwald." *Prospect,* May 22. https://www.prospectmagazine.co.uk/essays/46323/the-errors-of-edward-snowden-and-glenn-greenwald.

Parker, Ian. 2018. "The Bane of Their Resistance." *New Yorker,* Aug. 27. https://www.newyorker.com/magazine/2018/09/03/glenn-greenwald-the-bane-of-their-resistance.

Parks, Miles. 2021. "Outrage as a Business Model: How Ben Shapiro Is Using Facebook to Build an Empire." *All Things Considered,* Jul. 19. https://www.npr.org/2021/07/19/1013793067/outrage-as-a-business-model-how-ben-shapiro-is-using-facebook-to-build-an-empire.

Pasquale, Frank. 2014. "The Dark Market for Personal Data." *New York Times,* Oct. 16. https://www.nytimes.com/2014/10/17/opinion/the-dark-market-for-personal-data.html.

Pasquale, Frank. 2015. "Reforming the Law of Reputation." *Loyola University Chicago Law Journal* 47, 515–30. https://lawecommons.luc.edu/luclj/vol47/iss2/6.

Pasquale, Frank. 2016. *The Black Box Society: The Secret Algorithms That Control Money and Information.* Cambridge, Mass.: Harvard University Press.

Pasquale, Frank. 2020. *New Laws of Robotics: Defending Human Expertise in the Age of AI.* Cambridge, Mass.: Harvard University Press.

Pasquale, Frank. 2021. "Licensure as Data Governance: Moving toward an Industrial Policy for Artificial Intelligence." Knight First Amendment Institute at Columbia University, Sep. 28. https://knightcolumbia.org/content/licensure-as-data-governance.

Pattillo, Ulric. 2021. "Financial Protestants: How the Bitcoin Revolution Resembles the Reformation." *Bitcoin Magazine,* Jul. 28. https://bitcoinmagazine.com/culture/why-bitcoin-resembles-the-protestant-reformation.

Paxton, Robert O. 2004. *The Anatomy of Fascism.* New York: Knopf.

Peck, Robert. 2020. "The Hate-Fueled Rise of r/The_Donald—and Its Epic Takedown." *Wired,* Aug. 3. https://www.wired.com/story/the-hate-fueled-rise-of-rthe-donald-and-its-epic-takedown/.

"Peer-to-Peer." 2021. Wikipedia. Last modified Jul. 15. https://en.wikipedia.org/w/index.php?title=Peer-to-peer&oldid=1033755835.

Pein, Corey. 2014. "Mouthbreathing Machiavellis Dream of a Silicon Reich." *The Baffler,* May 19. https://thebaffler.com/latest/mouthbreathing-machiavellis.

Pein, Corey. 2016. "Everybody Freeze!" *The Baffler,* Mar. https://thebaffler.com/salvos/everybody-freeze-pein.

Pein, Corey. 2017. "The Moldbug Variations." *The Baffler,* Oct. 9. https://thebaffler.com/latest/the-moldbug-variations-pein.

Pein, Corey. 2018. *Live Work Work Work Die: A Journey into the Savage Heart of Silicon Valley.* New York: Metropolitan Books.

Pepitone, Julianne. 2012. "SOPA Explained: What It Is and Why It Matters." *CNN Money,* Jan. 20. https://money.cnn.com/2012/01/17/technology/sopa_explained/.

Perens, Bruce. 2005. "The Emerging Economic Paradigm of Open Source." *First Monday* S2 (Oct. 3). https://doi.org/10.5210/fm.v0i0.1470.

Pettit, Thomas. 2012. "Bracketing the Gutenberg Parenthesis." *Explorations in Media Ecology* 11(2) (Aug.): 95–114. https://doi.org/10.1386/eme.11.2.95_1.

Pettit, Thomas. 2019. "The Gutenberg Parenthesis Research Forum: An Internet Archive." University of Southern Denmark Department for the Study of Culture. https://www.academia.edu/38284215/The_Gutenberg_Parenthesis_Research_Forum_an_Internet_Archive.

Pickard, Victor. 2014. *America's Battle for Media Democracy: The Triumph of Corporate Libertarianism and the Future of Media Reform.* New York: Cambridge University Press.

Pickard, Victor, and David Elliot Berman. 2019. *After Net Neutrality: A New Deal for the Digital Age.* New Haven, Conn.: Yale University Press.

Plant, Sadie, and Nick Land. 1994. "Cyberpositive." In Matthew Fuller, ed., *Unnatural: Techno-Theory for a Contaminated Culture.* London: Underground, n.p.

Popper, Karl. 1945. *The Open Society and Its Enemies.* 2 vols. London: Routledge.

Popper, Nathaniel. 2018. "A Cryptocurrency Millionaire Wants to Build a Utopia in Nevada." *New York Times,* Nov. 1. https://www.nytimes.com/2018/11/01/technology/nevada-bitcoin-blockchain-society.html.

Postigo, Hector. 2012. *The Digital Rights Movement: The Role of Technology in Subverting Digital Copyright.* Cambridge, Mass.: MIT Press.

Potter, Claire. 2021. "Glenn Greenwald Punches Down." *Public Seminar,* Apr. 1. https://publicseminar.org/essays/glenn-greenwald-punches-down/.

Poulsen, Kevin. 2018. "Defector: WikiLeaks 'Will Lie to Your Face.'" *Daily Beast,* May 9. https://www.thedailybeast.com/defector-wikileaks-will-lie-to-your-face.

Poulsen, Kevin. 2019. "Mueller Report: Assange Smeared Seth Rich to Cover for Russians." *Daily Beast,* Apr. 18. https://www.thedailybeast.com/mueller-report-julian -assange-smeared-seth-rich-to-cover-for-russians.

Powers, Shawn M., and Michael Jablonski. 2015. *The Real Cyber War: The Political Economy of Internet Freedom.* Urbana: University of Illinois Press.

Powles, Julia. 2014. "Jimmy Wales Is Wrong: We Do Have a Personal Right to Be Forgotten." *The Guardian,* Aug. 8. https://www.theguardian.com/technology/2014/aug/ 08/jimmy-wales-right-to-be-forgotten-wikipedia.

Powles, Julia. 2015. "Results May Vary: Border Disputes on the Frontlines of the 'Right to Be Forgotten.'" *Slate,* Feb. 25. https://www.slate.com/articles/technology/future_ tense/2015/02/google_and_the_right_to_be_forgotten_should_delisting_be_global _or_local.html.

Powles, Julia, and Enrique Chaparro. 2015. "How Google Determined Our Right to Be Forgotten." *The Guardian,* Feb. 18. https://www.theguardian.com/technology/ 2015/feb/18/the-right-be-forgotten-google-search.

Prasanna. 2022. "What Is Monero (XMR) Crypto? Is Edward Snowden behind This Project Too?" *CryptoTicker,* Jul. 28. https://cryptoticker.io/en/what-is-monero-xmr -edward-snowden/.

"PROTECT IP Act." 2020. Wikipedia. Last modified Sep. 11. https://en.wikipedia.org/ w/index.php?title=PROTECT_IP_Act&oldid=977889274.

"Protests against SOPA and PIPA." 2020. Wikipedia. Last modified Sep. 29. https:// en.wikipedia.org/w/index.php?title=Protests_against_SOPA_and_PIPA&oldid=9 81004629.

Prud'homme, Rémy. 1995. "The Dangers of Decentralization." *World Bank Research Observer* 10(2) (Aug.): 201–20.

Purnell, Newley, and Jeff Horwitz. 2021. "Facebook Services Are Used to Spread Religious Hatred in India, Internal Documents Show." *Wall Street Journal,* Oct. 23. https://www.wsj.com/articles/facebook-services-are-used-to-spread-religious-hatred -in-india-internal-documents-show-11635016354?mod=article_inline.

Purtill, James. 2019. "Fuelled by a Toxic, Alt-Right Echo Chamber, Christchurch Shooter's Views Were Celebrated Online." *TripleJ Hack,* Mar. 15. https://www.abc .net.au/triplej/programs/hack/christchurch-shooters-views-were-celebrated-online/ 10907056.

"Quick Facts." n.d. United States Census Bureau. Last modified Jan. 23, 2024. https:// www.census.gov/quickfacts/fact/table/US/HSD410219.

Rao, Leena. 2011. "Wael Ghonim: If You Want to Liberate a Government, Give Them the Internet." *TechCrunch,* Feb. 11. https://techcrunch.com/2011/02/11/wael-ghonim -if-you-want-to-liberate-a-government-give-them-the-internet/.

Rasmussen, Scott, and Douglas Schoen. 2010. *Mad as Hell: How the Tea Party Movement Is Fundamentally Remaking Our Two-Party System.* New York: HarperCollins.

Ratcliffe, Jonathan. 2020. "Rebooting the Leviathan: NRx and the Millennium." *b2o: An Online Journal* 4(2) (Apr. 2). https://www.boundary2.org/2020/04/jonathan-rat cliffe-rebooting-the-leviathan-nrx-and-the-millennium/.

Raymond, Eric S. 1999. *The Cathedral and the Bazaar: Musings on Linux and Open Source by an Accidental Revolutionary.* Sebastopol, Calif.: O'Reilly Media.

Raymond, Eric S. 2012. "Why I Think RMS Is a Fanatic, and Why That Matters." Armed and Dangerous, Jun. 11. http://esr.ibiblio.org/?p=4386.

Read, Max. 2011. "What Happened to Encyclopedia Dramatica?" *Gawker,* Apr. 16. https://web.archive.org/web/20110514145854/http:/gawker.com/5792738/what-hap pened-to-encyclopedia-dramatica.

Redman, Jamie. 2020. "$2 Trillion for Surveillance Capitalism: US Government Promises $1,200 to Every American." Bitcoin.com, Mar. 25. https://web.archive.org/ web/20200329001553/https:/news.bitcoin.com/2-trillion-surveillance-capitalism -government-promises-1200/.

Reitman, Rainey. 2011. "Bitcoin: A Step toward Censorship-Resistant Digital Currency." Electronic Frontier Foundation, Jan. 20. https://www.eff.org/deeplinks/2011/ 01/bitcoin-step-toward-censorship-resistant.

Reitman, Rainey. 2021. "The Cryptocurrency Surveillance Provision Buried in the Infrastructure Bill Is a Disaster for Digital Privacy." Electronic Frontier Foundation, Aug. 2. https://www.eff.org/deeplinks/2021/08/cryptocurrency-surveillance-provision -buried-infrastructure-bill-disaster-digital.

Renda, Matthew. 2021. "Ninth Circuit Deals 3rd Blow to NSA Spying Case." *Courthouse News,* Aug. 17. https://www.courthousenews.com/nsa-spying-case-is-dismissed -again/.

Reynolds, Glenn. 2006. *An Army of Davids: How Markets and Technology Empower Ordinary People to Beat Big Media, Big Government, and Other Goliaths.* New York: Thomas Nelson.

Reynolds, Simon. 2005. "Simon's Interview with CCRU (1998)." *K-punk,* Jan. 20. http://k-punk.abstractdynamics.org/archives/004807.html.

Riccardi, Nicholas. 2021. "Zuckerberg's Cash Fuels GOP Suspicion and New Election Rules." *AP News,* Aug. 8. https://apnews.com/article/elections-facebook-mark-zuck erberg-d034c4c1f5a9fa3fb02aa9898493c708.

Rider, Karina, and David Murakami Wood. 2019. "Condemned to Connection? Network Communitarianism in Mark Zuckerberg's 'Facebook Manifesto.'" *New Media and Society* 21(3) (Mar.): 639–54. https://doi.org/10.1177/1461444818804772.

Riley, Duncan. 2015. "Edward Snowden: Bitcoin Is Flawed but the Basic Principles Combined with Tokenization Are Interesting." *SiliconANGLE,* Aug. 16. https://sili conangle.com/2015/08/16/edward-snowden-bitcoin-is-flawed-but-the-basic-princi ples-combined-with-tokenization-are-interesting/.

Rivlin, Gary. 2002. "The Madness of King George." *Wired,* Jul. 1. https://www.wired .com/2002/07/gilder-6/.

Roberts, Russ. 2009. "Jimmy Wales on Wikipedia." *EconTalk,* Mar. 9. https://www .econtalk.org/wales-on-wikipedia/.

Roberts, Sarah. 2019. *Behind the Screen: Content Moderation in the Shadows of Social Media.* New Haven, Conn.: Yale University Press.

Robinson, Nathan J. 2021. "How to End Up Serving the Right." *Current Affairs,* Jun. 17. https://www.currentaffairs.org/2021/06/how-to-end-up-serving-the-right.

"Roko's Basilisk." 2021. RationalWiki. Last modified May 10. https://rationalwiki.org/ w/index.php?title=Roko%27s_basilisk&oldid=2323690.

Romano, Aja. 2018. "A New Law Intended to Curb Sex Trafficking Threatens the Future of the Internet as We Know It." *Vox,* Jul. 2. https://www.vox.com/culture/2018/4/13/17172762/fosta-sesta-backpage-230-internet-freedom.

Romm, Tony. 2019. "Zuckerberg: Standing for Voice and Free Expression." *Washington Post,* Oct. 17. https://www.washingtonpost.com/technology/2019/10/17/zuckerberg-standing-voice-free-expression/.

Rosenbach, Marcel, and Holger Stark. 2010. "'The Only Option Left for Me Is an Orderly Departure': Interview with 'Daniel Schmitt.'" *Der Spiegel,* Sep. 27. https://www.spiegel.de/international/germany/wikileaks-spokesman-quits-the-only-option-left-for-me-is-an-orderly-departure-a-719619.html.

Ross, Alexander Reid. 2017. *Against the Fascist Creep.* Chico, Calif.: AK Press.

Ross, Janell. 2019. "Civil Rights Leaders Criticize Zuckerberg's Free Speech Address." *NBC News,* Oct. 17. https://www.nbcnews.com/news/nbcblk/civil-rights-leaders-rebuke-zuckerberg-s-free-speech-address-n1068461.

Roszak, Theodore. (1969) 1995. *The Making of a Counter Culture: Reflections on the Technocratic Society and Its Youthful Opposition.* 2nd ed. Berkeley: University of California Press.

Roszak, Theodore. (1986a) 1994. *The Cult of Information: A Neo-Luddite Treatise on High-Tech, Artificial Intelligence, and the True Art of Thinking.* 2nd ed. Berkeley: University of California Press.

Roszak, Theodore. 1986b. *From Satori to Silicon Valley: San Francisco and the American Counterculture.* San Francisco: Don't Call It Frisco Press.

Rothbard, Murray. 2000. *Egalitarianism as a Revolt against Nature, and Other Essays.* Auburn, Ala.: Ludwig von Mises Institute.

Rozen, Jacob. 2021. "Code Isn't Law—Law Is Law." *CoinGeek,* Mar. 24. https://coingeek.com/code-isnt-law-law-is-law/.

Rozsa, Matthew. 2017. "Is Julian Assange a Misogynist, or Just Seething with Rage against Hillary Clinton? We Wonder." *Salon,* Apr. 16. https://www.salon.com/2017/04/16/is-julian-assange-a-misogynist-or-just-seething-with-rage-against-hillary-clinton-we-wonder/.

Ruane, Kathleen Anne. 2014. *Freedom of Speech and Press: Exceptions to the First Amendment.* Washington, D.C.: Congressional Research Service. https://sgp.fas.org/crs/misc/95-815.pdf.

Sacasas, L. M. 2013a. *The Borg Complex* (Tumblr blog). Last modified Sep. 11. https://borgcomplex.tumblr.com/.

Sacasas, L. M. 2013b. "Borg Complex: A Primer." *Frailest Thing,* Mar. 1. https://thefrailestthing.com/2013/03/01/borg-complex-a-primer/.

Sandifer, Elizabeth. 2017. *Neoreaction A Basilisk: Essays on and around the Alt Right.* n.p., Eruditorum Press.

Sankin, Aaron. 2021. "What Does Facebook Mean When It Says It Supports 'Internet Regulations'?" *The Markup,* Sep. 16. https://themarkup.org/the-breakdown/2021/09/16/what-does-facebook-mean-when-it-says-it-supports-internet-regulations.

Sauerberg, Lars Ole. 2009. "The Encyclopedia and the Gutenberg Parenthesis." Paper presented at "Stone and Papyrus: Storage and Transmission," Media in Transition 6, Cambridge, Mass., Apr. 24–26. https://web.mit.edu/comm-forum/legacy/mit6/papers/sauerberg.pdf.

"Save the Internet: Join Us." 2007. SavetheInternet.com Coalition. Last modified Oct. 12. https://web.archive.org/web/20071012025915/http:/www.savetheinternet.com/=coalition.

"Save the Internet: Members." 2007. SavetheInternet.com Coalition. Last modified Oct. 12. https://web.archive.org/web/20071011164621/http:/savetheinternet.com/=members.

Schmidt, Eric, and Jared Cohen. 2013. *The New Digital Age: Reshaping the Future of People, Nations, and Business.* New York: Knopf.

Schneider, Nathan. 2019. "Decentralization: An Incomplete Ambition." *Journal of Cultural Economy* 12(4): 265–85. https://doi.org/10.1080/17530350.2019.1589553.

Schneiderman, Eric T. 2017. "A.G. Schneiderman: I Will Sue to Stop Illegal Rollback of Net Neutrality." Press release, New York Office of the Attorney General, Dec. 14. https://ag.ny.gov/press-release/2017/ag-schneiderman-i-will-sue-stop-illegal-roll back-net-neutrality.

Schradie, Jen. 2019. *The Revolution That Wasn't: How Digital Activism Favors Conservatives.* Cambridge, Mass.: Harvard University Press.

Schrager, Nick. 2017. "WikiLeaks Founder Julian Assange Is an Egomaniacal, Sexist Creep in *Risk.*" *Daily Beast,* May 6. https://www.thedailybeast.com/wikileaks -founder-julian-assange-is-an-egomaniacal-sexist-creep-in-risk.

Schriever, Leigh Anne. 2018. "Uber and Lyft Lobby Their Way to Deregulation and Preemption." *Regulatory Review,* Jun. 28. https://www.theregreview.org/2018/06/28/ schriever-uber-lyft-lobby-deregulation-preemption/.

Schrodt, Paul. 2016. "Edward Snowden Just Made an Impassioned Argument for Why Privacy Is the Most Important Right." *Business Insider,* Sep. 15. https://www.business insider.com/edward-snowden-privacy-argument-2016-9.

Schwarz, Mattathias. 2008. "The Trolls among Us." *New York Times,* Aug. 3. https:// www.nytimes.com/2008/08/03/magazine/03trolls-t.html.

Scott, Allen. 2018. "Vitalik Buterin: I Quite Regret Adopting the Term 'Smart Contracts' for Ethereum." *Bitcoinist,* Oct. 14. https://bitcoinist.com/vitalik-buterin-ethe reum-regret-smart-contracts/.

Seetharaman, Deepa, and Emily Glazer. 2020. "How Mark Zuckerberg Learned Politics." *Wall Street Journal,* Oct. 16. https://www.wsj.com/articles/how-mark-zucker berg-learned-politics-11602853200.

Segal, David. 2013. "A Moment for Aaron." In Moon, Ruffini, and Segal 2013, vii–xiv.

Selinger, Evan, and Woodrow Hartzog. 2019. "What Happens When Employers Can Read Your Facial Expressions?" *New York Times,* Oct. 17. https://www.nytimes.com/ 2019/10/17/opinion/facial-recognition-ban.html.

Selwyn, Neil. 2013. *Education in a Digital World: Global Perspectives on Technology and Education.* New York: Routledge.

Shapiro, Gary. 2011. "The Copyright Lobby Comeuppance." *The Hill,* Dec. 11. https:// thehill.com/blogs/congress-blog/technology/100024-the-copyright-lobby-come uppance/.

Shaw, Aaron. 2012. "Centralised and Decentralised Gatekeeping in an Open Online Collective." *Politics and Society* 40, 349–88, https://doi.org/10.1177/0032329212449009.

Shaw, Aaron, and Benjamin Mako Hill. 2014. "Laboratories of Oligarchy? How the Iron Law Extends to Peer Production." *Journal of Communication* 64(2) (Apr.): 215–38. https://doi.org/10.1111/jcom.12082.

Shaw, Tamsin. 2018. "Edward Snowden Reconsidered." *New York Review of Books,* Sep. 13. https://www.nybooks.com/online/2018/09/13/edward-snowden-reconsidered/.

Sherman, Cary. 2012. "What Wikipedia Won't Tell You." *New York Times,* Feb. 7. https://www.nytimes.com/2012/02/08/opinion/what-wikipedia-wont-tell-you.html.

Shillingsburg, Peter L. 2006. *From Gutenberg to Google: Electronic Representations of Literary Texts.* New York: Cambridge University Press.

Shirky, Clay. 2008a. *Here Comes Everybody: The Power of Organizing without Organizations.* New York: Penguin.

Shirky, Clay. 2008b. "Why Abundance Is Good: A Reply to Nick Carr." *Encyclopedia Britannica Blog,* Jul. 17. https://web.archive.org/web/20150227155605/http:/blogs.britannica.com/2008/07/why-abundance-is-good-a-reply-to-nick-carr/.

Silverman, Jacob. 2021. "What if the idyllic, before-the-fall internet . . ." X, May 29. https://twitter.com/SilvermanJacob/status/1398836476109000713. [Tweet since deleted.]

Skocpol, Theda, and Vanessa Williamson. 2012. *The Tea Party and the Remaking of Republican Conservatism.* New York: Oxford University Press.

Slobodian, Quinn. 2019. "Anti-'68ers and the Racist-Libertarian Alliance: How a Schism among Austrian School Neoliberals Helped Spawn the Alt Right." *Cultural Politics* 15(3) (Nov. 1): 372–86. https://doi.org/10.1215/17432197-7725521.

Smith, Harrison, and Roger Burrows. 2021. "Software, Sovereignty, and the Post-Neoliberal Politics of Exit." *Theory, Culture, and Society* 38(6): 143–66. https://doi.org/10.1177/0263276421999439.

"Snowden Revelations." 2014. *Lawfare,* Jan. 22. https://www.lawfaremedia.org/article/catalog-snowden-revelations.

Snyder, Timothy. 2017. *On Tyranny: Twenty Lessons from the Twentieth Century.* New York: Crown.

Soave, Robby. 2021. *Tech Panic: Why We Shouldn't Fear Facebook and the Future.* New York: Simon & Schuster.

Soldatov, Andrei, and Irina Borogan. 2015. *The Red Web: The Kremlin's War on the Internet.* Washington, D.C.: PublicAffairs.

Solon, Olivia. 2020. "Child Sexual Abuse Images and Online Exploitation Surge During Pandemic." *NBC News,* Apr. 23. https://www.nbcnews.com/tech/tech-news/child-sexual-abuse-images-online-exploitation-surge-during-pandemic-n1190506.

Southern Poverty Law Center. n.d. "Andrew 'Weev' Auernheimer." SPLC Extremist Files. https://www.splcenter.org/fighting-hate/extremist-files/individual/andrew-%E2%80%9Cweev%E2%80%9D-auernheimer.

Southern Poverty Law Center. 2015. "Third Positionism on the Web." SPLC Intelligence Report. https://www.splcenter.org/fighting-hate/intelligence-report/2015/third-position-web.

Srinivasan, Balaji S. 2013. "Balaji Srinivasan at Startup School 2013." YouTube, Oct. 25. https://www.youtube.com/watch?v=cOubCHLXT6A.

Srinivasan, Balaji S. 2020a. "Guy who has built nothing . . ." X, Apr. 20. https://twitter.com/balajis/status/1252276198983385090.

Srinivasan, Balaji S. 2020b. "Read the news . . ." X, Apr. 20. https://twitter.com/balajis/status/1252283233032482816.

Srinivasan, Balaji S., and Leland Lee. 2017. "Quantifying Decentralization." *Earn,* Jul. 27. https://news.earn.com/quantifying-decentralization-e39db233c28e.

St. Laurent, Andrew M. 2004. *Understanding Open Source and Free Software Licensing.* Sebastopol, Calif.: O'Reilly Media.

Stallman, Richard M. n.d. "What Is Free Software?" GNU Operating System. Last modified Jan. 1, 2024.

Stallman, Richard M. 2002. *Free Software, Free Society: Selected Essays of Richard M. Stallman.* Boston: Free Software Foundation / GNU Press.

Stanley, Jason. 2018. *How Fascism Works: The Politics of Us and Them.* New York: Random House.

Stanley, Manfred. 1978. *The Technological Conscience: Survival and Dignity in an Age of Expertise.* Chicago: University of Chicago Press.

Stark, Luke, and Jevan Hutson. 2022. "Physiognomic Artificial Intelligence." *Fordham Intellectual Property, Media and Entertainment Law Journal* 32(4) (May). https://ir.lawnet.fordham.edu/iplj/vol32/iss4/2/.

Steele, Robert David. 2012. *The Open-Source Everything Manifesto.* Berkeley, Calif.: Evolver Editions.

Stoller, Matt. 2019. "Tech Companies Are Destroying Democracy and the Free Press." *New York Times,* Oct. 17. https://www.nytimes.com/2019/10/17/opinion/tech-monopoly-democracy-journalism.html.

Stoltz, Mitch, Andrew Crocker, and Christoph Schmon. 2022. "The EU Digital Markets Act's Interoperability Rule Addresses an Important Need, but Raises Difficult Security Problems for Encrypted Messaging." Electronic Frontier Foundation, May 2. https://www.eff.org/deeplinks/2022/04/eu-digital-markets-acts-interoperability-rule-addresses-important-need-raises.

Stop Hate for Profit. 2021. "Recommended Next Steps." Last modified Jan. 6, 2024. https://www.stophateforprofit.org/productrecommendations.

"Stop Online Piracy Act." 2020. Wikipedia. Last modified Oct. 24. https://en.wikipedia.org/w/index.php?title=Stop_Online_Piracy_Act&oldid=985113808.

Strömbäck, Per. 2016. *21 Digital Myths: Reality Distortion Antidote.* Stockholm: Volante.

Sullivan, Danny. 2014. "How Google's New 'Right to Be Forgotten' Form Works: An Explainer." *Search Engine Land,* May 30. https://searchengineland.com/google-right-to-be-forgotten-form-192837.

Sveiby, Karl-Erik. 2017. "Unintended Consequences of Innovation." In Godin and Vinck 2017, 137–55.

Swanson, Ana, and Jim Tankersley. 2020. "Trump Just Signed the USMCA: Here's What's in the New NAFTA." *New York Times,* Jan. 29. https://www.nytimes.com/2020/01/29/business/economy/usmca-deal.html.

Sylvain, Olivier. 2017. "'AOL v. Zeran': The Cyberlibertarian Hack of §230 Has Run Its Course." In Goldman and Kosseff 2020, 78–80.

Sylvain, Olivier. 2018. "Intermediary Design Duties." *Connecticut Law Review* 50(1): 204–74. https://papers.ssrn.com/sol3/papers.cfm?abstract_id=2997141.

Szóka, Berin, and Ashkhen Kazaryan. 2020. "Section 230: An Introduction for Antitrust and Consumer Protection Practitioners." Global Antitrust Institute, Nov. 11. https://dx.doi.org/10.2139/ssrn.3733746.

Szóka, Berin. 2020. "Bill Barr Declares War on the Internet as We Know It." *Morning Consult,* Feb. 19. https://morningconsult.com/opinions/bill-barr-declares-war-on-the-internet-as-we-know-it/.

Tabarrok, Alexander, and Tyler Cowen. 1992. "The Public Choice Theory of John C. Calhoun." *Journal of Institutional and Theoretical Economics / Zeitschrift für die gesamte Staatswissenschaft* 148(4) (Dec. 1992): 655–74. https://www.jstor.org/stable/40 71557.

Taleb, Nassim Nicholas. 2022. "A Clash of Two Systems." *Medium,* Apr. 19. https://medium.com/incerto/a-clash-of-two-systems-47009e9715e2.

Tapscott, Don, and Alex Tapscott. 2018. *Blockchain Revolution: How the Technology behind Bitcoin and Other Cryptocurrencies Is Changing the World.* New York: Portfolio.

Tapscott, Don, and Anthony D. Williams. 2013. *Radical Openness: Four Unexpected Principles for Success.* New York: TED Conferences.

Tech Transparency Project. 2017a. "Google Academics Inc." Jul. 11). https://www.tech transparencyproject.org/articles/google-academics-inc.

Tech Transparency Project. 2017b. "Google Funds Dozens of Groups Fighting Sex Trafficking Bill." Sep. 27. https://www.techtransparencyproject.org/articles/google -funds-dozens-groups-fighting-sex-trafficking-bill.

Tech Transparency Project. 2020. "White Supremacist Groups Are Thriving on Facebook." May 21. https://www.techtransparencyproject.org/articles/white-suprema cist-groups-are-thriving-on-facebook.

Tech Transparency Project. 2022. "Funding the Fight against Antitrust: How Facebook's Antiregulatory Attack Dog Spends Its Millions." May 17. https://www.tech transparencyproject.org/articles/funding-fight-against-antitrust-how-facebooks -antiregulatory-attack-dog-spends-its-millions.

Tenney, Claudia. 2021. "New Information Confirms Zuckerberg-Connected Group Funneled Majority of Election Payments to Democrat-Leaning Counties." Press release, Dec. 20. https://tenney.house.gov/media/press-releases/new-information-con firms-zuckerberg-connected-group-funneled-majority-election.

Thiel, Peter. 2009. "The Education of a Libertarian." *Cato Unbound,* Apr. 13. https://www.cato-unbound.org/2009/04/13/peter-thiel/education-libertarian/.

Thierer, Adam. 2014. "Embracing a Culture of Permissionless Innovation." Cato Online Forum, Nov. 17. https://www.cato.org/cato-online-forum/embracing-culture -permissionless-innovation.

Thierer, Adam. 2016. *Permissionless Innovation: The Continuing Case for Comprehensive Technological Freedom.* Arlington, Va.: Mercatus Center.

Thierer, Adam. 2018. "GDPR Compliance: The Price of Privacy Protections." *Technology Liberation Front,* Jul. 9. https://techliberation.com/2018/07/09/gdpr-compliance -the-price-of-privacy-protections/.

Thierer, Adam. 2019. "The Great Facial Recognition Technopanic of 2019." *The Bridge,* May 17. https://www.mercatus.org/economic-insights/expert-commentary/ great-facial-recognition-technopanic-2019.

Thierer, Adam, and Berin Szóka. 2009. "Cyber-Libertarianism: The Case for Real Internet Freedom." Technology Liberation Front, Aug. 12. https://techliberation .com/2009/08/12/cyber-libertarianism-the-case-for-real-internet-freedom/.

Thompson, Alex. 2020. "Why the Right Wing Has a Massive Advantage on Facebook." *Politico*, Sep. 26. https://www.politico.com/news/2020/09/26/facebook-con servatives-2020-421146.

Tkacz, Nathaniel. 2012. "From Open Source to Open Government: A Critique of Open Politics." *Ephemera* 12(4): 386–405.

Tkacz, Nathaniel. 2015. *Wikipedia and the Politics of Openness.* Chicago: University of Chicago Press.

Topinka, Robert. 2019. "'Back to a Past That Was Futuristic': The Alt-Right and the Uncanny Form of Racism." *b2o: An Online Journal* 4(2) (Oct. 14). https://www .boundary2.org/2019/10/robert-topinka-back-to-a-past-that-was-futuristic-the-alt -right-and-the-uncanny-form-of-racism/.

"Tor Project: Overview." 2019. Tor Project. https://2019.www.torproject.org/about/ overview.html.en.

Turkewitz, Neil. 2018. "Freedom House Report on Internet Freedom: How Can You Rank What You Don't Understand?" *Medium,* Nov. 6. https://medium.com/@ntur kewitz_56674/freedom-house-report-on-internet-freedom-how-can-you-rank-what -you-dont-understand-74495f1d5e6f.

Turner, Fred. 2006a. *From Counterculture to Cyberculture: Stewart Brand, the Whole Earth Network, and the Rise of Digital Utopianism.* Chicago: University of Chicago Press.

Turner, Fred. 2006b. "How Digital Technology Found Utopian Ideology: Lessons from the First Hackers Conference." In David Silver and Adrienne Massanari, eds., *Critical Cyberculture Studies: Current Terrains, Future Directions.* New York: NYU Press, 345–61.

Turner, Fred. 2018. "Trump on Twitter: How a Medium Designed for Democracy Became an Authoritarian's Mouthpiece." In Boczkowski and Papacharissi 2018, 143–50.

Turner, Fred. 2019. "Machine Politics: The Rise of the Internet and a New Age of Authoritarianism." *Harper's Magazine,* Jan. https://harpers.org/archive/2019/01/ machine-politics-facebook-political-polarization/.

United Nations. 2022. "Social Media Poses 'Existential Threat' to Traditional, Trustworthy News: UNESCO." *UN News,* Mar. 10. https://news.un.org/en/story/2022/ 03/1113702.

UnKoch My Campus. n.d. "Austrian Economics: A Gateway to Extremism." Part of *Advancing White Supremacy through Academic Strategy.* https://static1.squarespace .com/static/5400da69e4b0cb1fd47c9077/t/636934fb4d078058a8292ee3/1667839 235779/Academic+White+Supremacy+Report.pdf.

UK Ofcom. 2010. "Ofcom's Approach to Net Neutrality." Nov. 24. https://www.ofcom .org.uk/__data/assets/pdf_file/0011/50510/statement.pdf.

U.S. House Committee on Energy and Commerce. 2019. "Fostering a Healthier Internet to Protect Consumers." Hearing of the Subcommittee on Consumer Protection and Commerce, Oct. 16. https://docs.house.gov/Committee/Calendar/ByEvent.aspx?EventID=110075.

U.S. House Intelligence Committee. 2016. "Review of the Unauthorized Disclosures of Former National Security Agency Contractor Edward Snowden." Sep. 16. https://s3.documentcloud.org/documents/3245804/Hpsci-Snowden-Review-Declassified.pdf. [Unclassified version of congressional report.]

U.S. White House. 2021. "Statement by Press Secretary Jen Psaki on the Occasion of the United States Joining the Christchurch Call to Action to Eliminate Terrorist and Violent Extremist Content Online." Press release, May 7. https://www.whitehouse.gov/briefing-room/statements-releases/2021/05/07/statement-by-press-secretary-jen-psaki-on-the-occasion-of-the-united-states-joining-the-christchurch-call-to-action-to-eliminate-terrorist-and-violent-extremist-content-online/.

Vaidhyanathan, Siva. 2004. *The Anarchist in the Library: How the Clash between Freedom and Control Is Hacking the Real World and Crashing the System.* New York: Basic Books.

van Alsenoy, Brendan, and Marieke Koekkoek. 2015. "The Extra-Territorial Reach of the EU's 'Right to Be Forgotten.'" CiTiP Working Paper, Jan. 20. https://ssrn.com/abstract=2551838.

Vinsel, Lee, and Andrew L. Russell. 2020. *The Innovation Delusion: How Our Obsession with the New Has Disrupted the Work That Matters Most.* New York: Currency / Random House.

Vogel, Kenneth P. 2017. "Google Critic Ousted from Think Tank Funded by the Tech Giant." *New York Times,* Aug. 30. https://www.nytimes.com/2017/08/30/us/politics/eric-schmidt-google-new-america.html.

Walch, Angela. 2017. "Blockchain's Treacherous Vocabulary: One More Challenge for Regulators." *Journal of Internet Law* 21(2) (Aug.): 1, 10–16. https://commons.stmarytx.edu/cgi/viewcontent.cgi?article=1514&context=facarticles.

Walch, Angela. 2019. "Deconstructing 'Decentralization': Exploring the Core Claim of Crypto Systems." In Chris Brummer, ed., *Crypto Assets: Legal and Monetary Perspectives.* New York: Oxford University Press, 39–68. https://doi.org/10.1093/oso/9780190077310.003.0003.

Walch, Angela. 2021. "Testimony: 'Cryptocurrencies: What Are They Good For?'" Testimony before the U.S. Senate Committee on Banking, Housing, and Urban Affairs, Jul. 27. https://www.banking.senate.gov/imo/media/doc/Walch%20Testimony%207-27-21.pdf.

Wales, Justin S., and Richard J. Ovelmen. 2019. "Bitcoin Is Speech: Notes toward Developing the Conceptual Contours of Its Protection under the First Amendment." *University of Miami Law Review* 74(1) (Fall): 204–75. https://repository.law.miami.edu/umlr/vol74/iss1/6.

Wallace, Jonathan, and Michael Green. 1997. "Bridging the Analogy Gap: The Internet, the Printing Press, and Freedom of Speech." *Seattle University Law Review* 20, 711–48.

Wang, Claire. 2016. "Stanford's History with Eugenics." *Stanford Daily,* Dec. 7. https://stanforddaily.com/2016/12/07/stanfords-history-with-eugenics/.

Warner, Michael. 1990. *The Letters of the Republic: Publication and the Public Sphere in Eighteenth-Century America.* Cambridge, Mass.: Harvard University Press.

Warner, Michael. 2002. *Publics and Counterpublics.* New York: Zone.

Watson, Libby. 2017. "Group That Takes Money from Tech Industry Complains That Tech Coverage Is Too Negative." *Gizmodo,* Feb. 23. https://gizmodo.com/tech-think -tank-whines-that-journalists-are-too-mean-1792673883.

Watters, Audrey. 2014. "From 'Open' to Justice." *Hacked Education,* Nov. 16. https:// hackeducation.com/2014/11/16/from-open-to-justice.

Weber, Max. 2004. *The Vocation Lectures: "Science as a Vocation"; "Politics as a Vocation."* Edited by David Owen and Tracy B. Strong. Translated by Rodney Livingstone. Indianapolis: Hackett.

Weber, Steven. 2004. *The Success of Open Source.* Cambridge, Mass.: Harvard University Press.

Weber, Tripp. 2014. "How the Internet and Advertising Technology Destroyed Newspapers." *Leader's Edge,* Jan. 27. https://jhucle.wordpress.com/2014/01/27/how-the -internet-and-advertising-technology-destroyed-newspapers/.

The Week Staff. 2016. "Peter Thiel's 6 Favorite Books That Predict the Future." *The Week,* May 2. https://theweek.com/articles/443683/peter-thiels-6-favorite-books-that -predict-future.

Weyl, E. Glen. 2022. "Sovereign Nonsense: A Review of *The Sovereign Individual* by James Dale Davidson and Lord William Rees-Mogg." *RadicalxChange,* Jan. 18. https://www.radicalxchange.org/media/blog/sovereign-nonsense/.

Wheeler, Marcy. 2021a. "Insurance File: Glenn Greenwald's Anger Is of More Use to Vladimir Putin Than Edward Snowden's Freedom." *Emptywheel,* May 21. https:// www.emptywheel.net/2021/05/21/insurance-file-glenn-greenwald-is-of-more-use -to-vladimir-putin-than-edward-snowden/.

Wheeler, Marcy. 2021b. "Liar's Poker: The Complexity of Julian Assange's Extradition." *Emptywheel,* Dec. 10. https://www.emptywheel.net/2021/12/10/liars-poker-the -complexity-of-julian-assanges-extradition/.

Wheeler, Marcy. 2021c. "WikiLeaks and Edward Snowden Champion Sociopathic Liars and Sloppy Thinking." *Emptywheel,* Jun. 27. https://www.emptywheel.net/20 21/06/27/wikileaks-and-edward-snowden-champion-sociopathic-liars-and-sloppy -thinking/.

White, Nathan. 2017. "The Internet as We Know It Is at Risk." AccessNow, Jul. 12. https://www.accessnow.org/internet-know-risk/.

Whitehead, Laurence. 2002. *Democratization: Theory and Experience.* New York: Oxford University Press.

Wilentz, Sean. 2014. "Would You Feel Differently about Snowden, Greenwald, and Assange If You Knew What They Really Thought?" *New Republic,* Jan. 19. https:// newrepublic.com/article/116253/edward-snowden-glenn-greenwald-julian-assange -what-they-believe.

Wille, Matt. 2022. "Facebook Might Stop Removing So Much COVID-19 Misinformation." *Input,* Jul. 26. https://www.inverse.com/input/tech/facebook-covid19-mis information-oversight-board.

Williams, Sam. 2002. *Free as in Freedom: Richard Stallman's Crusade for Free Software.* Sebastopol, Calif.: O'Reilly Media.

Williamson, Kevin D. 2021. "Mark Zuckerberg's Facebook Fight Is Really about Silencing Right-Wing Voices." *New York Post,* Oct. 30. https://nypost.com/2021/10/30/facebooks-fight-is-really-about-silencing-right-wing-voices/.

Wilson, Cody. 2016. *Come and Take It: The Gun Printer's Guide to Thinking Free.* New York: Gallery Books.

Winn, Joss. 2012. "Open Education: From the Freedom of Things to the Freedom of People." In Michael Neary, Howard Stevenson, and Les Bell, eds., *Towards Teaching in Public: Reshaping the Modern University.* London: Continuum, 133–47.

Winner, Langdon. 1986. *The Whale and the Reactor: A Search for Limits in an Age of High Technology.* Chicago: University of Chicago Press.

Winner, Langdon. 1997. "Cyberlibertarian Myths and the Prospects for Community." *ACM SIGCAS Computers and Society* 27(3) (Sep.): 14–19.

Wolfe, Liz. 2021. "Elon Musk: Government Is 'The Biggest Corporation, with a Monopoly on Violence, Where You Have No Recourse.'" *Reason,* Dec. 8. https://reason.com/2021/12/08/elon-musk-government-is-the-biggest-corporation-with-a-monopoly-on-violence-where-you-have-no-recourse/.

Wong, Julia Carrie. 2021. "Revealed: The Facebook Loophole That Lets World Leaders Deceive and Harass Their Citizens." *The Guardian,* Apr. 12. https://www.theguardian.com/technology/2021/apr/12/facebook-loophole-state-backed-manipulation.

Wozniak, Steve, and Michael Copps. 2017. "Ending Net Neutrality Will End the Internet as We Know It." *USA Today,* Sep. 29. https://www.usatoday.com/story/opinion/2017/09/29/ending-net-neutrality-will-end-internet-we-know-steve-wozniak-michael-copps-column/704861001/.

Wu, Tim. 2002. "A Proposal for Network Neutrality." University of Virginia, Jun. http://www.timwu.org/OriginalNNProposal.pdf.

Wu, Tim. 2003. "Network Neutrality, Broadband Discrimination." *Journal of Telecommunications and High Technology Law* 2, 141–79. https://scholarship.law.columbia.edu/faculty_scholarship/1281/.

Wu, Tim. 2019. "Beyond First Amendment Lochnerism." Knight First Amendment Institute at Columbia University, Aug. 21. https://knightcolumbia.org/content/beyond-first-amendment-lochnerism-a-political-process-approach.

Wyett, Todd A. 1991. "State Lotteries: Regressive Taxes in Disguise." *Tax Lawyer* 44(3) (Spring): 867–83. https://www.jstor.org/stable/20771362.

Wylie, Christopher. 2019. *Mindf*ck: Inside Cambridge Analytica's Plot to Break the World.* New York: Random House.

Yates, Andy. 2020. "Liberal Mark Zuckerberg's Facebook Platform Silences Trump and Republican Candidates." *Washington Times,* Sep. 16. https://www.washingtontimes.com/news/2020/sep/16/liberal-mark-zuckerbergs-facebook-platform-silence/.

York, Jillian C. 2021. *Silicon Values: The Future of Free Speech under Surveillance Capitalism.* New York: Verso.

Zara, Christopher. 2017. "The Most Important Law in Tech Has a Problem." *Wired,* Jan. 3. https://www.wired.com/2017/01/the-most-important-law-in-tech-has-a-problem/.

Zuboff, Shoshana. 2019. *The Age of Surveillance Capitalism: The Fight for a Human Future at the New Frontier of Power.* New York: PublicAffairs.

Zuboff, Shoshana. 2021. "Shoshana Zuboff Speaks on Big Tech Regulation: Who Knows? Who Decides Who Decides?" Observer Research Foundation America, May 21, YouTube video, 00:42:46. https://youtu.be/7W9Teyj_yFo?.

Zucchi, Kristina. 2020. "Is Bitcoin Mining Profitable?" *Investopedia,* Jun. 30. https://www.investopedia.com/articles/forex/051115/bitcoin-mining-still-profitable.asp.

Zwolinski, Matt. 2016. "The Libertarian Non-Aggression Principle." *Social Philosophy and Policy* 32(2) (Spring): 62–90. https://doi.org/10.1017/S026505251600011X.

Index

Abboud, Antoinette, 80
Abella, Alex, 57
Abelson, Hal, 253, 254, 255
accelerationism, 382, 385, 387
access, 46, 137, 254, 262; denying, 211,
  263; digital book, 248
Access Now, 137
accountability, 45, 105, 117, 122, 159, 162,
  165, 166, 167, 173, 177, 325, 366;
  increase in, 232; open government
  and, 231
ACLU. *See* American Civil Liberties
  Union
activism, xxiii, 6, 19, 32, 34, 59, 108, 120,
  147, 262, 398; anticopyright, 249; antidemocratic, 129, 255; antigovernment,
  255, 282, 283; civil rights, 270, 359;
  cyberlibertarian, 247, 262, 318;
  cypherpunk, 318; digital, xxiii, 35–36,
  90, 100, 109–14, 268–69, 291, 297,
  340; internet, 33, 36, 317; NN, 261,
  268; Occupy, 375; political, 57; protofascist, 114; social, 5; social media-
  based, 224
Acxiom, 53
ADL. *See* Anti-Defamation League
"Against Technocratic Authoritarianism.
  A Short Intellectual History of the
  Cypherpunk Movement" (Beltramini),
  112

Age of Surveillance Capitalism, The
  (Zuboff), 83
AGI. *See* artificial general intelligence
agitation, xiii; anticopyright, 242, 246;
  antigovernment, 135, 314; cyberliber-
  tarian, 36, 43, 105, 131, 178; NN, 264
AI. *See* artificial intelligence
AI Now Institute, 104
AIDS, 65, 382
Airbnb, 15, 31, 52, 54
algorithms, 102, 275, 317, 333
All In with Chris Hayes (MSNBC), 137
*All Watched Over by Machines and Loving
  Grace* (Curtis), 4
Allen, Paul, 6
Alliance to Counter Crime Online, 163
Allow States and Victims to Fight
  Online Sex Trafficking Act, 95
alt-right, 127, 345, 346, 370–81, 371, 387;
  cyberfascism and, 339; libertarianism
  and, 341; rise of, 340–41
Altman, Sam, 349, 373, 374
Amadae, S. M., 57
Amazon, 83, 103, 104, 133, 137, 148, 150,
  320, 321, 323, 395
America First, 325
America Online, 152
American Civil Liberties Union
  (ACLU), 52, 53, 90, 97, 98, 109, 148,
  269, 307, 319, 398; donations to, 99;

449

blockchain, 85, 114, 194, 281, 288–89, 293, 295, 300, 313, 314, 333, 357; applications, 278; communities, 84, 86; decentralization in, 291; development, 294; discourse, 278; law, 290; permissionless, 290; software, 114, 288, 289, 293, 294, 295, 314
Blockchain Revolution, The (Tapscott and Tapscott), 23
Blockchains (company), 278
Blue, Violet, 23
Book of the Dead (Lovecraft), 111
Bookchin, Murray, 282
Boorstin, Bob, 34
Booz Allen Hamilton, 117
Border Gateway Protocol (BGP), 286, 287
Borgman, Christine, 192
Borogan, Irina, 119, 120
Borsook, Paulina, 3; cyberlibertarianism and, 11; on Gilder, 13; philosophical cyberlibertarianism and, 14; on philosophical libertarianism, 10–11; ravers and, 12, 14
boyd, danah, 104, 106, 107–8, 318
Boyle, James, 242
Brand, Stewart, 58, 60, 61, 62, 63, 67, 101, 200; computers and, 66; cyberlibertarianism and, 59; Media Lab and, 100; "new communalist" vision of, 100; political libertarianism of, 66; Turner on, 65–66
Brandom, Russell, 140
Breitbart, 50, 52
Brexit, 18, 40, 51, 83, 387
Brin, Sergey, 220
Brooke, Heather, 23
Brown v. Board of Education (1954), 5, 351
Buffalo, mass murder in, 180
Burning Man festival, 14
Burrows v. Superior Court (1974), 301
Buterin, Vitalik, 289, 290, 333, 377
BuzzFeed, Squire and, 44
BuzzFeed News, 44

cable television packages, NN and, 264–65
CALEA. *See* Communications Law Enforcement Assistance Act
Calhoun, John C., 352, 353
California ideology, 7, 66
"California Ideology, The" (Barbrook and Cameron), 3, 238
California Privacy Protection Act, 184
Cambridge Analytica, 51, 96–97, 133
Cameron, Andy, 3, 7, 59, 70; anti-statism and, 16
Canadian Centre for International Governance Innovation, 315–16
capital: accumulation of, 52; business power and, 218; dark will of, 384; democratizing, 278
capitalism, 20, 66, 67; accelerating, 385; communicative, 387; digital transcendence of, 239; free-market, 49, 142, 241; frontier zones of, 384; hegemony of, 387; liberal, 21; runaway, 383; unregulated, 234, 249. *See also* surveillance capitalism
Carlson, Tucker, 51, 115, 116
Carolan, Jennifer, 193
Carr, Nicholas, 194, 276, 211, 275
Carusone, Angelo, 51
Casey, Michael, 85, 86
Castro, Daniel, 162, 184
Cathedral, 373, 385, 386
Cathedral and the Bazaar, The (Raymond), 241
Catholic Church, 194, 195, 204, 205, 214, 216, 354; colonialism/violence and, 208; Reformation and, 208
Catholicism, Protestantism and, 204, 206
Cato Institute, 27, 130, 144, 371, 374
CCDH *See* Center for Countering Digital Hate
CCRU. *See* Cybernetic Culture Research Unit
CDA. *See* Communications Decency Act

counterculture, 6, 60, 61, 112, 387
Covid–19 pandemic, 18, 65, 86, 121, 135, 246, 277; misinformation about, 47, 48, 138
Cowen, Tyler, 26, 190, 353
Cox, Christopher, 150, 152; CDA and, 149; digital technology and, 151; free speech and, 158; Section 230 and, 157, 158
Cox-Wyden Amendment, 149
Crawford, Susan, 137
Creative Commons, 318
creative destruction, 143–44, 226; theory of, 142
crime syndicates, 112, 355
Crisis Text Line (CTL), 106, 107
critical legal studies, 69
critical race theory, 69
crypto-anarchism, 109, 110, 111, 113, 190, 249–50, 282, 290; fascism and, 114; interest in, 112
"Crypto-Anarchist Manifesto" (May), 109, 113, 128, 134, 190, 389
Crypto Anarchy, Cyberstates, and Pirate Utopias (Ludlow), 250, 396
cryptocurrency, 84, 85, 114, 139, 194, 250, 278, 290, 291, 293, 294, 333, 356, 357, 385; digital rights and, 88; industry, 300–301; investment in, 295; surveillance capitalism and, 86, 88, 89; taxability of, 88
Crypto-Current: Bitcoin and Philosophy (Land), 385
cryptography, 128, 249, 250, 310, 365, 394
CTL. *See* Crisis Text Line
Cult of the Constitution (Franks), 97
Cultural Logic of Computation, The (Golumbia) 338
culture, 246, 319, 342, 353; chan, 360; changes in, 207; computer, 57; democratic, 22, 221; development of, 60; exploitative, 235; hacker, 235; literate, 198; oral, 198; political, 224; technology and, 4. *See also* digital culture; print culture

Curtis, Adam, 4
Cyber Civil Rights, 98
cyber-collectivism, 28, 333
cyber-communism, 238, 239, 241
"Cyber-Libertarianism: The Case for Real Internet Freedom" (Szóka), 27–28
Cyber Policy Center (Stanford), 147
cyberfascism, 339, 345–46, 359–63, 395; cyberlibertarianism and, 393, 394
cyberlibertarian discourse, 9, 16, 21, 24–25, 189, 195, 225, 226, 228, 271, 290, 291, 322, 369
"Cyberlibertarian Myths and the Prospects for Community" (Winner), 3
cyberlibertarian principles, 21, 156, 371
cyberlibertarian rhetoric, 79, 229, 330, 370
Cybernetic Culture Research Unit (CCRU), 381–82, 383–84
cybernetics, 383
cyberpathology, 383
"Cyberpositive" (Plant and Land), 382
Cyberselfish (Borsook), 3, 10
cyberspace, 12, 174, 327, 329, 346, 347; architecture of, 331; discourse of, 326; placelessness of, 348
"Cyberspace and the American Dream: A Magna Carta for the Knowledge Age" (Gilder and Toffler), xxi, 13
"Cyphernomicon, The" (May), 110, 111, 113, 134, 298, 365, 389
cypherpunks, 25, 93, 128, 134, 190, 252, 253, 255, 290, 358, 364, 371, 394; digital activism and, 109–14; encryption and, 249; fascist opinions and, 111; mailing list, 94, 100, 111, 136, 250, 312, 359, 365, 385, 388; Nazism/white supremacy and, 111
Cypherpunks: Freedom and the Future of the Internet (Assange et al.), 364

Dahlberg, Lincoln, 280–81
Daily Kos, 319
Daily Stormer, 394

Mill, John Stuart, 20, 133, 237, 314, 327, 351
Milton, John, 314
Minsky, Marvin, 382
MIRI. *See* Machine Intelligence Research Institute
Mirowski, Philip, 28, 57, 73, 76, 77, 81, 104, 284, 324, 326; climate change and, 80; climate denialists and, 131; "double truth" doctrines and, 233; on Hayek, 74; on marketplace of ideas, 74; murketing by, 234–35; neoliberalism and, 54, 72, 74; on neoliberals/double truth, 77; open-source/free software and, 235–36; on populist philosophy, 74; on technology, 54; Wikipedia and, 77, 241
Mises, Ludwig von, 26, 28, 30, 73, 326
misinformation, 36, 39, 40, 47–48, 50–51, 181; public, 269
MIT. *See* Massachusetts Institute of Technology
Mitchell, William, 329
modernization theory, 323
Moglen, Eben, 214, 215, 216–17, 218, 243; corporate power and, 219; print-digital parallel and, 219
Moldbug, Mencius, 357, 371, 372, 373, 374, 375, 385, 386, 387
money: dark, 104; democratizing, 278
money is speech, 308
money laundering, 134, 135
Mont Pelerin Society (MPS), 20, 30, 35, 73, 77, 233, 326, 351
moral panic, 131–34
Moravec, Hans, 382
Morozov, Evgeny, 53, 205, 228–29, 325; law/economics tradition and, 326; on open government/accountability, 231; solutionism and, 52; on technology/anti-technology, 52; on technology/neoliberalism, 54
Morrison, Aimée Hope, 12
Morrison, Toni, 218
Mosaic web browser, 349

Mother of All Demos, 61
Motherboard, 106
Mozilla, 9, 35, 52
MPS. *See* Mont Pelerin Society
MSI Integrity, research methodology and, 168
Mueller, Milton, 174, 179; analysis by, 169; anarcho-capitalism and, 172; far-right ideas and, 169–70; globalism and, 170; on ICANN, 167, 168; liberalism and, 170, 171–72; on multi-stakeholderism, 173; Russia hoax and, 115
Multi-stakeholder Initiative Integrity, 168
multistakeholder initiatives (MSIs), 168
multistakeholder processes (MSPs), 166
multistakeholderism, 149, 155, 164, 165, 174; criticism of, 170–71; democratic, 177; digital roots of, 166–67; internet governance and, 168; language, 166; policymaking and, 173; politics and, 169; promoting, 175; vision of, 166
"Multistakeholderism vs. Democracy" (Gurstein), 177
Multnomah County Common Law Court, 399
Mumford, Lewis, 199, 200, 340
murketing, concept of, 234–35
Musiani, Francesca, 287
Musk, Elon, 17, 2930, 36
Mussolini, Benito, 342, 343, 383
Myth of Digital Democracy, The (Hindman), 281

NAACP, 41, 45
NAACP Legal Defense Fund, 38, 40
Nakamoto, Satoshi, 194, 195, 296; Bitcoin and, 291, 293
Nameless World, 360
Nanashii Warudo, 360
Napoleon Bonaparte, 217
Narula, Neha, 293
National Center for Supercomputing Applications, 349

Northern Renaissance, 207
nostalgia, false, 139–41
Nozick, Robert, 12, 26, 28, 30
NRC. *See* Nuclear Regulatory
  Commission
NRx. *See* neoreaction
NSA. *See* National Security Agency
NTC. *See* Neoliberal Thought Collective
nuclear energy, 81
Nuclear Regulatory Commission
  (NRC), 328, 399

Obama, Barack, 102, 126, 323
Obamacare, 27, 137, 282
Objectivism, 357
Occupy Wall Street, 375
Ochigame, Rodrigo, 102, 103
Ofcom rules (UK), 264
Ohanian, Alexis, 318
Oklahoma City bombing, 393–94
Old Left, 376
OneZero, 266
Ong, Walter, 200, 202, 225
onion sites, 256, 258
open, 130, 288; democracy and, 229;
  digital rhetoric and, 232; free and, 235;
  ideology of, 9; term, 30, 92, 228–38
open access, 7, 211; NN and, 269
Open Data, 231
open government, 7; accountability and,
  231
open internet, 145, 272, 316, 317, 319, 321
Open Internet Order (FCC), 266; NN
  and, 267
Open Internet Rules (FCC), 138, 139,
  264, 265, 266, 270
Open Knowledge Foundation, 91
Open Markets Institute, 87, 300
Open Media, 316
Open Society, 233, 234, 283
Open Society and Its Enemies (Popper),
  232, 233
Open Society Foundation, 52
open source, 7, 230–31; corporate, 240;
  free and, 238–41; term, 236, 238

Open-Source Everything Manifesto
  (Steele), 231
Open Source Initiative, 230, 241
open-source movement, promotional
  techniques of, 235
open-source software, xix, xxiii, 24, 218,
  235–36, 242, 359; gun printing and,
  394
Open Technology Institute, 9192, 318
openness, xxi, xxii, 68, 229, 231–32, 233,
  281, 319, 333, 369; concerns about, 83
openwashing, 229
OR Books, 364
O'Reilly Media, 241
Oreskes, Naomi, 64, 130
organized crime, 135, 350, 355
OSI Reference Model, 285
othering, 345
Overcoming Bias, 372, 376, 377
Oversight Board, 47
Oyama, Katherine, 163

Packer, George, 126, 128, 129
Page, Larry, 373
Pai, Ajit, 137, 265
Paine, Thomas, 217
Palantir, 183
Pallone, Frank, 163
paranoia, diffusing, 251–52
"Partnership on AI to Benefit People and
  Society," 103
Pasquale, Frank, 130n1, 181, 236, 402–3
Patel, 309
paternalism, 105, 323
patriarchal system, 105
Patriot Act (2001), 72
Paul, Rand, 15, 26, 370, 399
Paul, Ron, 15, 26, 126, 170, 340, 341, 370,
  375, 399; civil liberties and, 72
Paxton, Robert, 343, 345
PayPal, SOPA/PIPA and, 35
pedophiles, 134
peer-to-peer, 292, 293
Pein, Cory, 372, 373, 374
Peloponnesian War, 232

DAVID GOLUMBIA (1963–2023) was associate professor in the English department and the Media, Art, and Text PhD program at Virginia Commonwealth University. He was author of *The Cultural Logic of Computation* and *The Politics of Bitcoin: Software as Right-Wing Extremism* (Minnesota, 2016).